# Histories of Transnational Criminal Law

# Histories of Transnational Criminal Law

*Edited by*

NEIL BOISTER
SABINE GLESS
FLORIAN JESSBERGER

OXFORD
UNIVERSITY PRESS

OXFORD
UNIVERSITY PRESS

Great Clarendon Street, Oxford, OX2 6DP,
United Kingdom

Oxford University Press is a department of the University of Oxford.
It furthers the University's objective of excellence in research, scholarship,
and education by publishing worldwide. Oxford is a registered trade mark of
Oxford University Press in the UK and in certain other countries



First Edition published in 2021

Impression: 1



Published in the United States of America by Oxford University Press
198 Madison Avenue, New York, NY 10016, United States of America

British Library Cataloguing in Publication Data

Data available

Library of Congress Control Number: 2021933265

ISBN 978–0–19–284570–2

DOI: 10.1093/oso/9780192845702.001.0001

Printed and bound by
CPI Group (UK) Ltd, Croydon, CR0 4YY

# Foreword

In the not too distant past crime was considered a local matter—local in commission and effect—to be governed by a local response. But with the changes technology has brought to our global landscape, nothing could be further from our reality today. Grave crimes recognized as international in nature, because of the threat they pose, tragically continue to be perpetrated in many corners of the world. Moreover, many crimes once considered 'domestic' in nature now by scope, manner of perpetration or impact have become transnational. Further, individual criminals and organized groups easily traverse borders to evade detection and hide the evidence and profits of their crimes rendering local responses highly ineffective. These realities have driven a multitude of initiatives over the last few decades designed to respond to the internationalization of crime.

Looking back on these with the perspective of a practitioner, I think it fair to say some of the most important outcomes have been in the context of the evolution of a framework to address international crimes which affect us as a global community. Prominent examples are the rapid expansion and development of international criminal law including the establishment of landmark ad hoc courts and tribunals such as the International Criminal Tribunal for the former Yugoslavia, the International Criminal Tribunal for Rwanda and, of course, the first permanent International Criminal Court.

Unquestionably, the developments have been ground-breaking and well merit the attention paid to them on both a practical and academic level. Tragically far too much of the world's population today is touched by conflicts—insurrections, wars—with horrific crimes still being committed in the context of the same. For that, advancing international criminal law is imperative.

At the same time, this highly visible progress has tended to overshadow the equally remarkable achievements in the efforts to find global solutions to combat 'common' crime which by its nature, scope or effect creates a transnational threat. Transnational crime is pervasive, touching all of us in different ways, in every corner of the world, posing a grave threat as well to the safety and security of all our communities. The progression of transnational criminal law is of equal importance in our global village.

For this reason, it is imperative that we 'shine a light' on the significant initiatives and achievements in this lesser known field of transnational criminal law. Careful reflection on where we have been and where we are now, on the progress and the challenges, is fundamental to safeguarding the gains made and ensuring future progression.

With that aim, *Histories of Transnational Criminal Law* is a seminal work presenting a comprehensive and detailed overview of the substantive fields—terrorism, organized crime, cybercrime and human trafficking, to name a few—as well as the procedural mechanisms—multilateral suppression, institution building and norm development. Due attention is also paid to the often neglected field of international cooperation in criminal matters—including extradition and law enforcement cooperation.

Each chapter provides a discrete overview of a substantive issue or procedural development that can quickly inform a practitioner or researcher with a targeted subject in mind. Collectively the text paints a compelling picture of the global initiative against transnational crime exposing both its success and failures, identifying progress and the challenges we face today and will face in future.

In the course of my career I have participated directly in development of some of the initiatives related to the fight against transnational crime and I worked at the United Nations Office on Drugs and Crime where they formed part of everyday practice. Thus I consider I have a pretty good knowledge base in the field. Yet I can assure you I was captivated by this text. It is a credit of course to the impressive group of scholars and practitioners who have contributed to it. I learnt about subjects I had never considered in the context of this field and as a whole it provided a unique overview of the important interrelated components of this rapidly developing subject area. I invite you to carry out a similar exploration of this important work so relevant in the context of international law and criminal law in our times.

Kimberly Prost
Judge, International Criminal Court

# Preface

The book goes back to a conference held in October 2019 at Schloss Herrenhausen in Hannover, Germany. The chapters of this volume are edited papers presented and discussed at this conference. The conference has been made possible through generous funding and administrative support from the *Volkswagenstiftung*.

We would like to acknowledge the support of the whole team of the *Lehrstuhl Jeßberger* during the conference, in particular of Luca Hauffe. Antonia Gillhaus in Berlin as well as Claudine Abt and Lia Börlin in Basel helped with copy-editing the manuscript. Our gratitude also lies with our publishers, Merel Alstein and Jack McNichol, for their valuable support.

All websites cited in this volume have last been accessed on 1 December 2020.

Christchurch, Basel and Berlin
December 2020

# Table of Contents

*List of Abbreviations* xiii
*List of Contributors* xvii
*List of Treaties* xix

Introduction 1
*Neil Boister, Sabine Gless and Florian Jeßberger*

1. Norms, Procedures and Practices of Transnational Criminal Law in 18th and Early 19th-Century Europe 14
*Karl Härter*

2. Criminological Reformism and Transnational Criminal Law (1870s–1930s) 27
*Michele Pifferi*

3. The Growth of the Multilateral Suppression Conventions in the First Half of the 20th Century 39
*Neil Boister*

4. Transnational Epistemic Communities: From the League of Nations to the United Nations War Crimes Commission 57
*Kerstin von Lingen*

5. Gerhard Mueller's Role in Developing the Concept of Transnational Crime for the United Nations 70
*Mangai Natarajan*

6. The Emergence of Criminal Law Norms in International Organizations 84
*Frank Meyer*

7. Transnational Criminal Courts: A Partially Realized Idea 101
*Sara Wharton and Robert J Currie*

8. A History of Maritime Piracy: A Transnational Crime in Need of Transnational Substantive Criminal Law 115
*Masha Fedorova and Piet Hein van Kempen*

9. British Anti-Slave-Trade Treaties with African and Arab Leaders as Precursors of Modern Suppression Conventions 128
*Roger S Clark*

10. Social Anarchy, 'Common Danger' or Political 'Terrorism'? Origins of Transnational Legal Suppression of Terrorism in the Unification of Criminal Laws, 1927–35 138
*Ben Saul*

11. The History of the Global Anti-Human Trafficking Agenda, with a Focus on Prostitution and Sexual Exploitation 151
*Heli Askola*

12. A Short History of Smuggling of Migrants in International Law 162
*Andreas Schloenhardt*

13. Organized Crime: The Road to the Palermo Convention 177
*Serena Forlati*

14. The Origins of International Anti-Corruption Law: The Failed Negotiation of an International Agreement on Illicit Payments 187
*Cecily Rose*

15. Corporate Liability for Economic Crimes: A Contested Transnational History 202
*Michael Elliot and Felix Lüth*

16. The Illicit Trade in Cultural Objects: From Marginalization to the Current Surge in Attention by Transnational Criminal Policymakers 220
*Arianna Visconti*

17. The Emerging History of Transnational Criminal Law Relating to Cybercrime 236
*Dominik Brodowski*

18. A Historical Perspective on Modes of Liability in Transnational Criminal Law 249
*Anneke Petzsche*

19. A Short History of Jurisdiction in Transnational Criminal Law 261
*Florian Jeßberger*

20. The Making of Modern International Extradition Law 276
*Joanna Harrington*

21. The Historical Development of International Law Enforcement Cooperation—The Case of Interpol 287
*Saskia Hufnagel*

22. The Acquisition of Legal Status by Individuals in Transnational Criminal Proceedings in Europe 300
*Sabine Gless*

*Index* 319

# List of Abbreviations

| | |
|---|---|
| AICCM | Act on International Cooperation in Criminal Matters |
| AIDP | Association International de Droit Pénal |
| AML | Anti-Money Laundering |
| APG | Asia/Pacific Group |
| ASC | American Society of Criminology |
| AU | African Union |
| BGH | Bundesgerichtshof |
| CAT | Committee Against Torture |
| CCF | Commission for the Control of Interpol's Files |
| CCPCJ | UN Commission on Crime Prevention and Criminal Justice |
| CDPC | European Committee on Crime Problems |
| CFATF | Caribbean Financial Action Task Force |
| CIA | Central Intelligence Agency |
| CIRT | League of Nations' Drafting Committee for the International Repression of Terrorism |
| CISA | Convention implementing the Schengen Agreement |
| CJEU | Court of Justice of the EU |
| CLOUD | Clarifying Lawful Overseas Use of Data Act |
| CoE | Council of Europe |
| COPLA | Latin American and Caribbean Criminal Court Against Transnational Organized Crime |
| CPCJB | Crime Prevention and Criminal Justice Branch |
| CPI | Corruption Perceptions Index |
| CPT | European Committee for the Prevention of Torture and Inhuman or Degrading Treatment or Punishment |
| CTC | UN Security Council Counter-Terrorism Committee |
| CTS | Consolidated Treaty Series |
| DDoS | Distributed Denial of Service |
| ECHR | European Convention of Human Rights |
| ECLI | European Case Law Identifier |
| ECOSOC | United Nations Economic and Social Council |
| ECOWAS | Economic Community of West African States |
| ECST | European Convention on the Suppression of Terrorism |
| ECtHR | European Court of Human Rights |
| EPPO | European Public Prosecutor's Office |
| EU | European Union |
| FATCA | Foreign Account Tax Compliance Act |
| FATF | Financial Action Task Force |
| FCPA | Foreign Corrupt Practices Act |

| | |
|---|---|
| FIU | Financial Intelligence Unit |
| GRECO | Group of States against Corruption |
| HEUNI | European Institute for Crime Prevention and Control |
| IACC | International Anti-Corruption Court |
| IAF | International Abolitionist Federation |
| IBUCL | International Bureau for the Unification of Criminal Law |
| ICAO | International Civil Aviation Organization |
| ICC | International Criminal Court |
| ICCPR | International Covenant on Civil and Political Rights |
| ICJ | International Court of Justice |
| ICPC | International Criminal Police Commission |
| ICTY | International Criminal Tribunal for the former Yugoslavia |
| IGO | Intergovernmental Organization |
| IKV | Internationale Kriminalistische Vereinigung |
| ILA | International Law Association |
| ILC | International Law Commission |
| IMO | International Maritime Organization |
| IO | International Organization |
| IOM | International Organization for Migration |
| ISIL | Islamic State of Iraq and the Levant |
| ISPAC | International Scientific and Professional Advisory Council of the United Nations Crime Prevention and Criminal Justice Programme |
| ITT | International Telephone and Telegraph |
| ITU | International Telecommunication Union |
| LIA | London International Assembly |
| LNU | British League of Nations Union |
| MLA | mutual legal assistance |
| MNE | Multinational Enterprise |
| NAA | National Archives of Australia |
| NGO | non-governmental organization |
| NVA | National Vigilance Association |
| OAS | Organization of American States |
| OECD | Organisation for Economic Co-operation and Development |
| OHCHR | Office of the United Nations High Commissioner for Human Rights |
| PAC | Permanent Armaments Commission |
| PC-CY | Committee of Experts on Crime in Cyber-Space |
| PCDC | Preparatory Committee for the Conference on Disarmament |
| PC-OC | The Council of Europe's Committee of Experts on the Operation of European Conventions on Co-operation in Criminal Matters |
| SC | UN Security Council |
| SEC | US Securities and Exchange Commission |
| SLTD | Stolen and Lost Travel Documents Database |
| TCC | Transnational criminal courts |
| TCL | Transnational criminal law |
| TLO | Transnational Legal Orders |

| | |
|---|---|
| TMC | Temporary Mixed Commission on Disarmament |
| TNA | The National Archives, London |
| TNC | Transnational Corporations |
| TOC | Transnational Organized Crime |
| TREVI | Terrorisme, Radicalisme, Extrémisme, Violence Internationale |
| UK | United Kingdom |
| UN | United Nations |
| UNCAC | United Nations Convention against Corruption |
| UNCTAD | UN Conference on Trade and Development |
| UNCTC | United Nations Centre on Transnational Corporations |
| UN-CTS | Crime Trends and Operations of Criminal Justice Systems |
| UNESCO | United Nations Educational Scientific and Cultural Organization |
| UNGA | United Nations General Assembly |
| UNHCR | United Nations High Commissioner for Refugees |
| UNICEF | United Nations Children's Fund |
| UNICRI | United Nations Interregional Crime and Justice Research Institute |
| UNIDROIT | United Nations International Institute for the Unification of Private Law |
| UNTOC | United Nations Convention against Transnational Organized Crime |
| UNODC | United Nations Office on Drugs and Crime |
| UNOG | United Nations Office at Geneva |
| UNSCR | United Nations Security Council Resolution |
| UNWCC | United Nations War Crimes Commission |
| US | United States |
| USC | United States Code |
| USD | United States Dollar |
| VCLT | Vienna Convention on the Law of Treaties |
| WDC | World Disarmament Conference |
| WWI | World War I |
| WWII | World War II |

# List of Contributors

**Heli Askola**
Associate Professor of Law at Monash University, Melbourne, Australia.

**Neil Boister**
Professor of Criminal Law at the University of Canterbury, Christchurch, New Zealand.

**Dominik Brodowski**
Junior Professor of Criminal Law and Criminal Procedure at Saarland University, Saarbrücken, Germany.

**Roger S Clark**
Professor of Law at Rutgers University, Camden, United States.

**Robert J Currie**
Professor of Law at Dalhousie University, Halifax, Canada.

**Michael Elliot**
Researcher at Rights and Accountability in Development (RAID), London, United Kingdom.

**Masha Fedorova**
Professor of Criminal Law and Criminal Procedure Law at Radboud University, Nijmegen, the Netherlands.

**Serena Forlati**
Professor of International Law at the University of Ferrara, Italy.

**Sabine Gless**
Professor of Criminal Law and Criminal Procedure at the University of Basel, Switzerland.

**Joanna Harrington**
Professor of Law at the University of Alberta, Canada.

**Karl Härter**
Senior Researcher at the Max Planck Institute for European Legal History, Frankfurt am Main, Germany.

**Saskia Hufnagel**
Reader in Criminal Law at Queen Mary University of London, United Kingdom.

**Florian Jeßberger**
Professor of Criminal Law, International Criminal Law and Modern Legal History at Humboldt-University, Berlin, Germany.

**Piet Hein van Kempen**
Professor of Criminal Law and Criminal Procedure at Radboud University, Nijmegen, the Netherlands.

**Kerstin von Lingen**
Professor of Contemporary History at the University of Vienna, Austria.

**Felix Lüth**
Doctoral Researcher, Graduate Institute of International and Development Studies, Geneva, Switzerland.

**Frank Meyer**
Professor of Criminal Law, Criminal Procedure and International Criminal Law at the University of Zürich, Switzerland.

**Mangai Natarajan**
Professor of Criminal Justice at John Jay College of Criminal Justice, The City University of New York, United States.

**Anneke Petzsche**
Postdoctoral Researcher and Lecturer in Criminal Law at Humboldt-University, Berlin, Germany.

**Michele Pifferi**
Professor of Legal History at the University of Ferrara, Italy.

**Cecily Rose**
Assistant Professor of Public International Law at Leiden University, the Netherlands.

**Ben Saul**
Professor of International Law at the University of Sydney, Australia.

**Andreas Schloenhardt**
Professor of Criminal Law at the University of Queensland, Brisbane, Australia, Honorary Professor of Foreign and International Criminal Law, University of Vienna.

**Arianna Visconti**
Associate Professor of Criminal Law and Law & the Arts at the Catholic University Sacro Cuore, Milan, Italy.

**Sara Wharton**
Assistant Professor at the University of Windsor, Canada.

# List of Treaties

## Table of significant treaties and other international instruments (in chronological order)

19 November 1794, Treaty of Amity, Commerce and Navigation between Great Britain and the United States, 52 CTS 243 (**'Jay' Treaty**)

20 December 1841, Treaty for the Suppression of the African Slave Trade, 2 Martens Noveau Recueil General des Traités 392 (**Treaty of London**)

14 March 1884, Convention for the Protection of Submarine Telegraph Cables, 163 CTS 241 (**1884 Submarine Cables Convention**)

26 February 1885, The General Act of the Berlin Congo Conference (**Berlin General Act**)

18 May 1904, International Agreement for the Suppression of the White Slave Traffic, 35 Stat 1979, 1 LNTS 83 (**1904 White Slave Agreement**)

4 May 1910, The International Convention for the Suppression of the White Slave Traffic, 98 UNTS 101 (**1910 White Slave Convention**)

23 January 1912, Hague International Opium Convention, 8 LNTS 187 (**1912 Hague Opium Convention**)

30 September 1921, The International Convention for the Suppression of the Traffic in Women and Children, 9 LNTS 415 (**1921 Convention for the Suppression of the Traffic in Women and Children**)

12 September 1923, International Convention for the Suppression of the Circulation of and Traffic in Obscene Publications, 27 LNTS 214 (**1923 Obscene Publications Convention**)

25 September 1926, The Slavery Convention, 60 LNTS 253 (**1926 Slavery Convention**)

20 April 1929, The International Convention for the Suppression of Counterfeiting of Currency, 112 LNTS 371 (**1929 Counterfeiting Convention**)

28 June 1930, ILO Convention No 29: Convention Concerning Forced or Compulsory Labour, 39 UNTS 55 (**1930 Forced Labour Convention**)

11 October 1933, International Convention for the Suppression of the Traffic in Women of Full Age, 150 LNTS 431 (**1933 Convention for the Suppression of the Traffic in Women**)

26 June 1936, Convention for the Suppression of the Illicit Traffic in Dangerous Drugs, 198 LNTS 300 (**1936 Drugs Convention**)

16 November 1937, Convention for the Prevention and Punishment of Terrorism,19 LNOJ 23 (**1937 Terrorism Convention**)

16 November 1937, Convention for the Creation of an International Criminal Court, 7 Hudson 878 (**1937 International Criminal Court Convention**)

2 December 1949, Convention for the Suppression of the Traffic in Persons and of the Exploitation of the Prostitution of Others, 96 UNTS 271 (**1949 Convention for the Suppression of the Traffic in Persons**)

14 May 1954, Hague Convention for the Protection of Cultural Property in the event of Armed Conflict 249 UNTS 240 (**1954 Hague Cultural Property Convention**)

14 May 1954, Protocol for the Protection of Cultural Property in the Event of Armed Conflict, The Hague, 249 UNTS 251 (**1954 Hague Cultural Property Protocol**)

13 June 1956, ICPO-Interpol Constitution (**Interpol Constitution**)

7 September 1956, Supplementary Convention on the Abolition of Slavery, the Slave Trade and Institutions and Practices Similar to Slavery, 226 UNTS 3 (**1956 Slave Trade Convention**)

25 June 1957, ILO Convention No. 105: Abolition of Forced Labour Convention, 320 UNTS 291 (**1957 Forced Labour Convention**)

12 December 1957, European Convention on Extradition, ETS 24 (**1957 European Extradition Convention**)

29 April 1958, Convention on the High Seas, 450 UNTS 11 (**1958 High Seas Convention**)

20 April 1959, European Convention on Mutual Assistance in Criminal Matters, ETS No 30 (**1959 European Convention on Mutual Assistance**)

30 March 1961, Single Convention on Narcotic Drugs, 520 UNTS 151 (**1961 Single Convention on Narcotic Drugs**)

14 September 1963, Convention on Offences and Certain other Acts Committed on Board Aircraft, 704 UNTS 219 (**1963 Tokyo Convention**)

May 1966, Scheme for Extradition within the Commonwealth (as amended) (**Commonwealth Scheme for Rendition of Fugitive Offenders**)

14 November 1970, UNESCO Convention on the Means of Prohibiting and Preventing the Illicit Import, Export, and Transfer of Ownership of Cultural Property, 823 UNTS 231 (**1970 UNESCO Convention**)

16 December 1970, Convention for the Suppression of Unlawful Seizure of Aircraft, 860 UNTS 105 (**1970 Hague Hijacking Convention**)

21 February 1971, Convention on Psychotropic Substances, 1019 UNTS 175 (**1971 Psychotropic Substances Convention**)

23 September 1971, Convention for the Suppression of Unlawful Acts against the Safety of Civil Aviation, 974 UNTS 177 (**1971 Montreal Convention**)

25 March 1972, Protocol Amending the Single Convention on Narcotic Drugs, 1961, 976 UNTS 3 (**1972 Drugs Protocol**)

17 December 1979, International Convention against the Taking of Hostages, 1316 UNTS 205 (**1979 Hostage Taking Convention**)

25 February 1981, Inter-American Convention on Extradition, 20 ILM 723 (1981) (**1981 Inter- American Extradition Convention**)

10 December 1982, United Nations Convention on the Law of the Sea, 1833 UNTS 3 (**UNCLOS**)

10 December 1984, Convention against Torture and Other Cruel, Inhuman or Degrading Treatment of Punishment, 1465 UNTS 85 (**1984 Convention against Torture**)

1 August 1986, Scheme Relating to Mutual Assistance in Criminal Matters within the Commonwealth, 12 *Commonwealth Law Bulletin* (1986) 1118 (**Harare Scheme**)

10 March 1988, IMO Convention for the Suppression of Unlawful Acts Against the Safety of Maritime Navigation, 1678 UNTS 201 (**1988 SUA Convention**)

20 December 1988, United Nations Convention against Illicit Traffic in Narcotic Drugs and Psychotropic Substances, 1582 UNTS 95 (**1988 Drug Trafficking Convention**)

April 1990, Financial Action Task Force Forty Recommendations on Money Laundering (major updates in 1996, 2003, 2012 when they were integrated with the Special Recommendations on Terrorist Financing), and 2016 when they were subtitled the International Standards on Combating Money Laundering and the Financing of Terrorism and Proliferation (**FATF Recommendations**)

14 December 1990, UN Model Treaty on Extradition, annexed to GA Res 45/116 (1990) (**UN Model Extradition Treaty**)

14 December 1990, UN Model Treaty on Mutual Assistance in Criminal Matters, Optional Protocol to the Model Treaty on Mutual Assistance in Criminal Matters concerning the proceeds of crime, both annexed to GA Res 45/117 (1990) (as amended by GA Res 53/112 (1998)) (**UN Model Mutual Assistance Treaty**)

24 June 1995, UNIDROIT Convention on the International Return of Stolen or Illegally Exported Cultural Objects, 34 ILM 1322 (**UNIDROIT Convention**)

29 March 1996, Inter-American Convention against Corruption, 35 ILM 724 (**1996 Inter-American Corruption Convention**)

15 December 1997, International Convention for the Suppression of Terrorist Bombings 2149 UNTS 256 (**1997 Terrorist Bombings Convention**)

18 December 1997, OECD Convention on Combating Bribery of Foreign Public Officials in International Business Transactions, 37 ILM 1 (**1997 OECD Bribery Convention**)

9 December 1999, International Convention for the Suppression of the Financing of Terrorism 2178 UNTS 197 (**1997 Terrorist Financing Convention**)

25 May 2000, Optional Protocol to the Convention on the Rights of the Child on the Sale of Children, Child Prostitution and Child Pornography, 2171 UNTS 227 (**2000 Optional Protocol on the Sale of Children**)

15 November 2000, UN Convention against Transnational Organised Crime, 2225 UNTS 209 (**UNTOC or 2000 Palermo Convention**)

15 November 2000, Protocol to Prevent, Suppress and Punish Trafficking in Persons, Especially Women and Children, supplementing the United Nations Convention Against Transnational Organized Crime, 2237 UNTS 319 (**2000 Human Trafficking Protocol**)

15 November 2000, Protocol against the Smuggling of Migrants by Land, Sea and Air, Supplementing the United Nations Convention against Transnational Organized Crime, 2241 UNTS 507 (**2000 Migrant Smuggling Protocol**)

31 May 2001, Protocol against the Illicit Manufacturing of and Trafficking in Firearms, Their Parts and Components and Ammunition, supplementing the United Nations Convention against Transnational Organized Crime, 2326 UNTS 208 (**2001 Firearms Trafficking Protocol**)

23 November 2001, Convention on Cybercrime, ETS No 185 (**2001 European Cybercrime Convention or 2001 Budapest Convention**)

28 November 2002, EU Framework Decision on the strengthening of the penal framework to prevent the facilitation of unauthorised entry, transit and residence, 2002/946/JHA (**2002 EU Framework Decision on Unauthorised Entry, Transit and Residence**)

11 July 2003, African Union Convention on Preventing and Combating Corruption, 43 ILM 5 (**2003 AU Corruption Convention**)

31 October 2003, United Nations Convention against Corruption, 2349 UNTS 41 (**UNCAC**)

13 April 2005 International Convention for the Suppression of Acts of Nuclear Terrorism 2445 UNTS 89 (**2005 Nuclear Terrorism Convention**)

15 May 2005, Council of Europe Convention on the Prevention of Terrorism, CETS 196 (**2005 European Terrorism Convention**)

3 August 2005, Draft Comprehensive Convention against International Terrorism Annex, App II, UN Doc. A/59/894 (**draft UN Terrorism Convention**)

21 July 2007, Council of Europe Convention on the Protection of Children against Sexual Exploitation and Sexual Abuse, CETS 201 (**2007 Lanzarote Convention**)

11 May 2011, Council of Europe Convention on Preventing and Combating Violence Against Women and Domestic Violence, ETS 210 (**2011 Istanbul Convention**)

13 December 2011, Directive 2011/92/EU of the European Parliament and of the Council on combating the sexual abuse and sexual exploitation of children and child pornography, OJ L 335/1 (**2011 EU Directive on Sexual Abuse and Sexual Exploitation of Children**)

27 June 2014, Protocol on Amendments to the Protocol on the Statute of the African Court of Justice and Human Rights, 27 June 2014 (**2014 Malabo Protocol**)

22 October 2015, Additional Protocol to the Council of Europe Convention on the Prevention of Terrorism, ETS 217(**2015 European Terrorism Protocol**)

15 March 2017, Directive 2017/541 of the European Parliament and Council on combating terrorism, OJ L 88/6 (**2017 EU Terrorism Directive**)

28 June 2017, Directive 2017/1371 of the European Parliament and Council on the fight against fraud to the Union's financial interests by means of criminal law, OJ L 198/29 (**2017 EU Anti-Fraud Directive**)

# Introduction

*Neil Boister, Sabine Gless and Florian Jeßberger*

Over the last two and a half centuries, states have responded to real or feared transnational criminal activities by trying to coordinate their approaches to these activities. They have resorted to a range of legal measures: internal arrangements, informal bilateral arrangements, more formal bilateral arrangements and treaties, regional measures and treaties, global multilateral 'soft' laws and crime suppression conventions (large multilateral conventions for the suppression of crime with open or regional membership). They have used these measures to reform the substantive criminal law, defining and enacting new offences and treating with other states so that they adopt certain offences in their domestic law. They have also used them to reform the criminal procedural law, adopting new procedures such as legal assistance and extradition, and promising states that they will, on the basis of reciprocity, provide this assistance or even extradite, in the hope that their cooperating states will do likewise.

It is difficult to define transnational crime or to proceed against it without resorting to legal measures that frame domestic criminal and procedural laws in this way. Bruinsma, for example, resorts in part to legal distinctions to frame transnational crime:

> There is no clear definition in the criminological literature about what transnational crimes is. It can be distinguished from international crimes, crimes that are defined by international (criminal) law.... Transnational crimes have to do with crimes that are commissioned in more than one country, crossing national borders. Activities can be illegal in all nations where they occurred, or in one or more but not all countries (for instance in one country alcohol is forbidden by criminal law but not in its adjacent neighbours).[1]

The history of the international legal frameworks that have defined these transnational crimes is not well known nor understood. Nor is the predicament in which these frameworks left individuals as they became entangled in the web of rules of international or foreign origin of which they may not even have been

[1] Gerben Bruinsma, 'Criminology and Transnational Crime' in Gerben Bruinsma (ed), *Histories of Transnational Crime* (Springer 2015) 1.

Neil Boister, Sabine Gless and Florian Jeßberger, *Introduction* In: *Histories of Transnational Criminal Law*.
Edited by: Neil Boister, Sabine Gless and Florian Jeßberger, Oxford University Press.  DOI: 10.1093/oso/9780192845702.003.0001

aware. While there are works that have focused on the historical development of the transnational crimes themselves,[2] or of the policies that frame specific transnational crimes or particular institutions (which may touch on legal issues),[3] there has never really been an attempt to gather a number of histories of the evolution of these legal frameworks.[4] This book aims to fill that gap. While the various chapters touch on many different policies and crimes which may have been covered in other volumes, the focus here is on the histories of legal norms and institutions. It does not provide a comprehensive or exhaustive history of transnational criminal law; such a work must wait for another time. Instead, it provides a relatively short but in-depth account of the history of key developments in these legal frameworks. The idea is to furnish the reader with a distinctive perspective that will enable her to develop a deeper understanding of the mechanics and nature of the development of these frameworks. We seek inter alia to investigate

- why key policy decisions were taken to act through criminalization against particular trans-border activities and how these key policy decisions were transformed into law;
- how and why the resulting crimes took particular forms both in a material and mental sense;
- how and why particular procedural modes of international cooperation were developed in regard to these crimes;
- how and why these procedural modes of cooperation were developed using the particular elements we are now familiar with;
- how and why particular transnational institutions were developed to foster and supervise global legal cooperation against crime;
- what these histories of transnational criminal law reveal about ontological beliefs about the underlying reality of the structure of cross-border/purely domestic action against cross-border/purely domestic crime and the epistemologies developed to learn more about these problems.

[2] See eg Gerben Bruinsma (ed), *Histories of Transnational Crime* (Springer 2015).

[3] See eg Paul Knepper, *The Invention of International Crime. A Global Issue in the Making, 1881–1914* (Palgrave Macmillan 2010); Paul Knepper, *International Crime in the Twentieth Century: The League of Nations Era, 1919–1939* (Palgrave Macmillan 2011); Mark Lewis, *The Birth of the New Justice. The Internationalization of Crime and Punishment, 1919–1950* (OUP 2014) (hereafter Lewis, The Birth); Paul Knepper and Anja Johansen (eds), *The Oxford Handbook of the History of Crime and Criminal Justice* (OUP 2016).

[4] There are, in contrast, a number of works focusing on international criminal law in the core sense *stricto sensu*—see, for a recent example, Immi Tallgren and Thomas Skouteris (eds), *The New Histories of International Criminal Law. Retrials* (OUP 2019). Immi Tallgren and Frédéric Mégret (eds), *The Dawn of a Discipline: International Criminal Justice and its Early Exponents* (OUP 2020) touches on some of the issues of cross-border crime but it too tends to focus on the crimes under international law.

In order to provide some stability to our approach, the broad definitions of the concepts we use in this book (although not every author writing in the book uses these terms consistently) are as follows:

*Transnational crime* (transboundary crime, transborder crime, extraterritorial crime) we understand as consisting of crimes that have (i) actual or (ii) potential transboundary effects or (iii) transboundary moral impact.

*Transnational criminal law* is used here to mean the 'suppression by international law through domestic penal law of criminal activities that have (i) actual or (ii) potential transboundary effects or (iii) transboundary moral impact'.[5] To put it another way, transnational criminal law can be defined doctrinally as (a) horizontal international obligations between states to criminalize and cooperate, and (b) the vertical application of criminal law and procedures by those states to individuals in order to meet these international obligations. [6] Typically, although not necessarily, this international obligation arises in the form of a treaty between states (*suppression convention*)[7] and in this sense there is an overlap between the concept of 'treaty based crimes'[8] and transnational criminal law. The former, however, is really a subset of a broad transnational criminal law entailing all forms of international law designed to suppress transnational crimes through domestic penal law.

*International criminal law (stricto sensu)* 'encompasses all norms that establish, exclude, or otherwise regulate responsibility for crimes under international law'.[9] In the terminology used here, international criminal law has the same meaning as '*Völkerstrafrecht*',[10] '*droit international pénal*'[11] and '*derecho internacional penal*'[12] and can be distinguished from transnational criminal law.

[5] Neil Boister, 'Further Reflections on the Concept of Transnational Criminal Law' (2015) 6(1) Transnational Legal Theory 9, 13.

[6] See Neil Boister, *An Introduction to Transnational Criminal Law* (2nd edn, OUP 2018) 18; see also Florian Jeßberger, 'Transnationales Strafrecht, Internationales Strafrecht, Transnationale Strafrechtsgeltung—eine Orientierung' in G-P Calliess (ed), *Transnationales Recht* (Mohr Siebeck 2014).

[7] For a list of major suppression conventions referred to in this book see Appendix.

[8] See eg Mahmoud Cherif Bassiouni, 'The Sources and Content of International Criminal Law: A Theoretical Framework' in Mahmoud Cherif Bassiouni (ed), *International Criminal Law*, Vol I (2nd edn, Transnational 1999) 3, 32 et seq; William A Schabas, *An Introduction to the International Criminal Court* (5th edn, CUP 2017) 83 et seq; Neil Boister, 'Treaty-Based Crimes' in Antonio Cassese and others (eds), *The Oxford Companion to International Criminal Justice* (OUP 2009) 540.

[9] Gerhard Werle and Florian Jeßberger, *Principles of International Criminal Law* (4th edn, OUP 2020) para 97 (hereafter Werle and Jeßberger, *Principles*).

[10] See Gerhard Werle and Florian Jeßberger, *Völkerstrafrecht* (5th edn, Mohr Siebeck 2020) para 97 (hereafter Werle and Jeßberger, *Völkerstrafrecht*).

[11] See, also for the distinction from 'droit pénal international', Sandra Szurek, 'Historique: La Formation du Droit International Pénal' in Hervé Ascensio, Emmanuel Decaux and Alain Pellet (eds), *Droit International Pénal* (Pédone 2000) 7, 10 et seq (hereafter Ascensio and others, *Droit International Penal*).

[12] See also for the distinction from 'derecho penal internacional', Antonio Quintano Ripollès, *Tratado de Derecho Penal Internacional e Internacional Penal*, Vol I (1955) and Vol II (Instituto Francisco de Vitoria 1957).

*Crimes under international law (core crimes)* 'are any crimes that involve direct responsibility under international law'.[13] These so-called 'core crimes',[14] genocide, crimes against humanity, war crimes and aggression,[15] are the 'most serious crimes of concern to the international community'.[16] In contrast, the term 'international crime' is best reserved to include all crimes with an international element, no matter how peripheral.[17]

*International criminal law (lato sensu)* means all norms of criminal law that have some relationship with an international or foreign law norm whether direct or indirect (and thus include international criminal law *stricto sensu*, transnational criminal law and rules of extraterritorial jurisdiction).[18]

The concept of transnational criminal law as used in this book appears to have emerged out of transnational police cooperation in the 19th century. Building an international regime for police cooperation faced differences in jurisdiction, the absence of a universal system of extradition and unwillingness to expel political asylum seekers.[19] The concept of social defence became popular in organizations like the *Internationale Kriminalistische Vereinigung* (IKV) as a sociologically focused response to the doctrinal focus of classical schools of penal law.[20] While social defence in a general sense was concerned primarily with crime control, in a transnational context the specific objects of social defence were those cross-border criminals considered a threat to all societies. It justified the use of repressive measures against them by states acting together in a kind of collective effort to protect their own security. According to Lewis, leading scholars in the *Association International de Droit Pénal* (AIDP) such as Pella and Saldaña believed 'that economic and social interdependence necessarily created a form of international

[13] See eg Werle and Jeßberger, *Principles* (n 9) para 97.

[14] On the concept of 'core crimes', see, inter alia, Bruce Broomhall, *International Justice and the International Criminal Court* (OUP 2004) 10 (hereafter Broomhall, *International Justice*).

[15] See eg Robert Cryer and others, *An Introduction to International Criminal Law and Procedure* (4th edn, CUP 2019) 4; David Luban, Julie R O'Sullivan and David P Stewart, *International and Transnational Criminal Law* (Kluwer 2010) 4. For a broader concept see Antonio Cassese and others, *International Criminal Law* (3rd edn, OUP 2013) 21, who include, in addition to the crimes named in the text, torture outside of armed conflict or systematic attacks on civilian populations and international terrorism.

[16] See International Criminal Court Statute, Preamble (4), (9) and art 5.

[17] A number of writers distinguish between international crimes in the narrow sense (crimes under international law) and in the broad sense: see eg Ascensio and others, *Droit International Pénal* (n 11) 249 et seq ('les crimes contre la paix et la sécurité de l'humanité' and 'les autres infractions internationalement définies'); see also Broomhall, *International Justice* (n 14) 34 et seq; Luigi Condorelli, 'Présentation de la IIe partie', in Ascensio and others, *Droit International Pénal* (n 11) 241, 241; Charles C Jalloh, 'The Nature of the Crimes in the African Criminal Court' (2017) 15 JICJ 799, 802 et seq.

[18] See eg Mahmoud Cherif Bassiouni, *Introduction to International Criminal Law* (2nd edn, Nijhoff 2013) 1; Antonio Cassese, *International Criminal Law* (2nd edn, OUP 2008) 3. Interpreted in this broad way, the term 'international criminal law' corresponds to the German term 'Internationales Strafrecht': see Sabine Gless, *Internationales Strafrecht Grundriss für Studium und Praxis* (Helbing Lichtenhahn 2015) nos 8–34; Werle and Jeßberger, *Völkerstrafrecht* (n 10) para 131 et seq, See also Kai Ambos, *Internationales Strafrecht* (5th edn, CH Beck 2018) § 7, para 275.

[19] Lewis, *The Birth* (n 3) 21.

[20] ibid 22–26.

solidarity that must be codified in law'.[21] Saldaña's concept of 'universal social defence' was sufficiently broad to embrace a range of offences affecting state security.[22] Pella planned for an 'inter-state' criminal law to regulate interactions between states.[23] He considered counterfeiting, for example, to be an activity impacting upon the interest that every state possessed in safeguarding the security of the international monetary system.[24] The AIDP advocated for an international court to protect states against inter alia transnational crime[25] and for an international penal code, and for the reform of the law of extradition and police cooperation.[26] In 1931, in a preparatory report to a League Committee on the possible unification of criminal law, Pella made the grand claim that the multilateral suppression conventions then in vogue as a tool against cross-border crime revealed 'the tendency to secure international solidarity against criminality by the unification of certain forms of charges in the law of various countries'.[27] Against this we have Jessup's more pragmatic stock-taking of these histories in 1956:

> A certain amount of ... solidarity had developed, particularly over the last 100 years in regard to activities such as piracy, the ... slave trade, the narcotics traffic, and traffic in obscene publications and in woman and children.[28]

Unification was motivated in part out of need to ensure respect for *nullum crimen sine lege* in a transnational context.[29] The concern for this linchpin of criminal justice systems in cross-border cooperation marks one path of development eventually leading to the acknowledgement of individual rights in transnational criminal law.[30] At an early stage, Saldaña's concept of 'universal individual defence' could have provided a vision for a protection of individual rights within the transnational space but failed to gain traction in practice.[31] Although his ideas did not trigger a global advancement, other scholars encouraged an acknowledgment of

[21] ibid 7.

[22] Ignacio de la Rasilla del Moral, 'International Criminal Justice as Universal Social Defence: Quintiliano Saldaña (1878–1938)' in Immi Tallgren and Frédéric Mégret (eds), *The Dawn of a Discipline: International Criminal Justice and its Early Exponents* (OUP 2020) 118, 127 (hereafter del Moral, 'International Criminal Justice').

[23] In Vesapasian Pella, *La Criminalité Collective des États et le Droit Penal de L'Avenir* (Imprimerie de l'Etat 1925).

[24] Lewis, *The Birth* (n 3) 119.

[25] ibid 79, 108.

[26] ibid 101.

[27] League of Nations, *Penal and Penitentiary Questions: Improvements in Penal Administration, Report of the Fifth Committee*, LON Doc A.70.1931.IV, 21 September 1931, 1, fn 1.

[28] Philip Jessup, *Transnational Law* (Yale UP 1956) 58.

[29] MA Caloyanni, 'An International Criminal Court' (1928) 14 Transactions of the Grotius Society 69, 75; Lewis, *The Birth* (n 3) 115–16.

[30] Sabine Gless 'Bird's-eye View and Worm's-eye View: Towards a Defendant-based Approach in Transnational Criminal Law' (2015) 6(1) Transnational Legal Theory 117.

[31] Del Moral, 'International Criminal Justice' (n 22) 131–32.

treaty rights as individual entitlements.[32] Overall, however, individual rights were neglected in transnational criminal law until relatively recently. Recently, courts and legal scholars have been motivated mostly by practical dilemmas to think about individuals' legal position when subject to transnational prosecutions. At the same time there has been a growing understanding in recent times that transnational cooperation in criminal matters has collided with liberal principles like the principle of legality.[33] We have seen an increasing concern with reform of the system to accommodate individuals with the grant of transnational equivalents to judicial and defence rights that had already been established in domestic criminal justice systems in the 19th century. A fundamental shift is taking place with this human rights turn, a shift that reflects the changing status of the individual under international law: individuals can now claim rights under transnational criminal law.[34] Although this development is patchy and inconsistent, arguably the seeds had already been planted in the inter-war period.

The inter-war period also saw a growing division between the notion of internationalism, which found expression in the enforcement of 'crimes under international law' at the end of World War II (focused on external sovereignty/peace[35]), and transnationalism, the idea of the coordination of the enforcement of sovereign penal laws (focused on internal sovereignty/crime control).[36] The former was a muddy amalgam of victim-centred individualized justice hung on the distinct concept of criminalization of aggressive war, which evolved into international criminal law (*stricto sensu*) after 1942 (only in the 1990s did we see a real shift in the organizing principle to security of individuals from atrocity).[37]

The latter, which evolved into transnational criminal law, is not and has never been a homogenous category. From its early days it has contained within it a range

[32] See, however, Jean Spiropoulos, 'L'individu et le droit international' (1929) 30 RdC 191, 197 or Nicolas Politis, *Les nouvelles tendances du droit international* (Hachette 1927) 55–93, 76.

[33] See eg Monique Mann, Ian Warren and Sally Kennedy, 'The Legal Geographies of Transnational Cyber-prosecutions: Extradition, Human rights and Forum Shifting' (2018) 19(2) Global Crime 107; Neil Boister, 'The "Bad Global Citizen", "Naked" in the "Transnational Penal Space"' in Mikkel Jarle Christensen and Neil Boister (eds) *New Perspectives on the Structure of Transnational Criminal Justice* (Brill 2018) 12. There has been specific concern in the EU: Annika Suominen, 'What Role for Legal Certainty in Criminal Law Within the Area of Freedom, Security and Justice in the EU?' (2014) 2(1) Bergen Journal of Criminal Law & Criminal Justice 1–3; Sabine Gless, 'A New Test for Mens Rea? Safeguarding Legal Certainty in a European Area of Freedom, Security and Justice' (2011) 2 EuCLR 114; Valsamis Mitsilegas and Fabio Giuffrida, 'The European Public Prosecutor's Office and Human Rights' in Willem Geelhoed, Leendert Erkelens and Arjen Meij (eds), *Shifting Perspectives on the European Public Prosecutor's Office* (TMC Asser Press 2018) 59–98.

[34] See eg *Cox v Kanada*, Human Rights Committee Meeting 31 October 1994, CCPR/C/52/D/539/1993, No 539/1993, para 16.1: '[I]f a State party to the [UNO-Pakt II] takes a decision relating to a person within its jurisdiction, and the necessary and foreseeable consequence is that that person's rights under the [UNO-Pakt II] will be violated in another jurisdiction, the State party itself may be in violation of the [UNO-Pakt II]'; LaGrand *(Germany v United States of America)* (Judgment) [2001] ICJ Rep 466, para 77.

[35] Only in the 1990s did the focus of internationalism shift.

[36] See Lewis, *The Birth* (n 3) 124, 149.

[37] ibid 151, 180.

of different tendencies. For example, the inter-war period saw a growing tension between on the one hand the idea of social convergence and solidarity driving ever closer unification of criminal laws, and on the other hands particularist state interest in the suppression of different crimes. The unification movement championed by scholars like Pella was at the internationalist/universalist end of the transnational criminal law continuum but it failed to get real support in state practice. Indeed, while universalist language was common in what could be described as the zenith of transnational criminal law in the 1980s and 1990s, state practice still supported a transnational/particularist approach, and arguably the latter approach has grown even more dominant in the last three decades as influential states turned away from UN conventions to soft law instruments to control transnational crime emanating from other states.

The histories of transnational criminal law discussed in this volume, however, do reveal programmatic tendencies that idealized movement to a global community, a sense that international legal frameworks should be developed to drive reforms of domestic laws framing and dealing with cross-border crime towards something more effective from the perspective of a slowly unifying world. These histories also reveal that these programmatic communitarian tendencies existed in tension with a range of more or less familiar stumbling blocks which, in addition to simple impediments to change based on a widespread and enduring domestic sovereignty over both domestic criminal law and its enforcement, includes programmatic tendencies of a more particularistic kind, 'fake' international communities representing the interests of groups of powerful states as the interests of all. Perhaps most disruptive of the notion that a rapidly globalizing world should inevitably lead to a global social solidarity, the existence of which was established by a range of different agreements to suppress different types of crime, was the evidence that these agreements were largely developed in some greater or lesser degree of isolation from one another, by officials and civil society advocates who did not see themselves as working to some grand plan. The grand plan may only have existed in the eyes of scholars in the criminal sciences looking down upon the various efforts from a bird's eye view. The residue of these ideas were the elements or fragments of agreements that were subsequently used as negotiating elements for future conventions. So, not a grand plan, but a toolbox.

The structure of the book flows from its conceptual, substantive and procedural concerns: Chapters 1-7 are concerned with conceptual and institutional development, and the phases of legal development it covers flow in a roughly chronological order from very early precursors, through early practices in the 18th century, into the 19th century and the first wave of treaty-making, then into the League era. The punctuation point is World War II which divides much of these histories from the 1970s and the rise of modern transnational criminal law. In Chapter 1, Karl Härter explores the 18th- and 19th-century 'breeding ground' of many of the transnational criminal procedures dealt with later in this volume. His focus is on early modern

Europe and the *ius commune*, where, as he illustrates, acceptance of jurisdictional claims to enforce domestic law over conduct that occurred extraterritorially was driven by a shared interest in acting against certain kinds of criminals with loose connections to particular states. In Chapter 2, Michele Pifferi focuses his attention on the generally ignored fact that in the late 19th and early 20th century influential criminological reformers relied heavily on the notion of 'social defence', which provided a foundational conceptual justification for the modernization of approaches to the transformation of criminal law to meet transnational criminal threats. He shows how they used international associations such as the AIDP as venues for developing their ideas about modernization of practices and institutions, and then used these associations to influence state practice through treaty-making. In Chapter 3, Neil Boister surveys the history of the crime suppression conventions from the beginning of the 19th century but with the main focus being on the inter-war period in the 20th century. He shows how the indirect system of application through national criminal law and sustained respect for what might be called penal sovereignty made it difficult for scholars of the day to incorporate these offences within a grand scheme of international criminal law. In Chapter 4, Kerstin von Lingen explores the parallel development of international prohibitions on the use of force and the crime against humanity to the prosaic development of transnational criminal law in the League era concerned with drugs and humans. Her main concern is to show how representatives from small states, scholars and NGO activists, came to form a transnational epistemic community that pressed for change to first how state aggression is controlled under international law and then how crimes against civilians are to be dealt with in the latter phases of World War II. In Chapter 5, Mangai Natarajan explores the impact of the influential criminologist Gerhard Mueller on the formation of the concept of transnational crime and its institutionalization in the post- World War II period. She shows how he introduced the term transnational crime in the mid-1970s at the UN Crime Congress in Switzerland as a criminological term to describe cross-border crime, and how it slowly evolved into a legal rather than criminological descriptor and was taken up by the UN criminal justice bureaucracy. Frank Meyer's historical focus in Chapter 6 is on the post-World War II period and the activities of the UN, Council of Europe, OECD and the EU in transnational crime control. Advocating an expansion of the scope of transnational criminal law to include a broad range of law-making processes, he provides a detailed multi-dimensional map of these processes, based on a linear model of inputs into the legal process, conversion of these inputs into legal content, and outputs. In Chapter 7, Robert Currie and Sara Wharton examine the various failed or not fully realized attempts to establish an alternative to national criminal jurisdiction over transnational crimes, in the shape of various different models of transnational criminal court. They range from the mixed commissions against slavery in the 19th century to the criminal chamber of the African Court sketched out in the Malabo Protocol. A variety of reasons appear to drive these initiatives but they have one thing in common—an incapacity within the current system to deal with certain kinds of transnational crime at all or in a politically acceptable manner. The concern is not new. Donnedieu de Vabres imagined an international court solely concerned with crimes where the prosecution might result in 'complex and sensitive political situations between states'.[38]

Chapters 8–17 cover histories of specific crimes. Although they also reach back into the 19th century, the scope of attention tends to focus on the League era and the post-1945 era. In Chapter 8, Masha Fedorova and Piet Hein van Kempen eschew explorations of the nature of piracy to focus on whether there is some legal basis for an obligation in conventional and customary international law on states to criminalize piracy, concluding that such an obligation is absent. But the main thrust of the chapter is an historical survey which tries to decipher why this is the case. In Chapter 9, Roger Clark shifts attention to slave-trading, but rather than focusing on the late 19th century and early 20th century multilateral treaties against slave-trading he narrows the focus to early treaties entered into with African potentates by Great Britain. Clark illustrates how these treaties served as vehicles for the slow expansion of British enforcement power against slavers, suggesting that extraterritorial enforcement is a key driver in the expansion of transnational criminal law. In Chapter 10, Ben Saul takes us back to legal antecedents of modern terrorism laws, unfolding a story of how increases in the level and sophistication of law enforcement cooperation against anarchists led eventually to the attempted negotiation under League auspices of an anti-terrorism convention, the AIDP's attempts to draft a code of common offences for mankind including terrorism, and the work of the International Bureau for the Unification of Criminal Laws (IBUCL) in trying to unify national criminal laws under the League. In Chapter 11, Heli Askola examines the early history of international instruments for the suppression of the trafficking in women and children involved in so called 'white slavery' as precursors to the more recent developments relating to human trafficking. She challenges the notion of the linear progression in the development of the law and illustrates that the contests between various NGOs and government organizations meant that this development was neither smooth nor uncontested. In Chapter 12, Andreas Schloenhardt describes how the turn to criminalization of migrant smuggling has to be seen against the background of the Post-Cold War period and the clamp-down by Western states on smuggling across their borders, reconstructed now as a security threat. The fact that this criminalization remains in tension with the relative neglect of migrants' human rights he argues, reveals the true nature of the Protocol as a suppression convention.

[38] Frédéric Mégret, 'Henri Donnedieu de Vabres: Penal Liberal, Moderate Internationalist and Nuremberg Judge' in Immi Tallgren and Frédéric Mégret (eds), *The Dawn of a Discipline: International Criminal Justice and its Early Exponents* (OUP 2020) 146, 152 citing Henri Donnedieu de Varbes, *La Répression Internationale des Délits de Droit de Gens* (Les Editions internationals 1935) 17.

In Chapter 13, Serena Forlati examines a more recent development, the UN Convention against Transnational Organised Crime (UNTOC). Standing back from the treaty, she analyses how the converging concerns of European states with cross-border crime and US concerns about the post-Cold War threat posed by organized crime together with a willingness to adopt flexible solutions made agreement on such a broad programmatic instrument possible. In Chapter 14, Cecily Rose uses the failed negotiation of an agreement about illicit payments in the UN in the 1970s to throw light on how the international legal definition of corruption became constricted to a narrow focus on bribery even though developing states were seeking a broader instrument that included ethical standards for transnational corporations to control rampant corporate corruption and political interference in developing states. In Chapter 15, Michael Elliot and Felix Lüth examine the development of corporate criminal liability. Reaching back to its historical roots in the United States, they discuss how the Foreign Corrupt Practices Act was internationalized through organizations like the OECD and FATF and in a more diluted fashion through the UN, giving corruption its current character as a public-sector problem committed by corrupt individuals rather than by institutions as a whole. Trying to explain why it has taken so long, in Chapter 16, Arianna Visconti traces the relatively recent evolution of attempts to suppress the trafficking in cultural objects towards criminalization. She sets out how the halting attempts to criminalize in the failed Council of Europe's Delphi Convention have reached only potential fruition in the latest pure criminal law treaty, the Council of Europe's 2017 Nicosia Convention, and questions whether criminalization really is the solution. In Chapter 17, Dominik Brodowski digs through the early days of cybercrime's emergence emphasizing how it acquired a strong transnational element in various ways and how dominant legal frameworks such as the Budapest Convention emerged from soft law and national legislation. He examines the more recent shift from a prosecutorial focus to the pursuit of evidence held abroad, and the rising political tension around the Russian- and Chinese-backed initiative backing a UN convention on cybercrime.

Chapter 18, the scope of which spans the League and post-1945 eras, deals with attribution of liability. In Chapter 18, Anneke Petzsche explores, through analysis of the provisions on modes of responsibility in the suppression conventions, whether there is a general part of transnational criminal law. Interestingly, Saldaña postulated a global penal code that had both a general part and a special part.[39] While the suppression conventions have spelled out the conduct elements of the offences, and latterly paid more attention to differentiating perpetration and participation, nevertheless, she argues that the necessary margin of domestic

[39] Del Moral, 'International Criminal Justice' (n 22) 135.

appreciation given to states when criminalizing, a margin of appreciation that preserves domestic doctrinal coherency, disrupts the coherence of any general part.

Chapters 19-22 examine procedure and jurisdiction. Its scope is broader: back to early beginnings, across the 18th and 19th centuries, through the League era to the 1970s and 80s. In Chapter 19, Florian Jeßberger explores the development of criminal jurisdiction in multilateral suppression conventions. He identifies general trends, such as extension, specification and standardization, and shows that suppression conventions oscillate between simple replication of firmly settled bases of jurisdiction and integration of innovative, typically subject-matter-specific bases, often pushing the boundaries of the established law of criminal jurisdiction. He also points to the repercussions of jurisdictional rules in transnational criminal law on the ambit of domestic criminal law, by (as treaty practice) shaping the permissive rules under customary international law which limit domestic authority to punish. In Chapter 20, Joanna Harrington traces the development of modern extradition law back to the 19th century. Against a background of interactions between different states' legal systems, the impact of peace treaties, the impact of the law of asylum, the growing use of multilateral treaties, the importance of counter-terrorism law, she conducts us on a tour of the principal flash-points in extradition, and the measures such as the political offence exception, and exceptions to this exception, taken to defuse them. Drawing out the theme of conflict between practice of police cooperation and political imperatives, in Chapter 21, Saskia Hufnagel shows how modern police cooperation grew up in continental Europe from harmonized practices imposed during the Napoleonic era. She shows how minimal political engagement and the overriding concern with technical matters carried through to the founding conferences that led to Interpol. Finally, in Chapter 22, Sabine Gless highlights the individual's journey from an object of government caprice, susceptible to arrest on a foreign warrant without legal protection, to a legally protected defendant in the frameworks of transnational criminal law. Using in particular Germany and Switzerland as examples of different approaches taken in continental Europe, she maps the evolution of defendants' rights from domestic criminal justice to European Human Rights from the 19th to the 21st century, and the slow shift from a state-centred understanding of transnational criminal law to the acknowledgement of individual rights under a human rights narrative.

A number of general themes are identifiable in these histories:

*Roots in law enforcement*: The adoption of formal instruments for cooperation between states against transnational crime has usually been preceded by more informal law enforcement cooperation, and inevitably it is law enforcement practices which percolate into these formal legal obligations. In result movement to more formal cooperation has tended to involve pragmatic solution-seeking to specific incidents or specific trends in harmful activity, although it is not always clear what is actually being targeted. These roots in law enforcement have also tended to cement a quite narrowly drawn notion of the target category as cross-border criminals pursuing private gain or goals, which has only slowly expanded to include among those private goals activities like terrorism and cybercrime. Negotiating states have been at pains to try to avoid criminalizing the activities of other states but it has been difficult in regard to terrorism and cybercrime (criminalization of hacking for political reasons, some of which appear to support state strategic goals). Acting to control these groups has seen a continuity in the rationalization of justification in ideas ranging from social defence to crime control. These law enforcement roots do mean, however, that jurisdiction and more particularly the enforcement of jurisdiction is a more dominant purpose than harmonization of criminal laws; criminalization is a means to enforcement.

*The turn to suppression:* There is a perceptible drift from a range of approaches to the dominance of suppression through criminal law as the key to coordination of enforcement, and there are perceptible high points in this trend in the inter-war period and in the 1980s and 90s. However, this 'turn towards suppression' did not always coincide across different types of crime. The 'turn to suppression' was engineered through indirect reform of states' domestic criminal laws and the de-territorialization of jurisdiction and the enforcement of that jurisdiction, and through the neglect of individuals' rights.

*Incrementalism:* These histories show that international coordination against transnational crime was notoriously difficult because of concerns about preservation of sovereignty. It thus usually developed at a very slow pace with minimal rather than maximal standards relating to the extension of jurisdiction, direct police to police cooperation, legal assistance obligations and in particular extradition. Dramatic innovations have tended to fail when they lost focus on technical crime control or ushered in too dramatic a change. That appears to be why dress rehearsals or dry runs for regulation in crimes like human trafficking, terrorism and corruption appear to have been necessary precursors for successful treaty-making decades later.

*Isolationism*: Most of the particular suppression regimes (combinations of different measures against particular types of transnational crime) have developed in isolation from others. It is remarkable, for instance, how hermeneutic the seal was around the drugs regime until fairly late in the 20th century. Nevertheless, technical measures in one regime tend to cross-pollinate into others, resulting in the same or very similar tools being used against different crimes and criminals.

*Influence:* Transnational criminal laws touch on the lives of millions of people every day yet ironically they are the product of a handful of individuals who tend to turn up in different diplomatic conferences negotiating responses to different types of crimes. Identifying these influencers is sometimes difficult, but it may serve to explain the measure of convergence in approaches between different prohibition regimes. The use of transnational criminal law in the service of clubbable interests among powerful states is better understood. Certain states have responded through transnational criminal law to their concerns using domestic legislative precursors as models. They have also ensured that a narrow focus on illicit commerce prevents expansion into coverage of harmful activities of licit commerce.

*Changing methods of norm dispersion:* One of the more specific changes that is illustrated by these histories is that different methods of control have been resorted to by 'global policemen' such as Great Britain and the United States. Thus, we have—to put it very roughly—seen a shift from bilateral treaties, to limited, then broader participation multilateral treaties and then into soft law or limited participation treaties, a constant shifting that is reflective of the political struggle to maintain instruments effective in achieving crime control. The more recent shift to soft law results, for example, from a growing tension between more instrumental unilateral approaches and more mutual (but perhaps less effective) multilateral approaches under the auspices of the UN.

*Tension between statism (state interests) and globalism (individual interests)*: The characteristic indirect mechanism where criminalization/jurisdiction/legal assistance remains in the hands of the nation state and international instruments are used to outline criminal, jurisdictional and procedural norms, reflects the essentially functional nature of transnational nominal law and its importance to states. Attempts by scholars to sew the system more tightly into larger schemes of global criminalization such as penal denationalization or international criminal codification never really reached fruition in practice as the focus remained pragmatic and contingent on preservation of sovereign difference. The location of penal power remains in the state, and states are resistant to direct attempts to harmonize, which threatens their control.

These are not the only themes identifiable in these histories, but drawing them out here provides a useful way of framing what follows.

# 1

# Norms, Procedures and Practices of Transnational Criminal Law in 18th and Early 19th-Century Europe

*Karl Härter*

## I. Introduction

It is a common assumption that transnational criminal law emerged in the 19th century in the context of globalization, international law and the formation of nation states.[1] However, if we apply the definition of transnational criminal law as a 'system that attempts to suppress harmful activity that crosses borders or threatens to do so', comprised of various types of cross-border crime, transnationally agreed norms and a variety of procedures 'against harmful activity that affects a given state but occurs in part or whole beyond the state's territory', we can trace the historical roots farther into the past.[2] It allows us to study the formation of the still relevant norms, procedures and practices of transnational criminal law within the legal framework of early modern *ius commune* and their further development in the age of the French and European revolutions (1789–1848). This particularly concerns:

- the jurisdictions that could prosecute, adjudicate and punish extra-territorial/cross-border crimes and foreign perpetrators;
- transboundary cooperation such as mutual legal assistance, requisition proceedings, exchange of search and arrest warrants, immediate pursuit and police cooperation;
- criminal asylum and extradition, in particular the emergence of bilateral agreements, treaties, laws and the respective provisions and principles; and

[1] Neil Boister and Robert J Currie (eds), *Routledge Handbook of Transnational Criminal Law* (Routledge 2015) (hereafter Boister and Currie, *Handbook*); Neil Boister, *An Introduction to Transnational Criminal Law* (2nd edn, OUP 2018) (hereafter Boister, *Introduction*); for Germany: Florian Jeßberger, *Der transnationale Geltungsbereich des deutschen Strafrechts. Grundlagen und Grenzen der Geltung des deutschen Strafrechts für Taten mit Auslandsberührung* (Mohr Siebeck 2011) 42 (hereafter Jeßberger, *Geltungsbereich*).

[2] Neil Boister and Robert J Currie, 'Introduction' in Boister and Currie (eds), *Handbook* (n 1) 2.

Karl Härter, *Norms, Procedures and Practices of Transnational Criminal Law in 18th and Early 19th-Century Europe*
In: *Histories of Transnational Criminal Law*. Edited by: Neil Boister, Sabine Gless and Florian Jeßberger, Oxford University Press. © Karl Härter 2021. DOI: 10.1093/oso/9780192845702.003.0002

- legal concepts and narratives of transnational crime and transboundary operating criminals.

This chapter gives an overview about these areas with a spatial focus on the Holy Roman Empire (of the German Nation) characterized by hybrid jurisdictional structures and the European *ius commune*. Although the legal character changed considerably after the French and European revolutions, to some extent established norms, procedures and practices of pre-modern transnational criminal law persisted.[3] Hence, the focus here is on *ius commune* criminal law and jurisdiction[4] and therefore on *droit pénal international* (*Strafanwendungsrecht* or, traditionally, *internationales Strafrecht*) and not on *droit international pénal* (*Völkerstrafrecht*).[5] Although concerned with issues such as the principle of *aut dedere aut iudicare*, pre-modern international law only fragmentarily covered transnational criminal law, whereas the jurisprudence of continental common criminal law provides a systematic access to norms, procedures and exemplary cases of transboundary practices.[6]

## II. Jurisdiction, Inquisitorial Procedure and Transnational Criminal Law

The core elements of pre-modern transnational criminal law were shaped by *ius commune* and the inquisitorial system that established the principle of the public prosecution of any crime by any competent jurisdiction and/or public authority. These authorities were obliged to prosecute every crime and perpetrator they became aware of and investigate the material truth and substantive facts through a criminal procedure that included local investigative proceedings and the adjudication by a central judicial body. The inquisitorial system extended to crimes,

[3] Karl Härter and others (eds), *The Transnationalisation of Criminal Law in the Nineteenth and Twentieth Century. Political Crime, Police Cooperation, Security Regimes and Normative Orders* (Klostermann 2019) (hereafter Härter and others, *Transnationalisation*). For non-historians, the term pre-modern denotes the Middle Ages and early modern period, followed by the 'saddle period' (Sattelzeit) from 1750 to 1850, followed by the Modern period which begins in the 19th century.

[4] For the development of criminal jurisdiction in suppression treaties since the 19th century see Jeßberger, Chapter 19 in this book.

[5] Frédéric Mégret, 'International Criminal Justice History Writing as Anachronism: The Past that Did Not Lead to the Present' in Immi Tallgren and Thomas Skouteris (eds), *The New Histories of International Criminal Law. Retrials* (OUP 2019) 72, 77–81.

[6] Pasquale Fiore, *Trattato di diritto internazionale pubblico* (Unione Tipografico-Editrice 1879) (hereafter Fiore, *Trattato*); Carl Ludwig von Bar, *International Law: Private and Criminal* (Soule & Bugbee 1883) 620–75 (hereafter von Bar, *International Law*); Josef Kohler, *Internationales Strafrecht* (Ferdinand Enke 1917) (hereafter Kohler, *Internationales Strafrecht*); Friedrich Meili, *Lehrbuch des internationalen Strafrechts und Strafprozessrechts* (Füssli 1910) 30–69 (hereafter Meili, *Lehrbuch*); Henri Donnedieu de Vabres, *Introduction à l'étude du droit pénal international. Essai d'histoire et de critique sur la compétence criminelle dans les rapports avec l'étranger* (Paris 1922) (hereafter de Vabres, *Introduction*).

offenders and facts outside a country/jurisdiction and legally founded three competent and competing courts of jurisdiction:

- the criminal court in whose jurisdiction a crime had been committed: the *forum delicti commissi*,
- the criminal court in whose jurisdiction a criminal was born or residing: the *forum domicilii*, and
- the criminal court in whose jurisdiction a suspect had been apprehended: the *forum deprehensionis*.[7]

Based on the obligation that a competent judicial authority should prosecute every crime and investigate its facts and circumstances, the *forum deprehensionis* became of prime relevance for the development of transnational criminal law. Like a court in whose jurisdiction a crime was committed, the judicial authorities that had apprehended a fugitive or foreign perpetrator were obliged to *ex officio* start an inquisitorial investigation, since it was in the interest of every state that no crime should go unpunished. This dogmatic principle was widely adopted in criminal law.[8] If the court could identify a concrete crime and competent court, it could request the remission (transport or extradition) of the perpetrator to this jurisdiction. Italian and French jurisprudence stressed that the *forum delicti commissi* should have the higher priority and this was also a recurrent practice.[9] However, if a remission was refused, the *forum deprehensionis* was obliged to continue the inquisitorial procedure, which included the investigation of further crimes or accomplices, regardless of whether such crimes were committed in another territory or by a foreigner. Commonly the interrogation of a perpetrator who had committed a crime in the jurisdiction of the *forum deprehensionis* revealed accomplices or offenders in other territories. Categories of suspects such as vagrants, members of mobile robber gangs, ex-soldiers, deserters or other kinds of mobile and foreign perpetrators were labelled as transnational threats to public security and to the interests of the state because they were regarded as mobile and masterless. It was feared they would commit theft, robbery, murder and transboundary crimes such as smuggling, counterfeiting, illegal migration or desertion and would escape criminal prosecution by moving across borders into another jurisdiction or into a criminal asylum.[10] The actual transnational practice of prosecution was limited to

[7] Von Bar, *International Law* (n 6) 620–25; Kohler, *Internationales Strafrecht* (n 6) 39–67; Meili, *Lehrbuch* (n 6) 75 et seq.

[8] Benedict Carpzov, *Practica Nova Imperialis Saxonica Rerum Criminalium* (Wittenberg 1646) III q 110 (hereafter Carpzov, *Practica Nova*); Prospero Farinacci, *Praxis et theoricae criminalis* … (Frankfurt am Main 1622) lib I, tit 1, q VII; Giulio Claro (Julius Clarus), *Opera omnia sive practica civilis atque criminalis* (Geneva 1666) lib V, q XXXIX (hereafter Claro, *Opera omnia*).

[9] See de Vabres, *Introduction* (n 6) 353–67; Meili, *Lehrbuch* (n 6) 40–60.

[10] Karl Härter, 'Security and Cross-border Political Crime: The Formation of Transnational Security Regimes in 18th and 19th Century Europe' (2013) 38 Historical Social Research 96 (hereafter Härter, 'Formation of Transnational Security Regimes').

serious, extra-territorial and transboundary crimes and respective criminal groups involving a transnational dimension. Remission/extradition was something of an exception, since many states/jurisdictions preferred to exercise sovereign jurisdictional power in cases with a transnational dimension (or waived proceedings).[11]

Contemporary jurisprudence debated which law should be applied in such cases: that of the *forum deprehensionis* or that of the jurisdiction where a crime had been committed. However, in practice this hardly mattered, since adjudication could be based on a variety of legal sources from *ius commune* and imperial to domestic territorial, customary and even administrative law. Hence, the legal pluralism of early modern criminal law exacerbated the problem of the competent court and the question of punishment or extradition.[12]

The *forum deprehensionis* and the obligation to prosecute every crime legally founded a criminal power that according to Georg Friedrich von Martens extended

> to everyone in the territory, whether subject or foreigner.... A Sovereign can punish foreigners, whether they have committed a crime in his dominions, or whether, after having committed it in a foreign country, they seek shelter in his dominions. In neither case is the sovereign perfectly obliged to send them for punishment in their own country, nor the place where the crime was committed.[13]

He demonstrates that international law adopted the doctrine of the *ius commune* in the form of the general principle to punish crimes or extradite criminals: *aut dedere aut iudicare.*[14] However, from the perspective of pre-modern criminal law it seems inappropriate to characterize the *forum deprehensionis* as a 'universal jurisdiction' and an obligation of all nations to punish or extradite.[15] It was rather the product of the inquisitorial system and its principles, the diversity of jurisdictions and the increase of cross-border security threats—and it involved jurisdictional conflicts and collisions and triggered the development of specific norms and procedures of transnational criminal law.

[11] Ferdinand von Martitz, *Internationale Rechtshilfe in Strafsachen. Beiträge zur Theorie des positiven Völkerrechts der Gegenwart* . . . (Leipzig 1888/1897) vol 1, 154 et seq (hereafter von Martitz, *Internationale Rechtshilfe*).

[12] Kohler, *Internationales Strafrecht* (n 6) 58 et seq; von Bar, *International Law* (n 6) 620 et seq; from the perspective of modern transnational criminal law: Boister, *Introduction* (n 1) 246 et seq.

[13] Georg Friedrich von Martens, *Summary of the Law of Nations, founded on the Treaties and Customs of the Modern Nations of Europe* (Philadelphia 1795) 106 et seq (hereafter von Martens, *Law of Nations*).

[14] Christian Maierhöfer, *'Aut dedere—aut iudicare': Herkunft, Rechtsgrundlagen und Inhalt des völkerrechtlichen Gebotes zur Strafverfolgung oder Auslieferung* (Duncker & Humblot 2006).

[15] For this older approach see Kohler, *Internationales Strafrecht* (n 6) 58–64. Modern critical view: Jeßberger, *Geltungsbereich* (n 1) 282 et seq.

## III. Transboundary Practices: Requisition, Warrants, Hot Pursuit and Police Cooperation

In this early modern period transnational mutual legal assistance took the shape of so-called requisition proceedings which could include the exchange of search and arrest warrants, court records, interrogation protocols, evidence, transfer of witnesses and suspects or extradition requests.[16]

While Roman law had already formalized judicial requisition, it was further developed in early modern criminal law with regard to the specific nature of the inquisitorial procedure. As mentioned above, investigative proceedings constituted an integral part of the criminal process and were characterized by specific forms of written communication including the dispatch of records and interrogation protocols to other judicial authorities. Courts or administrative bodies also exchanged information in criminal matters across borders using formalized proceedings involving rogatory letters (*litterae requisitoriales*),[17] that became an established practice of international law.[18] We can also observe an increasing use and exchange of search and arrest warrants and comprehensive wanted lists, which various authorities issued in print and also distributed via requisition letters to other jurisdictions and neighbouring states. They often concerned foreign, fugitive and transboundary perpetrators who had committed offences in more than one territory. Most warrants were requests for the apprehension of the suspects, but only seldom requested extradition. Instead, they compiled information on criminals, their 'milieu' and the crimes committed in various jurisdictions into comprehensive lists and collections used to support identification, investigation and adjudication. Although contemporary jurisprudence and public law attempted to develop legal rules, the use as evidence was not clearly regulated by law, but became nevertheless a part of judicial and administrative practice.[19] These search warrants and wanted lists developed into a precursor of transboundary police cooperation and were widely adopted as a mode of transnational policing and exchange of intelligence in the 19th century.[20]

[16] Comprehensive overview: Christoph Carl Stübel, *Das Criminalverfahren in den deutschen Gerichten mit besonderer Rücksicht auf das Königreich Sachsen wissenschaftlich und zum praktischen Gebrauche dargestellt*, vols 1–5 (Leipzig 1811) vol 1, 189–200, vol 3, 223–89, vol 5, 106 et seq (hereafter Stübel, *Criminalverfahren*); Heinrich Lammasch, *Auslieferungspflicht und Asylrecht. Eine Studie über Theorie und Praxis des internationalen Strafrechtes* (Leipzig 1887) 821–70 (hereafter Lammasch, *Auslieferungspflicht*); von Martitz, *Internationale Rechtshilfe* (n 11).

[17] Christian Jacob von Zwierlein and Johann Anton Koethe, *De litteris requisitorialibus ex usu Romanorum antiquiori et recentiori* (Göttingen 1758).

[18] Philip F Sutherland, 'The Use of the Letter of Request (or Letter Rogatory) for the Purpose of Obtaining Evidence for Proceedings in England and Abroad' (1982) 31 ICLQ 784; Boister, *Introduction* (n 1) 312 et seq.

[19] Heinrich Samuel Eckhold, *Exercitatio inauguralis iuridica de literis incarcerationis patentibus s. arrestatoriis, vulgo Steck-Briefen* (Leipzig 1678 and 1702); Stübel, *Criminalverfahren* (n 16) vol 3, 267–89.

[20] Karl Härter, 'Security and Transnational Policing of Political Subversion and International Crime in the German Confederation after 1815' in Beatrice de Graaf and others (eds), *Securing Europe after*

Judicial practice and contemporary jurisprudence shaped a crucial exception from formal requisition proceedings: hot pursuit of perpetrators across borders of jurisdictions, territories and states.[21] Immediate pursuit was of particular relevance in the Empire and imperial law explicitly granted the right to engage in transboundary persecution in cases of revolt, violation of public peace criminals and gangs operating across borders. However, with the formation of sovereign states the crossing of borders to pursue and arrest suspects was increasingly regarded as a violation of the territory, in particular when public officers of the pursuing state were involved. As a result, transboundary pursuit was limited to crimes committed in a border region or a mixed jurisdiction, instances where perpetrators had been caught red-handed and were escaping to a neighbouring territory, and the pursuit of dangerous and mobile criminals who might threaten the security of the country into which they were about to escape. The authorities crossing a border were required to inform local authorities as soon as possible, and in case of an arrest the transportation of the perpetrator back across a border required the consent of the concerned territorial authority or an existing agreement.[22] In the 18th century increasing conflict and abuse of abduction or expulsion further triggered the regulation of immediate pursuit in bilateral (often local) agreements and in extradition treaties (mostly concerning deserters and robber gangs) which strictly limited immediate pursuit.[23] With the French Revolution and the solidification of sovereign nation states, cross-border pursuit began to fall into disuse in the first half of the 19th century. It revived from the middle of the 19th century, however, as several countries concluded agreements on hot pursuit and police cooperation. These included various German states among themselves, Spain and Portugal (1872), and Prussia and Russia (1882).[24]

*Napoleon. 1815 and the New European Security Culture* (CUP 2019) 193 (hereafter Härter, 'Security and Transnational Policing' and de Graaf and others, *Securing Europe*); Boister, *Introduction* (n 1) 316–32.

[21] From the angle of common and international law: Glanville L Williams, 'The Juridical Basis of Hot Pursuit' (1939) 20 BYBIL 83; Nicholas M Poulantzas, *The Right of Hot Pursuit in International Law* (2nd edn, Martinus Nijhoff Publishers 2002) 4 et seq.

[22] Christian Wildvogel and Andreas Simson Biechling, *De persecutione delinquentium. Von der Nacheile …* (Jena 1709); von Martens, *Law of Nations* (n 13) 109 et seq; Wilhelm Koch, *Die Nacheile im deutschen öffentlichen Recht und im Völkerrecht* (Greifswald 1917) (hereafter Koch, *Nacheile*); Karl Härter, 'Grenzübergreifende Kriminalität von Vaganten und Räuberbanden – interterritoriale Strafverfolgung und Landessicherheit im Alten Reich (1648–1806)' in Wolfgang Wüst (ed), *Historische Kriminalitätsforschung in landesgeschichtlicher Perspektive. Fallstudien aus Bayern und seinen Nachbarländern 1500—1800 …* (Erlangen 2017) 19 (hereafter Härter, 'Grenzübergreifende Kriminalität').

[23] Example: Cartel zwischen … Dännemarck / Norwegen und … Schweden … wegen derer Deserteurs … wie auch anderer Missethäter und Ueberläuffere Anhalt- und Auslieferung, Copenhagen 1738, art 4 and 8 in: Georg Friedrich von Martens (ed), *Recueil des principaux traités d'alliance, de paix, de trêve, de neutralité, de commerce, de limites, d'échange …*, 11 vols (Göttingen 1791–1808) supp 1, 249 et seq (hereafter von Martens, *Recueil*); Cartel entre sa Majesté trés chrétienne le Roy de France & le louable Cercle de Franconie touchant le renvoy reciproque des deserteurs & malfaiteurs (Nuremberg 1741), art 4 (hereafter Cartel entre le Roy de France & le Cercle de Franconie).

[24] Koch, *Nacheile* (n 22) 23.

Transnational policing thus consisted mostly in the exchange of search warrants and wanted lists, joint cross-border patrols, arranged hot pursuit and informal coordination of police activities and security measures such as expulsion. These practices were sometimes regulated through ordinances and agreements as well as elaborated by authors of public law and pragmatic-practical literature. However, criminal jurisprudence and international law hardly achieved a dogmatic implementation of these practices in trans- or international criminal law. During the 18th and early 19th centuries, crucial proceedings and forms of transboundary cooperation in criminal matters and mutual legal assistance may well have been established in practice but the level of legal regulation through transnational criminal law was rather low.

## IV. Criminal Asylum and Extradition

The development of extradition as a crucial element of transnational criminal law was closely related to the pre-modern practice of criminal asylum.[25] Different authorities could grant asylum to a variety of refugees that had committed crimes such as homicide, infanticide, fraudulent bankruptcy, desertion or *lese majeste* and often escaped across borders. During the early modern period many states started to legally regulate criminal asylum in a transnational context and negotiated agreements with the Holy See to limit church asylum. The respective papal bulls stipulated the crimes which qualified for asylum (or were extraditable) and regulated the procedure of request, safe conduct and delivery.[26] Similar developments can be observed for secular and diplomatic asylum and particularly for political crimes with a transboundary dimension. In the 18th century several states concluded conventions, comprising of the provision not to grant asylum nor protection for fugitive rebels, assassinators or deserters.[27] Between 1750 and 1850 nearly all European states concluded transnational agreements and issued laws that heavily restricted and then finally abrogated all forms of criminal asylum. This was underpinned by enlightened criminal jurisprudence, which claimed to abolish asylum in favour of national criminal justice systems that should interact by means of extradition (the denial of extradition had the effect of granting asylum). Although revolutionary France abrogated criminal asylum as well, the French Constitution of 1793 for the

[25] See von Bar, *International Law* (n 6) 707–09; Lammasch, *Auslieferungspflicht* (n 16); S Prakash Sinha, *Asylum and International Law* (Nijhoff 1971) (hereafter Sinha, *Asylum*).

[26] Karl Härter, 'Vom Kirchenasyl zum politischen Asyl: Asylrecht und Asylpolitik im frühneuzeitlichen Alten Reich' in Martin Dreher (ed), *Das antike Asyl. Kultische Grundlagen, rechtliche Ausgestaltung und politische Funktion* (Böhlau 2003) 301.

[27] Conventions between Russia and Austria, 22 May 1746, art 14, and 21 March 1760, art 15 in von Martens, *Recueil* (n 23) supp 1, 272 et seq and supp 3, 45 et seq; see also Sinha, *Asylum* (n 25) 12 et seq.

first time stipulated political asylum for all refugees that were prosecuted by their homeland as political offenders. Subsequently, many European states adopted the principle that political crimes should be treated differently to conventional crimes, and in the first half of the 19th century the privileging of political crimes, which implied political asylum and the non-extradition of political offenders, was included in several extradition treaties. Thus early modern criminal asylum was transformed (or limited) to the political offence exception, a transformation that influenced transnational extradition law, which adopted principles and practices for the identification of extraditable crimes and procedures for requisition and surrender.[28]

As already mentioned, European criminal law established as a basic principle the remission—transfer and/or extradition—to the jurisdiction in which a crime had been committed: *remissio delinquentium ad locum commissi delicti*.[29] Although most contemporary authors sustained remission to neighbouring jurisdictions, it seems that in practice it was rather the exception. There were various reasons for this. For one thing, the requesting and receiving jurisdiction had to compensate the expense of the previous investigation and of the transfer. Additionally, the obligation of a remission *ad locum delicti* was restricted to *delictis gravibus* (felonies). In several cases the *forum deprehensionis* prosecuted suspects for the crimes committed in the domestic as well as in foreign territories. Hence, it was more convenient to punish them in one procedure for every crime. Despite the fact that contemporary criminal jurisprudence elaborated basic legal principles in a variety of treatises, the proceedings were not thoroughly regulated.[30] In many cases authorities eschewed extradition and used expulsion as a form of arbitrary penalty for dealing with suspects whose crimes could not be properly established. Existing research seems to evince that since the 18th century expulsion and deportation became frequent transboundary criminal practices, particularly used against perpetrators, suspects and vagrants who had crossed borders.[31]

This also influenced the development of the more formal specific extradition agreements and conventions. This development had already started in the 16th century with the inclusion of remission/extradition provisions in conventions

[28] Karl Härter, 'The Circulation of Transnational Criminal Law between the Americas and Germany (1848–1914) in Extradition Treaties, Juridical Discourses and International Associations' (2019) 74 Revista da Faculdade de Direito da Universidade Federal de Minas Gerais 353 (hereafter Härter, 'Circulation').

[29] Carpzov, *Practica Nova* (n 8) III q 110 n 7–9; Kohler, *Internationales Strafrecht* (n 6) 64–67.

[30] Andreas Mylius and Christian Siegfried Fritsch, *De remissione facinorosorum, eorumque transportatione per territorium alienum* … (Leipzig 1690, 1720, 1729); Johannes Fridericus Wincop and Johannes Fridericus Grabo, *De remissione delinquentium ad locum perpetrati delicti* (Erfurt 1704); Edmund Büschleb, *Commentatio de principiis juris civilis, publici et gentium circa comprehensionem, punitionem vel remissionem peregrinorum qui in alieno territorio deliquerunt, praesertim ad requisitionem exterae gentis* (Göttingen 1800).

[31] Härter, 'Grenzübergreifende Kriminalität' (n 22).

such as the *Concordia* between the kingdoms of Castile and Portugal (1569) or the *Cartel* between Denmark and Sweden, which dealt with prisoners of war, deserters and robber-arsonists (1677).[32] In the 18th century, the number of specific bilateral extradition agreements steadily increased, and they were concluded by territories of the Empire as well as between neighbouring states such as France, Spain, Denmark, the Netherlands, Poland, Austria and Great Britain. These conventions were often initially concerned with the extradition of deserters, but were gradually extended to others *malfaiteurs*, rebels, robbers and cross-border operating perpetrators.[33] Hence, they dealt with crimes against the state and public security. In this regard, the narrative of public security influenced the juridification and formalization of extradition treaties, which in a few cases were also published in the concerned states through separate domestic laws. As a result, in late 18th-century Europe a variety of conventions, agreements, cartels, patents and a few international treaties dealt with extradition. This assortment of instruments also created multinormativity and legal uncertainty for the states and their authorities as well as the fugitives involved.

They further triggered juridical discourse on criminal and international law and after the turn of the century treatises and monographs appeared that specifically dealt with extradition as the most important procedure of mutual legal assistance and transnational criminal law. This discourse conceptualized dogmatic principles which finally differentiated 'internal transfer' between jurisdictions and external extradition between states, as well as delineating extraditable crimes and the proceedings of requisition and surrender. The norms and procedures of extradition exhibit the highest grade of continuity from early modern to modern transnational criminal law.[34]

[32] Concordia entre estos reynos de Castilla y el Portugal, acerca de la remission de los delinquentes que de vn reyno a otro … (Castilla 1569); Cartel zwischen Dänemark-Norwegen, Kriegsrath Herrn Meyer und Schwedischen General- Auditeur, 1677.

[33] Cartel Sweden and Denmark, 10.4.1738, art VIII, in von Martens, *Recueil* (n 23) suppl 1, p 254 et seq; Cartel Entre Sa Majesté Tres Chres. le Roy de France et le Louable Cercle de Souabe, touchant le renovoy reciproque des deserteurs et malfaiteurs (Straßburg 1732, renewed Stuttgart 1741); Cartel entre le Roy de France & le Cercle de Franconie (n 23); Traité de San Ildefonso between France and Spain 1765, art 3 (accord d'extradition); Patent die mit des Königs von Großbritannien Majestät, in Ansehung Dero deutschen Staaten, wegen Auslieferung der Delinquenten, geschlossene Convention betreffend vom 7ten Febr. 1794. See also Christopher L Blakesley, 'The Practice of Extradition from Antiquity to Modern France and the United States: A Brief History' (1981) 4 Boston College International and Comparative Law Review 39, 50 et seq.

[34] Whereas the historiography of 'modern' extradition almost exclusively refers to extradition treaties; see Ivan A Shearer, *Extradition in International Law* (Manchester UP 1971); Joanna Harrington, 'Extradition of Transnational Criminals' in Boister and Currie, *Handbook* (n 1) 153.

## V. Early Concepts of Transnational Crime

The extradition agreements and jurisdiction of the *forum deprehensionis* that extended to *delictis extra territorium*[35] formed the basis for early modern criminal jurisprudence to engage in the rudimentary conceptualization of 'transnational crimes' and to create narratives of 'transnational criminals'.[36] It was thought that serious felonies should be punished or qualified for extradition if they were *equidem multum interest reipublicae*, meaning they violated general laws and common interests of all nations. Most authors denominated piracy, desertion, rebellion, violation of public peace (*Landfriedensbruch*), smuggling, counterfeiting and thieving vagrants forming networks and 'organized gangs'. In particular vagrants were considered as the most dangerous mobile criminals who would commit crimes in different countries and therefore should be punished by every competent jurisdiction instead of extraditing them.[37] According to Benedict Carpzov, this was a general practice in Europe; other authors underlined that in addition every *crimen publicum* of an evil nature such as piracy should be punished by every competent jurisdiction.[38] This principle was later adopted by international law: although von Martens denied a general obligation of states to prosecute foreign perpetrators who had committed crimes in other countries, he nevertheless stressed that 'the general good seems to require that those who attack immediately the safety of the state should not go unpunished; and accordingly, in case of requisition, no sovereign refuses directly to take cognizance of such crimes'.[39] From the viewpoint of the *forum deprehensionis* and the *crimen publicum*, early modern criminal law shaped notions and narratives of transnational crime which involved:

- Offenders who operated across borders, formed criminal gangs, intruded countries and committed crimes such as robbery, thieving and arson. Although they were regarded as somehow 'organized' and 'professional' criminals it was rather their social status—marginal groups, mobile, migratory, 'stateless'—that made them 'transnational criminals'.
- Suspects and refugees who had escaped across borders and sometimes found criminal asylum.
- Crimes related to borders and border regions such as smuggling, illegal migration and trafficking (humans, weapons and coins).

[35] Georg Ludwig Böhmer and Johann Martin Ruppel, *De delictis extra territorium admissis* (Göttingen 1748); Johann Achaz Rudolph, *De poena delictorum extra territorium admissorum* (Erlangen 1790).

[36] For a discussion of the concept see Boister, *Introduction* (n 1) 3–11; Gerben Bruinsma, 'Criminology and Transnational Crime' in Gerben Bruinsma (ed), *Histories of Transnational Crime* (Springer 2015) 1.

[37] Carpzov, *Practica Nova* (n 8) p III q 110 n 69; see Meili, *Lehrbuch* (n 6) 41.

[38] Claro, *Opera omnia* (n 8) p III q 39 n 7.

[39] von Martens, *Law of Nations* (n 13) 109.

- Political and state crimes with a transboundary dimension and related to security such as rebels, conspirators and assassinators operating from a neighbouring country as well as ex-soldiers, deserters and dissidents who had escaped to other countries/jurisdictions.
- Public crimes (of an evil nature) that endangered the common or Christian order such as piracy.[40]

However, early modern criminal law did not establish a comprehensive legal concept of trans- or international crime to protect humankind through universal justice. Jurisprudence, legal norms and judicial practice were rather concerned to maintain public security and common interests against a variety of transnational threats. Thus, early modern transnational crime may be characterized as a historically flexible concept and regime that allowed early modern authorities and states to label and prosecute various emanations of harmful activity that crossed borders or threatened to do so.[41] Early modern criminal law created various narratives of 'transnational (organized, professional) crime' that underwent further changes, in particular at the turn of the century.

## VI. Changes 1789–1848 and Conclusion

The French Revolution led to an increase of transnational threats, offences and groups that challenged the political order and security of more than one state. These ranged from smuggling to political exiles and movements operating across borders by means of violence and sedition. The emerging nation states regarded them as specific offences against their sovereignty as well as a general threat to order and security in Europe. In particular, the authoritarian regimes of the Holy Alliance labelled seditious and violent cross-border political activities as international conspiracy and political crime, which, in the long run, influenced the concept of international crime and transnational criminal law, specifically with regard to political asylum and extradition.[42] The Congress of Vienna (1814–15) further shaped the notion of a new transnational security culture that besides political crimes also included smuggling, counterfeiting, slave trade and illegal immigration as

[40] On the various crimes see Gerben Bruinsma (ed), *Histories of Transnational Crime* (Springer 2015); Härter, 'Grenzübergreifende Kriminalität' (n 22); Cornel Zwierlein and Beatrice de Graaf (eds), *Security and Conspiracy in History, 16th to 21st Century* (2013) 38 Historical Social Research 96-106; Mark Chadwick, *Piracy and the Origins of Universal Jurisdiction. On Stranger Tides?* (Brill 2019).

[41] Härter, 'Security and Transnational Policing' (n 20).

[42] BartonL Ingraham, *Political Crime in Europe. A Comparative Study of France, Germany, and England* (Berkeley 1979); Karl Härter, 'Legal Responses to Violent Political Crimes in Nineteenth Century Central Europe' in Karl Härter and Beatrice de Graaf (eds), *Vom Majestätsverbrechen zum Terrorismus: Politische Kriminalität, Recht, Justiz und Polizei zwischen Früher Neuzeit und 20. Jahrhundert* (Klostermann 2012) 161.

transnational threats. These gradually became issues of the changing transnational criminal law and the 'invention of international crime'.[43]

Most new nation states in Europe abrogated *ius commune* criminal law and therefore the *forum deprehensionis*. Following the example of France, they established national criminal justice systems that claimed the power to punish all crimes and all kind of perpetrators within the national jurisdiction (territoriality principle), all citizens who would commit crimes in foreign countries (personality principle) and foreigners involved in crimes against one's own nation while being in a foreign country. The last principle was explicitly expressed in the French *Code d'instruction criminelle* (1808, article 6) and displays continuities with early modern criminal law, in particular as regards the prosecution of cross-border criminal activities endangering the security of a state and the request for the extradition of the respective perpetrators. The 'nationalization' of criminal justice also intensified the need for cross-border cooperation in criminal matters. Most states developed transnational norms, procedures and practices through new agreements (particularly extradition treaties), transboundary cooperation and domestic laws regulating asylum, mutual assistance and requisition proceedings, while still using pre-existing practices such as exchange of information, the distribution of arrest warrants and wanted lists, requests and expulsion.[44]

Continuity and change produced contradictions and collisions that can be observed, for instance, in the abrogation of the criminal asylum, its transformation to transnational political asylum and the inclusion of the political offence exception in extradition treaties along with the principles of reciprocity, identical norm, speciality, lenity and the non-extradition of nationals. This partly contradicted the increasing demand for the cross-border prosecution of political offenders and led to further modifications of extradition treaties through the Belgian *attentat clause* (1856).[45]

At the same time, a renewed jurisprudence of criminal law started to systematize the contradictory developments from *ius commune* to modern transnational criminal law, discussing intensely, for instance, the punishment of crimes committed in foreign states, the ambit of criminal law, criminal justice, asylum and extradition from the perspective of international law, thus, gradually forming the new discipline of international criminal law *lato sensu* that finally emerged in the second half of the 19th century.[46] However, up to the middle of the century, neither

[43] De Graaf and others, *Securing Europe* (n 20); Paul Knepper, *The Invention of International Crime. A Global Issue in the Making, 1881–1914* (Palgrave Macmillan 2010).

[44] Härter, 'Security and Transnational Policing' (n 20); Härter, 'Formation of Transnational Security Regimes' (n 10).

[45] Härter, 'Circulation' (n 28) 358 et seq.

[46] Carl August Tittmann, *Die Strafrechtspflege in völkerrechtlicher Rücksicht*... (Dresden 1817); Julius Friedrich Abegg, *Über die Bestrafung der im Auslande begangenen Verbrechen* ... (Landshut 1819); Albert Friedrich Berner, *Wirkungskreis des Strafgesetzes nach Zeit, Raum und Personen. Besonders von der Bestrafung der im Auslande begangenen Verbrechen, vom Asylrecht und von der Auslieferung der Verbrecher*... (Berlin 1853); Robert von Mohl, *Revision der völkerrechtlichen Lehre vom Asyle* (Tübingen

criminal jurisprudence nor the various transnational norms established a coherent concept of 'modern' transnational criminal law and still had to deal with procedures, practices and difficulties that were related to *ius commune* criminal law and its historical transformation. Similar developments can be observed for the prevailing narratives of 'transnational criminals' and notions of 'international crime' that particularly justified transnational legal assistance, policing and security measures.[47] The contradictory development from *ius commune* to modern transnational criminal law and the transnationalization of criminal law in the early 19th century resulted in transnational security and criminal law regimes with a low level of 'juridification' (*Verrechtlichung*). This would only change after the emergence of international congresses, organizations and conventions in the last decades of the 19th century which still, however, had to deal with norms, procedures, practices and narratives of transnational criminal law rooted in early modern traditions.[48]

1853); August von Bulmerincq, *Das Asylrecht in seiner geschichtlichen Entwickelung. Beurtheilt vom Standpunkte des Rechts und dessen völkerrechtlicher Bedeutung für die Auslieferung flüchtiger Verbrecher*... (Dorpat 1853). About this discourse see Jeßberger, *Geltungsbereich* (n 1) 42 et seq.

[47] cf Donnedieu de Vabres, *Introduction* (n 6) 2, 127 et seq, 402 et seq; Fiore, *Trattato* (n 6) 81 et seq; Kohler, *Internationales Strafrecht* (n 6) 97 et seq.

[48] Härter and others, *Transnationalisation* (n 3).

# 2

# Criminological Reformism and Transnational Criminal Law (1870s–1930s)

*Michele Pifferi*

## I. Introduction

The framework of this chapter is the reformist legal doctrine developed in the later 19th century, which advocated criminological reorganization and transformation of criminal law based on the key notions of social defence and offenders' social dangerousness.[1] Both the methodological and theoretical bases of this movement were not entirely homogeneous and national peculiarities also contributed to different implementations of new ideas.[2] Nonetheless, from 1876 Lombroso's *Criminal Man* to the 1930s, a 'criminological wave' contributed to rethinking the foundations of Western criminal law tenets.[3] While this subject and the contribution of the most influential reformers such as Cesare Lombroso, Enrico Ferri, Franz von Liszt and Adolphe Prins have been thoroughly investigated, the impact of their views on the specific field of what we now consider transnational criminal law has only been partially considered.[4]

At the end of the 19th century the response to transborder crimes, till then mostly regulated by extradition treaties,[5] became intertwined with the building of

[1] In this chapter I refer to 'criminology' (and 'criminologists') as to the knowledge (and experts, mostly jurists) which, since the last decades of the 19th century, dealt with criminal law and penology with a new approach, based on the centrality of the criminal man rather than the crime and on an interdisciplinary methodology emphasizing the contribution of sociology, anthropology, physiology, psychology, psychiatry, statistics, economics etc to both the reform of criminal law and the elaboration of penal policies.

[2] See Michele Pifferi, 'Global Criminology and National Tradition: The Impact of Reform Movements on Criminal Systems at the Beginning of the 20th Century' in Thomas Duve (ed), *Entanglements in Legal History: Conceptual Approaches* (Max Planck Institute for European Legal History 2014) 543.

[3] See eg David Garland, *Punishment and Welfare: A History of Penal Strategies* (Gower 1985); James Q Whitman, 'The Case for Penal Modernism: Beyond Utility and Desert' (2014) 1(2) Critical Analysis of Law 143; Michele Pifferi, *Reinventing Punishment: A Comparative History of Criminology and Penology in the 19th and 20th Centuries* (OUP 2016) (hereafter Pifferi, *Reinventing Punishment*).

[4] See eg Paul Knepper, *The Invention of International Crime. A Global Issue in the Making, 1881–1914* (Palgrave Macmillan 2010) 159–87; Willem Hendrik Nagel, 'International Collaboration in the Field of Criminology' in Jacob Maarten van Bemmelen (ed), *Le droit pénal international. Recueil d'études en hommage a Jacob Maarten Van Bemmelen* (Brill 1965) 193.

[5] See Härter, Chapter 1 in this book.

Michele Pifferi, *Criminological Reformism and Transnational Criminal Law (1870s–1930s)* In: *Histories of Transnational Criminal Law*. Edited by: Neil Boister, Sabine Gless and Florian Jeßberger, Oxford University Press. © Michele Pifferi 2021.
DOI: 10.1093/oso/9780192845702.003.0003

an international criminal law system,[6] and was also affected by international legal discourse on 'penal modernism'. This chapter will begin by providing some comments on how criminological positivism dealt with the problem of transnational criminality. It will then analyse how some key notions of criminological positivism characterized the international and transnational criminal law debate in the early decades of the 20th century. Then it will briefly refer to the issue of security measures in the process of international unification/codification of criminal law.

## II. 'Les gendarmes ne devaient pas continuer à aller à pied, quand les voleurs courraient à bicyclette'[7]: The New Challenges of Transnational Criminality

In 1931 Jean-André Roux, professor at the University of Strasbourg and Secretary general of the International Association of Penal Law (Association Internationale de Droit Pénal, AIDP), stressed that sovereignty-centred theories should not be an obstacle to the organization of super- and international social defence. At that time, it was a common opinion among criminologists that, given the enormous increase in professional delinquents exploiting the opportunities of international trade, technological inventions and the ease of global mobility, the internationalization of the fight against criminality was unavoidable and set the agenda of international penal reformism.

A brief survey of the works of some international legal groups and associations committed to reforming criminal law shows how the criminological movement exerted a significant influence over the understanding of transnational crime. The congresses of the International Prison and Penitentiary Commission, held from 1872 (in London) to 1950 (in The Hague), were particularly interested in the problem of transnational and international crime.[8] The Institute of International

[6] Mark Lewis, *The Birth of the New Justice. The Internationalization of Crime and Punishment, 1919–1950* (OUP 2014) (hereafter Lewis, *The Birth of the New Justice*). It is worth noting that the two fields were not yet finely conceptualized as distinct, and that many scholars discussed problems related to what we now consider transnational criminal law as part of the broader notions of international criminal justice and international crimes; see eg Quintiliano Saldaña, 'La Justice Pénale Internationale' (1925) 10 Recueil des Cours de l'Académie de Droit International 223 (hereafter Saldaña, 'La Justice'). On the conceptual definition of transnational criminal law as an autonomous field from international criminal law see Neil Boister, 'The Concept and Nature of Transnational Criminal Law' in Neil Boister and Robert J Currie (eds), *Routledge Handbook of Transnational Criminal Law* (Routledge 2015) 11.

[7] Jean-André Roux, 'L'entr'aide des États dans la lutte contre la criminalité' (1931) 36 Recueil des Cours de l'Académie de Droit International 89.

[8] The congresses addressed the following issues: the need to collect reliable international penal statistics and the utility of extradition treaties (London 1872); the creation of a network among police forces of different states in order to facilitate criminals' arrest (Stockholm 1878); mutual exchange of procedural files between government of different states and, again, extradition (Rome 1885); unification of the anthropometrical measurement procedures to verify the criminal's identity (Paris 1895); extradition of national citizens (Brussels 1900); effects and enforcement of penal judgments given against a foreigner (Washington 1910); how the struggle against international delinquency can be made more effective

Law dealt with extradition in its 1877 meeting in Zurich and 1880 meeting in Oxford, while in Heidelberg in 1887 it discussed how states should share information in order to identify legal gaps of potential advantage to criminals. The first International Criminal Police Congress held in Monaco in 1914, where practical measures to contrast international criminality were discussed, and the foundation of the International Criminal Police Commission in 1923, were expressions of the need to adjust international policing to the internationalization of crime.[9]

The International Union of Penal Law (Internationale Kriminalistische Vereinigung, IKV),[10] founded in 1889 by Adolphe Prins, Gerhard van Hamel and Franz von Liszt, also debated many problems related to international and transnational criminality. At the Hamburg meeting in 1905, police cooperation to fight against international criminality was discussed and the following resolutions were adopted: (a) it was recognized that as a consequence of the modern development of relationships between states and populations, a form of international criminality had arisen, which demanded that modern methods for investigating and responding to these crimes extended to all countries; (b) in order to respond appropriately to this criminality it was important for every state to create central services that: (i) were connected with police authority of the capital of each country, (ii) collected and permanently shared all the available information about international crimes to achieve a more effective prevention and (iii) had the right to directly interact; (c) the material collected by the central police service should be the object of scientific investigation aimed at laying the foundations for the future development of actions against international crimes.

The modern criminological approach characterizing the IKV also permeated some of the reports presented on this topic. Hopff, the chief police officer in Hamburg, in adherence to the principle of social defence claimed by reformers, argued that the barycentre of criminal justice should shift from the offence to the offender.[11] He provided a definition of international crime, based on two elements: the criminal activity should be disseminated in different countries and the offender should be a professional criminal. In his view, the simple fact of multiple violations committed in different countries was not enough to constitute international delinquency, because this did not imply that the offender was particularly dangerous to society and that special security measures were necessary. Extradition treaties were only to be conceived as extreme remedies. To effectively

through inter-state cooperation (London 1925); and international cooperation to face the transformation of criminality and analysis of its causes (Prague 1930).

[9] Mathieu Deflem, 'Bureaucratization and Social Control: Historical Foundations of International Police Cooperation' (2000) 34(3) Law & Society Review 739; see also Clive Emsley, *Crime Police and Penal Policy: European experiences 1750–1940* (OUP 2007).

[10] See Elisabeth Bellmann, *Die Internationale Kriminalistische Vereinigung (1889–1933)* (Lang 1994).

[11] Gustav A Hopff, 'La lutte contre la criminalité internationale' (1906) 13 Mitteilungen der IKV 295.

repress international crimes other measures had to be adopted including: (a) in drafting penal codes, each legislator should provide that in order to determine the penalty, judges could take into consideration previous convictions in other countries; (b) universal extradition treaties should be signed; (c) the mutual exchange of information between judicial authorities of different countries should be facilitated; (d) central organizations to contrast international criminality should be created; and (e) police information about arrests, crimes, relevant circumstances should be published every two weeks in different languages.[12]

In another report, the French jurist Feuilloley, general attorney at the Court of Cassation, criticized the traditional notion of the unity of crime, according to which any act preparatory or subsequent to the crime but which did not represent a distinct crime per se, if committed in a country different from the *locus commissi delicti*, was neither indictable nor punishable, unless with extradition (this was a consequence of the principles of territoriality and sovereignty).[13] The new criminological school, he argued, provided a solution to this problem, because, by taking into consideration the psychical and subjective elements of any offence, it saw in the plurality of agents-offenders the coexistence of a plurality of crimes for which, therefore, each accomplice-perpetrator could be autonomously prosecuted in his own country.

The AIDP, founded in 1924 as a reaction to the post-war crisis of the IKV, was particularly committed to both the unification of penal law through a process of international codification and the creation of an international criminal court (it held congresses in Warsaw in 1927, Rome in 1928, Brussels in 1930 and Paris in 1931). Its purpose was to reform international criminal law applying social defence theory, oriented more to protect society against criminals than rehabilitate or re-educate them.[14] As was clearly stated in a Project of the Association, published in the first issue of the *Revue Internationale de Droit Pénal*, the war had caused an increase of criminality because of the moral and material instability following the catastrophe. Moreover, foreign criminals were identified as a particular threat to public opinion; 'the interpenetration of people and the presence on many territories of more and more foreigners' had multiplied the forms of international criminality.[15] The AIDP explicitly chose not to embrace any scientific credo, either positivist or classical.[16] Its more active members included certain more conservative and retributivist jurists such as Roux, and others who were pro-social defence reformers. The latter included the Romanian Vespasian Pella (1897–1960),

[12] ibid 328–32.

[13] G Feuilloley, 'La lutte contre la criminalité internationale' (1906) 13 Mitteilungen der IKV 247.

[14] Mark Lewis, 'The History of the International Association of Penal Law, 1924–1950: Liberal, Conservative, or Neither?' in Morten Bergsmo, Cheah Wui Ling, Song Tianying and Yi Ping (eds), *Historical Origins of International Criminal Law: Volume 4* (Torkel Opsahl 2015) 599.

[15] Henry Berthélemy and others, 'Projet d'une Association Internationale de Droit Pénal' (1924) 1(1) Rev Int de Droit Pénal 1.

[16] ibid 2.

one of the founders of the AIDP and a member of its Board of Directors, the Spanish criminologist and professor of criminal law and criminal anthropology at the University of Madrid Quintiliano Saldaña (1878–1938) and the Pole Emil Stanislaw Rappaport (1877–1965), another of the AIDP's founders and its vice-chairman between 1924 and 1939.

Even though in the 1920s the time of the struggle between classical and positivist schools had been replaced in criminological thinking by eclectic and compromising approaches, some ideas of the new school had taken root into the criminal law culture of the 'civilized nations'. It would be misleading to overemphasize the 'positivism' of some prominent figures of the building of international and transnational criminal law and, consequently, to label this process as determined by Ferri's or Liszt's ideas. However, the legacy of 'penal modernism' on the makers of the 20th century transboundary criminal law seem no less significant than its influence on national penal culture and legislation.

## III. Elements of an International Social Defence Criminal Policy

The ideas of criminological positivism were based on scientific premises whose methodology and substance were potentially universal: anthropological knowledge, categorization of criminal types, dangerousness assessment criteria and methods of individualization of punishment could be applied regardless of national boundaries and national legislation. Despite the global circulation of penal reformism, its impact on transnational criminal justice was more of an indirect effect than a specific goal. The intensification of comparative legal studies and comparative criminology seemed primarily directed towards triggering uniform reforms at a national level. Given the growing interest in international criminal law, however, some reformers examined how this field could be affected by their key principles—principles such as social defence, punishments based on the dangerous character of the criminal rather than on the abstract seriousness of the offence, special prevention as a rationale and purpose of penal measures and social understanding of the aetiology of crime, individualization of punishment.[17]

[17] See eg Willem Adriaan Bonger, 'Rapport sur la question Une coopération internationale en vue de l'observation des changements dans la criminalité et de l'examen de leurs causes est-elle possible et dans quelles conditions?' in *Actes du Congrès Pénal et Pénitentiaire International De Prague, Août 1930, Rapports Sur Les Questions du Programme de la Troisième Section: Prévention,* vol IV (Bureau de la Commission internationale pénale et pénitentiaire 1931) 195; Henri Donnedieu De Vabres, 'Rapport sur la deuxième question' in *Actes du Congres Pénitentiaire International de Londres. Août 1925. Rapports sur les questions du programme de la Troisième section: Prévention,* vol IV (Bureau de la Commission Pénitentiaire Internationale 1925) 159.

Raffaele Garofalo drafted an outline of an international penal code[18] built around his idea of natural (or social) crimes (ie 'such acts as offend the sentiment of humanity or violate the rules of conduct exacted by the common or average probity of present-day civilized peoples' (§ 2)) which could be perpetrated by specific classes of criminals (§ 6: these included murderers, violent criminals, criminals deficient in probity and lascivious criminals).[19] Extradition of these categories of delinquents should, he thought, be a duty of each state regardless of whether they were a national citizen or not.[20] Mutual solidarity between states should extend to the execution of punishment as well. He thought internment for indefinite period in penal colonies overseas the most effective measure to eliminate dangerous criminals, and that in result those states without colonial territory should be allowed to send their criminals to foreign penal colonies (§ 3(c)). Retribution was to be replaced by punishment as 'a means calculated to effect the cessation of the criminal's harmfulness to society' (§ 5). This was to be proportional not to the objective gravity of the offence nor the moral responsibility of the offender but 'adapted to the criminal aptitude of the wrong-doer' (§ 11) and aimed at striking 'the criminality of the agent as revealed by the fact' (§ 12). Fixed and predetermined terms of imprisonment were abolished (§ 5(d)) and replaced by punishments aimed at the elimination of the offender 'incapable of adaptation to the social coexistence' (the death penalty or relative elimination with forms of indeterminate internment/confinement, §§ 17–19).

In 1897, Prospero Fedozzi, professor of international law at the University of Padua, employed positivist notions to support the nationality principle. He argued that if, as the new school maintained, both crime and punishment were strictly dependent upon the social conditions of the state in which the offender grew up, the judge better placed to assess the criminal's anthropological and social traits as well as determine the proper individualized sentence was the judge of the criminal's country rather than the one of the *locus commissi delicti*.[21] He thought extradition

[18] Raffaele Garofalo, 'Outline of Principles Suggested as a Basis for an International Penal Code' in Raffaele Garofalo (ed), *Criminology* (Little, Brown & Co 1914) 402 (hereafter Garofalo, *Criminology*); Raffaele Garofalo, 'De la solidarité des nations dans la lutte contre la criminalité' (1909) 17(1) Revue Internationale de Sociologie 1.

[19] As he wrote in the *Preface* to the English edition of 1914, 'the idea of "natural crime" as opposed to crime which is merely legal or conventional ... furnishes the means of establishing an international penal code—an undertaking which is awaited by the civilized world' see Garofalo, *Criminology* (n 18) xxxv.

[20] Similarly see also Alfredo Pozzolini, 'L'Organizzazione giuridica internazionale della difesa sociale contro la delinquenza' (1929) 1(1) Il pensiero giuridico penale 68.

[21] Prospero Fedozzi, *Delle Possibili Conseguenze del Positivismo Penale nel Sistema di Diritto Penale Internazionale* (Bocca 1897) 14–15 (hereafter Fedozzi, *Delle possibili conseguenze*). The same position was claimed with different arguments by Adolphe Prins, 'De quelques Idées Modernes en Matière D'extradition' (1879) 11 Revue du Droit International et de Législation Comparée 85: to leave citizens to be judged by foreign jurisdictions would mean to divest them of the most precious safeguards: 'même dans notre civilisation moderne qui n'a encore su faire disparaître ni les différences d'organisation judiciaire ni les antipathies de race'.

should also be regulated accordingly: theoretically all criminals should be extradited, but, in the light of the positivist distinction between occasional delinquents and 'born' delinquents, only the latter should be returned to the requesting state. As social defence was the true purpose of punishment, the fact that the occasional offender was already living in a foreign country far from the conditions which led him to violate the law could in itself be considered as a measure sufficient to prevent further crimes.[22]

More or less radical though such proposals were, they had little or no effect on the formation of a new international criminal law regime. As Ferri recognized in 1926, the solidarity between states in the defence against criminality was still too fragile and reliant on the 'old' notions of state sovereignty and territorial penal jurisdiction. Idealism should be combined with realism in proposing gradual progress towards the realization of an international justice.[23] Nonetheless, some of the most influential and active jurists involved in this theoretical and pragmatic challenge in the 1920s demonstrated that certain positivist beliefs had shaped their views on some tenets of criminal justice, even if conceived in a super-national perspective. To provide a few examples, I refer here to works of Pella and Saldaña.

Pella sent a proposal to the League of Nations concerning the creation of an international system for the elimination of dangerous and habitual criminals, which was published in 1924 in the first issue of the *Revue Internationale de Droit Penal*. In this essay Pella's arguments were clearly influenced by criminological reformism. He argued that (a) crime should not be considered as a legal entity but as a social phenomenon, which should be opposed by severe and general prophylactic measures; (b) the 'ordinary' criminal was the same in all the civilized countries and everywhere presented the same antisocial characteristics; (c) social and biological factors of crime were also the same in all the civilized countries, therefore (d) the criminal should not be considered as the citizen of a specific state, but as a human being who could not conform his behaviour to the general and permanent condition of social life; (e) the problem of 'ordinary' or 'common' criminality should be scientifically solved employing universal methods directed against the human being in general. Pella contended that one of the main problems of international criminality concerned the elimination of habitual and/or professional criminals, that is the problem of recidivism. Following Garofalo's proposal, he suggested that, given the abolitionist trend against death penalty, social defence against 'unreformable' delinquents (particularly depraved murderers, offenders who had repeatedly attempted to escape from prison or to kill their wardens; serious crime recidivists) should be achieved by means of a common system of social elimination, such as transportation of dangerous and incorrigible offenders into

[22] Fedozzi, *Delle possibili conseguenze* (n 21) 26–30.

[23] See eg Enrico Ferri, 'La Solidarietà degli Stati Nella Lotta Contro la Delinquenza' (1926) 36 La Scuola Positiva 19.

lands far from the European continent; in so doing, even states without colonies could resort to a measure of artificial selection.[24] The Romanian jurist, whose role in the building of the 'new justice' was significant,[25] cannot be considered a strict positivist: in his contributions, though, there are often discourses, references and reasoning that connote a criminological imprint.[26]

Saldaña was among those reformers more dedicated to the building of an international and supranational criminal law system. Grounded upon a universalist and cosmopolitan doctrine, he advocated the conception of a 'universal social defence',[27] proposed a universal penal de-nationalization and drafted an international penal code based on these ideas.[28] Inspired by Ferri's and by Liszt's point that punishment should be directed to the offender rather than to the offence, Saldaña argued that the science of universal social defence was based on the principle of non-territoriality, namely that the prosecution and repression of every crime—except for international crimes whose jurisdiction was of the permanent tribunal of international justice—should be given to the *iudex deprehensionis*, whether the perpetrator is a national citizen or a foreigner. Therefore, an international criminal proceeding should aim not at the surrender of the fugitive detainee, but at the guarantees of a fair trial and rational and humane treatment, supposing the same level of civilization between the states involved. The extradition system, thus, should be substituted by what he defined the 'international request of penal guarantee'.[29] Analysing the international social defence's historical developments and achievements, Saldaña claimed that the powerful force of international criminality was opposed by nothing but a useless national repression, even though provided with the old legal tool of extradition.[30] He consequently elaborated an articulated system of international criminal justice, which he fully developed at a course he gave in 1925 at the Academy of International Law in The Hague.

At the outset of the course, the Spanish criminologist presented the difference between what he considered the old and outdated idea of 'international judicial

[24] Vespasien Pella, 'Proposition adressée a la Société des Nations en vue de l'organisation d'un Système international d'élimination des criminel dangereux et des délinquants d'habitude' (1924) 2(1) Rev Int de Droit Pénal 141. See also Vespasian Pella, 'Mémorandum présenté par le Secrétariat' Document A/CN.4/39 [Memorandum Concerning a Draft Code of Offences Against the Peace and Security of Mankind] (1950) II Yearbook of the International Law Commission 289.

[25] See Lewis, *The Birth of the New Justice* (n 6) 100–06, 131–35, 195–99.

[26] John AE Vervaele, 'The IUPL/IAPL: 125 Years of Serving Criminal Justice, Human Rights, and Humanity' (2015) 86(3) Rev Int de Droit Pénal 768, pinpoints that Pella 'is using basic notions of the modern positivistic school' in his study of the collective psychology of states and war crimes as well as in his categorization of offenders as purely political offenders or anti-social criminals (Vespasien Pella, 'Discours' in Vespasien Pella (ed), *Union Interparlementaire. Compte rendu de la XXIIe conférence tenue a Berne et Genève du 22 au 28 Août 1924* (Payot 1925), reprinted in (2015) 86(3) Rev Int de Droit Pénal 841–50, esp at 843 and 846).

[27] Quintiliano Saldaña, *La Defensa Social Universal (Conferencias de Paris, Roma y La Haya* (Góngora 1926) (hereafter Saldaña, *La Defensa*).

[28] Saldaña, 'La Justice' (n 6) 387–424.

[29] Saldaña, *La Defensa* (n 27) 46–47.

[30] ibid 52.

assistance'—linked to the classical notion of sovereignty, voluntary and freely exerted, whose typical examples are extradition and enforcement of foreign judgments—and the progressive idea of 'supranational legal existence', embedded in the League of Nations, which implemented international justice rather than abstract theoretical elaboration and in which national sovereignty was replaced by mutual interdependence among states.[31] He then divided the evolution of international criminal justice into the 'evolution of facts' and 'evolution of ideas'. The first category referred to the shift from a traditional national criminality to international criminality as a consequence of social and technological progress. By following a kind of autonomous approach, different from the classical school which was exclusively centred on the offence as well as from the positivist school which was criminal-oriented, Saldaña suggested applying his approach of a pragmatic criminal justice—based on the centrality of the human being and their legal safeguards rather than on the offence—even to international criminal justice. There was an international community of dangerous subjects—he argued—characterized by an *internationale Gemeingefärlichkeit* (international social dangerousness): the international awareness of a universal criminal threat led states to sign conventions and treaties and stimulated cooperation between police forces.[32] Saldaña then identified four categories of international crimes: crimes of international law (such as violations of the law of war, aggression between states), crimes against international law (such as violations of personal immunity, international regicide, anarchic crimes, crimes against the law of nations), extra-national crimes created by international law (eg piracy, unlawful interference with—or crime against—submarine cables, illegal boarding of vessels or airplanes), and what he considered the international crimes (typical examples of which we would label transnational crimes). Indeed, he defined them as offences prepared, perpetrated or participated in the territories of different states or across borders, in which any cooperation was given by a foreigner, or in which a foreigner had concealed stolen goods, or offences initiated in one country and then carried on in a different one.[33] This kind of crimes, which raised a criminological problem, he thought should be solved directly by the international criminal justice rather than by diplomatic or administrative activities. They were offences whose legal, sociological and anthropological elements were spread into different countries, nationalities or races; they prejudiced rights and interests of different populations, victims belonged to different countries; they could be cosmopolitan offences (international banditry), multinational offences (international forgery; counterfeit money) and xenophobic offences (border fights).[34]

[31] Saldaña, 'La Justice' (n 6) 228–42.
[32] ibid 287–88.
[33] ibid 292.
[34] Crimes encompassed within these categories are eg slavery, traffic in 'white' women and children, international banditry, illegal traffic of opium or other drugs, obscene publications, unfair competition, contraceptive or pro-abortion propaganda (ibid 319–35).

Saldaña's view of extradition was that it lacked any foundations in principles of modern criminal law, because, on the one hand, the retributivist theory on which it rested was not followed anymore and, on the other, the theory of social defence did not require any control beyond borders because criminals stopped being a social danger as soon as they crossed borders and left the country. 'Personal' extradition, an institution of national law, should be replaced by the notion of 'real' extradition, according to which the offender should remain in the country of refuge if and when this was able to apply measures of moral and social reform; the stolen goods should be returned; and the victim should be paid a compensation. While, in the past, extradition was imposed because of an obsession with the offender's impunity—he contended—in the 20th century this approach had no value because what really mattered were criminals' rehabilitation and correctional treatment, which had nothing to do with surrendering the culprit to the requesting state. In opposition to what was maintained by Enrico Pessina, an Italian champion of penal liberalism who thought that extradition was beneficial to all states insofar as the repressive defence of one state represented the preventive defence of all the others,[35] Saldaña believed that the universal repression exercised by the *iudex deprehensionis*, with regard to all offenders and for all offences, was the only effective way to achieve universal prevention; extradition, in contrast, only constituted a way to facilitate the offender's potential escape during the often long and complicated handover.[36]

The foundation of Saldaña's universal penal jurisdiction lay neither in an idea of absolute supreme justice nor in any universal human morality, but in the idea of common utility, namely in a sort of universal social solidarity, whose realization—he concluded—depended more on governments' political decisions than on legal theories.[37] At the time his theory was considered too utopian, naïve and not without inconsistencies.[38] What is worth noting, however, is Saldaña's resort to typical criminological concepts and discourses to elaborate his system.

## IV. Security Measures and the Unification of International Criminal Law

Influences of 'penal modernism' are visible also in the attempts, drafts and schemes for the unification and codification of international criminal law. Rappaport observed in 1929 that the 19th-century national ideology of codification was

[35] Enrico Pessina, *Elementi di diritto penale* (Marghieri 1871) 115.

[36] Saldaña, 'La Justice' (n 6) 355. Arguments for the jurisdiction of the *iudex deprehensionis*, even though more moderate and not grounded on positivist views, were also made by Henry Donnedieu de Vabres, *Les Principes Modernes du Droit Pénal International* (Librairie du Recueil Sirey 1928) 167–70.

[37] Saldaña, 'La Justice' (n 6) 357.

[38] See eg Alfredo De Marsico, *Principi Informatori del Diritto Penale Internazionale* (Laterza 1929) 31–38.

moulding the international criminal law debate, in an effort to reproduce on an inter- and transnational scale the same rationalizing, simplifying and unifying political process that from the Napoleonic Code onward characterized the legal orders of almost all the European countries (as well as of the countries all over the World influenced by the civil law system).[39] After Garofalo's draft, in the 1920s the pace of the unification of international law accelerated.[40] It is noteworthy that the second conference for the unification of penal law held in Rome in 1928 tried to unify national rules concerning measures of security. This conference represented, in Rappaport's opinion, the effort to profit from the fifty-year struggle of the positivist school to introduce into penal legislation special means of social defence against particularly dangerous criminals, criminals considered dangerous because of their vicious inclinations which they had either inherited biologically or developed within a bad social milieu.[41]

The issue of implementation and codification of security measures dated back to late 19th-century criminological debate.[42] The fascist Italian Code of 1930 introduced an articulated discipline of such measures, provided them with the guarantee of the principle of legality and judicialized their application.[43] It was considered the most important practical achievement of penal positivism, or at least the most significant compromise it was able to achieve.[44] Its reappraisal within the debate on the international criminal law code was celebrated,[45] somewhat opportunistically,[46] as a trademark of the impact of the new school. Other important emblematic 'criminological' themes such as the attention given to the executive phase of punishment (which also needed to be codified)[47] and the application of preventive measures of social defence to collectivities (more precisely to the offending states),[48] were also discussed but only found partial recognition in the criminal law internationalization process. Only the introduction into this process of preventive

[39] Emil Stanislaw Rappaport, *Le Problème de l'unification Internationale du Droit Pénal* (Varsovie 1929) esp 6–10 (hereafter Rappaport, *Le Problème de l'unification*). On the 'myth' of the codification see eg Paolo Grossi, *Mitologie Giuridiche della Modernità* (Giuffrè 2001), and, for a comparative survey, Paolo Cappellini and Bernardo Sordi (eds), *Codici. Une riflessione di fine millennio* (Giuffrè 2002).

[40] See Lewis, *The Birth of the New Justice* (n 6) 113–17.

[41] Rappaport, *Le Problème de l'unification* (n 39) 21.

[42] Pifferi, *Reinventing Punishment* (n 3) 86–142.

[43] Emil Rappaport, 'Mesures de sûreté. Nature et garanties juridiques. Rapport' in *Deuxième Conférence Internationale d'Unification du Droit Pénal. Rome 21–25 Mai 1928. Actes de la Conférence* (Istituto poligrafico dello Stato 1931) 23.

[44] Marc Ancel, 'The Collection of European Penal Codes and the Study of Comparative Law' (1958) 106(3) University of Pennsylvania Law Review 329, esp 364–65.

[45] See eg Enrico Ferri, 'Il trionfo della scienza italiana al Congresso penitenziario internazionale di Londra' in Enrico Ferri (ed), *Studi Sulla Criminalità* (2nd edn, Utet 1926) 801.

[46] Emil Rappaport, 'Les deux faces de la carrière scientifique d'Enrico Ferri' in Rappaport, *Le problème de l'unification* (n 39) 87.

[47] Emil Rappaport, 'Le Nouveau Système de Codification de la Législation Criminelle' (1931) 8(1) Rev Int de Droit Pénal 34.

[48] Emil Rappaport, 'The Problem of the Inter-State Criminal Law' (1932) 18 Transactions of the Grotius Society 53.

security measures reached a broad consensus among scholars and lawmakers, both at a national and supranational level.[49]

## V. Conclusion

The formation of an international and transnational criminal law regime has been described as a gradual process of the widening of human rights' protection,[50] or as an 'organic outgrowth of lower-level transnational networks that have reached critical mass through the process of governmentality … a matrix of local-global/global-local horizontal capacity building, multi-layered enforcement techniques, and convergences of rules and strategies … geared toward providing security for vulnerable populations'.[51] The sketch provided in this chapter does not necessarily contradict these interpretations. The imprint of 'penal modernism' on the mentality and doctrine of some of the most influential architects of transnational criminal law does not imply a negative connotation. It rather means that historiographical consideration of the legacy, achievements and limits of criminological positivism, of how penal reformism transformed the constitutional framework of liberal criminal law, should also be extended to a supranational dimension.

A deeper cultural comprehension of the idea (or ideal) of transnational and international criminal law that was projected or implemented, calls for the pinpointing of some of its criminological underpinnings. These include: (1) the spread and pervasiveness of the notion of social defence; (2) the notions of particularly dangerous international criminals (to be eliminated or neutralized with indeterminate treatment-punishments such as transportation in oversea penal colonies) as well as of incorrigible offenders due to biological or socially ineradicable characteristics; (3) the claim that preventive security measures should be adopted; and (4) the idea that criminals and crimes, even international or transnational ones, could better be responded to by relying upon a scientific, experimental and sociological approach to criminality methodologically unaffected by any geographical peculiarities.

[49] See eg Louis Braffort, 'L'Unification du Droit Pénal et le Droit Comparé' (1935) 21 Revue Trimestrielle 61.

[50] M Cherif Bassiouni, 'IAPL: Over a Century of Dedication to Criminal Justice and Human Rights' (2015) 86(3) RiDP 1069.

[51] Gregory S Gordon, 'Transnational Governmentality Networking: A Neo-Foucauldian Account of International Criminal Law' in Morten Bergsmo and Emiliano J Buis (eds), *Philosophical Foundations of International Criminal Law: Correlating Thinkers* (Torkel Opsahl 2018) 675, quotations at 676, 752.

# 3

# The Growth of the Multilateral Suppression Conventions in the First Half of the 20th Century

*Neil Boister*

## I. Introduction

The legal systems framing transnational crime and those establishing the core international criminal law rest on different principles. In 1955, former Tokyo War Crimes Tribunal Justice Bert Röling identified the principles of the core international criminal law as:

1. The principle of the individual responsibility for the violation of the law of nations, including the responsibility for the acts of state;
2. The principle of the threefold individual responsibility, for crimes against peace, war crimes and crimes against humanity;
3. The principle that individuals have international duties which transcend the national obligations of obedience imposed by the individual state.[1]

The principles of the laws that frame transnational crime—what has come to be called transnational criminal law—were also, it is proposed, settled by the mid-20th century as follows:

1. The principle of individual responsibility only applies to the violation of the laws of participating states;
2. The principle of individual responsibility applies to a range of transnational crimes governed by treaty, IGO resolution or recommendation;
3. The scope of the duties and obligations is narrowly owed to participating states.

[1] Bert Röling, 'On Aggression, on International Criminal Law, on International Criminal Jurisdiction' (1955) Nederlandse Tijdschrift voor Internationale Recht 167, 185.

Neil Boister, *The Growth of the Multilateral Suppression Conventions in the First Half of the 20th Century*
In: *Histories of Transnational Criminal Law*. Edited by: Neil Boister, Sabine Gless and Florian Jeßberger,
Oxford University Press. © Neil Boister 2021. DOI: 10.1093/oso/9780192845702.003.0004

The divergence between these two systems can be traced back to two early phases in the historical evolution of transnational criminal law, when multilateral treaties against crime gradually became the instrument of choice for suppression of transnational crime.

In the first phase, in the 18th, 19th and early 20h centuries, most transnational criminal law was either a product of the domestic articulation of legal systems in Europe or of law enforcement cooperation or of extradition relations which demanded some articulation of legal systems,[2] or the subject-matter of judicial and scholarly discourse.[3] However, some early examples of multilateral crime suppression conventions were developed, prototypes of what was to come.

The second phase, the inter-war period of the 20th century, was a normative melting pot out of which modern transnational criminal laws emerged (alongside core international criminal laws). Building upon earlier models, treaties were developed with the goal of greater substantive alignment of and procedural articulation among cooperating states, in order to suppress transnational crime.

To illuminate the use of these conventions to structure transnational relations on cross-border threats today, this chapter explores these early phases. It examines selected early examples of the suppression conventions, the kinds of provisions they contained and the way contemporary scholars understood them. It then goes on to examine scholarly attempts to construe these early phases from the post-war perspective, in the building of an 'omnibus' all-inclusive concept of international criminal law.

## II. The First Phase: The Late 19th and Early 20th Centuries

### 1. The Suppression of Crime Becomes a Multilateral Issue

While examples of bilateral suppression conventions can be found as far back as the 'Jay' Treaty of 1794 between Britain and the United States,[4] in the 19th century suppression of crime became a multilateral issue. A profusion of international gatherings focused their attention on novel crimes enabled by new technologies and transport methods such as the telegraph, steam train and ship.[5]

[2] See Härter, Chapter 1 in this book.

[3] See Karl Härter, 'The Circulation of Transnational Criminal Law between the Americas and Germany (1848–1914) in Extradition Treaties, Juridical Discourses and International Associations' (2019) 74 Rev Fac Direito UFMG, Belo Horizonte 353 (hereafter Härter, 'Circulation').

[4] See Roger S Clark, 'Some Aspects of the Concept of International Criminal Law: Suppression Conventions, Jurisdiction, Submarine Cables and the Lotus' (2011) 22 Crim LF 519, 523 (hereafter Clark, 'Some Aspects') pointing to the significance of the promise by both parties in art 20 to apply 'condign punishment' to those who 'receive, protect, harbour, conceal or assist [pirates] in any manner'.

[5] Paul Knepper, *The Invention of International Crime: A Global Issue in the Making, 1881–1914* (Macmillan 2010) 5 (hereafter Knepper, *Invention*).

Attempts to suppress the slave trade had to rely on treaties because, as Wheaton noted in 1866, attempts to analogize slavery to the customary law of piracy had failed.[6] Early anti-slave trade treaties were limited. The legality of the seizure of alleged slave-ships, for example, was generally dependent on the domestic law of the flag state.[7] By 1879, however, Phillimore thought slavery a crime[8] and praised the Great Britain Egyptian Treaty for the Suppression of Slave Trade of 4 August 1877,[9] which provided inter alia that 'any person engaged in the traffic' would be held by the government of the Khedive as guilty of 'stealing with murder', and if subject to Egyptian jurisdiction, tried by court-martial. The treaty also provided for rights of visit and for a penalty of hard labour from five months to five years.

The United States had first mooted a treaty for the protection of sub-ocean telegraph cables in 1869 but had been frustrated by the Franco-Prussian war. The idea was picked up first in 1879 by the Institute of International Law and then in 1882 by a conference in France.[10] The 1884 Submarine Cables Convention is a still operative innovation with a broad scope. In 1905, Oppenheim drew attention to article II, a provision that proclaimed 'it is a punishable offence to break or injure a submarine cable, wilfully or by culpable negligence'.[11] Although apparently directly created by the treaty, article XII revealed the indirect mechanism for creation of this offence:

> The High Contracting Parties engage to take or to propose to their respective legislatures the necessary measures for insuring the execution of the present Convention, and especially for punishing, by either fine or imprisonment, or both, those who contravene the provisions of articles II, V and VI.

The Convention adopted a structure for international coordination that became the standard: the treaty outlined an inter-state norm and the parties promised to criminalize it. Further provisions set out the ambit of these laws and their enforcement. Article VIII made provision for flag-state jurisdiction and failing that jurisdiction based on nationality or other 'general rules of jurisdiction prescribed by the laws of the particular state'. The jurisdiction to enforce under article X included a revolutionary power to demand that the master of a vessel reasonably believed to have committed an offence prove the nationality of the vessel.[12]

6 Henry Wheaton, *Elements of International Law* (1866; reproduced Clarendon Press 1936) 125.

7 See Hugo Fischer 'The Suppression of Slavery in International Law' (1950) 3(1) ILQ 28, 34–36.

8 Sir Robert Phillimore, *Commentaries upon International law: Volume 1* (3rd edn, Butterworths 1879) 410–411 (hereafter Phillimore, *Commentaries*).

9 (Adopted 4 August 1877) Hertslet's Commercial Treaties, vol XIV, 321; Phillimore, *Commentaries* (n 8) 422–23.

10 Lassa Oppenheim, *International Law: A Treatise: Volume One: Peace* (4th edn by Arnold McNair, Longmans 1928) 754 (hereafter Oppenheim, *International Law*, 4th edn).

11 Lassa Oppenheim, *International Law: A Treatise: Volume One: Peace* (1st edn, Longmans 1905) 354 (hereafter Oppenheim, *International Law*, 1st edn).

12 Clark, 'Some Aspects' (n 4) 527–28.

In contrast, an attempt in the late 1890s to police anarchism through secret protocols did not have the desired effect of harmonizing offences because of qualms about political policing.[13]

Scholars and diplomats cooperating in a number of new NGOs drove development of new laws through the turn of the century. For example, action against the *traité des blanches* (white slavery) was driven by NGOs and international congresses.[14] Press exposés in the early 1880s that leading British girls into prostitution in Belgium was not a crime in Britain,[15] triggered moral panic and multilateral action. In 1899, the National Vigilance Association helped organize an International Congress on the White Slave Traffic held in London. The first inter-state conference took place in 1902 in Paris. The 1904 White Slave Agreement, concerned with information exchange and victim protection, was followed by the 1910 White Slave Convention, which sought to align substantive criminal offences. Article 1, for example, provides:

> Whoever, in order to gratify the passions of another person, has procured, enticed, or led away, even with her consent, a woman or girl under age, for immoral purposes, shall be punished, notwithstanding that the various acts constituting the offence may have been committed in different countries.

Explicitly transnational in scope, it anticipates that the commission of the offence, although not necessarily cross-border, might cross borders; if it did so, the parties promised to punish it as an offence in their own law. Responding to the potential transnationality of crime in this way has been typical of suppression conventions ever since. Article 3 clarifies that criminalization is through national law, and article 5 deems these offences to be contained within any of the parties' extant extradition treaties, another innovation.

## 2. Attempts to Conceptualize Early Suppression Conventions

The first steps towards recognizing an international criminal law in the sense of international law concerned with crime had already been taken in Germany by von Bar and Beling in the early 1890s.[16] By 1898 Von Lizst had a concept of offences against international law.[17] The difficulty, accentuated by positivism's divorce of

[13] Knepper, *Invention* (n 5) 156–58; Richard Bach Jensen, 'The International Anti-Anarchist Conference of 1898 and the Origins of Interpol' (1981) 16(2) Journal of Contemporary History 323.

[14] Marlou Schrover, 'History of Slavery, Human Smuggling and Trafficking 1860–2010' in Gerben Bruinsma (ed), *Histories of Transnational Crime* (Springer 2015) 41, 45, 51; Knepper, *Invention* (n 5) 98, 111 et seq.

[15] Knepper, *Invention* (n 5) 101.

[16] Carl Ludwig von Bar, *Lehrbuch des internationalen Privat- und Strafrechts* (Enke 1892) and Ernst Beling, *Die strafrechtliche Bedeutung der Exterritorialität* (Schletter 1896).

[17] Frans von Liszt, *Das Völkerrecht systematisch dargestellt* (Haering 1898) 125–30.

the national law from the *ius gentium*,[18] was the disconnection between the international 'rule' and the national norm. In a strongly dualistic analysis, in 1899 Triepel pointed out that the so-called crimes against nations were offences in domestic law and thus had no point of contact with international law.[19]

However, as early as 1882, citing agreements for punishment of anarchist attacks, Von Lizst stated that international criminal law could include among other things (extradition, extraterritorial jurisdiction) '[t]he legal clauses created by international agreement for the purpose of protecting certain legal interests against international attacks.'[20] At the turn of the century, contemporary scholarship continued to categorize these treaties within a broad international criminal law. In 1905, Oppenheim noted that

> 'International Crimes' refers to crimes like piracy on the high seas or the slave trade, which either every state can punish on the seizure of the criminals, of whatever nationality they may be, or which every state has by the law of nations a duty to prevent.[21]

By 1920, Oppenheim had added the drug, slavery, white slavery and pornography treaties as examples.[22] Individuals who fell within the scope of these treaties were considered by some to be, as Manner noted in 1952 (citing Adler writing in 1907)

> subjects both of national and international law. For, this argument continues, the duty of the individual to abstain from these acts is not only a national, but a 'national international' municipal duty or an obligation imposed upon men both by national and international law.[23]

Focusing on the need to increase transnational cooperation, others thought of these treaties as administrative in nature. Van Hamel characterized them in 1911 as an effort 'to obtain efficient international relations for mutual assistance of police authorities, extradition, and other measures.'[24] In 1928, Brierly described them as

[18] See Ziv Bohrer, 'International Criminal Law's Millennium of Forgotten History' (2016) 34(22) Law & Hist Rev 393, 427 et seq.

[19] Heinrich Triepel, *Völkerrecht und Landesrecht* (Hirschfield 1899) 331–35.

[20] Franz von Lizst, 'Sind gleiche Grundsätze des internationalen Strafrechts für die europäischen Staaten anzustreben und eventuell welche?' (1882) 2 Zeitschrift für die Gesamte Strafrechtswissenschaft 50 et seq (author's translation).

[21] Oppenheim, *International Law*, 1st edn (n 11) 201.

[22] Lassa Oppenheim, *International Law: A Treatise: Volume One: Peace* (3rd edn, Longmans 1920) 767–68.

[23] George Manner, 'The Object Theory of the Individual in International Law' (1952) 46 AJIL 428, 434 citing Adler, 'Über die Verletzung völkerrechlicher Pflichten durch Individuen" (1907) 1 Zeitschrift für Völkerrecht 614.

[24] See Joost Adriaan van Hamel, 'The International Union of Criminal Law' (1911) 2(1) JCLC 22, 26.

special forms of international cooperation 'limited to an agreement to coordinate national laws or to introduce uniform methods into the national administration'.[25]

## III. The Second Phase: The Proliferation of Suppression Conventions in the Inter-War Period

### 1. The Institutionalization of Transnational Crime Suppression

After its establishment in 1919, the League of Nations became the centre for dealing with global social issues including crime control.[26] A transnational crime control administration was built around the advisory committees on opium and trafficking in women.[27] Even non-members of the League like the United States and Japan (after their withdrawal) participated fully in these organizations.

The 1923 Obscene Publications Convention was one of the first multilateral treaties adopted in this period. Attacking the supply chain, it required parties to criminalize trade and distribution as well as importation, conveyance and exportation, dealing in, distributing or advertising of obscene matter.[28] Jurisdictional innovations included a permissive nationality jurisdiction and expansion of territoriality if any one of the constitutive elements of the offence occurred within a state party's territory.[29] Provision was also made for the direct transmission of rogatory commissions between judicial authorities or through the diplomatic channel directly to a judicial authority.[30]

Counterfeiting of stamps and smuggling through the mail had been a concern of the Universal Postal Union (UPU) from 1878[31] and in the 1924 UPU Convention,[32] counterfeiting stamps and smuggling of drugs through the post were finally subject to a criminalization obligation.[33] Counterfeiting of foreign currency was also a concern. The US Supreme Court's determination in 1887 in the *US v Arjona*[34] that international law obliged states to prevent the counterfeiting of foreign currency

[25] JL Brierly, *The Law of Nations: An Introduction to the International Law of War and Peace* (Clarendon 1928) 202.

[26] See Ernestine Fitz-Maurice, 'The Convention for the Suppression of Counterfeiting Currency: An Analysis' (1932) 26 AJIL 533, 536 (hereafter Fitz-Maurice, 'Counterfeiting').

[27] Paul Knepper, *International Crime in the Twentieth Century: The League of Nations Era, 1919–1939* (Palgrave Macmillan 2011) 67 et seq. (hereafter Knepper, *League of Nations*).

[28] Art 1.

[29] Art 2.

[30] Art 3.

[31] Art 11 of the 1878 Universal Postal Union Convention (adopted 1 June 1878, entered into force 1 April 1879) 20 Stat 734.

[32] 1924 Universal Postal Union Convention (adopted 28 August 1924, entered into force 1 October 1925) 44 Stat 2221.

[33] Arts 41 and 79.

[34] *US v Arjona* [1887] 120 US 479.

within their jurisdictions had had little practical impact. In 1925, for example, France complained in vain to Hungary about the large quantities of French francs counterfeited in Hungary apparently with the complicity of Hungarian officials.[35] The difficulty according to Fitz-Maurice was how to 'internationalize' the crime while still respecting sovereignty.[36] She describes a characteristic split between maximalist and minimalist views of cooperation, and why practicality dictated minimalism:

> There were two main currents of thought, one, which favoured the unification of national laws to a maximum degree, and the other, which sought the reconciliation of national legal diversity if only to a limited extent. Since the application of the former idea would have far exceeded the limits of possibility and hence have spelled the failure of the convention as a practical measure, it was the latter idea of minimum modification which prevailed.[37]

The 1929 Counterfeiting Convention was considered the model convention on 'harmonization' of criminal laws.[38] It tackled the transnationality of offences using the model pioneered in the 1923 Obscene Publications Convention: if the fabrication occurred in one state while the uttering of the currency occurred in another, both were to be treated as independent offences giving each state jurisdiction.[39] For extraterritorial counterfeiters, the treaty provided for nationality jurisdiction and for an extradite or prosecute mechanism.[40] The Convention also made provision for the establishment of national central offices to foster transnational cooperation and serve as clearing houses.[41] There was no absolute obligation to extradite, however (a victory for those states keen to preserve asylum). An optional protocol was adopted requiring parties not to treat extradition for counterfeiting as limited by political asylum; in order to obtain 'really effective suppression of crime' the Conference recommended the adoption of a general extradition convention.[42]

The League also assumed a prominent role in international drug suppression. It revived the 1912 Hague Opium Convention which laid down basic regulation of licit drug activities.[43] Criminalizing illicit drug-related activities proved

35 Fitz-Maurice, 'Counterfeiting' (n 26) 535; Mark Lewis, *The Birth of the New Justice: The Internationalization of Crime and Punishment, 1919–1950* (OUP 2014) 114 (hereafter Lewis, *Birth of the New Justice*).

36 Lewis, *Birth of the New Justice* (n 35) 114.

37 ibid 114; also JW Garner, 'International Convention for the Repression of Counterfeiting' (1930) 24 AJIL 135, 136.

38 League of Nations, *Penal and Penitentiary Questions: Improvements in Penal Administration, Report of the Fifth Committee*, LON Doc A.70.1931.IV, 21 September 1931, 2, fn 1.

39 Art 4; Fitz-Maurice, 'Counterfeiting' (n 26) 539.

40 Arts 8 and 9; Fitz-Maurice, 'Counterfeiting' (n 26) 544.

41 Art 12; Fitz-Maurice, 'Counterfeiting' (n 26) 546; Lewis , *Birth of the New Justice* (n 35) 118.

42 Rec 12 and 14.

43 Art 295 of the League Covenant provided that ratification of the Covenant also means ratification of the 1912 Hague Opium Convention. See Knepper, *League of Nations* (n 27) 68.

more difficult. Consider, for example, Dutch objections to an Opium Advisory Committee recommendation that the 1925 Opium Convention's[44] offences should be extraditable:

> It would be very difficult to find a definition which would be recognised internationally for offences against the opium laws in respect of which extradition should be granted and which should give rise to international co- operation. Every State which signed the 1925 Geneva Convention ... has framed its own legislation in such a way as to give effect to the provisions of that Convention. The penal stipulations contained in those laws are directed against acts which have been made punishable by the Administration in accordance with the special circumstances of the country.[45]

The 1936 Drugs Convention tried to bring suppression of illicit drug activities into line with earlier innovations. 'Some unification' of domestic drug crimes, as well as agreement to heavy penalties, extradition and jurisdiction and police cooperation, was considered appropriate to respond to the scale and relative impunity of drug trafficking.[46] The 1936 Drugs Convention incorporated the main features of the 1929 Counterfeiting Convention.[47] Again, a minimalist approach to the modification of domestic law was adopted because of the diversity of drug laws, differences in scale of penalties, terminology and distinctions in matters of principle.[48] Under article 2, parties promised to punish severely a number of listed acts, something considered a great advance by most[49] except the United States which thought harmonization too difficult.[50] Employing the 1929 Counterfeiting Convention approach, article 4 provided that each of these acts if committed in different states shall be considered a distinct offence. Provision was made for extradition or prosecution where that was not on option, but the United States' proposal for the seizure of the profits from drug trafficking was rejected as too difficult in practice.[51] It also protested against the failure to regulate the sale of opium or cannabis and the 'worthless' extradition provision as it permitted refusal in insufficiently serious cases.[52] These protests echoed the US

[44] International Convention, Adopted by the Second Opium Conference (League of Nations), and Protocol thereto, Geneva, 19 February 1925, 81 LNTS 317.

[45] Reply from the Netherlands government [Translation.] The Hague, 29 August 1932, League of Nations Doc 12/38670/20950, League of Nations Official Journal, Jan 1933, 160.

[46] JG Starke, 'The Convention of 1936 for the Suppression of the Illicit Traffic in Dangerous Drugs' (1937) 31(1) AJIL 31, 32 (hereafter Starke, '1936 Convention').

[47] See Recommendation V of the Final Act of the Convention.

[48] See Starke, '1936 Convention' (n 46) 34.

[49] See Starke, '1936 Convention' (n 46) 38.

[50] 1936 Drugs Convention Communication from the Government of the United States of America, 3 December 1936, LON Doc C.530.M.341.1936.XI., 3–4.

[51] ibid 3–4; see also Starke, '1936 Convention' (n 46) 41–42.

[52] ibid 4–5.

position in the Opium Advisory Committee, one pursued vigorously after the war.[53]

## 2. The Nature of the Inter-War Development of the Suppression Conventions

During the inter-war period, organizations like the International Police Commission[54] used the notion of 'international crime' not for war crimes but for crimes that were the product of inter-connectedness, where threats originating 'elsewhere' crossed boundaries freely and could only be effectively dealt with by cooperating states.[55] Increasingly, treaties were resorted to in order to counter this alien threat to sovereignty. The Counterfeiting Convention, for example, was designed to permit parties to try an alien for extraterritorial crimes under the principle of protection/self-defence of their security and independence.[56] Thus while these conventions were viewed in abstract by contemporary scholars as meeting a general social interest in human welfare,[57] the conventions were responses to specific problems. Rather than a progressive development based on general principles, agreed measures adopted in earlier conventions were built on in later conventions. Starke distilled this nicely in 1937:

> It is curious to reflect how the small existing body of international criminal law has grown; not out of wide general principles, but *inductively*, step by step, in respect to particular offences which called for action of an international character. When such action has been taken, it has invariably been restricted by considerations of national sovereignty. In the international agreements which have dealt with criminal offences, *e.g.*, the Geneva Conventions as to slavery, counterfeiting, and traffic in women and children, the contracting states shrank from incurring obligations of a wide or general character and limited themselves to undertakings co-extensive only with the necessities of the situation.[58]

Negotiating states only agreed to as much as they needed to because each suppression convention had a purely utilitarian law enforcement rationale: to cut the source of supply in order to achieve domestic suppression.[59] Starke comments that

[53] See David Bewley-Taylor, *The United States and International Drug Control* (Continuum 1999) 54 et seq.

[54] Knepper, *League of Nations* (n 27) 77–78.

[55] Knepper, *League of Nations* (n 27) 72–73.

[56] PE Corbett, *Law and Society in the Relations of States* (Harcourt Brace 1951) 171.

[57] Charles G Fenwick, *International Law* (Allen and Unwin 1924) 65–66; Oppenheim, *International Law*, 4th edn (n 10) 800; William M Hepburn, 'International Legislation on Social Questions' (1931) 9 New York University Law Quarterly Review 198 (hereafter Hepburn, 'Social Questions').

[58] Starke, '1936 Convention' (n 46) 31.

[59] Hepburn, 'Social Questions' (n 57) 200.

the 1936 Drug Convention demonstrated that 'international legislation tends to be fullest and most extensive in application where utilitarian interests are strongest'.[60]

Only a limited number of states participated in this development because the threatening activity was considered to be the work of aliens not nationals; to originate in Africa, Asia and South America. The early treaties were adopted by states that had more in common than they had with the world at large.[61] In 1928, McNair described the efforts to abolish slavery as products of Christian civilization. [62] The label the 'Gentleman's club', given to the League's Opium Advisory Committee, characterizes the authors of the drug treaties fittingly.[63] The laws these states agreed on had a paternalistic nature. Mandate holders under the League were, for example, permitted to impose them for the benefit of the locals.[64] Finally, the appetite for treaty-making among these states was driven by their selective interests: the League rejected calls from the *Association International de Droit Pénal* (AIDP) for conventions in universal jurisdiction over acts of terrorism and piracy in 1926 and 1927 before the successful negotiation of the Counterfeiting Convention.[65]

## 3. Inter-War Attempts to Categorize the Suppression Conventions

Contemporary scholars recognized that crime was becoming increasingly 'international' in the sense that it impacted across borders. For example, speaking at the League Assembly in 1927, the Romanian delegate Professor Vespasian Pella in a sociological observation noted that crime was becoming international.[66] However, they did not agree about how to categorize the crimes in the suppression conventions. McNair, writing in 1928, for example, noted that the antislavery treaties had the limited goal of ensuring 'international cooperation'.[67] In 1929, Fischer Williams identified a clear ambiguity in the term 'international criminal law':[68]

[60] Starke, '1936 Convention' (n 46) 43.

[61] George Schwarzenberger, *A Manual of International Law* (5th edn, Stevens 1967) 14.

[62] Oppenheim, *International Law*, 4th edn (n 10) 522–23.

[63] Kettil Bruun, Lynn Pan and Ingemar Rexed, *The Gentlemen's Club: International Control of Drugs and Alcohol* (University of Chicago Press 1975).

[64] William Edward Hall, *A Treatise on International Law* (8th edn, Clarendon 1924) 162.

[65] Andrei Mamolea, 'Vespasian V. Pella: International Criminal Justice as a Safeguard of Peace, 1919–1952' in Frederic Mégrét and Immi Tallgren, *The Dawn of a Discipline: International Criminal Justice and its Early Exponents* (CUP 2020) 49, 72 (hereafter Mamolea, 'Pella').

[66] See LON Doc C.548.M.196.1925.V, 40.

[67] Oppenheim, *International Law*, 4th edn (n 10) 590.

[68] Sir John Fischer Williams, *Chapters on Current International Law and the League of Nations* (Longmans 1929) 243. Fischer Williams was one of the main opponents of attempts in the negotiation of the Counterfeiting Convention to impose an obligation to extradite—see Lewis, *Birth of the New Justice* (n 35) 119.

> In what sense in this connection is the expression 'international crime' used? It would appear to have at least two meanings: one, a crime against international law, and the other, a crime which brings or may bring the offender into conflict with the laws of more than one country. It is the second sense which is the most popular use of the phrase, and which is associated with the 'international criminal' who is known to the authorities of more than one police force. An example of 'international crime' in this second sense would be the printing in country A of forged paper currency of country B with intent to pass it off in country C. Although respectable political authority may be cited for the use of the words 'international crime' as a description of an offence of this class, all such offences fall within the province of municipal law, and do not acquire their delictual quality from international law, whether conventional or original. Such offences may properly call for the close co-operation of the police forces of several countries with a view to their more effectual repression and may, equally with all other crimes whose authors may be outside the limits of the local jurisdiction primarily concerned, emphasise the urgent necessity in modern international intercourse for the adoption of rules for extradition affecting nationals as well as aliens, but they do not constitute 'international crimes' in the sense that they are violations of the Law of Nations.

Fischer William's procedural goal of more effectual suppression of specific transnational criminality stands in stark contrast to the attempts by scholars in the AIDP to use the suppression conventions as a foundation for a grander systemic change.[69] In 1924 the AIDP voted in favour of a proposal by Pella for the unification of penal law.[70] Pella advocated unification in order to suppress offences like terrorism and counterfeiting particularly damaging to the international legal order; unification would remove national inconsistencies that operated as obstacles to extradition and jurisdiction.[71] Another supporter, Rappaport, saw unification as a step towards universalism over crimes under international law because he considered extradition as insufficient to deal with these crimes.[72] With a similar destination in mind, Saldaña argued for the progressive denationalization of the international order from national to extra-national to supranational, with the abandonment of discretionary tools such as extradition along the way.[73] For the advocates of unification, the ultimate goal—a kind of global common criminal law—would ensure respect

[69] Lewis, *Birth of the New Justice* (n 35) 112.

[70] 'Resolutions of the Congresses of the International Association of Penal Law' (2015) 86 RiDP 253. See Mamolea, 'Pella' (n 65) 56.

[71] See Mamolea, 'Pella' (n 65) 49–50.

[72] Patrycja Grzebyk, 'Emil Stanislaw Rappaport: His Road from Abolition to Prosecution of Nations' in Immi Tallgren and Frédéric Mégret (eds), *The Dawn of a Discipline: International Criminal Justice and its Early Exponents* (OUP 2020) 93, 106 (hereafter Tallgren and Mégret, *Dawn of Discipline*).

[73] Ignacio de la Rasilla del Moral, 'International Criminal Justice as Universal Social Defence: Quintiliano Saldaña (1878–1938)' in Tallgren and Mégret, *Dawn of Discipline* (n 72) 118, 130.

for *nullum crimen sine lege* in a transnational context.[74] They were not, however, that interested in articulating the response of states to cross-border crime; unification was a step on the road to supranationalism. Ironically, only de Vabres, a founder member of the AIDP who was to sit as a judge at Nuremberg, was actually concerned to address the problems of transnationalism.[75] In response to transnational crime's increased potential for jurisdictional conflict, he sought to develop what Mégret terms a 'sort of meta-private international criminal law, or at least an international public law of private international law' that would provide solutions by both simultaneously permitting states to extend extraterritorial jurisdiction and limiting that extension.[76]

International Conferences on the Unification of Criminal Law held in 1927 and 1928 first tried to unify the forms of charges for the offences in the Opium, Counterfeiting and Obscene Publications Conventions.[77] In 1928, the International Bureau for the Unification of Criminal Law was founded, with the goal of identifying which questions of criminal law could be harmonized.[78] In 1931, the League of Nations Fifth Committee reported to the League Assembly on the limits of intensification of international cooperation against crime. The rapporteur, Pella, identified three perspectives on this problem: 'progressive unification of penal law, the co-operation between States for the prevention and suppression of crimes, and the execution of the penalty'.[79] He noted that in the Fifth Committee civil law states comfortable with unification had cited the suppression conventions as activity towards unification concerning 'offences of an international character';[80] the conventions were the first step in progressive unification of penal laws.[81] Pella also noted a similar unification concerning 'fundamental principles of criminal law' through these conventions, citing the Counterfeiting Convention's provisions on attempts and complicity.[82] In his preparatory report, he had even speculated:

[74] MA Caloyanni, 'An International Criminal Court' (1928) 14 Transactions of the Grotius Society 69, 75; Lewis, *Birth of the New Justice* (n 35) 115–16.

[75] Frédéric Mégret, 'Henri Donnedieu de Vabres: Penal Liberal, Moderate Internationalist and Nuremberg Judge' in Tallgren and Mégret, *Dawn of Discipline* (n 72) 146, 153.

[76] ibid 152.

[77] First International Conference for the Unification of Penal Law, Warsaw, 1–5 November 1927, Actes de la Conférence (1929, Recueil Sirey) 1; Second International Conference for the Unification of Penal Law, Rome, 21–25 May 1928, Actes de la Conférence (1931, Juris-Classeurs) 1.

[78] International Bureau for the Unification of Criminal Law, Draft Statues, art 1, annex to Joint reply submitted to the secretary general by the seven organisations consulted on questions of the gradual unification of criminal law and the cooperation of states in the prevention and suppression of crime, LON Doc C.L.174.1932.IV. Annex. A.P.4, 20 October 1932.

[79] League of Nations, *Penal and Penitentiary Questions: Improvements in Penal Administration, Report of the Fifth Committee*, LON Doc A.70.1931.IV, 21 September 1931, 1.

[80] ibid 2.

[81] ibid 3.

[82] ibid 2, fn 1. See also Jeßberger, Chapter 19 and Petzsche, Chapter 18 in this book..

> At a more distant date, the possibility might even be contemplated of embodying all the provisions of the existing conventions in a *general convention*, which would include all the rules relating to the punishment of offences declared to be international offences by treaty provisions. All other offences which Governments might agree to regard as international in character could be inserted within the framework of such a Convention, without it being necessary to draft new conventions.[83]

When the League Assembly approached a number of penal NGOs asking them how the League might help to achieve the goal of 'a gradual unification of criminal law and the cooperation of states in the prevention and suppression of crime', they were a little less sanguine. In their joint reply, they said that the League could do so through standardized definitions of offences and of fundamental rules of criminal law in national penal law, under obligations in international conventions,[84] a development that would have had obvious benefits for individuals, as it would have ensured adherence to the principle of legality in a transnational context. The NGOs also suggested improvements for cooperation between states on extradition and policing.[85] The responses of members of the League to these ideas was mixed. Civil law states used to codification were more receptive, common law states were not. Britain, for example, thought standardization should only be sought about specific topics where there was some prospect of unanimity such as the traffic in women and drugs. Unification was not the goal; the goal was to address the problem of policing crime.[86] Similarly, Hungary suggested the object should be regulation '[o]n a wide international basis, of the punishment of crimes and offenses committed in a foreign country'.[87] Kuhn articulated this opposing view:

> The crux of the problem is that the divergences of law and procedure be fully recognized and yet that the administration of criminal police and criminal justice be coordinated throughout the world by a full exchange of information, by active co-operation in apprehending criminals, and in a logical and just division among the various countries of their sovereign jurisdiction to punish for crime.[88]

[83] ibid 2, fn 1.

[84] Joint reply submitted to the secretary general by the seven organisations consulted on questions of the gradual unification of criminal law and the cooperation of states in the prevention and suppression of crime, LON Doc C.L.174.1932.IV. Annex. A.P.4, 20 October 1932, para 1.

[85] ibid para 2.

[86] League of Nations, *Gradual Unification of Criminal Law and Co-operation of States in the Prevention and Suppression of Crime*, 30 May 1933, LON Doc A.7.1933.V, 4; Arthur K Kuhn, 'International Cooperation in the Suppression of Crime' (1934) 28(3) AJIL 541, 543 (hereafter Kuhn, 'International Cooperation').

[87] Kuhn, 'International Cooperation' (n 86) 543.

[88] ibid.

The maximalist-minimalist division within responses to transnational crime articulated by Fitz-Maurice is patent in these views, and it was to persist in the post-war debate about the role suppression conventions played in a broad concept of international criminal law.

## IV. The Suppression Conventions in a Post-War 'Omnibus' International Criminal Law

At the close of World War II, there was little clarity as to just how the suppression conventions fitted into the newly minted international criminal law.[89] In 1945, Levy listed a range of 'international law crimes' including piracy, protection of submarine cables, slave trading, arms trafficking, trafficking in obscene publications and counterfeiting, as special grounds of state jurisdiction.[90] That same year, Wright went further and identified piracies and offences defined in general treaties as offences 'against universal law'.[91] However, in 1947, Wright labelled the 1937 Terrorism Convention as an exercise in national jurisdiction to try aliens for certain offences against the laws of nations outside that state's territory.[92] In 1952, Jessup opined that the crimes in the suppression conventions were 'acts significant enough to warrant placing their punishment under international auspices',[93] while Kelsen analogized criminal liability under the provisions of the Submarine Cables Convention to piracy and thus subject to international obligation.[94] In 1955, Lauterpacht claimed that pirates, slave-traders and the Nuremberg accused were subjects of international law but omitted other crimes in the suppression conventions.[95]

The idea that the suppression conventions constitute a part of an 'omnibus' international criminal law in the sense of an undifferentiated all-inclusive system, received its clearest articulation and support in the 1960s and 70s, when the number of suppression conventions began to grow but the practical application of the core international criminal law weakened. Conscious as van Bemmelen put it in 1973 that '[i]nternational criminal law is only in its infancy'[96] various scholars tried

[89] See eg Hersch Lauterpacht, 'The Law of Nations and the Punishment of War Crimes' (1944) 21 BYIL 63.
[90] Albert GD Levy, 'Criminal Responsibility of Individuals and International Law' (1945) 12 UChiLRev 313, 326.
[91] Quincy Wright, 'War Criminals' (1945) 39 AJIL 257, 282.
[92] Quincy Wright, 'The Law of the Nuremberg Trial' (1947) 41 AJIL 38, 43.
[93] Philip C Jessup, *A Modern Law of Nations* (Macmillan 1952) 178.
[94] Hans Kelsen, *Principles of Public International Law* (Reinhart 1952) 127.
[95] Oppenheim, *International Law: A Treatise: Volume One: Peace* (8th edn by Hersch Lauterpacht, Longmans 1955) 341.
[96] JM Van Bemmelen, 'Reflections and Observations on International Criminal Law' in M Cherif Bassiouni and Ved P Nanda, *A Treatise on International Criminal Law; Volume I Crimes and Punishment* (Thomas 1973) 77 (hereafter Bassiouni and Nanda, *Treatise*).

to buttress it with as much normative weight as possible. In 1968 Kunz noted the 'quasi-universal' nature of the suppression conventions.[97] In 1970, Falk boosted the gravity of their offences when he referred to 'other phenomena that shock the conscience and undermine the common interests of states [such as] trading and slaves and narcotics, genocide, and apartheid'.[98] In 1972, Starke labelled the suppression conventions 'normative' rather than mere contractual treaties and concluded that through concerted action by states international drug traffickers, counterfeiters and hijackers had 'become subjects of conventional rules of international criminal law in much the same way as pirates jure gentium under customary rules'.[99] In 1973, Mueller and Besharov thought them 'lesser offences' than for example war crimes but nevertheless falling within the 'larger jurisdictional unit' of international criminal law to which states had given up sovereignty.[100] In the same collection of essays, Jescheck included treaty crimes within international crimes but noted that they have 'enjoyed quite different degrees of protection by international criminal law'.[101] Ryu and Silving identified an expansive tendency to treat international criminal law as all international law dealing with criminal matters but then to confine the label to crimes under international law and to use international criminal law in this sense to stand in place of all variations of criminal law with an international aspect.[102]

Criticism of the notion that the suppression conventions buttressed international criminal law in this narrower sense had, however, been made as early as the 1940s. In 1944, the Stalinist jurist Trainin thought that the suppression conventions failed to provide evidence of an international criminal law:

> Selection of ... crimes as the object of the provisions of international conventions is necessitated, not by theoretical considerations concerning the nature of international crime, but by various political motives, the interests of one country or a group of countries in the combat against a given crime, material facilities for organization of such combat and other reasons of that nature. Because of their juristic nature and because of their factual significance, conventions for certain common criminal offences appear to be one of the various forms of reciprocal support for criminal law by governments having in view a realistic combat against

[97] Joseph L Kunz, *The Changing Law of Nations: Essays on International Law* (Ohio State UP 1968) 29–30.

[98] Richard Falk, *The Status of International Society* (Princeton UP 1970) 139.

[99] JG Starke, *An Introduction to International Law* (6th edn, Butterworths 1972) 47, 72.

[100] GOW Mueller and Douglas Besharov, 'The Existence of International Criminal Law and its Evolution to the Point of its Enforcement Crisis' in Bassiouni and Nanda, *Treatise* (n 96) 7.

[101] Hans Heinrich Jescheck 'International Criminal Law—Its object and Recent Developments' in Bassiouni and Nanda, *Treatise* (n 96) 49, 50–72.

[102] Paul K Ryu and Helen Silving, 'International Criminal Law—Search for Meaning' in Bassiouni and Nanda, *Treatise* (n 96) 22.

> crime. The reciprocal action of governments is not connected directly with the problem of international crimes.[103]

By 1950, Pella, was also eager to

> dispel the confusion of the group of international crimes consisting of acts against the peace and security of mankind and another group of so-called international crimes, such as piracy, slave trade, traffic in women and children, [etc]. [104]

He noted that the latter did not generally prejudice international relations and were unsuited to the jurisdiction of an international criminal court; given states were interested in their repression they should he thought be left to national courts with expanded jurisdictions.[105] In 1950, after pointing out that one of the claimed subject matters of international criminal law by its proponents was rules imposing on each state a duty to include in its municipal law rules for punishing certain acts in its jurisdiction, Schwarzenberger argued that this was not part of an international criminal law because the penal rules in each were municipal.[106] In 1955, former Tokyo International Military Tribunal judge Radhabinod Pal distinguished what he called crimes 'under' international law, in which he included piracy, slavery and counterfeiting from crimes in international law itself (which like Schwarzenberger he considered an empty category).[107] The former were in his view *delicta juris gentium*, crimes defined by international law but brought into national legal systems by domestic legislation, the condition precedent to an obligation on individuals to observe these laws. He continued:

> If such acts are criminal it is because they are made so by the several national states for their respective national systems. They may be brought *under* international law for various political motives, for considerations other than the infringement of the order, if any, established by international law. The interests of a country or of a group of countries in the combat of a given crime, material facilities for organization of such combat and the like might have been responsible for such crimes having been brought under international control. But for this reason they cannot juristically be called crimes in international relations in the strict sense.[108]

[103] AN Trainin, *The Criminal Responsibility of the Hitlerites* (Moscow 1944).
[104] Vespasian V Pella, 'Towards an International Criminal Court' (1950) 44(1) AJIL 37, 54–55.
[105] ibid 55.
[106] G Schwarzenberger, 'The Problem of International Criminal Law' 1950 (3) CurrLegProb 263.
[107] Radhabinod Pal, *Crimes in International Law* (University of Calcutta Press 1955) 1.
[108] ibid 1.

## V. Conclusion

The separation of international criminal law in a strict sense from transnational criminal law occurred in the immediate post-war period at Nuremberg and Tokyo when war crimes, joined by the newly minted crimes of aggression and humanity, scaled the formidable barrier of state sovereignty. What we now call transnational criminal law, the product of prudential motives and technical enforcement capacity was left behind that barrier. The history of the suppression conventions illustrates that in the development of these crimes, grander schemes to produce a uniform global penal code faltered in the face of the need to accommodate sovereign interests and the absence of the required solidarity. Saldaña's dream of global codification was not realized with regard to cross-border crime. The suppression conventions were simply a step in the process of codification but they never abandoned sovereignty, so in a sense transnational criminal law is a residue of nationalism. It retains, indeed is designed to foster the use of discretionary remedies like extradition and extraterritorial jurisdiction. Today, transnational criminal law has more in common with de Vabres' notion of a meta-private international criminal law, designed to permit and control sovereign extensions of extraterritorial jurisdiction. Nevertheless, within this system it is important to recognize that the 'maximalists' tend to lose out in their constant battle with the 'minimalists' because the cross-border nature of the targeted activities sustains a strong domestic interest in their suppression.

Post-war attempts to build the suppression conventions into a viable 'omnibus' concept of international criminal law strongly identified with the core international crimes were never entirely convincing. The label was uncomfortable because of the dualistic nature of the legal obligations involved (identified by Triepel in 1899): an inter-state tortious obligation to establish criminal offences according with the conventional definition, and a domestic penal obligation imposing individual criminal liability for violation of an offence. It is difficult to call the individual criminal subject to the latter obligation an international criminal because they are not a criminal in international law. Moreover, the 'omnibus' model neglected the sociological nature of these crimes. In a negative sense, they did not have the element of state involvement so characteristic of a true international crime. In a positive sense, they were all actually or potentially cross-border in nature and this potential cross-border harm was what led to state interest in coordination of efforts against these activities, and the development of different modes of cooperation against them. These crimes are better described as transnational criminal law, building on Jessup's view of 'transnational law' as including 'all law which regulates actions or events that transcend national frontiers'.[109] That is not to say that

[109] ibid 2–3.

a differently more broadly formulated omnibus concept of international criminal law which includes international criminal law in the strict sense of crimes under international law, transnational criminal law, mutual legal assistance, issues of extraterritorial jurisdiction … in effect all criminal law with some international aspect, is not a useful concept. It is just to say that we should avoid too close an identification of transnational criminal law with the crimes under international law because of their varying legal and social natures.

# 4

# Transnational Epistemic Communities

## From the League of Nations to the United Nations War Crimes Commission

*Kerstin von Lingen*

## I. Introduction

The development of legal concepts relating to transboundary crimes—as war is—has to be seen in conjunction with the growth of internationalism in the first half of the 20th century. During this period, a transnational circle of lawyers who followed through with their aim of settling violence against civilians, thus forming an epistemic community of lawyers, became agents of a new, supranational policy.[1] In this chapter I explore the emergence of networks of likeminded people who first convened during the League of Nations era to draft conventions relating to minority rights and disarmament conventions, and who during World War II met again in the United Nations War Crimes Commission (UNWCC), concerned to coin concepts relating to crimes against civilians, namely 'crimes against humanity' or 'genocide'. I argue that the transboundary dimension of both, crimes and actors, formed a learning system towards what could be termed 'global justice'. 'Global' is understood here not only with a view to the planetary scale of their endeavour. Following Bhabha's notion of 'public space',[2] I argue that the most fruitful debates were created by the exile situation. Defining the earlier trajectories of thinking at Geneva as well as the boundaries of this 'exile' space is crucial to thinking about the space in which these exiled lawyers operated.[3]

According to Mazower the inter-war years and the advent of internationalism showed the importance of global encounter and arenas of debate as provided, for

[1] This chapter builds on thoughts first discussed in Kerstin von Lingen, 'Legal Flows: "Crimes against Humanity" in Transnational Legal Thought, 1899–1945' (2018) 3 Forum of Modern Intellectual History <https://doi.org/10.1017/S1479244318000239> (hereafter Lingen, 'Legal Flows'); Kerstin von Lingen, 'Setting the Path for UNWCC. The Representation of European Exile Governments on LIA and Cambridge Commission, 1941–1944' (2014) 25(1) Crim Law Forum 45, 46 (hereafter Lingen, 'Setting the Path').

[2] Homi Bhabha, *The Location of Culture* (Routledge 1994).

[3] Martin H Geyer and Johannes Paulmann, 'Introduction: The Mechanics of Internationalism' in Martin H Geyer and Johannes Paulmann (eds), *The Mechanics of Internationalism: Culture, Society, and Politics from the 1840s to the First World War* (OUP 2001) 1, 11.

Kerstin von Lingen, *Transnational Epistemic Communities* In: *Histories of Transnational Criminal Law*. Edited by: Neil Boister, Sabine Gless and Florian Jeßberger, Oxford University Press. © Kerstin von Lingen 2021.
DOI: 10.1093/oso/9780192845702.003.0005

example, in the *League of Nations* and later in the *United Nations*.[4] Sluga has highlighted, when observing the framework of international organizations, how they formed an arena of engagement especially for nations that were not yet or newly sovereign, or for minorities that were still sidelined.[5] Following the dismantling of the Habsburg empire, smaller states from Central Europe rose to the international stage. 'Small' does not refer to size, but to an element of 'secondness' deeply rooted in earlier perceptions of statehood, as was a noteworthy imbalance of access to power, expressed in the distinction of 'greater' and 'smaller' states.[6] In the inter-war years, actors like Poland, and Czechoslovakia, but also Belgium and the Netherlands, were eager to make their voices heard in international bodies, and this desire became more acute when in 1939 their statehood was threatened again by their German neighbours. I argue here that older hierarchies and existing power structures persisted even in apparently supranational bodies and continued to cause friction and frustration, especially with actors from smaller states. Organizations like the League and later the UNWCC could thus serve as what Herren describes (with a view to Swiss foreign policy endeavours) as a 'back door to power' for smaller states and during a period of exile.[7] Another recurring feature is that because of the small size of their delegations, the same representatives of small states seem to attend nearly all committees, while larger powers tend to send in more narrowly focused experts. The notion of 'impulses from the margins' is thus also applicable to European states, if their access to power and resources are similarly limited, as Fassbender and Peters have argued.[8]

This chapter proposes to zoom in on the epistemic communities[9] involved, communities characterized by the intellectual history of the emergence of concepts relating to crimes against civilians, and the actor-centred network behind these debates. Three groups can be distinguished: high-level diplomats and statesmen at diplomatic conferences, legal scholars interested in the advance of international law in an orthodox sense, and national civil servants and mid-level internationalists, who were open to compromise and not limited by a too narrow interpretation of international law. These three categories of actors bridge the two main concerns of the League of Nations: prevention and settlement of political disputes (which

[4] Mark Mazower, *No Enchanted Place: The End of Empire and the Ideological Origins of the United Nations* (Princeton University Press2009).

[5] Glenda Sluga, *Internationalism in the Age of Nationalism* (University of Pennsylvania Press 2013) 8.

[6] Georgios Varouxakis, '"Great" versus "Small" Nations: Size and National Greatness in Victorian Political Thought in Duncan Bell (ed), *Victorian Visions of Global Order. Empire and International Relations in Nineteenth Century Political Thought* (CUP 2007) 136, 136.

[7] Madeleine Herren, *Hintertüren zur Macht. Internationalismus und modernisierungsorientierte Aussenpolitik in Belgien, der Schweiz und den USA 1865–1914* (De Gruyter2000) 129.

[8] Bardo Fassbender and Anne Peters, 'Introduction: Towards a Global History of International Law' in Bardo Fassbender, Anne Peters and Simone Peter (eds), *The Oxford Handbook of the History of International Law* (OUP 2012) 1, 9.

[9] Kerstin von Lingen, *'Crimes against Humanity': Eine Ideengeschichte der Zivilisierung von Kriegsgewalt 1864–1945* (Schoeningh 2018) 23.

touches questions of core international criminal law) and furthering social and economic development (where questions of criminal law like drug-trafficking and counterfeiting of concern to states were dealt with).[10] There even seems to be a trans-scalar dimension to the phenomenon, vertical and horizontal, where actors move between international, national and local levels. Remarkably, in these committees it was often small states representatives as well as lower-level social activists representing international NGOs that really influenced opinion, working in harness with law enforcement officials rather than diplomats.

When assessing the records of the most prominent voices of international law in the inter-war years who had a record also at the League at Geneva, we see actors like Romanian minister and scholar Vespasian Pella, or his French colleague Henri Donnedieu de Vabres, a later Nuremberg judge, emerge. Kreß identifies others, including Edouard Descamps, Hugh Bellot, Quintiliano Saldano, as he focuses on other important inter-war platforms like the International Law Association (ILA) and the Association de Droit International Penal (AIDP).[11] However, this chapter zooms into the global historical dimension of the inter-war internationalist scene at Geneva and its legacy within the exile community later at London, by focusing on the circles involved with settling accounts with war criminals. A number of hitherto unfamiliar names is thus brought to the fore.

## II. From the League of Nations to London

After its establishment in 1920, the League of Nations was an 'imagined community', to borrow a term from Anderson.[12] Although Anderson used this term to refer to the nation, it also seems applicable to international organizations like the League of Nations. Pedersen observes that the League was to be 'something more than a meeting ground for sovereign states; it was to rise above national hatreds and defend nothing less than "civilisation" itself'.[13] The League was perceived as a 'democratic diplomatic arena' (McCarthy), in which, unlike in previous international politics characterized by secret diplomacy, other actors were finally allowed to raise their voices and much value was placed on transparent decision-making processes and publicity. But it turned out that transnational cooperation reached its limits where it touched the security interests of the great powers.

In the League of Nations, in trying to answer the question of containment of wartime violence, a double strategy of finding political consensus and meeting

[10] I would like to thank Neil Boister for comments on an early draft, which I take up.

[11] Claus Kreß, *Towards a Truly Universal Invisible College of International Criminal Lawyers* (2014) 2 <https://www.toaep.org/ops-pdf/4-kress>. See Pifferi, Chapter 2 in this book.

[12] Benedict Anderson, *Imagined Communities: Reflections on the Origin and Spread of Nationalism* (Verso 1983).

[13] Susan Pedersen, *The Guardians: League of Nations and the Crisis of Empire* (OUP 2015) 6.

civil society demands became important; a strategy recognizable, for example, in the committees on questions of armaments control.[14] The commission consisted of a (solely military) Permanent Armaments Commission (PAC) and a (primarily civilian) Temporary Mixed Commission (TMC) on Disarmaments, as well as a Preparatory Committee for the Conference on Disarmament (PCDC), which convened between 1926 and 1930.[15] While the earlier circles were seen as technical expert groups, the PCDC was clearly seen as a political and diplomatic endeavour, composed of delegates who expressed their nation's views.[16]

As Webster's research shows, for most of these countries the same people tended to be assigned to deal with disarmament in the various commissions, resulting in a core of individuals who 'set themselves apart over time as the main voices and chief experts on disarmament'.[17] It looks as if the disarmament committees became the breeding ground for the later legal circles debating war crimes issue, as the experiences made (and failures witnessed) in the disarmament commissions[18] formed a learning system. Lord Robert Cecil of Chelwood (Great Britain), Edvard Benes (Czechoslovakia), Paul Hymans (Belgium), Eric Colban (Norway) and Nicolas Politis (Greece) represented their countries on the PCDC. All were later to play a role in the legal debates and the UNWCC meetings of the 1940s in London. Lord Cecil was also a member of the TMC, which convened a sub-group on chemical warfare, giving him a platform for several remarkable speeches.[19]

What this group had in common was that although they represented their nation-state positions, they remained oriented towards the common goal—arms restrictions—and were prepared to make concessions. This vision was characteristic of a transnational group of experts and in this case became the driving force behind the disarmament chapters in the League of Nations. Webster summarizes:

> The contradiction that emerged in the League-sponsored disarmament process was between the 'international' approach preferred by the governments of the major powers in particular, who viewed disarmament from the viewpoint of their own strategic interests, and the 'transnational' ambitions of those League

[14] The question of international armaments control is the topic of a new research project by historian Daniel Stahl at the University Jena, see <https://www.gw.uni- jena.de/fakult%C3%A4t/historisches+institut/bereiche/neuere+und+neueste+geschichte/dr_+daniel+stahl>.

[15] Andrew Webster, 'The Transnational Dream; Politicians, Diplomats and Soldiers in the League of Nations' Pursuit of International Disarmament, 1920–1938' (2005) 14(4) Contemporary History 493, 495–97 (hereafter Webster, 'Transnational Dream').

[16] ibid 513. 'The consequence was that the members of the PCDC had very little room to depart from their formal instructions, with their primary identities as national delegates overpowering the alternative role of transnational disarmament experts.'

[17] ibid 495.

[18] See for a complete account on the failures Andrew Webster, 'From Versailles to Geneva: The Many Forms of Interwar Disarmament' (2006) 29(2) Journal of Strategic Studies 225 (hereafter Webster, 'Versailles to Geneva').

[19] ibid 237.

enthusiasts who viewed disarmament as an issue which the world war had shown intimately to affect all humanity regardless of nationality.[20]

It becomes clear that the long-standing personal cooperation of the delegates contributed a great deal to the transborder dimension and an ability to understand divergent national positions and seek compromises.

The fifth General Assembly of the League of Nations in September 1924 seems to have been something of a founding moment for the anti-war movement, whether fuelled by the development of the disarmament protocols or the need to find legal grounds to punish crimes against civilians. If we look at the members list of the fifth Assembly, we see that it includes number of individuals who proved to be influential personalities such as Benes, Hymans, Politis, Masaryk and Cassin. However, the Geneva Conference on Disarmament in May 1925 also revealed the old national reservations about internationalist efforts. The result was the 'Geneva Protocol' which embodied the formula of security, disarmament and arbitration.[21] As had been the case in Paris in 1919, there were deep differences in the insistence on the principle of sovereignty on the part of the great powers, for whom armament was a very sensitive part of their national security policy, and the interest of the smaller states in disarmament, which led to the failure to reach agreement.[22]

Two committees worked on the details, and both were chaired by men who in World War II would again play a leading role in coining post-war justice: Czech delegate Edvard Benes chaired the (third) committee on security, and Greek delegate Nicolas Politis the first committee on legal and constitutional questions, which also dealt with compulsory arbitration.[23] The third committee of the League was on disarmament, and formed the nucleus of later legal circles at London. It was chaired by Benes, Lord Cecil played a vital part in it, as did Nicolas Politis.[24]

It is interesting to focus on the representatives in these committees, and upon Edvard Benes in particular. Benes, the 'most conspicuous figure of Geneva' (Sally Marks),[25] or, as Steiner calls him, the 'calculating realist' who favoured 'a middle-of-the road approach to diplomacy',[26] was determined to establish Czechoslovakia as a mediator between Britain and France, to the advantage of Czech interests. Benes consulted only with his president, Masaryk, and was distrusted by the British

[20] Webster, 'Transnational Dream' (n 15) 498.

[21] Zara Steiner, *The Lights that Failed. European International History, 1919–1933* (OUP 2005) 380 (hereafter Steiner, *Lights*).

[22] David R Stone, 'Imperialism and Sovereignty: The League of Nations' Drive to Control the Global Arms Trade' (2000) 35(2) Journal of Contemporary History 213, 229 (hereafter Stone, 'Imperialism and Sovereignty'); Webster, 'Transnational Dream' (n 15) 504–06.

[23] Webster, 'Transnational Dream' (n 15) 506.

[24] ibid 508.

[25] Sally Marks, *The Illusion of Peace: International Relations in Europe, 1918–1933* (Palgrave Macmillan 2003) 89 (hereafter Marks, *Illusion*).

[26] Steiner, *Lights* (n 21) 298.

government.[27] Then British Foreign Secretary Austen Chamberlain was so wary of Benes that he strongly opposed his candidature as secretary general of the League in 1925. Benes was, however, the man of Geneva, six times chairman of the League Council, president of the Assembly and chairman and rapporteur of innumerable committees.[28] He was, together with Nicolas Politis, key in drafting and mobilizing support for the 1924 Geneva Protocol. Benes had a pragmatic approach and saw security policy as an assurance to the small states most at risk of revisionism.[29] This was exactly the agenda of the exile lawyers and UNWCC in London, twenty years later. The committees on disarmament at the League were the core committees used to voice both the concerns of small states and an expert community's view on security politics free from national restraints.

The fact that the epistemic community of lawyers was very creative in mobilizing support of public relations through politically instrumentalized expertise must be underlined.[30] In Geneva, the League of Nations encouraged the creation of its own civil society organizations, the so-called League of Nations Societies, to advance the creation of 'international minds', as Carnegie secretary Nicolas Butler once framed it.[31] League secretary Eric Drummond described the officials of these groups as 'scouts sent out ahead by the army of international progress', and the General Assembly confirmed that the Societies should inform the public about the humanitarian work of the League of Nations.[32] The British League of Nations Union, chaired by the aforementioned representative Lord Robert Cecil, was particularly active and tried to intervene through resolutions, memos and letters to parliamentarians and ministers as well as League of Nations representatives.

Support was needed, as the power of small states representatives was always limited in the realm of diplomacy, and this was even more so when in October 1925 at Locarno Germany was called back into the circle, and the earlier attempts to settle European disputes quietly ceased. The atmosphere changed rapidly and Locarno's tea parties 'morphed into hotel diplomacy of the great powers', as Marks observes.[33] The smaller states, amongst them Czechoslovakia (Benes), Belgium (Paul Hymans) and Nansen (Norway) protested, but to no avail.[34] Steiner

[27] ibid, quoting Gábor Bátonyi, *Britain and Central Europe, 1918–1933* (Clarendon Press 1999) 183. The Foreign Office shared Lord Curzon's dictum he 'travelled too much and chaptered too hard'.

[28] Steiner, *Lights* (n 21) 298.

[29] Steiner, *Lights* (n 21) 299.

[30] Katharina Rietzler, 'Experts for Peace: Structures and Motivations of Philanthropic Internationalism in the Interwar Years' in Daniel Laqua (ed), *Internationalism Reconfigured: Transnational Ideas and Movements between the World Wars* (Bloomsbury 2011) 45, 46.

[31] Nicolas Murray Butler, *The International Mind. An Argument for the Judicial Settlement of International Disputes* (Scribner's 1912).

[32] Helen McCarthy, 'The Lifeblood of the League? Voluntary Associations and League of Nations Activism in Britain' in Daniel Laqua (ed), *Internationalism Reconfigured. Transnational Ideas and Movements between the World Wars* (Bloomsbury 2011) 187, 194.

[33] Marks, *Illusion* (n 25) 89.

[34] ibid.

concludes: 'League diplomacy was often little more than great power diplomacy dressed in Wilsonian clothes, and the importance of representatives of small states, however active, was necessarily limited.'[35]

The end of the 'transnational dream' (Webster) came with the failure of the World Disarmament Conference (WDC), which took place between 1932 and June 1934. It opened with representatives from fifty-nine nations. Six commissions were quickly created to deal with various aspects of the question. At their heads were key experts from the previous decade of League efforts,[36] amongst them again Benes and Politis, and Hymans as head of the disarmament section.[37] Even after the final collapse of the WDC in June 1934, attempts continued to be made in Geneva to secure limited arms control initiatives: on the regulation of the trade in and manufacture of armaments, on publicizing national budgetary expenditure on armaments and on the creation of a permanent international disarmament commission. Unsurprisingly, these too met with no success.[38]

When the WDC reconvened at the 1936 Assembly, some familiar faces were still in the front row: Nicolas Politis represented Greece and was the provisional chairman of the WDC following the death of Arthur Henderson in 1935. Once again it was the smaller European powers (Belgium, Denmark, Finland, Netherlands, Norway, Sweden and Switzerland) that made a final effort in the Assembly to achieve some amount of disarmament. It was still hoped that small steps might serve as a means to restart a wider disarmament process, but it was too late. When the League Council met at the end of September 1938, in the midst of the crisis over Czechoslovakia and the 'Munich agreement', secretary-general Joseph Avenol reported that the planned reconvening of the conference's executive bureau had been put off due to 'the political situation'.[39]

## III. Debating International Justice during World War II: The UNWCC

The war offered a new chance to bring the debate to a close. During the 1940s in London, exiled lawyers within the UNWCC were among the main protagonists to coin the concept of 'Crimes against humanity'. The UNWCC was a hub of transnational legal thought during the war, an epistemic community initially formed from European protagonists forced into exile by German occupation, as well as from Chinese representatives who suffered under Japanese occupation. I propose

[35] Steiner, *Lights* (n 21) 299.
[36] Webster, 'Transnational Dream' (n 15) 514.
[37] ibid 495.
[38] ibid 516.
[39] ibid 517.

here to speak of a 'London hub', which stresses the institutional connections at London.[40]

Most of the exiled lawyers were already prominent lawyers in their home countries who had been forced into exile by Nazi politics.[41] The Czech and Polish exile government representatives, echoed by their Belgian and Dutch counterparts, particularly hoped that the Nazis would be deterred from committing further crimes by establishing fierce legal guidelines.[42]

From 1941, legal circles advocated new ideas of post-war justice within the two forerunners of the UNWCC, the International Commission for Penal Reconstruction and Development, emanating from the Faculty of Law at the University of Cambridge (Cambridge Commission), and the London International Assembly (LIA). Legal scholar Hersch Lauterpacht was particularly active in fostering the debate during the conference at Cambridge in November 1941.

The founding event was a scientific conference on 'Rules and Procedure to Govern the Case of Crimes against International Public Order' to debate urgent political questions on the punishment of war crimes; one is reminded of the conferences of St Petersburg and Brussels in the 19th century, but in this case, rather than diplomats, committees of experts were invited to a conference on exchange of ideas, with the clear aim of drawing up new guidelines. Two topics were discussed: first, the definition of war crimes with a view to new crimes and, secondly, the establishment of an international court. Probably following the practice in the League of Nations, the London committees gave preference to experts over the strict distribution of seats by nation. This can be seen, for example, in the fact that a German representative—the Jewish judge Otto Friedburg from Berlin, who was forced into emigration—also took part in the discussions.[43] The member list reveals two familiar names: Edvard Benes and Nicolas Politis, although we see also a younger generation emerge: Marcel De Baer for Belgium (instead of Hymans), René Cassin for France and Bohuslav Ečer for Czechoslovakia.

The second pioneering body to precede the UNWCC, the LIA, was founded in the autumn of 1941, on the initiative of the British League of Nations Union (LNU) under Lord Robert Cecil of Chelwood.[44] In the front row again: Edvard Benes, Marcel De Baer, René Cassin and Bohuslav Ečer. The LIA was an interesting approach from the margins, in that a non-governmental organization took the lead

[40] Lingen, 'Legal Flows' (n 1) 7.

[41] The National Archives, London (hereafter TNA), LCO 2/2973, Papers of the International Commission for Penal Reconstruction and Development, member list. Of sixteen members of exile countries, five were former Ministers of Justice, five were High Court judges, two were law professors, the others their assistants.

[42] Lingen, 'Setting the Path' (n 1) 50.

[43] See Member list, supra footnote 41.

[44] The papers of the LNU are kept at the LSE at London. Its library catalogue states: 'The League of Nations Union (LNU) was formed by the merger of the League of Free Nations Association and the League of Nations Society, two groups working for the establishment of a new world order based upon the ideals of the League of Nations.'

in providing a platform for debate. In contrast to the Cambridge Commission, the number of members had increased; members from Great Britain, the US, India, Brazil, Egypt and China and at least one observer from the Soviet Union were present.[45] In a partial abandonment of Eurocentrism, the involvement of non-European members demonstrated the potentially global approach and political implications of this legal endeavour. In this regard, the LIA can be seen as a blueprint for the later UNWCC.

Epistemic communities are defined by a shared understanding of terms. Thus defining crimes against civilians, as well as war crimes, was crucial. Contrary to the orthodox legal view, which maintained until 1939 that war crimes could only involve cases committed within a state's own territory or against its nationals,[46] the head of the LIA, Belgian representative Marcel De Baer, offered a new definition in 1942. In his definition, war crimes could—in a wider sense—be seen as 'offences against the *ius gentium*, or against international agreements' (such as The Hague and Geneva Conventions).[47]

The minutes of debates also show the problem of language used in the various committees' meetings, and thus the problem of translating concepts. Most of the lawyers were not familiar with English when they arrived in London, and first debates were actually held in French (as the proceedings of the Cambridge meetings show), and some even in German. The exile lawyers helped one another to frame memoranda, as we know from a letter of Ečer praising the English language skills of De Baer (De Baer occasionally shared his office with Ecer).[48] The exile lawyers were polyglot scholars, following the tradition of multi-lingual empires as the Austro-Hungarian one; Ečer for example spoke seven languages, but English was not amongst them when he arrived at London.

The most important transnational arena of codification was the UNWCC. It was officially founded in London, on 20 October 1943, and began functioning in early 1944. Its objectives were framed in three main spheres: the investigation of facts and evidence regarding war crimes, the enforcement of the law respecting the punishment of war criminals and legal opinions relating to war crimes and the penal liability of perpetrators.[49] As an organization, the UNWCC was composed of three committees, of which the Legal Committee in London gave the most important input towards the development of contemporary international law. Given the continuity of its members, the UNWCC went beyond its mandate and pushed for a real war crimes policy.[50]

45 London International Assembly, The Punishment of War Criminals. Recommendations of the LIA. List of Participants in appendix to the brochure.

46 Arieh J Kochavi, 'Britain and the Establishment of the UNWCC' (1992) 107 English Historical Review 323, 325.

47 TNA (n 41) TS 26/873, LIA, De Baer proposal, April 1942.

48 National Archive Prague, ÚD NAD 615. Ecer, Report No 14, 2 April 1944.

49 United Nations War Crimes Commission, *History of the United Nations War Crimes Commission and the Development of the Laws of War* (HMSO 1948) 169 (hereafter UNWCC, *History*).

50 Kirsten Sellars, *'Crimes against Peace' and International Law* (CUP 2013) 58.

The engagements of exile lawyers within the UNWCC and its forerunners was decisive for the finalizing of a century-long debate. In assessing the historical record of Nazi crimes, Ečer stated that the UNWCC had received several accounts on the planned nature of Nazi warfare especially in Eastern Europe, where not only Jews, but also other civilians were slaughtered by SS troops without prior trial.[51] He proposed the new term 'crimes against humanity' to cover these offences. By debating the Martens Clause and the Versailles achievements, Ečer underlined that the Preamble of the Hague Convention—the Martens Clause—was of immense value for the work of UNWCC, as it referred to the term 'humanity'.[52] The motivation of exile lawyers to accomplish the task of judging war criminals, something not achieved after 1919, is clearly visible.

It can be demonstrated that Ečer was not only inspired by his colleagues at London and thus the legal debates in the West, but also followed closely academic developments from the other war time ally, the Soviet Union. In 1944, the Soviet Union's leading legal scholar, Aron Trainin, had issued an English translation of his book on the criminal responsibility of the 'Hitlerites', where he advocated the crime of aggression as a main charge in war crimes, as well as the legal tool of complicity to bring the Nazi elites to judgment.[53] In scholarly debate, the contribution of the Soviet Union to the development of the legal framework of the war crimes trials after World War II and thus to a modern international law has only recently resurfaced.[54] Its influence had, however, been especially appealing to the Central European exile lawyers, who were deeply troubled by Nazi crimes of occupation in their home countries, or by anti-Semitic violence forcing them into exile. With growing disappointment about the tentative British support for new legal ideas (and prior to the experience of the Soviet's double standards at Nuremberg), the Soviet's approach to war crimes became an academic inspiration, and perhaps an alternative, for legal scholars like Ečer.[55]

For Ečer it was a personal victory when 'Crimes against Humanity' was laid down in the London Charter on 8 August 1945, although the UNWCC legal

[51] Ecer, Additional Note, 12 May 1944, UNWCC III/4, 'Scope of the Retributive action of the United Nations according to their official Declarations—The Problem of War Crimes in connection with the second World War' 7, 2 <https://www.legal-tools.org/doc/6335bd/>.

[52] ibid 4.

[53] Aron N Trainin, *Hitlerite Responsibility under Criminal Law* (Hutchinson 1944).

[54] Francine Hirsch, 'The Soviets at Nuremberg: International Law, Propaganda, and the Making of the Postwar Order' (2008) 2 American Historical Review 701, and her new book *Soviet Judgment at Nuremberg. A New History of the International Military Tribunal after World War II* (OUP 2020); Valentyna Polunina, 'The Human Face of Soviet Justice? Aron Trainin and the Origins of the Soviet Doctrine of International Criminal Law' in David Crowe (ed), *Stalin's Soviet Justice: 'Show' Trials, War Crimes Trials, and Nuremberg* (Bloomsbury 2019) 127.

[55] National Archives of Australia (NAA), A 2937/273, Note of meeting with General de Baer, by Wright, 1 December1944, 2. In this note, the later chairman of UNWCC reported fears that Ecer and Zivkovic had turned over to the Soviets: 'He had heard Ecer and Zivkovic express sentiments that they would prefer to remain on the Commission in London, but if things went on as at present they would certainly turn to the strong Russian Commission.'

experts were not invited to take part in the meetings.[56] It is clear that the different strands woven together into the concept derived from earlier war-time debates at London, as we have seen. It was one of the flaws of the legal debates that the concepts of 'crimes against humanity' and 'genocide' developed into two different tools, although Czech scholar Egon Schwelb had argued earlier that they formed 'two rivers flowing under two different names', and needed to be united after the war.[57]

In scholarship the emergence of the new term is loaded with mythical undertones, which this chapter opposes.[58] Although it has not yet been possible to prove how the American judge Robert Jackson[59] came to use the term 'crimes against humanity'[60] in the meeting, it seems feasible that Hersch Lauterpacht might be the missing link,[61] as he met with Jackson before the London Conference and might have summed up the ongoing debates he had had with his UNWCC colleagues, amongst them Ečer. Lauterpacht should be seen as the transmitter between exile circles and diplomatic circles and international lawyers.

Set up through the same structures, the UNWCC Pacific sub-commission, established in the Chinese war-time capital of Chongqing in 1944, was a failure. Although ten different Allied powers took part in the sub-commission meetings and they started with high hopes of it becoming the hub for war crimes prosecution in Asia, in the eyes of the other members the Chinese National Office was dysfunctional from the beginning.[62] In scrutinizing its work, we see the complete lack of transnationality, as no networks and preceding organization had established channels of cooperation, and thus we see this commission fail after a short while in 1946. According to Dutch ambassador Lovink and other delegates, many of the charges developed by the Pacific sub-commission lacked quality, were sloppy and showed indifference.[63] It became apparent that for the Chinese the main point

[56] The text of the Nuremberg Charter/London Conference can be found at <http://avalon.law.yale.edu/imt/jack60.asp>.

[57] UNOG library, letter Schwelb to Humphrey, 7 June 1947, cited in Mira Siegelberg, 'Unofficial Men, Efficient Civil Servants: Raphael Lemkin in the History of International Law' (2013) 15(3) Journal of Genocide Research 297, 304.

[58] David Luban, 'A Theory of Crimes against Humanity' (2004) 29 Yale J Int'l L 85. He states at 86 that 'no record exists of how the term crimes against humanity came to be chosen'.

[59] Robert Jackson, *Report on the International Conference on Military Trials at London, 1945* (Office of Public Affairs 1947) 416.

[60] A theory is presented in Kerstin von Lingen, 'Fulfilling the Martens Clause: Debating "Crimes Against Humanity", 1899–1945' in Fabian Klose and Mirjam Thulin (eds), *Humanity—A History of European Concepts in Practice from the 16th Century to the Present* (V&R 2016) 187.

[61] Martti Koskenniemi, *The Gentle Civilizer of Nations: The Rise and Fall of International Law, 1870–1960* (CUP 2002) draws on Lauterpacht's decisive role within the British prosecution, where he drafted the opening and closing speech, see the chapter: 'Lauterpacht: The Victorian tradition in International Law' 388–89. This view is bolstered by Philippe Sands, *East West Street: On the Origins of 'Genocide' and 'Crimes Against Humanity'* (Random House 2016) 109–11 (hereafter Sands, *East West Street*).

[62] 'Minutes of the Seventh meeting of the Far Eastern and Pacific Sub-Commission of the UNWCC' 27 July 1945, 2 via Legal Tools <https://www.legal-tools.org/en/browse/record/a236c3/>.

[63] Lisette Schouten in her forthcoming book on Dutch War Crimes Policy cites: NIOD, collectie 400 IC, inv.no. 5190, 'Letter from A.H. Lovink to Minister Kleffens' 27 August 1945; see on Chinese views Anja Bihler, 'The Legacy of Extraterritoriality and the Trials of Japanese War Criminals in the Republic

was the sustaining of the image as a 'big power'. The British representative wrote to London:

> Those of us who took an active interest in trying to get Japanese criminals properly dealt with, namely the Australian, Netherlands, United States and United Kingdom delegates had the devil of a time trying to keep the Chinese authorities up to scratch, and we all felt at the end that we came out second best in the war of passive resistance conducted against us by the Chinese military authorities concerned (not by our Chinese colleagues on the sub-commission who seemed to share our sense of frustration).[64]

So, we see again a friction between governmental and transnational communities, as had already occurred in Geneva. However, we can also detect the notion of 'legal flows' between London and Chongqing (which were unsuccessful in producing results), and the impact of Western legal experts' distrust of their unknown Asian colleagues. One can only surmise whether this would have been different if they had met with old Geneva networks, and actors like The Hague's international judge and later sub-committee chairman Wang Chonghui, Tokyo judge Mei Ru'ao or the Chinese top diplomat at London, Yale-educated Wellington Koo.

## IV. Conclusion

To sum up, two points need to be underlined.

First, the 'Geneva and London hub' during the first half of the century created the framework for the advancing of a victim-centred 'new justice', to borrow from Lewis's expression.[65] In terms of a learning system, the League committees were a decisive formative moment for transnational cooperation. The internationalists first at Geneva and later at London formed an epistemic community involving some of the most renowned lawyers of the time, a truly transnational intellectual network. When analysing the frictions and alliances between governmental bodies and transnational communities established by political exile elites, their impact becomes even more remarkable.

When assessing the record of transnational epistemic communities involved, the notion of space and generation is crucial. In the inter-war years, a likeminded

of China' in Kerstin von Lingen (ed), *War Crimes Trials in the Wake of Decolonization and Cold War in Asia, 1945–1956. Justice in Time of Turmoil* (Palgrave Macmillan2016) 93.

[64] TNA (n 41) FO 371/66570, No S/O 568 (8316/976/47), British Embassy Nanking, 14 July 1947, Coghill for LH Lamb to War Crimes Section.

[65] Mark Lewis, *The Birth of New Justice: The Internationalization of Crimes and Punishment, 1919–1950* (OUP 2014).

community formed at the League of Nations at Geneva, and during World War II, some of them met again in London in exile. I argue that the noteworthy characteristic of those who met in London is less the regional affiliation and Central European background[66] than the early experience of violence and anti-semitism, together with the internationalist approach to working together in commissions to solve legal problems of transnational concern. Belonging to a cohort of likeminded people is a decisive factor, as is the notion of a group—which in Geneva and London included Asian actors, and in Chongqing did not work out due to a perceived 'otherness'.

Finally, within the epistemic community of lawyers, the motivation and distinguishing feature is the common goal: although they represented their nation-state positions, they remained oriented towards a compromise to reach arms restriction and secure peace. This vision characterized this transnational group of experts and became the driving force behind the disarmament attempts in the League of Nations, and later the UNWCC. We must not forget that the debates stemmed from an experience of political powerlessness; these exiled politicians and experts keenly felt the low position their agendas and authority to punish war criminals held amongst their British hosts. During the early 1940s, the 'exile space' itself created a 'global moment', a catalyst to bring the nearly century-long debate about war violence towards civilians to a close.

[66] Although I agree with Sands, *East West Street* (n 61) that this was a formative factor.

# 5
# Gerhard Mueller's Role in Developing the Concept of Transnational Crime for the United Nations

*Mangai Natarajan*

## I. Introduction

In the 1970s, UN congresses on the prevention of crime and the treatment of offenders focused attention on the need to define crimes that transcend national borders. Gerhard O W Mueller (1926–2006), a US legal scholar of German origin with an extensive knowledge of criminology, was appointed in 1974 as head of the United Nations Crime and Criminal Justice Branch. He charted a course for the UN to follow in dealing with the contentious issues surrounding the definition of these crimes that transcend national borders. He participated in the Fourth UN Crime Congress held in 1970, which declared 'hijacking of airplanes' a new form of crime requiring international intervention (1970 Hague Hijacking Convention). At the Fifth UN Crime Congress in 1975,[1] he introduced the term 'transnational' to refer to these new dimensions of criminality. He maintained that 'transnational crime' did not have a juridical meaning but was a criminological term, under which may be lumped what is variously and differently defined in the penal codes of states, although with the common attribute of transcending the jurisdiction of any given state.[2] A quarter of a century later, the criminological term 'transnational crime' became a legal term in article 3(2) of the United Nations Convention against Transnational Organized Crime (UNTOC), adopted by the UN General Assembly Resolution 55/25 of 15 November 2000. Gerhard Mueller, and his legal and criminological scholarship, had a large hand in this transformation of transnational crime from a criminological to legal term.

[1] Professor GOW Mueller was the chief of the Crime Prevention and Criminal Justice Branch and the executive secretary of the Fifth Congress which was held in Geneva, Switzerland, 1–12 September 1975.

[2] Gerhard OW Mueller, 'Transnational Crime: Definitions and Concepts' in Phil Williams and Dimitri Vlassis (eds), *Combating Transnational Crime* (Frank Cass 2001) 13 (hereafter Mueller, 'Transnational Crime').

Mangai Natarajan, *Gerhard Mueller's Role in Developing the Concept of Transnational Crime for the United Nations* In: *Histories of Transnational Criminal Law.* Edited by: Neil Boister, Sabine Gless and Florian Jeßberger, Oxford University Press. © Mangai Natarajan 2021. DOI: 10.1093/oso/9780192845702.003.0006

This chapter is about Mueller's key role in the institutional development of the term 'transnational crime'. The chapter is in two sections. The first describes Mueller's intellectual background that made him—as a legal scholar, though one well versed in criminology—uniquely suited to guiding the UN in the control and prevention of transnational crime. The second section is a history of the various steps taken by Mueller, as the head of the UN's Crime Branch, to map out a substantive role for the UN in dealing with transnational and international crimes.

## II. Gerhard Mueller and International Criminology and Criminal Justice

On completing schooling in Germany in 1947, Mueller then spent two years in the University of Kiel Law School, where he specialized in criminal law and procedure, criminology, forensic sciences and legal history. On emigrating to the United States, this broad educational background secured his admission to the JD degree programme at the University of Chicago (where he obtained one of the top marks in his cohort) as well as into the LLM programme at Columbia University. He served two quarters as assistant professor, and later associate professor, at the University of Chicago, doing comparative law research. During 1953–54 he was instructor of law, in the School of Law, University of Washington and served in 1954–55 as Huger W Jervey Fellow of Comparative (Criminal) Law in Columbia University, School of Law.[3]

His teaching in criminology and criminal justice began when he served as professor of law, University West Virginia (1955–58); this was followed by two decades at New York University (1958–77). From 1974 to 2006, he served as a distinguished professor at the school of criminal justice, Rutgers, The State University of New Jersey.[4] While at Rutgers, he was awarded DrJur (honoris causa) by the University of Uppsala, Sweden. He also held a post as vice president of the Association International de Droit Pénal (AIDP) between 1964 and 2006 and was a member of the board of directors of the International Institute of Higher Studies in Criminal Sciences in Siracusa, Italy.[5]

Mueller encouraged criminal law professors to integrate a comparative perspective into their teaching. To do so, the lecturer should have a basic understanding of codified criminal law and its workings; should have an understanding

[3] Gerhard OW Mueller, 'Tort, Crime and the Primitive' (1955) 46 J Crim L Criminology & Police Sci 303.

[4] I am one of the beneficiaries of Professor Mueller's teaching on comparative criminal law. It was an honour to be his teaching and research assistant at Rutgers. I am proud to say that he was the supervisor of my PhD dissertation, a comparative cross-cultural study of women in law enforcement.

[5] M Cherif Bassiouni, 'In Memoriam: Gerhard OW Mueller, March 15, 1926–April 21, 2006' (2006) 77(1) RiDP 9 (hereafter Bassiouni, 'In Memoriam').

of comparative law method; should select the topics of greatest need; and should learn a foreign language to put comparative law to the best possible use in teaching, adjudication and especially legislation. He also advocated for the establishment of an American Institute of Comparative Criminal Law for enhancing international thinking.[6] His comparative cross- cultural expertise in criminal law and criminology dating from the 1950s, and specifically, his vast knowledge of jurisdictional issues, was to prove extremely valuable in developing international strategies against cross-border crimes.

A good example is provided in Mueller and Poole-Griffiths' book on comparative criminal procedures, where they devoted a chapter to jurisdiction over crimes committed aboard an aircraft.[7] They engaged in an extensive discussion of the case of *United States v Cordova*,[8] a case that led to a domestic law change in the United States that percolated into international law. It concerned two passengers aboard an American commercial aircraft over the high seas who assaulted one another, and when the captain intervened also assaulted him. Cordova was brought to trial under 18 USC § 7 (1)–(4), which deals with the special maritime jurisdiction of the United States. The court dismissed the case for lack of jurisdiction, as the plane was not a vessel within the terms of the statute.[9] However, this decision led to the enactment of a new subsection (5) to 18 USC § 7 extending federal jurisdiction to aircraft owned by the United States, its citizens and corporations while such aircraft is in flight over the high seas or over any other waters within the admiralty and maritime jurisdiction of the United States, and out of the jurisdiction of any particular state.[10] Subsequently, similar provision was made in the 1963 Convention on Offences and Certain Other Acts Committed on Board Aircraft (the 1963 Tokyo Convention). Article III(2) authorizes each flag state to exert jurisdiction over its aircraft, even when above the territory of a foreign nation.

A comparison of different national laws showed that mere national legislation cannot provide a satisfactory solution to the jurisdictional problems involved in dealing with cross-border crimes. Mueller emphasized the use of treaty or multipartite conventions to maximize the amount of judicial assistance in criminal matters; he argued that satisfactory solutions to problems of cross-border crimes cannot be achieved solely by written laws but only by a combination of statute or

[6] Gerhard OW Mueller, 'Teaching of Comparative Law in the Course on Criminal Law' (1958) 11 J Legal Educ 59.

[7] Gerhard OW Mueller and Fré Le Poole-Griffiths, *Comparative Criminal Procedure* (New York UP 1969) (hereafter Mueller and Poole-Griffths, *Comparative Criminal Procedure*).

[8] 89 F Supp 298 (1950).

[9] Mueller and Poole-Griffiths, *Comparative Criminal Procedure* (n 7) 146.

[10] ibid 147.

treaty and customary law. He believed in a treaty on international judicial assistance which would codify mutual respect for other states' systems.[11]

In 1968, Mueller was the first legal scholar to become president of the American Society of Criminology (ASC). In his presidential address[12] Mueller stated that the millennium had begun with the criminal law, but he highlighted the role of criminology in defining crime control and in translating the social and psychological stimuli of crime into law. He said:

> No amateurish legislature can provide us with laws for the governance of human beings unless it acts with the guidance of specialists in criminal justice.... The mission of criminology is in the transmission of professional information to colleagues in all contributing professions, the transmission of their ideas into the mainstream of criminological development, and the direction of valid criminological theories into governmental practices.[13]

He was one of the five members of the editorial board of the journal *Criminologica* in 1970 when it was renamed as *Criminology: An Interdisciplinary Journal*, which became the official publication of the ASC. Mueller's lectures in criminology were always inspirational (particularly notable were his contributions on the criminological significance of fairy tales and their lessons for punishment[14]).

The second major contribution he made to the responses to cross-border crime was the study he and Freda Adler[15] undertook in 1985 on maritime criminal activities (including modern-day piracy, ocean pollution, marine insurance fraud, theft, killing marine animals and smuggling aliens).[16] Their discussion also included terrorism, a neglected topic in mainstream criminology, both then and now.[17] They concluded that all eras of crime on the high seas are marked by conflicts of jurisdiction as well as unresolved questions about who can and should intervene to

[11] Gerhard OW Mueller, 'International Judicial Assistance in Criminal Matters' (1962) 7 Vill L Rev 193.

[12] Gerhard OW Mueller, 'A Presidential Communication, G. O. W. Mueller' (1968) 6(2) Criminologica 59.

[13] Gerhard OW Mueller, 'The Millennium of Criminology' (1967) 5(1) Criminologica 2.

[14] Gerhard OW Mueller, 'The Criminological Significance of the Grimm's Fairy Tales' in Ruth B Bottigheimer (ed), *Fairy Tales and Society—Illusion, Allusion, and Paradigm* (The University of Pennsylvania Press 1986) 217.

[15] Gerhard OW Mueller and Freda Adler, *Outlaws of the Ocean: The Complete Book of Contemporary Crime on the High Seas*, (Hearst Marine Books 1985) (hereafter Mueller and Adler, *Outlaws of the Ocean*).

[16] Mueller's interest in maritime crimes was no doubt stimulated by the period he spent at the close of World War II, when he was assigned by the British military government in Germany to command a seagoing patrol vessel, which took him around the Baltic shores, Kiel Canal, Elbe River and parts of the North Sea coastline.

[17] Mainstream criminology focuses predominantly on street crimes and only a minority of criminologists study transborder crimes, especially terrorism. Mueller and Adler, *Outlaws of the Ocean* (n 15) state that criminologists had no part in drafting the UNCLOS.

do something about a particular problem and by the lack of operational capacity to do something about it. In their view, the 1982 UN Convention on the Law of the Sea (UNCLOS) was a colossal achievement. Three centuries in the making, the product of the work of thousands of lawyers from 160 countries, they regarded it as the first step towards ending lawlessness on the oceans.[18]

Criminologists were at the time customarily focused on local crimes, but a few scholars in the 1960s embarked on comparing crimes and justice systems in other countries under the rubric of comparative criminology/criminal justice.[19] In the 1970s cross-border crimes became a focus of criminological concern with the phrase, 'transnational crime' being introduced by Mueller at the Fifth UN Crime Congress. As noted, in his view, 'transnational crime' was not a legally defined category of crime but rather referred to criminal activities, transactions or schemes that violate the laws of more than one country or have a direct impact on a foreign country.[20] Mueller explained further how 'transnational crimes' are distinguishable from 'international crimes', the crimes recognized by international law and in which the entire world is harmed and which fall within the jurisdiction of international war crimes tribunals, the (then) projected permanent international criminal court and national criminal courts adhering to international conventions. Writing in 2016 Bassiouni[21] commends Mueller's 'natural law' philosophical approach to international crimes, founded on higher values and overarching principles that should control states. He notes that after World War II, the establishment of the UN and the development of international human rights law sought to reconcile conflicting and competing state interests while at the same time identify commonly shared interests that reflect certain higher values and enduring principles. He draws attention to Mueller and Wise's *International Criminal Law*,[22] a seminal 1965 publication dedicated to the Swiss section of the AIDP, in which the existence, dilemmas and the progress of international criminal law and international criminal justice are discussed.[23]

18 Mueller and Adler, *Outlaws of the Ocean* (n 15*), 19.*

19 Hermann Mannheim, *Comparative Criminology* (Taylor & Francis US 1965).

20 See Mueller, 'Transnational Crime' (n 2) 13.

21 Mahmoud Cherif Bassiouni, 'Challenges to International Criminal Justice and International Criminal Law' in William A Schabas (ed), *The Cambridge Companion to International Criminal Law* (CUP 2016) 353.

22 Gerhard OW Mueller and Edward M Wise, *International Criminal Law* (Fred B Rothman 1965). This was the first set of teaching materials on the subject in English and was the basis for a popular course at New York University from the mid-1960s on.

23 Mahmoud Cherif Bassiouni, 'Chronology of Efforts to Establish an International Criminal Court' (2015) 86(3) RiDP 1163 (hereafter Mueller, 'Chronology of Efforts'). Interestingly, the book uses as its departure point Schwarzenberger's critique of the existence of international criminal law—see Georg G Schwarzenberger, 'The Problem of International Criminal Law' 1950 (3) Curr Leg Prob 263, and goes on to include pieces on legal cooperation, extradition, jurisdiction and aviation offences.

The globalized world economy of the 21st century promotes transnational outcomes and increasing numbers of crimes span borders, leaving very few local crimes that are not somehow impacted by foreign factors.[24] The three types of the 21st-century crime highlighted in Figure 5.1 are fluid hence the concepts overlap but they can be distinguished based on criminological understanding of the crime opportunity structure.[25] Crime theorists say all crimes have local origin and border crossing is merely a sequence in transnational crime. But in the sequential process, legal steps are necessary for controlling and prevention of the crime especially when it violates the law of another country.[26] 'Local crime' impacted by 'foreign factors' fluidly moves into the category of transnational crime, namely when the country of origin, by legislation, turns the impacting activity into a crime by change of legislation.[27] Where a universal interest is engaged, transnational crimes may evolve into international core crimes.

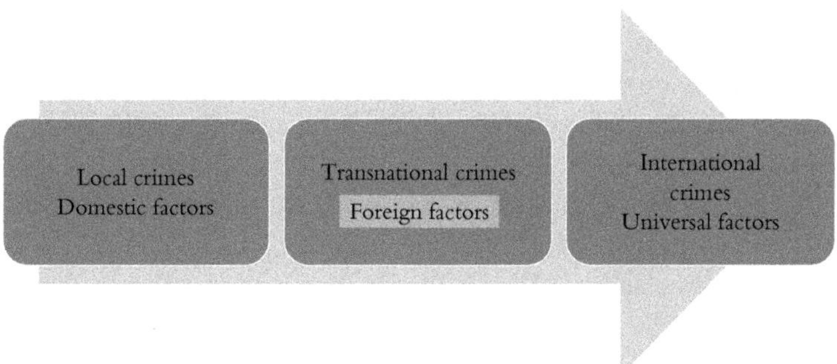


**Figure 5.1** Trajectory of Crime Types

Identifying transnational and international crimes serves two important criminal justice purposes: first, it encourages the international community to focus its resources on the gravest crimes that threaten the peace and wellbeing of the world; and second, it encourages criminal justice, including law enforcement, to narrow its focus on cross-national-border crimes that affect the safety and security of specific countries or regions.[28]

[24] Gerhard OW Mueller, 'Transnational Crime: An Experience in Uncertainties' in Stanley Einstein and Menachem Amir (eds), *Organized Crime: Uncertainties and Dilemmas* (Office of International Criminal Justice 1999) 4 (hereafter Mueller, 'Transnational Crime').

[25] Phil Williams, 'Emerging Issues: Transnational Crime and its Control' in Graeme Newman (ed), *Global Report on Crime and Justice* (UN ODCCP 1999) 225.

[26] Marcus Felson, 'Routine Activities and Transnational Crime' in Mangai Natarajan (ed), *International Crime and Justice* (2nd edn, CUP 2019) 229.

[27] Mueller, 'Chronology of Efforts' (n 23).

[28] Mangai Natarajan, 'Introduction' in Mangai Natarajan (ed), *International and Transnational Crime and Justice* (CUP 2019). See also M Cherif Bassiouni, *International Criminal Law* (Transnational 1996) and Neil Boister, 'Transnational Criminal Law' (2003) 14(5) EJIL 953.

## III. Mueller, the UN and the Transnational Crime

Many distinguished scholars have played important roles in the UN, but Mueller's contribution is unique in the realm of criminal justice.[29] He was appointed as the chief of the Crime Prevention and Criminal Justice Branch (CPCJB)[30] of the UN in 1974—the international administrative unit that, at the time, directed the UN's crime agenda worldwide[31]—and held that post until 1981. It is important to note that Professor Mueller was also a long-standing and distinguished member[32] of the AIDP.[33] Since 1955, the AIDP enjoyed consultative status with the UN along with three other NGOs: the International Society of Criminology, the International Society of Social Defense and the International Penal and Penitentiary Foundation. Its large membership, wide-ranging activities on every continent, the work of its Siracusa Institute and the influence of its board of directors and members have had a marked effect on international criminal law, comparative criminal sciences and the shaping of criminal justice policy all over the world.[34] Further, at all UN congresses AIDP members have played a major role in its scientific contributions, and were frequently chairs or vice-chairs of these meetings. Mueller was a part of this epistemic community of likeminded people,[35] instrumental in influencing the development of UN congresses.

In addition, he was a permanent representative to the United Nations of the AIDP (1967–74) and of the Instituto Superiore Internazionale di Scienze Criminali, Siracusa, Italy (1982–2005). He also served as chairman of the International Scientific and Professional Advisory Council of the United Nations Crime Prevention and Criminal Justice Programme (ISPAC) in Milan and to the United Nations Interregional Crime and Justice Research Institute (UNICRI).[36] He was one among the five members that supported the establishment of the European Institute for Crime Prevention and Control (HEUNI), established in 1981 in Finland. In 1983 Friedlander noted that the fact that the UN Crime Prevention

[29] Slawomir Redo, *Blue Criminology: The Power of United Nations Ideas to Counter Crime Globally: A Monographic Study* (HEUNI 2012).

[30] Gerhard OW Mueller, 'The United Nations and Criminology' in Elmer Johnson (ed), *International Handbook of Contemporary Developments in Criminology* (Greenwood 1983) 63.

[31] Now subsumed in the UN Office of Drugs and Crime, still located in Vienna.

[32] Freda Adler and Gerhard OW Mueller, 'A Very Personal and Family History of the United Nations Crime Prevention and Criminal Justice Branches' in M Cherif Bassiouni (ed), *The Contributions of Specialized Institutes and Non- Governmental Organizations to the United Nations Criminal Justice program* (Nijhoff 1995) 3.

[33] Edward M Wise, 'Foreword: The International Association of Penal Law and the Problem of Organized Crime' (1998) 44 Wayne L Rev 1281.

[34] Mahmoud Cherif Bassiouni, 'AIDP: Over a Century of Dedication to Criminal Justice and Human Rights' in (2015) 86(3) RiDP 1095.

[35] On similar communities see von Lingen, Chapter 4 of this book.

[36] Bassiouni, 'In Memoriam' (n 5) 1–2.

Branch had been placed under the direction of Professor Mueller, a noted authority in the field of international criminal law, signified the UN's interest in establishing the importance of this field.[37]

Joutsen identifies three major transitions of the UN's Crime Prevention and Criminal Justice Programme.[38] The first was a transition from a forum for intellectual debate to a truly global programme (1950s–60s). The second was a transition in the 1970s–80s from an expert-driven programme to a government-driven programme in the 1990s. The third was a transition from a soft law programme to a programme based on hard law treaties (the 2000s). He remarks that during the 1970s the topics of transnational and organized crime began to make more frequent appearances on the agenda, in the form of issues such as corruption, trafficking in cultural property and terrorism.

The growing world-wide concern with transnational organized crime and terrorism led policymakers to see crime as a national security issue. Records indicate that Mueller played a major role in all three transition periods in varying capacities and roles.

## 1. UN Congresses on Crime Prevention and Criminal Justice

The UN Congresses on Crime Prevention and Criminal Justice[39] are the world's largest and most diverse gathering of policymakers, practitioners, academics, intergovernmental organizations and civil society organizations in the field of crime prevention and criminal justice. Held every five years and attended by most UN member states, individual experts and numerous civil society representatives, their purpose is to discuss and develop criminal justice standards and model treaties (see Table 5.1 below).[40] Over the years, the increased participation of governments, NGOs and individual participants reflects the international community's burgeoning interest in crime.

Transnational crime was frequently discussed at these congresses, a topic of discussion which culminated in the adoption in 2000 of the UNTOC, the main international instrument in the fight against transnational organized crime. Gerhard Mueller attended the Third UN Crime Congress (1965) as a representative of the AIDP (he was vice-president of the AIDP and its chief UN representative in

[37] Robert A Friedlander, 'The Foundations of International Criminal Law: A Present-Day Inquiry' (1983) 15 Case W Res J Intl L 13.

[38] Matti Joutsen, 'Four Transitions in the United Nations Crime Programme' (2017) Agenda 22, 26.

[39] See generally Roger S Clark, *The United Nations Crime Prevention and Criminal Justice Program* (University of Pennsylvania Press 1994) 73.

[40] Roger S Clark, 'The Role of the United Nations' in Mangai Natarajan (ed), *International and Transnational Crime and Justice* (2nd edn, CUP 2019) 397.

New York). At the Fourth UN Crime Congress he served as a consultant and as a member of AIDP. At the Fifth (1975) and Sixth (1980) Crime Congresses he served as executive secretary of the Congress and he continued to play a significant role in the UN criminal justice machinery until the Tenth Congress, the congress that lead to General Assembly resolution 55/25 of 15 November 2000 on Transnational Organized Crime, adopting the UNTOC.

## 2. The Tipping Point for Transnational Crime at the UN

Fijnaut argues that transnational crime is a 'container' concept which covers many different types of crime including organized crime, corporate crime, professional crime and political crime.[41] He also contends that the term 'transnational' recognizes no national boundaries.[42] As noted in the introduction to this chapter, the term 'transnational crime' was first discussed at the Fifth UN Crime Congress in 1975. At that meeting, the general rapporteur Sir Arthur Peterson noted that the 'increasing vulnerability of all countries' to 'transnational manifestations of crime', enabled by 'the spread of the mass media and of high-speed communication and travel facilities (highly desirable in themselves)', was 'a universal concern'.[43] The topics discussed under transnational criminality were:

1. Crime as business: organized crime, white-collar crime and corruption;[44]
2. Offences involving works of art and other cultural property;[45]
3. Criminality associated with alcoholism, drug abuse and illicit traffic in drugs;[46]
4. Violence and terrorism of transnational and comparative international significance;[47] and
5. Criminality associated with migration and flight from natural disasters and hostilities.[48]

[41] Cyrille Fijnaut, 'Transnational Crime and the Role of the United Nations in its Containment through International Cooperation: A Challenge for the 21st Century' (2000) 8(2) Eur J Crime Cr L Cri J 119.
[42] ibid.
[43] Fifth United Nations Congress on the Prevention of Crime and Treatment of Offenders, Geneva, 1–12 September 1975: Report prepared by the Secretariat, Chapter III, UN Doc A/Conf.56/10, para 383.
[44] ibid ch II, paras 51–59.
[45] ibid ch II, paras 60–64.
[46] ibid ch II, paras 65–77.
[47] ibid ch II, paras 84–95.
[48] ibid ch II, paras 98–106.

As the executive secretary at the Fifth UN Crime Congress, Gerhard Mueller played an important role in preparing the agenda and facilitating the discussions on the above transnational aspects of crime. This paved the way for discussion on organized transnational crimes in subsequent congresses.

When Mueller was the chief of the UN's International Crime Prevention and Criminal Justice Branch, the Surveys of Crime Trends and Operations of Criminal Justice Systems (UN-CTS) were begun.[49] Their major purpose was seen to be the collection of data on the incidence of reported crime and the operations of criminal justice systems with a view to improving the analysis and dissemination of that information globally. The Fourth UN-CTS provided the data for an extended discussion of transnational crimes at the Ninth UN Crime Congress in Cairo in 1995 (see Table 5.1). The survey asked respondents to report the transnational crime categories that were dealt with in the legal instrument and the legislation in which the crime categories were defined in the reporting member states. With 55 out of 193 states reporting, it was concluded that defining transnational crime was difficult because the national legislation did not refer to the transnational dimensions of the offences.[50] Mueller described the nineteen categories of transnational crime identified by the UN survey:[51] (i) money laundering, (ii) terrorist activities, (iii) theft of art and cultural objects, (iv) theft of intellectual property, (v) illicit traffic in arms, (vi) sea piracy, (vii) hijacking on land, (viii) insurance fraud, (ix) computer crime, (x) environmental crime, (xi) trafficking in persons, (xii) trading in human body parts, (xiii) illicit drug trafficking, (xiv) fraudulent bankruptcy, (xv) infiltration of legal business, (xvi) corruption, (xvii) bribery of public officials, and (xviii) other offences committed by organized criminal groups.

[49] RW Burnham and Helen Burnham, *United Nations World Surveys on Crime Trends and Criminal Justice Systems, 1970–1994: Restructured Five-Wave Data* (2006) <https://doi.org/10.3886/ICPSR02513.v1>.

[50] Sixth United Nations Congress on the Prevention of Crime and Treatment of Offenders, Caracas, Venezuela, 25 August–5 September 1980: Report prepared by the Secretariat, UN Doc A/Conf.87/14/Rev.1.

[51] Mueller, 'Transnational Crime' (n 24) 4. See also Frieda Adler, Gerhard OW Mueller and William S Laufer, *Criminology* (McGraw Hill 1995) 359–60 (hereafter Adler and others, *Criminology*); Gerhard OW Mueller, 'Transnational Crime: Definitions and Concepts' in Phil Williams and Dimitri Vlassis (eds), *Combating Transnational crime* (Transnational 2001) 13.

**Table 5.1** UN Congresses on Crime Prevention and UNTOC[52]

| UN Crime Congress | Place | Focus | Outcome | Participants |
|---|---|---|---|---|
| 1st (1955) | Switzerland | Treatment of prisoners | Research on juvenile delinquency | 51 governments<br>43 NGOs<br>512 participants |
| 2nd (1960) | England | Police cooperation for juveniles | Measures to prevent juvenile delinquency | 68 governments<br>50 NGOs<br>1046 participants |
| 3rd (1965) | Sweden | Social change and criminality | Criminological research on technical assistance; comparative crime and delinquency; UNICRI-Research | 74 governments<br>39 NGOs<br>1083 participants |
| 4th (1970) | Japan | Crime and development | Discussion of terrorism and hijacking, organized crime; cross national issues | 79 governments<br>31 NGOs<br>998 participants |
| 5th (1975) | Switzerland | New dimensions of crime—transnational and national violence; torture and cruel punishments | Discussion of female criminality; formulation of international code for law enforcement | 101governments<br>33 NGOs<br>909 participants |
| 6th (1980) | Venezuela | Crime prevention | Crime statistics | 102 governments<br>38 NGOs<br>920 participants |
| 7th (1985) | Italy | Crime as a global concern | Action against organized crime | 125 governments<br>58 NGOs<br>1395 participants |
| 8th (1990) | Cuba | International dimensions of crime | Research on organized crime structure; tools | 127 governments<br>46 NGOs<br>1127 participants |
| 9th (1995) | Egypt | Seeking security action against organized crime | Action based research, national, regional and international | 138 governments<br>73 NGOs<br>1899 participants |
| 10th (2000) | Austria | Combating TOC, rule of law, international cooperation | Legal instrument—UNTOC; speedy measures | 137 governments<br>58 NGOs<br>1902 participants |

[52] UNODC, *United Nations Congresses on Crime Prevention and Criminal Justice 1955–2010: 55 Years of Achievement* <https://www.un.org/en/conf/crimecongress2010/pdf/55years_ebook.pdf>.

Prior to 2003, the UN used the term 'transnational organized crime' to encompass all profit-motivated criminal activities of organized crime groups with international implications, but did not give a precise definition of the term because these criminal activities are constantly changing. However, in the UNTOC, the UN adopted a comprehensive, treaty-based legal instrument that applied to 'transnational organized crime', which it defined in article 3(1) as an offence that is transnational in nature and involves an organized criminal group.[53] Although it did not define organized crime but rather an organized criminal group,[54] the UNTOC does provide a definition of transnational crime in article 3(2):

> [A]n offence is transnational in nature if it is (a) committed in more than one State; (b) committed in one State but a substantial part of its preparation, planning, direction or control takes place in another State; (c) committed in one State but involves an organized criminal group that engages in criminal activities in more than one State; or (d) committed in one State but has substantial effects in another State.

This is essentially a jurisdictional definition rather than a criminological definition. To some extent it reflects the essence of Mueller's original concept of transnational crime which focused on transnationality of activity rather than on organization.

Since change is constantly happening around the world, definitions of transnational organized crime are needed not just for standardizing norms for law enforcement and judicial cooperation[55] but also for criminological understanding of the nature, extent and magnitude of these crimes in order to develop control and prevention measures. According to criminologists, 'neither individually, nor by type, nor collectively by category, do transnational crimes conform to the definitions and categorizations found in penal codes'.[56] Though the UNTOC's use of 'transnational' (as defined in article 3(2)) and 'organized group' (as defined in article 2(a)—see Table 5.2 below) is explicit, it is still not entirely clear what the compound term 'transnational organized crime' (TOC) means. Is it, for example, transnationally organized crime or crime committed by organized crime groups transnationally (see Table 5.2)? In fact, clear definitions of 'transnational' and 'organized' in TOC are a recurring concern in arriving at any global level assessments and initiatives. Table 5.2 lays out TOC elements to illustrate the challenges in including organized crime since there are about 200 definitions of this concept in the literature.[57]

[53] For more on the language of the Palermo Convention, see Roger S Clark, 'The United Nations Convention against Transnational Organized Crime' (2004) 50 Wayne L Rev 161 and sources cited there.

[54] See further Forlati, Chapter 13 in this book.

[55] See Council for Foreign Relations, 'The Global Regime for Transnational Crime' (no date) <https://www.cfr.org/report/global-regime-transnational-crime>.

[56] Adler and others, *Criminology* (n 51) 354.

[57] Klaus von Lampe, *Organized Crime: Analyzing Illegal Activities, Criminal Structures, and Extra-Legal Governance* (Sage 2015).

Table 5.2 Explanations of UNTOC Elements

| Transnational Organized Crime | Transnational Crime | Organized Group | Organized Crime |
|---|---|---|---|
| An offence is transnational if: *It is committed in more than one state; *It is committed in one state but a substantial part of its preparation, planning, direction or control takes place in another state; *It is committed in one state but involves an organized criminal group that engages in criminal activities in more than one state; or *It is committed in one state but has substantial effects in another State. | Criminal activities extending into, and violating the laws of, several countries. | 'Organized criminal group' is *a group of three or more persons that was not randomly formed; *existing for a period of time; *acting in concert with the aim of committing at least one crime punishable by at least four years' incarceration; *in order to obtain, directly or indirectly, a financial or other material benefit | Organized crime is a continuing criminal enterprise that rationally works to profit from illicit activities that are often in great public demand. Its continuing existence is maintained through corruption of public officials and the use of intimidation, threats or force to protect its operations. |

Gerhard Mueller warned us of the uncertainties of the definition of 'transnational crime'. As mentioned earlier, it is commonly used by criminologists, criminal justice officials and policymakers, but its complementary term, 'transnational criminal law', is still relatively unknown and although becoming more common is generally not yet part of the curricula of institutions. This is in part because the specific knowledge of how to solve the difficulties of investigating and prosecuting criminal cases affecting more than one jurisdiction has not usually been part of traditional legal training.[58]

## IV. Conclusion: The Tipping Point of Transnational Crime

The review above of the criminological and criminal justice expertise of Gerhard Mueller has shown that his involvement in the UN Crime Congresses, especially the Fifth Congress in 1975, led to a tipping point in the usage of the term 'transnational' in the UN's discussions of five major types of crimes that span the borders

[58] Sabine Gless and John Vervaele, 'Law Should Govern: Aspiring General Principles for Transnational Criminal Justice' (2013) 9 Utrecht L Rev 1.

of two or more countries. This usage advanced the future agenda for the fourth UN crime trends survey on transnational crimes worldwide. The Ninth UN Crime Congress held in Cairo in 1995 recognized the challenges in coming to a legal consensus in measuring transnational crime. The use of the term 'transnational' was institutionalized in the UNTOC although ambiguity remained about what constituted transnational organized crime. Freda Adler's presidential address at the 1995 American Society of Criminology[59] drew attention to the nature and prevalence of nineteen transnational crimes and their burgeoning global impact. She argued that the UN data on transnational crime considerably advanced the study of 'transnational crime' in criminology. She called for an updated inventory of all transnational (organized) crimes and how they are defined in the domestic laws of all UN member states. That inventory would help in coming to some agreement about universal definitions and would set the platform for developing solid transnational criminal law. As Professor Mueller has argued, just as international criminal law was taught in some universities so should transnational criminal law be taught. Such teaching would help in identifying the formidable challenges cooperation against cross-border crime entails.

[59] Freda Adler, 'Our American Society of Criminology, the World, and the State of the Art—the American Society of Criminology 1995 Presidential Address' (1996) 34(1) Criminology.

# 6

# The Emergence of Criminal Law Norms in International Organizations

*Frank Meyer*

## I. Introduction

The development of transnational criminal law is influenced by a multitude of actors convening and interacting in a dazzling variety of settings, compositions and manifestations. International organizations have played a particularly dominant role in this cycle. While many studies have paid attention to their influence and activities with respect to specific areas of crime or particular forms of international cooperation, these organizations have attracted considerably less attention in terms of cross-policy and cross-organization analysis and comparison, especially from a legal point of view. This lack of interest stands in stark contrast with the passion and dedication found in the study of the field of international criminal law *stricto sensu*. Admirable intellectual efforts to broaden the scope of international criminal law by extending it to the most serious treaty-based crimes[1] have not gained track. Apparently there is a strong sense of otherness which separates their spheres.[2] The imbalance also appears to be influenced by the low visibility of many jurisgenerative processes in the international sphere and, as a result, a wide-spread general impression that these processes are unproblematic because (and as long as) criminal law norms do not become binding without the formal consent of the national sovereign. The rather technical definition of transnational criminal law focusing on treaty-based crimes, which is being used by many scholars in the wake of Boister, might have compounded the problem.[3]

While this understanding has the structural advantage of clarity, simplicity and historical tradition, it appears not to be sensitive enough to the many ways in which law evolves in the transnational sphere and seems ill-equipped to process its

[1] See in particular, the seminal work of Cherif Bassiouni, 'International Criminal Justice in the Age of Globalization' in *International Criminal Law: Quo Vadis?* (2004) 19 Nouvelles Études Pénales 79, 82, who denied fundamental theoretical differences between transnational criminal law; see also Cherif Bassiouni (ed), *International Criminal Law, Vol. 1: Sources, Subjects and Contents* (3rd edn, Brill 2008).

[2] On the perceived differences, Claus Kreß, 'International Criminal Law' in *Max Planck Encyclopedia of Public International Law* (OUP, last updated March 2009) paras 6 et seq.

[3] See Neil Boister, 'Transnational Criminal Law?' (2003) 14(5) EJIL 953 (hereafter Boister, 'Transnational Criminal Law?').

Frank Meyer, *The Emergence of Criminal Law Norms in International Organizations* In: *Histories of Transnational Criminal Law*. Edited by: Neil Boister, Sabine Gless and Florian Jeßberger, Oxford University Press. 
DOI: 10.1093/oso/9780192845702.003.0007

complexity. There are manifold instruments and mechanisms in the transnational realm (other than treaties) that have emerged during the last fifty years which impact on the legal situation at the national level; for instance Security Council resolutions that order national legislation, FATF recommendations, monitoring bodies that compile and enforce transnational best practices. Yet, it is unclear whether such mechanisms should fall under the heading of transnational criminal law proper. While the narrow technical definition as treaty-based crimes, which has become standard,[4] might be flexible enough as to encompass some of these examples, it has not encouraged a broader and more subtle debate about the forms, nature, animating ideas and boundaries of transnational criminal law.[5] Delineating its scope and contents, thus, remains an unsettled matter.

Assuming that many jurisgenerative processes beyond suppression conventions could be qualified as transnational criminal law and that they are not completely irrelevant with respect to the legitimacy of the criminal laws they produce, one is immediately confronted with the unpleasant reality that accountability and legitimacy concerns with respect to state sovereignty, democratic self-determination, rule of law and human rights cannot be addressed cogently due to a lack of understanding of how these laws came about and how to typify and qualify law-generating processes. These uncertainties cast a shadow over transnational criminal law. And they challenge any lawyer who wishes to tell a history of law-making in international organizations.

This contribution will discuss how such a history could be told and what methodological and theoretical obstacles loom in this path. The chapter might therefore differ from others as it does not give a historical account of transnational criminal law's contents and architects but intends to enrich the debate with some conceptual and methodological reflections. It will elaborate on referential frameworks, concepts and standards that could help to integrate these accounts, put them in perspective to overarching legitimacy questions and kindle further differentiated analysis in the field of transnational criminal law. In doing so, however, the jurisgenerative processes analysed will be presented in historical perspective to highlight contingencies and institutional trajectories.

The starting points for this analysis are three central research questions developed in an extensive study from 2011.[6] The first research question is, obviously, what is actually going on. This, first and foremost, means to analyse and categorize.

[4] William Schabas, *An Introduction to the International Criminal Court* (5th edn, CUP 2017) 75; Boister, 'Transnational Criminal Law?' (n 3) 955): indirect suppression by international law through domestic penal law of criminal activities that have actual or potential transboundary effects.

[5] That is not to say that legitimacy is not being discussed by experts in the field; see, for instance, Neil Boister, *An Introduction to Transnational Criminal Law* (OUP 2012) 20 et seq. (hereafter Boister, *Introduction to TCL*); Boister, 'Transnational Criminal Law?' (n 3) 955, 957, notes that criminalization processes and the social construction of transnational crime threats receive too little attention.

[6] Frank Meyer, *Strafrechtsgenese in Internationalen Organisationen* (Nomos 2011) 39 et seq. (hereafter Meyer, *Strafrechtsgenese*).

The second research question addresses the 'why and when'. Looking beyond form and process, it is highly informative and important to take a deeper look at the purposes behind international organizations' (IO) activities (in addition to the rather vague criterion of 'transboundary effect'). It is imperative to develop a better understanding of the (organization-specific) internal and political logic of actions in order to make sense of the law-making processes. Such an approach would allow us to stake out the legal and political limits of IOs' actions and offers a clearer vision as to which IO is best suited for a given transnational-crime-related issue. As to 'when' IOs resort to criminal law one would assume that the answer will quite often be linked up with the objectives (of IO policies) that actual internal or external events trigger and which are significant enough to prompt the IO (or its member states) into action. Other potential causes to be analysed could be cross-pollination (whereby IOs borrow ideas and tested practices from others), policy-laundering[7] or the evolving self-conception and operational maturity of an IO. Both questions will be combined and some tentative timelines suggested as to the when and in what circumstances certain mechanisms gained track, spread or fell out of fashion with the growing influence and evolution of IOs after 1945. In this context it will also be scrutinized whether the incrementalism that characterizes the development of many treaty crimes[8] is visible with respect to the toolbox of law-generation as well.

The third research question deals with the meta-question of legal legitimacy which encapsulates the various preconditions in international, constitutional and criminal law doctrine that attach to the exercise of a *ius puniendi* by all public authorities. Shifting law-generating capacities (once the exclusive domain of the nation state) to IOs over time inevitably causes concerns about accountability and sovereignty. The legitimacy debates of today about democratic self-determination, human rights and compatibility with basic criminal law concepts testify to the different phases of development these IOs have gone through.

It is beyond the scope of the chapter to analyse driving forces and decisive actors within these processes. Such meta-study would complement this chapter wonderfully, but one suspects that the group of key players is hugely diverse, comprising epistemic communities and influential individuals[9] as well as civil society and individual or like-minded states whose agenda might, of course, have been guided by powerful expert groups or imposing figures. Instead this chapter looks at the gateways available for the use of different types of stakeholders.

[7] Eg Paul de Hert and Angela Aguinaldo, 'A Leading Role for the EU in Drafting Criminal Law Powers? Use of the Council of Europe for Policy Laundering' [2019] NJECL 99 et seq (hereafter De Hert and Aguinaldo, 'A Leading Role').

[8] Boister, *Introduction to TCL* (n 5) 275.

[9] See von Lingen, Chapter 4 and Natarajan, Chapter 5 respectively in this book.

## II. Methodological Challenges

Any attempt to categorize or typify jurisgenerative processes runs the risk of being either too formalistic (by focusing on traditional manifestations of law and law creation such as treaties) or vulnerable to methodological distortions as histories of transnational criminal law can be legal, sociological, political, philosophical, even geographical narratives. The primary interest of lawyers is in legal mechanisms and legal effects. Yet, most lawyers working in this field will be fully aware that the creation of legal norms in IOs is not limited to traditional treaty-making but features other phenomena that defy established categories of international law and legal theory. What is much less clear is how to gauge and treat these processes to make them amenable to legal assessments.

Methodologically drawing on the concept of 'governance', which prior studies adapted for the purposes of legal research,[10] two insights will define this chapter. First, to fully understand the evolution of norms it is of the essence to look beyond the formal legislative process and learn to think in policy cycles. The evolution of norms has an input, a conversion and an implementation phase. Jurisgenerative processes may stretch across all phases or merely occur in one of them. In addition, the policy process is not necessarily linear, but often cyclical. Policy cycle output may become input and might be converted into more binding or differentiated forms of law which adds a diachronic dimension to this method.

Second, to find better descriptions and coin better terms to capture the essence of what IOs are doing, governance studies suggest analysing the role of legal norms as an instrument and product of the coordination of international and national actors.[11] Applied to the development of transnational criminal law this approach urges us to look into how and by what legal means (norms, institutions and structures including the actors' institutional and organizational framework) the relationships and interactions of relevant actors are coordinated and influenced in the process of moulding and shaping criminal norms. To look beyond legal form into legal impact and implicit normativity is equally pertinent for this approach.

[10] Meyer, *Strafrechtsgenese* (n 6) 48.

[11] Meyer, *Strafrechtsgenese* (n 6) 53; a different path was chosen in Terence Halliday and Gregory Shaffer (eds), *Transnational Legal Orders* (CUP 2015) (hereafter Halliday and Shaffer, *Transnational Legal Orders*) which used socio-legal case studies. These highly informative studies did not aim at discerning and pinpointing a general and comprehensive framework of jurisgenerative processes; for an overview of different formations and structures of transnational criminal law actors see Terence Halliday and Gregory Shaffer, 'Researching Transnational Legal Orders' in Halliday and Shaffer, *Transnational Legal Orders* 475, 504–05.

## III. Overview of Jurisgenerative Processes

Travelling down this road one quickly realizes a host of idiosyncratic and innovative modes that steer jurisgenerative processes and even compel nation states to act in a certain direction. When looking at these jurisgenerative processes through a governance lens three stages of the policy-cycle must be distinguished: input, conversion and implementation.

### 1. Input

At the input level four distinct modes influence the emergence of new legal content. The first is framing (of issues), which signifies the controlling of policymaking and negotiations through the identification of problems and possible solutions by expert committees, task forces or the organs of IOs themselves (agenda-setting). Based on a claim of expertise (eg impact assessments) they cast legal problems and their nature in a certain light and stake out the scope of possible and wished for solutions and, at least mildly, predetermine ensuing deliberations. This mode is present in all IOs. But only the more integrated and established IOs have introduced standing committees in the area of criminal law over time, which provide a permanent basis for law reform (from the perspective of the IO's mission as set forth in its charter). The United Nations Congress on Crime Prevention and Criminal Justice, held every five years since 1955, is an early example of this institutionalization phenomenon. The establishment of a standing European Committee on Crime Problems (CDPC) by the Committee of Ministers of the Council of Europe (CoE) in 1958 has allowed it to continually oversee and coordinate activities in the field of crime prevention and crime control until now.

Pro-Palestinian terrorism later brought about significant changes. The task of identifying problems and ways forward was entrusted to those UN organizations whose areas of responsibility had been particularly affected by terrorist attacks.[12] The threat of international terrorism emerging in the late 1990s moved the UN to a new level of activity and ultimately led the Security Council to establish dedicated sub-committees in charge of different groups and aspects of terrorism after 2001 such as the ISIL (Da'esh) and Al-Qaida Sanctions Committee, CTC (Security Council Counter-Terrorism Committee) and '1540'-Committee. This shift exemplifies a general trend towards more specific and advanced designs once matters of international security become involved.

[12] IMO (International Maritime Organization), 1988 SUA Convention; International Civil Aviation Organization (ICAO), 1963 Tokyo Convention, 1970 Hague Hijacking Convention; the latter introduced the so-called 'Hague model' which emerged as the template for subsequent suppression conventions.

In the EU both legislative organs have their own standing committees for criminal matters and civil liberties to foster and initiate debate. Even more important, the EU Commission shapes the debate via impact assessments and other types of working documents. The emergence of these structures since the beginning of the Schengen Cooperation in 1985 is a necessary consequence of growing European integration and especially the conferral of law-making competences to the EU. This evolution was further propelled by the entry into force of the Lisbon Treaty in 2009 which vastly expanded the criminal law powers of the EU. As these structures result from the conversion of the EU into a supranational entity it is obvious why other organizations could not follow the same trajectory.

Of course, not all input is generated internally and autonomously. Ideas migrate or are deliberately funnelled into organizations whose tasks and institutional make-up make them a supposedly more receptive or ideal multiplier.[13] Terrorism is a case in point. Measures against foreign fighters adopted at the UN recently trickled down to regional organizations such as the CoE (or the EU) for adoption and further implementation.[14] Some experts have dubbed this phenomenon the internalization of external ideas.[15] However, history tells us that it does not always work so smoothly. Vulnerability to political obstruction and conflicts between the global South and Western world have derailed many universal initiatives and precipitated a change of venue. An illustrative example for such policy transfers is bribery of foreign officials. After much frustration and facing an impasse at the UN in the late 1970s, like-minded states and their experts turned to the OECD to pick up the slack in order to shape ideas and mutually acceptable solutions for a new economic era after the end of the Cold War.[16] There may be instances of cross-pollination as well. The OECD Convention, for instance, has inspired a cascade of activities against corruption in the UN, CoE and EU alike.

Finally, input, as Chapters 4 and 5 have shown, might originate in epistemic communities and civil society groups from outside the IO's internal world and find their way on to the international agenda.[17]

[13] The Council of Europe has become a particularly versatile actor. It cooperates with the UN to transform Security Council resolutions into conventions, interacts with the EU to spread EU law among its state parties or to ensure equivalent standards in Europe. But it also promotes legal reforms of pan-European concern on its own motion from prison reform to artificial intelligence; especially where the EU lacks competences to legislate; crit De Hert and Aguinaldo, 'A Leading Role' (n 7) 99, 101 et seq.

[14] The evolution of the measures against foreign fighters is a good recent example; see Valsamis Mitsilegas, '"Security Law" and Preventive Justice in the Legal Architecture of the European Union' in Ulrich Sieber and others (eds), *Alternative Systems of Crime Control: National, Transnational, and International Dimensions* (Duncker & Humblot 2018) 203, 208 (hereafter Mitsilegas, 'Security Law and Preventive Justice'); on the UN origins John Ip, 'Reconceptualising the Legal Response to Foreign Fighters' (2020) 69 ICLQ 103, 110 et seq.

[15] Mitsilegas, 'Security Law and Preventive Justice' (n 14) 203, 208, 212.

[16] 1997 OECD Bribery Convention. Some observers have cast doubt on the true character of this forum-shifting and consider it a telling example of local globalism as it was supposedly driven by US interests in levelling the playing field through internationalizing the Foreign Corrupt Practices Act.

[17] For a case study on human trafficking see Paulette Lloyd and Beth Simmons, 'Framing for a New Transnational Legal Order' in Halliday and Shaffer, *Transnational Legal Orders* (n 11) 400 et seq.

The second related mode captures the drafting and adoption of policy guidelines by the government or parliamentary bodies of IOs, which demand legal developments in certain areas and can point in the direction of normatively preferable solutions (policy formulation) by way, for example, of policy programmes, global agendas, recommendations etc.[18] Their scope, intrinsic quality and internal legal status may differ markedly among IOs. In its more basic forms policy formulation has been around since the inception of IOs. We can see, for example, the Compendium of United Nations standards and norms in crime prevention and criminal justice published in its first edition in 1992 by the newly founded UN Commission on Crime Prevention and Criminal Justice. It is the closest many international actors get to passing government-like policy programmes and to exercising some influence over member states. In this sense the duration, ambition and authority of these programmes reflect integration and institutional maturity, with the European Council's multi-year programmes in the area of freedom, security and justice (starting with the Tampere Conclusions in 1999) being the most advanced example. The EU Security Agenda and implementing Commission action plans are further examples. However, this mode is not immune to outside influence. In particular, security law has repeatedly bridged the external-internal divide, indicating that other actors like the Security Council at least in some areas like international security have started to formulate a global security agenda.

Looked at from a historical perspective, the growing importance of international institutions and expanding law-making competences has led to more sophisticated forms of policy formulation. These range from comprehensive Recommendations of the CoE Committee of Ministers which have resulted in numerous CoE conventions[19] to the Tampere Conclusions which called on member states to introduce joint investigative teams to combat trafficking in drugs and human beings as well as terrorism.[20] In retrospect, it seems that particular issues at the heart of states' sovereignty and security concerns such as terrorism have led to more intensified and advanced uses of this mode whereas other prima facie equally important concerns like public health or environmental protection have drawn less attention.

A third mode of increased practical importance is the preparation of treaties, resolutions and other legal documents, quite often in permanent or ad hoc subsidiary organs (such as the PC-OC, ICAO, IMO, ECOSOC) staffed with experts, government officials and other stakeholders and hidden from public scrutiny. Options are weighed and chosen for adoption by the state parties without participation

[18] Eg Recommendation CM/Rec(2017)6 of the Committee of Ministers to member States on 'special investigation techniques' in relation to serious crimes including acts of terrorism.

[19] Eg Recommendation No R (91) 11 concerning sexual exploitation, pornography and prostitution of, and trafficking in, children and young adults and Recommendation Rec(2001)16 on the protection of children against sexual exploitation were instrumental in the negotiation of CoE Convention No 201 on the Protection of Children against Sexual Exploitation and Sexual Abuse.

[20] Tampere Council 1999, Presidency Conclusions, para 43.

of parliamentarians as traditional holders of the *ius puniendi*. Institutional arrangements vary from state conferences via specialized bodies to genuine law-making bodies. In historical perspective their development has broadly speaking been shaped by two forces. First, it is inextricably intertwined with the history of IOs. Institutional maturation enables them to tap the full institutional potentials of their charters (to concentrate and develop expertise). Outside events are the second driver. For example, terrorist attacks in the 1970s prompted expansions of the mandates of the ICAO and IMO[21] while a host of ad hoc bodies sprang up in the aftermath of 9/11. Only the EU installed permanent specialized committees within its legislative bodies and in the Commission, after criminal matters became a union policy in 1993. Overall, this mode is more often influenced by or is the product of the evolution of the IO itself than of crime-specific necessities. In some instances, both strands may converge. In the field of terrorism, the push by the Security Council might be interpreted as an attempt to bypass General Assembly subsidiary organs and force other international actors into action more directly.

The fourth input mode is value communication. As a result of lack of competence or political restraint, many actors formulate normative targets by communicating legal positions and underlying principles. Like pastoral letters they convey what would be good, reasonable legal solutions and why they should be adopted, using the institutional and legal framework of organizations as points of reference. Often such communications qualify as soft law. Resolutions of the CoE Parliamentary Assembly are a prime example.[22] Other influential examples include the European Prison Rules (adopted by the CoE's Committee of Ministers)[23] and the UN General Assembly's Mandela Rules.[24] The prominence of this mode waxes and wanes. It is used in an ad hoc manner in times of crisis or to corroborate ongoing developments, and it may have different functions over the course of time. Value communication can offer a substitute or propose a compromise where political majorities in (executive) bodies are lacking. It may provide guidance where more incisive instruments have met resistance from member states or nudge member states towards particular practices where a legal framework already existed. In the long run, such value communication may contribute to the emergence of customary law, becoming a mode of conversion. Overall, it seems that only few organizations firmly rooted in universal values and principles have acquired the

[21] See above, text at n 12.

[22] For instance on renditions: Parliamentary Assembly, Resolution 1838 (2011), Abuse of state secrecy and national security: obstacles to parliamentary and judicial scrutiny of human rights violations; in the same vein European Parliament, Resolution of 11 September 2012 on alleged transportation and illegal detention of prisoners in European countries by the CIA: follow-up of the European Parliament TDIP Committee report (2012/2033(INI)).

[23] Recommendation Rec(2006)2 of the Committee of Ministers to member states on the European Prison Rules.

[24] United Nations Standard Minimum Rules for the Treatment of Prisoners (the Nelson Mandela Rules), A/RES/70/175.

authority to use this mode effectively (eg the UN, CoE, and EU but perhaps not the OECD). Internal institutional crisis inevitably leaves its mark on its frequency and potency. In the temporal dimension, this aspect might better explain action or inaction in transnational criminal law than law enforcement necessity.

In terms of substance the input phase features several typical ingredients. Criminalization requirements, definitions of offences, rules on participation and jurisdiction and obligations to cooperate can all be found in varying levels of scope and detail. Duties to cooperate have become more sophisticated than in the past. And asset recovery and financial regulation have become staples of the fight against organized crime and terrorism. A tendency to include institutional arrangements which range from monitoring and investigative bodies (like Financial Intelligence Units and the European Public Prosecutor) to courts is of more recent origin. It is found very rarely though and never gained the same traction in transnational criminal law as in international criminal law.[25] There is no visible interest among powerful member states in expanding the standard toolkit in this direction. As of now, it seems that enforcement courts require a state-like constitutional stature which only the EU exhibits. Much more common is the proposal of monitoring bodies, which play a double role throughout the conversion and implementation phase. In historical perspective this innovation has come to full fruition in the past twenty years. Hardly any criminal control treaty or regulation is proposed these days without ancillary mechanisms to ensure effective enforcement. Increasingly, these obligations are embedded in and promulgated as components of more comprehensive security, economic or social-political packages underscoring the objectives pursued with a transnational criminal law initiative.

## 2. Conversion

Conversion denotes the transformation of input into legal content. In this phase different modes come into play. Almost all IOs still rely on horizontal multilateralism. Its main products remain crime control treaties. In terms of adoption and ratification multilateral treaties are probably the least problematic type of law-making, even though parliaments have limited influence during the drafting period.

A hidden (though well-established), more troubling form of conversion that sometimes goes hand in hand with treaty-making is the adoption of explanatory memoranda or guidance notes, for example by the CoE Committee of Ministers or assemblies of state parties. This mechanism allows governments to provide

[25] The failed establishment of an MH17 tribunal in the UN highlights the political impasse debilitating any effort at strengthening judicial accountability <https://www.un.org/press/en/2015/sc11990.doc.htm>.

explanations and substantiations of treaty content that not only influences or even predetermines the implementation process but create new legal content. It has been common practice for a long time but seems problematic in view of the vague terminology found in many treaties. Recent examples include provisions against travelling jihadists or corruption. At the other end of the spectrum vertical directives that order national states to amend, change or expand their criminal laws mark the most controversial law-making mechanism. In this case, the law-making powers of an international actor supersede national sovereignty and the supposedly exclusive *ius puniendi* of the nation state. In this area emotions run high. This mode remains the preserve of the most powerful and integrated organizations. It is a natural corollary of the supranationalization of the EU and the high levels of harmonization put in place since 2009. The Security Council has claimed similar powers after 9/11 for selected threats.[26] Its limited self-empowerment follows a different logic though. Not being a legislative body at all, the Security Council's authority rests on a creeping long-term diversification of the concept of 'peace' and the array of Chapter VII measures starting after the end of the Cold War, which emboldened the Security Council to take drastic measures in response to urgent security concerns about violent groups of non-state actors.

Diachronically speaking, the EU's powers follow a predictable trajectory whereas the Security Council has no coherent agenda but avails itself of the most effective powers when international security demands and political feasibility permit such interventions. This helps explain why plans for drastic measures and judicial accountability mechanisms for Syria have ground to a halt. However, and despite these stark differences both examples do share an equally recent, less obvious function. Both the EU and Security Council have activated their legislative authority as fall-back implementation tools to enforce already binding international or supranational norms.[27]

Another, methodologically fraught mechanism is the constructive creation of customary law. IOs and international tribunals sit at the juncture of policy, soft law and binding international law. We have seen in the past that UN bodies inaugurated customary law by fiat in the area of international criminal law (to facilitate the establishment of international tribunals).[28]

More often, however, targeted resolutions frame international consensus and try to move the international community successively towards an aspired practice.[29]

[26] SC Res 1373 (28 September 2001); SC Res 1540 (28 April 2004).

[27] Eg Recitals 3–5 Directive 2009/123/EC of the European Parliament and of the Council of 21 October 2009 amending Directive 2005/35/EC on ship-source pollution and on the introduction of penalties for infringements, OJ L 280, 52; SC Res 1373, para 3 (Calls upon all States to ... (d) Become parties as soon as possible to the relevant international conventions and protocols relating to terrorism, including the 1999 Terrorist Financing Convention).

[28] Security Council, Report of the Secretary General Pursuant to Paragraph 2 of Security Council Resolution 808 (3 May 1993), para 35.

[29] Eg SC Res 2125 (2013), paras 8 (*Calls upon* States to cooperate ... on the issue of hostage taking, and the prosecution of suspected pirates for taking hostages) and 17 (*Calls upon* all States to criminalize

Less obvious, but a constant source of rancour in many countries, is something that could be dubbed value standardization and enforcement by courts based on human rights catalogues and fundamental freedoms guaranteed in the charters (constitutions) of the IOs. It is not easy to ascertain to what extent this mechanism is institution-driven or induced by individuals or pressure groups. But without setting up an institutional framework that makes TCL-related activities subject to direct or indirect forms of judicial review (for their human rights compatibility) hand in hand with doctrines (devised by courts) that encourage individual complaints[30] it would not have got off the ground. Even today, mechanisms to counter structural and systemic deficiencies (eg ECHR pilot procedure; positive obligations) evolve internally and intend to enlist individuals as agents of change. At the same time, the adoption of international human rights treaties after World War II has nurtured greater awareness and willingness (encouraged by early successes and receptive courts) of individuals and civil liberties movements to pursue their interests in court. The sky-rocketing case load of the European Court of Human Rights (ECtHR) after 1990 demonstrates this beneficial interrelation. Introducing human rights complaints which empower individuals to drag nation states in front of international tribunals to have their actions declared illegal is the single most important booster for the evolution of human rights law and its extension to ever new settings. This thrust allowed the ECtHR to derive upper limits and minimum punishment thresholds from the ECHR. The Strasbourg court punches holes into national criminal statutes through calling out the incompatibility of certain elements of crime or interpretations thereof with human rights guarantees.[31] While this appears to be the regular job of a human rights tribunal, the sometimes-erratic methodology of the ECtHR (notions like the margin of appreciation, European consensus and overall fairness) puzzles academic observers and respondent states alike.

From a diachronic perspective, the ECtHR's jurisprudence is nevertheless becoming more and more assertive. The Strasbourg court has been developing the notion of positive obligations into a highly versatile doctrinal tool for more than a decade now. It comes into play to impose duties of investigation and even international cooperation in the last couple of years.[32] It provides the doctrinal basis for duties to enact criminal prohibitions and to guarantee certain criminal justice

piracy under their domestic law and to favourably consider the prosecution of suspected, and imprisonment of those convicted, pirates apprehended off the coast of Somalia, and their facilitators and financiers ashore).

[30] The ECtHR, eg, is directly accessible by individual complaints, something parties were bound to introduce by virtue of Additional Protocol XI of 1994. The court facilitates this evolution through positive obligations to investigate potential violations at the national level and starting in the late 1990s/early 2000s to lower the admissibility bar and alleviate evidence problems of the potentially aggrieved.

[31] ECtHR, *Dudgeon v United Kingdom*, App no 7525/76, 22 October 1981.

[32] ECtHR, *Güzelyurtlu and Others v Cyprus and Turkey*, App no 36925/07, 21 January 2019.

standards where the court has repeatedly used the formulation of positive obligations to convert soft law (eg European Prison Rules, CPT reports) into hard law.[33] Overall, it is fair to say that this expansion is of the court's own doing.

The second case in point is the Court of Justice of the EU (CJEU) which introduced EU fundamental rights as general principles of EU law and defended fundamental freedoms against national incursions in order to strengthen the legitimacy of EU law. Interestingly, it encouraged EU citizens to defend their rights in court. The CJEU has been more reluctant in regard to positive obligations. Instead, the Luxembourg court resorts to the principle of effectiveness to enforce obligations to comply with EU law (including the use of criminal law).[34] There are good constitutional reasons for this judicial self-restraint since the EU, unlike the CoE, has legislative competences and processes at its disposal that do the same job in a much more democratic way.

Overall, both examples demonstrate that this mode is a privilege and trademark of IOs with integrated judicial review systems.

The final and least obvious jurisgenerative process is policy evaluation. This governance by information does not intend to create new law directly. Rather, IO organs, task forces or committees propose solutions, model rules and toolkits to tackle transnational crime-related problems at the national level. These suggestions are not binding. Yet they still exert a quantum of persuasion based on expertise and subtle (economic) peer pressure and will not go unnoticed by national actors. Like framing, governance by information can decisively shape and predetermine national debates. This process (after sporadic prior use) took off in the latter part of the 1990s and is now ubiquitous in the OECD, the UN, the CoE and in the practice of the EU Commission. It has evolved into an often-used substitute for law-making where treaty-making has failed, proved too cumbersome or was never entertained as it seemed easier to reach political compromise using policy evaluation. The OECD has raised this mode of law-creation to new heights. Negotiating a protocol to the OECD bribery convention was not seriously attempted. Instead, soft law recommendations and monitoring were used to achieve improvements to the legal anti-corruption framework.[35] Other phenotypical examples include model rules for MNEs (first versions date back to 1976) or cooperation and information exchange in tax matters (since 2000). The strength of this mechanism is well documented by the fact that it has triggered a cascade of law-making activities in better integrated IOs with stronger law-making toolkits or specific regional focus.[36] The

[33] ECtHR, *Ananyev and Others v Russia*, App nos 42525/07 and 60800/08, 10 January 2012.

[34] It is often overlooked that CJEU interventions have led to decriminalization in many areas of regulatory criminal law; mostly based on fundamental freedoms jurisprudence and the effective EU-wide enforcement of harmonized market rules; eg ECJ, *Dassonville* [1974], ECLI:EU:C:1974:82; ECJ, *Ratti* [1979] ECLI:EU:C:1979:110.

[35] 2009 Recommendation of the Council for Further Combating Bribery; 2009 Recommendation on the Tax Deductibility of Bribes to Foreign Public Officials and other related instruments.

[36] The Council of Europe has adopted multiple instruments in the wake of the OECD Convention: Criminal Law Convention on Corruption of 27 January 1999 (ETS 173; entry into

OECD's clout does not immunize it against occasionally being bypassed via bilateral or multilateral treaties propagated by powerful states. In tax matters, for instance, the US established its own parallel cooperation regime (FATCA) using its control over the dollar as a lever to strong-arm other states into more one-sided agreements. Another crucial actor that has become more and more influential in lockstep with European integration and which makes rich use of policy evaluation is the EU Commission. In comparative and historical perspective it is important to note that while any organization might pursue ulterior goals, the Commission's crime-related activities are pervaded by an overarching interest to adjust and strengthen the protection of EU norms in their own specific political and economic ecosystem. This aim (which predates the Lisbon Treaty and goes as far back as the Greek Maize case [1988]) is not shared by other organizations.

A typical product of policy evaluation is the identification and promulgation of best practices. It goes hand in hand with the devolution of policymaking to specialized bodies and the growing use of monitoring by groups of experts that can be witnessed over the past twenty-five years. A further factor contributing to its rise lies in its impact. Despite their non-binding nature, they are relatively effective, especially when coupled with strong monitoring powers. Best practices in many cases ring in the conversion phase and set pertinent (if not compelling) benchmarks. They are part and parcel of a policy cycle in that they frame and may be converted into model rules, directives or new law-making initiatives. Best practices also very easily spread to other organizations. Money laundering is a good example. Over the past two decades the number of policymaking and monitoring bodies that are mutually influenced by each other's assessments has multiplied (eg the assessments of the FATF, Caribbean Financial Action Task Force (CFATF), Asia/Pacific Group (APG), Moneyval, and EU Commission in regard to money laundering).

## 3. Implementation

The implementation phase receives comparatively less attention, perhaps because there is a general presumption that the law-making work is completed once a legal instrument has been adopted. Yet, this would understate the magnitude and complexity of issues that wait to be resolved in the implementation process (eg devising technical solutions, seamless integration into national legal frameworks, discretionary selection of optional choices, substantiation of abstract concepts

force: 1 July 2002), Civil Law Convention on Corruption of 4 November 1999 (ETS 174; entry into force: 1 November 2003), Additional Protocol to the Criminal Law Convention on Corruption of 15 May 2003 (ETS 191; entry into force: 1 February 2005), Resolution (97) 24 Concerning Twenty Guiding Principles on the fight against Corruption, Rec(2000)10E on Codes of Conduct for Public Officials, Rec(2003)4 of the Committee of Ministers to member states on Common Rules against Corruption in the Funding of Political parties and electoral campaigns.

and effective enforcement). Besides the technical implementation process at the national level, this phase features mechanisms as diverse as monitoring/mutual evaluation and, once more, policy evaluation and judicial enforcement/protection.

In modern-day transnational criminal law, monitoring has become commonplace. Security Council resolutions, UN treaties, CoE conventions etc are coupled with institutional frameworks setting up supervisory bodies and procedures. Such committees or expert bodies (eg the Committee against torture (CAT), Group of Experts (GRECO) or the FATF) periodically review technical compliance and effective application in contracting states. The strength of this mechanism is contingent on the actual expertise of the committees and their backing in charter or auxiliary regulations. While the Security Council's ad hoc bodies draw authority from Chapter VII, CoE bodies find support in founding documents or rules of procedure like Rule 30 GRECO Rules of Procedure, which requires compliance with recommendations. Here the decisive enforcement leverage comes from prior state consent. In historical perspective, this mode grows ever stronger. Most recent examples are Grevio (Group of Experts on Action against Violence against Women) and FATF-style EU black and grey lists. Further indicators are signs that the EU contemplated setting up its own corruption monitoring body. The pinnacle of the evolution is embodied in the EU's multi-level, multi-agency enforcement structures, which did not exist fifteen years ago.

While these look like very reasonable arrangements one must not miss two important aspects of mutual evaluation. It goes hand in hand with benchmarking and identification of best practices. Frequently, monitoring bodies also review adherence to non-binding articles and still reprimand states for non-compliance (naming and shaming). In this way monitoring bodies decisively substantiate treaty provisions and jostle member states to adjust their laws beyond what was consented to. The mode is particularly forceful when coupled with other enforcement tools such as grey lists or blacklists. As a result, mutual evaluation can become a powerful alternative to more direct law-making competences, making for instance, the FATF a considerably influential body. The second pitfall that is hardly ever discussed is the methodology employed by monitoring bodies. It was only when the EU Commission threatened to put strategically important states like Saudi-Arabia on a new blacklist in 2019 that its listing process was castigated for bad methodology, albeit apparently out of political calculus. The compilation of Transparency International's Corruption Perceptions Index also deserves closer examination.

Policy evaluation pulls in the same direction, yet in a non-institutionalized manner and free from direct peer pressure. This governance by information is intended to convince states to opt for certain solutions. To achieve its goals, the IO resorts to soft communicative power and a claim to superior expertise (less arm-twisting). A special form of policy evaluation is the adoption of policy documents such as action plans by expert committees or transnational governing bodies.

While policy evaluation is a trademark of IOs like the OECD, this approach reflects a certain long-term outlook and institutional maturity that the EU Commission embodies much more than any other international actor.

With respect to judicial enforcement, access to courts plays a crucial role in safeguarding individual rights as was already explained for the conversion phase. With respect to the enforcement of binding transnational criminal law, especially treaties and secondary law, enforcement usually works through national courts, simply because IOs generally do not have an integrated judicial system at their disposal. The only exception is the CJEU with its preliminary ruling procedure and infringement proceedings. Interestingly, very few actions are brought before it either by the Commission or other member states. So far, no infringement proceedings concerning the sluggish implementation of mutual legal assistance framework decisions have been instituted.

## IV. Some Final Thoughts on Legitimacy

As should have become clear by now, the picture is much more colourful than one would expect. Taxonomies of this kind are more differentiated and closer to reality than traditional formalistic legal descriptions. They consequently establish a much better basis for discussions about the legitimacy of transnational criminal law. Legitimacy requirements are contingent on how particular governance modes work. The legitimacy concerns they pose are equally as diverse as these modes themselves. Unfortunately, the matter of legitimacy gives rise to its own set of problems. Traditional standards are inextricably linked with the nation state and integrated national constitutional orders. When applied in transnational contexts these standards need to be transformed themselves. This operation is of a highly delicate nature as the heated debates surrounding the EU's criminal legislation competence and Chapter VII resolutions of the Security Council ordering member states to expand their criminal laws in the pursuit of peace have vividly shown. As a result, one not only struggles with finding proper categories for new jurisgenerative processes but is also confronted with vexing uncertainty about the parameters of their legal legitimacy.[37]

The most compelling jurisgenerative processes are Chapter VII resolutions and EU directives. Both command the highest degree of justification as they deeply encroach on the terrain of national autonomy. While EU member states have partially transferred their *ius puniendi* to the EU Parliament and Council and, thus, more or less resolved the most intricate problem (provided one agrees that democratic self-determination at the supranational EU level is basically possible and the

[37] In more detail Meyer, *Strafrechtsgenese* (n 6) 597 et seq.

EU stays within bounds),[38] the UN's situation remains precarious. The Security Council cannot claim that it has assumed the role of national parliaments to legislate in criminal matters as a power implied in Chapter VII. As an executive body it lacks (internal and external) constitutional authority to order criminal legislation. Despite the need for decisive action in the areas of environmental protection, preservation of species, tax justice etc we should be wary of any attempt of the Security Council to usurp criminal law competences for these purposes.

With respect to the many non-binding mechanisms one must not underestimate the subtle pressure they can develop. To direct this influence into legitimate channels three steps are necessary. The methodology and procedures employed for monitoring purposes deserve more rigorous scientific scrutiny. In the same vein, the expertise of those behind best practice guidance and impact assessments is not beyond question. Transparency requirements regarding composition of bodies, study design, relevant documentation etc would help determine whether such mechanisms should be credited with elevated cogency. The ultimate antidote against undue pressure is self-assertion. Alas, parliaments are often misled by their own government about the inevitability of voting international standards into law. FATF recommendations are the most striking example. In all these cases national parliaments should seek more effective control of jurisgenerative processes and make their voices heard. There are many ways to achieve this.

Last but not least, human rights doctrine and evolutive interpretation by the ECtHR are not sacrosanct. Although we might like the results, we should be more sceptical whether the reasoning of the court holds water.

To conclude, the history of law-making in IOs is also a history of asymmetry and asynchronicity between constant expansion of criminal laws and transnational steering mechanisms on one side and efforts to examine their legitimacy on the other. Despite the growth and diversification of law-making processes over the past thirty years only few modes have kindled a profound academic debate.

## V. Conclusions

This chapter has offered a different methodologic path to tell a history of transnational criminal law and discuss its legitimacy. The study has sketched the evolution of the toolkit of IOs and identified its components. While a general tendency towards extension and diversification of jurisgenerative processes is visible across IOs, their scope and impact may diverge as a consequence of growth or limitation of tasks and policy responsibilities, deeper integration, maturity of organization

38 Frank Meyer, *Demokratieprinzip und Europäisches Strafrecht* (Nomos 2009). The conferral of powers does not alleviate other procedural deficits like depriving the European Parliament of a right to introduce a bill.

and the finalities pursued. It will surprise nobody that matters of transnational security have come to justify particularly far-reaching competences. Institutionally, it visibly contributed to the evolution of transnational criminal law norms when IOs interlinked with other IOs, forming what others have come to call transnational legal orders.[39] It also proved beneficial that some organizations were flexible enough to vary their law-generating techniques to fend off challenges and overcome stalemates. Alas, this contribution could only scratch the surface of many problems that rattle transnational criminal law. It appears that transnational criminal law, unlike international criminal law, is still lacking in animating ideas for its analysis and legitimization. It remains an expansive collecting tank that lacks a distinct DNA or foundational matrix. The contribution will end here but not without a plea for a concerted quest for future concepts that might guide and constrain the emergence of criminal law norms in IOs.

[39] See n 13.

# 7
# Transnational Criminal Courts
## A Partially Realized Idea

*Sara Wharton and Robert J Currie*[*]

## I. Introduction

At one point during the proliferation of international criminal tribunals being established in the late 20th and early 21st centuries, commentators could be heard complaining of 'tribunal fatigue'.[1] This comment betrayed scepticism about the utility of such courts to deal with the aftermath of conflict, and that the political and financial will in the international community were wearing thin. Yet in the second decade of the 21st century there have been developments which might prove to confound the idea of tribunal fatigue, in that they show the will to create new international tribunals—albeit courts geared towards the prosecution not of the 'core' international crimes or crimes under international law, but of transnational crimes (the subject matter of this volume).

In 2013, Argentinian NGO *Democracia Global* initiated a proposal to establish a Latin American and Caribbean Criminal Court Against Transnational Organized Crime (COPLA). The proposal seeks to establish a regional criminal court with jurisdiction over transnational crimes, including: drug trafficking, firearms trafficking, human trafficking, migrant smuggling, trafficking in cultural property, money laundering and transnational bribery.[2] The following year, in 2014, the African Union adopted the Protocol on Amendments to the Protocol on the Statute of the African Court of Justice and Human Rights ('Malabo Protocol') which seeks to add criminal jurisdiction to the African Court of Justice and Human and Peoples' Rights.[3] In addition to the core international crimes, this African criminal

* Sara thanks Maria Stellato and Amanda Hawkins for their research assistance.

[1] Luc Coté, 'International Criminal Justice: Tightening up the Rules of the Game' (2006) 88(861) IRRC 133, 143.

[2] See Robert J Currie and Jacob Leon, 'COPLA: A Transnational Criminal Court for Latin America & the Caribbean' (2019) 88 Nordic JIL 587.

[3] 27 June 2014, Assembly of the African Union, Assembly/AU/Dec.529(XXIII). See Charles C Jalloh, Kamari M Clarke and Vincent O Nmehielle, *The African Court of Justice and Human and Peoples' Rights in Context: Development and Challenges* (CUP 2019); Gerhard Werle and Moritz Vornbaum, *The African Criminal Court: A Commentary on the Malabo Protocol* (TMC Asser Press 2017) (hereafter Werle and Vornbaum, *African Criminal Court*).

Sara Wharton and Robert J Currie, *Transnational Criminal Courts* In: *Histories of Transnational Criminal Law*. Edited by: Neil Boister, Sabine Gless and Florian Jeßberger, Oxford University Press. © Sara Wharton and Robert J Currie 2021.
DOI: 10.1093/oso/9780192845702.003.0008

court would have jurisdiction over recognized and emerging transnational crimes including: drug trafficking, human trafficking, money laundering, corruption, terrorism, piracy, trafficking in hazardous wastes and illicit exploitation of natural resources. More recently, an International Anti-Corruption Court (IACC) has been proposed.[4]

COPLA is still essentially a proposal, the IACC just an idea; and the Malabo Protocol, while signed, is not yet in force. The significance of such courts is that they would provide a new avenue for accountability for transnational crime, at the *supra*national level. However, these 'new' developments have deep historical roots. This chapter will provide a history of transnational criminal courts (TCCs), both as an idea and as a task that still has only been partially executed. 'Transnational' here does not speak to the legal character of the courts, which would be constituted under international law, but rather indicates that such courts would adjudicate 'transnational crimes' as they are understood in this volume. Starting with the British slavery courts and the 1937 League of Nations Convention for an international court to prosecute terrorism, it will move to discuss: the International Law Commission's consideration of the question of an international criminal jurisdiction, taken up at its very first session; the proposal to establish a court to prosecute apartheid; and the establishment of the International Criminal Court (ICC)—which was proposed to address transnational drug trafficking yet, ultimately, came into being with jurisdiction over core international crimes alone. It will then look at proposals to establish a piracy court, and finally provide an account of the Malabo Protocol. Attentive to the historical dynamics and legal needs that drive the discourse about the need for TCCs, we will observe that the continued vitality of the idea suggests that it is simply geopolitical conditions, rather than any weakness in principle, that has prevented it from being fully realized.

We will generally not be dealing with international or internationalized courts that have or have had jurisdiction over crimes under international law; while the manner in which such courts were formed had some resonance in transnational criminal law generally, our focus here is on efforts directed towards transnational crimes specifically.

## II. History of an Idea: Why Have Transnational Criminal Courts?

As shown below, ideas for TCCs have taken various forms and responded to various sorts of needs— geographic/regional and political needs not least among them. However, in our view the impulse to found TCCs shares with the transnational

[4] Lloyd Axworthy and Allan Rock, 'Let's Hold the Kleptocrats to Account' *Globe and Mail* (22 June 2020) <https://www.theglobeandmail.com/opinion/article-lets-hold-the-kleptocrats-to-account/>.

criminal law system itself a fundamental, driving *legal* practicality that derives from the decentralized sovereign order of states it seeks to serve. To wit, in order to combat transnational crime effectively, inter-state cooperation is required. Simply put, the interests of many states in crime suppression are best served when there is a shared idea of what conduct merits criminalization, as well as mechanisms which relax the limitations imposed by the bar on exercising extraterritorial enforcement jurisdiction.[5] A TCC would be a venue for such cooperation, by externalizing it from the jurisdiction of any particular state.

That said, a supranational venue for the prosecution of transnational crimes would be a departure from the 'ordinary' forms of cooperation in transnational criminal law regimes, which rest on horizontal mutual assistance between states. Indeed, this is one of the fundamental characteristics of transnational criminal law, where the targeted conduct is criminalized only under domestic laws, and prosecutions proceed before domestic courts. This is seen not only as a practical necessity but as a selling point—in that criminal law is highly domesticized and states often prefer to apply their own substantive criminal law and procedure and maintain their prosecutorial goals and strategies as much as possible.

However, various rationales for using a TCC as a cooperative machine have presented themselves over the years and in the literature.[6] As Boister notes, the transnational criminal law system has various fracture points:

> States ... may be unwilling to cooperate because they are broadly sympathetic for some reason with the alleged criminals, or because they are politically antagonistic towards the requesting state, or because they are implicated in the offence themselves ... [S]tates may not be inclined to help with what they consider to be some other state's problem. They may have strong moral objections to extradition. They may be apprehensive about facilitating the imposition of foreign law and foreign punishment (often-times more severe) on their fellow countrymen, which they might regard with suspicion. They may find themselves between rich and violent criminals and a very profitable criminal market.[7]

He further notes that these problems are particularly profound for smaller states 'with weak internal sovereignty',[8] since they may both need to resist political

[5] That is, the customary rule of international law to the effect that states cannot exercise enforcement powers (investigation, arrest) on the territories of other sovereign states. See Robert J Currie and Joseph Rikhof, *International & Transnational Criminal Law* (3rd edn, Irwin Law 2020) 97–99.

[6] See eg Faiza Patel, 'Crime Without Frontiers: A Proposal for an International Narcotics Court' (1990) 22 NYU JIntl L & Pol 709; Craig Thedwall, 'Choosing the Right Yardarm: Establishing an International Court of Piracy' (2010) 41 Ga J Intl & Comp L 501; Erin Creegan, 'A Permanent Hybrid Court for Terrorism' (2011) 26 Am U Int L Rev 237; Neil Boister, 'Treaty Crimes, International Criminal Court?' (2009) 12 New Crim L Rev 341 (hereafter Boister, 'Treaty Crimes').

[7] Boister, 'Treaty Crimes' (n 6) 301.

[8] ibid 300.

pressure from more powerful states, on the one hand, and be compromised in terms of their ability to conduct complex investigations and run numerous, large-scale trials, on the other. The impairment of domestic criminal justice systems by corruption and other pressures levied by organized crime gangs was a driving force behind both the COPLA project and, as we will see, the original proposal for the ICC.

Accordingly, in some situations a system of transnationalized adjudication recommends itself as an efficient and potentially effective way of dealing with the legal and political problems that might stem from conventional transnational criminal law-based cooperation. A third-party, external court with an agreed-upon substantive jurisdiction and procedure can serve a number of policy needs. However, what emerges from the historical review below is a picture of an idea that has had spotty uptake, suffered opposition at various points and, in the end, has never quite been fully realized.

## III. Earlier Efforts

### 1. The UK Slavery Courts

The UK-led movement against the slave trade in the late 18th and early 19th centuries gave birth to perhaps the earliest entity that might qualify as a TCC: the Courts of Mixed Commission.[9] These courts were created by bilateral treaties between Britain and a number of sea-going states (Spain, the Netherlands, Portugal, Brazil), under which ships accused of slave trade were tried by 'Commissioners' appointed by each state. Adverse findings would result in condemnation and forfeiture of the ship and, in some cases, repatriation of the crew to the flag state for prosecution under domestic slavery laws. It is debateable (and debated) whether these courts were criminal in nature, given the nature of the remedies; US insistence that they *were* criminal held up the US-UK treaty until 1862, by which time the outcome of the Civil War made the treaty irrelevant for that state's domestic purposes.[10]

In the end it was growing international opposition to the slave trade, driven by an aggressive British maritime foreign policy that brought an end to both slavery and the courts. Britain 'augment[ed], and then replace[d] the mixed court system

[9] See Jenny S Martinez, 'Antislavery Courts and the Dawn of International Human Rights Law' (2008) 117 Yale LJ 550, 579–95 (hereafter Martinez, 'Antislavery Courts'); Edward Keene, 'A Case Study of the Construction of International Hierarchy: British Treaty-Making against the Slave Trade in the Early Nineteenth Century' (2007) 61 Int'l Org 311. And see Jenny S Martinez, *The Slave Trade and the Origins of International Human Rights Law* (OUP 2012) ch 4.

[10] Eugene Kontorovich, 'The Constitutionality of International Courts: The Forgotten Precedent of Slave Trade Tribunals' (2009) 158 U Penn LR 39, esp 82–86.

with a combination of military force and domestic courts'.[11] The anti-slavery pressure this produced led to domestic criminalization and enforcement by the sea-going states, and consequent inability of slave ships to use their flags. The court established by the US-UK treaty heard no cases, but removal of the US flag as an option for slavers killed the already-declining Cuban slave trade.[12] The Mixed Courts ended because they were no longer needed, their jurisdiction happily ceded to domestic courts.

## 2. The League of Nations Convention

Perhaps the most notable effort at creating a TCC prior to the Malabo Protocol was the League of Nations' 1937 Convention for the Creation of an International Criminal Court (1937 International Criminal Court Convention),[13] which was designed to prosecute terrorist crimes. The effort to create the Convention was not primarily due to abstract state interest in suppressing terrorism; it was directed at defusing tensions on the European continent arising from the assassination in France, in October 1934, of King Alexander I of Yugoslavia, allegedly at the hands of terrorist groups based in Italy and trained in Hungary. Two months later, a memorandum from the government of France proposed points that would support the conclusion of an anti-terrorism suppression treaty, as well as a separate treaty creating an international criminal court to try terrorist acts. The memorandum 'was purposely ambiguous and incomplete', so as to facilitate continued inter-state discussion and reduce political tensions.[14] However, it dovetailed with existing interest on the part of some member states and organizations of jurists in creating an international criminal jurisdiction as a means of advancing international peace through multilateralism.[15]

A League-appointed committee of experts produced drafts of both a suppression treaty that focused on state-sponsored terrorism, and a treaty creating a permanent international tribunal to try accused terrorists. A conference in 1937 produced completed versions of both conventions. The 1937 Terrorism Convention was signed by only twenty-five League member states, and the 1937 International Criminal Court Convention by only thirteen. Most states were reluctant on the basis that the project was premature, and some (like the UK) were simply opposed in principle.[16] This also reflected significant disagreement on the

[11] Martinez, 'Antislavery Courts' (n 9) 621.
[12] ibid 628.
[13] See also Saul, Chapter 10 in this book.
[14] Michael D Callahan, 'Terrorism Court (1937)' in *Max Planck Encyclopedia of International Procedural Law*, Oxford Public International Law (OUP, updated October 2018) para 27.
[15] ibid para 7.
[16] ibid paras 15, 19, 20.

substantive underpinning of the court—whether and how to criminalize terrorism. The League's dissolution and the outbreak of World War II pushed terrorism further down the list of priorities, and no state ever ratified the 1937 International Criminal Court Convention.

The kinds of problem-solving displayed by the mechanics of the court still resonate in the overall context of international tribunals today,[17] particularly insofar as they dealt with the axes between the court and party states on questions of jurisdiction, inter alia.[18] In the end, however, the 1937 International Criminal Court Convention was the victim of the political motives and lukewarm enthusiasm behind its inception, as well as historical happenstance that diverted energy from the overall effort.

## IV. Post-War Bridging: The Work of the ILC

In 1948, the General Assembly invited the International Law Commission (ILC) to study the 'desirability and possibility' of establishing an international criminal jurisdiction.[19] This resolution was passed in conjunction with the adoption of the Convention on the Prevention and Punishment of the Crime of Genocide, which contemplated the existence of an international penal tribunal.[20] However, the General Assembly's mandate to the ILC was not limited to consideration of a genocide court.[21]

The ILC took up this mandate at its very first session in 1949. At that time, it was presented with a memorandum submitted by the Secretary-General on the 'Historical Survey of the Question of International Criminal Jurisdiction', demonstrating that this was clearly not a novel question. While the ILC necessarily considered the question of *how* such a court might be established,[22] it focused more on the question of the substantive jurisdiction of such a court which was, in turn,

[17] Mark Lewis, *The Birth of the New Justice: The Internationalization of Crime and Punishment, 1919–1950* (OUP 2014) 150–80.

[18] Boister has proposed that the convention is worth considering as the starting point for how to structure a standing transnational criminal court, Neil Boister, 'International Tribunals for Transnational Crimes: Towards a Transnational Criminal Court?' (2012) 23 Crim LF 295, 308 et seq. (hereafter Boister, 'International Tribunals').

[19] GA Res 260(III)B, 9 December 1948.

[20] Adopted Paris, 9 December 1948, entered into force 12 January 1951, 78 UNTS 277, art VI (hereafter Genocide Convention).

[21] The General Assembly invited the ILC to consider the establishment of an 'international judicial organ for the trial of persons charged with genocide *or other crimes over which jurisdiction will be conferred upon that organ by international conventions*'. GA Res 260(III)B, 9 December 1948 (emphasis added).

[22] Ricardo J Alfaro, Special Rapporteur, 'Question of International Criminal Jurisdiction', 3 March 1950, Document A/CN.4/15 in *Yearbook of the International Law Commission 1950*, Vol II, A/CN.4/SER.A/1950/Add.1, paras 128–34.

the subject of its parallel project, the Draft Code of Offences against International Peace and Security ('Draft Code').

In the early 1950s, the ILC focused on the so-called 'political element' of crimes and included the Nuremberg crimes alongside a list of variations on the concept of aggression within its discussion on the Draft Code.[23] Thus, it excluded 'such matters as piracy, traffic in dangerous drugs, traffic in women and children, slavery, counterfeiting currency, damage to submarine cables, etc.', offences more generally characterized today as transnational crimes.[24]

Based on the ILC's work, in the early 1950s the General Assembly established two committees comprised of seventeen states 'for the purpose of preparing one or more preliminary draft conventions and proposals relating to the establishment and the statute of an international criminal court'.[25] Early work by these committees considered including such 'minor crimes' as 'counterfeiting currencies, traffic in persons, traffic in narcotics, damaging of submarine cables',[26] but they were ultimately excluded.

In 1954, the ILC's work on this topic was put on hold by the General Assembly until the definition of aggression could be resolved.[27] When the Draft Code appeared on the ILC's agenda again in 1982, the general sentiment was that its scope should be expanded beyond the 1954 version to take into account international instruments that had come into effect in the interim period. The ILC now stated that the Draft Code should cover 'the most serious international crimes' and that '[t]his seriousness may be measured either by the extent of the calamity or by its horrific character, or by both at once'.[28] The ILC also took an inductive approach, surveying relevant developments in international law. It enumerated twenty-four relevant and important international instruments including five suppression conventions, alongside General Assembly resolutions, human rights instruments and other treaties.

Through the 1980s, the Commission considered the addition of colonialism, apartheid, hostage taking, violence against internationally protected persons, aircraft hijacking, mercenarism and acts causing serious damage to the environment.[29] There was also some discussion of the crime of piracy but the general

[23] Mr J Spiropoulous, Special Rapporteur, 'Draft Code of Offences against the Peace and Security of Mankind' in *Yearbook of the International Law Commission 1951* (United Nations Publishing 1957) 58.

[24] ibid.

[25] GA Res 489(V), 12 December 1950; GA Res 687(VII), 5 December 1952.

[26] Report of the Committee on International Criminal Jurisdiction on its second session held from 1 to 31 August 1951, UNGAOR, Seventh Session, Supplement, No 11 (A/2136), paras 30–34.

[27] UN GA Res 897 (1954); UN GA Res 1186 (1957).

[28] Report of the International Law Commission on the Work of its thirty-fifth session (3 May–22 July 1983), Document A/38/10 in *Yearbook of the International Law Commission 1983*, Vol II, Part Two (United Nations Publications 1985) 14.

[29] Report of the International Law Commission on the Work of its thirty-sixth session (7 May–27 July 1984), Document A/39/10 in *Yearbook of the International Law Commission 1984*, Vol II, Part Two (United Nations Publications 1985) 17.

sentiment at the time was that 'it [was] not at present a scourge of mankind'.[30] By 1989, following the adoption of the 1988 Drug Trafficking Convention, the perspective on drug trafficking had shifted and more members favoured, or at least accepted, its inclusion.

In 1993–94, the ILC's final proposal for a draft statute for an international criminal court envisioned a court with inherent jurisdiction over genocide and consent-based jurisdiction over others, including crimes under six listed sectoral terrorism treaties, apartheid, torture and crimes involving illicit traffic in narcotics as per the 1998 UN Convention.[31]

The key moment in the ILC's work respecting the potential inclusion of transnational crimes occurred from about the mid-late 1980s to the early 1990s. In 1991 the Commission adopted on first reading a Draft Code listing twelve crimes that included: colonial domination and other forms of domination; apartheid; offences relating to mercenaries; international terrorism; illicit traffic in narcotic drugs; and wilful and severe damage to the environment. However, the final Draft Code in 1996 included only five: the four 'core' crimes alongside crimes against United Nations and associated personnel.[32]

Despite the fact that, at times, the Commission considered an expansive approach to the Draft Code, the final product was much more limited. Attacks against UN personnel proved the only (and very late) addition to the list of crimes in the 1996 Draft Code beyond those recognized in the immediate post-World War II period (although some transnational crimes were captured in some form under the heading of crimes against humanity).[33] Despite the ILC's pragmatic drive for securing consensus, it included the following caveat in its commentary on article 1 of the Draft Code: 'This provision is not intended to suggest that the Code covers exhaustively all crimes against the peace and security of mankind.' Throughout its work, much consideration was given to the severe impacts of transnational crimes, but these were ultimately omitted—a pattern to be seen again as the international community worked towards establishing an international criminal court.

[30] ibid.

[31] Report of the International Law Commission on the work of its forth-sixth session (2 May–22 July 1994), Document A/49/10 in *Yearbook of the International Law Commission 1994*, Vol II, Part Two (United Nations Publishers 1997) 38–42, 68.

[32] Report of the International Law Commission on the work of its forty-eighth session (6 May–26 July 1996), Document A/51/10 in *Yearbook of the International Law Commission 1996*, Vol II, Part Two (United Nations Publishers 1998) 42–56.

[33] 1996 Draft Code, art 18(d) and (f).

## V. Modern Efforts: Mid-20th and 21st Centuries[34]

### 1. The Apartheid Convention

Similarly to article VI of the Genocide Convention,[35] article V of the 1973 Apartheid Convention[36] provided that jurisdiction over the crime might be established not just by state parties to the convention, but by 'an international penal tribunal'. This mandate was taken up by the UN Commission on Human Rights, which in 1981 produced a draft convention for the establishment of such a tribunal with jurisdiction over 'grave breaches' of the Apartheid Convention and other international crimes.[37] While the proposal sat as a dead letter so far as creating a TCC, it eventually served as one of the models for the creation of the ICC.[38] This shifting of apartheid into the core crimes space seems to have removed any enthusiasm for a TCC, though as explained below the idea saw a resurgence with the Malabo Protocol.

### 2. The International Criminal Court

In 1989, the UN General Assembly asked the ILC to take up the question of establishing an international criminal court, following a push by Trinidad and Tobago and the Caribbean Community to do so.[39] The primary concern of these small Caribbean island states was not with the core crimes but, rather, with transnational criminality and, in particular, with the crime of drug trafficking.[40] Challenges faced by domestic jurisdictions in adequately addressing large-scale transnational criminality, alongside a desire to reassert a degree of sovereignty and prevent the extraterritorial application of the laws of certain foreign states, contributed to the proposal to establish an independent international institution to hold

[34] We exclude here the arrangement that led to the 'Lockerbie Trial' (ie an agreement leading to a Scottish trial being held in the Netherlands), because in our view it was more of an ad hoc transfer of proceedings scheme.

[35] See n 20.

[36] International Convention on the Suppression and Punishment of the Crime of Apartheid, GA Res 3068 (XXVIII) (adopted 30 November 1973, entered into force 18 July 1976).

[37] Study on ways and means of insuring the implementation of International instruments such as the International Convention on the Suppression and Punishment of the Crime of Apartheid, including the establishment of the international jurisdiction envisaged by the Convention, UN Doc E/CN.4/1426 (19 January 1981) 21, art 4.

[38] Carola Lingas, 'The Crime against Humanity of Apartheid, in a post-Apartheid World' (2015) 2 Oslo L Rev 86, fn 24 and accompanying text.

[39] UN GA Res 44/39, 4 December 1989. See Boister, 'International Tribunals ' (n 18) 343; Delia Chatoor, 'The Role of Small States in International Diplomacy: CARICOM's Experience in the Negotiations of the Rome Statute of the International Criminal Court' (2001) 7 International Peacekeeping 295, 296–301 (hereafter Chatoor, 'The Role of Small States').

[40] UNGAOR 6th Comm, 44th Sess, UN Doc A/C.6/44/SR.38–41 (1989).

perpetrators accountable.[41] The ILC took up this mandate and completed a draft code for an international criminal court in 1994.[42] This effort was considered by an ad hoc committee established by the UN General Assembly in 1995 and, subsequently, by a preparatory committee which worked to produce a draft statute to be submitted to the diplomatic conference of plenipotentiaries in Rome in 1998.

The draft submitted to the Rome Conference proposed a court with inherent jurisdiction over the core international crimes as well as consent-based jurisdiction over other crimes including drug trafficking and terrorism.[43] While some states advocated for the inclusion of transnational crimes, many preferred a narrower jurisdiction limited to three or four core crimes. Some argued for the inclusion or exclusion of transnational crimes on a normative basis, debating their seriousness (in particular when compared to the core international crimes).[44] However, pragmatic arguments favouring a more limited subject-matter jurisdiction dominated. States argued that limiting the number of crimes would make the court more feasible and more affordable, allow for more straightforward jurisdictional rules and attract more states to ratify.[45] Ultimately, attempts to secure widespread ratification of the Rome Statute favoured a more conservative approach. Boister has also pointed out the political influence of certain powerful states, as crimes like drug trafficking and terrorism were 'more likely to affect the political interests of Western states'.[46]

While the Rome Statute ultimately excluded transnational crimes (other than those incorporated under the rubrics of crimes against humanity or war crimes), a resolution passed at the conclusion of the Rome Conference in 1998 recommended that the parties revisit the inclusion of the crimes of drug trafficking and terrorism at the future mandated review conference.[47] However, the 2010 Kampala Conference focused on securing consensus on a definition for the crime of aggression and the possible expansion of the subject-matter jurisdiction was left off of the agenda.

Following the Review Conference, a Working Group on Amendments was established to consider substantive amendments to the Rome Statute, including proposals to incorporate the crimes of terrorism and drug trafficking. However,

[41] Chatoor, 'The Role of Small States' (n 39) 297.

[42] Report of the International Law Commission on the work of its forty-sixth session, 2 May–22 July 1994, GAOR, 49th Sess, Supp No 10, 26–74.

[43] Report of the Preparatory Committee on the Establishment of an International Criminal Court, Addendum, Draft Statute for an International Criminal Court, UN Doc A/CONF.183/2/Add.1 (1998).

[44] See eg Report of the Ad Hoc Committee on the Establishment of an International Criminal Court, UNGAOR, 50th Sess, Supp No 22, UN Doc A/50/22 (1995), paras 54-55 and 81.

[45] Eg, ibid 54; Neil Boister, 'The Exclusion of Treaty Crimes from the Jurisdiction of the Proposed International Criminal Court: Law, Pragmatism, Politics' (1998) 3 JCS & L 27, 37 (hereafter Boister, 'Exclusion of Treaty Crimes').

[46] Boister, 'Exclusion of Treaty Crimes' (n 45) 38.

[47] Final Act of the United Nations Diplomatic Conference of Plenipotentiaries on the Establishment of an International Criminal Court, UN Doc A/CONF.183/10 (1998), Resolution E.

states generally still favour securing universal ratification of the Statute.[48] The Netherlands withdrew its proposed amendment to include the crime of terrorism in 2013.[49] In recent years, the court has faced many challenges and it is unlikely that expansion of its subject-matter jurisdiction will happen any time soon. The original proposal to address pressing criminal justice needs of small states has been lost in the political shuffle.

## 3. Piracy

In response to a 21st-century resurgence in piracy off the coast of Somalia, there were calls within the international community for new enforcement and accountability mechanisms. In particular, the UN Security Council expressed concerns about the lack of capacity within the judicial systems of Somalia and other states in the region to adequately prosecute those accused of piracy and armed robbery at sea.[50] In his responding report, the Secretary-General explored multiple options for pursuing piracy prosecutions including three involving supranational courts: the establishment of a regional tribunal by multilateral agreement, the establishment of an international tribunal by multilateral agreement or the establishment of an international tribunal by the Security Council acting under its Chapter VII powers.[51]

With respect to the possibility of establishing either a regional or an international court, the Secretary-General highlighted the salutary potential for capacity-building in the host state engendered by more substantial funding.[52] Nonetheless, the report also highlighted that these options involved more complex legal issues when compared to situating the proposed court within a national jurisdiction, would be more expensive than resorting to national courts and, particularly in the case of a regional or international court established by agreement with the UN, would be time-consuming to establish.[53]

Ultimately, these options for an international or regional court were not taken any further. It was left to national courts, primarily those in Kenya and the Seychelles, to pursue prosecutions based on universal jurisdiction with some international support in the form of transfer of detainees from the EU and other naval

[48] ICC Assembly of States Parties, Tenth Session, Report on the Working Group on Amendments, ICC Doc ASP/10/32 (2001), para 5.

[49] ICC Assembly of States Parties, Twelfth Session, Report of the Working Group on Amendments, ICC Doc ASP-12/44 (213), para. 4.

[50] UN SC Res 1918, 27 April 2010, S/RES/1918(2010).

[51] S/2010/394, 26 July 2010, 2. See Florian Jeßberger, 'Piracy (art 28F), Terrorism (art 28G) and Mercenarism (art 28H)' in Werle and Vornbaum, *African Criminal Court* (n 3) para 85 (hereafter Jeßberger, 'Piracy, Terrorism and Mercenarism').

[52] Jeßberger, 'Piracy, Terrorism and Mercenarism' (n 51) paras 80–104.

[53] ibid.

patrolling states, financial support, capacity building and technical assistance and international policing via the multi-national naval forces.[54]

## 4. Malabo Protocol

As noted in the introduction, the 2014 Malabo Protocol would add criminal jurisdiction to an amalgamated African Court of Justice and Human and Peoples' Rights. While the Malabo Protocol is not yet in force (and may never be), it creates, at least on paper, the first regional criminal court and the first multi-national court with jurisdiction over transnational crimes. The Malabo Protocol is particularly noteworthy for its expansive subject-matter jurisdiction. In addition to jurisdiction over the four 'core international crimes', the Malabo Protocol envisions a court with jurisdiction over recognized and emerging transnational crimes, including: trafficking in persons, trafficking in drugs, money laundering, corruption, piracy, terrorism, mercenarism, trafficking in hazardous wastes and illicit exploitation of natural resources.[55]

As with all efforts to establish international or multi-national criminal institutions, states are motivated by concerns of impunity and 'enforcement gaps' for certain forms of criminality and the Malabo Protocol is no exception.[56] In this particular case, the expansive subject-matter jurisdiction was designed to capture the range of crimes of particular importance on the African continent.[57] While the unique crime of Unconstitutional Change of Government is most commonly pointed to in this regard,[58] this holds true for all the added crimes. Other noteworthy examples include the newly resurgent crime of piracy[59] as well as the more novel additions of trafficking in hazardous waste and illicit exploitation of natural resources, which reflect the colonial and post-colonial legacies on the continent.[60]

[54] UNODC, 'Maritime Crime Programme—Indian Ocean' <https://www.unodc.org/unodc/en/piracy/indian-ocean- division.html> .

[55] Statute of the African Court of Justice and Human and Peoples' Rights, Annex to Protocol on the Amendments to the Protocol on the Statute of the African Court of Justice and Human Rights (Malabo Protocol).

[56] Neil Boister, 'Transnational Crimes Jurisdiction of the Criminal Chamber of the African Court of Justice and Human and Peoples' Rights' in Charles C Jalloh and others (eds), *The African Court of Justice and Human and Peoples' Rights in Context* (CUP 2019) 341–42 (hereafter Boister, 'Transnational Crimes Jurisdiction'); Jeßberger, 'Piracy, Terrorism and Mercenarism' (n 51) 75.

[57] The failure to establish the apartheid court, as discussed above, is of particular note; see Ademola Abass, 'Historical and Political Background to the Malabo Protocol' in Werle and Vornbaum, *African Criminal Court* (n 3) 15–16, 18–20 (hereafter Abass, 'Historical and Political Background'); Boister, 'Transnational Crimes Jurisdiction' (n 56) 340.

[58] Abass, 'Historical and Political Background' (n 57) 18–20.

[59] Jeßberger, 'Piracy , Terrorism and Mercenarism ' (n 51) 78; 'The Gulf of Guinea is now the World's Worst Piracy Hotspot' *The Economist* (29 June 2019) < https://www.economist.com/international/2019/06/29/the-gulf-of-guinea-is- now-the-worlds-worst-piracy-hotspot>.

[60] Martin Heger, 'Trafficking in Hazardous Wastes (art 28L) and Illicit Exploitation of Natural Resources (art 28L*bis*)' in Werle and Vornbaum, *African Criminal Court* (n 3) 127.

Other potential motivations for such a broad range of crimes that have been identified include the desire to see corporate criminal responsibility in relation to these crimes (one of the other unique elements of the proposed statute)[61] and a reclamation of a degree of sovereignty by addressing such matters regionally as opposed to in foreign states.[62]

Despite the potential significance of the Malabo Protocol, the court is a long way from actually coming into existence, if indeed it ever does. Currently the Malabo Protocol has only been signed by fifteen of fifty-five AU member states and has yet to be ratified by any.[63] This is a long way from the fifteen required ratifications necessary to bring the Protocol into operation[64] and the actual establishment of the proposed institutions, requiring the raising of sufficient funds, the hiring of personnel, amongst many other logistical efforts.

Critiques of the Malabo Protocol, which may potentially prevent the proposed court from ever coming into existence, are many. The Protocol creates a mega-court with tripartite jurisdiction of which its criminal jurisdiction is only one part. The proposed criminal jurisdiction itself is unwieldy with a significant number of crimes alongside very broad bases for the exercise of jurisdiction[65] and for criminal liability. Thus, it would be a very costly institution to establish (likely too costly)[66] and would likely be 'fraught with myriad substantive and procedural problems'.[67] Additionally, concerns about 'limited buy in'[68] from states suggest that this significant effort to establish a regional multi-national criminal court for the prosecution of transnational crimes (alongside core international crimes) may never see actual operation.

## VI. Conclusion

The threads of the foregoing history are difficult to tie together. There is really no single theme which animates the motivations behind the attempted and successful

[61] Boister, 'Transnational Crimes Jurisdiction' (n 56) 341.

[62] ibid 342.

[63] African Union, Protocol on the Amendments to the Protocol on the Statute of the African Court of Justice and Human Rights Status List <https://au.int/sites/default/files/treaties/36398-sl- PROTOCOL%20ON%20AMENDMENTS%20TO%20THE%20PROTOCOL%20ON%20THE%20STATUTE%20OF%20THE%20AFRICAN%20COURT%20OF%20JUSTICE%20AND%20HUMAN%20RIGHTS.pdf>0.

[64] African Union, Protocol on the Amendments to the Protocol on the Statute of the African Court of Justice and Human Rights, art 11(1).

[65] Statute of the African Court of Justice and Human and Peoples' Rights, Annex to Malabo Protocol, art 46E*bis*(2).

[66] Charles C Jalloh and others, 'Introduction' in Charles C Jalloh and others (eds), *The African Court of Justice and Human and Peoples' Rights in Context* (CUP 2019) 42–43 (hereafter Jalloh and others, 'Introduction').

[67] Abass, 'Historical and Political Background' (n 57) 14, 23–24.

[68] Jalloh and others, 'Introduction' (n 66) 44.

efforts to establish TCCs, though a combination of addressing practical difficulties (the slavery and piracy courts, the original ICC proposal) and underscoring international consensus on the seriousness of some crimes (the League of Nations and Apartheid Conventions, the Malabo Protocol) cover a good deal of that ground. Significant at all times was agreement—either settled or prospective—on the importance of the subject-matter jurisdiction, both in terms of which crimes fell within the substantive jurisdiction of a TCC and how they were to be defined. The ILC's work was consumed by this question, while the League's effort foundered in part on the lack of success on it. All of this suggests that a TCC with jurisdiction over transnational crimes need not necessarily be structurally distinct from an international court with jurisdiction over crimes under international law, despite some differences in what might motivate their founding.

In the end, it is noteworthy that recent efforts to establish TCCs, such as the Malabo Protocol or the COPLA and IACC proposals, may seem novel but they actually follow more than a century of similar efforts. However, most of the previous attempts to create TCCs either stalled before getting off the ground, fell victim to changing practical realities or political priorities, suffered from a lack of genuine political will in the first place or, in the case of the ICC, morphed into a core crimes court instead. In the case of the proposed piracy court, it was felt that national courts operating on the basis of universal jurisdiction with some international support would prove sufficient. Nonetheless, the assumption that domestic courts will always be adequate for prosecution of transnational crimes, which lies at the heart of the transnational criminal law regime, may ultimately prove to be incorrect. The historical record shows that the idea of a TCC is one that consistently re-emerges, which is unsurprising in that the policy rationale ultimately seems sound. It is hardly speculative to say that the right time for some type of international enforcement of transnational crimes will probably arrive at some point, and that we may yet see the idea fully realized.

# 8

# A History of Maritime Piracy

## A Transnational Crime in Need of Transnational Substantive Criminal Law

*Masha Fedorova and Piet Hein van Kempen*

### I. Introduction

The history of the maritime crime of piracy is long and opaque. The notion of pirates as *hostes humani generis* (enemies of mankind) resonates through a daunting amount of historical primary and secondary sources that take different perspectives on the phenomenon.[1] Rather than summarize or replicate the numerous explorations and conceptualizations of piracy as a criminal activity, this contribution offers a substantive criminal law perspective and focuses on the obligation to criminalize piracy under international law.

The inspiration for this approach came mainly from two sources. First, as this book intends to address the histories of transnational criminal law, Boister's conceptualization of transnational criminal law is taken as a point of departure: it entails the indirect suppression by international law through domestic penal law of criminal activities that have actual or potential transboundary effects or transboundary moral impacts.[2] A necessary condition is the international component of this definition: through a transnational transfer of the norm and the shared purpose of the states involved via some legal form, international law orders states to involve domestic criminal law to suppress certain criminal activity. Arguably, from a normative perspective, this involves an international duty to criminalize this activity in domestic criminal law. A second source that inspired our investigation into the crime of maritime piracy is Rubin's conclusion in his elaborate study into the primary sources of the law of piracy, stating that: 'It is possible to assert with some

[1] Cicero (106–43 BCE) qualified the pirate as a common enemy of all (*communis hostis omnium*), see Alfred P Rubin, *The Law of Piracy* (Naval War College Press 1988) 10–11 (hereafter Rubin, *Law of Piracy*); Edwin D Dickinson, 'Is the Crime of Piracy Obsolete?' (1924–25) HLR 351 (hereafter Dickinson, 'Is the Crime of Piracy Obsolete?'); Jacob WF Sundberg, 'The Crime of Piracy' in M Cherif Bassiouni (ed), *International Criminal Law, Volume I: Sources, Subjects and Contents* (Martinus Nijhoff Publishers 2008) 799 (hereafter Sundberg, 'The Crime of Piracy' and Bassiouni, *International Criminal Law I*).

[2] Neil Boister, 'Transnational Criminal Law?' (2003) 14 EJIL 953; Neil Boister, *An Introduction to Transnational Criminal Law* (2nd edn, OUP 2018) 17 (hereafter Boister, *An Introduction*).

Masha Fedorova and Piet Hein van Kempen, *A History of Maritime Piracy* In: *Histories of Transnational Criminal Law*. Edited by: Neil Boister, Sabine Gless and Florian Jeßberger, Oxford University Press.  DOI: 10.1093/oso/9780192845702.003.0009

confidence that there is no international law of "piracy" at all and that it is possible that there never has been any such law.'[3]

This somewhat disenchanting conclusion on a phenomenon that is considered to be one of the first international crimes has prompted us to address the following: (1) Does transnational criminal law entail a duty to specifically criminalize piracy? (2) What are the main historical factors that have affected the development of transnational criminal law on piracy? These questions are discussed in the second and third sections of this chapter respectively. In the final section we conclude. The focus is on transnational substantive criminal law aspects and not on domestic criminalization of piracy.

## II. Does Transnational Criminal Law Entail a Duty to Specifically Criminalize Piracy?

### 1. Possible First Steps

It has been noted that the history of piracy as a legal phenomenon is a confused one.[4] Historically, piracy refers to various malpractices united by a common geography: the open seas. Many uses of the term piracy in classical texts do not reflect any legal connotation as a criminal activity.[5] Possibly a first cautious step towards positive transnational criminal law relating to piracy may be seen in the Treaty of Étaples of 3 November 1492,[6] a French/English peace treaty requiring the parties to repress piracy along their own coasts and amongst their own subjects[7] and in the bilateral British/United States treaty of 1794 requiring them to punish their subjects for acts or offences associated with assistance to pirates.[8] Although no clear obligation to specifically criminalize piracy can be derived from the wording of these treaties, the use of the term 'punish' indicates a criminal justice enforcement orientation for piratical and associated acts.

[3] Rubin, *Law of Piracy* (n 1) 343.

[4] Douglas Guilfoyle, 'Piracy' in Neil Boister and Robert J Currie (eds), *Routledge Handbook of Transnational Criminal Law* (Routledge 2015) 366 (hereafter Guilfoyle, 'Piracy').

[5] Rubin, *Law of Piracy* (n 1) 6–8 (also endnote 37) and 12–13; see eg also 32–33; Guilfoyle, 'Piracy' (n 4) 366.

[6] See the Latin text of the treaty in Jean Dumont, *Corps universel diplomatique du droit des gens; contenant un recueuil des traitez* (vol III, part II) (Brunel Wetstein 1726) 291–95. The treaty was confirmed by the English Parliament in 1495 and again in 1498; see Anne Curry, 'Étaples, treaty of' in John Cannon and Robert Crowcroft (eds), *The Oxford Companion to British History* (OUP 2015) 345.

[7] See Adam Anderson, *An Historical and Chronological Deduction of the Origin of Commerce, from the earliest accounts. Vol I* (Walter 1787) 552–53; Patrick Pringle, *Jolly Roger, The Story of the Great Age of Piracy* (Museum Press 1953) 25; Philip Gosse, *The History of Piracy* (Dover Publications 2007 [1932]) 315 (Appendix IV).

[8] Roger S Clark, 'Some Aspects of the Concept of International Criminal Law' (2011) 22 Crim LF 519, 523, referring to art 20 of the 'Jay' Treaty.

## 2. Conventional Basis for a Duty to Criminalize Piracy?

The general international—instead of national or bilateral—legal relevance of piracy as a criminal conception seems to have been acknowledged as early as the 16th century. Yet, it is questionable whether positive international law on piracy—let alone on piracy as a criminal offence—actually existed before the 20th century.[9] By that time only the universal criminal jurisdiction that applies to piracy was generally recognized by the law of nations.[10] Even now it is difficult to ascertain what positive international law on the crime of piracy encompasses.

Presently, the international instrument most relevant to piracy is the 1982 UN Convention on the Law of the Sea (UNCLOS). It holds first of all a duty for states in article 100 to cooperate to the fullest possible extent in the repression of piracy on the high seas. However, this article does not expressly and unambiguously obligate states to criminalize piracy, nor does any other provision in the UNCLOS. Secondly, article 101 authoritatively defines piracy as acts of violence, detention or depredation by private ships or aircrafts, conducted for private ends against another ship at the open sea. Notably, the definition refers to 'acts' of piracy rather than 'crimes' or 'offences', in contrast to article 113 of the UNCLOS (breaking or injury of a submarine cable or pipeline) or as is common in transnational criminal law treaties in other areas, such as narcotic drugs, terrorism, corruption and human trafficking.[11] Thirdly, the Convention lays down the principle of permissive universal jurisdiction over piracy on the high seas (article 105).

Since the Convention does not contain any explicit obligation for states to criminalize piracy in their domestic jurisdiction, the question arises whether such obligation follows implicitly from the duty to cooperate in article 100 of the UNCLOS and/or the universal jurisdiction in article 105 over piracy. These articles are based on the 1958 High Seas Convention and on the 1956 ILC High Seas articles.[12] The preparatory history (*travaux preparatoires*) of these provisions does not offer much guidance. The most significant observation is the ILC's comment on the duty to cooperate laid down in article 38 of the ILC articles, where the ILC observed that a state fails a duty under international law when it does not take measures against piracy having an opportunity to do so.[13] The ILC does not clarify what kind of measures it has in mind, whether these measures only have to be taken within the

[9] Rubin, *Law of Piracy* (n 1) 186, 309–10, 321.

[10] See eg Harvard Law School, 'Research in International Law; IV. Piracy' (1932) 26(1) AJIL, Supplement, 739–885, 756–63 (hereafter Harvard Law, 'Piracy'); Malcolm Evans, 'The Law of the Sea' in Malcolm Evans (ed), *International Law* (OUP 2010) 651, 666.

[11] See Robin Geiß and Anna Petrig, *Piracy and Armed Robbery at Sea* (OUP 2011) (hereafter Geiß and Petrig, *Piracy and Armed Robbery*).

[12] Arts 14 and 19 of the 1958 High Seas Convention; and arts 38 and 34 of the ILC's 'Articles concerning the Law of the Sea with commentaries' (1956) *Yearbook ILC* (vol II) 265 (hereafter ILC, 'Commentaries').

[13] ILC, 'Commentaries' (n 12) 282.

existing national law framework, what international law demands, or how this comment on unilateral state action relates to state cooperation (the subject of article 38).

One could argue that cooperation 'to the fullest possible extent' in article 100 requires states to fully implement the provisions relating to piracy in the UNCLOS, including the criminalization of piracy as defined in article 101. Such extensive interpretation is not asserted explicitly in the ILC's commentary. In fact, the wording of article 43 on universal jurisdiction and the ILC's commentary to it point towards an opposite interpretation, as they refer to a 'right' ('States may') rather than a duty of states to take action against piracy. That a fundamental difference exists between an obligation and a right is also acknowledged by the ILC.[14] Moreover, the rejection during the official deliberations on the 1958 High Seas Convention of a farther-reaching provision obliging states to take proceedings against and to punish acts of piracy also points towards a more limited interpretation of the said clause.[15] Notably, international efforts to formulate a duty to criminalize piracy had failed before. During the drafting of the 1926 Draft Provisions on the Suppression of Piracy,[16] the ILC rejected the Romanian proposal to include an obligation 'to take proceedings against and to punish acts of piracy'.[17] Neither was an international duty to criminalize or prosecute piracy accepted by the Harvard researchers who drafted the 1932 Harvard Draft Convention on Piracy, a document of major significance for the development of the international law on piracy.[18]

According to the Harvard Draft, 'piracy is not a crime by the law of nations', but merely 'a special, common basis of jurisdiction beyond the familiar grounds', which jurisdiction 'may or may not be exercised by a certain state', depending on 'the municipal law of the state, not on the law of nations'. Thus, according to article 2 of the Harvard Draft, every state 'has jurisdiction to prevent piracy and to seize and punish persons' because of piracy.[19] Importantly, the Harvard Draft makes clear that defining the crime of piracy is up to states that (want to) exercise universal jurisdiction, therewith implying that there is no international duty on states to criminalize piracy in the first place or for states criminalizing piracy to adopt the definition in article 3 of the Draft. This definition merely specifies the extent of states' right to exercise universal jurisdiction.[20] Arguably, the attribution of universal criminal jurisdiction to piracy implies that piracy is considered

[14] See ILC, 'Commentaries' (n 12) 382 (commentary to art 39, para 2).

[15] Albania and Czechoslovakia: proposal, 21 March 1958, A/CONF.13/C.2/L.46 in United Nations Conference on the Law of the Sea, Official records Vol IV, Geneva 1958, A/CONF.13/40, 84, 128.

[16] Geneva, 26 January 1926, League of Nations C.196.M.70.1927.V, 119, also in (1932) 26(1) AJIL, Suppl, 873 (Appendix 1).

[17] League of Nations C.196.M.70. 1927.V, 220–21, also in (1932) 26(1) AJIL, Suppl, 874–75 (Appendix 2).

[18] Harvard Law, 'Piracy' (n 10) 756, 759, 760.

[19] ibid 743, 768.

[20] See ibid 785–87, 790.

to be felonious conduct by the law of nations. But this does not mean that states are under the obligation to criminalize it. It is difficult to argue otherwise in respect of definitions in article 101 of the UNCLOS, article 15 of the 1958 High Seas Convention and article 39 of the ILC High Seas articles. Although conventional international law thus provides an authoritative definition of piracy, it leaves states free as to whether to criminalize piracy or not, the extent to which they may criminalize it and the elements of the crime of piracy.

The duty to cooperate is the only positive convention obligation in relation to piracy. Considering the rather vague wording of this duty in article 100 of the UNCLOS, article 14 of the 1958 High Seas Convention and article 38 of the ILC High Seas articles, it is very possible to read a whole pallet of operational and legal obligations into these provisions. However, we argue that there is good cause to read these provisions in a restrictive way. Considering the vagueness of the formulation of the duty to cooperate, a direct or otherwise clear footing for a criminal law obligation is absent. It is also difficult to derive such obligation from the system of the piracy provisions considered as a whole, most importantly because it does not contain a duty to either extradite or prosecute. Furthermore, the object and purpose of these Conventions is to regulate the use of the sea, rather than to suppress piracy. Finally, the preparatory history of the Convention and the earlier codification efforts indicate a cautious approach to states' duties, considering that there have been several rejections of even limited proposals that implied duties to criminalize piracy. In fact, reading such a duty into the Convention's provisions would disregard accepted law-creating processes of international legal norms. Although the challenges to consensualism as a sole foundation for the validity of international legal obligations are growing, state consensus continues to be the bottom line and an important yardstick of the legitimacy of international law. In addition, a more substantive argument against deriving an international obligation short of explicit or implicit state agreement to that end lies within the subject matter of such an obligation, that is to criminalize conduct in national law. Criminal law touches upon the core of a state's prerogative to punish individuals within its jurisdiction for norm-breaking behaviour as a sovereign expression of the social contract in a particular political community. The rationale that criminal law measures infringe on people's freedom stands in the way of assuming obligations to criminalize conduct in national law on the basis of a vague agreement between states. The inevitable conclusion then must be that there exists no conventional obligation, explicit or implicit, to criminalize piracy.[21]

[21] The 1988 SUA Convention obliges state parties to criminalize certain acts that could overlap with acts of piracy, but it does not criminalize piracy as such.

## 3. Customary Law Basis for a Duty to Criminalize Piracy?

The next question is whether a customary law basis for a duty to criminalize piracy can be identified. In fact, many writers assert that international law on piracy even has the status of *jus cogens*, but without making sufficiently clear to what obligation that status exactly applies and on what it is based.[22] It seems undisputed that the UNCLOS provides for a legal framework for the repression of piracy in international law and that many provisions in the Convention related to piracy are considered to reflect customary international law.[23] The fact that this Convention does not explicate a duty to criminalize piracy in national law is a first important indication of the absence of a customary rule to that effect. Rather than a duty under international law, enacting national legislation—whether or not of criminal nature—is considered merely an important step a state can take to be able to effectively cooperate in the repression of piracy.[24]

Furthermore, piracy is not within the jurisdiction of any international court,[25] nor is it expressly mentioned by the ICJ as an act to which *jus cogens* or *erga omnes* obligations apply.[26] Since most of the international norms that do have *jus cogens* status are human rights or are related to them,[27] it is also noteworthy that no international or regional human rights convention specifically addresses piracy. Obviously, piracy can involve acts the prohibition of which has the status of *jus cogens* (such as murder, torture, slavery), but that does not mean that the prohibition of piracy itself has that status. Furthermore, although piracy has a distinct extraterritorial element and is a matter of general international concern,[28] it seems hard to argue that piracy in principle threatens peace and security and/or shocks

[22] See eg M Cherif Bassiouni, 'Universal Jurisdiction for International Crimes' (2001) 42(1) Va J Intl L 82, 108–12 (hereafter Bassiouni, 'Universal Jurisdiction'); Michael Mulligan, 'Piracy and Empire' (2017) 19 J Hist Int L 70, 87–89 (hereafter Mulligan, 'Piracy and Empire'); Michael J Kelly, 'The Pre-History of Piracy as a Crime & Its Definitional Odyssey' (2013) 46 Case W Res J Intl L 25, 27–28.

[23] According to its Preamble, UNCLOS achieved 'the codification and progressive development of the law of the sea'. See also the preamble of the 1958 High Seas Convention, and furthermore: International Maritime Organization, 'Piracy: elements of national legislation pursuant to the United Nations Convention on the Law of the Sea' (UN-DOALOS), LEG 98/8/8 (2011) para 1 (hereafter IMO, 'Piracy: elements'); UNODC, *Maritime Crime* (UN 2020) 114; Guilfoyle, 'Piracy' (n 4) 370; Tulio Treves, 'Piracy, Law of the Sea, and Use of Force' (2009) 20 EJIL 399, 401 (hereafter Treves, 'Piracy, Law of the Sea and the Use of Force'); José E Alvarez, *International Organizations as Law-Makers* (OUP 2005) 217; Patricia W Birnie, 'Piracy, Past, Present and Future' (1987) Marine Policy 163, 168 (hereafter Birnie, 'Piracy, Past, Present and Future').

[24] IMO, 'Piracy: elements' (n 23) para 2.

[25] See also ILC, 'A/49/10: Report of the International Law Commission on its forty-sixth session' (2 May–22 July 1994)' (1994) *Yearbook ILC* (vol II-2) 68, where the 'Commission decided not to include piracy as a crime under general international law' in the Draft statute for an international criminal court.

[26] See eg the examples of such obligations given in *Barcelona Traction, Light and Power Company (Belgium v Spain, Second Phase)* (Judgment) [1970] ICJ Rep 3, 32 (paras 33–34).

[27] In that sense see also Forrest Martin, 'Delineating a Hierarchical Outline of International Law Sources and Norms' (2002) 65 Saskatchewan L Rev 333, 347.

[28] ILC, 'Survey of international law' (1971) *Yearbook ILC* (vol II, part two) 3–99, 21.

the conscience of humanity.[29] Nevertheless, as mentioned above, the international acknowledgement of universal criminal jurisdiction for piracy implies that piracy is considered to be felonious conduct by the law of nations. As follows from the ILC commentaries on article 53 Vienna Convention on the Law of Treaties (VCLT[30]),[31] a treaty contemplating or conniving at piracy, 'in the suppression of which every State is called upon to co-operate', possibly constitutes an example of a violation of a *jus cogens* norm. Adopting such a treaty would also clearly be contrary to states' obligation to cooperate to the fullest possible extent in the repression of piracy. Following the ILC, the peremptory norm is that states may not promote piracy or engage in it,[32] but it falls short of a duty to criminalize piracy.

## 4. UN Security Council Resolutions

A last possible basis for an international obligation to criminalize piracy that we shall address here are resolutions of the UN Security Council. The 'Somalia experience' at the beginning of the 21st century marked a turning point in the law of piracy and generated increasing activity on the part of the Security Council. During the peak of piracy off the coast of Somalia between approximately 2005 and 2013, the Security Council adopted a vast number of resolutions addressing piracy. By 2010 the Council, acting under Chapter VII of the UN Charter, was calling upon all states 'to criminalize piracy under their domestic law'.[33] Since then this call has been regularly repeated using similar wording in the operative part of the resolution; the Security Council 'calls upon' or 'urges' states to criminalize piracy under their domestic law.[34] The text of the resolutions signifies that the SC is keen on having all states criminalize piracy in their national laws. However, the language of the text falls short of a legislative act creating an abstract and general obligation

[29] See similar ibid 97–98; M Cherif Bassiouni, 'International Crimes: Jus Cogens and Obligation Erga Omnes' (1996) 59(4) Law & Contemp Probs 63, 70; Marta Bo, 'Piracy at the Intersection between International and National' in Harmen van der Wilt and Christophe Paulussen (eds), *Legal Responses to Transnational and International Crimes* (Edward Elgar 2017) 71, 73–74 (hereafter Bo, 'Piracy at the Intersection' and Van der Wilt and Paulussen, *Legal Responses*). See also Human Rights Committee, General Comment No 36, art 6: Right to life (2018), CCPR/C/GC/36, para 35.

[30] (Signed Vienna, 23 May 1969; entered into force 27 January 1980) 1155 UNTS 331.

[31] 'ILC Draft Articles on the Law of Treaties with commentaries' (1966) *Yearbook ILC* (vol II) 187, 248. See also K Schmalenbach, 'Article 53' in Oliver Dörr and Kirsten Schmalenbach (eds), *Vienna Convention on the Law of Treaties, A Commentary* (Springer 2012) 897, 901–03 (hereafter Dörr and Schmalenbach, *Commentary*).

[32] ILC Draft Articles Law of Treaties, *Yearbook ILC* (n 31) 248. See also Schmalenbach, 'Article 53' in Dörr and Schmalenbach, *Commentary* (n 31) 901–03. Piracy needs to be distinguished here from privateering, see ILC Reference Guide to the Articles concerning the Law of the Sea, A/C.6/L.378 (1956) 146; Robert C Beckman, 'The Piracy Regime under UNCLOS' in Robert C Beckman and James A Roach (eds), *Piracy and International Maritime Crimes in ASEAN* (Edward Elgar 2012) 22.

[33] SC Res 1950(2010) para 13

[34] SC Res 2015(2011) preamble and para 9; SC Res 2382(2017) para 19; SC Res 2442(2018) para 19; SC Res 2500(2019) para 18.

on all states to criminalize piracy. This is particularly evident when the resolutions on piracy are compared to resolutions where the SC decided that states 'shall' criminalize certain terrorist acts.[35] In view of the above exploration of the state of affairs on a duty to criminalize piracy under transnational criminal law, it is hard to argue that the Security Council's strong and specific 'call' for criminalization of piracy in domestic law either reiterates a pre-existing duty or creates a duty to that effect.

## III. Historical Factors that Have Affected the Development of Transnational Criminal Law on Piracy

The way piracy was conceived by states varies when we look at different historical periods: piracy in the Ancient World, piracy from the Middle Ages to the 19th century and the modern crime of piracy.[36] This rough categorization serves merely as orientation in the following sketch of the historical development of piracy, from which a number of interrelated and interconnected principled and pragmatic factors can be identified that help to explain why states never came to agree on an international legal duty to criminalize piracy. To us, at least three factors seem greatly relevant.

The first concerns the nature of the crime of piracy. Traced back to the beginnings of navigation, piracy in the Ancient World equated to warfare or a condoned way of living and acquiring wealth, rather than a criminal act.[37] Famous 'piratical' communities, such as the Vikings from Scandinavia or the Moors in the Mediterranean, operated widely into the Middle Ages.[38] From the late Middle Ages into the 19th century, state-sponsored piracy—so-called privateering—was used as a convenient instrument of warfare by colonizing states to protect their claims to overseas territories and to enrich their treasury.[39] Piracy was forbidden unless authorized by a recognized sovereign. Interestingly, Cicero's infamous labelling of

[35] See eg SC Res 1373(2001) and SC Res 1540(2004). In contrast, see eg SC Res 1269(1999).

[36] For an elaborate historical account see Rubin, *Law of Piracy* (n 1). For a typology of historical and modern pirates, see Hua-Lun Huang, 'Who Are Sea Cutthroats? A Typological Analysis of Pirates' (2010) 53 Crime Law Soc Chang 277.

[37] See eg Henry A Ormerod, *Piracy in the Ancient World* (Johns Hopkins UP 1997 [1924]); Philip de Souza, *Piracy in the Graeco-Roman World* (CUP 1999); Joshua Michael Goodwin, 'Universal Jurisdiction and the Pirate' (2006) 39 Vand J Transnatl L 973 (hereafter Goodwin, 'Universal Jurisdiction and the Pirate').

[38] Eg Rubin, *Law of Piracy* (n 1) 12.

[39] Paul Hallwood and Thomas Miceli, 'Piracy and Privateers in the Golden Age: Lessons for Today' (2018) 49(3) Ocean Dev & Intl L 236; Nikolas Jaspert, '"Piracy," Connectivity and Seaborne Power in the Middle Ages' in Michel Balard (ed), *The Sea in History: The Medieval World* (Boydell & Brewer 2017) 45; Theodore M Cooperstein, 'Letters of Marque and Reprisal: The Constitutional Law and Practice of Privateering' (2009) 40(2) J Mar L & Com 221; Virginia West Lunsford, *Piracy and Privateering in the Golden Age Netherlands* (Palgrave MacMillan 2005); George F Dow and John H Edmonds, *The Pirates of the New England Coast, 1630–1730* (Dover Publications 1996) (hereafter Dow and Edmonds, *The Pirates of the New England Coast*); Rubin, *Law of Piracy* (n 1) 13–50; John Franklin Jameson (ed), *Privateering and Piracy in the Colonial Period, Illustrative Documents* (Kelly 1970 [1923]).

the pirate as *communis hostis omnium*, although not intended as a legal opinion, strongly influenced legal thinking on piracy in later times.[40] The depiction of pirates as common enemy of all has generated a certain confusion, conflating the substantive nature of the crime of piracy and international core crimes such as genocide and crimes against humanity. Moreover, by analogy to piracy, universal jurisdiction was also attributed to these core crimes.[41] As a result, nowadays piracy is often seen as the prototype international crime that has formed an important precedent for the analogical construction of modern international criminal law *stricto sensu*.[42] This neglects the substantive difference between the nature of piracy and international crimes in a strict sense. Many authors emphasize that this labelling in case of piracy does not relate to the heinous nature of the crime that is and should be condemned by all nations. Historically, pirates are enemies of mankind because they operate on the open sea beyond any states' jurisdiction and endanger the security of trade and travel of all nations.[43] Here, universal jurisdiction is not based on substantive reasons concerning the exceptional gravity of the acts as such but rather came about in order to provide for a legal tool that enables states to suppress such activity.[44] Thus, labelling pirates *hostis generis humani* is based on primarily jurisdictional reasons[45] but does not entail the international criminalization of piracy as such.

A second factor which helps to explain why historical developments regarding piracy have not resulted in an international duty to criminalize piracy concerns the primary interests and needs of sovereign powers operating at sea. As mentioned, the practice of privateering as an instrument of warfare was used by the

[40] See William Blackstone, *Commentaries on the Laws of England, Book the Fourth* (OUP 1770) 71; Rubin, *Law of Piracy* (n 1) 10; David Luban, 'The Enemy of All Humanity' (2018) 47(2) Neth J Leg Philos 112 (hereafter Luban, 'Enemy of All Humanity'); Sundberg, 'The Crime of Piracy' (n 1) 799.

[41] The first step towards extending the *hostis generis humani* category was to declare slave trade as piracy in order to be able to lawfully board a slave ship in peacetime; see eg Luban 'Enemy of All Humanity' (n 40) 112–37; Joaquín Alcaide Fernández, 'Hostes humani generis: Pirates, Slavers, and Other Criminals' in Bruno Fassbender and Anne Peters (eds), *The Oxford Handbook of History of International Law* (OUP 2014) 120; Stephen Macedo (ed), *Universal Jurisdiction* (University of Pennsylvania Press 2006).

[42] In a Joint Separate Opinion to the Yerodia Arrest Warrant Case, Judges Higgins, Kooijmans and Buergenthal mention piracy as 'the classical example' of a crime 'regarded as the most heinous by the international community' ((*Congo v Belgium*) [2002] ICJ Rep 63 para 61). See also Anna Tarwacka, 'Piracy in Roman Law and the Beginnings of International Criminal Law' (2012) 1(1–2) Pol Rev Int & Eur L 57; Gerry Simpson, 'Piracy and the Origins of Enmity' in Matthew Craven, Malgosia Fitzmaurice and Maria Vogiatzi (eds), *Time, History and International Law* (Martinus Nijhoff 2006) 219, 219; M Cherif Bassiouni, 'International Crimes: The *Ratione Materiae* of International Criminal Law' in Bassiouni, *International Criminal Law I* (n 1) 149; Bassiouni, 'Universal Jurisdiction' (n 22) 110–11.

[43] See eg Dickinson, 'Is the Crime of Piracy Obsolete?' (n 1) 357–59; Goodwin, 'Universal Jurisdiction and the Pirate' (n 37); Eugene Kontorovich, 'The Piracy Analogy: Modern Universal Jurisdiction's Hollow Foundation' (2004) 45 Harv Intl LJ 183; Anne H Geraghty, 'Universal Jurisdiction and Drug Trafficking' (Legal Series Working Paper 55, 2003) 19.

[44] Luban 'Enemy of All Humanity' (n 40) 126; Claus Kress, 'International Criminal Law' in *Max Planck Encyclopedia of Public International Law* (OUP, last updated 2009) para 9.

[45] Luban 'Enemy of All Humanity' (n 40) 131. See Judge Moore's Dissenting Opinion in the Lotus Case [1927] PCIJ Series A, No 10, 65, 70.

colonizing states from the Middle Ages into the 19th century. After the 1494 Treaty of Tordesillas, in which Spain and Portugal divided newly discovered lands, the great naval powers England, France and the Netherlands opposed a Spanish monopoly on trade with those regions and openly promoted piracy off the shores of Spanish America.[46] Authorization of a sovereign through the issuance of letter of marque and reprisal marked the difference between privateers and pirates. The practical distinction between pirates and privateers was, however, vague.[47] At that time, states operating at sea and benefiting from the privateer system were not particularly interested in a precise definition of piracy, let alone in defining a transnational crime of piracy or accepting an international duty to criminalize piracy. It seems, moreover, doubtful that a need for such duty actually existed since various criminal offences in domestic law, such as theft, robbery, hijacking, murder or manslaughter, could and can cover piratical acts. Sovereigns that had the power and interest to suppress piracy had already designed their laws appropriately.[48] It is telling that with the development of nation states, the increased importance of trade by sea and recognition that more peaceful relations at sea were better for all, a process of prohibition of the privateer system began, continuing the gradual process of domestic criminalization of the pirate.[49] The fact that privateers turned to piracy after the conclusion of peace treaties was one of the causes of the rise of piracy during the so-called 'Golden Age of Piracy' in the late 17th to mid-18th centuries.[50] It was the British Royal Navy and British colonial tribunals handing out harsh punishments—death in many instances—that strongly contributed to suppressing piracy by the end of the 18th century.[51] Central to the international law perspective is that any state is justified to operate on the high seas in order to prevent, disturb and bring an end to piratical activities. The permissive rather than obligatory nature of universal jurisdiction in case of piracy also aligns with the rather opportunistic state practice: major maritime nations openly tolerated even large-scale piracy when it was directed at their enemies. In addition, the enforcement of

[46] Jon Latimer, *Buccaneers of the Caribbean: How Piracy Forged an Empire* (Harvard UP 2009); Violet Barbour, 'Privateers and Pirates of the West Indies' (1911) 16(3) Am Hist Rev 529 (hereafter Barbour, 'Privateers and Pirates of the West Indies').

[47] Dow and Edmonds, *The Pirates of the New England Coast* (n 39) 19.

[48] For an early example, see the British 1536 Offences at Sea Act; about the Act, see Rubin, *Law of Piracy* (n 1) 36–38, see 359–61 for the text of the Act.

[49] Louis Sicking, 'God's Friend, the Whole World's Enemy' (2018) 47(2) Neth J Leg Philos 176; Mulligan, 'Piracy and Empire (n 22) 70–92; Jan Martin Lemnitzer, *Power, Law and the End of Privateering* (Palgrave Macmillan 2014); Michael Bahar, 'Attaining Optimal Deterrence at Sea: A Legal and Strategic Theory for Naval Anti-Piracy Operations' (2007) 40(1) Vand J Transnatl L 11; Clive M Senior, *A Nation of Pirates: English Piracy in Its Heyday* (Cane Russak 1976) 151; Barbour, 'Privateers and Pirates of the West Indies (n 46) 529–66.

[50] Stephen Barnett, 'Monsters of Their Own Making: Understanding the Context of the Rise of the "Golden Age of Piracy"' (2012) LOGOS 19, 26 (hereafter Barnett, 'Monsters of Their Own Making').

[51] See eg Joel H Baer (ed), *British Piracy and the Golden Age: History and Interpretation, 1660–1730* (Vol I) (Routledge 2007); Barnett, 'Monsters of Their Own Making' (n 50) 19. The system of privateering was formally abolished by the Paris Declaration Respecting Maritime Law, 16 April 1856.

piracy was historically in the hands of a few states that had the maritime power to protect their own interests at sea.[52] A right to do so based on universal jurisdiction was in their interest, an international obligation to criminalize and perhaps even a subsequent duty to prosecute was not.

A third important factor that has coloured the history of the development of piracy as a legal phenomenon concerns the reoccurrence of piracy as a factual phenomenon. The exploration of oceans and maritime trade have been important drivers of the rise and fall of piracy throughout history. Periods with large-scale piracy notwithstanding, there were long intervals where piracy did not present a challenge to a great proportion to states. In fact, the perception that piracy was a thing of the past dominated the process of codification of international law on piracy in the 20th century.[53] This perception seems to explain the absence of particular attention to a duty to criminalize piracy in the UNCLOS or any other convention, as explained above. The return of piracy in its modern shape—as a complex and multidimensional phenomenon involving transnational, oftentimes organized criminal activity that endangers the security of maritime navigation and international trade by sea[54]—has prompted renewed attention to piracy as a legal phenomenon. However, the transnational interest that would lead to the adoption of a general duty to criminalize piracy is as yet not strong enough. This is shown by the inadequate international support for the creation of a general treaty on piracy proposed by Ukraine in its Draft Comprehensive Convention on the Suppression of Acts of Piracy at Sea.[55]

[52] Magdelena Satora, 'Piracy from the Middle Ages to the 19*th* Century' (2012) 1(1–2) Pol Rev Int &Eur L 75, 79; Frank Lambert, *The Barbary Wars: American Independence in the Atlantic World* (Hill and Wang 2005); Nicholas B Harding, 'North African Piracy, the Hanoverian Carrying Trade and the British State, 1728–1828' (2000) 43(1) Hist J 25, 30, 32; Thomas Wemyss Fulton, *The Sovereignty of the Sea* (Blackwood 1911).

[53] Harvard Law, 'Piracy' (n 10) 739–885, 755–57, 759–60; Birnie, 'Piracy, Past, Present and Future' (n 23) 163–83,169; Geiß and Petrig, *Piracy and Armed Robbery* (n 11) ch 2; James F Warren, 'A Tale of Two Centuries: The Globalisation of Maritime Raiding and Piracy in Southeast Asia at the end of the Eighteenth and Twentieth Centuries' (2003) Asia Research Institute Working Paper Series No 2; Dickinson, 'Is the Crime of Piracy Obsolete?' (n 1) 334–60.

[54] See eg Rubin, *Law of Piracy* (n 1) 337–46; Adam J Fenton and Ioannis Chapsos, 'Prosecuting Pirates: Maritime Piracy and Indonesian Law' (2019) 19 Aust J Asian L 19(2) 1–16; Douglas Guilfoyle (ed), *Modern Piracy: Legal Challenges and Responses* (Edward Elgar 2013); Elizabeth Nyman, 'Modern Piracy and International Law: Definitional Issues with the Law of the Sea' (2011) 5(11) Geography Compass 863; Silvia Ciotti Galletti (ed), *Piracy and Maritime Terrorism* (IOS 2012).

[55] See Annex to Letter dated 1 October 2010 from the Permanent Representative of Ukraine, A/65/489. Art 5 of the Draft Convention introduces an obligation to criminalize piracy. Critical of the contemporary international legal piracy regime and arguing for a separate piracy convention or tribunal, see eg Treves, 'Piracy, Law of the Sea, and the Use of Force' (n 23) 399–414; Andreas von Arnauld, 'Die Moderne Piraterie und das Völkerrecht' (2009) 47 Archiv des Völkerrechts 454.

## IV. Conclusion

The definition of transnational criminal law employed in the introduction above entails that international law orders states to suppress transnational crime through national criminal law. Normatively, this implies a legal duty for states to criminalize certain conduct. It follows from the expedition through numerous legal sources on piracy that there is insufficient ground to conclude that historically there exists a duty to criminalize piracy. Considering the historical development of piracy, we have identified at least three plausible factors that help explain why states have never agreed on such a duty. The question remains what implication this weak state of transnational substantive criminal law on piracy has or should have from a more general perspective. Two observations seem appropriate.

On the one hand, the development of transnational criminal law with regard to one of the oldest crimes that attract universal jurisdiction exposes the challenges to transnational law-making that we face today and underscores the institutional limitations of global governance. It is debatable whether the use of executive law-making power by the Security Council would in fact strengthen the transnational law regime for piracy or rather emphasize the democratic deficit in the development of transnational criminal law. As has been observed before, the hegemonic protection of self-interest of states plays a central role in the development of transnational criminal law.[56] The self-interested way in which states have gone about developing universal agreements on cyber-security, for example, seems to mirror to some extent the development of transnational criminal law on piracy.

On the other hand, the history on maritime piracy supports the argument that for a proper development of transnational criminal law as a coherent and legitimate system of law, some measure of harmonization of national substantive criminal law should underpin the duty on states to cooperate in the suppression of transnational crimes. In fact, the enhancement of procedural cooperation between states in the fight against transnational crime—something that has been argued to constitute 'the main focus of transnational criminal law' [57]—is preconditioned upon a certain amount of harmonization of national substantive criminal law. The suppression of piracy seems to have suffered because many states have either not criminalized it or have done so very differently, as the recent rise and fall of piratical activity near Somalia has shown.[58] The strong call of the Security Council for criminalization of piracy in domestic law bears witness to that.

[56] Boister, *An Introduction* (n 2) 19.

[57] Neil Boister, 'Responding to Transnational Crime: The Distinguishing Features of Transnational Criminal Law' in Van der Wilt and Paulussen, *Legal Responses* (n 29) 27, 39.

[58] Beatriz López Lorca, 'Harmonisation of National Criminal Laws on Maritime Piracy: a Regulatory Proposal for the Crime of Piracy and its Penalties' (2017) 23 Eur J Crim Policy Res 115; Bo, 'Piracy at the Intersection' (n 29) 71–91; J Ashley Roach, 'Countering Piracy off Somalia: International Law and International Institutions' (2010) 104(3) AJIL 397.

This should not be read as a plea for a far-reaching duty to criminalize piracy. Where the criminalization of conduct is problematic per se, because criminalization by definition infringes upon individual's rights, criminalization through transnational substantive criminal law should be viewed even more critically. The necessarily subsidiary role of transnational substantive criminal law, the political and cultural nature of criminalization, the democratic deficit within transnational criminal law and the particular difficulties to amend it later on are all, inter alia, relevant in this regard. A possible transnational criminalization of even the old crime of piracy must thus be approached in a careful, informed and principled manner.

# 9

# British Anti-Slave-Trade Treaties with African and Arab Leaders as Precursors of Modern Suppression Conventions

*Roger S Clark*

## I. Introduction

Having proscribed its own participation in the slave trade in 1807, Great Britain embarked on an ambitious international campaign to halt the slave trade globally.[1]

European and American slave traders lacked capacity to invade the African continent to carry off sufficient slaves to the New World. They relied on indigenous leaders to capture slaves, by war or raids on other groups, and to transport them to or near the coast, where European shippers could take over. This chapter examines one tool used by Britain to attack the trade, negotiating treaties with Arab and African leaders through whose territory the trade passed. Beginning in 1817, British diplomatic, consular and (especially) naval representatives negotiated scores of bilateral suppression treaties for the abolition of the trade with East and West African leaders (variously described as 'Kings', 'Chiefs' or 'Potentates'), and with Arab leaders (typically 'Sheiks'). The treaties were early examples of what, in the 20th century, came to be called 'Suppression Conventions'.[2] Unlike the (hesitant) colonial efforts later in the nineteenth century at ending slavery itself, which are the subject of significant literature,[3] these treaties have received sparse attention

[1] See eg Hugh Thomas, *The Slave Trade* (Touchstone/Simon & Schuster 1997) ch 31 ('Active Exertions') (hereafter Thomas, *The Slave Trade*).

[2] See Neil Boister, *An Introduction to Transnational Criminal* Law (OUP 2012) 14. Most modern suppression treaties are multilateral, typically with 150–90 parties; the older ones, like those in this chapter, were bilateral. The instruments discussed here are variously titled 'Treaty', 'Agreement', 'Convention' or 'Engagement'. The difference in nomenclature has no legal significance.

[3] See eg Suzanne Miers, *Britain and the Ending of the Slave Trade* (Longmans 1975) (hereafter Miers, *Britain*); Trevor R Getz, *Slavery and Reform in West Africa: Toward Emancipation in Nineteenth Century Senegal and the Gold Coast* (Ohio UP 2004); Paul E Lovejoy, *Transformations in Slavery: A History of Slavery in Africa* (2nd edn, CUP 2000).

Roger S Clark, *British Anti-Slave-Trade Treaties with African and Arab Leaders as Precursors of Modern Suppression Conventions* In: *Histories of Transnational Criminal Law*. Edited by: Neil Boister, Sabine Gless and Florian Jeßberger, Oxford University Press. © Roger S Clark 2021. DOI: 10.1093/oso/9780192845702.003.0010

in either legal[4] or historical[5] literature. This chapter aims to fill the gap in knowledge of these instruments.

The slave trade suppression genre began with British practice with European and American powers, initially with Portugal[6] and Spain.[7] The focus of this chapter is on treaties with African and Arab leaders that began to appear, at first sporadically, shortly after those first European models. I have located about a hundred of them, printed alongside treaties with recognized European and American states in the Consolidated Treaty Series (CTS). I also found manuscript copies of many of the published ones in the British National Archives in Kew outside London—Britain had a bureaucracy devoted to the slave trade (the Slave Trade Department).[8] They span the period 1817 to 1893, underscoring that they were no passing fancy and that British officials obviously thought them worthwhile. Only a sample can be examined in the space available, but the sample reflects the tone.

Considerable resources were devoted to negotiation and implementation[9]—salaries and expenses of negotiators; contributions in coin or goods to the leaders; enforcement, especially by naval patrols and the stationing of British 'agents'. The treaties seldom attempted to impose British sovereignty, or even some lesser colonial relationship, over all or part of the entities concerned.[10] The non-British party was treated as an 'equal' sovereign.[11] The British were interested in trade

[4] Apart from some earlier thoughts on a more limited sample of the treaties, Roger S Clark, 'Steven Spielberg's *Amistad* and other Things I Have Thought About in the Past Forty Years: International (Criminal) Law, Conflict of Laws, Insurance and Slavery' (1998–99) 30 Rutgers LJ 371, 428–32, and some references in Howard Hazen Wilson, 'Some Principal Aspects of British Efforts to Crush the African Slave Trade, 1807–1929' (1950) 44 AJIL 505, there is little on them in the legal literature. Similar treaties with European states are discussed in Jenny S Martinez, *The Slave Trade and the Origins of International Human Rights Law* (OUP 2012). Martinez, however, misses the significance of these treaties as suppression conventions.

[5] Miers, *Britain* (n 3) 43–55 is the best discussion I found of the significance of the treaties. Thomas, *The Slave Trade* (n 1) 669–70 mentions the treaties generally but does not discuss the contents; Christopher Lloyd, *The Navy and the Slave Trade* (Frank Cass 1968) (hereafter Lloyd, *The Navy*) has several references but no systematic discussion, see eg 149–56.

[6] Additional Convention between Great Britain and Portugal for the Prevention of the Slave Trade, 28 July 1817, 67 CTS 373.

[7] Treaty between Great Britain and Spain for the Abolition of the Slave Trade, 23 September 1817, 68 CTS 45.

[8] The manuscripts are in the Foreign Office Archives, FO 97/432 (Slave Trade Department). They are mostly handwritten, copies rather than originals, and sometimes, in spite of copperplate penmanship, hard to decipher. I discovered some of them when looking for something else in the *British and Foreign State Papers* in the 1960s and much later searched in the CTS. Since the titles did not always say 'slave trade' I missed some at this point, but found more in the Archives and then in Clive Parry and Charity Hopkins, *Index of British Treaties 1101–1968*, Vol II, pt four (HMSO 1970).

[9] There are examples of associated costs (especially 'salaries and incidentals') in FO 96/34 at the British National Archives, Foreign Office, Chief Clerk's Department 1824–43.

[10] An exception: Additional Articles, to the Treaty with Cartabar (Gambia), 23 April 1841 (same date) 92 CTS 336 (ceding to the Queen one square mile of territory and asking her to become the 'protecting sovereign' of the whole).

[11] Space constraints preclude entering into the important debate about the 'legality' of such instruments under international law. But there is no doubt that the British took them seriously. For some useful thoughts and references on the African and comparable Pacific treaties, see Tom Bennion, 'Treaty-Making in the Pacific in the Nineteenth Century and the Treaty of Waitangi' (2004) 35 VUWLR 6. In form, the treaties appear to be effective for both parties upon signature, without any further

and soft-power influence rather than formal colonial acquisition. By the 1890s, however, the agreements had run their course; they were superseded by the more familiar, but legally varied, instruments of colonial control, namely straight annexation or creation of a 'protectorate' or 'protected state' status. Newly revised Instructions for the captains and commanding officers of Her Majesty's ships of war employed in the suppression of the slave trade, issued in 1892, noted the effective demise, through territorial colonization, of the instruments with East and West African leaders discussed here.[12] Dahomey succumbed to the French the following year, completing 'civilized' control of the West Coast. Agreements with Arab leaders continued into the twentieth century.

Typically, the leaders were obliged by the treaties to adopt and enforce a law banning the slave trade in their territories and to authorize the Royal Navy to search their ships in their waters and on the high seas, and sometimes ships of all nations within their territorial and internal[13] waters. Slave 'factories', or 'barracoons', could be destroyed; the slaves freed. The aim was to cut off supply of slaves[14] to the Americas or the Persian Gulf. In return, leaders earned the pleasure of the British Crown, trading expectations (for goods other than slaves, such as palm oil), and, in many earlier treaties, a one-time or recurring 'present' of goods. This chapter examines the language of a sample of these instruments and seeks to place them in their historical context. Of particular interest is that the British characterized the issues as legal ones, using the tools of international law. For the most part, even as the dominant hegemon of the time, Britain regarded itself as required by the rule of law to act through such instruments rather than naked force.[15]

'ratification'. I did, however, find two related unpublished Agreements banning human sacrifice which note that 'Her Majesty has been graciously pleased to confirm and ratify the same'. Despatch No 43 from Lord Stanley in FO 97/432.

[12] London, HMSO, 1892. These Instructions asserted:

> The partition of the Coasts of Africa between European Powers has altered the position of the 'Uncivilized States' on the West Coast with whom Great Britain has Treaties for the Suppression of the Slave Trade. The waters of that Coast, with the exception of the coast line belonging to Dahomey, have, within the limits recognized by International Law, become the territorial waters of some Civilized State. You will consequently be guided in regard to vessels within these limits by the instructions relating to Territorial Waters.

[13] Many of the leaders had territories abutting or enclosing rivers or creeks, rather than the ocean. The British right to patrol territorial or internal waters is comparable with modern US agreements empowering patrols for drug traffickers. See Ellen S Podgor, Roger S Clark and Lucian Dervan, *International Criminal Law* (4th edn, CAP 2016) 232–33.

[14] Modern suppression treaties often deal with both supply and demand. See eg 1988 Drug Trafficking Convention.

[15] In a debate with Viscount Palmerston, who had argued for more unilateral power, Sir Robert Peel insisted that 'No doubt we are a powerful country, and it is possible to land on the coast of Africa and destroy these places, but it is important for us to ascertain whether the Laws of Nations or Conventions justify such acts as these.' *Hansard*, House of Commons, 16 July 1844. Peel also referred to a legal opinion of the Queen's Advocate: 'Unless you have a convention with the native African princes, you are not entitled to destroy the barracoons; [the slave trade] is not an act of piracy which the Law of Nations would take notice of, and if a murder be committed, you will be responsible for the act.'

## II. The Treaties

What follows is a discussion of a sample of the treaties up to the early 1850s, by which time the language was largely standardized.

The first was a treaty of 23 October 1817 with Radama, King of Madagascar,[16] article 2 of which provided:

> that Radama, King of Madagascar, will make a Proclamation and Law, prohibiting all his Subjects, or Persons depending on him or his Dominions, to sell any Slave, to be transported from Madagascar; or to aid, abet, or assist in such sale, under penalty, that any Person so offending, shall be reduced to slavery himself.

The last line hits home, does it not? Like nearly all the treaties in my sample, this is not a treaty forbidding slavery; it is the *trade* that is banned; and, to underscore the point, slavery is the penalty for trading.

Radama had a price. Article 3 promised that 'articles' (money and goods) would be given annually to the King 'in consideration of this concession on the part of' the King, 'and in full satisfaction for the same, and in consideration of the loss of revenue thereby incurred by Radama'. A pattern was established: an obligation to criminalize and to enforce, and the giving of material incentives.

The second, more complex, example is the 'General Treaty between the East India Company (Great Britain) and the Friendly Arabs (Trucial Sheikdoms of Oman and Bahrein)' of 8 January 1820.[17] Its main focus was suppressing piracy in the Persian Gulf, but it addressed other matters, including the slave trade.

Article 9, the nub for our purposes, provided that 'The carrying off of slaves, men, women, or children, from the coasts of Africa or elsewhere, and the transporting them in vessels, is plunder and piracy, and the friendly Arabs shall do nothing of this nature.'[18] There were no 'presents' on this occasion, I suspect because the

[16] Treaty between Great Britain and Madagascar, 23 October 1817, 68 CTS 115.

[17] 70 CTS 463, signed initially by entities called Ras-al-Khaimah, Zyah, Shargah, Abu Dhabi, Ajman and Umm-al-Quaiwaim, and acceded to by Bahrein on 5 February; Translation from the Arabic original. The Treaty Series contains numerous agreements entered into by the East India Company, regarded as an instrument of the Crown for treaty purposes. For another early East India Company suppression treaty, see Treaty between the East India Co. (Great Britain) and the Imam of Muscat for the Suppression of Slavery, signed 10 September 1822, 72 CTS 473 (Imam promises to prevent his subjects from selling slaves to 'Christians of all nations', but apparently not to non-Christians); permit stationing a British slave trade intelligence-gathering official in Zanzibar, where the Imam also held sway; and allow British seizure of slave ships in certain contingencies). Zanzibar and Muscat became the prime focus of British efforts late in the 19th century before colonial control was exercised over them, and many additional treaties with Arab entities followed. See Raymond Howell, *The Royal Navy and the Suppression of the Slave Trade* (St Martin's 1987) (mentioning the treaties discussed here only in passing).

[18] There is no explicit criminalization of the trade in this provision, unless the reference to piracy is meant to imply that the slave trade is equally criminal and perhaps even amenable to British (universal) jurisdiction. Throughout the 19th century, the British sought to conflate the slave trade with piracy. This also occurred sometimes in US usage. The British/American conflation of the slave trade and piracy never garnered widespread acceptance, although the British were still trying to make the piracy/slave

British were mindful of the long experience of European and American powers forced to pay ransom to the Barbary States for the rescue of 'Christian' slaves and did not want to establish another precedent for payment.

The first treaty in West Africa was the 'Treaty with the Chiefs of the Soombia Soosoos', in the hinterland of Sierra Leone, 18 April 1826,[19] signed by the Acting Governor of Sierra Leone.[20] Its fourth article provided that:

> The said Chiefs and Headmen promise and engage to abolish the slave trade and not to allow any exportation of slaves from their respective countries nor to allow any vessels, craft, boats or canoes to enter any of their rivers, creeks, bays or waters for the purpose of buying or selling slaves or being in any manner engaged in the slave trade nor to allow factories or other establishments to be found by any means whatsoever for the purchasing or selling of slaves.

This, again, seeks abolition of the trade, but not abolition of slavery within the realms of the Soombia Soosoos. As in other treaties, there is an assumption on the British side that even a 'primitive' legal system had the capacity to take the necessary legislative and executive action to give effect to the agreements, even though the British negotiators must have been hazy about how the chiefly system actually functioned.

These early treaties just noted are random in drafting technique and sporadic in negotiation. 1841, however, was a banner year for treaty negotiation, accompanying a general increase in British anti-slave-trade patrols on the African coast.[21] The CTS[22] contains a group of nine treaties described as 'made by the British anti-slavery patrols with native potentates' in West Africa during that year.

trade connection in the negotiations on the 1926 and 1956 Slavery Conventions, CWW Greenidge, *Slavery* (Allen & Unwin 1958) 183, 196. Some slave traders moonlighting as pirates were captured by the British naval squadron on slave patrol and executed for piracy rather than slave-trading, Lloyd, *The Navy* (n 5) 64–67.

[19] 76 CTS 185.

[20] In 1808, Great Britain established a small colony on the coast, at the estuary of the Sierra Leone River, mainly the city of Freetown, where freed slaves were sent. Not until 1893 was a much larger protectorate established over the interior of what is now Sierra Leone. As well as those with chiefs in the interior of Sierra Leone, many of the treaties discussed here were with chiefs from the area near the, also small, Gambia colony. The Gambia, Sierra Leone, Gallinas, Senegal, Niger and Congo Rivers were common routes for the export of slaves.

[21] Thomas, *The Slave Trade* (n 1) 659–64.

[22] Treaties etc between Great Britain and New Cestos, the Timmanees, Cape Mount, Cartabar, Kings Bell and Acqua, Aboh, Egarra and Old Calebar (West Africa) signed 11 January, 13, 21 February, 23 April, 7 May, 28 August, 6 September and 6 December 1841, 92 CTS 315. Orders for enforcing most of this batch appear in the *Instructions for the Guidance of her Majesty's Naval Officers Employed in the Suppression of the Slave Trade* 90–98 (London, both Houses of Parliament, 1844) (issued by 'the Commissioners for executing the Office of the Lord High Admiral', presumably after consultation with the Foreign Office). This document also contains negotiating instructions for new agreements (15–16) and a 'Draft of Engagement' (168), used as a model for several subsequent agreements in the 1840s. Lloyd, *The Navy* (n 5) 92–93 attributes the drafting of this model Engagement to ardent opponent of the slave trade Captain Joseph Denman, son of the Lord Chief Justice.

Typical is a Treaty with the Chiefs of the Timmanees (in the hinterland of Sierra Leone), 13 February 1841.[23] Article II provides that no persons whatever shall be taken out of the Timmanee country as slaves; and no person in the Timmanee country shall be concerned in any way in seizing, keeping, carrying or sending away any persons for the purpose of their being taken out of the country as slaves. The Chiefs were obligated to 'punish severely all who break this law'. Criminalization and punishment were now firmly established as central to the treaties.

I have found no useful data about how well these and similar leaders complied with obligations to criminalize and punish, and suspect the real nub of the treaties was British enforcement power. Article III, indeed, contained a dramatic, and novel, delegation of enforcement power to the British:

> The officers of the Queen of England may seize every vessel or boat of the Timmanees found anywhere carrying on the trade in slaves in the waters belonging to the Timmanees, and may also seize every vessel or boat of other nations found carrying on the trade in slaves in the waters of the Timmanees. And the vessels and boats so seized shall be taken to an English possession to be tried by English law.[24] And the officers of the Queen of England may destroy all barracoons, buildings, fences and inclosures, used in keeping or detaining persons when taken away to another country as slaves. And they may seize all goods, merchandize, in such barracoons, buildings, fences, or inclosures, or which shall have been imported into the Timmanee country, for the purpose of buying or being exchanged for persons to be carried away as slaves. And the goods and merchandize so seized shall be taken to a British territory to be tried by English law. And the proceeds shall be disposed of between the Queen of England and the Alikarlie,[25] or other Chiefs of the Timmanees, in the manner provided by the existing treaty with Spain;[26] but the officers of the Queen of England shall not

[23] 92 CTS 316. Art I insists that no British born subjects or liberated Africans shall be enslaved in Timmanee country. It also contains an unusual example of British exercise of nationality jurisdiction, which also appears in several later treaties: But no British born subjects, or liberated Africans, shall engage in war, or excite or provoke to war, in the Timmanee country; and if any British born subjects, or liberated Africans, shall engage in war or excite or provoke war, they shall be sent for by the Governor of Sierra Leone and punished.

For an example of nationality jurisdiction over slave trade offences committed by British citizens anywhere in the world, see 6 & 7 Victoria, c XCVIII (24 August 1843). The prohibition on British nationals engaging in war may well have involved a kind of quid pro quo—enforce your slave trade laws and we will keep our nationals out of your affairs and even guarantee your territorial inviolability.

[24] There was British legislation empowering the relevant naval and judicial action. Vice-Admiralty courts had jurisdiction.

[25] Apparently an inner group of chiefs.

[26] The reference must be to the 1817 Treaty with Spain (n 7) which provided, in art VII of its Regulations for Mixed Commissions, that duly seized vessels and their cargo, apart from slaves, were to be sold at public sale 'for the profit of the two Governments'. Slaves would be freed. Such provisions were a precursor of, eg, art 5 of the 1988 Drug Trafficking Convention which contemplates seizure of proceeds and of 'materials and equipment and other instrumentalities used in or intended for use in any manner' in the drug traffic, and sharing of the proceeds with other parties.

> destroy any barracoons, buildings, fences, or inclosures, without the authority of the Chief or headman of the district; nor shall they carry away any goods or merchandize which they find on land, without his authority; but they may take all persons whom they find detained in the barracoons, or other buildings or enclosures, as well as in all vessels or boats, and place them under the protection of the Queen of England, that they may be made free.

Apparently the British could seize any slave vessel belonging to a Timmanee person 'anywhere'—within Timmanee waters (including rivers and creeks) or on the high seas.[27] Vessels of other nations plying their trade in Timmanee waters could also be seized. Timmanee territorial jurisdiction over such vessels had been delegated to the British.[28] British enforcement power, with local acquiescence, extended also beyond the waters to the land territory of the Timmanees. Buildings, goods and chattels could be seized and sold (with acquiescence of the local leader) and proceeds shared out. Above all, the slaves were to be made free.

But there was more: 'presents'. Article XIII provided that the Queen of England, 'out of friendship for the Chief of the Timmanees, and because the said Chief, with the consent of the proper Chiefs, has made this agreement', gives him and thirty-six other Chiefs and leaders, various quantities of baft (fabric), tobacco and rum, to be payable every year.[29]

Some of the treaties contemplated British action if there was non-compliance. Thus the Aboh Treaty[30] states that 'Any infringement of this Treaty will subject the Chief of Aboh to the severe displeasure of the Queen of Great Britain, and the loss of duties herein stipulated for.'[31]

[27] See also Treaty with Aboh, reproduced in next note, which is even clearer about 'anywhere'.

[28] Not every sovereignty would be comfortable about the British boarding their boats. The territorial sovereign would have power under international law to search anyone's vessels in its waters and could presumably delegate that power to the World's Policeman. But would all agree with either part of this proposition? Some of the later treaties were a little more cautious on this front. For example, the Treaty with Obi Osai, Chief of Aboh (in modern Nigeria), 28 August 1841, 92 CTS 328, provided:

> The officers of the Queen of Great Britain may seize every vessel or boat of Aboh, found anywhere carrying on the Trade in Slaves, and may also seize every vessel or boat *of other nations with whom a similar Agreement has been made*, carrying on the Trade in Slaves in the waters belonging to the Chief of Aboh. Upon such seizure and after regular condemnation, according to the provisions of this Agreement, the slaves shall be made free, and the vessels or boats shall be destroyed. (Emphasis added.)

By the 1850s, limiting language like that italicized was boilerplate. Condemnation under the Agreement normally meant an examination made by the naval officer in charge in the presence of a Chief or headman (art III).

[29] 'Every year' seems to mean indefinitely, but other treaties promised only a single payment or payments for say five years.

[30] 92 CTS 328 at 330 (art XV).

[31] The reference to 'duties' is apparently to the Chief's power under the treaty to collect duties of up to one-twentieth the value of British imports. Aboh had also obtained many presents, but they were one-off not repeating. There was no threat to take them back. An identical duties provision appears in the Treaty with Egarra, 92 CTS 331 at 334. This Chief also received a one-time set of goods, including a dozen snuff boxes, a dozen padlocks, a dozen pairs of spectacles, one drum and one tambourine.

British naval presence, in the rivers and off the coast, was extensive, but information was still useful so that ships could be deployed most effectively. Thus some of the treaties, in an early form of Mutual Legal Assistance, have the relevant African leader promising that 'should any slave-vessels arrive in the river, he will inform any of Her Britannic Majesty's cruizers thereof that may be in the neighbourhood'.[32] The enterprise was a cooperative one.

The suppression obligation in some of the treaties is quite stark. The Treaty with the King of Cartabar,[33] for example, asserts that:

> The King of Cartabar shall, within 48 hours of the date of this Treaty, make a law for carrying the whole of it into effect, and shall proclaim that law; and the King of Cartabar shall put that law into force from that time for ever.[34]

A batch of almost identical slave trade treaties done in 1852[35] represent what were effectively adhesion treaties. They now include provisions forbidding human sacrifice and the killing of prisoners of war.[36] Beyond that, they forbid the export of slaves, and people within the jurisdiction from so doing, on pain of punishment; no European or other person may be permitted to reside in the land as a slave-trader; slave buildings are to be destroyed; if the slave trade re-emerges, the British may use force and seize boats of the entity concerned (but not those of other

[32] Treaty with King Bell, 92 CTS 325. To same effect, Treaty with King Acqua, 92 CTS 326, 327; Treaty with King Eyamba, 92 CTS 335. Among others, the Treaty with the King of Cartabar, CTS 323, 324, went further and provided for an agent: 'The Queen of England may appoint an agent to visit or to reside in the Cartabar country, and this agent is to watch over the fulfilment of this treaty; he shall always receive honour and protection in the Cartabar country, and the King will pay attention to what he says. The person and property of this agent shall be sacred.' On agents, see also, Timmanees (n 23); Aboh (n 28); Egarra (n 31).

[33] 92 CTS 323, Cartabar, art XI.

[34] The treaty has obligations concerning such matters as trade and the rights of English residents as well as forbidding 'white slavery' and the slave trade, so the King's 'law' could be quite complex if it followed British legislative practice where Parliament would give effect to it in Parliament's own words. I suspect that African constitutional practice was most often merely some sort of proclamation of the Treaty. The forty-eight-hour requirement is striking—these are not necessarily constitutional monarchies requiring consultation with Parliament. But some agreements on their face required consultation with other leaders under local customs.

[35] Engagements for the Abolition of the Traffic in Slaves etc between Great Britain and the Chiefs of the Egba Nation, Dahomey, Porto Novo, Little Popoe, Goom Cork-way, Abo-Den Arfo, Afflowhoo, Adinnar Cooma, Adaffie, Block-ouse, Aghwey, Grand Popoe, Jaboo, King Akitoe of Lagos, the Chiefs of Bussama and Badagry (West Africa), signed 5, 13, 17, 24, 26, 27, 28, 29, 30 January, 2, 25, 28 February, 9, 18 March 1852, 107 CTS 423 et seq. Most of these treaties were signed on behalf of the Queen by Thomas George Forbes, Commander of Her Majesty's Ship *Philomel* and witnessed, among others, by Louis Fraser, Her Majesty's Vice-Consul for the Kingdom of Dahomey. Provision was made in these treaties for France to accede should it wish (and it did join several of them). Fraser, whose main task was to obtain a slave treaty with the King of Dahomey, failed in this endeavour, although Forbes was able to negotiate one that did not include the abolition of human sacrifice. See Robin Law (ed), *Dahomey and the Ending of the Trans-Atlantic Slave Trade: The Journals and Correspondence of Vice-Consul Louis Fraser 1851–1852* (OUP for British Academy 2012). Lloyd, *The Navy* (n 5) discusses, 154, the joy of the King of Dahomey in human sacrifice.

[36] Slaves and prisoners of war were commonly used in human sacrifice.

states);[37] slave-traders are to be expelled; the British may trade freely; missionaries may follow their vocation. Interestingly, the era of compensation for the loss of slave revenue is over; there is no provision for gifts to the leadership in any of them.

This remained the basic pattern for the treaties though the remainder of the century.[38]

## III. Conclusion

The British crusade to end the slave trade, and ultimately slavery itself, focused on both demand and supply. Until slavery was entirely abolished in the United States, Cuba and Brazil,[39] efforts in tandem with those countries emphasized discouraging re-supply by their merchant marines or rogue ships of other nations. The efforts with the African and Arab potentates endeavoured to cut off supply at the source, before it crossed the ocean, undoubtedly with some success, although how much success is debated. Nevertheless, the British would hardly have persisted with such a dramatic programme of treaty negotiation unless they thought it was having some effect. I have found no statistics that disaggregate the captures made pursuant to treaties with major powers from those with African leaders, but there are some interesting joint figures available, obviously entailing some guesswork. An 1849 Report from the House of Commons Select Committee on the Slave Trade asserts that, from 1814 to 1847, 963,582 slaves were exported from Africa; between 1810 and 1846, 116,862 slaves were liberated and landed alive; and that between 1819 and 1849, 1,020 slaving vessels were captured and condemned.[40] A later Report has testimony about the destruction of up-river barracoons, and (lower) figures for vessels captured and slaves aboard them in East and West Africa and on the coasts of Brazil and Cuba between 1849 and 1852.[41] This was when the trade was diminishing and Brazil had practically stopped receiving slaves. Ultimately, abolition in the Americas in the last third of the 19th century spelled the end of the Trans-Atlantic Trade, as demand faded.[42] It is hard to dispute Suzanne Miers's

[37] cf nn 30–34. Treaties with other Chiefs or with European and American states may have permitted such seizures.

[38] A House of Commons, *Report from the Select Committee on Slave Trade Treaties*, 1852–53, paras 3 and 4 (hereinafter 'House of Commons Report'), gives an official tally. In 1849–50 here were 'forty-two treaties for the Suppression of the Slave Trade existing between Great Britain and native Chiefs on the Coast of Africa'. Since May of 1850, twenty-three more treaties had been concluded with 'native Chiefs'. My research suggested at least 100 by the 1890s.

[39] 'The House of Commons report' (n 38) indicates that the trade to Brazil had largely dried up by 1852, and that the whole trade would be 'extinct' if the Cuban market could be closed off.

[40] Cited in Lloyd, *The Navy* (n 5) 117.

[41] 'House of Commons Report' (n 38) 223.

[42] Some African domestic traffic continued through the century, however. See Allen M Howard, 'Nineteenth Century Coastal Slave Trading and the British Abolition Campaign in Sierra Leone' (2006) 27 Slavery and Abolition 23.

conclusion that the naval operations associated with the treaties 'forced up the costs of slaving, harassed slavers and led to the recapture and liberation of perhaps eight percent of the victims shipped from Africa. They doubtless also prevented many more from ever embarking. But they failed to stop the traffic.'[43] Nobody guarantees full enforcement of the criminal law!

The treaties did not attempt to abolish slavery as such.[44] Much of abolitionist work entailed compromise and weighing of what could be done at a particular time. Did it just prove too difficult to navigate issues of total abolition within Africa so early? Lacking administrative capacity, or perhaps political will, Britain must have found it a bridge too far until colonial annexation made abolition possible. Indeed, even as late as 1890, the states that signed the crowning glory of slave trade suppression treaties, the multilateral General Act of Brussels[45] (the Europeans, the United States, the Ottoman Empire, Persia, Zanzibar and the Congo Free State) were promising only to counteract the slave trade in the interior of Africa and to criminalize capturing and dealing in slaves. It was not until the 1926 League of Nations Slavery Convention that there was general treaty suppression of the institution of slavery itself.[46]

[43] Miers, *Britain* (n 3) 46 (footnote omitted).

[44] One outlier instrument was a unilateral declaration by King Makasane of Mapoota (now Maputo in Mozambique) dated 23 August 1823, FO 97/432 (Foreign Office, Slave Department). I have not found a printed version and it apparently became a dead letter: 'No human creature shall ever be a slave in Mapoota.'

[45] 2 July 1890, 173 CTS 293.

[46] 82 UNTS 51. Even then, the undertaking was '[t]o bring about, progressively and as soon as possible, the complete abolition of slavery in all its forms.'

# 10

# Social Anarchy, 'Common Danger' or Political 'Terrorism'? Origins of Transnational Legal Suppression of Terrorism in the Unification of Criminal Laws, 1927–35

*Ben Saul*

## I. Introduction

While the political origins of the term 'terrorism' are normally traced to the French revolution at the end of the 18th century, it only emerged as legal concept over a century later. A League of Nations counter-terrorism convention of 1937 is usually seen as the earliest crystallization of 'terrorism' as a transnational legal category. That starting point obscures, however, legal antecedents which helped to produce legal ideas about terrorism. This chapter first briefly charts two early influences (both of which are well known in the scholarship): the depoliticization of political offences in extradition and subsequent, related efforts to counter transnational anarchist violence (as social and *apolitical* crime). The second part focuses on less well-known initiatives of private associations of international jurists in the 1920s and 30s.

The International Bureau for the Unification of Criminal Law (IBUCL) was founded in 1928 as an offshoot of the International Association of Penal Law (AIDP, *Association Internationale de Droit Pénal*), founded in 1924. The IBUCL held six international conferences for the unification of penal law from 1927 to 1935, four of which sought to define 'terrorism' for the purpose of uniform or harmonized codification in national criminal law. The conferences were the first transnational attempt to suppress 'terrorism' as a discrete legal category. They in turn were influenced by the earlier challenges of extraditing political offenders and cooperating against anarchist violence, as well as by pre-war German jurists who advocated suppressing crimes against 'common safety' and Italian criminologists concerned about 'social crime'. With the coming of World War II, the IBUCL's texts did not influence national laws, and even though they did partly align with the

Ben Saul, *Social Anarchy, 'Common Danger' or Political 'Terrorism'? Origins of Transnational Legal Suppression of Terrorism in the Unification of Criminal Laws, 1927–35* In: *Histories of Transnational Criminal Law*. Edited by: Neil Boister, Sabine Gless and Florian Jeßberger, Oxford University Press. © Ben Saul 2021. DOI: 10.1093/oso/9780192845702.003.0011

League's contemporaneous draft texts (from 1934 to 1937), the League's treaty also never entered into force because of the war. This chapter explores the conference records to illuminate the emerging notion of terrorism in the 1920s and 30s and the political and ideological attitudes it embodies.

## II. Depoliticizing Political Offences in Extradition

In the tumult of 19th-century Europe, violence was variously used by political rebels against monarchical or authoritarian regimes, ethnic separatists against imperial powers, socialist revolutionaries against capitalist regimes, and anarchists against governments of all stripes. Some acts were narrowly targeted at state agents while others deliberately or indiscriminately harmed civilians. Perpetrators sometimes escaped across national borders, triggering demands from the victim state for their surrender and producing inter-state tensions.

The possibility of extradition was left to national law, facilitated by bilateral agreements but without any common international law of extradition.[1] National legal systems developed their own criteria to decide whether a suspect should be surrendered or extradition refused. Starting with Belgium in 1833[2]—which became independent in 1830 through rebellion—it became common in western European democracies and the United States to refuse extradition for foreign 'political offences',[3] in order to safeguard political asylum and so as not to interfere in internal political struggles in other states.

What constituted a political offence (even where recognized in bilateral treaties) remained a sovereign discretion, with diverse approaches being taken particularly to 'relative', 'connected' or 'mixed' offences involving common criminal aspects (such as violence against persons or property) with political purposes.[4] Some terrorist-type conduct *might* be excluded under some legal tests, such as where violence was disproportionate, too remote, indiscriminate, barbarous and so on, but practice was highly inconsistent. The political offence exception created a risk of impunity for genuinely terrorist atrocities where extradition was refused, since the state of custody would seldom possess extraterritorial jurisdiction over foreign crimes, and there were no treaty obligations to 'extradite or prosecute' such offenders.

Some national laws responded by narrowing the political offence exception, whether by tightening the definition of 'political offences' or introducing explicit exceptions, even if acts were still politically motivated. The Belgian *attentat*

[1] Christine van den Wijngaert, *The Political Offence Exception to Extradition* (Kluwer 1980) 21 (hereafter van den Wijngaert, *The Political Offence*).

[2] Belgian Extradition Act 1833.

[3] M Cherif Bassiouni, *International Extradition and World Public Order* (Sijthoff 1974) 370–428.

[4] Van den Wijngaert, *The Political Offence* (n 1) 108–11.

('attempt') clause of 1856 rendered extraditable, as not political, certain archetypally terrorist acts—'the attempt against the person of a foreign head of state or against the person of his family members, whether the attempt be by means of murder, assassination or poisoning'[5]—regardless of their political motive.

## III. Transnational Cooperation against Anarchy

A catalyst of efforts to better systematize and harmonize *transnational* legal cooperation on political violence, that is, beyond national laws and bilateral treaties, was the growth of anarchism in Europe from the 1870s to 1914, peaking in the 1890s.[6] Anarchism imagined a non-hierarchical society without government.[7] Influential anarchists initially advocated collective revolution,[8] but the failure of communal uprisings after the Paris Commune was suppressed in 1871 (with 25,000 killed[9]) turned some anarchists towards individual action. A tactic of violence known as 'propaganda by the deed' gained currency in the 1880s and 90s.[10] It aimed to maximize publicity through the psychological effects of using new technology such as dynamite bombs,[11] although pistols and daggers remained more common. While some anarchists confined violence to state institutions (such as police and officials), others called for its indiscriminate use against the bourgeoisie.[12]

Anarchist violence reached its zenith in the 1890s and early 1900s, with seven heads of state or government assassinated in Europe, Russia and the US, hundreds of officials and civilians killed in sixteen countries and anarchist groups active in Egypt, China, Japan and India.[13] Whereas the public reacted relatively calmly to sporadic assassinations in the 1880s, the more widespread violence against the innocent in the 1890s triggered greater consternation.[14] Anarchism increasingly came to be described as 'terrorism',[15] particularly after 1904.[16]

5 ibid 14–16, 135–38.

6 Richard Bach Jensen, 'The International Campaign against Anarchist Terrorism, 1880–1930s' (2009) 21 Terrorism and Political Violence 89, 89–90 (hereafter Jensen, 'Campaign').

7 Richard Bach Jensen, *The Battle against Anarchist Terrorism: An International History, 1878–1934* (CUP 2014) 8 (hereafter Jensen, *The Battle*).

8 ibid 13–15 (including leading theorist Mikhail Bakunin).

9 Martin Miller, *The Foundations of Modern Terrorism: State, Society and the Dynamics of Political Violence* (CUP 2013) 105.

10 Jensen, *The Battle* (n 7) 16; Whitney Kassel, 'Terrorism and the International Anarchist Movement of the Late Nineteenth and Early Twentieth Centuries' (2009) 32 Studies in Conflict and Terrorism 237, 241.

11 Jensen, *The Battle* (n 7) 25.

12 ibid 18.

13 ibid 36; Jensen, 'Campaign' (n 6) 90; see also Gotelind Mueller, 'China and the "Anarchist Wave of Assassinations": Politics, Violence and Modernity in East Asia around the Turn of the Twentieth Century' in Carola Dietze and Claudia Verhoeven (eds), *The Oxford Handbook of the History of Terrorism* (OUP 2014) <www.oxfordhandbooks.com/view/10.1093/oxfordhb/9780199858569.001.0001/oxfordhb-9780199858569> (hereafter Mueller, 'China').

14 Jensen, *The Battle* (n 7) 31, 33–34.

15 ibid 7; Mueller, 'China' (n 13).

16 Jensen, *The Battle* (n 7).

Special national laws to counter anarchist violence proliferated between 1883 and 1910,[17] although anarchism was often still treated as common crimes or political offences.[18] Some laws prohibited the use of explosives, while thirteen states suppressed propaganda by the deed; and three states—Switzerland, Spain and Italy—responded in 1894 with the earliest 'terrorism' laws,[19] following the assassination of French President Carnot by an Italian. Anarchism also stimulated the modernization of national policing.[20] At the transnational level, it prompted the intensification of informal technical cooperation (as on information exchange and border controls) between police and intelligence agencies in the 1890s.[21] It also led to two more structured multilateral initiatives.

First, the assassination of the Austrian Empress in Switzerland by an Italian anarchist in late 1898[22] led to the twenty-two-state Rome Anti-Anarchist Conference in 1898. It defined an 'anarchist act' as one 'whose objective is the destruction of all social organisation by violent means'.[23] The definition followed that in a resolution of the Institute of International Law in 1892,[24] which aimed to facilitate extradition and recast anarchist violence as social not political crime.[25] The Conference did not address socialist or other political violence.[26] Transnational cooperation was politically possible (albeit still difficult) because anarchists were regarded as the enemies of all governments, not just particular political systems, and as offenders against social order, thus avoiding disagreement about the treatment of political offenders—even if the anarchist label was often conveniently applied to all who used violence.[27]

The Conference did not conclude formal agreements but its Final Protocol recommended, inter alia, criminal suppression of violent anarchist acts and preparatory conduct, and the elimination of the political offence exception in extradition for anarchist violence and *attentat* generally.[28] It also recommended administrative measures of surveillance, the creation of central agencies and information

[17] ibid 92; Jensen, 'Campaign' (n 6) 91–92.

[18] Tina Hannappel, 'Extradition and Expulsion as Instruments of Transnational Security Regimes against Anarchism in the Late Nineteenth Century' in Karl Härter, Tina Hannappel and Conrad Tyrichter (eds), *The Transnationalisation of Criminal Law in the Nineteenth and Twentieth Century: Political Crime, Police Cooperation, Security Regimes and Normative Orders* (Klostermann 2019) 65, 70 (hereafter Härter and others, *Transnationalisation*).

[19] Jensen, *The Battle* (n 7) 92.

[20] ibid 5.

[21] ibid 93–102.

[22] Jensen, 'Campaign' (n 6) 94.

[23] Jensen, *The Battle* (n 7) 157, 366.

[24] Institute of International Law, 'Resolution Revising arts 13 and 14 of the Resolution of Oxford (Extradition)' (Geneva 8 September 1892) art 4.

[25] Paul Knepper, *International Crime in the 20th Century: The League of Nations Era, 1919–1939* (Palgrave Macmillan 2011) 145.

[26] Jensen, *The Battle* (n 7) 179.

[27] ibid 7.

[28] Final Act of the Anti-Anarchist Conference of Rome 1898, part V(A).

exchange.[29] Secret side-meetings of police further agreed on expulsions, police cooperation and scientific methods (*portrait parlé*) to identify criminals.[30] The Conference stimulated few new laws, but influenced depoliticization in extradition, practice on expulsions, the use of *portrait parlé* and police cooperation.[31]

Secondly, a more formal (and secret) arrangement was the binding St Petersburg Anti-Anarchist Protocol of 1904, prompted by the assassinations of the Italian King, Umberto I, in 1900 and US President William McKinley in 1901. The Protocol avoided defining anarchism or addressing national law or extradition and instead focused on administrative improvements, such as establishing central police bureaus to monitor anarchists and exchange information with other states,[32] and regulating expulsions.[33] Nine European states (mainly from the reactionary Eastern empires) were original signatories and four other states later joined,[34] but most Western European states and the US did not participate. In practice the Protocol improved police cooperation, information exchange and the use of central agencies.[35] However, rising political tensions, culminating in World War I, spelled the end of the Protocol.

## IV. Unification of Criminal Laws in the 1920 and 30s

After World War I, elements of the preceding developments—the political offence exception in extradition, and anti-anarchist cooperation—were fused with a new emphasis on crimes constituting a 'common danger' and the related notion of 'terrorism'. As anarchist violence subsided after World War I, concern shifted to other kinds of intensifying political violence, including ultra-nationalist, communist and separatist attacks, some arising from post-war settlements on territorial and minority issues.[36] The League was often incapable of dealing with these threats, or threats from state sponsorship of transnational violence and tensions arising from the grant of asylum.[37]

Police cooperation continued to solidify, for example, through the creation of the International Criminal Police Commission in 1923 in Vienna (the forerunner of today's Interpol). It was, however, private associations of civil law jurists in the

[29] ibid part III.
[30] Jensen, *The Battle* (n 7) 163–67.
[31] ibid 168–74.
[32] St Petersburg Protocol 1904, parts II–VI.
[33] ibid part I.
[34] The original signatories were Russia, Romania, Serbia, Bulgaria, Ottoman Turkey, Austria-Hungary, Germany, Denmark, and Sweden-Norway; Spain, Portugal, Switzerland and Luxembourg later endorsed it in various forms.
[35] Jensen, 'Campaign' (n 6) 99; Jensen, *The Battle* (n 7) 296.
[36] Mark Lewis, *The Birth of the New Justice: The Internationalization of Crime and Punishment, 1919–1950* (OUP 2014) 123, 126 (hereafter Lewis, *Birth*).
[37] ibid 126–27.

1920s and 30s which took the lead in conceptualizing new categories of transnational crime, and promoted codification through treaty-making and uniform national legislation, which in turn informed belated League efforts to draft a counter-terrorism convention from 1934 to 1937.[38]

## 1. International Criminal Justice and Terrorism

There were two broad strands to these post-war efforts. One strand, concerned at impunity for crimes committed during the war,[39] pursued the codification of international criminal law, with an emphasis on war crimes, crimes against humanity and aggression. These included initiatives of the International Law Association (1922–26)[40] and the French-dominated AIDP. In preparing a code of crimes under international law, the AIDP looked beyond core crimes under international law to also consider peacetime crimes 'liable to disrupt peaceful relations between states'.[41] These included piracy, drug or sex trafficking, counterfeiting, cross-border theft, sabotaging undersea telegraph cables or railways, distribution of obscene publications and crimes that created 'a common danger' (such as political assassinations and bombings).[42]

The AIDP never finalized its code, although one member, the Romanian jurist Vespasian Pella, issued his own draft in 1935, which included terrorist-type offences such as attacks on foreign officials and international transport, and the use of chemical, incendiary or biological weapons.[43] The AIDP's interest in transnational crime was a pragmatic recognition that states would be reluctant to punish state officials for crimes under international law.[44] It was also influenced by concerns to prevent the misuse of modern global technologies (such as communications and transport) by criminals.

Theoretically the AIDP was influenced by Italian criminological 'social defence' or 'social crime' theories.[45] Such theories circulated in Europe from the 1860s to the mid-1930s to categorize threats (particularly external ones) to society, in contrast to (political) crimes against a particular state and its political order (and

[38] See Ben Saul, 'The Legal Response of the League of Nations to Terrorism' (2006) 4 Journal of International Criminal Justice 78.

[39] Lewis, *Birth* (n 36) 78.

[40] ibid 96–97.

[41] ibid 110; Mark Lewis, 'The History of the International Association of Penal Law, 1924–1950: Liberal, Conservative, or Neither?' in Morten Bergsmo, Cheah Wui Ling, Song Tianying and Yi Ping (eds), *Historical Origins of International Criminal Law: Volume 4* (Torkel Opsahl Academic EPublisher 2015) 610, 612–18.

[42] Lewis, *Birth* (n 36) 101, 108–10.

[43] Vespasian Pella, 'Plan d'un code repressif mondial' (1935) 12 RiDP 348.

[44] Lewis, *Birth* (n 36) 79.

[45] ibid 113–14, 122, 126. See eg Adolphe Prins, *La défense sociale et les transformations du droit pénal* (Misch et Thron 1910).

which may justify refusal of extradition) or (common) crimes against individuals.[46] For French jurists it primarily meant violent anarchist threats, whereas for Italian and Spanish jurists it extended to revolutionary workers' strikes.[47] Such theories were also advocated by the German jurist Johann Bluntschli at the Institute of International Law and influenced its 1892 resolution on depoliticizing anarchist crimes.

The related notion of 'crimes constituting a common danger'—potentially including terrorism—was developed by jurists in the 1920s out of a pre-war concept of the German-based International Union of Criminal Law (IKV, *Internationale Kriminalistische Vereinigung*), established in 1888. The conservative IKV contemplated strong state action to prevent crime by those who endangered 'common safety', such as 'habitual criminals', vagrants and 'inebriates'.[48] One of the AIDP's influential members, Pella, was also interested in transnational suppression of group crime,[49] whether social or political or perpetrated by gangs, socialist revolutionaries or terrorists.

Pella separately suggested in 1926 that an international criminal court should deal with terrorists.[50] Romania duly proposed the idea at the League of Nations that year, to punish terrorism as 'a means of imposing certain social doctrines by force or intimidation'.[51] Terrorism was thus conceived of as 'not anti-governmental [that is, political], but rather anti-social in character, and . . . it does not aim at subverting the political order of any specific country but the public law and order of all civilized States'.[52] There was little support for the Romanian proposals in the League, including other proposals to eliminate asylum in extradition for political assassination and terrorism.[53]

## 2. Unification of National Criminal Laws and Terrorism

As proposals for international criminal justice floundered at the League, the AIDP pivoted towards promoting the 'unification' of national criminal laws,[54] from

[46] Lewis, *Birth* (n 36) 603, 609, 611; Richard Bach Jensen, 'The Rise and Fall of the "Social Crime" in Legal Theory and International Law: The Failure to Create a New Normative Order to Regularize Terrorism, 1880–1930s' in Härter and others, *Transnationalisation* (n 18) 197, 197–99.

[47] See eg Juan Cristóbal Marinello Bonnefoy, 'Los delitos sociales en la España de la Restauración (1874–1931)' (2016) 86 Anuario de historia del derecho español 521.

[48] Lewis, *Birth* (n 36) 23–24.

[49] ibid 103.

[50] AIDP, *Premier Congrès International de Droit Pénal, Bruxelles (26–29 juillet 1926): Actes du Congrès* (Librarie des Juris–Classeurs–Éditions Godde 1927) 562 (hereafter AIDP, *Premier Congrès*).

[51] League of Nations, Committee of Experts for the Progressive Codification of International Law (CIRT), 'Report to the Council, 3rd session' (20 April 1927) LoN Doc C.196.M.70.1927.V annex II, 196, 221.

[52] ibid 229.

[53] Lewis, *Birth* (n 36) 101, 124.

[54] ibid 113.

the late 1920s to the mid-1930s, at a time when states were revising their penal codes. In 1928, the AIDP established the IBUCL to influence debate in the League. The IBUCL grew beyond European jurists to include jurists from the Middle East, South America and Soviet Union, and became part of the League in 1936. Unification was, however, divisive; jurists from authoritarian states hoped it would promote suppression of political crime against all governments, whereas other states were concerned about intrusion on their legal sovereignty or safeguarding political liberties.[55]

The concept of terrorism emerged at four International Conferences for the Unification of Criminal Law between 1927 and 1935, in which its meaning fluctuated. At the first conference in Warsaw in 1927, offences against the law of nations (*delicta juris gentium*) were proposed to include, inter alia, 'intentional use of any means capable of producing a common danger', without definition (including whether it covered terrorism). A report of an AIDP sub-commission proposed that 'anarchist offences', being 'social offences' or 'crimes against human rights' should be treated as extraditable common crimes not political offences,[56] following the 1892 Institute resolution. The plenary did not, however, adopt the proposal.

Another offence supported at the Conference, counterfeiting, was described by Pella as a new kind of 'terrorism'—potentially more harmful than assassination or bombing—which imposes social doctrines by intimidation or pursues collective political or chauvinist vengeance,[57] and undermines confidence in and security of the international exchange of money.[58] The work of the Conference contributed to the drafting[59] of the 1929 Counterfeiting Convention, an initiative of France in response to the counterfeiting of its currency in Hungary in 1926, as part of agitation to revise the post-war territorial settlement in the Treaty of Trianon.[60]

At the third Conference in Brussels in 1930,[61] the discussion of 'means capable of producing a common danger' was fused with the first explicit discussion of 'terrorism'.[62] A Rapporteur, Belgian law professor Niko Gunzburg, objected that the term 'terrorism' 'tragically colours the subject', since (unlike piracy or drug trafficking) it involves 'episodes of political, economic and social struggles, and, indeed, of the great revolutions [such as legitimate workers' struggles] which

[55] ibid 116–17.

[56] Michel Potulicki (ed), *Actes de la Conférence Internationale d'Unification du Droit Pénal (Varsovie, 1–5 Novembre 1927)* (Recueil Sirey 1929) part V, annex I, 149–50.

[57] Vespasian Pella, *La Coopération des États dans la lutte contre le faux monnayage: Rapport et projet de convention présentés à la Société des nations* (Pedone 1928).

[58] Lewis, *Birth* (n 36) 119.

[59] Ernestine Fitzmaurice, 'Convention for the Suppression of Counterfeiting Currency: An Analysis' (1932) 26 AJIL 533, 536.

[60] Lewis, *Birth* (n 36) 117.

[61] Simon Sasserath (ed), *IIIe conférence Internationale pour l'unification du droit penal, Bruxelles, 26–30 juin 1930: Actes de la conference* (Office de Publicité 1931) (hereafter Sasserath, *IIIe conférence*).

[62] ibid 17; Raphael Lemkin, 'Terrorisme', in *V Conferencia Internacional para La Unificación del Derecho Penal, Madrid, Octubre 1933* (Imprenta de Galo Sáez 1933) 3.

constitute the origin of new states'.[63] He cautioned against deploying terrorism as 'a governmental weapon against the worst enemies of a particular state' when such offenders are limited to defending political or economic ideals.

While Gunzburg accepted that national law may punish citizens who undermine the state's security, he argued that such crimes are not offences against the law of nations, unless an act is directed not against a specific state but against 'humanity' and the foundations of any social organization (invoking the Institute resolution). His report limited 'common danger' offences to acts endangering people or property through arson, explosion, flood or toxins, or the interruption of communications, transport, utilities or infrastructure. There was no reference to political motives. His offences were based on Bulgarian and Italian legislation, draft Czech legislation and the older penal codes of France and Belgium.

Initially Gunzburg's approach was supported, but jurists from Italy, Yugoslavia and Poland insisted on including terrorism as crimes committed for *political* or social ideas.[64] A compromise was reached whereby one offence would exclusively deal with common danger, while a new offence would address 'terrorism' *through* means capable of producing a common danger *and* where done 'in order to manifest or realize political or social ideas'.[65] The defining characteristics of terrorism were thus harm to people or property, for a political or social purpose, using methods capable of endangering the public.

At the fourth Conference in Paris in 1931,[66] there was much debate about terrorism, following two reports by Jean Radulesco, a professor at the University of Cernautzi (then part of Romania, now Ukraine) and the Polish jurist Raphael Lemkin. There were three key developments at Paris. First, terrorism was decoupled from means producing a common danger and was treated as an autonomous offence, since it was a 'scourge that threatens the whole of humanity'.[67] The terrorist offence was defined as follows:

> Whoever, for the purpose of terrorizing the population, uses against persons or property bombs, mines, incendiary or explosive devices or products, fire arms or other deadly or deleterious devices, or who provokes or attempts to provoke, spreads or attempts to spread an epidemy, a contagious disease or other disaster, or who interrupts or attempts to interrupt a public service or public utility will be punished.[68]

[63] Niko Gunzburg, 'Acts of Terrorism' in Sasserath, *IIIe conférence* (n 61) 43–48.

[64] AIDP, *Premier Congrès* (n 50) 114–16.

[65] Quoted in Raphael Lemkin, 'Terrorisme: Emploi intentionnel de moyens capables de faire courir un danger commun' in Henri Donnedieu De Vabres (ed), *IVe Conférence internationale pour l'unification du droit pénal, Paris, 27–30 décembre 1931: actes de la Conférence* (Librairie du Recueil Sirey 1933) 9 (hereafter Lemkin, 'Terrorisme' and De Vabres, *IVe Conférence*).

[66] De Vabres, *IVe Conférence* (n 65) generally.

[67] ibid 133, 147.

[68] ibid 480.

Despite lack of reference to means producing a common danger (against the recommendation of Radulesco), the definition implicitly incorporates many of the means mentioned at Brussels.

Secondly, a special intent element was added, namely 'for the purpose of terrorizing the population', based on articles 420–21 of the Italian Penal Code (*publico timore*—terrorizing a population)[69] and supported by Lemkin's report.[70] Thirdly, the Conference did not embrace the recommendations of both Radulesco and Lemkin to define terrorism by its distinctive purpose of imposing a *political* or *social* policy through violence or intimidation[71] (so as to capture, for instance, both communism and anarchism[72]). The Conference thought that such an element would be under-inclusive, as in the case of profit-driven gangsters who terrorize;[73] be too vague; or incriminate political offenders.[74] Also rejected was Radulesco's view that counterfeiting is terrorism,[75] as not being sufficiently dangerous.[76]

Ongoing disagreement in the Conference plenary led to the establishment of a commission to consider terrorism ahead of the fifth conference. The Madrid Conference in 1933 then focused on terrorism, in part because some thought common danger offences should not be crimes under international law.[77] Two rapporteurs presented reports: the president of the AIDP, French law professor Jean-André Roux, and Lemkin again. There were two key developments at Madrid. First, unlike at Paris, terrorism was redefined by reference to its *social* (but not political) purpose, while retaining the special intent to terrorize (from Paris). The Conference thereby assimilated terrorism to anarchy[78] and rejected the preference of both Lemkin and Roux to focus instead on the intent to terrorize. Addressing *political* terrorism was seen as too controversial because of disagreements over the political offence exception,[79] whereas social terrorism was agreed to be a common crime. Some delegates, however, criticized the exclusion of political terrorism.[80]

Secondly, the definition omitted the enumeration of the physical means in the Paris definition (such as by explosives, disease and the like) and simply referred to commission by 'any means', endorsing Roux's suggestion[81] and rejecting Lemkin's

69 ibid 133, 156, 253, 255, 258.
70 ibid 64.
71 ibid 52, 57.
72 Radulesco, 'Terrorisme' in De Vabres, *IVe Conférence* (n 65) 48, 49.
73 De Vabres, *IVe Conférence* (n 65) 133, 253, 255.
74 ibid 253, 255.
75 ibid 253, 255.
76 ibid 253, 254.
77 Luis Jimenez de Asua and Vespasien Pella (eds), *Ve Conférence International Pour L'Unification du Droit Penal, Madrid, 14–20 Octobre 1933: Actes de la Conference* (Pedone 1935) 241, 243 (hereafter de Jimenez de Asua and Pella, *Ve Conférence*).
78 ibid 137, 146, 481.
79 ibid 245.
80 ibid 137, 143, 248, 249.
81 Henri Roux, 'Terrorisme' in Jimenez de Asua and Pella, *Ve Conference* (n 77) 42, 45.

articulation of means in an even more detailed manner than at Paris (including 'the vile or savage destruction of arts and cultural works ... (vandalism)' and 'barbarous actions, including massacres, pogroms, collective cruelties against women and children'[82]). The Madrid definition thus read: 'Whoever, with a view to destroying any [all] social organization, employs any means to terrorize the population, will be punished.'[83] Lemkin also unsuccessfully sought to recast terrorism as 'crimes against human rights' (*crimina juris gentium*), borrowing the latter concept from French professor Henri Donnedieu de Vabres.[84]

The sixth (and last) conference at Copenhagen in 1935 considered four terrorism reports by Gunzburg, Lemkin, Thomas Givanovitch (a professor at the University of Belgrade) and Quintiliano Saldaña (a professor at Madrid and social crime theorist).[85] The Conference met after the League had commenced (but not completed) drafting a terrorism treaty in 1934 following the assassination of the Yugoslav King Alexander I in France, and had the benefit of the League's texts before it.[86] Seven members of the AIDP or IBUCL represented their states on the League's drafting Committee for the International Repression of Terrorism (CIRT), including the CIRT's chair (the Belgian lawyer and AIDP president, Henri Carton de Wiart) and one of its rapporteurs (Pella).[87] The Conference nonetheless decided not to refocus on the League's goal of a convention but to continue its work on model national legislation.[88]

The Conference thus proposed model laws for the suppression of 'offences creating a public danger or a state of terror'.[89] Article 1 proposed the offence of 'intentional acts directed against the life, body, health, or liberty' of specified internationally protected persons (largely reflecting the League's draft text prepared by France), where the perpetrator has 'created a common [public] danger or state of terror of a nature to cause a change in or impediment to the operation of the public authorities or to disturb international relations'. Article 2 then details the means which create a common danger or provoke terror, involving serious harms to transport, communication and public services, utilities or buildings; endangering life by poison or disease; public use of explosives; or other act imperilling life and creating a public danger.

[82] Lemkin, 'Terrorisme' (n 65) 12–17.
[83] Jimenez de Asua and Pella, *Ve Conference* (n 77) 335.
[84] Lemkin, 'Terrorisme' (n 65) 5–6, 12–17.
[85] CB Ingwersen and others (eds), *VIe Conférence internationale pour l'unification du droit pénal: actes de la Conférence: Copenhague, 31 août–3 septembre 1935* (Pedone 1938) (hereafter Ingwersen, *VIe Conférence*).
[86] ibid 180, 182.
[87] The others were Givanovitch, Simon Sasserath (a Belgian criminal lawyer), Ugo Aloisi (an Italian judge), Lucien Bekerman (a Polish jurist) and Ernst Delaquis (a Swiss professor).
[88] Ingwersen, *VIe Conférence* (n 85) 369, 371–78.
[89] League (CIRT), 'Texts adopted by the Sixth International Conference for the Unification of Criminal Law (Copenhagen, 31 August–3 September 1935)' (7 January 1936) LoN Doc CRT.17.

The Copenhagen Conference thus defined two alternative crimes (public danger or terrorism, as suggested by Gunzburg) based on shared underlying conduct (harm to persons, through specified means), thus satisfying those who wished to criminalize both harms as well as those who wished to maintain a distinction between them (since not all common dangers amounted to terrorism, and vice versa). Maintaining separate offences was recommended at Paris and Madrid; whereas the League Convention omitted common danger altogether. At the same time, the Copenhagen offences replicated the enumerated means of producing a common danger in its underlying physical elements (as had been done implicitly at Paris, and explicitly at Brussels). The specification of means also departed from the open-ended approach at Madrid.

Finally, the Copenhagen definition retained a specific intent to provoke a state of terror (identical to the contemporaneous League draft, and similar to the Paris and Madrid formulas of terrorizing the population), while abandoning any requirement of a social (anarchist) purpose (from Madrid) or social or political purpose (from Brussels, and also advocated in Givenovitch's report at Copenhagen). The intent to provoke a state of terror was, however, augmented by a further requirement that it be 'of a nature to cause a change in or impediment to the operation of the public authorities or to disturb international relations'. That element narrows terrorism to conduct which not only terrorizes but thereby coercively affects governments (even if only domestically) or international relations. A more specific reference to disturbing the territorial integrity of the state, suggested by Gunzburg, was not included; nor was Lemkin's proposal to create separate offences for domestic and international terrorism.

The Copenhagen Draft (like the League Convention which followed) did not remove the political offence exception to extradition. However, a recommendation appended to it suggested an 'extradite or prosecute' formula: where extradition is refused, the offender should be referred to an international criminal jurisdiction (court), unless the requested state prefers to judge him or her in its own courts.[90] The principle of 'extradite or prosecute' had first found its way into treaty law a few years earlier in the 1929 Counterfeiting Convention[91] (albeit only if an extradition request has been received and refused).

## V. Conclusion

A spectrum of violent challenges to state or imperial authority in Europe from the mid-19th to the early 20th centuries—anarchist, socialist, separatist and democratic—stimulated numerous efforts to improve transnational criminal

[90] Ingwersen, *VIe Conférence* (n 85) 369, 421.
[91] Art 9.

and police cooperation. Initially, national laws and bilateral agreements narrowed the political offence exception to extradition, so as to exclude assassinations of high officials, but common agreement on further narrowing the exception proved more difficult. Informal technical cooperation between police developed, but was still impeded by political differences and a lack of formal legal arrangements. Legislative and administrative measures to suppress anarchism specifically stemmed from the Rome Anti-Anarchist Conference 1898 and the St Petersburg Anti-Anarchist Protocol 1904, but participation and implementation were limited, particularly due to political differences.

By the 1920s, civil law jurists unofficially sought to unify or harmonize criminal laws but disagreement persisted over the conceptualization of political violence, whether as terrorism, common danger or (social) anarchism, as well as how to treat such violence in extradition. While private unification efforts were somewhat marginal because they largely occurred outside the League, their proponents were well connected to states and some of them (and their ideas) played key roles in the League's drafting of the first international counter-terrorism treaty from 1934 to 1937, when terrorism became viewed as a higher order international security problem and as ripe for criminalization and formal cooperation.

# 11

# The History of the Global Anti-Human Trafficking Agenda, with a Focus on Prostitution and Sexual Exploitation

*Heli Askola*

## I. Introduction

The genesis of the Protocol to Prevent, Suppress and Punish Trafficking in Persons, Especially Women and Children (2000 Human Trafficking Protocol), supplementing the UN Convention against Transnational Organized Crime (UNTOC), is well known.[1] It is also widely recognized that despite the success of the Protocol in garnering state support and influencing policy responses to trafficking in human beings, its definition of trafficking is a compromise that is deliberately vague, masking differences of opinion over issues such as consent, the meaning of exploitation and the role of cross-border activity for establishing criminal liability.[2] In relation to prostitution and sexual exploitation, these issues are sources of disagreement both within and between groups of feminists, civil society organizations and states.

This chapter shows that lack of clarity and consensus are not new issues for anti-trafficking law. It traces the early history of the global anti-trafficking movement, which focused on the issue of prostitution (now discussed under the label 'sexual exploitation'). The initial emphasis placed on prostitution by the campaigns against the 'white slave trade' or 'traffic' in women and girls is reasonably familiar to many, but the standard legal outline that frames international law as arising as a response to a moral panic, or a crusade against 'vice', is simplistic. It detaches the development of the law from its historical context, erasing both the complex disagreements between the actors involved in the early campaigns (including civil society associations) and the shifts that occurred in the social understanding of prostitution in the first half of the 20th century.

[1] Anne Gallagher 'Human Rights and the New UN Protocols on Trafficking and Migrant Smuggling: a Preliminary Analysis' (2001) 23(4) Hum Rights Q 975.

[2] Ibid. See also Prabha Kotiswaran (ed), *Revisiting the Law and Governance of Trafficking, Forced Labor and Modern Slavery* (CUP 2017).

Heli Askola, *The History of the Global Anti-Human Trafficking Agenda, with a Focus on Prostitution and Sexual Exploitation*
In: *Histories of Transnational Criminal Law.* Edited by: Neil Boister, Sabine Gless and Florian Jeßberger, Oxford University Press. © Heli Askola 2021. DOI: 10.1093/oso/9780192845702.003.0012

This chapter argues instead that the history of anti-trafficking in this early period is full of contestations between groups of activists, civil society associations (as precursors to NGOs) and states over sexuality, morality, work and migration, and that these still-relevant disagreements caution against overstating the development of the law in linear terms. Using recent literature on the history of the early debates on trafficking, the chapter traces the evolving positions of campaigners and states, highlighting two phases in the adoption of the first international instruments. Due to space limitations, the focus is on European states that dominated the developments in this period.[3]

## II. The Usual Overview

The standard legal narrative of anti-trafficking history is brief, suggesting a more or less coherent path from the identification (or social construction) of a problem to legal solutions, which are then refined over time. It highlights the problem as having its roots in 19th-century problematization of 'white slavery' or 'export of prostitutes'[4] or, more neutrally, the recruitment of young European (ie white) women for prostitution abroad, using force or deceit.[5] The term 'moral panic' is often used in this context.[6] It is argued that moral crusaders used the alleged luring of young women for 'immoral purposes' to build a campaign using the sensationalist term 'white slavery', drawing from 'the sensationalized image of young and innocent white women being coerced into prostitution in foreign lands'.[7] Growing public concern over this phenomenon then prompted the subsequent adoption of international law to address this concern.[8] These resulting legal instruments are usually summarized as a chronology.[9] The first, the 1904 White Slave Agreement targeted 'procuring of women and girls for immoral purposes abroad' (article 1), but had a limited scope, involving measures such as collection of information

[3] The racial/colonial aspects of the early anti-trafficking law are discussed, eg by Philippa Levine, 'The White Slave Trade and the British Empire' in Louis A Knafla (ed), *Crime, Gender and Sexuality in Criminal Prosecutions* (Greenwood 2002) 133 (hereafter Levine, 'The White Slave Trade'); Stephen Legg, 'Stimulation, Segregation and Scandal: Geographies of Prostitution Regulation in British India, between Registration (1888) and Suppression (1923)' (2012) 46(6) Modern Asian Studies 1459.

[4] Laura Reanda, 'Prostitution as a Human Rights Question: Problems and Prospects of United Nations Action' (1991) 13 Hum Rights Q 202, 207 (hereafter Reanda, 'Human Rights Question').

[5] Anne Gallagher, *The International Law of Human Trafficking* (CUP 2010) 55 (hereafter Gallagher, *Human Trafficking*); Levine, 'The White Slave Trade' (n 3) 134.

[6] Gallagher, *Human Trafficking* (n 5) 56.

[7] ibid 55; also Nora Demleitner 'Forced Prostitution: Naming an International Offense' (1994) 18 Fordham Intl Law J 163, 166 (hereafter Demleitner 'Forced Prostitution').

[8] Gallagher, *Human Trafficking* (n 5) 57–58. See also Janie Chuang, 'Redirecting the Debate over Trafficking in Women: Definitions, Paradigms, and Contexts' (1998) 11 Harv Hum Rights J 65, 74 (hereafter Chuang, 'Redirecting the Debate').

[9] Gallagher, *Human Trafficking* (n 5) 57–58; Reanda, 'Human Rights Question' (n 4) 207–09; Demleitner 'Forced Prostitution' (n 7) 167–72; Chuang, 'Redirecting the Debate' (n 8) 74–75.

and supervision of train stations. However, the subsequent 1910 White Slave Convention required states to criminalize the procurement of minors regardless of consent and procurement of adults by violence or deceit (articles 1–2). The 1921 Convention for the Suppression of the Traffic in Women and Children abandoned the 'white slavery' rhetoric and expanded the scope of criminalization to children of either sex (article 2), and the 1933 International Convention on the Suppression of the Traffic in Women eliminated age requirements and included consensual movement across borders under the crime of international trafficking (article 1). These legal developments are framed as culminating in the adoption of the 1949 Convention for the Suppression of the Traffic in Persons, which penalizes procurement and exploitation of prostitution, irrespective of both consent and the crossing of international borders.

This sparse legal summary suggests a rather linear expansion of the scope of international law: in response to a (possibly overblown) concern ('moral panic') linked to the transnationalization of prostitution, states initially targeted non-consensual movement across international borders, but later come to reach a broader agreement on recruitment for and exploitation of prostitution as requiring suppression, regardless of the role of consent or border-crossing. However, scratch the surface and complexities emerge. While the 1949 Convention for the Suppression of the Traffic in Persons is often framed as significant because of its reach into the domestic sphere,[10] it is also considered a failure because this move arguably lost it the support of many states.[11] Regarding non-state actors, it is interesting that the early legal trajectory can be simultaneously celebrated as resulting in a set of international agreements adopted 'under feminist impetus',[12] yet its products dismissed as laws that 'neither ended prostitution nor improved prostitutes' working conditions', leading to the conclusion that 'increased state power to repress prostitution ends up being used against prostitutes themselves'.[13] These differing representations suggest that much depends on one's interpretation of the historical context.

The historical debates and developments in relation to dealing with prostitution have been elaborated by scholars who note, for instance, that the early 19th-century campaigns brought together 'vigilance societies, church groups, Jewish and Catholic protection societies, moral purity crusaders, feminists and women's groups'.[14] They highlight the influential role of individuals, such as journalist WT

[10] Reanda, 'Human Rights Question' (n 4) 209; Demleitner 'Forced Prostitution' (n 7) 172; Chuang, 'Redirecting the Debate' (n 8) 75.

[11] Gallagher, *Human Trafficking* (n 5) 61–63.

[12] Barbara Sullivan, 'Trafficking in Women' (2003) 5(1) International Feminist Journal of Politics 67, 68.

[13] Jo Doezema, 'Who Gets to Choose? Coercion, Consent, and the UN Trafficking Protocol' (2002) 10(1) Gender & Development 20, 24.

[14] Paul Knepper, *The Invention of International Crime: A Global Issue in the Making, 1881–1914* (Macmillan 2010) 98 (hereafter Knepper, *Invention of International Crime*).

Stead with his investigation 'The Maiden Tribute of Modern Babylon' and William Alexander Coote, the secretary of the National Vigilance Association (NVA).[15] Feminists are familiar with the role of women's rights campaigners, especially Josephine Butler, famous for her work against the Contagious Diseases Acts and state policies of regulationism (spread across Europe by French armies in an attempt to control venereal disease).[16] These accounts often mention legal developments, but their analysis does not often focus on the specifics of the subsequently adopted international law.[17]

This chapter contextualizes the simple legal narrative with the help of historical scholarship. Though the 'moral panic' served to prompt action, the campaigns on prostitution and trafficking were characterized by competing positions and priorities put forward by rival civil society organizations seeking to convince states to adopt their preferred policies. Rather than involving united efforts, the picture entails discord and dissenting voices. Nor is the translation of these various demands into law smooth, as states seek to reconcile their ideological and practical interests as well as domestic and international priorities. While the resulting law generally has an expanding scope (with relaxed age limits and less focus on consent/international movement), these developments are always contested but also highly contingent on the changing realities and attitudes in relation to prostitution/sex work, morality, women's status and international migration. The evolution of the law is thus neither smooth nor uncontested.

## III. Lead-Up to the Adoption of the First International Instruments

It is, of course, broadly speaking, true that the growing alarm over the international movement of women for prostitution, sparked in the late 19th century, led to the adoption of the 1904 White Slave Agreement and the 1910 White Slave Convention.[18] In fact, both of these instruments were negotiated in substance at the 1902 International Conference on the White Slave Traffic, with the 1904 White Slave Agreement dealing with mostly administrative matters and 1910 White Slave Convention with the more complex and contested legislative aspects.[19] Despite the

[15] ibid; Marlou Schrover, 'History of Slavery, Human Smuggling and Trafficking 1860–2010' in Gerben Bruinsma (ed), *Histories of Transnational Crime* (Springer 2015) (hereafter Schrover, 'History of Slavery').

[16] Knepper, *Invention of International Crime* (n 14) 100; Anne Summers, 'Which Women? What Europe? Josephine Butler and the International Abolitionist Federation' (2006) 62 History Workshop Journal 214 (hereafter Summers, 'Which Women?').

[17] See eg Knepper, *Invention of International Crime* (n 14); Schrover, 'History of Slavery' (n 15).

[18] Knepper, *Invention of International Crime* (n 14) ch 4.

[19] Jean Allain, 'White Slave Traffic in International Law' (2017) 1 Journal of Trafficking and Human Exploitation 1 (hereafter Allain, 'White Slave Traffic').

'slavery' rhetoric employed in the 19th century, neither document uses the term 'white slave traffic' except in the title.[20] The 1904 White Slave Agreement includes measures against 'procuring' of women or girls for prostitution 'abroad' (article 1) while the 1910 White Slave Convention seeks to criminalize the actions of those who 'procured, enticed, or led away' underage girls or women (the latter through fraud or violence, threats, abuse of authority) even where the various actions constituting the offence have taken place in different countries (articles 1–2).[21] Both refrained from any discussion of the treatment of prostitution within a state's borders, suggesting a concern over coercive and/or deceptive cross-border movement.

This limited scope might be taken to imply that the initial motivations of anti-trafficking actors were specifically limited to women's (coerced) movement across borders and that domestic or consensual prostitution was not part of the picture. In fact, as those familiar with Josephine Butler's involvement know, the push to tackle trafficking in the international arena was in part an offshoot of the various domestic struggles over sexual morality and, specifically, the British controversies over the state control of prostitution referred to as regulationism.[22] Regulationism operated in most European countries and was based on prostitution being seen as a necessary outlet for male sexuality (especially for military troops), yet also in need of control in the form of brothels, the registration of prostitutes, medical check-ups and police checks.[23] Without getting into whether the 'panic' was overblown, a careful analysis of the campaigns against 'white slavery' reveals important divisions on sexual morality, masculinity/femininity and views on the state's role in exercising control over women in prostitution that challenge any easy characterizations of the 'campaign' as a single movement with uniform aims.[24]

This lack of a unified agenda can be illustrated by comparing the views of the two main civil society coalitions involved in the early campaigns. The above-mentioned (and perhaps most well-known) NVA was an organization formed by British religious purity reformers in 1886—it later became the International Bureau for the Suppression of the White Slave Traffic (the Bureau). Its aim was to 'eradicate all forms of vice', and it worked in cooperation with national police and officials.[25]

[20] ibid 7–8.

[21] See further Nicole J Siller, 'Human Trafficking in International Law before the Palermo Protocol (2017) 64 NILR 407 (hereafter Siller, 'Human Trafficking').

[22] Summers, 'Which Women? (n 16).

[23] On systems of prostitution and the development of systems of traffic see Stephanie A Limoncelli, *The Politics of Trafficking: the First International Movement to Combat the Sexual Exploitation of Women* (Stanford UP 2010) ch 2 (hereafter Limoncelli, *Politics of Trafficking*); see also Summers, 'Which Women?' (n 16).

[24] Limoncelli, *Politics of Trafficking* (n 23) 7. Also Stephanie A Limoncelli 'International Voluntary Associations, Local Social Movements and State Paths to the Abolition of Regulated Prostitution in Europe, 1875–1950' (2006) 21(1) International Sociology 31 (hereafter Limoncelli, 'International Voluntary Associations').

[25] Laura Lammasniemi, 'International Legislation on White Slavery and Anti-trafficking in the Early 20th Century' in Jackie Jones and John Winterdyk (eds), *The Palgrave International Handbook of Human Trafficking, Volume 1* (Palgrave Macmillan 2019) 69 (hereafter Lammasniemi, 'International Legislation').

The NVA/Bureau was essentially a conservative force that pressed the claims of 'social purity' and demanded the repression of all manifestations of illicit or illegal sexuality, advocating for strong state action to control all forms of immorality.[26] As the NVA/Bureau worked closely with states to uphold the moral order, it was pragmatic about the existing systems to control and suppress prostitution, and did not denounce state-regulated prostitution.[27] Once concerned with female emigration, the NVA/Bureau made a distinction between the innocent ('slaves') and the not-innocent (ie prostitutes) and focused in the international arena on increasing state control of the international movement of 'female foreigners', following a gendered and class-based logic.[28]

In contrast, activists like Butler had started campaigning earlier. To begin with they were concerned with regulationism, which involved states exercising control over women working in prostitution.[29] Butler's campaigns to abolish regulationism was initially successful in Britain (the Contagious Diseases Acts were suspended in 1883 and repealed in 1886) and further international campaigns to create change across Europe took place under the International Abolitionist Federation (IAF).[30] Despite their religious inspiration, rather than being focused on (im)morality as such, Butlerites were concerned with the condition of working-class women working as prostitutes, and opposed them being placed on a police register, subjected to regular and invasive checks (for signs of venereal disease) and confined to licensed brothels.[31] The stated aim of abolitionists was to repeal regulationism and abolish the sexual double standards that sought to control prostitutes (and all women) as a group for the benefit of men, without respecting the rights of women.[32] For the IAF, the concern over trafficking was bound with these domestic battles, and 'traffic' was seen as existing because of the demand for licensed brothels.[33]

Given the complexity of views held by civil society actors, the differences between the two camps can also be overstated.[34] However, it is clear that tensions between (broadly) conservative and feminist campaigners played out in various ways both in the international civil society sector and across European states, and mapped onto whether actors sought the abolition of regulationism or more limited

[26] Rachael Attwood, 'Stopping the Traffic: the National Vigilance Association and the International Fight Against the 'White Slave' Trade (1899–c.1909)' (2015) 24(3) Women's History Review 325 (hereafter Attwood, 'Stopping the Traffic').

[27] Limoncelli, *Politics of Trafficking* (n 23) 56–58.

[28] Lammasniemi, 'International Legislation' (n 25) 69–71; further, Attwood, 'Stopping the Traffic' (n 26).

[29] Summers, 'Which Women?' (n 16).

[30] Limoncelli, 'International Voluntary Associations' (n 24).

[31] Lammasniemi, 'International Legislation' (n 25) 70.

[32] Limoncelli, 'International Voluntary Associations (n 24) 37.

[33] Limoncelli, *Politics of Trafficking* (n 23) 44–47.

[34] Magaly Rodríguez García, 'The League of Nations and the Moral Recruitment of Women' (2012) 57(S20) International Review of Social History 97, 102 (hereafter Rodríguez García, 'League of Nations').

controls on the movement of women involved in prostitution. The Netherlands, for instance, was heavily influenced by Butler and abolitionism.[35] Overall, however, 'Butler's personal fusion of liberalism with Christianity was not easily reproduced' in other countries with different religious and political dynamics.[36] In France, the birthplace and stronghold of regulationism, the movement met with predictable resistance;[37] in Germany, conservative forces held sway and kept abolitionism at bay;[38] and in Italy regulationism was restored after some initial moves towards abolitionism.[39]

Moreover, these different perspectives and demands played differently into states' agendas both domestically and in the international arena. In terms of concerns over the 'traffic' in women, abolitionism was a more controversial/far-reaching approach that opposed states' existing policies and challenged their moral standing, while the NVA/Bureau's more modest and limited focus on the international arena (and its legacy of supporting state action) placed it in a better position to influence states' policies.[40] Indeed, when it came to initiating and assisting in the shaping of the first treaties, the NVA was more pragmatically oriented and better at connecting their aims with states' interests than the IAF, thanks to the NVA having maintained strong semi-official links to officials and its more conservative/nationalist outlook.[41] It was thus the NVA that hosted the unofficial International Congress on the White Slave Trade (the 1899 Congress), which created the momentum among (initially largely reluctant) states for the first international conference of states (1902 Conference).[42]

At the 1902 Conference in Paris, with sixteen European states represented, treaties were only made about the question of international movement, as framed by the 1899 Congress and supported by the newly established Bureau.[43] Despite

35 Petra de Vries 'Josephine Butler and the Making of Feminism: International Abolitionism in the Netherlands (1870–1914)' (2008) 17(2) Women's History Review 257; Limoncelli, *Politics of Trafficking* (n 23) ch 5.

36 Anne Summers, 'Introduction: the International Abolitionist Federation' (2008) 17(2) Women's History Review 149, 150.

37 Karen Offen, 'Madame Ghénia Avril de Sainte-Croix, the Josephine Butler of France' (2008) 17(2) Women's History Review 239 (hereafter Offen, 'Madame Ghénia'); Limoncelli, *Politics of Trafficking* (n 23) ch 6.

38 Kerstin Wolff, 'Herrenmoral: Anna Pappritz and Abolitionism in Germany' (2008) Women's History Review 225; Victoria Harris, 'In the Absence of Empire: Feminism, Abolitionism and Social Work in Hamburg (c. 1900–1933)' (2008) 17(2) Women's History Review 279 (hereafter Harris, 'Absence of Empire').

39 Bruno PF Wanrooij, 'Josephine Butler and Regulated Prostitution in Italy' (2008) 17(2) Women's History Review 153; Marjan Schwegman, 'Comment: Amazons in Italy; Josephine Butler and the Transformation of Italian Female Militancy' (2008) 17(2) Women's History Review 173; Limoncelli, *Politics of Trafficking* (n 23) ch 7.

40 Limoncelli, *Politics of Trafficking* (n 23) ch 3; Attwood, 'Stopping the Traffic' (n 26).

41 Limoncelli, *Politics of Trafficking* (n 23) ch 4; see also Knepper, *Invention of International Crime* (n 14).

42 Siller, 'Human Trafficking' (n 21) 412–13; Attwood, 'Stopping the Traffic' (n 26) 331; Knepper, *Invention of International Crime* (n 14) 111–12.

43 Knepper, *Invention of International Crime* (n 14) 113; Attwood, 'Stopping the Traffic' (n 26).

the involvement of some abolitionist campaigners, states' domestic approach to prostitution was largely framed to be outside the scope of the negotiations, in recognition of differences in states' views about the continuance of regulationism. Some states suggested the criminalization of all procuring for immoral purposes, regardless of age and consent, but others (including France and Russia) successfully resisted the adoption of international rules touching on domestic traffic/prostitution on grounds of sovereignty.[44] The process for refining the 1910 White Slave Convention visited the same ground, with similar results.[45] The early treaties are thus best understood as a product of states starting to see the value of cooperating to regulate 'undesirable' international movement (eg because underage or immoral, however defined) and creating certain minimum procedural rules to make that possible, without harmonizing states' laws on prostitution.

## IV. League of Nations Period and the Turn Towards Suppression of Prostitution

After World War I, the anti-trafficking agenda was taken up by the League of Nations.[46] Its 1921 and 1933 Conventions continued to focus on transnational recruitment and transportation for prostitution (now regardless of colour or sex). However, they also raised the age limit for consent to prostitution (1921 Convention for the Suppression of the Traffic in Women and Children, article 5) and then abolished it altogether (1933 Convention for the Suppression of the Traffic in Women, article 1). Moreover, the negotiations of the so-called Draft Convention for Suppressing the Exploitation of the Prostitution of Others (1930–37) show 'a broader push to unify criminal law' by repealing the regulation of prostitution and creating a criminal law framework targeting third parties involved in exploiting prostitution.[47] These efforts, interrupted by World War II, eventually culminated in the adoption of the 1949 Convention. Ostensibly, this suggests that the early IAF aim of uniform abolition of regulationism was gradually achieved from the 1930s onwards—yet this was considered a failure by many concerned with women's rights. How did this come about?

[44] About the negotiations, see Allain, 'White Slave Traffic' (n 19); Siller, 'Human Trafficking' (n 21).

[45] Allain, 'White Slave Traffic' (n 19).

[46] Barbara Metzger, 'Towards an International Human Rights Regime during the Interwar Years: the League of Nations' Combat of Traffic in Women and Children' in Kevin Grant, Philippa Levine and Frank Trentmann (eds), *Beyond Sovereignty: Britain, Empire and Transnationalism, c.1880–1950* (Palgrave 2007) 54 (hereafter Metzger, 'Human Rights Regime'); Stephen Legg, '"The Life of Individuals as well as of Nations": International Law and the League of Nations' Anti-Trafficking Governmentalities' (2012) 25 LJIL 647 (hereafter Legg, 'The Life of Individuals').

[47] Philippa Hetherington and Sonja Dolinsek, 'Socialist Internationalism and Decolonizing Moralities in the UN Anti-Trafficking Regime, 1947–1954' (2019) 21 Journal of the History of International Law 212 (hereafter Hetherington and Dolinsek, 'Socialist Internationalism').

The answer lies in changed circumstances: the disruption of the war, shifts in attitudes to sexual morality, new medical discourses on sex and disease all challenged the assumptions and aims of the early campaigns.[48] In the inter-war period, prostitution was increasingly framed as a social evil, rather than an inevitability to be tolerated, gradually challenging the accepted role of states in regulating it. Laite has tracked shifts between support for state control of prostitution, abolitionism, social purity and, later, social hygiene, resulting in contestations over the use of criminal law to repress prostitution in the UK context.[49] The fall of regulationism in Germany after the establishment of the Weimar Republic was connected to the rise of a nationalist, conservative approach that framed prostitutes as degenerates in need of correction and intervention.[50] France, in contrast, maintained regulationism, despite continuing abolitionist struggle.[51] The inter-war positions and interactions of international civil society organizations, such as the IAF and the Bureau, were also increasingly marked by the lasting disagreements over policies on prostitution and the role of the state in controlling it.[52]

These shifts can also be traced at the international level via the League's Advisory Committee on Traffic in Women and Children, formed in 1921. As Legg notes, the League's work on trafficking is part of the emergence of global governance, including both the expansion of international law and the use of informal mechanisms to shape the discourse on trafficking.[53] The League's 1921 Convention expanded the scope of trafficking slightly but otherwise brought no dramatic change in the law.[54] The Advisory Committee, which incorporated representatives of states as well as the international voluntary organizations, emerged as the site of a struggle between those who supported continued state regulation of prostitution, those advocating for a prohibitionist approach to all forms of prostitution and control of the movement of all women, and feminist abolitionists who opposed regulationism.[55] Pliley has argued that abolitionists were influential in the 1920s during the Committee's investigative work into brothels and state involvement, but that towards the end of the 1920s, feminist voices in the Committee were muted, and policies became ever more paternalistic.[56]

[48] Summers, 'Which Women?' (n 16) 221.

[49] Julia Ann Laite 'The Association for Moral and Social Hygiene: Abolitionism and Prostitution Law in Britain (1915– 1959)' (2008) 17(2) Women's History Review 207.

[50] Harris, 'Absence of Empire' (n 38).

[51] Offen, 'Madame Ghénia' (n 37); Limoncelli *Politics of Trafficking* (n 23) ch 6.

[52] Limoncelli, *Politics of Trafficking* (n 23) 64; Limoncelli, 'International Voluntary Associations' (n 24).

[53] Legg, 'The Life of Individuals' (n 46).

[54] Siller, 'Human Trafficking' (n 21) 435–36.

[55] Jessica Pliley, '"Claims to Protection: the Rise and Fall of Feminist Abolitionism in the League of Nations" Committee on the Traffic in Women and Children, 1919–1936' (2010) 22(4) Journal of Women's History 90 (hereafter Pliley, 'Claims to Protection'). See also Rodríguez García, 'League of Nations' (n 34).

[56] Pliley, 'Claims to Protection' (n 55); but see also Rodríguez García, 'League of Nations' (n 34) and Metzger, 'Human Rights Regime' (n 46).

By the 1930s, the tide at the Committee turned in a more repressive direction, with prostitution seen as a problem or a threat in need of suppression.[57] Pliley has documented the rise of conservative men (including those representing the Bureau, which had a prominent position in the Committee), who advocated for state control over prostitution but eventually came to reject regulation while advocating for measures that limited women's freedoms, including migrants' freedom of movement.[58] Limoncelli also identifies growing nationalism as influencing the work of the Committee (and the Bureau) in creating a push to try and prohibit the participation of foreign women in prostitution altogether.[59] The 1933 Convention for the Suppression of the Traffic in Women, which covered international recruitment regardless of consent, further shifted the emphasis towards suppressing prostitution by eradicating the involvement of intermediaries.[60] This increasingly punitive focus singled out pimping/procuring as needing international legal definition.[61] At the same time, discourses that highlighted the use of criminal law to deal with sexual exploitation obscured broader (and enduring) questions about consent to sex work and the exploitation of women's work.[62]

The 1933 Convention for the Suppression of the Traffic in Women and the 1937 draft convention were thus negotiated in a context where prostitution was increasingly pathologized. Agreement was achieved on the criminalization of intermediaries once the Bureau and France changed their preference from regulationism towards prohibition.[63] By the time what eventually became the 1949 Convention for the Suppression of the Traffic in Persons was returned to after the war, there was 'remarkable agreement' on the desirability of suppressing prostitution, despite other ideological tensions between, for example, Soviet and capitalist states.[64] As a result, the Convention both abandoned regulationism and took a 'notably carceral approach' to the coercive rehabilitation of women in prostitution.[65] Anti-trafficking law thus moved away from regulating international movement to the suppression of undesirable commercial sex ('traffic', whether domestic or interstate) in general. Seeking to strike a compromise between states' remaining differences, the 1949 Convention calls for the criminalization of the exploitation of the prostitution of another.[66] Regardless of this compromise, the Convention was met

[57] Limoncelli, *Politics of Trafficking* (n 23) ch 4.

[58] Pliley, 'Claims to Protection' (n 55). See further Rodríguez García, 'League of Nations' (n 34); Limoncelli, *Politics of Trafficking* (n 23) ch 4.

[59] Limoncelli, *Politics of Trafficking* (n 23) 78–89.

[60] Siller, 'Human Trafficking' (n 21) 438–40.

[61] ibid 440.

[62] Julia Laite, 'Between Scylla and Charybdis: Women's Labour Migration and Sex Trafficking in the Early Twentieth Century' (2017) 62(1) International Review of Social History 37.

[63] Limoncelli, *Politics of Trafficking* (n 23) 89–92.

[64] Hetherington and Dolinsek, 'Socialist Internationalism' (n 47) 214.

[65] Hetherington and Dolinsek, 'Socialist Internationalism' (n 47) 218.

[66] Siller, 'Human Trafficking' (n 21) 445.

with limited interest by states whose differences of opinion soon re-surfaced, resulting in low ratification.

Ostensibly, the abandonment of regulationism, long resisted by social conservatives concerned about controlling the immorality of prostitution, led to what many early feminists had wanted (the uniform abolition of state-led management of prostitution), but in fact the change replaced regulationism with a new form of control, as prohibitionism emerged as the dominant ideology. This ideology, however, turned out to be equally divisive among states and was rejected and resisted by many civil society organizations. Insofar as the 1949 Convention for the Suppression of the Traffic in Persons was the outcome of a rising (if short-lived) consensus among states to repress prostitution by increasingly employing criminal law, it was also a defeat for those campaigning for an approach recognizing the complexity of sexual exploitation. The fact that the 1940 Convention is not popular with states shows the limits of unification in this highly contested area. While enough states were convinced to get behind the push for unification in the 1930s–40s, the history of the 1949 Convention for the Suppression of the Traffic in Persons suggests that fundamental conflicts about prostitution are enduring. While states may be willing to coordinate some of their actions, it is difficult to nail down a permanent consensus in support of any particular model in relation to the treatment of prostitution.

## V. Conclusion

One can detect a certain evolution in the character of the treatment of trafficking in law in its early phase of development; however, that evolution is neither smooth nor uncontested. The early European history of anti-trafficking law shows that both states' and civil society's positions on prostitution were in flux in the first half of the 20th century. As noted, the campaigns and processes leading to the adoption of early international law in this area raised a number of controversies still relevant today. These include the significance of issues such as consent, fraud, power differentials and international movement in defining what counts as prohibited conduct; the role of international law in coordinating international action and/or unifying states' positions on substantive issues; and the framing of prostitution/sexual exploitation as a 'special' form of oppression which is nonetheless connected to entrenched inequalities. Disagreements over these questions help explain why terminological clarity is so hard to establish in this area, often leading to the use of vague discourses and conceptual imprecision, such as that now seen in the context of 'modern slavery'.

# 12
# A Short History of Smuggling of Migrants in International Law

*Andreas Schloenhardt*

## I. Introduction

Smuggling of migrants is a relatively new addition to the offences covered in international law. It came into existence with the Protocol against the Smuggling of Migrants by Land, Sea and Air, supplementing the United Nations Convention against Transnational Organized Crime (Smuggling of Migrants Protocol). Drafted in the years 1999 and 2000, the Protocol was opened for signature on 15 November 2000 and entered into force on 28 January 2004. As of 1 October 2020, 149 states are parties to the Protocol, 112 states have also ratified it.[1] Many states, especially in Asia and the Pacific, have yet to accede to the Protocol and some states parties have yet to criminalize smuggling of migrants in their domestic law. Seen this way, the international law on smuggling of migrants is still in its adolescence.

A closer look at the history of smuggling of migrants paints a different picture. For as long as states have sought to control and fortify their borders, people have tried to circumvent border controls and immigration requirements, often with the aid of smugglers. Out of necessity, desperation or choice, throughout modern history migrants have resorted to smugglers to flee from persecution, war or poverty in order to find a better life abroad, often in return for large payments and in conditions that are degrading or exploitative. Put simply, smuggling of migrants, that is 'the procurement, in order to obtain, directly or indirectly, a financial or other material benefit, of the illegal entry of a person into a State Party of which the person is not a national or a permanent resident',[2] is not a new phenomenon but merely a new label.

[1] United Nations Treaty Collection, Chapter XVIII Penal Matters, 12.b Protocol against the Smuggling of Migrants by Land, Sea and Air, supplementing the United Nations Convention against Transnational Organized Crime <https://treaties.un.org/Pages/ViewDetails.aspx?src=TREATY&mtdsg_no=XVIII-12-b&chapter=18&clang=_en>.

[2] The terms 'smuggling of migrants' and 'migrant smuggling' are used interchangeably throughout this chapter. See also, Anne Gallagher and Fiona David, *The International Law of Migrant Smuggling* (CUP 2014) 44–47 (hereafter Gallagher and David, *International Law of Migrant Smuggling*).

Andreas Schloenhardt, *A Short History of Smuggling of Migrants in International Law* In: *Histories of Transnational Criminal Law*. Edited by: Neil Boister, Sabine Gless and Florian Jeßberger, Oxford University Press. © Andreas Schloenhardt 2021.
DOI: 10.1093/oso/9780192845702.003.0013

This chapter sheds light on the evolution of smuggling of migrants from the 20th century to today. After a brief look at historical manifestations of smuggling of migrants, the chapter turns to the events of the 1990s that shaped the concepts and content of the Smuggling of Migrants Protocol. Developments since the inception of the Protocol at the regional level are looked at briefly before the chapter closes with a short reflection on the future of smuggling of migrants in international law.

## II. Smuggling of Migrants in the 20th Century

Throughout the 20th century, smuggling of migrants repeatedly surfaced as a major humanitarian and political concern. Until quite recently, however, the international community did not consider it necessary—or simply failed—to agree on collective responses to prevent and suppress smuggling of migrants and to protect smuggled migrants.

### 1. Holocaust and Nazi Germany

The assistance rendered to those seeking to flee the Shoah and National-Socialism involved, inter alia, the acquisition of fraudulent passports, visas, immigration papers and guarantees, the hiring of boats and other vehicles, the provision of accommodation, food and the like.[3] Various clubs, Zionist associations and political parties played a major role in facilitating the smuggling of refugees, as did many private individuals who became involved in such activities.[4] Few of these were celebrated as heroes; many were arrested and prosecuted. Those caught by Nazi authorities were sent to the death camps, much like the people the smugglers sought to assist.

Not all smugglers acted for altruistic reasons; some asked for payment to recover costs, others sought to profit from the services they offered. The so-called 'Jew smuggler' Josef Schleich, for instance, sold fraudulent certificates about work qualifications which the bearer could use to emigrate to the United States. Others charged refugees for smuggling them along with contraband across the border. Some smugglers demanded payment merely for connecting would-be emigrants with organizations and individuals abroad.[5] Instances of fraud and deception were

[3] Lucia Reinisch, 'Fluchthilfe aus Österreich in der NS-Zeit 1938 bis 1945' in Andreas Schloenhardt (ed), *Schlepperkriminalität in Österreich* (NWV 2017) 81, 90 (hereafter Reinisch, 'Fluchthilfe aus Österreich').

[4] Pertti Ahonen, 'Europe and Refugees: 1938 and 2015–16' (2018) 52(2–3) Patterns of Prejudice 135, 142 (hereafter Ahonen, 'Europe and Refugees'); Reinisch, 'Fluchthilfe aus Österreich' (n 3) 91–95.

[5] Reinisch, 'Fluchthilfe aus Österreich' (n 3) 96.

not uncommon and some smugglers abandoned their 'clients' before crossing the border but after accepting their money and taking their sparse belongings.[6]

Despite the scale of the genocide and cruelty inflicted by the Nazis, the international community failed to come to the rescue of those displaced, much less develop coordinated efforts to provide legal avenues for asylum and prevent the smuggling of migrants. The Evian Conference, which brought together representatives of thirty-two states in July 1938 to discuss the plight of refugees from Germany, failed to produce any tangible outcomes and all but shut the door for Jews seeking protection abroad.[7]

## 2. Indochina

Smuggling of migrants became a major concern for the countries in Southeast Asia and beyond in the context of the wars in Indochina in the 1960s and 70s when tens of thousands of people sought to flee from Vietnam and Cambodia, many of them by sea, bringing the term 'boat people' into the language.

Many departures from Vietnam were facilitated by smugglers who demanded payment for transporting refugees to countries of first asylum in the region. From 1975 to 1978, some 62,000 Vietnamese refugees had fled to other Southeast Asian countries. By mid-1979, that number grew to 550,000 when smuggling syndicates started to use steel-hull vessels carrying up to 2,500 people at a time. Vietnamese officials were often involved in these journeys, accepting bribes or demanding payment from emigrants or for 'turning a blind eye' to irregular departures.[8]

The rise in irregular arrivals from Vietnam quickly led to 'compassion fatigue' in the countries of first asylum. Singapore, for instance, refused to allow sea arrivals to disembark unless they had secured resettlement in another country, which few of them had. Malaysia and Thailand began to push boats back to sea in order to stop any further arrivals. By June 1979, five Southeast Asian countries declared that they had 'reached the level of their endurance' and decided not to accept any new arrivals.[9]

The Conference on Indochinese Refugees held in Paris in July 1979 led to a temporary respite when Western nations pledged to increase resettlement places, Indonesia and the Philippines established regional processing centres and Vietnam agreed to halt and penalize irregular departures.[10] But the exodus of 'boat people'

[6] ibid 97.

[7] Ahonen, 'Europe and Refugees' (n 4) 139–40.

[8] Claire Higgins, *Asylum by Boat: Origins of Australia's Refugee Policy* (UNSW Press 2017) 106.

[9] Sten A Bronée, 'The History of the Comprehensive Plan of Action' (1993) 5(4) International Journal of Refugee Law 534, 534–35.

[10] W Courtland Robinson, 'The Comprehensive Plan of Action for Indochinese Refugees, 1989–1197: Sharing the Burden and Passing the Buck' (2004) 17(3) Journal of Refugee Studies 319, 319.

and the smuggling of migrants from Vietnam surged again from 1983 onwards. With states all the more reluctant to assist irregular migrants and some states pushing boats back to sea, many boats fell victim to pirates.[11] Much like the situation in the Mediterranean in the 2010s, NGOs and merchant vessels became involved in rescuing irregular migrants from unseaworthy vessels and taking them to safety.

## 3. Cold War Period

The Cold War and its 'Iron Curtain' that separated Western and Eastern blocs made movements between these blocs all but impossible and thus triggered the smuggling of migrants of another kind. The crackdown on dissidents and free speech, restrictions placed on the freedom of travel, the inability to acquire passports and permissions to leave one's country, often combined with dire economic situations, created the wish by many people in the Soviet bloc, especially in Eastern Europe, to emigrate to Western countries.[12]

As the borders between East and West became increasingly sealed, with shoot-to-kill orders given by some countries for persons attempting to flee, it became increasingly difficult for would-be emigrants to leave. 'Fluchthelfer' or 'refugee agents' were needed to make the dangerous journey which involved methods such as concealment in trucks or cars. Some of the methods used to smuggle migrants involved sophisticated planning and special equipment, such that payment of the smugglers became necessary. Some smugglers charged fees above and beyond their own expenses, seeking to profit materially from their operations, thus establishing quasi-commercial migrant smuggling networks.[13]

Sympathy for smuggled migrants and their smugglers grew or declined depending on the number and circumstances of these irregular arrivals. For the most part, Western nations viewed these arrivals as evidence of Soviet repression and as proof that Communism was cruel and failing. In a landmark decision, Germany's Federal Court of Justice, the Bundesgerichtshof (BGH), held that contracts between smugglers and smuggled migrants were legally valid and not against common, reasonable standards. As a result, smugglers could demand payment from their 'clients' if it had been agreed that they would pay a fee upon their

[11] See further, Arthur Helton, 'The Comprehensive Plan of Action for Indo-Chinese Refugees: An Experiment in Refugee Protection and Control' (1990) 8 NYL Sch J Hum Rts 111, 112–14.

[12] See further, Andreas Schloenhardt, *Migrant Smuggling: Illegal Migration and Organised Crime in Australia and the Asia Pacific Region* (Nijhoff 2003) 67–69 (hereafter, Schloenhardt, *Migrant Smuggling*); Guy S Goodwin-Gill, *The Refugee in International Law* (2nd edn, OUP 1996) 53.

[13] Erich Heimeshoff, 'Der Streit um die kommerzielle Fluchthilfe' [1978] 5 Zeitschrift für Rechtspolitik 97, 98; Marion Detjen, *Ein Loch in der Mauer: Die Geschichte der Fluchthilfe im geteilten Deutschland 1961–1989* (Siedler 2005) 95–162, 253–63.

arrival in Western Germany.[14] In a further decision, the same court held that it is permissible for the smugglers to demand payment of an advance for their services.

Reimbursement of the advance in the event that the smuggling venture remained unsuccessful was held to be legally required only if the failure was based on the smugglers' gross negligence.[15]

## 4. Post-Cold War Period

The development of an international treaty against the smuggling of migrants has its roots in the early 1990s when European countries became increasingly concerned about irregular migration. The opening of the 'Iron Curtain' was followed by a significant flow of people across borders from East to West. Taking advantage of routes and transit points that were previously unavailable, the smuggling of migrants emerged as a growing business to assist those who wanted or needed to migrate but did not meet the legal requirements for entry into transit and destination countries.[16]

At the same time, North America experienced a string of smuggling ventures in which irregular migrants, most of them Chinese, were brought clandestinely by boat across the Pacific to the United States and Canada (and in the late 1990s also to Australia, albeit in very small numbers). These boats were mostly large freight vessels that carried groups of Chinese nationals concealed in containers or other hidden compartments and released them clandestinely in the main ports along the Pacific Coast of the United States.[17] One of the most infamous incidents involved the *Golden Venture*, a cargo vessel that carried 286 Chinese migrants who boarded the boat in Bangkok, Thailand and en route in Mombasa, Kenya. In an attempt to avoid coastal patrols along the US West Coast, the *Golden Venture* sailed across the Atlantic to New York, where it was meant to be met by rendezvous vessels offshore. When these smaller vessels failed to show, the smugglers ran the ship aground in

[14] BGH III ZR 185/77 (Nuremberg), Neue Juristische Wochenschrift 1980, 1574

[15] BGH III ZR 118/76 (Berlin).

[16] Andree Kirchner and Lorenzo Schiano di Pepe, 'International Attempts to Conclude a Convention to Combat Illegal Migration' (1998) 10 International Journal of Refugee Law 662, 668 (hereafter, Kirchner and di Pepe 'Attempts to Conclude a Convention to Combat Illegal Migration'); Peter Andreas, 'The Rise of the American Crimefare State' (1997) 14(3) World Policy Journal 37, 37; Susan Martin, *Global Migration Trends and Asylum* New Issues in Refugee Research, UNHCR Working Paper 41 (30 April 2001) 8, 13.

[17] Ryan Chan, 'Ships & Snakeheads: The Brief Phenomenon of Fujianese-Chinese Boat Arrivals in Australia' (2018) 1 Re:Locations: Journal of the Asia-Pacific World 24, 30–33; Ronald Skeldon, 'Migration from China' (1996) 49 Journal of International Affairs 434, 442; Ko Lin Chin, *Smuggled Chinese: Clandestine Immigration to the United States* (Temple UP 1999) 28; Sheldon Zhang and Mark Gaylord, 'Bound for the Golden Mountain: The Social Organization of Chinese Alien Smuggling' (1996) 25 Crime, Law & Social Change 1.

Queens. Ten people died when they attempted to leave the stranded ship and swim ashore.[18]

The uncontrolled arrival of irregular migrants in Europe and North America combined with the involvement of criminal elements in these arrivals were quickly portrayed as threats to national security and state sovereignty over immigration and border control.[19] Countries determined to combat the smuggling of migrants and prosecute and punish smugglers slowly realized that international cooperation was essential in their quest. Critical gaps in their ability to cooperate across borders, non-existing anti-migrant smuggling laws in many countries and fragmented domestic law enforcement efforts, however, meant that governments were not in a position to easily cooperate to stop migrant smuggling and prosecute migrant smugglers.

## III. Towards an International Agreement

### 1. 'Alien Smuggling' and the United Nations

The United Nations (UN) General Assembly first addressed the topic of smuggling of migrants in December 1993 when it 'condemned the practice of smuggling of aliens in violation of international and national law and without regard for the safety, well-being and human rights of the migrants' and called on member states to enhance their efforts and cooperate to prevent and combat this phenomenon.[20]

The General Assembly requested the UN Commission on Crime Prevention and Criminal Justice (CCPCJ) to give special attention to the issue of migrant smuggling at its third session, held between 26 April and 6 May 1994. In discussing the issue, the Commission noted that '[a]lien smuggling was considered a matter of grave concern for many Governments' and suggested that '[c]riminal legislation should be enacted and enforced to combat the abominable practice'.[21] During the meeting, the United States introduced the first draft for a resolution on 'criminal justice action to combat the organized smuggling of illegal migrants across

[18] Cindy Yik-Yi Chu, 'Human Trafficking and Smuggling in China' (2011) 20(68) Journal of Contemporary China 39, 44; Cleo J Kung, 'Supporting the Snakeheads: Human Smuggling from China and the 1996 Amendment to the U.S. Statutory Definition of "Refugee" ' (2000) 90(4) Journal of Criminal Law and Criminology 1271, 1280.

[19] John Backers-Morrison and Sharone Backers-Morrison, 'The Dark Side of Globalisation: The Criminalisation of Refugees' (2001) 43(1) Race & Class 71; Anne Gallagher, 'Human Rights and Human Trafficking: Quagmire or Firm Ground? A Response to James Hathaway' (2009) 49 Va J Intl L 789, 790.

[20] UN General Assembly, Prevention of the smuggling of aliens, UN Doc A/RES/48/102 (20 December 1993) [1], [3] (hereafter UN General Assembly, Prevention) . See also, Gallagher and David, *International Law of Migrant Smuggling* (n 2) 30–31.

[21] UN Commission on Crime Prevention and Criminal Justice, Report of the Commission on Crime Prevention and Criminal Justice on its 3rd session, UN Doc E/CN.15/1994/12 (1994) 66 [29].

national boundaries'.[22] This draft was slightly revised[23] and later presented as Draft Resolution III for adoption by the UN Economic and Social Council (ECOSOC). The draft specifically

> [c]alls upon all States to take effective and expeditious measures, such as the enactment or amendment if necessary of domestic criminal law, providing appropriate penalties to combat all aspects of organized crime activities constituting the smuggling of illegal migrants, including all elements of the organization of smuggling and transport of illegal migrants, such as the production or distribution of false travel documents, money laundering, systematic extortion and misuse of international commercial aviation and maritime transport, in violation of international standards.[24]

ECOSOC adopted the Commission's proposed resolution on 25 July 1994.[25] Between 1994 and 1997, the General Assembly, [26] the CCPCJ[27] and ECOSOC[28] revisited the topic of migrant smuggling on multiple occasions, thus paving the way for greater international cooperation in this field.

## 2. Italy's and Austria's Proposals

In mid-1997, Italy submitted a proposal for a draft convention to define and target the smuggling of migrants by sea to the International Maritime Organization

22 UN Commission on Crime Prevention and Criminal Justice, Criminal justice action to combat the organized smuggling of illegal migrants across national boundaries, UN Doc E/CN.15/1994/L.8 (4 May 1994).

23 UN Commission on Crime Prevention and Criminal Justice, Criminal justice action to combat the organized smuggling of illegal migrants across national boundaries, UN Doc E/CN.15/1994/L.8/Rev.1 (6 May 1994).

24 UN Commission on Crime Prevention and Criminal Justice, Report of the Commission on Crime Prevention and Criminal Justice on its 3rd session, UN Doc E/CN.15/1994/12 (1994) 12 [9].

25 UN Economic and Social Council, Criminal justice action to combat the organized smuggling of illegal migrants across national boundaries, UN Doc E/1994/14 (25 July 1994).

26 UN General Assembly, Crime Prevention and Criminal Justice: Measures to combat alien smuggling; Report of the Secretary-General, UN Doc A/49/350 (30 August 1994) 22 [99]; UN General Assembly, Measures for prevention of the smuggling of aliens, UN Doc A/RES/61/62 (28 January 1997) 2 [3].

27 UN Commission on Crime Prevention and Criminal Justice, Report of the Commission on Crime Prevention and Criminal Justice on its 4th session, UN Doc E/CN.15/1995/13 (1995) 17–20; UN Commission on Crime Prevention and Criminal Justice, Measures to combat the smuggling of migrants, Report of the Secretary-General, UN Doc E/CN.15/1996/4 (21 March 1996) 7 [71]; UN Commission on Crime Prevention and Criminal Justice, International Cooperation in Combatting Transnational Organized Crime: Smuggling of Illegal Migrants, UN Doc E/CN.15/1997/8 (18 February 1997), and UN Doc E/CN.15/1997/8/Add.1 (8 April 1997); UN Commission on Crime Prevention and Criminal Justice, Report on the 6th session, UN Doc E/CN.15/1997/21 (1997) 130 [74]–[75].

28 UN Economic and Social Council, *Criminal justice action to combat the organized smuggling of illegal migrants across national boundaries*, UN Doc E/RES/1995/10 (24 July 1995).

(IMO).[29] It was at that time that Italy started to become particularly affected by seaborne smuggling from North Africa, the Balkans and the Eastern Mediterranean; a situation that persists today. In 1997, the primary concern of the Italian government was the heavy loss of life when crowded, unseaworthy smuggling vessels sank en route to Italy.[30]

A separate initiative by Austria, a country greatly affected by irregular migration after the end of the Cold War, pursued a similar goal. On 16 September 1997, Austria submitted a letter to the UN Secretary-General presenting a draft 'International Convention Against the Smuggling of Illegal Migrants'.[31] The letter noted that the 'efforts of the international community to cope in an efficient manner with the phenomenon of smuggling of migrants for criminal purposes' were significantly impeded by a 'legal lacuna under international law'. It was proposed 'that the problem should be dealt with in a special convention' and the letter stressed that

> the action to be undertaken under the aegis of the Commission [on Crime Prevention and Criminal Justice] urgently needs to be complemented by the elaboration of an appropriate international instrument ensuring that perpetrators as well as instigators and accomplices of this transnational crime will be effectively brought to justice.[32]

Italy subsequently expressed its support of the Austrian proposal and the two initiatives were combined by including special measures relating to the smuggling of migrants by sea into the Austrian draft.[33]

## IV. The Smuggling of Migrants Protocol

The proposals by Austria and Italy found strong support in various UN bodies and coincided with moves by the UN General Assembly to establish an open-ended

[29] IMO Legal Committee, Proposed Multilateral Convention to Combat Illegal Migration by Sea, IMO Doc LEG 76/11/1 (1 August 1997).

[30] See further, Patricia Mallia, *Migrant Smuggling by Sea: Combatting a Current Threat to Maritime Security through the Creation of a Cooperative Framework* (Nijhoff 2010) 112–16 (hereafter, Mallia, *Migrant Smuggling by Sea*); Kirchner and di Pepe 'Attempts to Conclude a Convention to Combat Illegal Migration' (n 16) 664–68; Schloenhardt, *Migrant Smuggling* (n 12) 347–48.

[31] UN General Assembly, Letter dated 16 September from the Permanent Representative of Austria to the United Nations addressed to the Secretary-General, UN Doc A/52/357 (17 September 1997).

[32] UN General Assembly, Prevention (n 20) 2 [2], [4]. See further, David McClean, *Transnational Organized Crime: A Commentary on the UN Convention and its Protocols* (OUP 2007) 21–22 (hereafter, McClean, *Transnational Organized Crime*); Kirchner and di Pepe 'Attempts to Conclude a Convention to Combat Illegal Migration' (n 16) 662, 670.

[33] See also, Anne Gallagher, 'Migrant Smuggling' in Neil Boister and Robert J Currie (eds), *Routledge Handbook on Transnational Organized Crime* (Routledge 2015) 187, 190–91 (hereafter, Gallagher, 'Migrant Smuggling'); Gallagher and David, *International Law of Migrant Smuggling* (n 2) 33.

intergovernmental Ad Hoc Committee for the Elaboration of a Convention against Transnational Organized Crime (AC.154).[34] The combined Austrian-Italian proposal constitutes the main textual influence of the Smuggling of Migrants Protocol.[35] Over the following two years, the Ad hoc Committee developed the Convention against Transnational Organized Crime,[36] along with three supplementing protocols, including the Protocol against the Smuggling of Migrants by Land, Sea, or Air.

## 1. Objectives

On the surface, the Smuggling of Migrants Protocol pursues three equally important objectives: to stop the smuggling of migrants, foster international cooperation and protect the rights of smuggled migrants.[37] A closer look, however, reveals that the criminal justice focus of the Protocol trumps human rights considerations. Indeed, early drafts of the Protocol were limited to criminalization and international cooperation and made no reference to the protection of smuggled migrants.[38]

During the fifth session of the Ad Hoc Committee in October 1999, several delegations suggested adding the words 'as well as to protect the victims of such smuggling, including their human rights' to the stated purposes of the Protocol or, alternatively, in a separate article,[39] but the draft text remained unchanged at that time.[40] An intervention by several United Nations agencies eventually led to a formal, albeit modest, recognition of the rights of smuggling of migrants in the text of the Protocol. At the eighth session of the Ad Hoc Committee in February and March 2000, the Office of the United Nations High Commissioner for Human Rights (OHCHR), along with UNHCR, the United Nations Children's Fund (UNICEF) and the International Organization for Migration (IOM) submitted a note stressing the

[34] UN General Assembly, Report of the Ad Hoc Committee on the Elaboration of a Convention against Transnational Organized Crime on the work of its first to eleventh sessions; Addendum: Interpretative notes for the official record (travaux préparatoires) of the negotiations for the United Nations Convention against Transnational Organized Crime and the Protocols thereto, UN Doc A/55/383/Add.1 (3 November 2000) xxv (hereafter UN General Assembly, Interpretative Notes); UN General Assembly, Resolution on Transnational Organized Crime, UN Doc A/RES/53/111 (9 December 1998).

[35] UNODC, *Travaux Préparatoires of the negotiations of the United Nations Convention against Transnational Organized Crime and the Protocols thereto* (United Nations, 2006) 451 (hereafter UNODC, *Travaux Préparatoires*) .

[36] See Forlati, Chapter 13 in this book.

[37] Smuggling of Migrants Protocol, art 2.

[38] UNODC, *Travaux Préparatoires* (n 35) 459.

[39] ibid.

[40] McClean, *Transnational Organized Crime* (n 32) 379.

> clear need to ensure that the individuals falling victim to such practices are protected. The vulnerability of migrants, in particular irregular migrants, as a result of their precarious situation in society often leads to violations of their most basic human rights.... It is imperative, therefore, that the Protocol should preserve and seek to uphold the fundamental human rights to which all persons, including smuggled migrants, are entitled.[41]

With the support of most delegations, the purpose 'to promote international co-operation in the interest of the protection of such trafficking and respect for their human rights' was included in a revised draft.[42] In October 2000, the words 'victims' and 'trafficking' were removed and substituted with the final text of article 2, which refers to 'protecting the rights of smuggled migrants'.[43]

Despite this inclusion, the Smuggling of Migrants Protocol is a criminal justice instrument that remains 'problematic from a human rights perspective'.[44] The Protocol is not an independent treaty: it supplements the UNTOC.[45] Through this Convention, states gain access to a range of criminal law and law enforcement tools designed to combat organized crime and foster international cooperation. The Protocol and the Convention add little to protect the rights of persons fleeing from persecution or poverty. The human rights of smuggled migrants were not the preeminent drivers of those developing the Protocol and remain secondary goals compared to the strong criminal justice focus of this instrument.

## 2. Final Text

The Smuggling of Migrants Protocol's central feature is the obligation in article 6 to comprehensively criminalize the smuggling of migrants and related conduct. Article 6(1) identifies three offences that must be established in domestic law, including: (a) a smuggling of migrants offence (b) an offence relating to fraudulent travel and identity documents, and (c) an offence of enabling of illegal stay. Article 6(2) expands liability for these offences to attempts, participation and incitement. Article 6(3) creates an obligation to legislate aggravating circumstances '(a) that endanger, or are likely to endanger, the lives or safety of the migrants concerned; or

41 UNGA, Ad Hoc Committee on the Elaboration of a Convention against Transnational Organized Crime, Note by the Office of the United Nations High Commissioner for Human Rights, the Office of the United Nations High Commissioner for Refugees, the United Nations Children's Fund and the International Organization for Migration on the draft protocols concerning migrant smuggling and trafficking in persons, UN doc A/AC.254/27 (8 February 2000) para 15.

42 UNODC, *Travaux Préparatoires* (n 35) 461.

43 ibid. See also Gallagher and David, *International Law of Migrant Smuggling* (n 2) 47–48.

44 Tom Obokata, 'Smuggling of Human Beings from a Human Rights Perspective: Obligations of Non-State and State Actors under International Human Rights Law' (2015) 17(2) International Journal of Refugee Law 394, 395.

45 Smuggling of Migrants Protocol, art 1(1).

(b) that entail inhuman or degrading treatment, including for exploitation, of such migrants.' It is open to states parties to legislate additional aggravations.

The Smuggling of Migrants Protocol does not prescribe specific penalties or sanctions. Article 6(4) merely notes that '[n]othing in this Protocol shall prevent a State Party from taking measures against a person whose conduct constitutes an offence under its domestic law.' The Interpretative Notes to the Protocol indicate that the reference to 'measures' is to be interpreted broadly to include both administrative and criminal sanctions. Article 11(1) of the UNTOC may be relevant in this context as it provides that states parties are required to adopt sanctions within domestic law that reflect, and are proportionate to, the gravity of the offences.[46]

The Protocol does not intend to criminalize humanitarian or altruistic activities to save or protect the life of the smuggled migrant. For these reasons, the Protocol limits the definition of smuggling of migrants and the criminalization requirement under article 6(1) to instances in which the offender seeks 'to obtain, directly or indirectly, a financial or other material benefit'. Acts that facilitate the illegal entry or stay of another but that are not done for this purpose are, by definition, not smuggling of migrants.

Furthermore, under article 5, 'migrants shall not become liable to criminal prosecution under this Protocol for the fact of having been the object of conduct set forth in article 6 of this Protocol'. The purpose of this provision is to shield smuggled migrants from criminal prosecution arising from the fact of having been smuggled. The provision upholds the cardinal principle that irregular migration is not per se criminal and that smuggled migrants must not be punished for using the services offered by migrant smugglers.[47]

The prevention and suppression of the smuggling of migrants by sea is specifically addressed in articles 7–9. Articles 10–14 of the Protocol require the adoption of general prevention measures targeted at improving border control capabilities, information gathering and law enforcement. Despite the Protocol's strong criminal justice focus, the stated purpose of protecting the rights of smuggled migrants in article 2 is reflected in several provisions. Article 4 extends the scope of the Protocol to 'the protection of the rights of persons who have been the object of [migrant smuggling]'. Under article 9(1), states parties are obliged to 'ensure the safety and humane treatment of the persons on board' suspected smuggling vessels. Article 16 sets out a number of 'protection and assistance measures'. Article 19 contains a 'saving clause' to ensure that 'other rights, obligations and responsibilities of States and individuals under international law' remain unaffected and that the Protocol is applied in a way 'that is not discriminatory to persons on the ground that they are

[46] Compare McClean, *Transnational Organized Crime* (n 32) 396.

[47] UNODC, Legislative Guide for the Implementation of the Protocol against the smuggling og Migrants by Land, Sea and Air, Supplementing the United Nations Convention against Transnational Organized Crime (UN 2004) 323, 347 ≤https://www.unodc.org/pdf/crime/legislative_guides/04%20 Legislative%20guide_Smuggling%20of%20Migrants%20 Protocol.pdf>.

the object of' migrant smuggling. In article 18, the Protocol sets out a framework for receiving states for the repatriation of smuggled migrants. It concludes with a range of final clauses that are mainly administrative in nature.[48]

## V. Regional Developments in Europe

Presently, the only binding regional measures pertaining to smuggling of migrants are those developed by the European Union (EU) in the early 2000s. These measures are part of a framework to develop common policies on asylum and immigration across member states and to combat immigration-related crime and abuse of asylum systems.[49]

The earliest reference to an offence similar to smuggling of migrants can be found in article 27(1) of the Convention implementing the Schengen Agreement (CISA) of 14 July 1985 which requires states parties 'to impose appropriate penalties on any person who, for financial gain, assists or tries to assist an alien to enter or reside within the territory of one of the Contracting Parties in breach of that Contracting Party's laws on the entry and residence of aliens'. On 28 November 2002, the Council of the European Union adopted Directive 2002/90/EC 'defining the facilitation of unauthorised entry, transit and residence',[50] followed by Framework Decision 2002/946/JHA 'on the strengthening of the penal framework to prevent the facilitation of unauthorised entry, transit and residence'.[51] These two interconnected documents[52] replace article 27 of CISA. Council Directive 2002/90/EC provides the definition of facilitation of unauthorized entry, transit and residence and the cases of exemption. Framework Decision 2002/946/JHA sets out the 'minimum rules for penalties, liability of legal persons and jurisdiction' of the offences under the Council Directive.[53]

The EU framework departs from the Smuggling of Migrants Protocol in several ways. One main point of difference is the lack of any reference to the purpose of obtaining a financial or other material benefit in the Council Directive. This is explained by the overall purpose of the Directive, which is to combat the facilitation

[48] Smuggling of Migrants Protocol, arts 20–25. For an outline of the Protocol see also, Andreas Schloenhardt and Jessica E Dale, 'Twelve Years On: Revisiting the UN Protocol against the Smuggling of Migrants by Land, Sea and Air' (2012) 67 Zeitschrift für öffentliches Recht 127.

[49] See further, Mallia, *Migrant Smuggling by Sea* (n 30) 200–22.

[50] EU Council Directive 2002/90/EC of 28 November 2002 defining the facilitation of unauthorised entry, transit and residence OJ L238/17, 5 December 2002.

[51] EU Council Framework Decision 2002/946/JHA of 28 November 2002 on the strengthening of the penal framework to prevent the facilitation of unauthorised entry, transit and residence, OJ L238/1, 5 December 2002.

[52] Compare Samuli Miettinen, *Criminal Law and Policy in the European Union* (Routledge 2007) 161, who refers to this as a 'dual approach'.

[53] Preamble, EU Council, Framework Decision 2002/946/JHA on the strengthening of the penal framework to prevent the facilitation of unauthorised entry, transit and residence [3].

of illegal immigration in all its forms. This is reinforced by a statement in paragraph (2) of the Directive's Preamble, which states that '[m]easures should be taken to combat the aiding of illegal immigration both in connection with unauthorised crossing of the border in the strict sense and for the purpose of sustaining networks which exploit human beings.' Thus, 'Directive 2002/90/EC does not limit the targets it is aimed at, potentially punishing those who are assisting irregular migration for honourable reasons as harshly as those who do so for financial gain, such as organised crime.'[54] The financial or material benefit is an aggravation under article 1 of the Framework Decision 2002/946/JHA, which envisages higher penalties (1) if the offence under article 1(1)(a) of the Council Directive is committed for financial gain and endangers the lives of the smuggled migrants, and (2) if the offence is committed for financial gain and is part of the activities of a criminal organization.

Whereas the Smuggling of Migrants Protocol is clear about its intention not to criminalize persons who engage in the smuggling of migrants for humanitarian purposes with no financial gain, the Council Directive leaves this matter to the discretion of member states. Article 1(2) allows member states 'not to impose sanctions with regard to the behaviour defined in paragraph 1(a) by applying its national law and practice for cases where the aim of the behaviour is to provide humanitarian assistance to the person concerned'.

## VI. The Way Ahead

Smuggling of migrants is one of the most recent additions to the range of crime types covered by transnational criminal law. The Smuggling of Migrants Protocol provides a global framework to criminalize this phenomenon, foster international cooperation and, albeit rudimentarily, protect the rights of smuggled migrants. The Protocol sets global standards in an area that historically has been guarded fiercely by states as a matter of state sovereignty reserved exclusively for national responses. It is remarkable that the Protocol has been signed and ratified by a great range of states from around the globe, with further signatories expected to follow. Most states worldwide now sanction smuggling of migrants under domestic law; an offence that did not exist in most jurisdictions twenty years ago.

The majority of non-states parties are presently in Asia and the Pacific. Among the twenty-nine non-parties from that region are several states with significant histories of irregular migration, such as China, Iran, the Democratic People's Republic of Korea, Malaysia, Nepal, Pakistan and Vietnam. In the Americas and Europe, nearly all states are parties to the Protocol. The Protocol has also found significant

[54] Matilde Ventrella, *The Control of People Smuggling and Trafficking in the EU* (Routledge 2010) 45; see also Valsamis Mitsilegas, 'Immigration Control in an Era of Globalization: Deflecting Foreigners, Weakening Citizens, Strengthening the State' (2012) 19(1) Ind J Global Legal Stud 3, 10

support across Africa, with only Chad, Comoros, Eritrea, Morocco, Somalia, South Sudan and Zimbabwe having yet to accede.

In the absence of express opposition or explicit statements rejecting the Smuggling of Migrants Protocol, it is difficult to say with certainty why individual states, or groups of states, have not, or not yet, ratified the Protocol. A study of the geographic, political, and socio-economic circumstances of non-states parties, and their exposure to irregular migration, published in 2015, reveals a number of commonalities that indicate why some states may be unwilling or unable to commit themselves to the obligations under the Protocol.[55] The financial costs and the material and human resources needed to implement and adhere to international treaties were found to be one impediment for some countries. The Protocol requires states parties to introduce complex legislative provisions into their domestic laws, establish mechanisms that protect the rights of smuggled migrants and facilitate or engage in international law enforcement, prosecutorial and judicial cooperation that can be costly and involve technical equipment and know-how that some countries, especially small, developing nations, do not have and cannot afford. Reservations about the Protocol further stem from the perception that destination countries gain greater benefits from—and are more likely to sign and ratify—the Protocol.[56] It has also been argued that states that are not or not significantly affected by the influx of irregular migrants have fewer incentives to ratify the Protocol.[57] The reluctance of some non-party states to accede to the Protocol may also be explained by the fact that they participate in non-binding multinational initiatives against irregular migration and formed the view that their involvement in these initiatives makes accession to and ratification of the Protocol unnecessary. Some states may lack the confidence in their capacity to fulfil Protocol obligations, or because they prefer to address the issue on their own terms and not under international obligation. This may explain the small number of states parties in some parts of Asia.

The smuggling of migrants creates a complex national security, international relations and human rights problem. Smuggling of migrants is the subject of fierce and controversial debate, polarizes public opinion and features prominently in political contests and media coverage. Combatting the smuggling of migrants poses unique challenges to the international community and to national governments. Adding to the complexity is the role many countries play in the web of smuggling routes that connect sending, transit and destination points by land, sea and air.

[55] See further, Andreas Schloenhardt and Hamish Macdonald, 'Barriers to Ratification of the United Nations Protocol against the Smuggling of Migrants' (2017) 7 Asian Journal of International Law 13.

[56] Peter Andreas and Ethan Nadelman, *Policing the Globe: Criminalization and Crime Control in International Relations* (OUP 2006) 105; Mireille Delmas-Marty, *Ordering Pluralism: A Conceptual Framework for Understanding the Transnational Legal World* (Hart 2009) 107; Neil Boister, 'The Concept and Nature of Transnational Criminal Law' in Neil Boister and Robert Currie (eds), *Routledge Handbook of Transnational Criminal Law* (Routledge 2015) 11, 23.

[57] Gallagher, 'Migrant Smuggling' (n 33) 188.

In international law, the Smuggling of Migrants Protocol is presently the best available tool to suppress the smuggling of migrants, but it does little to protect smuggled migrants and address the root causes of displacement. In many states, the Protocol has been used to justify tougher border controls and measures to stop smugglers and migrants alike.

History, however, shows that restrictions placed on the free movement of people are playing into the hands of migrant smugglers who can offer clandestine methods of migration and supply fraudulent documents, while taking advantage of those willing or forced to migrate. For many smuggled migrants, the illegal services offered by the smugglers represent the only way to escape persecution, violence, discrimination or other forms of threat and harm. For others, migrant smuggling is seen as the only or most immediate avenue to escape poverty and unemployment and find a better life for themselves, their families and friends.

The shortcomings of the Protocol are addressed, to some extent, by the Global Compact for Safe, Orderly and Regular Migration, which was adopted by the UN General Assembly on 19 December 2018.[58] It seeks to improve cooperation on international migration, enhance migration governance, human mobility and the rights of migrants. The Global Compact contains specific sections on smuggling of migrants that echo the obligations under the Protocol but also place smuggling into the broader migration context. Importantly, the Global Compact contains a range of measures aimed at creating durable solutions to irregular migration in all its forms, something the Protocol failed to consider.

The future of international law against smuggling of migrants thus lies in a combination of criminal justice and human rights frameworks that balance the desire to prevent and combat migrant smuggling with the need to protect smuggled migrants, facilitate human movement and recognize the causes of international migration.

[58] UN General Assembly, Global Compact for Safe, Orderly and Regular Migration, UN Doc A/RES/73/195 (11 January 2019).

# 13

# Organized Crime

## The Road to the Palermo Convention

*Serena Forlati*

## I. Introduction

The United Nations Convention against Transnational Organized Crime (UNTOC, 2000 Palermo Convention), adopted by the United Nations (UN) General Assembly on 15 November 2000 and entering into force on 29 September 2003,[1] has rapidly become one of the most widely ratified international treaties—it currently has 190 Contracting Parties[2]—and is increasingly resorted to as a basis for international cooperation against very different manifestations of transnational organized crime.

A wealth of documentation on the steps leading to this fairly recent document—from the 1975 United Nations Congress on the Prevention of Crime and the Treatment of Offenders[3] to the establishment of the Commission for Crime Prevention and Criminal Justice (CCPCJ) in 1992,[4] the adoption of the Political Declaration and Plan of Action at the Naples Ministerial Conference of 1994,[5] and the work of the Ad Hoc Committee on the Elaboration of a Convention against Transnational Organized Crime (Ad Hoc Committee) established in 1998[6]—is

[1] On the High-Level Political Signing Conference in Palermo see Gualtiero Michelini and Gioacchino Polimeni, 'Il fenomeno del crimine transnazionale e la Convenzione delle Nazioni Unite contro il crimine organizzato transnazionale' in Elisabetta Rosi (ed), *Criminalità organizzata transnazionale e sistema penale italiano—La Convenzione ONU di Palermo* (IPSOA 2007) 1, 21 (hereafter Michelini and Polimeni, 'Il fenomeno' and Rosi, *Criminalità*).

[2] Information available at <www.treaties.un.org>.

[3] Fifth United Nations Congress on the Prevention of Crime and the Treatment of Offenders, Geneva, 1 –12 September 1975. See further UNODC, *Travaux préparatoires of the negotiations for the elaboration of the United Nations Convention against Transnational Organized Crime and the Protocols thereto* (United Nations 2006) ix (hereafter UNODC, *Travaux préparatoires*); Mahmoud Cherif Bassiouni and Eduardo Vetere (eds), *Organized Crime: A Compilation of UN Documents, 1975–1998*, (Transnational Publishers 1998) Introduction, xvii et seq.

[4] ECOSOC Res 1992/1, 6 February 1992. ECOSOC acted upon request of the UN General Assembly (see GA Res 46/152 of 18 December 1991, para 11) and later identified transnational crime as one of the priority areas for the CCPCJ in Res 1992/22, 30 June 1992, VI(1)(a). See again UNODC, *Travaux préparatoires* (n 3) xii–xiii.

[5] World Ministerial Conference on Organized Transnational Crime, held at Naples, Italy, 21–23 November 1994, para 34. The Naples Political Declaration and Plan of Action was endorsed by the UN General Assembly in Res 49/159 of 23 December 1994.

[6] See UN General Assembly Res 53/111, 9 December 1998.

Serena Forlati, *Organized Crime* In: *Histories of Transnational Criminal Law*. Edited by: Neil Boister, Sabine Gless and Florian Jeßberger, Oxford University Press. © Serena Forlati 2021. DOI: 10.1093/oso/9780192845702.003.0014

widely available in official repositories[7] and several accounts on the negotiations have been provided, including by experts directly involved in the exercise.[8] Rather than attempting a complete review of those materials, this contribution will, firstly, put the UNTOC in the broader context of the construction of transnational criminal law; it will then seek to identify the main inputs and driving forces that led to the adoption of the Convention; thirdly, it will focus on the background of some provisions that arguably explain the Convention's success or innovations as compared to previous suppression conventions. Some concluding remarks will follow.

## II. The Palermo Convention and the Evolution of 'Transnational Criminal Law'

The Palermo Convention is among the most recent examples of multilateral suppression conventions contributing to the system of transnational criminal law.[9]

In the wake of the UNTOC's adoption, Clark observed that the

> most noticeable antecedent of the Convention against Transnational Crime is … the Declaration concerning the Slave Trade adopted at the Congress of Vienna in 1815. That Declaration introduced into multilateral State practice the notion of programmatic obligations, obligations to move in a particular direction without all the modalities spelled out. State practice was, at about the same time, beginning to experiment with the notion of an obligation to suppress some

[7] See UNODC, *Travaux préparatoires* (n 3); 'Report of the Ad Hoc Committee on the Elaboration of a Convention against Transnational Organized Crime on the work of its first to eleventh sessions', UN Doc A/55/383, 3 November 2000. See further <https://www.unodc.org/unodc/en/treaties/CTOC/travaux- preparatoires.html>.

[8] See eg Gerhard Kemp, 'The United Nations Convention against Transnational Organized Crime: A Milestone in International Criminal Law' (2001) 14 SACJ 152; Dimitri Vlassis, 'Drafting the United Nations Convention against Transnational Organized Crime' in Phil Williams and Dimitri Vlassis, *Combating Transnational Crime—Concepts, Activities and Responses* (Frank Cass 2001) 373 (hereafter Vlassis, 'Drafting' and Williams and Vlassis, *Combating*); Anne Gallagher, 'Human Rights and the New UN Protocols on Trafficking and Migrant Smuggling: A Preliminary Analysis' (2001) 23 Hum Rights Q 975 (hereafter Gallagher, 'Human Rights') discussing the parent convention alongside with the Protocols; Michelini and Polimeni, 'Il fenomeno' (n 1); Peter Gastrow, 'The Origins of the Convention' in Hans-Jörg Albrecht and Cyrille Fijnaut, *The Containment of Transnational Organized Crime—Comments on the UN Convention of December 2000* (iuscrim 2002) 19 (hereafter Gastrow, 'The Origins'); Stefano Betti, 'New Prospects for Inter-State Cooperation in Criminal Matters: The Palermo Convention' (2003) 3 International Criminal Law Review 151 (hereafter Betti, 'New Prospects'); David McLean, *Transnational Organized Crime: A Commentary on the UN Convention and its Protocols* (OUP 2007) 1 et seq (hereafter McLean, *Transnational*); Andreas Schloenhardt, 'Transnational Organized Crime and International Criminal Law' in Mahmoud Cherif Bassiouni (ed), *International Criminal Law Volume I—Sources, Subjects and Contents* (3rd edn, Nijhoff 2008) 939 (hereafter Schloenhardt, 'Transnational'); Neil Boister, 'The UN Convention against Transnational Organised Crime 2000' in Pierre Hauck and Sven Peterke, *International Law and Transnational Organized Crime* (OUP 2016) 126 (hereafter Boister, 'UN Convention').

[9] See Boister, Chapter 3 in this book, also for further references.

proscribed activity through the criminal law, usually imposed by treaty, but sometimes by customary law.[10]

The UNTOC differs from these earlier instruments in many ways, some of which are discussed below. However, other elements are in clear continuity with such antecedents.

Notably, the Palermo Convention is based on the assumption that criminalization of offences must find its basis in domestic law. Moreover, respect for state sovereignty is expressly safeguarded beyond the realm of criminalization *stricto sensu* under article 4, which stipulates:

> *Protection of sovereignty:* 1. States Parties shall carry out their obligations under this Convention in a manner consistent with the principles of sovereign equality and territorial integrity of States and that of non-intervention in the domestic affairs of other States.
>
> 2. Nothing in this Convention entitles a State Party to undertake in the territory of another State the exercise of jurisdiction and performance of functions that are reserved exclusively for the authorities of that other State by its domestic law.[11]

This provision is modelled after article 2(2) and (3) of the 1988 Drug Trafficking Convention. In the case of the *Immunities and Criminal Proceedings (Equatorial Guinea v France)*,[12] the International Court of Justice (ICJ) emphasized this link, interpreting article 4 in the light of the work of the Ad Hoc Committee[13] but also of the Commentary to the 1988 Drug Trafficking Convention, which it deemed 'relevant to the Court's examination of article 4 of the Palermo Convention'.[14] In rejecting Equatorial Guinea's construction, the ICJ highlighted that the rationale underlying article 2(2) was to reiterate 'universally accepted and well-established principles of international law' in an instrument going 'much further than previous drug control treaties in matters of law enforcement and mutual legal assistance'.[15] Moreover,

[10] Roger S Clark, 'The United Nations Convention against Transnational Organized Crime' (2002) 50 Wayne L Rev 161, 164 (hereafter Clark, 'Convention').

[11] The same rationale underlies the requirement of transnationality under art 3, which aims at avoiding 'pervasive practices of interference' by other states: see Gioacchino Polimeni, 'The Notion of Organised Crime in the United Nations Convention against Transnational Organized Crime' in Stefania Carnevale, Serena Forlati and Orsetta Giolo, *Redefining Organised Crime—A Challenge for the European Union?* (Hart 2017) 57, 64 (hereafter Polimeni, 'The Notion' and Carnevale and others, *Redefining*).

[12] *Equatorial Guinea v France* (Judgment) [2018] ICJ Rep 292 (hereafter *Equatorial Guinea v France*).

[13] ibid 322 paras 96 et seq.

[14] ibid 322 para 99.

[15] United Nations, 'Commentary on the United Nations Convention against Illicit Traffic in Narcotic Drugs and Psychotropic Substances 1988', Doc E/CN.7/590, New York 1998, 41–42, paras 2.1–2.3; cf *Equatorial Guinea v France* (n 12) 322 para 99.

> [t]he protection of the sovereignty, territorial integrity and domestic jurisdiction of a State is the purpose of article 2 (2) of the Convention against Illicit Traffic in Narcotic Drugs. Article 4 (1) of the Palermo Convention shares that purpose. Neither of these provisions is concerned with the related, but separate, question of the immunities of individuals, or of State property, in foreign territory.[16]

In fact, the line of continuity between the 1988 Drug Trafficking Convention and the Palermo Convention goes well beyond article 4 of the UNTOC. The 1988 Drug Trafficking Convention was 'a milestone on the path to coordinated international action against transnational crime',[17] as it targeted one of its most lucrative activities; David McLean notes that '[a]t least 15 of the operative articles (as opposed to the formal Final Clauses) are derived in whole or in part from the Vienna Convention'.[18]

If, therefore, the link to the 1988 Drug Trafficking Convention explains the origin of certain legal and technical solutions embraced in the UNTOC, the establishment of the G-7 Financial Action Task Force on Money Laundering in 1989 was also an important antecedent,[19] along with developments at the domestic level and in the area of mutual legal assistance.[20] With this in mind, the next section will identify the actors and driving factors which provided the impetus for negotiating the UNTOC.

## III. The Driving Forces behind the Adoption of the Palermo Convention

There is a tendency in Italy to see the Palermo Convention as an 'Italian' endeavour. This assumption has a grain of truth: on the one hand, the Sicilian mafia, with its rigid hierarchical structure and code of conduct, epitomizes the notion of organized crime—although of course similar structures exist in many areas of the world, with or without any historical connection to the Italian experience.[21] On the

[16] ibid 322 para 101.

[17] UNODC, *Travaux préparatoires* (n 3) xi. See Gastrow, 'The Origins' (n 8) 22–23. On the link between drug trafficking and organized crime see Richard Vogler and Shahrzad Fouladvand, 'The Convention against Illicit Traffic in Narcotic Drugs and Psychotropic Substances 1988 and the Global War on Drugs' in Pierre Hauck and Sven Peterke, *International Law and Transnational Organized Crime* (OUP 2016) 106, 108.

[18] McLean, *Transnational* (n 8) 11. Michelini and Polimeni, 'Il fenomeno' (n 1) 13, note that the UNTOC nonetheless puts a much stronger emphasis than the 1988 Drug Trafficking Convention on prevention and technical assistance (see at 12, as regards its relationship with the 1997 Terrorist Bombings Convention and of the 1999 Terrorist Financing Convention).

[19] Gastrow, 'The Origins' (n 8) 22–23.

[20] ibid.

[21] See, among many others, Federico Varese, *Mafias on the Move* (Princeton UP 2011); Mitchel P Roth, *Global Organized Crime—A 21st Century Approach* (2nd edn, Routledge 2017); and the contributions collected in Williams and Vlassis, *Combating* (n 8); Heinrich-Böll-Stiftung and Regine Schönenberg (eds), *Transnational Organized Crime—Analyses of a Global Challenge to Democracy*

other hand, the experience of cooperation between the United States of America and Italy in the field of drug trafficking—with the direct participation of Judge Giovanni Falcone, one of the most prominent Italian anti-mafia figures[22] and an advocate of international cooperation in this field[23]—led not only to important legislative and operational reforms in the fight against organized crime in Italy, but also to a strong political engagement of the Italian government in the elaboration of international instruments in this field, including the UNTOC.[24]

It goes without saying that the Palermo Convention could eventually be adopted only because a much broader consensus emerged around this project.[25] The political blueprint for the development of the new instrument came from the UN General Assembly in 1991. In setting out the scope of the UN crime prevention and criminal justice programme the General Assembly indicated that it 'may also include ... further development and promotion of international instruments on crime prevention and criminal justice'.[26] This input proved fruitful. Soon thereafter, the Report of the CCPCJ's First Session recorded:

> All speakers emphasized their serious concern about organized crime, including drug trafficking, the arms trade and terrorism, which was increasingly assuming new forms and transnational dimensions. Organized Crime was a world-wide problem, which affected both developing and developed countries and was

(Transcript Verlag 2013) (hereafter Heinrich-Böll-Stiftung and Schönenberg, *Transnational Organized Crime*); Letizia Paoli (ed), *The Oxford Handbook of Organized Crime* (OUP 2014) (hereafter Paoli, *Handbook*).

[22] On the contacts between Giovanni Falcone and US law enforcement authorities in the framework of operation 'Pizza connection' see Leonardo Guarnotta, 'La Convenzione di Palermo 3/Alle origini. Il ruolo di Palermo e di Giovanni Falcone' (2019) 5 Studi e ricerche sulla criminalità organizzata 43, 57–58. Shortly before his assassination, Falcone attended the first meeting of the CCPCJ as a member of the Italian delegation (Andreas Schloenhardt, 'Transnational Organized Crime' in Neil Boister and Robert J Currie, *Routledge Handbook of Transnational Criminal Law* (Routledge 2015) 409, 410 (hereafter Boister and Currie, *Routledge Handbook*). cf also Cyrille Fijnaut, 'Twenty Years Ago: The Assassinations of Giovanni Falcone and Paolo Borsellino' in André Klip and Hans-Jörg Albrecht (eds), *Crime, Criminal Law and Criminal Justice in Europe: A Collection in Honour of Cyrille Fijnaut* (Nijhoff 2013) 61 (hereafter Fijnaut, 'Twenty Years').

[23] Giovanni Falcone, 'La criminalité organisée: un problème mondial. La mafia italienne en tant que modèle pour la criminalité organisée opérant au niveau international' (1992) 45 Revue internationale de criminologie et de police technique 391, 398.

[24] Gualtiero Michelini, 'La Convenzione di Palermo 2/Il ruolo dell'Italia nella redazione del testo finale' (2019) 5 Studi e ricerche sulla criminalità organizzata 21.

[25] Pino Arlacchi noted that '[n]o United Nations Convention has ever had so many signatories immediately upon its opening for signature and less than one month after its formal adoption by the General Assembly. The implication is clear: the Palermo Convention strikes a chord that echoes throughout the world.' ('Keynote Speech' in Brice De Ruyver, Gert Vermeulen and Tom Vander Beken (eds), *Strategies of the EU and the US in Combating Transnational Organized Crime* (Maklu 2002) 25 (hereafter Arlacchi, 'Keynote' and De Ruyver and others, *Strategies*).

[26] Res 46/152, Annex—Statement of principles and programme of action for the UN crime prevention and criminal justice programme, principle 20. The Statement of principles is based on work and proposals elaborated at the Paris Ministerial Conference on the same topic of 21–23 November 1991: see Michelini and Polimeni, 'Il fenomeno' (n 1) 1.

> capable of threatening the institutional structure of countries and paralyzing national administrations.[27]

Among other factors explaining the expansion of organized crime, the Report identified 'free movement across frontiers'.[28] Indeed, members of what is now the European Union were sensitive to this facilitating factor at a time when the European Single Market was being completed and the Maastricht Treaty adopted—with the early steps of cooperation in criminal matters being regulated under Title VI.[29] This development helped convince some EU member states which had until then doubted the concept of organized crime and its relevance to their domestic communities.[30] Thus, according to Michelini,

> The Italian approach in the *Ad Hoc* Committee, which aimed at overcoming diffidence on the need to develop criminal cooperation against organized crime, had been elaborated—one may say, disseminated—within EU Institutions. Considerations had been shared and understood in Brussels on the opening of European interior borders as a factor facilitating transnational conduct and relocation of criminal groups in other States; on the emergence of organized crime in Eastern European Countries; on issues raised by economic crime and money laundering, which are typically organized criminal phenomena.[31]

This perceived need in Europe intersected with similar beliefs on the other side of the Atlantic. The consequences of the end of the Cold War were giving rise to further causes for concern as previously state-sponsored insurgents or extremist

[27] CCPCJ, 'Report on the First Session, 21–30 April 1992', ECOSOC Official Records, 1992, Supp no 10, UN Doc E/1992/30, para 60. Already the second CCPCJ session led to the organization of the Naples Ministerial Conference, and from this point onwards the process of elaborating the UNTOC was relatively swift (see McLean, *Transnational* (n 8)); nonetheless, diverging views emerged as to whether the emphasis of the new instrument should be on the 'transnational' or on the 'organized' nature of crime, which left traces in some linguistic versions of the 2000 Palermo Convention: see Michelini and Polimeni, 'Il fenomeno' (n 1); Gastrow, 'The Origins' (n 8) 26.

[28] CCPCJ, 'Report on the First Session' (n 27) para 60.

[29] Treaty on European Union, Maastricht, 7 February 1992, Title VI—Provisions on Cooperation in the Fields of Justice and Home Affairs, OJ C 191, 29 July 1992, 4; see Cyrille Fijnaut, 'Transnational Organized Crime and Institutional Reform in the European Union: The Case of Judicial Cooperation' in Williams and Vlassis, *Combating* (n 8) 276, 281.

[30] Michelini and Polimeni, 'Il fenomeno' (n 1) 9. See Gastrow, 'The Origins' (n 8) 26; Fijnaut, 'Twenty Years' (n 22).

[31] 'L'approccio italiano nel Comitato ad hoc, mirato a superare diffidenze sulla necessità di sviluppare la cooperazione penale contro il crimine organizzato, era stato sperimentato, per così dire disseminato, nelle istituzioni dell'Unione europea. A Bruxelles erano state diffuse e recepite considerazioni sull'apertura delle frontiere infra-europee anche come fattore di facilitazione delle condotte transnazionali e della dislocazione in altri Stati dei gruppi criminali; sull'emergere del crimine organizzato nei paesi dell'Europa dell'Est; sulle questioni suscitate dai crimini economici e dal riciclaggio, fenomeni criminali tipicamente organizzati' (Gualtiero Michelini, 'La Convenzione di Palermo 2/Il ruolo dell'Italia nella redazione del testo finale' (2019) 5 Rivista di studi e ricerche sulla criminalità organizzata 21, 25, translation by this author). See also Cyrille Fijnaut, 'European Union Organized Crime Control Policies' in Paoli, *Handbook* (n 21) 572, 575.

groups turned to criminal endeavours such as drug trafficking in order to finance their activities.[32] Thus, the Clinton administration identified the fight against transnational crime as a top national security interest of the United States of America.[33] After 'externalizing' their approach to drug trafficking in the 1980s[34] and taking the lead in the negotiation of the 1988 Drug Trafficking Convention, the United States thus also sought to internationalize their policies in the field of organized crime.[35]

In light of this picture, the outcome of the 1994 World Ministerial Conference is seen as 'represent[ing] a coincidence of interests between the United States, the member states of the European Union and the internal politics of the UN itself'.[36] The Convention would, however, not have been achieved in the same terms had the challenge of combating 'grand criminality' not been taken up also in other areas of the world,[37] with the UN serving 'as a clearing house and coordinator of new ideas that went beyond addressing domestic interests'.[38]

## IV. Behind the Specifics of the Palermo Convention: A Flexible and Integrated Approach in the Fight against Transnational Crime

The UNTOC's purpose, as stated in article 1, is to 'promote cooperation to prevent and combat international crime more effectively'.

At the time of the UNTOC's adoption there was a belief that this would require '[f]lexible multilateral agreements that allow law enforcement agencies in our many countries to pursue criminals and time-sensitive investigative leads in

[32] Bryan Sonderholm, 'US Presentation on the International Criminal Threat' in De Ruyver and others, *Strategies* (n 25) 43 (hereafter Sonderholm, 'US Presentation').

[33] On Presidential Directive 42 of 1995 see W Chamberlin, 'Remarks before the EU-US Conference on Strategies to Combat Transnational Organized Crime' in De Ruyverand others, *Strategies* (n 25) 31, 33; MM Richard, 'International Assistance in Combating Crime' in De Ruyver and others, *Strategies* (n 25) 227, 229; Gastrow, 'The Origins' (n 8) 29–30.

[34] Margaret Beare and Michael Woodiwiss, 'US Organized Crime Control Policies Exported Abroad' in Paoli, *Handbook* (n 21) 545, 551 (hereafter Beare and Woodiwiss, 'US'). For a critical appraisal of the motivations behind the US approach, Bruce Bullington and Alan A Block, 'A Trojan Horse: Anti-Communism and the War on Drugs' (1990) 14 Contemporary Crises 39, reprinted in Nikos Passas (ed), *Organized Crime* (Dartmouth 1995) 501.

[35] Beare and Woodiwiss, 'US' (n 34) 552. See further Bruce Zagaris, 'US Practice in Cross-Border Operations against Transnational Crime' in De Ruyver and others, *Strategies* (n 25) 155. On the US policies targeting corruption see Rose, Chapter 14 in this book. On the role of the Organization of American States see Vlassis, 'Drafting' (n 8) 359.

[36] Bere and Woodiwiss, 'US' (n 34) 552 arguing that 'Nations that have ratified the UNTOC Convention have committed themselves to the type of American measures deemed to be effective in combating organized crime by the UN.'

[37] Michelini and Polimeni, 'Il fenomeno' (n 1) 9. On developments at regional level leading to the adoption of the Palermo Convention see 'Report of the Ad Hoc Committee' (n 7) paras 9 et seq. As to the work of the G8 on the topic and the role of the Lyon Group see Betti, 'New Prospects' (n 8); A Scherrer, *G8 Against Transnational Organized Crime* (Routledge 2009).

[38] Gastrow, 'The Origins' (n 8) 27.

foreign countries with minimal impediments'.[39] The negotiators pursued such flexibility, which is arguably one of the main reasons for the Convention's success. It emerges in different ways, well beyond the optional or hortatory clauses and qualifications by reference to the domestic legal systems of the parties that also featured in previous instruments.[40]

The UNTOC pursues harmonization of domestic law not only as a way to favour international cooperation: it also aims at reinforcing the capacity of domestic legal orders to fight organized crime, thus establishing a 'general criminal policy'.[41] Nonetheless, the obligations of criminalization enshrined in the Convention are framed in such a way as not to hinder acceptability to states with different legal traditions. Notably, this rationale underpins the formulation of article 5 on the obligation to criminalize participation in an organized criminal group: the formulation encompasses both the criminalization model based on the common law concept of conspiracy and the French notion of *association de malfaiteurs*, aiming at a 'functional synthesis'[42] rather than at a complete harmonization of the legal systems of the parties.

As to the definition of 'organized criminal group', at the Naples Ministerial Conference it was suggested 'to make participation in Mafia-like organizations a criminal offence'.[43] However, the—much criticized[44]—final wording of article 2(a) and (c) UNTOC targets not only highly structured criminal organizations but also looser criminal networks,[45] in line with the outcomes of criminological research at the time of the Convention's adoption.[46] Even the requirement that criminal groups pursue a 'financial or other material benefit' is flexible enough to encompass some

[39] Sonderholm, 'US Presentation' (n 32) 47. See also the views of the chief Canadian negotiator, Keith Morrill, as reported in Alexandra V Orlova and James W Moore, 'Umbrellas or Building Blocks: Defining International Terrorism and Transnational Organized Crime in International Law' (2005) 27 Hous J Int'l L 267, 285 (hereafter Orlova and Moore, 'Umbrellas').

[40] On these clauses see 'Legislative Guide for the Implementation of the United Nations Convention against Transnational Organized Crime' 3–4 paras 12–13 <https://www.unodc.org/unodc/en/treaties/CTOC/legislative- guide.html#_Full_Version_2>. See Neil Boister, 'Human Rights Protections in the Suppression Conventions' (2002) 2 Hum Rts L Rev 199, 211–12 (hereafter Boister, 'Human Rights').

[41] Gualtiero Michelini and Gioacchino Polimeni, 'Le linee guida della Convenzione di Palermo e la legge italiana di ratifica' in Rosi, *Criminalità* (n 1) 33, 35.

[42] Clark, 'Convention' (n 8) 170; see also Gioacchino Polimeni, and, on the EU legal framework, Francesco Calderoni, *Organized Crime Legislation in the European Union* (Springer 2010); Vincenzo Militello, 'The Notion of Organised Crime in EU Law' in Carnevale and others, *Redefining* (n 11) 191.

[43] UNODC, *Travaux préparatoires* (n 3) xv, 19 et seq.

[44] For a detailed analysis of this notion and that of 'structured group' under art 2(c) see Polimeni, 'The Notion' (n 11). See further Schloenhardt, 'Transnational' (n 8) 950; Tom Obokata, *Transnational Organised Crime in International Law* (Hart 2010); Orlova and Moore (n 39) 285 (recalling however that the negotiators' focus was on enhancing international cooperation rather than defining organized crime adequately). For a perspective from EU Law cf Francesco Calderoni, 'A Definition that Does Not Work : The Impact of the EU Framework Decision on the Fight against Organized Crime' (2012) 49 CML Rev 1365 ; Vincenzo Militello, 'Transnational Organized Crime and European Union: Aspects and Problems' in Heinrich-Böll- Stiftung and Schönenberg, *Transnational* (n 21) 255.

[45] See also the interpretative note to art 2(c) in UNODC, *Travaux préparatoires* (n 3) 17.

[46] Vlassis, 'Drafting' (n 8) 358; Boister, 'UN Convention' (n 8) 133.

criminal activities of politically motivated formations, that in principle would not fall within the scope of the offence.[47]

Another key element in this regard is that, besides the four offences established in articles 5, 6, 8 and 23, the Convention applies to any 'serious crime' which is transnational in nature and committed by an organized criminal group, under articles 3(1)(b) and 2(b). The choice not to set forth a closed list of offences could be agreed upon only in the final phase of the negotiations.[48] Taken together with the loose notion of 'organized criminal group' just discussed and with the UNTOC's almost-universal ratification, it implies that the Convention often provides a 'general' legal basis for targeting transnational crime,[49] overlapping with other instruments of transnational criminal law and *de facto* somehow superseding them.

Another specificity of the Palermo Convention is its integrated approach to the fight against crime. The UNTOC sets forth obligations not only of criminalization and mutual legal assistance but also of prevention—with notably article 31 engaging the parties in targeting risk factors, including social marginalization[50]—and protection of specific vulnerable groups such as victims, witnesses and those cooperating with law enforcement authorities.[51] The latter provisions were discussed from the outset of the negotiation process[52] and could be seen as a tool for effective law enforcement action. However, the Ad Hoc Committee made it clear that it 'was cognizant of the need for protection of the rights of individuals as accorded under applicable international law'[53]—an unequivocal albeit indirect reference to international human rights law. Moreover, the Palermo Convention was drafted in a context of growing awareness that international cooperation in the fight against crime may significantly affect internationally protected human rights of persons targeted by law enforcement measures, also in light of the European Court of Human Rights' stance in *Soering*.[54] While the parent Convention includes

[47] On the objections of notably Turkey and Egypt see UNODC, *Travaux préparatoires* (n 3) 15, 31. See also for further references Alessandra Annoni, 'The Relationship between Organized Crime and Terrorism: An International Law Perspective' in Carnevale and others, *Redefining* (n 11) 121; Antonio Balsamo (interview by Daniela Piana), 'Lutter contre le terrorisme et l'État de droit: les nouvelles frontières de la justice pénale' in Daniela Piana and François Molinié (eds), *La lutte contre le terrorisme et les droits fondamentaux en droit comparé* (Societé de législation compare 2018) 79, 81 et seq.

[48] See Vlassis, 'Drafting' (n 8) 359–60; Michelini and Polimeni, 'Il fenomeno' (n 1) 11. See for a critical appraisal the statement reported by Orlova and Moore, 'Umbrellas' (n 39) 285.

[49] Serena Forlati, 'The Contribution of UNODC to Ocean Governance' in David Joseph Attard, Malgosia Fitzmaurice and Alexandros MT Ntovas, *The IMLI Treatise on Global Ocean Governance Volume II—UN Specialized Agencies and Global Ocean Governance* (OUP 2018) 227, 233.

[50] UNTOC, art 31 (especially paras 3 and 7). See Arlacchi, 'Keynote' (n 25). Already the informal preparatory meeting of Buenos Aires in 1998 recorded 'widespread acceptance of the principle that the convention should include provisions on prevention'; the Netherlands later presented several drafts of what became art 31: UNDOC, *Travaux préparatoires* (n 3) 261 fn 1.

[51] UNTOC, arts 24, 25 and 26(4). Art 25 also sets forth obligations of *assistance* to victims.

[52] UNODC, *Travaux préparatoires* (n 3) xv, xxiii, 217 et seq.

[53] Interpretative Note to art 25, reproduced ibid 224.

[54] *Soering v the United Kingdom*, App no 14038/88, 7 July 1989. See Boister, 'Human Rights' (n 40) 203; Robert J Currie, 'The Protection of Human Rights in the Suppression of Transnational Crime' in Boister and Currie, *Routledge Handbook* (n 22) 27 (hereafter Currie, 'Protection').

few explicit safeguards for individual rights and no direct reference to international human rights law[55] the Supplementing Protocols on Trafficking and Smuggling take a different approach, thanks mainly to pressure from within the UN and from NGOs.[56] Civil society thus played a key role in ensuring systemic integration between the two sets of rules, which is indispensable for the correct implementation of the Palermo Convention.[57]

## V. Conclusion

The road to the Palermo Convention was long and complex. The resulting instrument is in line with the tradition of suppression conventions and has a direct connection with the developments in the 1980s in the fight against drug trafficking: bilateral cooperation in this area led to the adoption of the 1988 Drug Trafficking Convention, which in turn served as a model for the UNTOC. The fall of the Berlin wall and the ensuing developments in the patterns of organized crime were catalysing events, together with the process of European integration. The EU and the USA were among the main supporters of the new instrument, which also, however, found broad acceptance at the international level thanks to the role played by the UN, with pressure from civil society contributing to one of its most innovative aspects—that is, the integrated approach to the fight against crime, encompassing crime prevention and protection of human rights, particularly in the Supplementing Protocols. The final text reflects the need for a flexible instrument, matching the protean nature of organizations engaged in transnational crime; specifically the recourse to the notion of 'serious crime' rather than to a closed list of offences enables the Convention to work as a 'catch-all' legal basis for targeting transnational crime, often overlapping with sectoral instruments—including its precursor, the 1988 Drug Trafficking Convention.

[55] Boister, 'Human Rights' (n 40) 212 et seq.

[56] Gallagher, 'Human Rights' (n 8) 1002–03.

[57] Gallagher, 'Human Rights' (n 8) and, more extensively, Anne T Gallagher, *International Law on Human Trafficking* (CUP 2010); Anne T Gallagher and Fiona David, *The International Law of Migrant Smuggling* (CUP 2014); Boister, 'Human Rights' (n 40) 215–16; Currie, 'Protection' (n 54) 40.

# 14

# The Origins of International Anti-Corruption Law

## The Failed Negotiation of an International Agreement on Illicit Payments

*Cecily Rose*

## I. Introduction

International law has given the term 'corruption' a particular meaning that should be seen not as inevitable, but as a product of history. The meaning of corruption in international law is narrower than both the colloquial use of this word and the way in which it is understood by economists and social scientists.[1] Much of international anti-corruption law, which emerged only in the 1990s and early 2000s, conceives of corruption as encompassing specific crimes, in particular bribery.[2] To a lesser extent, this body of law also encompasses other crimes such as the embezzlement or misappropriation of public funds, illicit enrichment and other conduct that closely resembles bribery (trading in influence and abuse of functions).[3]

International anti-corruption law's present-day focus on corruption as bribery is a product of corporate scandals of the 1970s, and the way that the United States framed those scandals at the time. As in other areas of transnational criminal law, the US played a critical role in defining this problem and identifying a legal solution to it.[4] But the US response to these scandals in the 1970s was reactive, rather

[1] Michael Johnston, *Syndromes of Corruption: Wealth, Power, and Democracy* (CUP 2005) 10–13 (defining corruption as 'the abuse of public roles or resources for private benefit'); Susan Rose-Ackerman and Bonnie J Palifka, *Corruption and Government: Causes, Consequences, and Reform* (2nd edn, CUP 2016) 8–9 (identifying fraud, conflicts of interest and nepotism as forms of corruption).

[2] See eg OECD Anti-Bribery Convention; Council of Europe Criminal Law Convention on Corruption (adopted 27 January 1999, entered into force 1 December 2009) CETS No 173 (CoE Criminal Law Convention), arts 2–11.

[3] 1996 Inter-American Convention against Corruption (covering abuse of functions (art VI(c)) and illicit enrichment (art IX)); Council of Europe Criminal Law Convention, art 12 (covering trading in influence); UN Convention against Corruption (UNCAC), arts 17–20 (covering embezzlement and misappropriation of public funds in mandatory terms, and trading in influence, abuse of functions and illicit enrichment in semi-mandatory terms).

[4] Peter Andreas and Ethan Nadelmann, *Policing the Globe: Criminalization and Crime Control in International Relations* (OUP 2006).

Cecily Rose, *The Origins of International Anti-Corruption Law* In: *Histories of Transnational Criminal Law*.
Edited by: Neil Boister, Sabine Gless and Florian Jeßberger, Oxford University Press. © Cecily Rose 2021.
DOI: 10.1093/oso/9780192845702.003.0015

than proactive.[5] The US was responding to an expansive framing of the problem by Chile, which denounced the 'corruptive influence' of foreign multinational corporations in domestic politics. While the narrow framing put forward by the US ultimately prevailed, this did not occur until the 1990s. The meaning of corruption was contested to such an extent in the mid to late 1970s that UN member states could not agree on the scope of the problem, nor a solution to it, and the topic was temporarily abandoned.

While the origins of the 1997 Organisation for Economic Co-operation and Development (OECD) Anti-Bribery Convention and its relationship to the Watergate scandal of the 1970s in the United States have been studied extensively,[6] the failed negotiation of an international agreement on 'illicit payments' at the UN in the 1970s has not been the subject of a dedicated legal study.[7] In addition, the reactive posture of the US during these negotiations has also not been widely acknowledged or appreciated. The story behind these treaty negotiations is significant for our understanding of the contemporary international legal approach to corruption.

The second section of this chapter sets the historical context by describing the political aftermath of corporate scandals in Chile and the US and the politics surrounding corporate involvement in Southern Africa.[8] The third section explains that treaty negotiations at the UN failed in the 1970s because member states could not agree on the scope of the term 'illicit payments' or on the most appropriate way to regulate corrupt conduct. The fourth section concludes by observing how the politics of the 1970s is reflected in the existing body of international anti-corruption instruments, which emerged in the 1990s and 2000s.

## II. The Historical Context: Allende, Watergate and Apartheid

The treaty negotiations that took place at the UN in the mid to late 1970s can only be understood in the context of two major scandals involving misconduct by American multinational corporations. The first scandal involved attempts by

[5] Elitza Katzarova, *The Social Construction of Global Corruption: From Utopia to Neoliberalism* (Palgrave Macmillan 2018) 77 (examining these historical developments from an international relations perspective) (hereafter Katzarova, *The Social Construction*).

[6] See eg Kenneth W Abbott and Duncan Snidal, 'Values and Interests: International Legalization in the Fight Against Corruption' (2002) 31 J Leg Stud 141; Mike Koehler, 'The Story of the Foreign Corrupt Practices Act' (2012) 73 Ohio State Law Journal 929; Kevin E Davis, *Between Impunity and Imperialism: The Regulation of Transnational Bribery* (OUP 2019) (hereafter Davis, *Impunity*).

[7] See eg James Thuo Gathi, 'Defining the Relationship between Human Rights and Corruption' (2009-2010) 31 U Pa J Intl L 125, 138–40; Kenneth W Abbott, 'Corruption, Fight Against' in *Max Planck Encyclopedia of Public International Law* (OUP, last updated September 2009) para 3.

[8] For a discussion of these scandals from the perspective of corporate liability for corruption, see Elliot and Lüth, Chapter 15 in this book.

the American company, International Telephone and Telegraph (ITT), to prevent Salvador Allende's election as president of Chile in 1970. The second scandal involved revelations, in the wake of the Watergate scandal, that hundreds of American corporations had engaged in the bribery of foreign public officials. The involvement of foreign multinational corporations in apartheid Southern Africa also influenced the treaty negotiations that took place at the UN. The following briefly recounts these corporate scandals and the history of economic sanctions in relation to Southern Africa, before turning to the UN treaty negotiations in Section 3.

## 1. ITT's Covert Activities in Chile and Allende's Call for Action

In 1970, Salvador Allende was elected president of Chile.[9] Allende was a democratic socialist who had declared his intention, if elected, to nationalize foreign investments in Chile.[10] Allende's plans extended to service industries, including the national telephone company, which was a subsidiary of ITT. American corporations with investments in Chile were apprehensive about the prospect of such expropriations, and were opposed to Allende's election.[11]

In March 1972, the American syndicated journalist, Jack Anderson, reported that ITT had attempted to prevent Allende's election in 1970.[12] ITT had offered USD 1 million in financial assistance to the Central Intelligence Agency (CIA), so that the CIA could fund the candidate opposing Allende, Jorge Alessendri of the National Party.[13] The CIA had declined ITT's offer, though it had advised ITT on how to convey funds to Alessendri.[14] ITT ultimately passed at least USD 350,000 to the opposition campaign, with the awareness of the CIA, but without its assistance.[15] After Allende's election and before he took office, ITT also considered participating in a CIA plot to foment economic chaos in Chile and thereby trigger a military coup that would prevent Allende from coming into power.[16] US efforts to generate an economic crisis did not have their intended impact, and Allende took

[9] Allende was elected on 4 September 1970 and inaugurated on 3 November 1970.

[10] Giuliano Garavini, *After Empires: European Integration, Decolonization, & the Challenges from the Global South 1957–1986* (Richard R Nybakken tr, OUP 2012) 136–38.

[11] United States Senate, Select Committee to Study Governmental Operations with Respect to Intelligence Activities, Covert Action in Chile, 1963–1973 (1975) 12.

[12] Jack Anderson, 'Memos Bare ITT Try for Chile Coup' *The Washington Post* (21 March 1972) B13; Jack Anderson, 'ITT Pledged Millions to Stop Allende' *The Washington Post* (22 March 1972) C23; 'ITT is Accused of Having Tried to Influence U.S. Policies' *The New York Times* (23 March 1972).

[13] United States Senate, Select Committee to Study Governmental Operations with Respect to Intelligence Activities, Covert Action in Chile, 1963–1973 (1975) 12–13.

[14] ibid 12–13.

[15] ibid 12–13.

[16] ibid 25.

office in November 1970.[17] These revelations, as first reported by Anderson, reverberated within the US Congress,[18] and also within the UN Conference on Trade and Development (UNCTAD) and the UN General Assembly.

The third session of UNCTAD (UNCTAD III) took place in Santiago, Chile in April–May 1972, just weeks after the ITT scandal became public. In his inaugural address at UNCTAD III, Allende reportedly 'electrified' the audience by evoking the developing world's collective struggle against capitalism.[19] Allende obliquely referenced the ITT affair and described 'the increasingly obvious conflicts between the public interests of the wealthy nations ... and the private interests of their great corporations'.[20] He further characterized multinational corporations as having a '*powerful corruptive influence* on the public institutions in rich and poor countries alike'.[21] Allende urged UNCTAD to look into the 'flagrant intervention' of corporations in the 'internal affairs of States', and urged the international community to take action.[22]

While UNCTAD did not take up Allende's call, the UN Economic and Social Council (ECOSOC) took initiative, leading to the creation of the United Nations Centre on Transnational Corporations (UNCTC) in 1974.[23] The UN's Under-Secretary General for Economic and Social Affairs, Philippe de Seynes, was in the audience when Allende delivered his inaugural address.[24] De Seynes, an 'activist international civil servant', had a keen and long-standing interest in foreign direct investment and multinational corporations.[25] When ECOSOC met in Geneva, six weeks after UNCTAD III, de Seynes played a key role in securing a mandate from ECOSOC for the creation of an international body that would deal with the conduct of multinational corporations. In addition, Chile's ambassador, Santa Cruz, complained to ECOSOC about ITT's behaviour in Chile, and submitted a draft resolution urging the creation of a Group of Eminent Persons to study the

[17] ibid 25.

[18] The ITT scandal resulted in the creation of the Senate Subcommittee on Multinational Corporations chaired by Frank Church. It held hearings between March 1973 and September 1976.

[19] Khalil Hamdani and Lorraine Ruffing, *United Nations Centre on Transnational Corporations: Corporate Conduct and the Public Interest: With Reflections and Critical Commentary from Colleagues, Delegates and Participants* (Routledge 2015) 8 (hereafter Hamdani and Ruffing, *UNCTC*); Katzarova, *The Social Construction* (n 5).

[20] Address Delivered by Mr Salvador Allende Gossens, President of Chile at the Inaugural Ceremony on 13 April 1972, Proceedings of the United Nations Conference on Trade and Development, Third Session, Santiago de Chile, 13 April–21 May 1971, Vol I, Report and Annexes (UN 1973) 353, para 62. See also UN General Assembly, Twenty-Seventh Session, 2096th Plenary Meeting, Address by Mr Salvador Allende, President of the Republic of Chile, 4 December 1972, paras 36–59.

[21] Address Delivered by Mr Salvador Allende Gossens (n 20) para 58 (emphasis added).

[22] Address Delivered by Mr Salvador Allende Gossens (n 20) para 62.

[23] See generally Katzarova, *The Social Construction* (n 5) 77–81.

[24] Hamdani and Ruffing, *UNCTC* (n 19) 9.

[25] Tagi Sagafi-nejad in collaboration with John H Dunning, *The UN and Transnational Corporations: From Code of Conduct to Global Compact* (Indiana UP 2008) 50; Hamdani and Ruffing, *UNCTC* (n 19) 26.

role of multinational corporations and their impact on the process of development.[26] This resolution was unanimously adopted and, in 1974, the OECD Anti-Bribery Convention Group of Eminent Persons recommended the creation of the UNCTC,[27] which worked for years, unsuccessfully, on a United Nations Code of Conduct on Transnational Corporations.[28]

Chile's direct contribution to the regulation of corporate conduct ended in 1973, with the overthrow and death of Allende and the establishment of a corporate-friendly military dictatorship under Augusto Pinochet, all with the backing of the CIA.[29] But Allende's framing of the ITT scandal as one involving 'corruptive influence' had a lasting impact on the negotiations on a Code of Conduct on Transnational Corporations, as well as an anti-corruption treaty.[30]

## 2. The Watergate Scandal and the 1977 Foreign Corrupt Practices Act

Watergate was the second major scandal of 1972 that influenced the international anti-corruption negotiations at the UN in the 1970s. In June 1972, Carl Bernstein and Bob Woodward of *The Washington Post* reported an attempted burglary at the offices of the Democratic Party's National Committee, at the Watergate building in Washington, DC.[31] Bernstein and Woodward showed that the burglary was a part of a massive spying and sabotage operation run by US President Richard Nixon's re-election campaign, against all of the major the Democratic presidential candidates.[32]

Subsequent investigations by Special Prosecutor Archibald Cox and the US Securities and Exchange Commission (SEC) revealed that major US corporations had used secret 'slush funds' to make illegal contributions to Nixon's re-election campaign as well as 'questionable or illegal foreign payments' in the context of international business deals.[33] In 1975 the SEC launched a voluntary disclosure

[26] ECOSOC Res 1721 (LIII) The impact of multinational corporations on the development process and on international relations (28 July 1972).

[27] Report of the Group of Eminent Persons to Study the Impact of Multinational Corporations on Development and on International Relations in The Impact of Multinational Corporations on the Development and on International Relations, E/5500/Rev.1, 51–53.

[28] Karl Sauvant, 'The Negotiations of the United Nations Code of Conduct on Transnational Corporations' (2015) 16 The Journal of World Investment and Trade 11 (hereafter Sauvant, 'Negotiations').

[29] Seymour M Hersch, 'C.I.A. Chief Tells House of $8-Million Campaign Against Allende in '70–73' *The New York Times* (8 September 1974).

[30] Katzarova, *The Social Construction* (n 5) 81.

[31] See eg Carl Bernstein and Bob Woodward, 'FBI Finds Nixon Aides Sabotaged Democrats' *The Washington Post* (10 October 1972).

[32] Carl Bernstein and Bob Woodward, *All the President's Men* (Simon and Schuster 1974).

[33] US Senate, 'The Final Report of the Select Committee on Presidential Campaign Activities' (June 1974) 445–447.

programme, through which it invited companies to conduct internal investigations into questionable or illegal foreign payments and to disclose the results of their investigations to the SEC.[34] Ultimately more than 400 companies disclosed over USD 300 million in questionable or illegal payments made to foreign government officials, politicians and political parties.[35] Of these companies, 117 were in the top Fortune 500.[36]

Meanwhile, the US Senate undertook its own investigations, out of concern about the foreign policy implications of such 'questionable or illegal foreign payments' by American multinational corporations.[37] The Senate's hearings in 1975 led to particularly scandalous revelations about the conduct of Lockheed, the largest US defence contractor at the time, which had recently been saved from bankruptcy by the US government and was being monitored by a US government agency.[38] The conduct disclosed by Lockheed was on a massive scale, involving Lockheed's payment of between USD 30 to 38 million, between 1970 and 1975, to foreign officials in fifty foreign countries.[39] These revelations caused major political scandals in Italy, Japan and the Netherlands.[40]

The US Congress simultaneously pursued both international and domestic legal solutions to the corporate practices uncovered as a result of the Watergate scandal. In November 1975, the US Senate passed a resolution directing the executive branch to pursue international negotiations 'for the purpose of developing an international code of conduct to eliminate the practices of bribery, indirect payments, kickbacks, unethical political contributions, and other unethical payments which presently burden the international trade of the United States'.[41] The resolution specifically directed the executive to undertake negotiations within the framework of the General Agreement on Tariffs and Trade, although it left open the possibility of negotiations in 'other appropriate international forums'. The executive ultimately pursued negotiations at the UN and the OECD. The resolution notably portrayed 'bribery and other forms of illegal payments' as problems originating in the foreign, host states where US corporations were engaged in international business transactions. The resolution notes that such practices are 'frequently rooted in the

[34] US Senate, Report of the Securities and Exchange Commission on Questionable and Illegal Corporate Payments and Practices, Submitted to the Committee on Banking, Housing and Urban Affairs (May 1976) 6–13.

[35] US House of Representatives, Report No 95-640, Unlawful Corporate Payments Act of 1977 (28 September 1977) 4.

[36] ibid.

[37] The Hearings were held by the Subcommittee on Multinational Corporations of the Senate Foreign Relations Committee, which had also investigated ITT's activities in Chile two years prior.

[38] Davis, *Impunity* (n 6) 37.

[39] ibid.

[40] See eg Ronald Kroeze, 'Lockheed (1977) and Flick (1981–1986): Anticorruption as a Pragmatic Practice in the Netherlands and Germany' in Ronald Kroeze, Andre Vitoria and G Geltner (eds), *Anticorruption in History: From Antiquity to the Modern Era* (OUP 2018) 282 et seq.

[41] A Resolution to Protect the Ability of the United States to Trade Abroad, Report to Accompany S Res 265 (5 November 1975).

policies and practices of other countries and are widely regarded as an unpleasant but necessary cost of doing business in such countries'.

In December 1977, while treaty negotiations were ongoing at the UN, the US Congress passed the Foreign Corrupt Practices Act (FCPA).[42] The FCPA criminalizes the bribery of foreign public officials, and also establishes record-keeping and accounting requirements. In enacting the FCPA, the US criminalized foreign bribery 'unilaterally', before having successfully negotiated an international instrument. Congress was motivated in part by concerns about morality, in particular about how such business conduct runs counter 'to the moral expectations and values of the American public'.[43] In addition, Congress considered that such conduct erodes 'public confidence in the integrity of the free market system', which is distorted by bribery in the context of public procurement.[44] Finally, Congress was also motivated by the foreign policy problems created by such conduct (eg the Lockheed scandals in Italy, Japan and the Netherlands).

Following the enactment of the FCPA in 1977, and in the absence of an international instrument dealing with corrupt practices, the American business community considered itself to be at a competitive disadvantage in international business transactions, relative to multinational corporations based in countries that did not yet govern foreign bribery. In 1988, when the FCPA was amended for the first time, Congress again directed the executive branch to pursue international negotiations, with a view towards concluding an international agreement against foreign bribery.[45] The negotiations that ensued at the OECD ultimately led to the conclusion of the 1997 OECD Anti-Bribery Convention.

## 3. Economic Sanctions and Southern Africa

Another significant influence on anti-corruption treaty negotiations in the 1970s stemmed from the international politics surrounding the investments of foreign multinational corporations in Southern Africa, in particular Southern Rhodesia (Zimbabwe) and South West Africa (Namibia). Following the unilateral declaration of independence in November 1965 by the Rhodesian settler government under Ian Smith, the UN Security Council called for non-recognition of this 'illegal racist minority' regime.[46] In 1966, the Security Council began instituting, for the first time in its history, mandatory economic sanctions against Southern Rhodesia,

[42] 15 USC ss 78dd-1 to 78dd-3.

[43] US House of Representatives, Report No 95-640ma (n 35) 4; Davis, *Impunity* (n 6) 38–39.

[44] Daniel K Tarullo, 'The Limits of Institutional Design: Implementing the OECD Anti-Bribery Convention' (2004) 44 Va J Intl L 665, 673; Mark Pieth, 'Introduction' in Mark Pieth, Lucinda A Low and Nicola Bonucci (eds), *The OECD Convention on Bribery: A Commentary* (2nd edn, CUP 2013) 10–11.

[45] Pub L No 100-418, 102 Stat 1415.

[46] UN SC Res 216 (12 November 1965).

including an embargo on trade and investment.[47] South Africa and Mozambique (Portuguese territory until 1975) did not, however, comply with these sanctions, and continued to trade with Southern Rhodesia.[48] Most significantly, from the perspective of foreign direct investment, Western oil companies with subsidiaries in South Africa and Southern Rhodesia participated in this trade, which was legal in these states, though in conflict with the UN sanctions regime. These subsidiaries were not subject to the sanction regulations applicable in the home jurisdictions of their parent companies (eg the US and UK).

In the early 1960s, the Security Council also adopted resolutions concerning economic sanctions with respect to Namibia (then South West Africa), although these sanctions were not under Chapter VII of the UN Charter, and were therefore hortatory rather than mandatory in character. On 26 October 1966 the General Assembly terminated South Africa's Mandate with respect to Namibia, following South Africa's annexation and institution of apartheid policies in Namibia. In 1970, following South Africa's failure to withdraw, the Security Council called on all states, especially those with economic and other interests in Namibia, to refrain from dealings with South Africa where it acted on behalf of Namibia.[49] In addition, in a 1971 Advisory Opinion, the International Court of Justice determined that all UN member states were under an obligation to refrain from any dealings with the government of South Africa 'implying the recognition of the legality of, or lending support or assistance to' South Africa's continuing administration of Namibia.[50]

Finally, with respect to apartheid South Africa itself, the Security Council did not impose mandatory economic sanctions until the mid 1980s.[51] Although the situation in apartheid South Africa was on the agenda of the Security Council from 1960 onwards, the Security Council was slow to come to an agreement on an appropriate response. During the 1960s and 1970s, the three Western permanent members of the Security Council (France, the United States and the United Kingdom) repeatedly vetoed draft resolutions on the imposition of economic sanctions and South Africa's expulsion from the UN. In 1977, the Security Council imposed a mandatory arms embargo on South Africa,[52] and in 1985 it imposed economic sanctions against South Africa.[53]

[47] UN SC Res 232 (16 December 1966); UN SC Res 253 (29 May 1968); UN SC Res 277 (18 March 1970); UN SC Res 388 (6 April 1976).

[48] Martin Schaub, 'Rhodesia/Zimbabwe' in *Max Planck Encyclopedia of Public International Law* (OUP, last updated April 2013) para 16.

[49] UN SC Res 276 (30 January 1970).

[50] *Legal Consequences for States of the Continued Presence of South Africa in Namibia (South West Africa) notwithstanding Security Council Resolution 276 (1970)*(Advisory Opinion) [1971] ICJ Rep 16, para 133; UN SC Res 301 (1971).

[51] Julia Gebhard, 'Apartheid' in *Max Planck Encyclopedia of Public International Law* (OUP, last updated January 2018); John Dugard and John Reynolds, 'Apartheid, International Law, and the Occupied Palestinian Territory' (2013) 24 EJIL 867, 878–80.

[52] UN SC Res 418 (1977); UN SC Res 421 (1977).

[53] UN SC Res 569 (1985).

## III. Failed Treaty Negotiations at the United Nations

The ITT and Watergate scandals, together with the situation in Southern Africa, had a stultifying effect on anti-corruption treaty negotiations at the United Nations. Delegations struggled to reach agreement on the scope of the concept of 'illicit payments', a vague term which had the potential to encompass everything from bribery, to illegal campaign contributions, to the payment by corporations of taxes and royalties in violation of UN sanctions regimes. They also struggled to agree upon the most suitable approach to the problem of corruption or 'illicit payments'. While developing countries favoured a code of conduct governing the behaviour of multinational corporations in general, developed countries favoured a treaty that took a mainly criminal law approach.

### 1. The Scope of the Treaty: Competing Conceptions of 'Corruption'

Competing conceptions of the term 'corruption' emerged among UN member states as early as 1975, when three states (Iran, Libya and the United States) submitted draft resolutions on corruption, for adoption by the General Assembly.[54] The US proposal framed corruption relatively narrowly, as a term predominantly referring to bribery. This approach was in keeping with the type of corporate misconduct uncovered in the aftermath of the Watergate scandal. The US proposed that the General Assembly condemn the 'offering or solicitation of bribes and other corrupt practices by enterprises, or their encouragement by government officials by individuals'. While this proposal focused on the offering or solicitation of bribes, it still allowed for the possibility of 'other corrupt practices'. This proposal also emphasized the role of the bribe solicitor, who 'encourages' corporations to engage in such conduct. During debate in the Assembly, both the US and Germany emphasized that 'references to bribery should cover all aspects of the problem, including solicitation and acceptance'.[55] The Iranian proposal similarly called for a resolution dealing with 'corruptive practices', with a particular focus on bribery.

Libya's proposal, however, framed corruption broadly, as encompassing unethical conduct by corporations, as well as the involvement of their home governments (ie state sponsorship of corruption by corporations). Libya proposed condemnation of 'illegal and immoral acts practised by transnational corporations against the safety and security of peoples and States'. This proposal made no specific reference to bribery, but instead highlighted the practice of 'home states' in 'employing transnational corporations as an instrument for intervening in the internal affairs

[54] 1975 UN Yearbook 486–87.
[55] ibid 487.

of host countries for political purposes'. This framing of the problem was broad enough to encompass the type of interference in domestic politics that took place in Chile. When a group of developing countries (including Libya and Iran) sponsored a separate resolution on the subject of corruption, Iran, Libya and the US all withdrew their proposals, paving the way for the General Assembly's adoption of Resolution 3514 on 15 December 1975.[56]

Resolution 3514 condemns 'corrupt practices, including bribery, by transnational and other corporations, their intermediaries and others involved, in violation of the laws and regulations of the host countries'. The resolution does not define the term 'corrupt practices', although it clearly identifies bribery as one practice that falls under the umbrella of this concept. The resolution notably calls on both host and home states to regulate this conduct, and to cooperate with each other to prevent and to prosecute offenders.[57] The General Assembly also linked the issue of corrupt practices with the development of a code of conduct for transnational corporations by the CTC, within the framework of the New International Economic Order.[58] The General Assembly specifically requested that ECOSOC direct the CTC to include corrupt practices in its work and to make recommendations on preventing such conduct.[59] The resolution thereby reflected the view, held by developing countries at this time, that corruption was just one of many aspects of corporate conduct that required international regulation.[60]

In August 1976, ECOSOC established the Ad Hoc Intergovernmental Working Group on Corrupt Practices.[61] Its mandate was to examine the 'problem of corrupt practices, in particular bribery' and to draft an international agreement 'to prevent and eliminate illicit payments, in whatever form, in connexion with international and commercial transactions'. The Working Group, which was initially meant to consist of eighteen members, expanded in 1977 to include all interested states, approximately half of which were developing countries.[62] This mandate was broad insofar as it did not limit corrupt practices to corrupt payments (ie bribery) and it allowed for the consideration of the role of corporations as well as home and host governments.[63]

Fundamental disagreement among member states about whether corruption should be framed as a broad or narrow problem only grew more entrenched as treaty negotiations got underway. It manifested itself in a treaty draft encompassing

[56] The resolution was sponsored by Algeria, Argentina, Benin, Bolivia, Colombia, Costa Rica, Cuba, Democratic Yemen, Ecuador, Egypt, Gabon, Guyana, Iran, Iraq, the Libyan Arab Republic, Madagascar, Nigeria, Pakistan, Peru, Romania, Somalia, the Syrian Arab Republic, Togo, the United Republic of Tanzania, the Upper Volta, Venezuela and Yugoslavia. ibid 487.

[57] ibid paras 3, 5.

[58] ibid preambular paras 2–3.

[59] ibid para 6.

[60] Katzarova, *The Social Construction* (n 5) 90.

[61] 1976 UN Yearbook 460; ECOSOC Res 2041 (LXI).

[62] 1977 UN Yearbook; ECOSOC Res 2122 (LXIII) E/6048 (4 August 1977) para 4(b).

[63] Katzarova, *The Social Construction* (n 5) 89.

both the broad and the narrow approaches, in a manner which was ultimately unsatisfactory and unworkable. The resulting draft treaty was entitled 'draft international agreement to prevent and eliminate illicit payments in international commercial transactions'. The term 'illicit payments' referred to bribery 'as well as illegal political contributions as defined in national laws and regulations and any payment of royalties and taxes to illegal minority regimes in southern Africa in contravention of United Nations resolutions'.[64] The term 'bribery' encompassed both active bribery, meaning the giving or offering of a bribe by a private person, as well as passive bribery, meaning the demanding and receiving by a public official or any other public person. The draft agreement produced in 1977 shows a lack of agreement about what ought to be criminalized, as the terms 'bribery' and 'illicit payments' appear under the criminalization article in brackets beside each other, indicating that the drafters had yet to agree on whether to retain one or both of these terms.[65]

The references to both bribery and illicit payments proved to be so controversial that the Working Group never reached an agreement on the scope of the treaty. Several delegations considered that the agreement should extend not only to bribery, but also to other illicit payments, and that the focus should be on the improper activities of transnational and other corporations, rather than the improper activities of public officials.[66] The inclusion of both passive as well as active bribery evidently met with objections from states that wished to emphasize the misconduct of the corporations offering and giving bribes, rather than the misconduct of the public officials soliciting and receiving those bribes.

In addition, the African members of the Working Group attached great importance to the inclusion of provisions concerning royalty or tax payments to illegal minority regimes in Southern Africa, in contravention of UN resolutions.[67] The Security Council resolutions specifically referenced in the drafting history concerned Namibia (Res 301) and Southern Rhodesia (Res 232; Res 253). But the draft treaty uses the general term 'southern Africa', a term which had the potential to encompass South Africa itself, should the Security Council adopt mandatory economic sanctions in the future (which it eventually did in 1985). These provisions, which set out prohibition and disclosure requirements, remained in brackets, due to the lack of a consensus on their inclusion in the treaty. The drafting history

[64] ECOSOC, Report of the Ad Hoc Intergovernmental Working Group on the Problem of Corrupt Practices on its First, Second, Third and Resumed Third Sessions, E/6006 (5 July 1977); Ad Hoc Intergovernmental Working Group on the Problem of Corrupt Practices, Major Issues to be Considered in the Examination of the Problem of Corrupt Practices, in Particular Bribery, in International Commercial Transactions by Transnational and Other Corporations, Their Intermediaries and Others Involved: Report of the Secretariat, E/AC.64/7 (17 March 1977) para 19.

[65] ECOSOC, Report of the Ad Hoc Intergovernmental Working Group on the Problem of Corrupt Practices on its First, Second, Third and Resumed Third Sessions, E/6006 (5 July 1977), art III.

[66] ECOSOC, Report of the Ad Hoc Intergovernmental Working Group on the Problem of Corrupt Practices on its Fourth, Fifth and Resumed Fifth Sessions, E/1978/115 (7 July 1978) para 21.

[67] ibid paras 3–4, 18.

indicates that the Working Group failed to discuss this issue on multiple occasions, despite its 'crucial importance' to the African members of the Working Group, who considered that it 'would endow this draft agreement with greater meaning, relevance and significance'.[68] The Ugandan representative, speaking on behalf of the other African members, noted 'his firm understanding that this exercise was but one dimension of the current world pre-occupation with the fulfilment or realization of certain fundamental rights of humankind, in particular as it related to the grave situation in southern Africa'.[69] He also clearly indicated that the support of the African members of the Working Group for this treaty was conditional on the 'reciprocal attention and positive attitude' of the other members of the Working Group towards this article.[70] In other words, without the inclusion of these provisions, the support of the African members of the Working Group would not be forthcoming.

## 2. The Character and Approach of the Instrument

The predominantly criminal law approach adopted in the draft treaty also became a source of controversy during the treaty negotiations. Although the Working Group seems to have devoted most of its attention to a criminal law approach to the problem of illicit payments, it also considered other approaches. These entailed a code of conduct as well as the drafting of a model national law, the adoption of voluntary guidelines by enterprises and professional associations or other international organizations, the elimination of tax shelters and the disclosure by public officials of their net worth.[71] Since the 1990s, international organizations have taken a largely criminal law approach to corruption, but this drafting history shows that this was not always the case, and need not have been the case in the 1990s and 2000s.

During the Working Group sessions, many delegations stressed the importance of giving equal weight to these other approaches to the problem of illicit payments. In June 1978, delegations from the G77, and in particular Latin America, stressed that the formulation of a code of conduct by the CTC 'should be accorded the highest priority'.[72] The following year, in 1979, the tone of the G77 became more strident: without a code of conduct on transnational corporations, the treaty should not enter into force (regardless of the treaty's provisions on its entry into force).[73]

[68] ibid para 18.
[69] ibid para 18.
[70] ibid para 18.
[71] ibid paras 10–11.
[72] ECOSOC, Report of the Ad Hoc Intergovernmental Working Group on the Problem of Corrupt Practices on its Fourth and Fifth Sessions, E/1978/39 (24 April 1978) 11.
[73] ECOSOC, Report of the Committee on an International Agreement on Illicit Payments on its First and Second Sessions, E/1979/105 (25 May 1979) para 57.

The G77 thereby made their support for the treaty conditional on the support of the developed world for the code of conduct—support which never materialized.[74]

The linkage of the code of conduct to the treaty, by both the G77 and later ECOSOC, ultimately spelled the death of the treaty negotiations. In 1978 the Ad Hoc Intergovernmental Working Group recommended that ECOSOC consider convening a diplomatic conference for the purpose of concluding an agreement on illicit payments.[75] In August 1978, ECOSOC accordingly adopted a resolution in which it established a Committee on an International Agreement on Illicit Payments, which would negotiate the treaty.[76] At the same time, however, ECOSOC clearly prioritized the conclusion of a code of conduct by the CTC, which EOCOSC tasked with making 'expeditious progress' in fulfilling its mandate.[77] Most significantly, ECOSOC 'reaffirm[ed] that the formulation of a code of conduct by the Commission on Transnational Corporations should be given the highest priority and that the conclusion of an international agreement on illicit payments should in no way interfere with or delay that priority'.[78] In May 1979, the Committee transmitted a nearly complete draft treaty through ECOSOC to the General Assembly. At this point the US proposed convening a conference no later than 30 June 1980, while the G77 proposed convening a conference to adopt a treaty only after the completion of the code of conduct.[79] The General Assembly, however, never took action to convene a conference, and by December 1980, this treaty-making exercise was effectively dead.[80]

## IV. Conclusion: The Rebirth of the 1990s and the Legacy of the 1970s

The international politics of the 1970s were hardly conducive to the conclusion of an international anti-corruption treaty within the framework of the UN. This was an era of 'tension and antagonism' between foreign multinational corporations and developing countries.[81] Various corporate scandals of the early 1970s, involving the misconduct of ITT in Chile and the misconduct of hundreds of American corporations abroad, had the effect of polarizing the debate about what corruption is and how it should be combated. UN member states could not come to an agreement

[74] On the reasons for the failure to negotiate the Code of Conduct see Sauvant, 'Negotiations' (n 28) 56–62; Hamdani and Ruffing, *UNCTC* (n 19) ch 3.

[75] 1978 UN Yearbook 550.

[76] ECOSOC Res 1978/71 (4 August 1978).

[77] ibid para 3.

[78] ibid para 5.

[79] 1980 UN Yearbook 668.

[80] ibid General Assembly Decision 35/425 (5 December 1980).

[81] EOCSOC, Report of the Commission on Transnational Corporations on its Seventeenth Session, Addendum, Efforts by the United Nations to Address the Issue of Corrupt Practices: Report of the Secretary-General, E/1991/31/Add.1 (4 July 1991) para 4.

on the most fundamental issue: the problem to be addressed. On the one hand, developing states defined the problem broadly as the influence of foreign multinational corporations on domestic politics, and they identified a code of conduct as the most appropriate method for a holistic regulation of the conduct of these private actors. On the other hand, developed states, in particular the US, defined the problem narrowly as the bribery of foreign public officials by multinational corporations. The US identified domestic criminalization of both active and passive bribery as the most appropriate method for combatting this conduct committed by both corporations and public officials. The politics surrounding the involvement of multinational corporations in Southern Africa further complicated negotiations, as African members insisted that this conduct must also be seen as an illicit payment that falls within the developing world's broad conception of corruption.

During the 1980s, the issue of corruption lay almost entirely dormant at international organizations. But by the early 1990s, with the end of the Cold War and apartheid South Africa, global politics had shifted so considerably that successful international and regional negotiations on this issue became possible. By that time, the New International Economic Order had been abandoned, and the Global South was no longer pursuing the regulation of multinational corporations through a code of conduct. Instead, many developing countries were seeking to attract foreign direct investment. In addition, the US had a special incentive to reinitiate treaty negotiations, because of the perceived disadvantage of American corporations, compared to foreign corporations that were not subject to foreign bribery laws. The ensuing negotiations, which took place within the framework of the OECD, were ultimately successful, and resulted in the issuance of OECD recommendations on bribery in international business transactions in 1994 and 1997, followed by the conclusion of the 1997 OECD Anti-Bribery Convention.

During the same period, regional anti-corruption instruments were concluded under the auspices of the Organization of American States and the Council of Europe.[82] The UN was comparatively slow to take up the issue of corruption again. The treaty negotiations that took place in the early 2000s at the United Nations were prompted not by corruption scandals or any particular event, but by the negotiation of the UN Convention against Transnational Organized Crime (UNTOC), during which states decided that the issue of corruption merited separate treatment in a devoted treaty.[83] In 2003, these separate treaty negotiations culminated in the UN Convention against Corruption (UNCAC), the most comprehensive and widely ratified of the anti-corruption treaties.

[82] 1996 Inter-American Convention against Corruption ; Council of Europe Criminal Law Convention on Corruption; Council of Europe Civil Law Convention on Corruption.

[83] Ad Hoc Committee on the Elaboration of a Convention against Transnational Organized Crime, Report of the Ad Hoc Committee on the Elaboration of a Convention against Transnational Organized Crime on its Seventh Session, Held in Vienna from 17 to 28 January 2000 (8 February 2000) UN Doc A/AC.254/25, paras 20–21.

The regional and international anti-corruption instruments concluded in the 1990s and early 2000s can only be fully understood in light of the attempt to negotiate an international agreement on illicit payments in the 1970s. With the exception of the 1999 Council of Europe Civil Law Convention on Corruption, these instruments approach the problem of corruption from a relatively narrow criminal law perspective. For the most part, they focus on the criminalization of active and passive bribery. In embracing this narrow definition of the problem of corruption, the 1997 OECD Anti-Bribery Convention, the 1996 Inter-American Convention against Corruption and the 1999 Council of Europe Criminal Law Convention all reflect the US legacy of the 1970s. Although UNCAC's criminalization provisions extend beyond bribery, a number of the other acts of corruption set out in UNCAC can be seen as closely related to, or variants on, the crime of bribery. Meanwhile, the Chilean legacy of the 1970s is now hidden from view, and attempts to regulate the conduct of multinational corporations through binding international instruments have repeatedly faltered.[84]

[84] See eg the failure to negotiate the UN Code of Conduct on Transnational Corporations in the 1980s and the OECD Multilateral Agreement on Investment in the mid to late 1990s.

# 15

# Corporate Liability for Economic Crimes

## A Contested Transnational History

*Michael Elliot and Felix Lüth**

## I. Introduction

This chapter considers the development of corporate liability standards in the main international anti-corruption, anti-money laundering and counter-terrorist financing instruments. Corporate liability, which in general terms refers to the application of legal responsibility to legal persons, has become a key feature in responses to economic crime, including of a transnational nature.[1] Its growing prominence has been rationalized by its importance to the 'fight against foreign bribery and other complex economic crimes'.[2] Yet as we show here, historicizing its emergence enables identification of other accounts with significant explanatory power.

Following this introduction, the chapter proceeds in three sections. The second section covers the pre-treaty phase, focusing particularly on the international contest over transnational corporations (TNCs) and the United States' adoption of the Foreign Corrupt Practices Act (FCPA) during the 1970s, as well as key developments beginning in 1988 that brought corporate liability to the fore internationally. Drawing out law's narrative role, it argues that the emergence of corporate liability in this context has primarily been geared not to crime reduction or utilitarian justice considerations, but to the legitimization of transnational corporate power and delegitimization of governance by global South states.

The third section examines the introduction and development of corporate liability standards in the multilateral treaty regime. It begins with a pair of regional economic crime treaties adopted in 1997, traces their evolution in the key United Nations (UN) economic crime conventions and concludes with the revived emphasis on non-binding instruments. The ongoing influence of the legitimizing

* The authors are grateful for comments to the editors as well as Radha Ivory and Jason Sharman.

[1] Organisation for Economic Co-operation and Development (OECD), *The Liability of Legal Persons for Foreign Bribery: A Stocktaking* Report (OECD 2016) 11 (hereafter OECD, *Liability of Legal Persons*); Leonardo Borlini, 'Art 26: Liability of Legal Persons' in Cecily Rose, Michael Kubiciel and Oliver Landwehr (eds), *The United Nations Convention Against Corruption: A Commentary* (OUP 2019) 274 (hereafter Borlini, 'Art 26').

[2] OECD, *Liability of Legal Persons* (n 1) 11.

Michael Elliot and Felix Lüth, *Corporate Liability for Economic Crimes* In: *Histories of Transnational Criminal Law*. Edited by: Neil Boister, Sabine Gless and Florian Jeßberger, Oxford University Press. © Michael Elliot and Felix Lüth 2021.
DOI: 10.1093/oso/9780192845702.003.0016

and delegitimizing functions identified in Section II is observed throughout. Space limitations preclude empirical analysis of the domestic implementation of corporate liability standards, though as referenced briefly in Section IV, our contention would be that such implementation largely bears out the key arguments developed here.[3]

Finally, the fourth section offers some concluding reflections, situating the development of corporate liability standards within broader transnational (criminal) law themes.

## II. The Pre-Treaty Phase

Unlike corporate liability's emergence in domestic criminal law,[4] its international development has been carefully and proactively pursued by policymakers. Conventional explanations, reflected in international instruments and scholarly literature, mainly relate the added value of international corporate liability standards to their crime-combating function: economic crimes are frequently 'committed by, through or under the cover of legal entities'; corporate structures make it difficult to identify particular individuals as responsible; and corporations are well placed to take preventive measures.[5] Notions of justice and fairness may also be invoked.[6]

Yet despite their persuasive valence, these explanations struggle to account for the fact that the propagation of corporate liability has occurred without being demonstrably effective in achieving the ends conventionally claimed.[7] They also

[3] The same applies to the potential recursive influence of domestic implementation on the development of subsequent international and domestic law. For an explanation of norm diffusion processes not as 'unidirectional' or one-off but as ongoing, recursive interactions between actors at the international and state levels, see Gregory Shaffer, 'Transnational Legal Ordering and State Change' in Gregory Shaffer (ed), *Transnational Legal Ordering and State Change* (CUP 2013) 14; Terence C Halliday and Gregory Shaffer (eds), *Transnational Legal Orders* (CUP 2015) 37–42. See also, Neil Boister, *An Introduction to Transnational Criminal Law* (2nd edn, OUP 2018) 20 (hereafter Boister, *Introduction to Transnational Criminal Law*).

[4] See eg Thomas J Bernard, 'The Historical Development of Corporate Criminal Liability' (1984) 22 Criminology 3, 3, describing the development of corporate criminal liability in common law jurisdictions as 'a process of accretion that lacked any conscious or overall direction'.

[5] Kevin E Davis, *Between Impunity and Imperialism: The Regulation of Transnational Bribery* (OUP 2019) 127–28 (hereafter Davis, *Between Impunity and Imperialism*); Gemma Aiolfi and Mark Pieth, 'International Aspects of Corporate Liability and Corruption' in Stephen Tully (ed), *Research Handbook on Corporate Legal Responsibility* (Edward Elgar 2005) (hereafter Aiolfi and Pieth, 'International Aspects'); United Nations Office on Drugs and Crime (UNODC), *Legislative Guides for the Implementation of the United Nations Convention against Transnational Organized Crime* (UN 2004) 116; Financial Action Task Force (FATF) 40 Recommendations, October 2003 (incorporating all subsequent amendments until October 2004) 2 <https://www.fatf- gafi.org/media/fatf/documents/FATF%20 Standards%20-%2040%20Recommendations%20rc.pdf> (hereafter FATF 40 Recommendations 2003).

[6] Council of Europe (CoE), *Liability of Legal Persons for Corruption Offences* (CoE 2020) 5 (hereafter CoE, *Liability of Legal Persons*).

[7] See eg Jason C Sharman, *The Money Laundry: Regulating Criminal Finance in the Global Economy* (Cornell UP 2011) (hereafter Sharman, *The Money Laundry*); Simeon Obidairo, *Transnational Corruption and Corporations: Regulating Bribery through Corporate Liability* (Routledge 2013) (hereafter

do little to explicate why corporate liability standards were being pushed by many of the same powerful states that were simultaneously pursuing an international agenda of economic liberalization, of which reducing regulatory constraints on corporations formed an important part.[8] And they largely disregard international law's role in not simply devising solutions to 'global' problems, but in constructing the narratives that inform the problems themselves.[9] Attending more closely to both this narrative role and the positioning of corporations as transnational actors, this section identifies two key, related functions in the emergence of corporate liability in this context, neither of which prioritizes combating crime, but rather economic liberalization. The first is the legitimization of transnational corporate power; the second, the undermining of governance by global South states.

## 1. 1970s: Contest over Transnational Corporate Activities and the FCPA

Revelations in 1972 that the American International Telephone and Telegraph Company had sought with the CIA to prevent Salvador Allende's election in Chile exacerbated concerns over interference by Western companies in global South states' domestic politics.[10] Constraining TNCs became an increasingly important cause for many states of the global South, leading to the establishment of the UN Commission on Transnational Corporations and work on a Code of Conduct on Transnational Corporations (TNC Code).[11] This drive pitted efforts to constrain TNCs against those seeking to legitimize them.[12] Whereas global South states thus endeavoured to protect and affirm host states' regulatory capacity, powerful states

Obidairo, *Transnational Corruption*); Terence C Halliday, Michael Levi and Peter Reuter, *Global Surveillance of Dirty Money: Assessing Assessments of Regimes to Control Money Laundering and Combat the Financing of Terrorism* (Center on Law and Globalization, American Bar Foundation and University of Illinois College of Law 2014) <www.americanbarfoundation.org/uploads/cms/documents/report_global_surveillance_of_dirty_money_1.30.2014.pdf>.

[8] Muthucumaraswamy Sornarajah, 'Power and Justice: Third World Resistance in International Law' (2006) 10 SYBIL 19, 22. See also, Christine Schwöbel-Patel, 'Multilateralism's Tipping Point and the End of International Law's Years of "Voluptuousness"?' in Jean d'Aspremont and John Haskell (eds), *Tipping Points in International Law* (ASIL Studies in International Legal Theory, CUP forthcoming 2021) (hereafter Schwöbel-Patel, 'Multilateralism's Tipping Point').

[9] See generally, Anne Saab, *Narratives of Hunger in International Law: Feeding the World in Times of Climate Change* (CUP 2019).

[10] Doreen Lustig, *Veiled Power: International Law and the Private Corporation, 1886–1981* (OUP 2020) 205 (hereafter Lustig, *Veiled Power*). For a more detailed account, see also Rose, Chapter 14 in this book (Section II.1).

[11] Sundhya Pahuja and Anna Saunders, 'Rival Worlds and the Place of the Corporation in International Law' in Jochen von Bernstorff and Philipp Dann (eds), *The Battle for International Law: South-North Perspectives on the Decolonization Era* (OUP 2019) 141.

[12] Karl P Sauvant, 'The Negotiations of the United Nations Code of Conduct on Transnational Corporations: Experience and Lessons Learned' (2015) 16 JWIT 11, 16–18 (hereafter Sauvant, 'United Nations Code of Conduct').

such as the US worked to circumscribe host states' policy space and 'arrive at a code of conduct *for the governments of host countries* (especially developing countries) in the international investment area' that would facilitate corporate access to global South resources.[13]

In this context, competing conceptualizations of corruption as a 'global' problem emerged.[14] One was rooted, in Allende's words, in corporations' 'powerful corruptive influence on public institutions in rich and poor countries alike'.[15] This conceptualization embedded the anti-corruption project within broader efforts to constrain corporate power and reset the international economic order along more equal lines. Such contextualization is evident, for example, in the UN General Assembly's (UNGA) Resolution 3514 of 1975, sponsored by members of the Group of 77 (G-77), which condemned all corrupt practices, including but not limited to bribery, reaffirmed states' right to legislate and take legal action against TNCs and recalled the previous year's Declaration of a New International Economic Order.[16] Emphasis remained on host state capacity, with home state governments called upon 'to co-operate' with those of host states to prevent and prosecute corrupt practices.[17]

The US in particular sought to counter this conceptualization of corruption with a narrower one that effectively equated it with illicit payments or bribery.[18] By this conception, the problem resided in governmental, not corporate, power and its abuse.[19] The relationship between corruption and corporate regulation was thereby transfigured, with the latter a corollary of efforts to combat corruption. So too was the relative emphasis on regulatory and enforcement power: rather than cooperating with host states, home states became the prime movers, defining the lawfulness of their corporations' interactions with host state governments.

In 1977, the implications of this latter conceptualization became more tangible with the enactment of the FCPA, which criminalized corporate bribes to foreign officials following the unearthing of such bribes on a large scale in the aftermath of the Watergate scandal.[20] Various factors likely contributed to the FCPA's

[13] ibid 25 (emphasis in original).

[14] The analysis in this section is particularly indebted to Elitza Katzarova, *The Social Construction of Global Corruption: From Utopia to Neoliberalism* (Palgrave Macmillan 2019) (hereafter Katzarova, *Social Construction*).

[15] UN Conference on Trade and Development, Address Delivered by Mr. Salvador Allende Gossens, President of Chile at the Inaugural Ceremony on April 13, 1972 (Proceedings of UNCTAD Third Session, Vol 1, Annex VIII, 353, para 58).

[16] UNGA, Measures against corrupt practices of transnational and other corporations, their intermediaries and others, A/RES/3514, 15 December 1975.

[17] ibid 5.

[18] Katzarova, *Social Construction* (n 14) 77, 84-88. See eg the US draft resolution drawn up within the framework of the UN Commission on Transnational Corporations and presented to the UNGA during its 30th session in 1975 (reprinted in summarized form in UN, 'Chapter XIII: Questions Concerning Transnational Corporations' (1975) 29 UNYB 486, 487).

[19] Katzarova, *Social Construction* (n 14) 2.

[20] US Foreign Corrupt Practices Act of 1977, 15 USC § 78dd-1. For a more detailed account, see Rose, Chapter 14 in this book (Section II.2).

enactment, including conceptions of morality and anxiety as to the private sector's capacity to interfere with American foreign policy and national security objectives.[21] Yet key Congressional reports place particular significance, especially in relation to corporate (criminal) liability, on concern for American corporations and the US-led economic order. A strong anti-bribery law was necessary 'to restore public confidence in the integrity of the American business system',[22] for not only was corporate bribery of foreign officials unethical, '[i]t erodes public confidence in the integrity of the free market system'.[23] Moreover, with the US then headquarter to roughly 90 per cent of all multinational companies,[24] 'in many cases the resulting adverse competitive effects are entirely domestic'.[25] Corporate criminal liability was preferred to legalizing foreign bribery through disclosure because it was considered a more effective deterrent, no more difficult to enforce, and '[m]ost importantly, ... far less burdensome on business'.[26]

Three further functions served by provision of corporate liability within the FCPA may be distilled. First, it enframed corruption as a public sector phenomenon, occluding the corruptive influence of private sector power.[27] Second, it instituted the 'individual actor paradigm', with corruption being not a systemic problem but 'a problem of individuals making corrupt decisions', who are 'exceptions to the anti-corruption norm within their own community'.[28] Third, corporate liability provisions rested expansive regulatory power over corporations' interactions with foreign officials in the US, ensuring it a significant definitional role regarding what constituted lawful conduct and an extraterritorial reach regarding matters important to the sovereignty of other states.[29]

The FCPA was to be complemented by international action. A 1975 Senate resolution, for example, had directed the executive to pursue negotiations for an international code of conduct to eliminate corrupt payments under the General Agreement on Tariffs and Trade framework.[30] Ultimately, negotiations were pursued elsewhere, including at the United Nations, with corporate liability for

[21] Kenneth W Abbott and Duncan Snidal, 'Values and Interests: International Legalization in the Fight against Corruption' (2002) 31 JLS S141, S161, S167 (hereafter Abbott and Snidal, 'Values and Interests'); Davis, *Between Impunity and Imperialism* (n 5) 40.

[22] US Senate, 'Foreign Corrupt Practices and Domestic and Foreign Investment Improved Disclosure Acts of 1977' Report No 95-114 (2 May 1977) 3 (hereafter S Rep No 95-114).

[23] US House of Representatives, 'Unlawful Corporate Payments Act of 1977' Report No 95-640 (28 September 1977) 4 (hereafter HR Rep No 95-640).

[24] Katzarova, *Social Construction* (n 14) 83.

[25] HR Rep No 95-640 (n 23) 5.

[26] HR Rep No 95-640 (n 23) 6.

[27] This enframing is captured by the World Bank's definition of corruption as 'the abuse of public office for private gain' (Katzarova, *Social Construction* (n 14) 65).

[28] Blake Puckett, 'Clans and the Foreign Corrupt Practices Act: Individualized Corruption Prosecution in Situations of Systemic Corruption' (2010) 41 Georget J Intl Law 815, 818.

[29] See eg Davis, *Between Impunity and Imperialism* (n 5) 38.

[30] A Resolution to Protect the Ability of the United States to Trade Abroad, Report to Accompany S Res 265 (5 November 1975). See also, Rose, Chapter 14 in this book (Section II.2).

corruption 'at the forefront'[31] of the 1978 draft International Agreement on Illicit Payments prepared by a committee established by the UN Economic and Social Council.[32] Although US efforts to conclude an agreement on the issue stalled in 1980 after the G-77 conditioned progress on adoption of a TNC Code,[33] when the US reinvigorated its international anti-corruption initiative nearly a decade later, the FCPA's corporate liability paradigm formed the model.[34]

## 2. 1980s–1990s: Establishment of the FATF and Reappearance of the Anti-Corruption Agenda

Corporate liability remained on the international agenda, notably as part of the 1985 UN Congress on Prevention of Crime and the Treatment of Offenders' Guiding Principles.[35] In this context, it was tied not just to economic crime but to the 'restructuring of the international economic system' and host state capacity.[36] Disembedding it from those broader aims was largely the product of two developments. The first was a 1988 amendment to the FCPA obliging the president to pursue negotiations towards an international agreement against foreign bribery. It followed pressure from the US business sector that saw the FCPA as a competitive disadvantage absent corresponding legislation elsewhere, helping to entrench a market logic that continues to inform anti-corruption instruments of 'levelling the playing field'.[37] The US proposal to the OECD the following year for a feasibility study on illicit payments led eventually to the OECD Convention on Combating Bribery of Foreign Public Officials in International Business Transactions.[38] It did so, however, only after the US had secured support for its anti-corruption agenda from the Organization of American States (OAS), which adopted the 1996 Inter-American Corruption Convention.

[31] Obidairo, *Transnational Corruption* (n 7) 65.

[32] Report of the Economic and Social Council Committee on an International Agreement on Illicit Payments, E/1979,104, 25 May 1979, ch III, art 1(c). See generally, Katzarova, *Social Construction* (n 14) 109–10 and Rose, Chapter 14 in this book.

[33] On the reasons for the failure to negotiate the International Agreement on Illicit Payments and a TNC Code, see Rose, Chapter 14 in this book (Section III) and Sauvant, 'United Nations Code of Conduct' (n 12) 56–62, respectively.

[34] Alejandro Posadas, 'Combating Corruption under International Law' (2000) 10 Duke J Comp & Intl L 345, 367 (hereafter Posadas, 'Combating Corruption').

[35] UN Department of International Economic and Social Affairs, Seventh UN Congress on the Prevention of Crime and the Treatment of Offenders, Milan, 26 August–6 September 1985, Report prepared by the Secretariat (UN 1986) ch I, s A, para 9.

[36] ibid ch I, s A, para 2.

[37] Obidairo, *Transnational Corruption* (n 7) 13. See also, Mark Pieth, 'Introduction' in Mark Pieth, Lucinda A Low and Nicola Bonucci (eds), *The OECD Convention on Bribery: A Commentary* (2nd edn, CUP 2014) 12 (hereafter Pieth, 'Introduction'); Rachel Brewster, 'Enforcing the FCPA: International Resonance and Domestic Strategy' (2017) 103 Va L Rev 1611, 1630 (hereafter Brewster, 'Enforcing the FCPA').

[38] Katzarova, *Social Construction* (n 14) 133–34.

The second development was also an American 'internationalizing' initiative, in this case seeking to extend the reach of its 'war on drugs' and ensure that other states followed its lead in enacting laws like the 1986 Money Laundering Control Act.[39] In 1989, the Group of Seven established an ad hoc intergovernmental body, the Financial Action Task Force (FATF), initially focused on money laundering from the illicit narcotics trade.[40] A year later, the FATF issued a set of recommendations which included that '[w]here possible, corporations themselves—not only their employees—should be subject to criminal liability'.[41] The FATF is not formally a law-maker, but its recommendation nevertheless marked an important development due to the FATF's increasingly influential international role. In particular, its membership and modes of operation, described as 'a group of the world's most developed countries [seeking] to impose standards that they developed upon all other countries and jurisdictions',[42] have lent its recommendations weight and helped disseminate its policies across member and non-member states alike.[43]

The anti-corruption and AML initiatives aligned with what has been observed generally as a turn away at the UN from conceptualizing issues of transnational crime within the context of TNCs' abuse of power towards 'more narrowly defined crime control'.[44] In this, the initiatives benefitted from a transformed international order and altered perceptions of TNCs' role within it. The Cold War ended and resistance amongst global South states to the ascendancy of economic liberalization had been severely weakened.[45] Focus more firmly shifted to means used not to counter corporate power, let alone systematically alter the structures that enabled it, but to legitimize its exercise, partly through self-regulation.[46] Although corporate liability provisions ostensibly entailed binding constraints, they nevertheless fit comfortably within and contributed to this self-regulatory paradigm. Even the FCPA, which imposed criminal liability, was largely to be 'a self-enforcing,

[39] Cecily Rose, *International Anti-Corruption Norms: Their Creation and Influence on Domestic Legal Systems* (OUP 2015) 1–2 (hereafter Rose, *International Anti-Corruption Norms*); Sharman, *The Money Laundry* (n 7) 21.

[40] Since then, its scope has expanded to include a range of issues, such as terrorism financing (Mark T Nance, 'The Regime that FATF built: An Introduction to the Financial Action Task Force' (2018) 69 Crime, Law and Social Change 109, 115 (hereafter Nance, 'The Regime')).

[41] FATF 40 Recommendations (1990), Recommendation 7 <https://www.fatf- gafi.org/media/fatf/documents/recommendations/pdfs/FATF%20Recommendations%201990.pdf>. The recommendation sparked 'extensive discussion' as many member states lacked corporate criminal liability law and its enactment could contravene constitutional principles (FATF Report (1990–1991) 6 <https://www.fatf- gafi.org/media/fatf/documents/reports/1990%201991%20ENG.pdf> (hereafter FATF Report 1990–1991).

[42] Rose, *International Anti-Corruption Norms* (n 39) 214–15.

[43] Sharman, *The Money Laundry* (n 7) 7.

[44] Boister, *Introduction to Transnational Criminal Law* (n 3) 9.

[45] Sundhya Pahuja, *Decolonising International Law: Development, Economic Growth and the Politics of Universality* (CUP 2011) (hereafter Pahuja, *Decolonising International Law*); Pieth, 'Introduction' (n 37) 8–9.

[46] Lustig, *Veiled Power* (n 10) 216–18. See also, Grietje Baars, *The Corporation, Law and Capitalism: A Radical Perspective on the Role of Law in the Global Political Economy* (Brill 2019) 355–57.

preventative mechanism'.[47] And as noted, corporate liability, premised on the idea that corporate misconduct was anomalous, located the problem in the governmental sphere.

It also rested public regulatory power in the home state, which coincided with growing delegitimization of governance by global South states, including by the International Monetary Fund and World Bank, for whom it helped explain the failure of their policies to achieve their stated aims and to justify further policy prescriptions.[48] Corruption in this light necessitated an expanded role for corporations because, in the words of a 1997 World Bank report:

> In general, any reform that increases the competitiveness of the economy will reduce incentives for corrupt behavior. Thus policies that lower controls on foreign trade, remove entry barriers to private industry, and privatize state firms in a way that ensures competition will all support the fight.[49]

Corporate liability facilitated that expanded role, going some way to answering the question considered by Transparency International USA's managing director as to 'what moral obligation Western business owes the people in emerging economies'.[50] It assured that corporations, rather than governments, could be trusted as 'moral' actors.

Both the FATF and the 1996 Inter-American Corruption Convention bore out these narratives. For the FATF, for which the 'soundness of the international financial system' is an important objective,[51] corporate liability was situated within a broader delegation of responsibility for AML policy implementation, bringing companies further into the governance fold.[52] Meanwhile, diffusion of its policies,[53] according to Sharman, has been successful partly because their adoption serves 'to impress foreign firms ... not because the policy reduces risk or fits with local circumstances, but because it communicates that a country is within the fold'.[54]

The 1996 Inter-American Corruption Convention performed a different role in this regard. It prohibited transnational bribery, but without explicit reference to the liability of legal persons, referring instead to 'businesses domiciled' in the respective state.[55] Yet importantly, it permitted the US, whose extensive efforts

[47] S Rep No 95-114 (n 22) 10.

[48] Abbott and Snidal, 'Values and Interests' (n 21) S173–S174; Pahuja *Decolonising International Law* (n 45) 172.

[49] World Bank, *World Development Report 1997: The State in a Changing World* (OUP 1997) 105.

[50] Nancy Zucker Boswell, 'An Emerging Consensus on Controlling Corruption' (1997) 18(4) U Pa J Intl Econ L 1165, 1165.

[51] FATF Report 1990–1991 (n 41) 20; Nance, 'The Regime' (n 40) 115.

[52] Sharman, *The Money Laundry* (n 7) 45.

[53] ibid 7.

[54] ibid 160.

[55] 1996 Inter-American Corruption Convention, art VIII. 'Businesses domiciled' is broad enough to encompass legal persons, but the omission of explicit reference is considered significant regarding

laid the groundwork for the 1996 Inter-American Corruption Convention but which did not ratify it until 2000, to counter arguments that criminalizing corporate bribery of foreign officials unduly interfered in host state sovereignty.[56] For the theme which 'permeates' the 1996 Inter-American Corruption Convention is governmental corruption.[57] It thus set the stage for a corporate liability regime extending from powerful global North states, particularly the US, that could be presented as accounting for the governance, even moral, failings of global South governments.

## III. The Treaty (and Post-Treaty) Phase

This section turns to the introduction of corporate liability standards at the multilateral treaty level and presents some subsequent developments in light of the established legitimizing and delegitimizing narratives. The trajectory traced dovetails with the post-Cold War 'rise and fall' of international law, which Schwöbel-Patel explains by multilateralism's initial facilitation of the geographic expansion of capital, before receding in the face of increasing inter-state competition.[58]

### 1. 1997: Emergence of Corporate Liability at the Multilateral Treaty Level

The developments at the OAS, OECD and FATF appear to have motivated action at the European Union (EU). On 19 June 1997, the Council of the EU introduced the liability of legal persons in the Second Protocol of the Convention on the Protection of the European Communities' Financial Interests.[59] Article 3 obliges member states to take 'the necessary measures' to impose liability on legal persons 'for fraud, active corruption and money laundering committed for their benefit'. Adopting the 'identification theory [of attribution] although with a slightly broader scope',[60] it applies only where the conduct was by a person with 'a leading

the provision's applicability to corporate liability (CoE, *Liability of Legal Persons* (n 6) 111). Moreover, the dissemination of corporate liability standards throughout Latin American states is attributed to the 1997 OECD Bribery Convention (Guillermo Jorge, 'The Impact of Corporate Liability on Corruption in Latin America' (2019) Symposium on New Directions in Anticorruption Law <https://doi.org/10.1017/aju.2019.57> (hereafter Jorge, 'Latin America')).

[56] Katzarova, *Social Construction* (n 14) 198.

[57] Posadas, 'Combating Corruption' (n 34) 393–94.

[58] Schwöbel-Patel, 'Multilateralism's Tipping Point' (n 8).

[59] Second Protocol of the Convention on the protection of the European Communities' financial interests [1997] OJ C 221/12 (hereafter Second Protocol 1995 EU Financial Interests Convention).

[60] Julio Bacio Terracino, *The International Legal Framework against Corruption: States' Obligations to Prevent and Repress Corruption* (Intersentia 2012) 262.

position within the legal person', but extends to instances where the corporation's 'lack of supervision or control ... has made possible the commission' of the crime. Article 4 requires that sanctions be 'effective, proportionate and dissuasive'.

Only several months later, the OECD introduced the responsibility of legal persons in article 2 of the 1997 OECD Bribery Convention, albeit in a much more 'minimalist' fashion. Article 2 provides:

> Each Party shall take such measures as may be necessary, in accordance with its legal principles, to establish the liability of legal persons for the bribery of a foreign public official.

The 1997 OECD Bribery Convention both omits reference to any particular rule of attribution[61] and introduces a 'safeguard clause' ('in accordance with its legal principles') which, as we shall see, would become a cornerstone of future corporate liability standards. In keeping with that clause, it contemplates non-criminal responsibility where 'under the legal system of a Party, criminal responsibility is not applicable to legal persons'.[62] Such flexibility was important. The extension of criminal, as opposed to civil or administrative, liability to corporations was resisted by many states,[63] engaging as it does philosophical conceptualizations of criminal law's aims, the nature of criminal punishment and especially the available sanctions for legal persons and concerns over blurring of legal fields.[64] Instead, like the Second Protocol 1995 EU Financial Interests Convention, the 1997 OECD Bribery Convention obliges in all instances that sanctions be 'effective, proportionate and dissuasive'.[65]

Corporate liability provisions, therefore, surfaced for the first time in economic crime treaties which reflected the EU's financial interests or, in the case of the 1997 OECD Bribery Convention, the US interest in the globalization of the FCPA, of

[61] ibid 262. See also, Aiolfi and Pieth, 'International Aspects' (n 5) 398–99.

[62] Art 3(2). As regards art 2, see Commentaries on the Convention on Combating Bribery of Foreign Public Officials in International Business Transactions and Related Documents, art 20, para. 20.

[63] Katzarova, *Social Construction* (n 14) 178. Considering that criminal law 'traditionally focuses on personal blame, guilt and the infliction of loss', the principle that corporations cannot commit crimes (*societas delinquere non potest*) used to be widely accepted (Mark Pieth, 'Article 2' in Mark Pieth, Lucinda A Low and Nicola Bonucci (eds), *The OECD Convention on Bribery: A Commentary* (2nd edn, CUP 2014) 215 (hereafter Pieth, 'Article 2')).

[64] Aiolfi and Pieth, 'International Aspects' (n 5) 405. For a flavour of the debate over the merits and demerits of imposing criminal liability on corporations, see eg Brent Fisse and John Braithwaite, *Corporations, Crime and Accountability* (CUP 1994); Vikramaditya S Khanna, 'Corporate Criminal Liability: What Purpose Does It Serve?' (1996) 109(7) Harv L Rev 1477; Celia Wells, *Corporations and Criminal Responsibility* (2nd edn, OUP 2001); Thomas Weigend, '*Societas delinquere non potest*? A German Perspective' (2008) 6(5) JICJ 927; Albert W Alschuler, 'Two Ways to Think About the Punishment of Corporations' (2009) 46 ACLR 1359; Sara Sun Beale, 'A Response to the Critics of Corporate Criminal Liability' (2009) 46 ACLR 1481; William S Laufer, 'The Missing Account of Progressive Corporate Criminal Law' (2017) 14(1) NYU J L & Bus 71.

[65] Art 3(1) and (2).

which it is '[t]he true international child'.[66] As observed by Boister, with most major multinational companies domiciled in states parties to the 1997 OECD Bribery Convention and its exclusive focus on 'supply-side corruption', that is on the payor as opposed to recipient, 'compliance in the states that "host" the corruption is irrelevant'.[67] Such corruption would ostensibly be addressed through a combination of corporate self-regulation and the exercise of home state jurisdiction.

## 2. Subsequent Developments

Once established, corporate liability standards were rapidly diffused globally via the three major UN conventions on economic crime:[68] the International Convention for the Suppression of the Financing of Terrorism of 9 December 1999 (1999 Terrorist Financing Convention); the Convention against Transnational Organized Crime of 15 November 2000 (UNTOC); and the Convention against Corruption of 31 October 2003 (UNCAC). There are relevant textual differences between the corporate liability provision of the UN Financing of Terrorism Convention and those of the UNTOC and UNCAC. In particular, article 5 of the 1999 Terrorist Financing Convention narrows the scope for liability by mandating its applicability 'when a person responsible for the management or control of [the] legal entity has, in that capacity', committed the relevant offence. In contrast, the near-identical provisions of the UNTOC and UNCAC hew more closely to the 'minimalist' approach. All three provisions include a 'safeguard clause'; permit liability to be criminal, civil or administrative; and mandate 'effective, proportionate and dissuasive sanctions'.

The development of the UNTOC, the longest in the making, is instructive.[69] The Naples Political Declaration and Global Action Plan against Organized Transnational Crime, which emerged from the 1994 World Ministerial Conference on Organized and Transnational Crime, stated that '[s]ubstantive legislation ... imposing criminal liability on corporate bodies should be considered';[70] and in 1996, Poland proposed a draft framework convention against organized crime which included provision that contracting states 'shall consider establishing ... the

[66] Boister, *Introduction to Transnational Criminal Law* (n 3) 151. See also, Pieth, 'Introduction' (n 37) 31–32.

[67] Boister, *Introduction to Transnational Criminal Law* (n 3) 151 with reference to art 1 of the OECD Convention and Rose, *International Anti-Corruption Norms* (n 39) 60.

[68] Pieth, 'Article 2' (n 63) 225. At the time of writing, the UN Secretary-General lists 189, 190 and 187 states parties, <https://treaties.un.org/Pages/Treaties.aspx?id=18&subid=A&clang=_en>.

[69] For more details on the general development of the UNTOC, see Forlati, Chapter 13 in this book.

[70] UNGA, A/49/748, 2 December 1994, para 15, approved by UNGA, A/Res/49/159, 24 February 1995.

possibility of criminal liability of corporate persons'.[71] The focus was thus on criminal liability, which would be 'considered' as opposed to mandatory.

After 1997, OECD states began to throw their weight behind corporate liability standards framed in terms similar to those of the 1997 OECD Bribery Convention. In 1998, the Working Group of the Commission on Crime Prevention and Criminal Justice listed three proposals for a corporate liability provision as part of a draft convention on transnational organized crime.[72] Libya's proposal dispensed with specification that the liability be criminal, but required only that states 'consider ... the possibility' of corporate liability. By contrast, the proposals of Finland and France, both OECD members, made such liability mandatory, expressly permitted that it be criminal, civil or administrative (as well, in the Finnish proposal, as commercial), while stipulating that sanctions be 'effective, proportionate and dissuasive'.

France submitted a further draft, which was similar in structure and substance[73] and formed the basis for discussion.[74] While the 1998 draft convention published by the Ad Hoc Committee still featured the Libyan proposal,[75] the revised draft published the following year dropped it in favour of one that tracked more closely the French proposal.[76] The inclusion of a 'safeguard clause', according to McClean, removed opposition to the principle of corporate liability, leaving only the details of the provision to be agreed.[77]

Each convention developed according to its own dynamics but to put it briefly, the flexible approach represented by the French proposal in the UNTOC negotiations was adopted by the Ad Hoc Committee tasked by the UN General Assembly with elaborating anti-terrorism conventions.[78] Corporate liability was a core feature of the French initiative to extend that Committee's mandate to the financing of terrorism,[79] supported by the US.[80] As noted, its ultimate expression in article 5 made reference to attribution rules, but otherwise reflected the adaptable features that steered a path between proposals that would have made it more specific or

[71] Draft United Nations framework convention against organized crime, A/C.3/51/7, 1 October 1996, art 3.

[72] Report of the Working Group on the implementation of the Naples Political Declaration and Global Action Plan against Organized Transnational Crime, Annex III, E/1998/30, E/CN.15/1998/11, 21–30 April 1998, 86–87.

[73] Proposals and Contributions Received from Governments, A/AC.254/5, 19 December 1998.

[74] David McClean, *Transnational Organized Crime: A Commentary on the UN Convention and its Protocols* (OUP 2007) 127 (hereafter McClean, *Transnational Organized Crime*).

[75] Draft United Nations Convention against Transnational Organized Crime, A/AC/254/4, 15 December 1998, art 5.

[76] Revised draft United Nations Convention against Transnational Organized Crime, A/AC.254/4/Rev.4, 19 July 1999, art 5.

[77] McClean, *Transnational Organized Crime* (n 74) 127–28.

[78] UNGA, Measures to eliminate international terrorism, A/RES/51/210, 16 January 1997.

[79] Draft International Convention for the Suppression of the Financing of Terrorism, A/AC.252/L.7/Add.1, 11 March 1999.

[80] Michael Levi, 'Combating the Financing Threat of Terrorism: A History and Assessment of the Control of "Threat Finance"' (2010) 50(4) BJC 650, 652.

removed it altogether.[81] By the time the UN General Assembly formally decided to begin work on an anti-corruption international instrument in December 2000, the standards had been largely established, indicated by the UNCAC's effective adoption of the UNTOC's corporate liability provision.[82] Notably, such liability would only apply to bribery in the public sector: efforts to mandate criminalization of bribery in the private sector, supported by the EU and Latin American and Caribbean states, were successfully opposed by the US.[83] The problem to be solved remained governmental, not corporate, (abuse of) power.

While the UNCAC marked a divergence between the US and EU regarding the private sector, as the above shows, US and European states remained the key drivers behind the diffusion of corporate liability provisions. Indeed, it is noteworthy that subsequent treaties from regions outside North America and Europe either did not include corporate liability provisions[84] or simply replicated the established OECD/UN approach without further development.[85] Moreover, while the 'minimalist' approach facilitated diffusion, it also suggests that the primary objective in ensuring corporate liability provisions within the key economic crime treaties lay in establishing the norm in principle, and thereby making corporations 'responsible' actors and affirming home state regulatory power. Effectiveness would depend not simply on enforcement but on key legal principles, such as attribution, that were either left unaddressed or engaged with only at a general level.

[81] UNGA, Measures to eliminate international terrorism, A/C.6/54/L.2, 26 October 1999. See in particular, the proposals of Guatemala, India and Papua New Guinea (Report of the Ad Hoc Committee established by GA Res 51/210 of 17 December 1996, A/54/37, 5 May 1999, Annex III).

[82] UNGA, A/RES/55/61, 22 January 2001; UNODC, *Travaux Préparatoires of the negotiations for the elaboration of the United Nations Convention against Corruption* (UN 2010) 235.

[83] UNGA, A/AC.261/9, 26 November 2002; Philippa Webb, 'The United Nations Convention Against Corruption: Global Achievement or Missed Opportunity?' (2005) 8(1) JIEL 191, 213–14.

[84] On terrorism, see eg: Arab Convention on the Suppression of Terrorism of April 1998; Convention of the Organisation of the Islamic Conference on Combating International Terrorism of 1 July 1999; OAU Convention on the Prevention and Combating of Terrorism of 1 July 1999 and its Protocol of 8 July 2004; Treaty on Cooperation among States Members of the Commonwealth of Independent States in Combating Terrorism of 4 June 1999; Shanghai Convention on Combating Terrorism, Separatism and Extremism of 15 June 2001; Convention of the Cooperation Council for the Arab States of the Gulf on Combating Terrorism of 4 May 2004; ASEAN Convention on Counter Terrorism of 13 January 2007. On corruption, see eg: Agreement among the Governments of the Black Sea Economic Cooperation Participating States on Cooperation in Combating Crime, in Particular its Organized Forms of 2 October 1998 (and its two protocols of 15 March 2002 and 3 December 2004); SADC Protocol against Corruption of 14 August 2001; AU Convention on Preventing and Combating Corruption of 11 July 2003.

[85] For example, Additional Protocol to the South Asian Association for Regional Cooperation Regional Convention on Suppression of Terrorism of 6 January 2004, art 6; Arab Anti-Corruption Convention of 21 December 2010, art 5; ECOWAS Protocol on the Fight against Corruption of 21 December 2001, art 11.

## 3. Return to Non-Binding Instruments

Finally, we can observe a return to non-binding international instruments, especially in the FATF and OECD contexts, where membership is more exclusive and the screws on some of those key legal principles have begun to be turned further than was possible through formal treaty negotiations.[86] This may be seen, for example, with the OECD Council's adoption of a new version of its 1994 and 1997 Recommendations, forerunners to the OECD Convention, together with two annexed 'Good Practice Guidances' in 2009.[87] While emphasizing respect for national legal principles and state discretion, it contains important developments and details on corporate liability. Pieth explains that it finally defines the minimum standard of corporate liability. Whereas the Convention

> had merely asked for 'effective, proportionate and dissuasive' sanctions, the 'Good Practice Guidance' draws the bottom line. It defines the failure of supervision and failure to implement adequate ethics and compliance programmes as an alternative to strict liability. Annex II defines what an adequate ethics and compliance programme requires.[88]

It is apparent that this standard is 'very close to the US Sentencing Guidelines'.[89] It reflects US preferences for finding corporate liability in management failures to supervise, the absence of internal processes of control and general deficiencies in corporate

[86] Pieth explains that at the OECD the 'original method chosen was to develop "soft law" Recommendations to state Parties' (Pieth, 'Introduction' (n 37) 36–37). See also, Boister, *Introduction to Transnational Criminal Law* (n 3) 166; Rose, *International Anti-Corruption Norms* (n 39) 61. Similar 'soft law' initiatives can also be observed in other fora such as the G20 (see eg Annex to G20 Leaders' Declaration: G20 High-Level Principles on the Liability of Legal Persons for Corruption, 8 July 2017, <https://www.g20germany.de/Webs/G20/EN/G20/Summit_documents/summit_documents_node.html>).

[87] OECD, Recommendation of the Council for Further Combating Bribery of Foreign Public Officials in International Business Transactions (26 November 2009, amended on 18 February 2010) C(2009)159/Rev1/FINAL, C(2010)19, Annex I: Good Practice Guidance on Implementing Specific Articles of the Convention on Combating Bribery of Foreign Public Officials in International Business Transactions, Annex II: Good Practice Guidance on Internal Controls, Ethics, and Compliance (hereafter OECD, Recommendation).

[88] Pieth, 'Introduction' (n 37) 27. Interestingly, while the idea of attaching corporate liability to a 'lack of supervision or control' had been envisaged in the Second Protocol 1995 EU Financial Interests Convention in 1997, it was not included in the subsequent OECD and UN conventions, but only taken up again by the OECD in its 2009 Recommendation from which it proliferated. Also considering that the Second Protocol 1995 EU Financial Interests Convention required more than eleven years from its adoption to gather sufficient state support for its entry into force on 19 May 2009, only a few months prior to the OECD Recommendation, this may be seen as further evidence not only of the greater influence of the outward-looking OECD foreign bribery regime as compared to the inward-looking EU financial interests regime, but of the careful, strategic pursuit of the development of corporate liability standards by key actors at the international level (eg to ensure the internationalization of the FCPA before returning explicitly to the idea of control- or supervision-related liability within the established framework).

[89] Pieth, 'Introduction' (n 37) 27 with reference to USSG 2012, §8B2.1.

culture which are largely 'policed' through the corporation itself.[90] This delegation of responsibility to large corporations still mainly located in the global North seems to reflect a modern embrace of governance roles for corporations and another step in the delegitimization of alternative governance efforts, especially by global South states. Currently under review, it is expected that the revised version of the OECD Recommendation will in many ways continue these 'privatization' trends.[91]

Similar dynamics are evident in the AML and terrorism financing fields, in which the FATF has assumed a particularly important role.[92] For example, after 11 September 2001, the FATF started issuing special recommendations on the financing of terrorism. While emphasizing in Recommendation I (Ratification and implementation of UN instruments) that '[e]ach country should take immediate steps to ratify and to implement fully the 1999 United Nations International Convention for the Suppression of the Financing of Terrorism', it went significantly further than that Convention in Recommendation II (Criminalising the financing of terrorism and associated money laundering) where the interpretative note indicated a clear preference: 'Criminal liability for terrorist financing should extend to legal persons. Where that is not possible (i.e. due to fundamental principles of domestic law), civil or administrative liability should apply.'[93] In addition, as Boister explains, the FATF has in practice recently adopted a restrictive view of when solely civil liability is acceptable, thus compelling some mainly civil law states to enact corporate criminal liability.[94] Notably, it has done so in the context of a mandate that includes 'protecting the integrity of the global financial system'[95] and despite 'the informal and secretive nature of its decision-making process and standard setting with little or no input from the wider group of developing and emerging market countries'.[96]

[90] Borlini, 'Art 26' (n 1) 279–80; Jennifer Arlen and Samuel Buell, 'The Global Expansion of Corporate Criminal Liability: Effective Enforcement Policy Across Legal Systems' (2020) 93 S Cal L Rev 697, 706–09.

[91] See for an overview, <http://www.oecd.org/corruption/2019-review-oecd-anti-bribery-recommendation.htm>. The OECD Working Group on Bribery 'has agreed to revisit in the context of this review' the following topics as regards legal persons: Responsibility of legal persons for foreign bribery through intermediaries [Annex I, C]; Enhancing compliance [Rec X.C. and Annex II]; and Incentives for anti-bribery compliance [Rec X] (Public Consultation Document: Review of the 2009 OECD Anti-Bribery Recommendation, 22 March–30 April 2019, 4, 7–9).

[92] Navin Beekarry, 'International Anti-Money Laundering and Combating the Financing of Terrorism Regulatory Strategy: A Critical Analysis of Compliance Determinants in International Law' (2011) 31 NJILB 137 (hereafter Beekarry, 'Regulatory Strategy').

[93] Interpretive Note to Special Recommendation II, para 12. A similar provision was introduced on money laundering in Recommendation 2(b) FATF 40 Recommendations 2003 (n 5) and repeated in the Interpretive Note to Recommendation 3 (Money Laundering Offence) and Recommendation 5 (Terrorist Financing).

[94] Boister, *Introduction to Transnational Criminal Law* (n 3) 181.

[95] Bjørn S Aamo, Global Partnership for Financial Inclusion Conference on Standard-Setting Bodies and Financial Inclusion: Promoting Financial Inclusion through Proportionate Standards and Guidance, 29 October 2012 <http://www.fatf- gafi.org/publications/fatfgeneral/documents/fatfsfocusonfinancialinclusionprotectingtheintegrityoftheglobalfinancialsyst em.html#:~:text=FATF's%20interest%20in%20financial%20inclusion,committed%20to%20the%20FATF%20Recomm endations>.

[96] Beekarry, 'Regulatory Strategy' (n 92) 191.

## IV. Conclusion

In this final section, we briefly summarize the main developments identified above before offering some more general reflections. The pre-treaty phase occurred within a broader contest over corporations as transnational actors and efforts to reshape the international economic order. Corporate liability's emergence was thus primarily reactive, operating to legitimize corporations' transnational power and undermine global South states' governance.

The treaty phase formalized and disseminated these trends. Having first secured a consensus amongst a small group of powerful global North states, partly through agreeing on broad and flexible terms, corporate liability standards were diffused globally, especially through the UN. While relatively brief, this phase was important to establishing the norm, its consequences for the distribution of regulatory power and the dominant narrative it assured. Thereafter, the development of, and regulatory contests over, those standards returned to fora dominated by global North states including members of the OECD and FATF. Although implementation is beyond our scope, domestication of corporate liability standards continued, notably even where ill-suited to local circumstances,[97] and in some respects advanced the themes, such as privatization, developed internationally.[98] One can also observe those themes reflected in the interplay between the international standards and domestic enforcement. In particular, while the FCPA had been effectively 'shelved' for its first two decades, the number of cases brought under it, many of them against foreign companies, spiked dramatically after the OECD Convention was concluded.[99] Brewster persuasively explains this increase on the basis that the OECD Convention 'established a clear path for prosecuting American and foreign firms equally' and thereby supposedly leveled the playing field of international commerce, while solving 'an American political problem of jurisdictional aggressiveness'.[100]

We conclude with four observations, situating the development of corporate liability standards within broader transnational (criminal) law themes. First, that development exemplifies the manufacturing by powerful states of international norms that 'globalize' local developments.[101]

Second, it attests to changing methods of norm diffusion: the treaty phase, reflecting an important but functionally limited interlude, demonstrated a strategic and flexible approach by key actors to internationalize the norm, while non-binding

[97] Jorge, 'Latin America' (n 55) 321; Sharman, *The Money Laundry* (n 7) 160.

[98] Liz Campbell, 'Corporate Liability and the Criminalisation of Failure' (2018) 12(2) LFMR 57.

[99] Brewster, 'Enforcing the FCPA' (n 37) 1614, 1678.

[100] ibid 1659, 1663.

[101] This is not to overstate the ease with which the United States was able to secure agreement (Katzarova, *Social Construction* (n 14) 215). See also, Boaventura de Sousa Santos, *Toward a New Legal Common Sense: Law, Globalization, and Emancipation* (2nd edn, CUP 2002) 210, 214 (referring to 'globalized localism' in the context of the *lex mercatoria*).

instruments otherwise represented the driving force. Both observations offer insight into how dominant states interact with international law. For Krisch, these interactions commonly oscillate between the two poles of instrumentalization and withdrawal, with extraterritorial projection of domestic law and informal diffusion of rules contributing to the maintenance of power.[102] These dynamics map well onto those identified in this chapter.

Third, the development of corporate liability standards aligns with the embrace of private transnational governance analysed by those such as Cutler and Zumbansen.[103] Both the corporate sector and non-governmental expert groups such as the FATF have been central to the internationalization and development of corporate liability norms.[104] Increasing emphasis on compliance-oriented liability and self-regulation similarly provides evidence of the significant role afforded to private governance and rule-making.[105]

Finally, the development of corporate liability standards tests the limits of transnational criminal law as an analytical framework in at least two respects. First, the importance of the 'minimalist' approach, allowing for a 'safeguard clause' and administrative and civil liability, to that development indicates that a narrow criminal law paradigm may be unduly circumscribed. So too does the aforementioned increasing emphasis on compliance-oriented liability and self-regulation. Second, by illustrating law's narrative function, the development of corporate liability standards suggests a need to broaden the frame from the 'norm entrepreneurs' and prohibition regimes on which transnational criminal law tends to focus.[106] As Shaffer notes, transnational legal norms 'can shape the perception and definition of problems and appropriate responses to them'.[107] In this regard, the success

[102] Nico Krisch, 'International Law in Times of Hegemony: Unequal Power and the Shaping of the International Legal Order' (2005) 16(3) EJIL 369. See also, Nico Krisch, 'The Decay of Consent: International Law in an Age of Global Public Goods' (2014) 108(1) AJIL 1–40; Joost Pauwelyn, Ramses Wessel and Jan Wouters (eds), *Informal International Lawmaking* (OUP 2012).

[103] For example, A Claire Cutler, 'Locating Private Transnational Authority in the Global Political Economy' in Peer Zumbansen (ed), *The Many Lives of Transnational Law: Critical Engagements with Jessup's Bold Proposal* (CUP 2020) 321; A Claire Cutler, *Private Power and Global Authority: Transnational Merchant Law in the Global Political Economy* (CUP 2003); Peer Zumbansen and Dionysia Katelouzou, 'The Transnationalization of Corporate Governance: Law, Institutional Arrangements and Corporate Power' (2021) 38(1) Ariz J Intl & Comp L 1; ; Gralf-Peter Calliess and Peer Zumbansen, *Rough Consensus and Running Code: A Theory of Transnational Private Law* (Hart 2010).

[104] Pieth, 'Introduction' (n 37) 19; Jason C Sharman, 'Power and Discourse in Policy Diffusion: Anti-Money Laundering in Developing States' (2008) 52 ISQ 635, 640, 648. For a recent example of corporate influence, see OECD, *Public Comments: Review of the 2009 Anti-Bribery Recommendation*, Private Sector.

[105] Carolin Liss and Jason C Sharman, 'Global Corporate Crime-Fighters: Private Transnational Responses to Privacy and Money-Laundering' (2015) 22(4) Rev Intl Political Econ 693, 701–02.

[106] Both of these limits are recently explored by Ivory: Radha Ivory, 'Transnational Criminal Law or the Transnational Legal Ordering of Corruption? Theorizing Australian Corporate Foreign Bribery Reforms' (2019) 4 UCI J of Int'l Transnational, & Comp L 26; Radha Ivory, 'Beyond Transnational Criminal Law: Anti-Corruption as Global New Governance' (2018) 6(3) LRIL 413. See also, Cian C Murphy, 'Transnational Counter-Terrorism Law: Law, Power and Legitimacy in the "Wars on Terror"' (2015) 6(1) TLT 31.

[107] Gregory Shaffer, 'Transnational Legal Process and State Change' (2012) 37(2) LSI 229, 238.

of corporate liability standards since their first enactment at least partly lies in establishing a conventional wisdom such that leading scholars may conclude

> A cumulative approach is called for if the aim of making corporations liable for corruption is to deter and reduce bribery within a larger effort to tackle the pernicious effects of corruption *in 'southern' countries' governments* ... In practice this means not just waving the stick of criminal law sanctions *but also producing the carrots* to bring about real changes in corporate behaviour *on a voluntary basis.*[108]

The concomitant ends of legitimizing corporate power while delegitimizing governance by global South states appear thus established. Yet as this chapter shows, historicizing the international development of corporate liability standards with particular attention to the power and ideational dynamics at stake brings to light not just the contingency of such enframing, but the broader functions it serves.

[108] Aiolfi and Pieth, 'International Aspects' (n 5) 410 (emphasis added).

# 16

# The Illicit Trade in Cultural Objects

## From Marginalization to the Current Surge in Attention by Transnational Criminal Policymakers

*Arianna Visconti*

## I. Introduction

This chapter focuses on an issue—the illicit trade in cultural objects—to which different jurisdictions have long struggled, and are still struggling, to pay a uniform level of attention, and therefore an adequate level of international cooperation, including by way of shared prevention and suppression strategies.

Several structural factors contribute to this delay. It starts with a persisting 'property' framework, that is a prevailing consideration of these offences as (mere) offences against property[1] (albeit a property endowed with a peculiar 'cultural' value). This in turn plays between the lines of a market for artworks and antiquities, which, as we will see, is not only intrinsically transnational in nature, but also driven by a great imbalance between its offer and demand sides. Resistance to regulation by market operators, especially in importing countries,[2] an until recently very limited interest in public opinion (mostly concerned with crimes of a more immediately perceptible harmfulness) and the submerged nature of many offences against cultural heritage[3] have all played their part.

The highest visibility and destructiveness of (at least some) offences against cultural heritage occurring in wartime, coupled with an ongoing broader turn to a 'human rights framework'[4] which is likely most congenial to international

[1] See eg Lyndel V Prott and Patrick J O'Keefe, 'Cultural Heritage or Cultural Property' (1992) 1 IJCP 307; Manlio Frigo, 'Cultural Property v. Cultural Heritage: A "Battle of Concepts" in International Law?' (2004) 86 IRRC 367; Francesco Francioni, 'A Dynamic Evolution of Concept and Scope: From Cultural Property to Cultural Heritage' in Abdulqawi A Yusuf (ed), *Standard Setting in UNESCO*, Vol I (Martinus Nijhoff Publishers 2007) 221.

[2] See Simon Mackenzie, 'Illicit Deals in Cultural Objects as Crimes of the Powerful' (2011) 56 CLSC 133 (hereafter Mackenzie, 'Illicit Deals').

[3] See eg Neil Brodie, Jessica Dietzler and Simon Mackenzie, 'Trafficking in Cultural Objects: An Empirical Overview' in Stefano Manacorda and Arianna Visconti (eds), *Beni culturali e sistema penale* (Vita e Pensiero 2013) 19.

[4] See also Kimberly L Alderman, 'The Human Right to Cultural Property (2011) 20 MSILR 20 69–81; Yvonne Donders, 'Cultural Heritage and Human Rights' in Francesco Francioni and Ana Filipa Vrdoljak (eds), *The Oxford Handbook of International Cultural Heritage Law* (OUP 2020) 379.

Arianna Visconti, *The Illicit Trade in Cultural Objects* In: *Histories of Transnational Criminal Law*. Edited by: Neil Boister, Sabine Gless and Florian Jeßberger, Oxford University Press. © Arianna Visconti 2021. DOI: 10.1093/oso/9780192845702.003.0017

humanitarian law, contribute symmetrically to the explanation of why this branch of law first experienced a significant shift towards a broader use of criminalization. Also symmetrically, the recent awakening of public awareness, mostly due to growing concern about cultural property trafficking becoming intertwined with more serious crimes, such as organized crime and terrorism (which we will discuss in the third section), contributes to an explanation of why there have been increasing efforts to promote a measure of criminal law harmonization that goes beyond war crimes.

A new push towards criminalization of offences related to cultural property trafficking is actually gaining momentum, even in several traditionally reluctant states. As the risk to rush into symbolic over-penalization is always present (even more so in an emotionally loaded context such as that of conduct offensive to peoples' cultural heritages), however, the final section will discuss the possible setbacks of any oversimplifying criminal policy.

## II. At the Origins: Cultural Heritage and the Laws of War

### 1. Enlightenment Ideals and Napoleonic Wars

Objects of art and antiquities have always had a high value,[5] not just in monetary terms, but also for their aesthetic, historical and more broadly spiritual significance, as well as their testimonial value as to the status of their commissioners, patrons and owners. Consequently, they have always been coveted war spoils. At the same time, due to their strict link to peoples' identity, religious and civil monuments have always been the target of wilful destruction in order to demoralize or annihilate the enemy. These are probably the reasons why the first development of international rules specifically directed at cultural heritage can be traced back to (first) peace treaties and (afterwards) laws of war.

We see, for instance, that some provisions referring to reciprocal restitutions of 'archives, documents and other movable things' were introduced in the Treaties of Westfalia of 1648, at the end of the Thirty Years' War,[6] and also appeared in some subsequent peace treaties. The ideas that pillage and seizure of artworks, archives, books etc—all objects that today we consider 'cultural property'—was not permitted even in times of conflict and that, when it occurred, the looting state had a duty to reinstate, as far as possible, the previous situation, emerged in the 17th

[5] See eg Craig Forrest, *International Law and the Protection of Cultural Heritage* (Routledge 2010) 3–13 (hereafter Forrest, *International*).

[6] Art CXIV, *Instrumentum Pacis Monasteriensis*, IPM, 24 October 1648. cf Tullio Scovazzi, 'Diviser c'est détruire: Ethical Principles and Legal Rules in the Field of Return of Cultural Properties' 6 (UNESCO 2009) <https://unesdoc.unesco.org/ark:/48223/pf0000245254> (hereafter Scovazzi, 'Diviser').

and 18th centuries and began to receive theoretical support through the writings of Enlightenment thinkers.[7] Antoine-Chrysostome Quatremère de Quincy, in a well-known pamphlet (first published in 1796),[8] took a strong standing against the appropriation, as spoils of war, of objects to be considered as the heritage of all peoples.[9] More broadly, he presented the removal of cultural properties from their context as a way of destroying them.[10] He also criticized the commercialization and export of cultural objects for purposes of gain,[11] and thought that cultural properties could not be treated like ordinary commercial goods.[12]

Scholars' views, of course, did not avail against the massive and systematic seizure of artworks in occupied territories during the Napoleonic campaigns, usually legitimized by the subsequent peace treaties.[13] Notwithstanding the lack of specific provisions on the restitution of cultural objects in the treaties adopted following the Congress of Vienna, by the beginning of the 19th century the idea of a duty to give back items of cultural relevance to the despoiled party had taken further root.[14] This was mostly thanks to the successful and well-known diplomatic mission of Antonio Canova, who achieved the restoration to the Papal States of a great number of artworks and manuscripts,[15] and to the subsequent, consistent restitution, by the Papal States, of a set of ancient manuscripts, looted from the Bibliotheca Palatina in 1622, to Heidelberg University.[16]

## 2. Cultural Heritage Protection at the Dawn of Modern Humanitarian Law

It was only at the beginning of the 20th century that the prohibition of wilful destruction and pillage of civilian properties formally entered international law. Some provisions of the Hague Convention II, on the Laws and Customs of War on Land (29 July 1899, articles 28, 47 and 56), and of the revised Hague Convention IV of 18 October 1909, specifically addressed the protection of 'buildings dedicated to religion, art, science, … historic monuments, … not being used … for military

[7] See also references in Scovazzi, 'Diviser' (n 6) 4.

[8] Antoine C Quatremère de Quincy, *Lettres sur le préjudice qu'occasionneroient aux Arts et à la Science, le déplacement des monumens de l'art de l'Italie, le démembrement de ses Ecoles, et la spoliation de ses Collections, Galeries, Musées, etc.* (Rome sn 1815).

[9] ibid 3–4.

[10] ibid 25–87.

[11] ibid 65–84.

[12] Scovazzi, 'Diviser' (n 6) 4.

[13] ibid 3.

[14] Roger O'Keefe, *The Protection of Cultural Property in Armed Conflict* (CUP 2006) 13–16 (hereafter O'Keefe, *The Protection*).

[15] Scovazzi, 'Diviser' (n 6) 3–5.

[16] Tullio Scovazzi, 'La dimensione internazionale della tutela' in Stefano Manacorda and Arianna Visconti (eds), *Beni culturali e sistema penale* (Vita e Pensiero 2013) 76.

purposes' (article 27 Reg.), as well as of the 'property of . . . institutions dedicated to religion, . . . education, the arts and sciences' and all 'works of art and science' (article 56 Reg.).[17]

This first codification was proven ineffective by the massive loss of monuments, artworks, documents etc, that occurred during World War I.[18] Yet, the 1919 Treaty of Versailles reaffirmed, in a sense, the binding nature of the principles expressed in those conventions, by providing for the restitution of identified cultural objects to their countries of origin.[19] In addition, a first attempt was made to criminalize these breaches of the laws of war: Sub-Commission III, on Responsibilities for the Violation of the Laws and Customs of War, produced a draft list of war crimes, meant to reflect international customary law as well as the Hague rules, and included the wanton destruction of religious, charitable, educational and historic buildings and monuments.[20] For political reasons, however, no actual trial was ever initiated.[21]

In the following years, several attempts were made by the League of Nations at developing a more effective international protection regime for cultural heritage in times of war,[22] but the outbreak of World War II stopped any discussion, and led to a level of destruction and dispersal of cultural property in comparison to which the Great War paled. In the post-war trials[23] the seizure of public and private collections in German-occupied territories was classified as a war crime under article 6(b) of the Charter of the International Military Tribunal of Nuremberg.[24] The most famous prosecution led to the conviction of Alfred Rosenberg, held 'responsible for a system of organised plunder of both public and private property throughout the invaded countries of Europe'.[25]

## 3. After World War II: A New Focus on Cultural Property Protection

The experience of World War II lies at the roots of the Convention for the Protection of Cultural Property in the Event of Armed Conflict, adopted on 14 May 1954 in The Hague, which entered into force on 7 August 1956.[26] It also influenced two

[17] cf O'Keefe, *The Protection* (n 14) 22–34; Forrest, *International* (n 5) 67–69.

[18] O'Keefe, *The Protection* (n 14) 36–39.

[19] Scovazzi, 'Diviser' (n 6) 6–8.

[20] UNWCC, *History of the United Nations War Crimes Commission and the Development of the Laws of War* (1948) 34 <http://www.unwcc.org/wp-content/uploads/2017/04/UNWCC-history.pdf>.

[21] O'Keefe, *The Protection* (n 14) 43–44.

[22] Forrest, *International* (n 5) 70–73; Jiří Toman, *The Protection of Cultural Property in the Event of Armed Conflict* (UNESCO 1996) 16–19.

[23] O'Keefe, *The Protection* (n 14) 88–91.

[24] Agreed and in force 8 August 1945, 82 UNTS 279.

[25] Judgment of the International Military Tribunal for the Trial of German Major War Criminals, Nuremberg, 30 September and 1 October 1946, Misc No 12 (1946), Cmd 6964, 95.

[26] 249 UNTS 240. See O'Keefe, *The Protection* (n 14) 92–195; Forrest, *International* (n 5) 78–104.

Additional Protocols added to the corpus of the Geneva Conventions in 1977,[27] and which included specific protection for 'historic monuments, works of art or places of worship which constitute the cultural or spiritual heritage of peoples' (article 53 of Protocol I). However, in dealing with the flow of illicit trafficking in cultural objects fed (among other events) by armed conflicts,[28] these treaties presented two considerable weaknesses.

Firstly, there is little if any focus on the seizing and export of artworks and antiquities: the 1977 Protocols only deal (including by obligations of criminalization)[29] with intentional destructive attacks against cultural property (articles 53 and 86(4)(d), Protocol I, and article 16, Protocol II). In the 1954 Hague Cultural Property Convention, article 4(3) obliges state parties 'to prohibit, prevent and, if necessary, put a stop to any form of theft, pillage or misappropriation of, and any acts of vandalism directed against, cultural property', at least by their own troops (while it is contested whether the obligation also covers prevention of like actions by third parties, such as civilians or enemy militias),[30] and to 'refrain from requisitioning movable cultural property situated in the territory of another High Contracting Party'. The obligation 'to prevent the exportation', in accordance to local national laws,[31] 'from a territory occupied' is relegated into a separate (First) Protocol,[32] which received fewer ratifications, and at a slower rate.

Moreover, the 1954 Hague Cultural Property Convention and First Protocol do not provide very demanding obligations of criminalization. In fact, the only norm that 'comes within the punitive province'[33] is article 28, which requires state parties to 'take, within the framework of their ordinary criminal jurisdiction, all necessary steps to prosecute and impose penal or disciplinary sanctions upon those persons, of whatever nationality, who commit or order to be committed a breach' of the Convention. The provision fails to enumerate and detail specific criminal offences, thus leaving ample latitude for very different transpositions into national

[27] Protocol Additional to the Geneva Conventions of 12 August 1949, and relating to the Protection of Victims of International Armed Conflicts (Protocol I), (adopted 8 June 1977, entered into force 7 December 1978) 1125 UNTS 3 and Protocol Additional to the Geneva Conventions of 12 August 1949, and relating to the Protection of Victims of Non-International Armed Conflicts (Protocol II), (adopted 8 June 1977, entered into force 7 December 1978) 1125 UNTS 609. See O'Keefe, *The Protection* (n 14) 202–33; Forrest, *International* (n 5) 108–110.

[28] Joris D Kila, 'From Crimes against Art to Crimes against Cultural Property: New Perspectives and Dimensions in Art Crime' in Joris D Kila and Marc Balcells (eds), *Cultural Property Crime* (Brill 2015) 182.

[29] O'Keefe, *The Protection* (n 14) 224–29, 233; Stefano Manacorda, 'Criminal Law Protection of Cultural Heritage: An International Perspective' in Stefano Manacorda and Duncan Chappell (eds), *Crime in the Art and Antiquities World. Illegal Trafficking in Cultural Property* (Springer 2011) 17, 27–28 (hereafter Manacorda, 'Criminal' and Manacorda and Chappell, *Crime in the Art and Antiquities World*).

[30] O'Keefe, *The Protection* (n 14) 132–33; Forrest, *International* (n 5) 91–92.

[31] O'Keefe, *The Protection* (n 14) 198; Forrest, *International* (n 5) 105.

[32] Protocol for the Protection of Cultural Property in the Event of Armed Conflict (adopted, The Hague, 14 May 1954, entered into force 7 August 1956) 249 UNTS 358.

[33] Manacorda, 'Criminal' (n 29) 27.

laws, besides being in itself too general and allowing for the use of disciplinary sanctions in the framework of military Law.[34] As for export prohibition, paragraph III article 11(a) of the First Protocol rather generically requires states to 'take all necessary measures to ensure [its] effective application', thus in fact leaving the parties totally free to choose what kind of sanctions—if any—should be introduced to this effect.[35]

## 4. At the Turn of the Century: A Push Towards Criminalization

The many shortcomings of the 1954 Hague Cultural Property Convention revealed by the Iran-Iraq conflict in the 1980s and by the First Gulf War and the Balkan Wars of the 1990s[36] provided a new push for, amongst other things, a more intensive use of criminal law to prevent and punish offences against cultural heritage in wartime, including, to some extent, actions capable of feeding international trafficking.

The 1998 Rome Statute, which instituted the International Criminal Court (ICC) (endowed with direct, albeit subsidiary, penal jurisdiction over war crimes),[37] had no immediate effect on the illicit trade, as it only provides for an offence of intentional attack against cultural property (article 8(2)(b)(ix) and 8(2)(e)(iv)).[38] However, the 1999 Second Protocol to the Hague Convention[39] encompasses a broader set of penal provisions, binding state parties to criminalize, amongst others, the 'extensive ... appropriation of cultural property' (article 15(1)(c)) and its 'theft, pillage or misappropriation' (article 15(1)(e)). These behaviours are deemed 'serious violations' of the Protocol,[40] and, differently from the 1954 Convention, each state party is bound to 'adopt such measures as may be necessary to establish [them] as criminal offences under its domestic law ... and to make such offences punishable by appropriate penalties' (article 15(2)). However, other offences conducive to illicit trafficking in cultural property are subject to less stringent obligations of criminalization:[41] according to article 21, the parties undertake

[34] ibid.

[35] Forrest, *International* (n 5) 108.

[36] David Keane, 'The Failure to Protect Cultural Property in Wartime' (2004) 14 JATIP 20 (hereafter Keane, 'The Failure'); O'Keefe, *The Protection* (n 14) 236–40.

[37] Statute of the International Criminal Court (adopted Rome, 17 July 1998, entered into force 1 July 2002) 2187 UNTS 90.

[38] Jérémy Hall, 'Les défis culturels de la Cour pénale internationale' in Evelyne Lagrange, Stefan Oeter and Robert Uerpmann-Wittzack (eds), *Cultural Heritage and International Law* (Springer 2018) 209. In 2016 the court issued the first conviction under art 8(2)(e)(iv): *The Prosecutor v Ahmad Al Faqi Al Mahdi* (Judgment) ICC-01/12-01/15 (hereafter *The Prosecutor v Al Mahdi*).

[39] Second Protocol to the 1954 Hague Cultural Property Convention (adopted 26 March 1999, entered into force 9 March 2004) 38 ILM (1999) 769. See Keane, 'The Failure' (n 36) 27–36; Forrest, *International* (n 5) 110–21.

[40] O'Keefe, *The Protection* (n 14) 274–87; Manacorda, 'Criminal' (n 29) 28–29.

[41] See O'Keefe, *The Protection* (n 14) 287–88; Manacorda, 'Criminal' (n 29) 29.

to 'suppress', when 'committed intentionally', any 'illicit export, other removal or transfer of ownership of cultural property from occupied territory in violation of the Convention or [the] Protocol', but they are free to choose between 'such legislative, administrative or disciplinary measures as may be necessary'.

Several factors may account for this slow process of criminalization. It is likely that this is partly due to the same divergences between market and source countries that have slowed down the use of penal sanctions against peacetime offences.[42] It also appears related to the difficult development of the *jus in bello* in general (major military powers in particular are usually reluctant to commit to new and more stringent provisions and to a stricter control by the international community as shown, for example, by the US's and Russian Federation's refusals to ratify the Second Protocol to the Hague Convention or the ICC Statute), as well as to a lingering resistance to expand wartime penal protection for 'mere' property,[43] albeit of particular significance. Nonetheless, by the end of the 20th century a trend towards a broader use of criminal law for cultural heritage protection had gained a foothold within humanitarian law, and it was soon to expand its influence into other branches of international law.

## III. Licit and Illicit Circulation of Cultural Objects in Peacetime

### 1. The 1970 UNESCO Convention and the Marginalization of Criminal Law

In the wake of the extensive decolonization process started after World War II, several countries, which had been and still were (mostly involuntary) net exporters of cultural property (so-called source states), began expressing a need for a transnational response to the illicit trade.[44] During conflicts as well as in peacetime the illicit trade had been (and remains) characterized by a flow of art and antiquities towards richer market countries, where a relative scarcity of cultural objects, and

[42] See next section.

[43] Eg in assessing the proportionate penalty for the war crime of intentionally attacking ten religious monuments the ICC (*The Prosecutor v Al Mahdi*, n 38) highlighted the judges' duty 'to weight each [war crime] by distinguishing, for example, between those against persons and those targeting property'. For a critical evaluation see Pierfrancesco Rossi, 'The "Al Mahdi" Trial before the International Criminal Court: Attacks on Cultural Heritage between War Crimes and Crimes against Humanity' [2017] DUDI 87, who suggests that the crime against humanity of persecution would have been a more appropriate indictment in this case. About the broader trend to understanding harms to cultural heritage as violations of fundamental human rights see references in n 4.

[44] Forrest, *International* (n 5) 132–35.

the availability of economic resources, fosters a constant demand as well as, frequently, a 'no questions' attitude in professional dealers and potential buyers.[45]

Eventually, after long negotiations, in 1970 the United Nations Educational Scientific and Cultural Organization (UNESCO) adopted the Convention on the Means of Prohibiting and Preventing the Illicit Export, Import and Transfer of Ownership of Cultural Property (1970 UNESCO Convention), which provides minimum shared public law rules on the circulation of cultural property. Actually, however, the diverse interests and positions of the negotiating states[46] led to a not-so-workable compromise.[47] Despite recent increases in ratifications by market states, this Convention cannot be considered to have bridged the gap between strict (but often quite ineffective in practice) protectionist legislation in source countries, and the liberal approach of most importing states, which favour minimum, or no, import barriers, 'light' regulation on circulation, short time limitations, extended protection for 'good faith' possessors and no specific criminal law provisions.[48]

In addition to a large body of provisions on social, educational, civil, economic and institutional measures, and others referring to international cooperation, the 1970 UNESCO Convention obliges state parties to consider 'illicit' any 'import, export or transfer of ownership of cultural property effected contrary to the provisions adopted under [the] Convention' (article 3). This provides the setting for an obligation (article 6(b)) of prohibiting exportation of cultural objects 'unless accompanied by the ... export certificate' provided for in article 6(a). Parties are also required (article 7(b)(i)) 'to prohibit the import of cultural property stolen from a museum or a religious or secular public monument or similar institution in another state party ..., provided that such property is documented as appertaining to the inventory of that institution' (export restrictions are thus far more stringent than limitations to importing).[49] Finally, states have to oblige antique dealers to keep a register of traded objects, complete with information on provenance, and to inform the purchaser of possible export prohibitions (article 10(a)).

Each of these provisions must be backed up by sanctions, but the Convention leaves it to each party's discretion to decide between criminal or administrative ones (articles 8 and 10(a)). On the whole, 'the fulcrum of the system controlling

[45] See eg Janet Blake, *International Cultural Heritage Law* (OUP 2015) 23–37 (hereafter Blake, *International*); Simon Mackenzie, Neil Brodie, Donna Yates and Christos Tsirogiannis, *Trafficking Culture. New Directions in Researching the Global Market in Illicit Antiquities* (Routledge 2020) 1–121.

[46] See Ronald D Abramson and Stephen B Huttler, 'The Legal Response to the Illicit Movement of Cultural Property' (1973) 5 LPIB 932.

[47] See Patrick J O'Keefe, *Commentary on the 1970 UNESCO Convention on the Means of Prohibiting and Preventing the Illicit Import, Export and Transfer of Ownership of Cultural Property* (2nd edn, Institute of Art and Law 2007) 7; Forrest, *International* (n 5) 167.

[48] See also John H Merryman, 'A Licit International Trade in Cultural Objects' (1995) 4 IJCP 13; Eric A Posner, 'The International Protection of Cultural Property: Some Skeptical Observations' (2007) 8 CJIL 213; Blake, *International* (n 45) 12–22.

[49] At least in the interpretation and implementation of the Convention which prevails in market states: see Forrest, *International* (n 5) 176–81.

the illicit circulation of cultural assets lies … in instruments of an administrative or private law nature … , even when the transfer itself involved acts of penal significance, such as theft',[50] and the 1970 UNESCO Convention has therefore been rightly considered as marginalizing criminal law as a tool to fight illicit traffic in cultural objects.

Later efforts focused, through the 'enrolment' of the United Nations International Institute for the Unification of Private Law (UNIDROIT), mostly on issues of recovery of trafficked cultural property, that the 1970 UNESCO Convention was structurally unable to address. This led, in 1995, to the adoption of the UNIDROIT Convention.[51] This treaty, albeit aimed at contributing to the fight against illicit trafficking in cultural property, can have only a very indirect effect, as its own Preamble acknowledges that its 'implementation … should be accompanied by other effective measures for protecting cultural objects', amongst which, however, penal tools are not mentioned.

## 2. First Steps Towards Systematic Criminal Justice Responses

Notwithstanding the prevailing 'blindness' of the international community to the criminal stature of the phenomenon, the 1980s and the 1990s also saw the first significant attempts at encouraging some measure of harmonization of national penal laws. In 1990 the Eighth UN Congress on the Prevention of Crime and the Treatment of Offenders adopted a Model Treaty 'for the prevention of crimes that infringe on the cultural heritage of peoples in the form of movable property'.[52]

The Model Treaty's stated purpose was 'combating criminal activities which involve movable cultural property through the introduction of measures for impeding illicit transnational trafficking in movable cultural property whether or not it has been stolen, the imposition of appropriate and effective administrative and penal sanctions and the provision of a means for restitution' (Preamble). It is therefore a template for international agreements concerning actual criminalization obligations.[53] Its most interesting features are the parallel presence of an offence of illicit export and one of illicit import (articles 2(a) and 3(a)), the intended punishment of intentional acquisition of, or dealing in, stolen or illicitly imported

[50] Manacorda, 'Criminal' (n 29) 32.

[51] cf Lyndel V Prott, 'UNESCO and UNIDROIT: A Partnership against Trafficking in Cultural Objects' (1996) 1 ULR 59.

[52] Eighth United Nations Congress on the Prevention of Crime and the Treatment of Offenders, Havana, 27 August–7 September 1990: report prepared by the Secretariat (United Nations publication, Sales No E.91.IV.2), ch I, s B.1, annex.

[53] See Manacorda, 'Criminal' (n 29) 36–37; Simon Mackenzie, *Protection Against Trafficking in Cultural Property* [2009] background paper for the meeting of the Expert group on protection against trafficking in cultural property, Vienna, 24–26 November 2009, UNODC/CCPCJ/EG.1/2009/CRP.1, 10–14; Neil Boister, *Transnational Criminal Law* (2nd edn, OUP 2018) 227–228 (hereafter Boister, *Transnational*).

cultural property (articles 2(b) and 3(b)), the specific consideration given to the criminalization of 'international conspiracies' (articles 2(c) and 3(c)) given the role played by transnational (albeit often loosely based) trafficking networks in this field[54] and the intended possibility to apply sanctions not only to physical persons, but also to juridical ones (articles 2 and 3).

Even though this document is not binding, it is considered a model for bilateral and multilateral agreements: it has achieved renewed visibility in recent years, mostly thanks to recommendations by the UN Economic and Social Council (ECOSOC)[55] and by the Expert Group on Protection against Trafficking in Cultural Property.[56] Moreover, it was not the only effort made towards a more coordinated use of penal provisions. On 23 June 1985, in Delphi, the Council of Europe (CoE) adopted and opened for signature (including by non-member states) the first international treaty specifically and consistently aimed at criminalizing acts that impinge upon cultural property, both movable and immovable, that is the European Convention on Offences Relating to Cultural Property.[57]

Significantly, a first group of offences against cultural property (theft, appropriation through violence or menace and receiving of the two previous offences' objects: article 3 and Appendix III) were subject to an obligation of criminalization. A second group of offences (mainly including other acts of illicit appropriation and dispersion) were permitted to be made by state parties into criminal offences, so that other contracting parties could not object. Finally, state parties could at any time declare that they would deem offences against cultural property any other harmful act or omission not listed within the Convention. Contracting States were also to commit themselves (article 12) to 'take the necessary measures for adequate sanctioning' (being able to choose amongst custodial and noncustodial sanctions, including fines, bans and disqualifications). A set of detailed provisions regulated jurisdiction, plurality of proceedings, application of *ne bis in idem principle*, letters rogatory and restitution of cultural property (articles 6–19).

The Convention never entered into force, having failed to reach the minimum number of three ratifications (article 21), and having collected only six signatures, none by a primary market state. The reasons for this failure are likely twofold: firstly, the conflict between source states' and market states' interests in, and

[54] Peter B Campbell, 'The Illicit Antiquities Trade as a Transnational Criminal Network: Characterizing and Anticipating Trafficking of Cultural Heritage' (2013) 20 IJCP 113; Jessica Dietzler, 'On "Organized Crime" in the Illicit Antiquities Trade: Moving beyond the Definitional Debate' (2013) 16 TOC 329.

[55] ECOSOC Res 2003/29; ECOSOC Res 2004/34; ECOSOC Res 2008/23; ECOSOC Res 2010/19; ECOSOC Res 2011/42, adopted by the General Assembly as Res 66/180, United Nations A/RES/66/180.

[56] Report on the Meeting of the Expert Group on Protection against Trafficking in Cultural Property, Vienna, 24–26 November 2009, UNODC/CCPCJ/EG.1/2009/2; Report on the Meeting of the Expert Group on Protection against Trafficking in Cultural Property, Vienna, 27–29 June 2012, UNODC/CCPCJ/EG.1/2012/4.

[57] ETS No 119. cf James AR Nafziger, 'International Penal Aspects of Protecting Cultural Property' (1985) 19 IL 840;

legal approaches to, cultural property circulation was still too sharp in the 1980s and 1990s, and it was not yet counterbalanced by a shared awareness of, and concern for, the interlinked criminal dimension of illicit traffic; secondly, criminal law is the branch of any legal system more strictly related to state sovereignty, and the Delphi Convention asked too much in terms of concessions to an external 'interference'. Still, something was slowly going to change in this respect, too.

## IV. New Trends for a New Millennium

### 1. UNODC Takes a Hand: Revivals and New Tools

At the beginning of the new millennium the increasing concern for transnational organized crime which had prompted the adoption, in 2000, of a specific United Nations Convention against Transnational Organized Crime (UNTOC) influenced also the approach to cultural property trafficking, increasingly regarded as an attractive playground for criminal organizations, mostly due to the easy portability and high monetary value of cultural objects, the availability of consolidated smuggling channels, the limited penal risks and a wide inconsistency among national regulations.[58] ECOSOC thus began recommending[59] a direct involvement of the United Nation Office on Drugs and Crime (UNODC) in the development of joint strategies to combat trafficking in cultural property.

A first line of intervention focused on the employment of UNTOC in this field,[60] given the large number of ratifications of the treaty. The idea of a specific additional Protocol was discarded, due to the difficulty in re-mobilizing the international community over an issue still perceived as marginal by many states.[61] The path actually taken was to encourage and support contracting parties to the UNTOC to employ the UNTOC to tackle criminal offences against cultural property.[62] This was to be done particularly by inviting them to make such offences into 'serious crimes' in the meaning of the Convention (article 2(b)): thus for the states parties to make them punishable 'by a maximum deprivation of liberty of at least four years or a more serious penalty', in order to bring them, 'where the offence is transnational in nature and involves an organized criminal group' (article 3(1)), within

[58] cf references at n 54 and Report of the Eleventh United Nations Congress on Crime Prevention and Criminal Justice, Bangkok, 18–25 April 2005, A/CONF.203/18, 3–4, 34.

[59] ECOSOC Res 2004/34.

[60] ECOSOC Res 2004/34; Report of the Conference of the Parties to the United Nations Convention against Transnational Organized Crime on its fifth session, Vienna, 18–22 October 2010, CTOC/COP/2010/17, and Res 5/7 of 2010; UNODC/CCPCJ/EG.1/2009/2; UNODC/CCPCJ/EG.1/2012/4.

[61] Manacorda, 'Criminal' (n 29) 43.

[62] ibid 42–45; Greg Borgstede, 'Cultural Property, the Palermo Convention, and Transnational Organized Crime' (2014) 21 IJCP 281; Blake, *International* (n 45) 48–50. See also Conference of the Parties to the UNTOC, tenth session, Vienna, 12–16 October 2020, Res. 10/7.

the UNTOC's scope of application. This, in turn, would make available for use UNTOC provisions concerning, amongst others, criminalization and other measures against laundering of proceeds of crime, seizure and confiscation, extradition, special investigative techniques and measures to enhance the transfer of evidence and cooperation with law enforcement authorities.

A recommendation to this effect is also present (Guideline 13), together with one concerning the use of the Model Treaty (Guideline 14), in the second tool developed under the auspices of UNODC: the International Guidelines for Crime Prevention and Criminal Justice Responses with Respect to Trafficking in Cultural Property and Other Related Offences, adopted by the UN General Assembly on 18 December 2014 with Resolution 69/196. Albeit not binding in nature (allowing them to be more easily adopted), the Guidelines have the potential to be a useful instrument for improvement of national criminal laws and their harmonization (Guidelines 15–27), and the development of further bilateral or multilateral agreements, particularly with regard to police and judicial cooperation (Guidelines 30 and 32–47). A further advantage of this soft law instrument resides in its not being limited to penal measures, as it also includes a broad set (Guidelines 1–12) of pre-penal (educational, social, administrative) preventive measures intended to both reduce crime rates and facilitate investigations when an offence is committed.

## 2. Renewed Efforts by the Council of Europe and the 2017 Nicosia Convention

By the mid-2010s, mostly because of the extensive unrest and conflicts in the Middle East and the consequent large-scale destruction and scattering of cultural properties, a new concern entered the political debate:[63] the idea that trafficking in looted antiquities can be used to finance terrorist groups and armed militias.[64] Together with the worry about involvement of organized criminal groups and, to a lesser extent, a rising awareness of the links between offences against cultural property and a broader set of economic and white-collar crimes,[65] this prompted the CoE towards making renewed efforts to promote a specific criminal law convention.

[63] See UN SC Res S/RES/1267 (1999) (Afghan conflict); UN SC Res S/RES/2195 (2014) (on terrorism in Africa); UN SC Res S/RES/2199 (2015); UN SC Res S/RES/2322 (2016); UN SC Res S/RES/2347 (2017); Council of Europe Convention on Offences relating to Cultural Property, Nicosia, 19 May 2017, CETS No 221, Preamble.

[64] See Hans-Jakob Schindler and Frederique Gautier, 'Looting and Smuggling of Artifacts as a Strategy to Finance Terrorism: Global Sanctions as a Disruptive and Preventive Tool' (2019) 26 IJCP 331 (hereafter Schindler and Gautier, 'Looting').

[65] See eg World Custom Organization, Cultural Heritage Programme <http://www.wcoomd.org/zh-cn/topics/enforcement-and-compliance/activities-and-programmes/cultural-heritage-programme.aspx>. See also Mackenzie, 'Illicit Deals' (n 2) 133–53; Marc Balcells, 'Art Crime as White-Collar Crime' in Joris D Kila and Marc Balcells (eds), *Cultural Property Crime* (Brill 2015) 96.

The new Convention on Offences relating to Cultural Property was eventually adopted in 2017[66] and it has presently reached twelve signatures, of which three followed by ratifications (of the five, including at least three by CoE member states, required for its entry into force: article 27). Its prospectsthus appear rosier, mostly due to the aforementioned change of political attitudes, coupled with some significant differences in the Convention's outline. The number of criminal offences has been drastically reduced in comparison to the Delphi Convention and mostly focused on movable objects[67] and behaviour instrumental to trafficking (including falsification of documents: article 9), with the 'thorniest' issues left free for parties to be made into administrative instead of criminal offences (unlawful excavation and removal, article 4, and illegal importation, article 5). The Convention also provides for corporate liability (article 13)—probably its most innovative provision—[68] and a broad set of sanctions and security measures besides custodial and monetary ones, such as bans, disqualifications, judicial supervision etc (article 14). Besides measures on police and judicial international cooperation (articles 16 and 19), the Convention, also building on the UN Guidelines, provides for a broad set of non-penal preventive measures (articles 20–21), aimed at integrating and supporting criminal ones.[69]

## 3. The New Attitude of EU Lawmakers

Due to the founding Treaties' constraints, the European Union has limited competence in the matter of harmonization of cultural heritage law, basically confined to issues of circulation strictly linked to the functioning of the common market.[70] Thus, between the 1990s and the first half of 2010s, the only two issues addressed by EU secondary law have been export of cultural 'goods' outside the Union's borders,[71] and the return of illegally exported items amongst member states.[72] Yet, in

[66] See Mateusz M Bieczyński, 'The Nicosia Convention 2017: A New International Instrument Regarding Criminal Offences against Cultural Property' (2017) 3 SAACLR 255; Boister, *Transnational* (n 53) 225–27; Derek Fincham, 'The Blood Antiquities Convention as a Paradigm for Cultural Property Crime Reduction' (2019) 37 CAELJ 299.

[67] With the exception of the criminal offence of destruction and damage, art 10, which also covers immovable property.

[68] Boister, *Transnational* (n 53) 226.

[69] See Elisabetta Mottese, 'Preventive Measures in the Council of Europe Convention on Offences relating to Cultural Property: An Overview' (2018) 4 SAACLR 126.

[70] See Irini A Stamatoudi, *Cultural Property Law and Restitution: A Commentary to International Conventions and European Union Law* (Edward Elgar 2011) 112–32.

[71] Council Regulation (EEC) No 3911/92 of 9 December 1992 on the export of cultural goods, OJ L 395, repealed by Council Regulation (EC) No 116/2009 of 18 December 2008 on the export of cultural goods, OJ L 39.

[72] Council Directive 93/7/EEC of 15 March 1993 on the return of cultural objects unlawfully removed from the territory of a Member State, OJ L 74, repealed by Directive 2014/60/EU of the European Parliament and of the Council of 15 May 2014 on the return of cultural objects unlawfully removed from the territory of a Member State and amending Regulation (EU) No 1024/2012 (Recast), OJ L 159.

recent years, the European Union has started to share international concerns about links between trafficking in cultural property and other serious crimes, particularly organized crime, money laundering and terrorism.[73]

The first step in tackling these issues has been taken through the Fifth Money Laundering Directive of 2018,[74] which expanded its scope of application in the art and antiquities market beyond 'high value dealers' to any 'persons trading or acting as intermediaries in the trade of works of art, including when this is carried out by art galleries and auction houses, where the value of the transaction or a series of linked transactions amounts to 10.000 € or more', independently of the payment method (article 1(1)(c)(i)).

Far more 'revolutionary' has been the adoption, in 2019, of a new Regulation on the import of cultural property from non-member states.[75] The new rules, which are gradually entering into force (article 16), prohibit the importation of items 'removed from the territory of the country where they were created or discovered in breach of the laws and regulations of that country' (article 3.1) and introduce a system of import licensing for 'cultural goods' deemed at higher risk of trafficking (archaeological findings and parts of dismembered monuments, articles 3(2) and 4, Annex Part B), as well as of mandatory importer's statements for further types of cultural objects (articles 3(2) and 5, Annex Part C). Even if these provisions cannot be mandatorily backed by criminalization obligations, due to the principle of legality, the Regulation requires them to be supported by 'effective, proportionate and dissuasive' penalties (article 11), and it is likely that several member states (especially those who will also choose to ratify the Nicosia Convention) will opt for introducing new criminal offences.

[73] See European Commission, *Illicit Trade in Cultural Goods in Europe. Final Report* (2018) 108–15 <https://publications.europa.eu/en/publication-detail/-/publication/d79a105a-a6aa-11e9-9d01-01aa75ed71a1>; Sabrina Urbinati, 'The European Union Legal Framework and the Fight against the Illicit Trafficking of Cultural Property Coming from Situations of Armed Conflict' (2018) 4 SAACLR 51; Maja RJ Dehouck, 'Balancing Markets, Morals and Law: The Fight to Regulate Illicit Trafficking in Cultural Goods and the EU Regulation on the Import of Cultural Goods' (2019) 24 AAL 1 (hereafter Dehouck, *Balancing*).

[74] Directive (EU) 2018/843 of the European Parliament and of the Council of 30 May 2018 amending Directive (EU) 2015/849 on the prevention of the use of the financial system for the purposes of money laundering or terrorist financing, OJ L 156. See Cates Saleeby, 'Recent EU Developments in Art Law and Cultural Heritage' (Center for Art and Law 20 August 2019) <https://itsartlaw.org/2019/08/20/recent-eu-developments-in-art-law-and-cultural-heritage/>.

[75] Regulation (EU) 2019/880 of the European Parliament and of the Council of 17 April 2019 on the introduction and the import of cultural goods, OJ L 151.

## V. Some Final Observations

It is worth asking if the trends discussed above are justified by sufficient criminological data, and whether there are some caveats international lawmakers should heed.

Presently, we have more evidence of links between offences against cultural property and white-collar and corporate crime[76] than we have about intersections with organized crime[77]—at least when conceived in traditional, 'Mafia-like' terms—and we have even less hard evidence of links with terrorism.[78] In regard to the intersection with organized crime, however, we do have sufficient proof of the organized nature of the illicit market in art and antiquities and of its relying on some kind of international criminal networking:[79] enough to satisfy the loose definition of 'organized criminal group' in the UNTOC[80] and to justify advocacy for its application.[81] When it comes to the financing of terrorism and civil wars, we can only rely on correlations (increased archaeological looting in territories controlled by terrorist groups)[82] and some historical and well-documented examples (like the final stages of the Khmer Rouge guerrilla rule in Cambodia).[83] This is not to say that present concerns, albeit possibly exaggerated,[84] are totally unfounded. On

[76] See n 65. On specific (albeit indirectly proven) links with corruption cf Raymond Fisman and Shang-Jin Wei, 'The Smuggling of Art, and the Art of Smuggling: Uncovering the Illicit Trade in Cultural Property and Antiques' (2009) 1 AEJAE 82.

[77] Duncan Chappell and Kenneth Polk, 'Unravelling the "Cordata": Just How Organized Is the International Traffic in Cultural Objects?' in Manacorda and Chappell, *Crime in the Art and Antiquities World* (n 29) 103–06 (hereafter Chappell and Polk, 'Unravelling'); Petrus C van Duyne, Lena Louwe and Melvin Soudijn, 'Money, Art, and Laundering: Coming to Grips with the Risks' in Joris D Kila and Marc Balcells (eds), *Cultural Property Crime* (Brill 2015) 79.

[78] UN Security Council, Twenty-third report of the Analytical Support and Sanctions Monitoring Team submitted pursuant to resolution 2368 (2017) concerning ISIL (Da'esh), Al-Qaida and associated individuals and entities, 15 January 2019, S/2019/50,19; see also Dehouck, *Balancing* (n 73) 17–21.

[79] See n 54.

[80] Art 2(a) defines an organized criminal group as 'a structured group of three or more persons, existing for a period of time and acting in concert with the aim of committing one or more serious crimes or offences established in accordance with [the] Convention, in order to obtain, directly or indirectly, a financial or other material benefit'.

[81] Chappell and Polk, 'Unravelling' (n 77) 103. See also references in n 62.

[82] Schindler and Gautier, 'Looting' (n 64) 332. The recent increase of Middle-Eastern antiquities on the international—and particularly on the digital—market, with a shift of the model of trade from 'low-volume but high-cost objects to a trade which is higher in volume but lower in quality', is also considered consistent with the idea that trafficking is (also) financing local armed groups: cf Kenneth Polk and Duncan Chappell, 'Policing and Prosecution of Heritage Crime: Revisiting the 'Cordata'—Just How Organised Is the International Traffic in Cultural Heritage?' in Valsamis Mitsilegas, Saskia Hufnagel and Anton Moiseienko (eds), *Research Handbook on Transnational Crime* (Edward Elgar 2019) 409.

[83] Simon Mackenzie and Tess Davis, 'Cambodian Statue Trafficking Networks: An Empirical Report from Regional Case Study Fieldwork' in Stefano Manacorda and Arianna Visconti (eds), *Protecting Cultural Heritage as a Common Good of Humanity* (ISPAC 2014) 158.

[84] For a critical analysis (which, however, supports the conclusion of an increase in illegal traffic of cultural objects from conflict areas) see Matthew Sargent and others, 'Tracking and Disrupting the Illicit Antiquities Trade with Open-Source Data' (RAND Corporation 2020) <https://www.rand.org/pubs/research_reports/RR2706.html>.

the contrary, the very 'grey' nature of the art and antiquities market[85] with its lack of transparency, traditional and heavy 'pollution' by objects of illicit or questionable provenance, mingling of legal and illegal actors and regulatory inconsistency amongst states, makes it the perfect 'crossroad' for very different criminal typologies, from smuggling to insurance fraud, from tax evasion to money laundering, from bribery to financial fraud,[86] and thus also attractive to organized and terrorist groups.

However, a certain caution is required when choosing criminal policy strategies, so as not to overestimate the preventive potential of penal measures while setting aside more effective tools. Certainly, the field requires stronger efforts towards harmonization of national regulations: the present situation highly favours opportunistic behaviours such as 'forum shopping' and property (as well as money) laundering. A minimum convergence in penal approaches is therefore also necessary. But criminal law can effectively prevent and sanction only harmful behaviours which are comparatively rare: when cultural property trafficking is as prevalent as it currently appears to be, an excessive focus on punishment will result in more of a cheap show of symbolic expression (often at the expense of individual liberties and fundamental rights) than in practical results.

To make criminal law provisions work, an adequate investment must be made in educational, economic, organizational, civil and administrative measures. These range from widespread inventorying of cultural property to 'neighbourhood watching' over monuments and archaeological sites, from licensing of dealers to the implementations of codes of conduct and administrative regulation (and sanctions) and so on. This, in turn, requires a willingness to find adequate resources and to follow a (legal, as well as economic) solidarity principle between states, including those at the two ends of the market. This change of attitude, we are afraid, is still a work very much in progress. Thus, we must guard against the risk that transnational criminal law is used as a rug under which to conveniently sweep actual harms to the cultural heritage of humankind.

[85] Simon Mackenzie and Donna Yates, 'What is Grey about the "Grey Market" in Antiquities?' in Jens Beckert and Matías Dewey (eds), *The Architecture of Illegal Markets* (OUP 2017) 70.

[86] Georgina Adams, *Dark Side of the Boom* (Lund Humphries 2017) 146–48, 188–90.

# 17

# The Emerging History of Transnational Criminal Law Relating to Cybercrime

*Dominik Brodowski*

## I. Introduction

Compared to other areas of criminal law addressed in this volume, cybercrime is rather new and still evolving. But as modern information and communication technology is inherently transnational, it evidently requires a transnational response. That response has evolved quickly in the past four decades, and progressed from a rather regional to a global level. Besides defining a common minimum definition of cybercrimes, it focuses ever more on procedural and evidentiary issues. Contrasting these developments with other areas of transnational criminal justice, the transnational response to cybercrime has, while progressing speedily, largely followed traditional patterns. Nonetheless, in some aspects the response to cybercrime also disrupts—or, at least, transforms—transnational criminal justice, in particular by focusing more on state powers than on territoriality.

## II. The Evolution of Transnational Cybercrime

### 1. What is 'Cybercrime'?

In the search for an appropriate label for criminal activities in the context of information technology, the term 'cybercrime' has emerged as the common denominator, though it is both broad and ambiguous,[1] and better describes the regulatory challenge than a concrete legal concept.[2] In particular, the term merges the two

[1] On the history and the definition of the term 'cybercrime', just see Dominik Brodowski, 'Cybercrime, Human Rights and Digital Politics' in Ben Wagner, Kilian Vieth and Matthias C Kettemann (eds), *Research Handbook on Human Rights and Digital Technology. Global Politics, Law and International Relations* (Edward Elgar 2019) 98; Christopher Ram, 'Cybercrime' in Neil Boister and Robert J Currie (eds), *Routledge Handbook of Transnational Criminal Law* (Routledge 2015) 380 et seq (hereafter Ram, 'Cybercrime'), with further references.

[2] Dominik Brodowski, 'Transnational Organised Crime and Cybercrime' in Pierre Hauck and Sven Peterke (eds), *International Law and Transnational Organised Crime* (OUP 2016) 335 (hereafter Brodowski, 'TOC and Cybercrime').

Dominik Brodowski, *The Emerging History of Transnational Criminal Law Relating to Cybercrime* In: *Histories of Transnational Criminal Law*. Edited by: Neil Boister, Sabine Gless and Florian Jeßberger, Oxford University Press. © Dominik Brodowski 2021. DOI: 10.1093/oso/9780192845702.003.0018

historic viewpoints on and approaches to address cybercrime:[3] on the one hand, there are criminal activities which affect the information technology as such, including the data stored therein. This includes crimes against the confidentiality, integrity and/or availability of information technology, but also computer fraud where a computer instead of a human is deceived to transfer money. Such 'cybercrimes' relate to the viewpoint that computer crimes are a genuinely new criminal law problem requiring new statutes,[4] a perspective continuing today in discussions on how to deal with phenomena such as the 'blockchain', the 'darknet' or 'artificial intelligence'. On the other hand, information technology may serve as a tool to commit a crime, without affecting the technology or interfering with it as such. On such a basis, rooted in an understanding that computer crimes are conventional crimes committed by new means,[5] criminal activities such as the dissemination of illegal content, in particular child pornography but also hate speech and classic fraud and extortion, can be labelled as cybercrime, not necessarily requiring the adoption of new statutes. More recently, a third form of cybercrime—or, in particular, of criminal statutes—can be discerned. These are justified by specific features of information technology or its specific risks, though information technology is not affected 'as such'.[6] Prime examples are the criminalization of so-called 'cybergrooming', that is contacting children online with the intent of future sexual abuse, but also the criminalization of 'Darknet' marketplaces.[7]

Last but not least, the term 'cybercrime' is ambiguous as there is no clear consensus on which behaviour actually can or should be criminalized. Such lack of consensus is most obvious in the tension between the human rights protections on free speech and the online dissemination of various forms of hate speech and, more recently, fake news.[8] However, in this contribution I will not get into the details of the borders of criminalization, but instead focus on what the different legislatures, regional and international institutions have actually considered to constitute cybercrime.

[3] See Nir Kshetri, *The Global Cybercrime Industry* (Springer 2010) 3; Ram, 'Cybercrime' (n 1); Joachim Vogel, 'Towards a Global Convention Against Cybercrime' (2008) C-06 eRIDP <http://www.penal.org/en/reaidp-2008-e-riapl- 2008>; UNODC, *Comprehensive Study on Cybercrime* (United Nations 2013) 11 et seq (hereafter UNODC, *Cybercrime*).

[4] Just see Donn B Parker, 'Computer Abuse Research Update' (1980) 2 Computer LJ 329, 334; and, more recently, Susan W Brenner, 'Cybercrime Metrics: Old Wine in New Bottles?' (2004) 9 V J L & Tech 1, 4 et seq; see further the discussion by Ram, 'Cybercrime' (n 1) 381.

[5] See Michael Edmund O'Neill, 'Old Crimes in New Bottles: Sanctioning Cybercrime' (2000) 9 Geo Mason L Rev 237, 238; see further the discussion by Ram, 'Cybercrime' (n 1) 381.

[6] Such as anonymity, automatization or reduced psychological barriers. Notably, these features have already been highlighted in the debate whether cybercrime is new wine in old bottles, see n 4 and n 5 above.

[7] On this development, see Dominik Brodowski, 'The Role of Criminal Law in Regulating Cybercrime and IT Security' in Georg Borges and Christoph Sorge (eds), *Law and Technology in a Global Digital Society* (Springer+VS 2021, in press).

[8] On the terminological implications, just see Ram, 'Cybercrime' (n 1) 382 et seq.

## 2. From Computer Crimes via Transnational Cybercrime to Crime as a Transnational Service

### a. Cybercrime as a Parallel Problem

Information technology began at a local level, in a few sparsely interconnected data centres. Criminal activities therefore could only occur within this context. By and large, only highly skilled individuals with access to the scarce technology had the chance to commit such crimes, and most such acts were committed for economic purposes.[9] Although the first forms of cybercrime had no genuine transnational component, various jurisdictions faced the same problem in parallel: how to address these new forms of crime, both in relation to substantive criminal law and to criminal procedure. In particular, this meant the necessity to enact provisions to protect the confidentiality, integrity and availability of computer systems, to address the shift from human decision-making to automatization and the shift from tangible objects to intangible goods.[10]

### b. Cybercrime as a Common Problem

Later the interconnection of information technology gained track, culminating with the Internet.[11] This interconnection poses additional risks for information technology, such as distributed denial of service (DDoS) attacks as the most pronounced form of network-based attacks. Even more importantly, the interconnection facilitates the use of information technology in the commission of information-related crimes such as the dissemination of child pornography or online hate speech.[12] With the interconnection of information technology not stopping at the borders of national criminal justice systems, cybercrime gained a strong transnational element: the location of the offender, of the victim and of the IT utilized in the commission of the offence easily spans different jurisdictions. Owing to this development, cybercrime was soon described as a common problem, requiring judicial cooperation and coordination of criminal justice systems. In particular, with content on the Internet being readily available world-wide, the question arose as to which jurisdiction was to define whether content posted online is criminal

[9] Ulrich Sieber, 'Mastering Complexity in the Global Cyberspace' in Mireille Delmas-Marty, Mark Pieth and Ulrich Sieber (eds), *Les chemins de l'harmonisation pénale* (Legis Comparee 2018) 129 (hereinafter Sieber, 'Mastering Complexity'); on early uses for political protesting, see Ram, 'Cybercrime' (n 1) 384 in n 24.

[10] See Stein Schjolberg, *The History of Cybercrime 1976–2014* (BoD 2014) 16 et seq (hereinafter Schjolberg, *History*); Ram, 'Cybercrime' (n 1) 384 et seq with further references.

[11] Just see James Curran, 'Reinterpreting Internet History' in Yvonne Jewkes and Majid Yar (eds), *Handbook of Internet Crime* (Willan 2010) 17 et seq (hereafter Curran, 'Reinterpreting').

[12] See Sieber, 'Mastering Complexity' (n 9) 129 et seq; David S Wall, *Cybercrime: The Transformation of Crime in the Information Age* (Polity Press 2007) 45; Murugesan Srinivasan, Solomon Raja Pandian and Arockiasamy Enoch, 'International Crimes: Cyber Crime, Crimes against Cultural Heritage, Environmental Crimes, and Money Laundering' in Sesha Kethineni (ed), *Comparative and International Policing, Justice, and Transnational Crime* (Carolina Academic Press 2010) 390 et seq.

hate speech or legitimate freedom of speech. The *Toeben* case (2000) highlighted the issue early on, but the court only solved the case at hand, taking a highly pragmatic approach.[13]

### c. Cybercrime as a Genuinely Transnational Problem

Based on the ubiquity of information technology and increasing technical protection against cybercrime, the last two decades have seen a shift as cybercrime has become largely economically driven in a model described by Wall as a 'flat e-commerce business model',[14] where highly skilled individuals become 'crime service providers'. Specializing in specific aspects of committing an 'attack', these highly professionalized criminals collaborate on a loose and case-by-case basis with others for their individual economic gain.[15] Such collaboration can sometimes take forms similar to that of IT 'start-ups', yet mostly differs from classic forms of organized crime—though some reports state that the links between cybercrime and 'classic' transnational organized criminal groups are increasing.[16] Besides the high level of sophistication, the opportunities for a transnational division of labour—and a transnational reach of the cybercrimes committed—increasingly conflict with the traditional limitation of investigatory powers to the territory of each sovereign nation state.

### d. Cybercrime as an Activity for the Masses

In parallel to this evolution of highly professionalized crime, the ubiquity of information technology has also led to cybercrime becoming an activity for the masses. A first manifestation of that trend may be seen in illegal and, at least in some jurisdictions, criminalized file-sharing activities. More recently, the ever-growing cancer of (criminal) hate speech and the online buying of illegal substances illustrate the growth in the labelling of mundane criminal activity, at least under a broad definition, as cybercrime. Concurrently, electronic evidence has become an important factor in ever more criminal investigations and prosecutions, even those not related to cybercrime:[17] evidence such as the location of mobile phones,

[13] Bundesgerichtshof (German Federal Court of Justice), Judgment of 12 December 2000—1 StR 184/00; on this judgment, just see Markus D Dubber and Tatjana Hörnle, *Criminal Law. A Comparative Approach* (OUP 2014) 631 et seq.

[14] David S Wall, 'The Organization of Cybercrime and Organized Cybercrime' in Marcello Bellini, Phillip Brunst and Jochen Jähnke (eds), *Current Issues in IT Security* (Duncker & Humblot 2010) 54.

[15] Just see Susan W Brenner, 'Organized Cybercrime? How Cyberspace May Affect the Structure of Criminal Relationships' (2002) 4 North Carolina J L & Tech 1 (hereafter Brenner, 'Organized Cybercrime?'); Brian Krebs, *Spam Nation* (Sourcebooks 2014) 113 et seq; Jan Spoenle, 'Underground Economy' in Marcello Bellini, Phillip Brunst and Jochen Jähnke (eds), *Current Issues in IT Security* (Duncker & Humblot 2010) 67; Erika Kraemer-Mbula, Puay Tang and Howard Rush, 'The Cybercrime Ecosystem: Online Innovation in the Shadows?' (2013) 80 Technological Forecasting & Social Change 550.

[16] Brenner, 'Organized Cybercrime?' (n 15) 1; Brodowski, 'TOC and Cybercrime' (n 2) 338 et seq; Jonathan Lusthaus, 'How Organised is Organised Cybercrime?' (2013) 14 Global Crime 53 et seq.

[17] On electronic evidence and its use in criminal prosecutions and trials, see Matthias Jahn and Dominik Brodowski, 'Digitale Beweismittel im deutschen Strafprozess—Ermittlungsverfahren,

encrypted electronic messages used by perpetrators for their coordination or the browser search history showing the suspect having searched for a suitable poison to use in the commission of a murder. Increasingly such data is stored not locally but in the so-called 'Cloud'—that is, on data storage which may be located in various places and jurisdictions—often under the control of foreign corporations. Linked to the topic of electronic evidence, this adds a genuine transnational element to many crimes, even if the conduct and the effects are confined to a local or national level.

## III. Milestones of Transnational Cybercrime Regulation

By and large, the transnational criminal justice response has matched this evolution of cybercrime.

### 1. International 'Soft Law'

In the 1980s, a wave of national legislation addressed substantive cybercrime law, in particular computer misuse and computer fraud. In 1986, instigated mostly by the similarity of the problems caused by the use of information technology,[18] a body of the OECD recommended that computer-related activities should be covered in national laws, suggesting that these 'acts may be expressed as far as possible in terms of functions rather than technology'. Already these recommendations, however, were drafted with 'respect to the transnational aspects to computer-related activity', pointing to the beginning of the interconnection of information technology.[19] In a similar vein, the Council of Europe (CoE) Recommendation of 1989[20] referred to the frequently 'transfrontier character' of computer-related crime. These recommendations referenced a report drafted by the European Committee of Crime Problems and specifically a guideline to national legislation on substantive criminal law, but not the procedural issues also analysed in the report—a significant *lacuna* that was addressed subsequently in 1995 by another

Hauptverhandlung und Revision' in Elisa Hoven and Hans Kudlich (eds), *Digitalisierung und Strafverfahren* (Nomos 2020) 67 et seq, with further references.

[18] See Schjolberg, *History* (n 10) 18 et seq.

[19] OECD, *Computer-Related Crime: Analysis of Legal Policy, ICCP Series No. 10* (OECD 1986) 69 et seq. On its genesis, see Schjolberg, *History* (n 10) 35 et seq.

[20] Recommendation No R (89) 9 of the Committee of Ministers to Member States on computer-related crime (1989) <https://rm.coe.int/CoERMPublicCommonSearchServices/DisplayDCTMContent?documentId=09000016804f1094>.

CoE Recommendation.[21] In a similar vein, a number of UN General Assembly resolutions, especially those of 2001 and 2002,[22] and in particular a multitude of model laws[23] drafted around that time, provided for minimum standards of criminalization and—partly—investigation mechanisms. The focus of these steps on the international level therefore correlates nicely with the first and to some extent also with the second generation of cybercrime described above.

## 2. Regional Conventions on Cybercrime

### a. 2001 European Cybercrime Convention

With the growing interconnection of the 'cyberspace', the need for a common definition of what (at a minimum) constitutes criminal offences relating to cybercrime, and in particular a need for enhanced transnational cooperation in the investigation and prosecution of such offences, became evident. It is not clear, however, why a convention was not pursued on a global level, and why instead the CoE was chosen—also by the G-8[24]—as the forum.[25] Potential factors might have been that computer and in particular Internet use was then considered to be a primarily 'first world' problem, but also the availability of resources at the CoE, and a supposed higher like-mindedness of the major players—European states and the US, with Japan and South Africa as active 'observers'[26]—involved in the preparation of the convention.

The task of drafting the 'binding legal instrument' was given in 1997 to a Committee of Experts on Crime in Cyber-Space (PC-CY), consisting of expert members appointed by a number of states (in particular 'prosecutors or judges dealing with computer crime cases'), and two scientific experts appointed by the CoE. The 'terms of reference' already set out an ambitious and broad agenda,

[21] Recommendation No R (95) 13 of the Committee of Ministers to member states concerning problems of criminal procedural law connected with information technology (1995) <https://go.coe.int/Tizfc>.

[22] UN GA Res A/RES/55/63 of 22 January 2001; UN GA Res A/RES/56/121; UN GA Res A/RES/56/261 of 15 April 2002. See additionally Marco Gercke, *Understanding Cybercrime. Phenomena, Challenges and Legal Responses* (ITU 2012) 115 et seq; Schjolberg, *History* (n 10) 56 et seq.

[23] In particular, see various initiatives by the ITU on which see Brodowski, 'TOC and Cybercrime' (n 2) 351, the Association International de Droit Pénal on which see Sieber, 'Mastering Complexity' (n 9) 139 and in Curran, 'Reinterpreting' (n 11) as well as the XIXth World Congress of Penal Law 2013, and by the 'Stanford Draft International Convention to Enhance Protection from Cyber Crime and Terrorism of 2000', on which see Abraham D Sofaer and Seymour E Goodman (eds), *The Transnational Dimension of Cyber Crime and Terrorism* (Hoover Institution Press 2001).

[24] Katherine S Williams, 'Transnational Developments in Internet Law' in Yvonne Jewkes and Majid Yar, *Handbook of Internet Crime* (Willan 2010) 479 (hereafter Williams, 'Transnational Developments').

[25] Alexander Seger, 'The Budapest Convention 10 Years on: Lessons Learnt' in Stefano Manacorda (ed), *Cybercriminality: Finding a Balance Between Freedom and Security* (ISPAC 2012) 170 (hereafter Seger, 'Budapest Convention') merely points to a 'window of opportunity' utilized by the CoE.

[26] See Ryan MF Baron, 'A Critique of the International Cybercrime Treaty' (2001–02) 10 Comm Law Conspectus 265 et seq (hereafter Baron, 'A Critique').

covering what was described above as the first and second generation of cybercrime, as well as 'the use, including the possibility of transborder use, and the applicability of coercive powers in a technological environment', 'the question of jurisdiction' and 'questions of international co-operation in the investigation of cyber-space offences'.[27] The task therefore was to cover all three of the aforementioned generations of cybercrime. After mostly closed-door negotiations up to April 2000 and subsequent involvement of stakeholders, the 2001 European Cybercrime Convention was agreed upon in June 2001 and then tabled for signature in Budapest in November 2001.[28]

Mostly in line with its initial agenda, this 2001 European Cybercrime Convention contains minimum standards on criminalization of cybercrime, on procedural provisions relating to computer data, including traffic data, and on jurisdiction on cybercrime. The Convention also addresses aspects of international cooperation, in particular mutual legal assistance. Novel approaches were taken with regard to the expedited preservation of stored computer data and of preserved traffic data; a 24/7 network of contact points—previously created under the umbrella of the G-8—was established as a treaty obligation and expanded in territorial scope. Notably, article 32 allows for transborder access to stored computer data, without the authorization of the other state, but requiring instead 'the lawful and voluntary consent of the person who has the lawful authority to disclose the data'. However, one area where no clear consensus could be reached—the criminalization of acts of a racist and xenophobic nature committed through computer systems—is covered only by an Additional Protocol, which has gained far fewer ratifications and accessions.[29]

Since its entry into force in 2004, almost all member states of the CoE have ratified or acceded to the Convention—except Ireland, Sweden and in particular Russia which has been a 'persistent objector'. In addition, a steadily increasing number of non-member states have ratified or acceded to the Convention, numbering twenty-one as of 2020, including the United States, Canada and Australia, bringing the total number of ratifications to sixty-five. By its proponents, it is seen as *the* de facto international agreement on cybercrime, though regional and 'Western' in its genesis, with accession being 'by invitation only'.[30]

[27] European Committee on Crime Problems, Decision CDPC/103/211196, adopted by the CoE Committee of Ministers, 583rd Meeting of 4 February 1997 as Item 10.3.

[28] See Baron, 'A Critique' (n 26).

[29] On the content of the Convention and the Additional Protocol, see Brodowski, 'TOC and Cybercrime' (n 2) 341 et seq; Jonathan Clough, 'A World of Difference: The Budapest Convention on Cybercrime and the Challenges of Harmonisation' (2014) 40 Monash University Law Review 699 et seq (hereafter Clough, 'Budapest Convention'); Williams, 'Transnational Developments' (n 24) 479 et seq.

[30] Just see Clough, 'Budapest Convention' (n 29) 700, 723 et seq, 734 et seq.

### b. Further Regional Initiatives

A similar—competing but far more regional—initiative was launched at the same time by the Commonwealth of Independent States (2001). Later on, the Shanghai Cooperation Organisation (2009), the League of Arab States (2010), ECOWAS (2011) and the African Union (2015)[31] followed suit, partly based on the non-representation in the negotiation and the regional/'Western' character of the 2001 European Cybercrime Convention.[32] In the European Union, a number of Framework Decisions and nowadays Directives contain provisions regarding the criminalization of cybercrime very similar to the CoE Convention, although more enforceable.[33] Furthermore, 'computer-related' crime is one of the 'Eurocrimes' where the dual-criminality test has been abolished within the EU system of mutual recognition.

### c. US CLOUD Act, E-evidence and the Transnational Interaction with Internet Service Providers

In the last few years, the focus has shifted to the topic of 'electronic evidence' and on accessing such data, in particular when the location where such data is stored is unknown to the investigating authority—the so-called 'loss of location' of data stored 'in the cloud'. An increasing number of states opine that the location of the data does not matter. Instead, the location of the service provided to the user, or the seat of the service provider, is considered decisive. The underlying rationale is pragmatic: owing to the ubiquity of electronic evidence, even in cases not traditionally labelled as cybercrime but potentially purely 'local' crimes, practitioners point to their need to access such data irrespective of where it is currently located—and that many (but not all) users do not care sufficiently as to where their data is stored.

In this vein, the United States (in its CLOUD Act), Belgium and other states have unilaterally enacted legislation which authorizes their domestic authorities to require the production of data stored by service providers, regardless of where the data is stored. The EU Commission suggests enacting a similar, Union-wide provision under the name of a 'European Production Order', and is in negotiations with the United States on a legal framework on the compulsion of US-based service providers by authorities within the EU to disclose electronic evidence. On a transnational level, negotiations on this topic have been concluded between the UK and the US, and are ongoing at the CoE, with a view to the tabling of a second additional

[31] The African Union Convention on Cyber Security and Personal Data Protection, adopted 27 June 2014 <https://au.int/en/treaties/african-union-convention-cyber-security-and-personal-data-protection>, has not yet entered into force.

[32] See Brodowski, 'TOC and Cybercrime' (n 2) 348 et seq; Clough, 'Budapest Convention' (n 29) 730 et seq.

[33] See Brodowski, 'TOC and Cybercrime' (n 2) 347 et seq; Adrian Haase, *Computerkriminalität im Europäischen Strafrecht* (Mohr Siebeck 2017) 25 et seq, 129 et seq.

protocol to the 2001 European Cybercrime Convention in 2021.[34] However, at least some negotiating positions may best be described as bifurcated: on the one hand, states want easy access for their own prosecutors while on the other hand, they want high safeguards around foreign access concerning their own citizens' data. For instance, the US CLOUD Act seeks to minimize access to and use of data relating to 'United States persons' (18 USC § 2523 (a) (2), (b) (2)), and the rapporteur in the European Parliament seeks to involve the country where the suspected person is located.[35]

## 3. A Global Convention on Cybercrime?

Until recently, the majority viewpoint was that the '"window of opportunity" during which . . . an [international] agreement could be reached may have passed'.[36] Instead, it was predicted that the fragmentation into a number of binding and non-binding instruments—with the 2001 European Cybercrime Convention taking a leading role—would continue. Moreover, efforts at the UN level seemed to have stalled, with the UNODC and its Comprehensive Study on Cybercrime of 2013 not really pushing an international convention superseding the existing international legal framework.[37] This is further underlined by the fact that in the last five years, thirteen further states have acceded to the 2001 European Cybercrime Convention, and some other states use the Convention as a 'model law' without formally acceding to it.[38]

Yet, in December 2019, the UN General Assembly adopted with seventy-nine to sixty votes and thirty-three abstentions a resolution to launch the 'elaborat[ion of] a comprehensive international convention on countering the use of information and communications technologies for criminal purposes'.[39] This move was considered by the EU to 'be highly divisive' and leading to 'further polarization'; the US suggested that it actually 'undermine[s] international cooperation to combat cybercrime'. In contrast, Russia—though part of the CoE—pointed out that the 'era of club agreements must give way to a democratic negotiating process'. In a similar vein, China expressed the need to 'guarantee the inclusivity of the negotiating process on such an international convention'.[40] The resolution itself does not yet set out

[34] Just see Jennifer Laskal, 'Unpacking the CLOUD Act' [2018] eucrim 220 et seq; Lawrence Siry, 'Cloudy Days Ahead: Cross-Border Evidence Collection and its Impact on the Rights of EU Citizens' (2019) 10 NJECL 227 et seq. On the US-UK agreement, see <https://www.justice.gov/dag/cloudact>.

[35] European Parliament, PE642.987v00-01.

[36] Clough, 'Budapest Convention' (n 29) 734; Seger, 'Budapest Convention' (n 25) 170. On the most recent draft T-CY (2020) 7 of 12 April 2021, see < https://www.coe.int/en/web/cybercrime/t-cy-drafting-group>.

[37] UNODC, *Cybercrime* (n 3) 63 et seq.

[38] See Clough, 'Budapest Convention' (n 29) 734; Seger, 'Budapest Convention' (n 25) 173 et seq.

[39] UN GA Res A/RES/74/247 of 27 December 2019.

[40] UN A/74/PV.52 of 19 December 2019, 35 et seq.

the exact points at which such a potential UN convention would differ from the 2001 European Cybercrime Convention. However, Russia and China—as major proponents of this move—are known to object to cross-border access to data on the one hand, and to push for increased state control over Internet usage in their respective countries.[41] A convention drafted with a 'less free' Internet in mind, and backed by the UN, would provide greater formal legitimacy to such (over-)criminalization, and may marginalize the 2001 European Cybercrime Convention. Yet, with all EU member states and in particular the US strongly opposed to the adoption of a UN convention, the last word may not yet have been spoken on the actual impact such a potential convention may have in the future.

## IV. Trends and Patterns of Transnational Cybercrime Regulation

On the basis of this brief sketch of how (transnational) cybercrime—and the transnational legal response to it—emerged in the past few decades, a few trends, patterns and features can be discerned. These are partly similar, partly dissimilar to other histories of transnational criminal justice discussed in this volume.

### 1. Cybercrime as a Multi-dimensional and Global Challenge

'Cybercrime' is a transnational regulatory challenge covering far more than new 'computer crimes'. Instead, the minimum provisions on criminalization typically extend to some 'common' crimes where IT merely serves as a neutral tool to commit a crime.[42] Yet 'cybercrime' must not be reduced to substantive criminal law. Instead, this phenomenon also raises—as evidenced, for instance, by the 2001 European Cybercrime Convention, which is best described as 'comprehensive'[43]—intertwined questions of jurisdiction (on crimes, but in particular on electronic evidence or 'data'), of procedural law and of transnational cooperation. This mixture of aspects—and the obvious linkage to human rights, primarily freedom of speech, and democracy—increases the difficulty of international consensus, as underlined by the increasing tensions between the 'Western' 2001 European Cybercrime Convention and a Russian/Chinese push for a UN convention.

Though cybercrime has become a global phenomenon, the lack of a global convention on cybercrime can probably be best explained by this difficulty of aligning

[41] See Samuel Salton, 'UN Backing of Controversial Cybercrime Treaty Raises Suspicions' (*Euractiv*, 30 January 2020) <https://www.euractiv.com/section/digital/news/un-backing-of-controversial-cybercrime-treaty-raises-suspicions/>.
[42] See Brodowski, 'TOC and Cybercrime' (n 2) 346 et seq.
[43] See Clough, 'Budapest Convention' (n 29) 701 et seq.

the multitude of substantive and procedural questions with a common understanding of a sufficiently 'free' Internet and the protection of human rights. This has led to like-minded 'Western' states agreeing and pushing the 2001 European Cybercrime Convention, which has gained notable traction also beyond Europe, on the one hand, and, on the other hand, an increasing number of states pursuing a different agenda and utilizing the UN as their forum. In the future, this may well lead to two conventions on the same subject-matter, both backed by renowned international organizations, but based on incompatible understandings on the equilibrium between human rights, state sovereignty and coercive and penal powers of the states.

## 2. Largely Traditional, but Speedy Transnational Criminal Justice Responses to Cybercrime

Despite the transformative power of digitalization, the transnational reaction to cybercrime has—broadly speaking—followed traditional patterns. There are no vertical turns of integration, such as the International Criminal Court (ICC) for international criminal justice, or the European Public Prosecutor's Office (EPPO) for the protection of the financial interests of the EU. Instead, the transnational justice response relies heavily on existing international and supranational organizations (in particular the CoE, but also the EU and other regional players as well as the ITU and the UN); it was largely driven by nation states;[44] and it uses traditional forms ('soft law', model rules, international conventions) and largely also common types of content (minimum provisions on criminalization, (extraterritorial) jurisdiction, extradition, affording of mutual legal assistance, network of contact points) of transnational criminal justice.

This reliance on existing practices of transnational criminal justice has allowed for a quite speedy response to a new phenomenon, even in view of the extraordinarily fast evolution of digital technology and the accompanying opportunities for criminal misuse. It has also helped that with regard to substantive criminal law, the OECD Recommendations of 1985 had early on suggested a 'technology-neutral' drafting of statutes. Though some limitations exist based on the principle of *nullum crimen sine lege*, this approach means that many modern crime phenomena are covered by criminal offences drafted long ago. In contrast, procedural provisions typically tend to be less 'technology-neutral'. Nonetheless, the procedural toolbox available under the CoE Convention should not be underestimated, though much depends on the—oftentimes wanting—implementation in national criminal procedure. Last but not least, the transformative power can be seen—at least so

[44] See Sieber, 'Mastering Complexity' (n 9) 175.

far—less in the forms or types of international cooperation, but probably more in the content, which continues to set out a 'complex and global reform agenda for criminal law systems'.[45]

One such area of novel content can be seen in the extensive standards on specific investigation measures prescribed in international instruments on transnational criminal justice relating to cybercrime, such as articles 16 et seq of the 2001 European Cybercrime Convention. Similar to criminalization requirements, such a common minimum standard serves as a 'model' for bringing national criminal procedure for solely domestic cases into alignment with the new requirements of prosecuting cybercrime. What is more, such a standard is helpful for mutual legal assistance, as there is at least some shared understanding as to what investigation measures are (or should be) available.

## 3. Transformative Power of Cybercrime: From Territoriality to Control

The most striking transformation relates to the territorial reach of state powers. Article 32 of the 2001 European Cybercrime Convention contains a highly disputed provision on non-coercive transborder access to data,[46] without notification of the state where the data is stored. In recent years, the quest for 'transnational production orders' relating to 'e-evidence' means that traditional physical borders are transcended. In the US CLOUD Act and similar measures adopted by some European states, such an expansion of the states' reach was enacted unilaterally on the basis of what may be called re-nationalization or domestication: situations which are factually transnational (the data is stored abroad) are normatively defined to be national (by requiring the service provider to transfer the data inland). While efforts are ongoing—bilaterally between the EU and the US, and within the CoE—to create an international legal framework on transnational production orders, the same fundamental shift is also present in the draft negotiation materials: state protection over evidence located within each state's territory is reduced in favour of extended access to evidence located abroad. The territorial location of evidence, and state sovereignty over data located in its territory, is becoming less relevant. Instead, the focus shifts to a question of the powers states may exert on data, on its citizens, on people and private entities. This *shift from territoriality to control* seems to be the major transformative change cybercrime facilitates in transnational criminal justice.

[45] ibid 136 et seq.

[46] On the disputes relating to this provision, just see Ulrich Sieber, *Straftaten und Strafverfolgung im Internet* (CH Beck 2012) C 78 et seq. On the interpretation of the provision, see the guidance note T-CY (2013) 7 E.

The traditional focus of transnational criminal justice was on nation states and their territory. That included, originally more as a reflex than on purpose, a protection of the things (evidence) and the people (suspects) present on the territory of the state. If territoriality is no longer a valid factor—and it is indeed a rather weak argument when it relates to some types of data stored in the so-called 'Cloud'—such indirect protection is lost. Instead, it will become ever more important to focus on the real underlying questions: the reach of criminal jurisdiction, the protection of human rights including the freedom of speech and further limitations to overcriminalization, and adequate procedural protections in criminal investigations. In this sense, cybercrime may yet—and should—cause transformations in how transnational criminal justice is configured, with more focus on the people affected as suspects and witnesses, and less focus on nation states.

# 18
# A Historical Perspective on Modes of Liability in Transnational Criminal Law

*Anneke Petzsche*

## I. Introduction

Transnational criminal law[1] is an area of law with an increasing influence on domestic laws globally. It aims to suppress certain harmful activities of a transnational nature, effect or concern[2] through criminalization (including establishing jurisdiction) and cooperation (eg extradition, mutual assistance). International cooperation is needed to create transnational criminal law because of the criminal phenomena addressed. It is seldom the case that one person acting alone can produce the transnational element required. Due to the scale and effect of the criminal conduct targeted, transnational criminal law mostly aims at acts that are perpetrated by more than one person so that group structures and the extent to which it requires punishment are relevant. The (criminal) phenomena addressed typically do not target lone actors[3] but entail the cooperation of several persons; as with international criminal law there is a collective nature to the crimes. This establishes the need for the international community to act together and address them.[4] The ICTY's finding regarding international criminal law therefore also holds true regarding transnational criminal law:

> Most of these crimes do not result from the criminal propensity of single individuals but constitute manifestations of collective criminality: the crimes are often carried out by groups of individuals acting in pursuance of a common criminal design. Although some members of the group may physically perpetrate the

[1] See the definition by Neil Boister, 'Further Reflections on the Concept of Transnational Criminal Law' (2015) 6(1) Transnational Legal Theory 9, 13 (hereafter Boister, 'Further Reflections') and in the Introduction to this book.

[2] ibid 17.

[3] A recent exception is the single perpetrator, so-called lone wolf, in the context of terrorism.

[4] Cyrille Fijnaut, 'Transnational Crime and the Role of the United Nations in Its Containment through International Cooperation: A Challenge for the 21st Century' (2000) 2 Eur J Crime Crim Law Crim Justice 119, 124 (hereafter Fijnaut, 'Transnational Crime') argues that no single country is capable of containing them.

Anneke Petzsche, *A Historical Perspective on Modes of Liability in Transnational Criminal Law* In: *Histories of Transnational Criminal Law.* Edited by: Neil Boister, Sabine Gless and Florian Jeßberger, Oxford University Press. © Anneke Petzsche 2021. DOI: 10.1093/oso/9780192845702.003.0019

> criminal act (murder ...), the participation and contribution of the other members of the group is often vital in facilitating the commission of the offence in question.[5]

The relevance of collective criminality is reflected in the criminal acts addressed by transnational criminal law. In hijacking, terrorism, organized crime and human trafficking the single perpetrator seldom acts alone: she acts together with other individuals pursuing common designs.

This raises the question of how exactly transnational criminal law, through its different international instruments such as UN or CoE conventions, addresses this collective nature. In order to answer this question, the extent to which transnational criminal law requires criminalization and the different modes of liability it relies on to achieve this need to be examined. The modes of liability it entails is an area that so far has mostly been neglected.[6] The increasing influence of transnational criminal law makes it worthwhile to examine them more closely. The importance of modes of liability not only lies in the nature of transnational criminal law, it also informs the extent to which a particular form of conduct requires punishment and the extent to which states cooperate in criminal matters such as through extradition or mutual assistance.

It is a daunting exercise to shed more light on this area because of what it encompasses. In the following, I shall begin to develop a historic picture of modes of liability in transnational criminal law. Due to space constraints and because corporate liability is discussed in Chapter 15 of this volume,[7] my focus is on individual liability.

## II. Forms of Individual Liability

### 1. General Background

International society responded to the globalization of harmful conduct by beginning to develop so-called suppression conventions in the 19th century.[8] This approach has become more and more significant due to societal developments such as globalization and the appearance of different actors on the international stage such as the United Nations (replacing its forerunner the League of Nations), the

[5] Judgment, Tadic (IT-94-1-A), Appeals Chamber, 15 July 1999, § 191; Gerhard Werle, 'Individual Criminal Responsibility in Article 25 ICC Statute' (2007) 5(4) JICJ 953, 954 (hereafter Werle, 'Individual Criminal').

[6] Neil Boister, '"Transnational Criminal Law"?' (2003) 14(5) EJIL 14, 953, 958 (hereafter Boister, 'Transnational Criminal Law').

[7] See Elliot and Lüth, Chapter 15 in this book.

[8] Boister, 'Transnational Criminal Law' (n 6) 955.

CoE, and the European Union (EU). In 2008, Bassiouni, for example, identified 267 conventions with penal characteristics and 28 types of international crimes.[9]

These conventions rely on an indirect enforcement system.[10] They typically describe a specific (criminal) conduct (such as '[a]ny fraudulent making or altering of currency, whatever means are employed' in article 3(1) of the 1929 Counterfeiting Convention). In addition they create an obligation for the members to establish the conduct as a criminal offence under national law ('The following should be punishable as ordinary crimes' reads the rubric to article 3 of the 1929 Counterfeiting Convention).

They do not aspire to be a world criminal code but require incorporation into domestic laws. From the beginning, they have targeted individual acts and while not creating it, they have demanded individual criminal liability be established.

Thus far 'little attention has been paid to the scope of criminal liability in the sense of degrees of participation'.[11] It is important to examine this subject more closely because of the different degrees of guilt or individual criminal responsibility the different forms of participation reflect, and the relevance of these degrees of responsibility for sentencing decisions. In order to lay a stronger focus on this doctrinal question from an historical perspective, in what follows, I briefly describe which criminal phenomena are addressed in transnational criminal law and which type of obligations the international conventions contain. Using specific examples, I then identify which modes of liability exist, focusing on their historic development before coming to a conclusion.

## 2. Criminal Phenomena Addressed in Transnational Criminal Law

As Boister has expounded, transnational criminal law aims at the 'suppression by international law through domestic penal law of criminal activities that have (i) actual or (ii) potential transboundary effects or (iii) transboundary moral impact'.[12] Only certain criminal phenomena are ascribed such an effect.

These criminal activities all share a commonality in that they neither address low-level crime such as theft nor grave crimes that are best dealt with on a national level and do not concern the international community as a whole such as murder. Rather, they target criminal activities that are challenging to the international

[9] M Cherif Bassiouni, *International Criminal Law—Vol I Sources, Subjects and Contents* (3rd edn, Brill | Nijhoff 2008) 134 (hereafter Bassiouni, *International Criminal Law*).

[10] ibid 157.

[11] Boister, 'Transnational Criminal Law' (n 6) 958. But see the analysis of Roger S Clark, 'Offenses of International Concern: Multilateral State Treaty Practice in the Forty Years Since Nuremberg' (1988) 57(1) Nordic J Intl L 49, 78 et seq (hereafter Clark, 'Offenses') and Neil Boister *An Introduction to Transnational Criminal Law* (1st edn, OUP 2012), 129 et seq.

[12] Boister, 'Further Reflections' (n 1) 13.

community as a whole.[13] These normally are of a collective nature such as organized crime. While there are many different criminal activities targeted, it is important to note that each international legal instrument deals with a specific (criminal) phenomenon. There exists no comprehensive system; each treaty, in principle, stands on its own. However, there are some universal issues addressed in each of them: one of them being modes of liability.

## 3. Nature of Obligation the International Conventions Contain

It is important to clarify the nature of the obligation such transnational treaties contain. Transnational criminal law, unlike international criminal law, does not establish 'crimes'. It does not create individual criminal responsibility under international law.[14] Transnational crimes are no such thing—this term is only used for reasons of convenience—but the conventions establish the foundation for certain crimes. Suppression conventions contain obligations to enact certain crimes. They represent an 'indirect system of interstate obligations generating national penal laws'.[15] This is commonly recognized and stressed in the conventions themselves. Often a clear reference to the need for respecting domestic laws can also be found, such as that contained in article 3(11) of the 1988 Drug Trafficking Convention, which holds:

> Nothing contained in this article shall affect the principle that the description of the offences to which it refers and of legal defences thereto is reserved to the domestic law of a Party and that such offences shall be prosecuted and punished in conformity with that law.

The conventions therefore need to be transposed into domestic law. While they provide a normative outline, the specific form of implementation is left to national discretion.[16] The obligations therefore are mostly described in broad terms to leave enough room for compatibility with the general structure and basic principles of domestic laws.[17] This structure is especially relevant when it comes to modes of liability.

All suppression conventions therefore depend on a transposition on a national level by the members of said convention. So far, this holds true for all conventions and other legal instruments established by the different international and

[13] Fijnaut, 'Transnational Crime' (n 4) 124.
[14] Boister, 'Transnational Criminal Law' (n 6) 962.
[15] ibid 962.
[16] Therefore, Boister argues, undoing 'any claim to codification', Boister, 'Further Reflections' (n 1) 20.
[17] ibid 15.

European actors. However, there are differences in the level of enforcement among conventions and instruments. While, for example, the UN and CoE mainly depend on the willingness of their members to respect their obligations and on censure, the European Union has a clear and assertive enforcement mechanism in case the obligations are not met.

## 4. Which Forms Exist?

### a. General

As noted, suppression conventions need to be transposed into national law. They often contain broad terms and only provide for a normative outline. This holds especially true when it comes to modes of liability. As they require incorporation into national law, they contain little guidance on general principles of liability. However, they do offer some.

Because these suppression conventions normally target (one) specific form of criminal conduct, they contain more or less precise descriptions of said criminal conduct; they contain mainly specifications in the ambit of the Special Part. While suppression conventions contain provisions on the criminal conduct targeted, they are less precise when it comes to general principles of liability. However, even very early conventions included some provisions regarding the General Part and, more specifically, modes of liability.

Before we examine what they regulate more closely, it is useful to map out what they do not regulate. Unlike international criminal law (specifically the Rome statute[18]), there exists no General Part of (substantive) criminal law applicable to all suppression conventions. Instead each convention or treaty contains their own provisions so that there exists no organically grown and developed system (as in a national legal system). Instead, they often contain rather vague concepts or the choice between alternatives that can be filled by national legislators with their own understanding.

### b. Perpetration

Suppression conventions—if they are not only focused on procedural issues and cooperation—always describe some forms of perpetration, whether for crimes as various as terrorism or drug trafficking. To give an example: hijacking is described as 'Any person who on board an aircraft in flight unlawfully, by force or threat thereof, or by any other form of intimidation, seizes, or exercises control of, that aircraft, . . . commits an offence.'[19] The conduct of the principal, therefore, is—more

[18] See Werle (n 5) 953.
[19] 1970 Hague Hijacking Convention, art 1.

or less—clearly defined. It includes both conduct and circumstance elements—force/threats—on board an aircraft.

### c. Participation

In addition, most suppression conventions also contain some provision on participation. Few, especially very old treaties, contain provisions only dealing with the principal, for example articles 1–3 of the 1910 White Slave Convention. Since then most such conventions have included provisions on both perpetration and participation. For example, the 1929 Counterfeiting Convention provides in article 3 for provisions on perpetration and participation. Article 3 reads as follows:

> The following should be punishable as ordinary crimes: (1) Any fraudulent making or altering of currency, whatever means are employed; (2) The fraudulent uttering of counterfeit currency; (3) The introduction into a country of or the receiving or obtaining counterfeit currency with a view to uttering the same and with knowledge that it is counterfeit; (4) Attempts to commit, *and any intentional participation in*, [my emphasis] the foregoing acts;

While the first three subparagraphs deal with the principal, the fourth deals with the participant. As we see in this example, early suppression conventions differentiated between principal and participant—though they did not always use the same language.[20] Moreover, they do not usually use the terms perpetration or perpetrator in the convention but rather simply describe the criminal acts of the principal.

The obligation to punish participation appears in different guises: 'any intentional participation in, the foregoing acts',[21] 'is an accomplice of a person'[22] or 'participates as an accomplice in an offence ... or organizes or directs others to commit an offence'.[23] These linguistic differences beg the question of whether they reflect a difference in content. Are all forms of participation (in its broad sense) included? Is there a difference between participant or accomplice? Do both contain both aider and abettor? The conventions themselves offer little guidance on this point apart from their wording, which changes from one convention to another.[24] It is mainly left to the national legislator to interpret them.

One might speculate that the differences are caused by the difficulties that exist when drawing a convention on an international level. Many different states have to compromise and agree to the wording used in provisions and the drafters themselves may differ (and are usually diplomats not legal scholars). In addition, the

[20] Clark's finding of 1988 that there is much variation in the language used in these treaties therefore still holds true today, see Clark 'Offenses' (n 11) 81.

[21] 1929 Counterfeiting Convention, art 3(4).

[22] 1970 Hague Hijacking Convention, art 1.

[23] 1997 Terrorist Bombings Convention, art 2(3)(a) and (b).

[24] Clark, 'Offenses' (n 11) 81.

provisions might be purposefully vague to leave the transposition to national discretion. For example, even if one argues that the term 'accomplice' does not contain the concepts of instigator or abettor (which as a broad term in this context it might be difficult to do) because of the lack of guidance national legislators are free to interpret terms like this either narrowly or broadly[25] depending on their own domestic interests which can lead to different (national) interpretations. On the contrary, some patterns that do emerge seem to be brought about by the continuity in the drafting personnel rather than real conceptual communalities or differences.[26]

Though in most transnational criminal law instruments both modes of liability are mentioned, there is no specific system prescribed. They describe no precise ambit of liability. It is left to national law to 'decide' how and in which form to criminalize them[27]—which conduct is contained in the general term of participation, and whether to demand full subsidiarity or limited subsidiarity, whether to follow a 'differential participation model', or a 'unitary perpetrator model'[28] (though the differentiation itself lends itself more to a differential participation model). Doctrinal guidance is clearly lacking.

## 5. Group Responsibility

In addition to the classic questions of perpetration and participation, another form of liability is of importance in transnational criminal law. Because of the complex structures of the criminal conduct targeted, the question of a form of organizational liability arises. Where the question of group responsibility arises in transnational criminal law this is mainly dealt with in terms of individual liability.[29] The organization per se is not criminalized but membership in it is criminalized. Examples being the contribution to a group crime in the 1997 Terrorist Bombings Convention and the United Nations Convention against Transnational Organized Crime 2000 (UNTOC), which contains in article 5(1) the criminalization of participation in an organized criminal group.

[25] Of course, the national legislator also can go further in criminalizing conduct as the conventions represent a minimum standard. For example, the United States has added a conspiracy provision in its legislation giving effect to the treaties on aircraft offences and the Torture Convention. A domestic constitutional problem that can arise from the creation of such offences is the application of universal jurisdiction.

[26] Clark, 'Offenses' (n 11) 86.

[27] Unlike the unified perpetrator model followed by international criminal law in the beginning.

[28] On both terms, see Albin Eser, 'Individual Criminal Responsibility' in Antonio Cassese, Paola Gaeta and John RWD Jones (eds), *The Rome Statute of the International Criminal Court: A Commentary Vol 1* (OUP 2002) 768, 781 et seq.

[29] In this context, the question of corporate criminal liability also arises. Whereas corporate liability is contained in many more recent conventions, they do not necessarily contain corporate criminal liability.

The former shows the potential for influence such wide provisions in an international treaty have as it later influenced the drafting of article 25(3)(d) of the Rome Statute.[30] However, the latter also reflects the difficulties such international treaties face in creating obligations compatible with different legal systems. Article 5 of the UNTOC contains the obligation to either create an offence if the perpetrator agrees with one or more other persons to commit a serious crime[31] or for taking part in the activities of an organized criminal group[32] (or both). This reflects the approach of targeting such conduct in common law through conspiracy and in civil law through criminalizing membership in a criminal group.[33] This example reflects the emphasis that is placed upon the protection of state sovereignty as evidenced by the wide margin of appreciation afforded to states.[34]

## 6. Historical Development of Individual Liability

Knowing that provisions on modes of liability in suppression conventions lack clarity and given their long history, it is interesting to see whether there is any kind of development visible in this area and if so, what kind. This is not just an intellectual exercise, but these different forms of participation are important because of how they determine the scope of a convention and consequently the obligations and the extent of cooperation they contain.

To form a comprehensive historic picture analysing every transnational criminal law convention, treaty or other legal instrument would be interesting but because of the large number of these treaties this cannot be done here. As there exists no universal General Part applicable to all conventions, in order to delve deeper historically the development within specific areas need to be examined. For that, two specific examples are chosen and examined more closely: human trafficking and corruption. Both topics are addressed in other chapters,[35] however, my focus differs as I want to concentrate on the provisions dealing specifically with modes of liability in the different legal instruments in order to tease out any historic development.

[30] See Roger S Clark, 'Elements of Crimes in Early Confirmation Decisions of Pre-Trial Chambers of the International Criminal Court' (2008) 6 New Zealand Yearbook of International Law 209, 229 who calls it a classic example of the 'previously agreed text' principle.

[31] Art 5(1)(a)(i).

[32] Art 5(1)(a)(ii).

[33] See further on this difference Anna Sergi, 'Organised Crime in Criminal Law: Conspiracy and Membership Offences in Italian, English and International Frameworks' (2014) 25(2) King's Law Journal 185; Neil Boister, *An Introduction to Transnational Criminal Law* (2nd edn, OUP 2018) 138 et seq.

[34] Tom Obokata and Brian Payne, *Transnational Organised Crime: A Comparative Analysis* (Routledge 2017) 34.

[35] Schloenhardt, Chapters 12 and Forlati, Chapter 13 in this book.

### a. Trafficking in Human Beings

The transnational fight against trafficking in human beings and its forerunner slavery has a long history. There are numerous treaties and conventions dealing with this criminal phenomenon—both on the international and on the regional European level.[36] I do not examine all of them but focus on a representative selection.

Early international treaties like the 1910 White Slave Convention,[37] and the 1921 Convention for the Suppression of the Traffic in Women and Children did not differentiate modes of liability but only contained provisions on the principal. Later instruments, however, like the 1949 Convention for the Suppression of the Traffic in Persons, contained provisions on the principal and the participants establishing the obligation to punish 'participation in the acts' set out in the convention.[38] The most relevant modern suppression convention is the 2000 Human Trafficking Protocol. It contains the criminalization of trafficking in human beings as perpetrator who engages in the recruitment, transportation, transfer, harbouring or receipt of persons,[39] as well as the participation as an accomplice[40] and the organization or direction of other persons to commit an offence.[41] This convention is therefore broader in content than its historic predecessors.

As human trafficking is viewed as an important criminal phenomenon that needs to be dealt with above the national level, there also exist European legal instruments—both on the level of the CoE and of the European Union—devoted to its suppression in Europe.

The central legal instrument at the level of the CoE is the 2005 Convention on Action against Trafficking in Human Beings[42] which contains the criminalization of trafficking in human beings as perpetrator who engages in the recruitment, transportation, transfer, harbouring or receipt of persons,[43] and the criminalization of acts relating to travel or identity documents.[44] Article 21(1) adds that

> Each Party shall adopt such legislative and other measures as may be necessary to establish as criminal offences when committed intentionally, *aiding or abetting the commission of any of the offences established in accordance with articles 18 and 20* of the present Convention. [my emphasis]

[36] Bassiouni, *International Criminal Law* (n 9) 146 et seq.
[37] Art 1 or 2 in conjunction with art 3.
[38] Art 4.
[39] Art 5(1) in conjunction with art 3.
[40] Art 5(2)(b).
[41] Art 5(2)(c).
[42] Adopted 16 May 2005, entered into force 1 February 2008, CETS 197.
[43] Art 18 in conjunction with art 4.
[44] Art 20.

The Convention therefore differentiates between perpetration and participation. It also includes in the ambit of participation both aider and abettor, using different terminology than the UN Convention.

Addressing human trafficking has been a priority for decades in the EU. By 1997, the EU had already adopted a Joint Action to combat trafficking in human beings and sexual exploitation of children.[45] It contained provisions on the trafficker as principal and the 'participation in' trafficking.

The subsequent 2002 Framework Decision on combating trafficking in human beings[46] contained both in article 1 provisions on the trafficker as principal and in article 2 on participation, namely 'instigation of, aiding, abetting' of an offence referred to in article 1. While the 2011 Directive on Preventing and Combating Trafficking in Human Beings and Protecting its Victims which replaced the Framework Decision[47] broadened what conduct is to be viewed as trafficking, participation again was included in the same terms of 'inciting, aiding and abetting'.

These legal instruments dealing with human trafficking contain a development regarding modes of liability. While older instruments like the 1921 Convention for the Suppression of the Traffic in Women and Children do not contain a provision on participation, these newer documents differentiate between the principal and the participant—though they use different wording to do so. The term 'participation' was used in the UN's 1949 Convention for the Suppression of the Traffic in Persons and the EU's 1997 Joint Action. More modern conventions are more differentiated and name different specific forms of participation—though in specific terms that differ from one instrument to another.

A general trend, therefore, exists on both levels: a development towards specification and differentiation occurs. Early instruments only dealt with the principal, more modern instruments differentiate between perpetration and participation—even later clarifying which forms the latter contains. While this does not necessarily broaden the scope of these later conventions, it seems an attempt at clarifying that participation in its broadest form is targeted and all forms are to be included. The fact that on the European level the first step is absent does not negate this trend. It is probably because the first European instruments appear decades later than the first global conventions and the EU drafters work in their own way.

### b. Corruption

Another criminal phenomenon with a reasonably long history of being addressed by international legal instruments—though the conventions are somewhat newer than the ones addressing human trafficking—is corruption. Again, there are

[45] Joint Action of 24 February 1997 adopted by the Council on the basis of art K.3 of the Treaty on European Union concerning action to combat trafficking in human beings and sexual exploitation of children, 97/154/JHA.

[46] 1 August 2002, OJ L 203/1 (2002).

[47] 15 April 2011, OJ L 101/1 (2011).

different actors relevant in this area. On the global level, the key treaty is the 1997 OECD Bribery Convention. It contains provisions on the principal and the participant using the following wording: 'complicity in, including incitement, aiding and abetting, or authorisation of an act of bribery of a foreign public official'. The 2003 United Nations Convention against Corruption (UNCAC) contains different corruption offences[48] and the obligation to 'establish as a criminal offence, in accordance with its domestic law, *participation in any capacity such as an accomplice, assistant or instigator in*'. [my emphasis][49]

On the European level, the 1999 CoE Criminal Law Convention on Corruption[50] contains different bribery offences in articles 2–13 and in article 15 criminalizes 'aiding or abetting the commission of any of the criminal offences established'. The 1997 EU Convention on Fighting Corruption Involving Officials of the EU or Officials of Member States[51] contains passive and active corruption in articles 2 and 3 and in article 5(1) criminalizes 'participating in and instigating the conduct in question'. The subsequent 2003 Framework Decision on Combating Corruption in the Private Sector[52] speaks of active and passive corruption in the private sector in article 2 and 'instigating, aiding and abetting' in article 3.

All aforementioned legal instruments therefore differentiate between the principal and the participants—again using different wording to describe what is contained in the concept of participation. The fact that with a view to the breadth of the substantive conduct not only the principal is covered by the treaties but also any participant seems to be the norm in later instruments of the last decades. Also, all offer some form of description of what is covered as participating conduct. Given the fact that all these instruments are considerably more recent than the ones examined earlier, a similar trend towards providing more detail is visible. For example, at the level of the European Union again the first instrument only spoke of 'participating in' while the later clarified this in speaking of 'instigating, aiding and abetting'.

As can be gleaned from these two examples of human trafficking and corruption, there exists a development regarding modes of individual liability. While very early conventions only regulated the conduct of the principal, later conventions broadened their scope by also including a provision on participation. There is no consistent wording used which reflects a lack of doctrinal coherency. This is probably because the structure of perpetration and participation—and consequently the terminology—is specific to each legal system and therefore the necessity arises to use broad terms in the conventions. The terms used seem purposefully not to contain strict specifications or requirements but to leave it to national discretion

[48] Arts 15–25.
[49] Art 27.
[50] Strasbourg, 27 January 1999, ETS No 173, in force 1 July 2002.
[51] 26 May 1997, OJ C 195/2 (1997).
[52] 31 July 2003, OJ L 192/54 (2003).

to fill them. However, there has been a development from just using a broad term such as 'participation' to a more specific description of what is contained in this term. The aim seems to be to clarify that participation in its broadest form is targeted and all forms are to be included in order to expand the scope of these conventions as far as possible.

## III. Conclusion

The collective nature of the criminal phenomena addressed by transnational criminal law is recognized by conventions through the way in which their provisions establish liability not just for the perpetrator but also by including different modes of liability. Historically, at first no distinction was made but only the principal was targeted. Later, this changed. Legal instruments began to try to encompass the participant and in certain areas organizational conduct. The main aim seems to have been to broaden the scope of criminalization.[53] By specifying which participatory conduct should be criminalized, the drafters tried to ensure that all forms of participation in its general sense were included. To that end, there has been a discernible development towards a more detailed description of participation and the addition of group (and corporate) responsibility.

However, what has not been developed is doctrinal coherency. The wording differs from one instrument to another. The conventions only offer terminology that then can—and needs—to be filled by domestic law. It is left for the national legislator to fit the transposition into their own legal system. In that sense, transnational criminal law is still a poorly developed system, which is partly because of its nature. All that can be said is that a certain harmonizing impact on general principles of domestic criminal laws can be observed.[54] As treaties require national implementation, they are designed to make use of developed national legal systems.[55] However, the wide discretion left to states is problematic not just from a doctrinal perspective[56] but also because of its potential for 'massive variation in its application, in violation of the principle of legality'[57] and its potential for abuse.

[53] See for a similar development Jeßberger, Chapter 19 in this book.

[54] Neil Boister *An Introduction to Transnational Criminal Law* (1st edn, OUP 2012) 126 et seq.

[55] Here lies an advantage for a body such as the EU which is striving to harmonize the criminal law of its member states. However, the limits are obvious so that an emphasis is laid on the principle of mutual recognition in criminal matters.

[56] Boister criticizes a 'neglect of doctrinal coherency', Boister, 'Transnational Criminal Law' (n 6) 958.

[57] ibid 959.

# 19

# A Short History of Jurisdiction in Transnational Criminal Law

*Florian Jeßberger*

## I. Introduction

This chapter deals with the international regulation of transnational jurisdiction over crime, in particular in multilateral treaties ('suppression conventions'[1]). In these treaties, a state party typically undertakes to 'adopt such measures as may be necessary to establish its jurisdiction over the offences established' by the respective convention.[2] Unlike most of the other chapters in this volume, the present chapter focuses neither on a specific historical period nor on the subject matter of one or more specific suppression conventions. Rather, it takes a cross-sectoral perspective and explores the provisions on the establishment of jurisdiction, which all conventions—expressly or implicitly—contain.

The chapter proceeds in three sections.[3] The first section revisits efforts to regulate (domestic) criminal jurisdiction in international law, in particular treaty law. The second section chronologically traces the rules on jurisdiction in suppression conventions since the late 19th century in order to identify common elements and innovations. In the third section, I offer general reflections on trends and directions before I conclude with a few general considerations, inter alia, on the repercussions of treaty regulations on the domestic realm. The chapter begins, however, with presenting three basic observations in order to situate our topic in the broader framework of the theory of jurisdiction, transnational criminal law and its history.

First, the establishment of jurisdiction is fundamental to criminal law. Rules on jurisdiction are part of every criminal legal order. In national legislations, typically but not necessarily, jurisdiction is set out explicitly, as a matter of substantive law

[1] This chapter follows the terminology set out in the introduction to this book (transnational criminal law', 'suppression conventions').

[2] Palermo Convention, art 15.

[3] The limited space available led to the chapter missing out on important dimensions of the topic: we shall neither explore in detail (or rather: not at all) the drafting history (of the specific conventions) and enquire into the reasons *why* a certain jurisdictional principle made its way into a convention (or, often more telling: *why not*), nor will we discuss the *consequences of the subject matter* of specific conventions on the shaping of its jurisdictional regime. We shall also not cover *regional instruments*, such as, in particular, Council of Europe conventions and EU Framework Decisions and Directives.

Florian Jeßberger, *A Short History of Jurisdiction in Transnational Criminal Law* In: *Histories of Transnational Criminal Law.* Edited by: Neil Boister, Sabine Gless and Florian Jeßberger, Oxford University Press. 
DOI: 10.1093/oso/9780192845702.003.0020

(eg in Germany) or as a matter of procedure (eg in Spain). The determination of the ambit of the criminal law—that is to 'make a state's law applicable to the activities, relations, or status of persons or the interests of things'—is often referred to as prescriptive jurisdiction.[4] If jurisdiction relates to acts with a foreign element (territory, person, interest), we speak of 'transnational jurisdiction'.[5] Systematically, rules on jurisdiction give an answer to several questions, in particular they determine the ambit of the law (*Geltungsbereich*) and the applicable law (*Anwendungsbereich*).[6] In addition, they usually determine the competent court (*forum*); typically local courts apply local law (*lex fori*). The basis for the determination of the reach of criminal law is the state's authority to punish (*ius puniendi*). This authority does not exist without limitations. These can be negative (permissive rules) or positive (prescriptive rules creating positive obligations, such as in suppression conventions). Limitations result from both international law—based on the principle of non-interference and, more generally, sovereignty—and (principles of) criminal law, in particular rights and guarantees protecting the individual. Where the exact boundaries are located is not entirely clear though. While the details are still controversial, there is an agreement that *international law* requires at least a substantive connection for the exercise of jurisdiction.[7] *Individual (rights)-based* limitations are even more difficult to identify, partly due to the fact that they have received much less attention in modern scholarship.[8]

Secondly, over time, a set of jurisdictional principles, some more controversial than others, has emerged.[9] These principles can be categorized in various ways. A fundamental classification reflects whether a state exercises its own inherent

[4] See American Law Institute's Restatement (Third) of Foreign Relations Law of the United States.

[5] The term 'transnational jurisdiction' is preferable to the term 'extraterritorial jurisdiction'. The former includes the latter but extends also to additional aspects which raise similar concerns, such as the exercise of jurisdiction over offences committed only partly in the territory or committed by foreigners in the territory.

[6] In addition, they give an answer to the preceding question of whether a specific act is made subject to the assessment of the respective authority to punish at all (*Bewertungseinzugsbereich*); for details see Florian Jeßberger, *Der transnationale Geltungsbereich des deutschen Strafrechts* (Mohr Siebeck 2011) 12 et seq (hereafter Jeßberger *Der transnationale Geltungsbereich*).

[7] More specifically, and according to one, rather restrictive view, legitimate connections are embodied in a *numerus clausus* of jurisdictional principles which are acknowledged under customary international law. For details on the discussion see Jeßberger, *Der transnationale Geltungsbereich* (n 6) 191 et seq with further references.

[8] It is interesting to note that the scholarly discourse on jurisdiction shifted from the 'criminal law paradigm' which was dominant during the 19th and early 20th centuries to the 'international law paradigm' emphasizing the sovereignty-based limitations of jurisdiction.

[9] See eg Michael Akehurst, 'Jurisdiction in International Law' (1972–73) 46 BYBIL 145; FA Mann, 'The Doctrine of Jurisdiction in International Law' (1964) 111 RCADI 1, 15; Florian Jeßberger, *Der transnationale Geltungsbereich* (n 6) 232 et seq; Josef Kohler, *Internationales Strafrecht* (Enke 1917); Franz von Liszt 'Sind gleiche Grundsätze des internationalen Strafrechts für die europäischen Staaten anzustreben und eventuell welche?' (1882) 2 Zeitschrift für die Gesamte Strafrechtswissenschaft 50; Dietrich Oehler, *Internationales Strafrecht* (2nd edn, Heymanns 1983). Influential comparative studies on the law of jurisdiction include the Harvard Draft Convention on Jurisdiction with Respect to Crime ((1935) 29 AJIL 439 and the study of the European Committee on Crime Problems, *Extraterritorial Criminal Jurisdiction* (1990).

authority to punish ('original' jurisdiction) or an authority to punish which originally belongs to another state or entity ('derivative' or transferred jurisdiction); the transfer of jurisdiction can be based on a treaty or take place in a one-off action.[10] Another, more common classification, relates to the specific grounds for the exercise of jurisdiction. For the purposes of this chapter, it may be sufficient to recall that, in particular, territory (strict, quasi, subjective, objective territoriality), person (active/national, passive, resident, official personality), and the legal interest protected by the criminal norm (individual, state, regional, universal protection) form recognized grounds in this regard.[11]

Thirdly, it seems helpful to note that the emergence of this set of jurisdictional principles is a relatively new phenomenon. Roman law, for instance, claimed to be universal and hence required no rules to determine (and distinguish) applicable legal regimes. An early example of a 'modern' law on criminal jurisdiction can be found in the legislation of Northern Italian City States from the 12th century on, where the human being remained subject to the law he was born into ('*lex ossibus inhaeret*') and the *lex patriae* was the basis for punishment.[12] It was not before the time of the Enlightenment and the formation of nation states that the nationality principle was replaced by territorial jurisdiction as the major basis for jurisdiction. But even during the 19th century, the scholarly discourse on jurisdiction was shaped by the search for the one *exclusive* jurisdictional principle.[13] Only towards the end of the 19th century—and this is the period where our analysis of treaty law begins—the idea gained traction that a *combination* of jurisdictional principles rather than the exclusive application of one principle was not only an option, but in fact preferable.[14] Today, triggered in part by the efforts to regulate criminal jurisdiction internationally and notwithstanding variations in details and language,[15]

[10] For details see Jeßberger, *Der transnationale Geltungsbereich* (n 6) 38 et seq; see also, Roger S Clark 'Jurisdiction over Transnational Crime' in Neil Boister and Robert J Currie (eds), *Routledge Handbook on Transnational Criminal Law* (Routledge 2015) 100, fn 47 (hereafter Clark 'Jurisdiction over Transnational Crime'). Examples of derivative jurisdiction are the exercise of universal jurisdiction for crimes under international law (where the state exercises jurisdiction on behalf of the international community), of jurisdiction for crimes against the interests of the European Union or of treaty-based jurisdiction (where the state exercises authority on behalf of another state party).

[11] For details see, inter alia, Neil Boister, *Introduction to Transnational Criminal Law* (2nd edn, OUP 2018) 136 (hereafter Boister, *Transnational Criminal Law*); and Jeßberger, *Der transnationale Geltungsbereich* (n 6) with further references.

[12] For a concise account of this period and the role of scholars like Bartolus, Baldus and Grotius, see Friedrich Meili, *Die hauptsächlichen Entwicklungsperioden des Internationalen Strafrechts*, (Füssli 1908).

[13] The debate resulted in different 'camps' or 'schools' of thought, comprising 'territorialists' (eg Julius Abegg, *Über die Bestrafung der im Auslande begangenen Verbrechen* (1819)), 'personalists' (Ernst Immanuel Bekker, *Theorie des heutigen deutschen Strafrechts*, Vol 1, (1859)), 'cosmopolitanists' (eg Robert von Mohl, *Staatrecht, Völkerrecht und Politik*, Vol 1 (1860) and 'protectionists' (eg August Hegler, *Prinzipien des internationalen Strafrechts* (1906)).

[14] See, inter alia, Ludwig von Bar, *Das internationale Privat- und Strafrecht* (1862); Christian Reinhold Köstlin, 'Über die Bestrafung der im Auslöand begangenen Verbrechen' (1850) 22 Kritische Zeitschrift für Rechtswissenschaft und Gesetzgebung des Auslandes 47.

[15] Broadly speaking, Anglo-American law has always relied more on territoriality, while Romano-Germanic law has been more open to provide for the extraterritorial application of criminal law, based in particular on the nationality principle. See also Boister, *Transnational Criminal Law* (n 11).

we find relative uniformity as regards the scope and ambit of the domestic criminal laws around the world.

## II. Efforts to Regulate Transnational Jurisdiction Transnationally: Comprehensive Coordination vs Sectoral Suppression

Historically, efforts to regulate transnational jurisdiction in international instruments took two different routes. Since the second half of the 19th century, transnational regulation of criminal jurisdiction was not only addressed in conjunction with international private law and conflict of laws, but, in a parallel development, as one (yet essential) element of efforts to control cross-border crime through international regulation by way of suppression conventions. To some extent both routes share the objective of coordinating (and stimulating) domestic prosecution of (typically transnational) crime. Ironically, while one route intended the 'resolution' of concurring jurisdictional claims (thereby responding to *positive* conflicts of jurisdiction), the other has been eager to create a tight net of competing claims to avoid impunity of certain transnational crimes (thereby responding to *negative* conflicts of jurisdiction).

The first route emanated from efforts to establish and codify rules for international private law. As a 'by-product' of these efforts, states also agreed on certain rules of criminal jurisdiction. Such efforts to regulate transnational criminal jurisdiction can be found in regional agreements of the late 19th and early 20th centuries, in particular in Latin America.[16] Early notable efforts include the 1878 Treaty of Lima,[17] and the 1889 Montevideo Treaty.[18] Both treaties established basic rules for domestic criminal jurisdiction, such as territorial jurisdiction, flag-state jurisdiction and universal jurisdiction for piracy. In addition, the treaties provided for hierarchies between the principles and mechanisms of coordination in case of conflict.[19] Similarly, the 1928 Bustamante Code[20] included a 'Section on Criminal Jurisdiction' and provided for territorial, protective and quasi-universal jurisdiction (inter alia for piracy, the slave traffic, 'white slave trade' and destruction of submarine cables). Different from modern suppression conventions, these regional

[16] For details, eg Oehler, *Internationales Strafrecht* (n 9) 13 et seq.

[17] Treaty for the Establishment of Uniform Rules in Private International Law 1878.

[18] Treaty on International Penal Law, 23 January 1889; the Treaty was later replaced by the Treaty on International Penal Law (Revised), 19 March 1940.

[19] See eg art 3 of the Montevideo Treaty (n 18): 'When an offense affects different States, the jurisdiction of the State in whose territory the offender is caught shall prevail.'

[20] Arts 296 et seq. Annexed to the Convention on Private International Law, 20 February 1928, reprinted in (1935) 29 AJIL, 642–43.

treaties were not limited to specific offences but regulated criminal jurisdiction in general.[21]

The second route to regulate criminal jurisdiction internationally concerns provisions on jurisdiction in sectoral suppression conventions. Similar to the provisions on extradition and mutual legal assistance, rules on jurisdiction form an essential element of suppression conventions. In fact, modern suppression conventions share a triadic structure of conventional duties: criminalization of certain behaviours, establishment of jurisdiction and extradition/mutual assistance. As Boister explains: '[c]riminalisation in national law of the provisions in the suppression conventions will be of limited practical effect unless the state enacting the crime establishes an adequate criminal jurisdiction for that crime'.[22] Typically, in such conventions, states agree to the application of certain jurisdictional principles: 'Each State Party shall adopt such measures as may be necessary to establish its jurisdiction over the offences.' What kind of 'measures' a state party adopts, if necessary, is left to its discretion.

## III. Jurisdiction in Suppression Conventions: Evolution and Milestones

This section examines major suppression conventions in chronological order, while noting innovations[23] and enquiring into the development of jurisdiction in transnational criminal law.[24]

### 1. Establishment of Basic Structures

During the early period of transforming efforts to control transnational crime into international suppression conventions, the major innovation was the establishment of the 'jurisdictional pillar' as part of the suppression conventions in

[21] In some respects, these early treaties were precursors of modern instruments (again regional, again general and not restricted to specific criminal activity) which provide for the coordination of concurring jurisdictional claims, such as the EU Framework Decision of 30 November 2009 on the Prevention and Settlement of Conflicts of Exercise of Jurisdiction in Criminal Proceedings (OJ L 328/42, 15 December 2009.

[22] Boister, *Transnational Criminal Law* (n 11) 135.

[23] Admittedly, the approach applied to the mapping exercise in this subchapter is simplistic. It does not specifically take account of the status of ratification, it does not take account of the specific subject matter of the respective treaty (and possible repercussions on the issue of jurisdiction) and it does not inquire into what was *not*, perhaps intentionally, included in a certain convention—for the opposite approach see Boister's account of jurisdiction in suppression conventions (*Transnational Criminal Law* (n 11) 138 et seq): he starts from the jurisdictional principles and follows them into the conventions.

[24] See also Boister, *Transnational Criminal Law* (n 11) 135 et seq; Clark 'Jurisdiction over Transnational Crime' (n 10) 91 et seq; Oehler, *Internationales Strafrecht* (n 9) 19 et seq.

the first place. In substance, the rules on jurisdiction were rather conservative. Conventions were concerned primarily with territorial jurisdiction, its specification and cautious extension, as well as flag-state jurisdiction (which, at that time, many understood as a sub-category of territoriality, *territoire flottant*). The basic rationale was that states agreed to apply their pre-existing jurisdiction to the specific transnational crimes covered by the conventions. This conservative approach which characterized conventional law in this early phase—the very idea that domestic law on jurisdiction should be left untouched, but simply extended to the conventional offences—is further demonstrated by the inclusion of general saving clauses, for the first time in the 1929 Counterfeiting Convention.[25] We can observe the following details:

In the 19th century, multilateral conventions such as the 1884 Submarine Cables Convention, the 1887 Liquor Traffic Convention and the 1910 White Slaves Convention include rules on criminal jurisdiction. The Submarine Cables Convention, which in many respects established a structure of international coordination that became the standard,[26] provides for flag-state jurisdiction and, failing that, for jurisdiction based on nationality 'in accordance with the general rules of criminal jurisdiction prescribed by the laws of that particular State, or by international treaties'.[27] The Liquor Traffic Convention concerns the sale or purchase of liquor on board of fishing boats and also provided for flag-state jurisdiction.[28] The White Slave Convention includes an expanded notion of territorial jurisdiction and explicitly includes cases where any one of the constitutive elements of the offence occurred within a state party's territory (principle of ubiquity).[29]

The 1920s brought a growth in the number of suppression conventions. While relying mostly on territorial and nationality jurisdiction, these conventions incorporated innovations in three areas: they dealt with the problem when extradition of a suspect is not possible (for factual or legal reasons in the requested state); they, following the blueprint of the White Slave Convention, addressed the issue of multiple places of commission or elements committed in different jurisdictions;

[25] Art 17 reads: 'The participation of a High Contracting Party in the present Convention shall not be interpreted as affecting that Party's attitude on the general question of criminal jurisdiction as a question of international law.' (art 17).

[26] See Boister, Chapter 3 in this book.

[27] Roger S Clark, 'Some Aspects of the Concept of International Criminal Law: Suppression Conventions, Jurisdiction, Submarine Cables and Lotus, (2011) 22 Criminal Law Forum 527.

[28] Art IV reads: 'The High Contracting Parties engaged to take, or to propose to their respective Legislatures, the necessary measures for insuring the execution of the present Convention, and especially for punishing, by either fine or imprisonment, or by both, those who may contravene Articles II. and III.' Art V reads: 'The Tribunals competent to take cognizance of infractions of Articles II. and III. are those of the country to which the accused vessel belongs. If vessels of different nationalities should be implicated in the same infraction, the Powers to which such vessels belong will mutually communicate to each other the Judgments given by the Tribunals.'

[29] '[E]ven when the various acts which together constitute the offence were committed in different countries'; for a similar provisions see the 1933 Convention for the Suppression of the Traffic in Women.

and finally, they included specific provisions for suspects who received the nationality of the requested state only after the commission of the offence.

A first clear and unequivocal application of both the principle of territoriality and the optional nationality principle ('when the laws of the country shall permit it') can be found in the 1923 Obscene Publications Convention. It explicitly makes provision for nationality jurisdiction over extraterritorial offences ('even if the constitutive elements of the offence were committed outside such territories').

The 1936 Drugs Convention followed this model and provides for the nationality principle, although still subject to the 'equal treatment clause'.[30]

The 1929 Counterfeiting Convention signified a major step forward and in many regards formed the model for later conventions. The Convention not only permits parties to apply the principle of protection, but embraces a *forum deprehensionis* rule (principle of vicarious administration of justice), which inspired modern versions of extradite or prosecute mechanisms. According to this rule, '[f]oreigners in the territory who have committed the offence abroad' should be punishable under the threefold condition that the 'internal legislation recognises as a general rule the principle of the prosecution of offences committed abroad', that 'extradition has been requested', and 'that the country to which application is made cannot hand over the person accused for some reason which has no connection with the offence'.[31]

The 1936 Drugs Convention incorporated the main features of the Counterfeiting Convention and further elaborated and specified the requirements of jurisdiction for offences committed by foreigners abroad.[32] An innovation included in the 1936 Drugs Convention was the mandatory application of the nationality principle as a replacement for extradition in countries where extradition of nationals was not recognized.[33] A similarly innovative feature was the extension of the nationality principle to cases where the offender 'has acquired his nationality after the commission of the offence'. Here again, treaty law reacted to specific challenges of non-extraditability. The 1937 Terrorism Convention is noteworthy in two regards. It explicitly includes jurisdiction for certain acts (conspiracy, incitement, participation, assistance) of transnational terrorism committed 'on his own territory with a view to an act of terrorism ... directed against another High Contracting Party, whatever the country in which the act of terrorism is to be

[30] 'Parties who possess extra-territorial jurisdiction in the territory of another High Contracting Party undertake to enact the necessary legislative provisions for punishing such of their nationals.'

[31] Art 9.

[32] 'The law of the country of refuge considers prosecution for offences committed abroad by foreigners admissible as a general rule.' This mechanism was specified by art 10 of the 1937 Terrorism Convention with the additional requirement that 'the foreigner is a national of a country which recognises the jurisdiction of its own courts in respect of offences committed abroad by foreigners'. Similar provisions can be found in the 1961 Single Convention on Narcotic Drugs and the 1971 Psychotropic Substances Convention.

[33] This was taken verbatim to the 1937 Terrorism Convention.

carried out'. And, remarkably, it contains a limiting clause providing that in cases of vicarious administration of justice, the forum state shall not undertake 'to pass a sentence exceeding the maximum sentence provided by the law of the country where the offence was committed'.

Between the late 1930s and 1970s, relatively little happened in the area of suppression conventions; perhaps states and the newly founded United Nations were too busy codifying the laws of war and the Nuremberg principles (eg in the Geneva Conventions and the Genocide Convention). However, noteworthy exceptions include the 1958 High Seas Convention, which confirms mandatory flag jurisdiction for the transport of slaves and flag as well as nationality jurisdiction for the breaking or injury of a submarine cable beneath the high seas. Another important innovation was the transformation of traditional flag-state jurisdiction to registration-state jurisdiction with regard to aircraft which, as mandatory jurisdiction, is included in the 1963 Tokyo Convention. In addition, for the first time, the Tokyo Convention includes what became a standard saving clause in many later conventions: 'This Convention does not exclude any criminal jurisdiction exercised in accordance with national law.'[34]

## 2. Crystallization of a Model Framework

A new milestone was set by the 1970 Hijacking Convention, which represented a blueprint for many conventions to come. The Convention was innovative mainly in four respects. It introduces what subsequently has become the basic structure and language of jurisdictional rules in suppression conventions. It includes landing state jurisdiction as a separate and novel basis for jurisdiction. It embraces the modern version of the *aut derdere aut iudicare* clause for the first time: irrespective of where the offence was committed, if an alleged offender is found in the territory of a party it must either extradite or submit the case to its competent authorities for the purposes of prosecution.

Article 4

1. Each Contracting State shall take such measures as may be necessary to establish its jurisdiction over the offence . . ., in the following cases:
   (a) when the offence is committed on board an aircraft registered in that State;
   (b) when the aircraft on board which the offence is committed lands in its territory with the alleged offender still on board;

[34] For similar provisions see eg Terrorist Bombings Convention, art 6(5) and Palermo Convention, art 15(6).

(c) when the offence is committed on board an aircraft leased without crew to a lessee who has his principal place of business or, if the lessee has no such place of business, his permanent residence, in that State.

2. Each Contracting State shall likewise take such measures as may be necessary to establish its jurisdiction over the offence in the case where the alleged offender is present in its territory and it does not extradite him . . . .
3. This Convention does not exclude any criminal jurisdiction exercised in accordance with national law.

Article 7

The Contracting State in the territory of which the alleged offender is found shall, if it does not extradite him, be obliged, without exception whatsoever and whether or not the offence was committed in its territory, to submit the case to its competent authorities for the purpose of prosecution. Those authorities shall take their decision in the same manner as in the case of any ordinary offence of a serious nature under the law of that State.

In addition, the Convention was a pioneering treaty in yet another aspect: it establishes a duty to notify other states concerned. With the (deliberate) establishment of overlapping jurisdiction, there was a need to coordinate conflicts of jurisdiction and, ultimately, to create mechanisms for determining the 'best venue' for prosecution. The reporting system provided for in the Hijacking Convention was a first step in this direction. In later conventions, this duty was extended to a more comprehensive obligation to consult and coordinate.[35]

The 1971 Montreal Convention largely copied the Hijacking Convention, with the exception that it included the principle of territoriality again.[36] Similarly, the 1979 Hostage Taking Convention followed the Hague blueprint but included two significant innovations: optional resident jurisdiction—as an extension of the nationality principle—still, however, limited to stateless persons;[37] and passive

[35] See, inter alia, 1971 Convention, art 6 and 1979 Hostage Taking Convention, art 6(2), which reads: 'The custody or other measures referred to in paragraph 1 of this article shall be notified without delay directly or through the Secretary-General of the United Nations to: (a) the State where the offence was committed; (b) the State against which compulsion has been directed or attempted; (c) the State of which the natural or juridical person against whom compulsion has been directed or attempted is a national; (d) the State of which the hostage is a national or in the territory of which he has his habitual residence; (e) the State of which the alleged offender is a national or, if he is a stateless person, in the territory of which he has his habitual residence; (f) the international intergovernmental organization against which compulsion has been directed or attempted; (g) all other States concerned.' See also 1997 OECD Bribery Convention, art 4(3); 1999 Terrorist Financing Convention, art 7(5); Palermo Convention, art 15(5); and Budapest Convention, art 2(5).

[36] The Montreal Convention was 'updated' in the 2010 Beijing Convention on the Suppression of Unlawful Acts Relating to International Civil Aviation. See Clark, 'Jurisdiction over Transnational Crime' (n 10) 91.

[37] Art 5 reads: 'by any of its nationals or, if that State considers it appropriate, by those stateless persons who have their habitual residence in its territory'. See for similar provisions 1988 SUA Convention,

personality jurisdiction,[38] a particularly controversial jurisdictional principle. The principle of protection was also included to cover acts committed 'in order to compel that State to do or abstain from doing any act'.

The 1984 Convention against Torture and the 1988 SUA Convention (Maritime Navigation) confirmed this new model. In addition, the SUA Convention contained, for the first time, the language which from then on was simply copied by all modern conventions: Accordingly, '[e]ach State Party shall take such measures as may be necessary to establish its jurisdiction over the offences set forth in ... when the offence is committed: ... ; A State Party may also establish its jurisdiction over any such offence when:'. The 1988 Drug Trafficking Convention, while following the model as regards structure and content, explicitly extends territorial jurisdiction to intended effects or consequences.[39]

## 3. Consolidation and Extension

The 1990s and early 2000s brought a further series of major suppression conventions—on terrorism, organized crime, cybercrime and corruption—most of them drafted under the auspices of the United Nations.[40] They largely follow previous conventions. The 1997 Terrorist Bombings Convention, in addition, authorized (but did not require) the establishment of passive personality jurisdiction, protective jurisdiction and resident jurisdiction (however, again limited to stateless persons). The 1999 Terrorist Financing Convention provided for mandatory territorial, flag and nationality jurisdiction and included the standard *aut dedere* rule.[41] Optional jurisdiction was provided for under the principles of protection,[42] passive personality and residency (for stateless persons). Similarly, the 2000 Optional Protocol on the Sale of Children included optional passive personality jurisdiction.

The 2000 Palermo Convention established probably the most comprehensive jurisdictional regime in a modern suppression convention. In terms of providing

1997 Terrorist Bombings Convention and the 1999 Financing of Terrorism Convention. See also the 1988 Drug Trafficking Convention which, however, extends jurisdiction to *every* foreigner, and is not limited to *stateless* residents ('a person who has his habitual residence in its territory' (art 4); similarly art 5 of the 1996 Inter-American Convention against Corruption.

38 '[W]ith respect to a hostage who is a national of that State, if that State considers it appropriate.'

39 Art 4 reads: 'The offence ... is committed outside its territory with a view to the commission, within its territory.

40 ' In this respect, the 1997 OECD Bribery Convention is an exception. Noteworthy may be that it provides for mandatory nationality jurisdiction and applies a broad notion of territoriality (art 4: 'in whole or in part in its territory').

41 Art 7(4).

42 Art 7(2)(b) and (c) read: 'The offence was directed towards or resulted in the carrying out of an offence ... against a State or government facility of that State abroad, including diplomatic or consular premises of that State' or 'committed in an attempt to compel that State to do or abstain from doing any act' art 7(2)(c).

for mandatory jurisdiction, the Palermo Convention was, however, relatively narrow. State parties were obliged to establish territorial and flag-state jurisdiction; even the *aut dedere* mechanism as a mandatory rule was limited to specific offences, and beyond that the establishment of *aut dedere* jurisdiction was left to the discretion of the state parties. In terms of permissive jurisdiction, however, the Palermo Convention was remarkably comprehensive. One reason for this—relatively broad permissive, relatively narrow prescriptive jurisdiction—may be the broad definition of offences in this Convention.[43] In sum, article 15 of the Palermo Convention represents an up to date example of the elements of a jurisdictional regime in suppression conventions:

Article 15

1. Each State Party shall adopt such measures as may be necessary to establish its jurisdiction over the offences ... when:
   (a) The offence is committed in the territory of that State Party; or
   (b) The offence is committed on board a vessel that is flying the flag of that State Party or an aircraft that is registered under the laws of that State Party at the time that the offence is committed.
2. Subject to article 4 of this Convention, a State Party may also establish its jurisdiction over any such offence when:
   (a) The offence is committed against a national of that State Party;
   (b) The offence is committed by a national of that State Party or a stateless person who has his or her habitual residence in its territory; or
   (c) The offence is:
      (i) ... committed outside its territory with a view to the commission of a serious crime within its territory;
      (ii) ... committed outside its territory with a view to the commission of an offence ... within its territory.
3. For the purposes of article ... , each State Party shall adopt such measures as may be necessary to establish its jurisdiction over the offences covered by this Convention when the alleged offender is present in its territory and it does not extradite such person solely on the ground that he or she is one of its nationals.
4. Each State Party may also adopt such measures as may be necessary to establish its jurisdiction over the offences covered by this Convention when the alleged offender is present in its territory and it does not extradite him or her.
5. If a State Party exercising its jurisdiction under paragraph I or 2 of this article has been notified, or has otherwise learned, that one or more other States

[43] See for details Forlati, chapter 13 in this book.

> Parties are conducting an investigation, prosecution or judicial proceeding in respect of the same conduct, the competent authorities of those States Parties shall, as appropriate, consult one another with a view to coordinating their actions.

Adopted shortly after, the 2001 Budapest Convention (on Cybercrime) again followed the standard model. Here, we find a variation as regards the nationality principle which is made mandatory only 'if the offence is punishable under criminal law where it was committed or if the offence is committed outside the territorial jurisdiction of any State'. Again with only minor variation, the 2003 UNCAC (Corruption) and the 2005 Nuclear Terrorism Convention follow this blueprint. In particular, passive personality jurisdiction and active resident jurisdiction (limited to stateless persons, or not) now seem to be standard elements of suppression conventions.[44] Another innovation included in these recent conventions concerns the general protection of sovereignty through a specific provision (eg UNTOC, UNCAC).[45] Accordingly, states parties were obliged to carry out their obligations under the convention 'in a manner consistent with the principles of sovereign equality and territorial integrity of States and that of non-intervention in the domestic affairs of other States'.[46]

## IV. Jurisdiction in Suppression Conventions: Trends and Directions

From a historical perspective, the development of criminal jurisdiction in multilateral suppression conventions can be conceptualized as a linear process—along the lines of greater standardization, extension and uniformization. It developed in three phases: following the establishment of basic structures and the fundamental paradigm at the beginning of the 20th century, the blueprint for modern suppression conventions emerged in the 1970s before the turn from the 20th to the 21st century led to further consolidation and dissemination. Today, as a result of this process we find a 'toolbox' comprising standard elements from which the drafters of suppression conventions can pick.

In terms of *format*, we can observe the emergence, over time, of a standard language simply copied from one convention to another. This includes the concept of providing for a multitude of bases of jurisdiction which again were structured as obligatory bases (prescriptive jurisdiction) and optional bases (permissive

[44] See also the 2005 Draft Convention on Terrorism and the 2019 ILC Draft Articles on the Prevention and Punishment of Crimes Against Humanity.

[45] See also Forlati, Chapter 13 in this book. Compare art 2(2) and (3) of the 1988 Illicit Traffic in Narcotic Drugs and Psychotropic Substances Convention.

[46] UNCAC, art XX(1)..

jurisdiction).[47] The fact that the establishment of jurisdiction was sometimes left to the discretion of the state parties may indeed indicate a certain hesitation about the legitimacy or perhaps the necessity of the jurisdictional bases concerned.[48] This trend—standardization and specification—can also be observed in other areas of transnational criminal law.[49] Relatively recently, we see the emergence of saving clauses which are supposed to guarantee the sovereign decisions of state parties. While the early conventions attempted to take account of sovereignty by connecting the conventional duties to pre-existing (domestic) legislation, modern treaties operated with stricter conventional obligations but included general safeguard clauses protecting legitimate claims of sovereignty.[50]

In terms of *substance*, treaties oscillated between confirmation and innovation. We have seen two different developments. On the one hand, specific bases of jurisdiction were confirmed (by way of replication), further specified and/or elaborated and—as an overall trend—extended. As a result, we can observe the continuous extension of the jurisdictional reach, be it mandatory or optional.[51] On the other hand, novel bases of jurisdiction were included, providing for 'innovation by treaty'. Regarding these innovative elements we can further distinguish two different types. A first type is *transnational criminal law specific* and does not reflect (at the time) pre-existing concepts in (domestic) law. This type includes the *aut dedere aut iudicare* clauses and the notification/coordination mechanisms which are part of many more recent conventions. The need to provide for the latter results from the idea of creating a tight net of competing jurisdictional regimes through suppression conventions—an idea which indeed raises concerns such as double jeopardy and, ultimately, creates a need for determining priorities in the exercise of jurisdiction.[52] The second type of 'innovation by treaty' concerns elements which do reflect *pre-existing concepts in some domestic legislations*, which are then shared in a top down approach with other legislations. This type includes, inter alia, country (or rather: region) specific extensions of personal jurisdiction (such as passive personality and resident) and territorial jurisdiction (such as landing-state and effects), which were then, through the suppression conventions, globalized.

[47] Clark, 'Jurisdiction over Transnational Crime' (n 10) 95.
[48] See Boister, *Transnational Criminal Law* (n 11) 138.
[49] See eg Petzsche, Chapter 18 in this book, for the modes of liability.
[50] In the conventions we find two types of saving clauses. A (classical) saving clause for the protection of the authority of the state party to determine its criminal jurisdiction. A (more recent) safeguard clause for the protection of the sovereignty of other states parties (and actually third states).
[51] It may be interesting to note that a similar development towards a standardization and extension can be observed on the regional level, in particular in Europe, within the Council of Europe and the Union, eg in the 2005 European Terrorism Convention, the 2007 Lanzarote Convention (eg mandatory resident jurisdiction), the 2011 Istanbul Convention, the 2017 Terrorism Directive and the 2011 Sexual Abuse and Sexual Exploitation Directive (permisse active and passive resident jurisdiction).
[52] As Clark, 'Jurisdiction over Transnational Crime' (n 10) 103, correctly highlights, early expressions of a 'priority system' can be found in the various Status of Forces Agreements.

## V. Conclusion: Diffusion, Custom, Punitiveness

We have seen that during the past 150 years a significant corpus of rules on jurisdiction emerged in treaty law. Together they form a comprehensive regime of transnational jurisdiction in transnational criminal law. Over time, a standard approach developed which is, basically, part of every suppression convention: The state party as a *forum* state promises to establish (and eventually exercise) its jurisdiction. Conventional rules on jurisdiction can be prescriptive ('shall establish') or permissive ('may establish'). By their nature, the respective treaty obligations are (1) international, (2) positive (as opposed to negative/prohibitive) and (3) relative (as opposed to absolute). Furthermore, the function of the provisions on jurisdiction is—measured against the overall concern of the conventions to provide for the criminalization of specific offences—(4) ancillary and (5) affects implementation, interpretation and, ultimately, the shaping of custom. We have also seen that overall trends include standard setting and expansion of jurisdiction. As Boister points out, some of the jurisdictional grounds are very specific and difficult to categorize; often the grounds reflect national approaches.[53] Given the specific understanding of criminal jurisdiction inherent to every domestic legal system (and the respective preconception of those educated in this domestic legal system), the 'challenge' for the drafters of the conventions has been—similar to the one concerning the modes of liability and extradition, and often enough different from the one concerning the definition of crimes, which were 'new' or 'unique'—to agree on a common legal framework. Often enough, this need to integrate diverging preconceptions resulted in including not the 'best of both worlds', but 'both worlds'.[54]

To conclude, it seems useful to connect the historical developments with some broader criminal jurisdiction and transnational criminal law themes, some of them were addressed in the introduction. Generally, the diffusion of jurisdictional norms may be indicative of the general trend to internationalize legal concepts or specific norms through treaties. Our historical analysis has confirmed Boister's assumption of 'incremental and radical change'. As he noted, suppression conventions developed at slow pace with rather conservative obligations relating to the extension of jurisdiction, but occasionally, sparked by events, a change occurred with regard to extraterritorial jurisdiction. Examples for such 'innovation through international agreement' are passive personality jurisdiction, resident jurisdiction and landing-state jurisdiction. Certainly, the change is guided by the subject matter and reflects certain types of criminal activity. Terrorism may be an example. Yet, such 'radical change' becomes problematic when observed in light of another

[53] Boister, *Transnational Criminal Law* (n 11) 138.

[54] Examples are the inclusion of both, broad effects jurisdiction (which has its roots in the territoriality oriented Anglo-American tradition) and passive personality jurisdiction (which has its roots in the personality oriented Romano-Germanic tradition).

trend: the spill-over from (sectoral) transnational criminal law to (general) domestic criminal law. It appears namely as if the transnational criminal law serves as a catalyst of domestic law reform in the area of criminal jurisdiction—even beyond the specific offences provided for in the convention.

Indeed, it is important to understand that suppression conventions have repercussions on criminal jurisdiction in domestic law—directly, as regards the specific offences, but also indirectly. As treaty practice, quasi-universal provisions, such as those in UNTOC, significantly impact on the course of general limitations of (domestic) criminal jurisdiction under customary international law. Although the effect of the suppression conventions as treaty law is restricted *ratione materiae* and *personae* they do touch upon the formation of customary international law. In fact, there is a significant interaction between the three levels of regulating jurisdiction: national legislation, international treaty regimes and customary international law. It becomes apparent that rules on criminal jurisdiction in transnational criminal law are the product of a 'circle of trans-judicial dialogue'. Jurisdiction in transnational criminal law flows from domestic practice and legislation and in turn shapes the international law of jurisdiction. At the same time, the transnational law of jurisdiction (as expressed by the suppression conventions) speaks back to the domestic level since it shapes, as treaty practice, the permissive rules under (customary) international law which in turn limit the discretion of the national lawmaker.

Finally, this short history supports the assumption of a general increase in punitiveness—reflected, inter alia, in the continuous expansion of the ambit of the criminal law. In that, the transnational law of criminal jurisdiction follows suit with the troubling overall direction of criminal law reform in the majority of domestic jurisdictions.[55]

[55] Generally, we witness a trend of continuous extension and a decrease of safeguards since the 19th century; for details see Jeßberger, *Der transnationale Geltungsbereich* (n 6) 148 et seq.

# 20

# The Making of Modern International Extradition Law

*Joanna Harrington*

## I. Introduction

For many, extradition law is a highly technical field designed to accomplish a specific task. That task is the securing, upon request, of the transfer from one state to another of a person wanted for trial or imprisonment. For many states, these transfers are governed by a national law, the application of which inevitably connects to other areas of law, most notably criminal law, but also constitutional law and administrative law, as well as broader discussions about state sovereignty, comity between nations and questions of safe havens and asylum. Indeed, some extradition requests may lead to the calling into question of the very nature of another state's criminal justice system, with policy repercussions for inter-state relations. However, unlike expulsion or exile, extradition law was also designed to extend some protections to the person wanted for surrender, with this aspect often downplayed by those who focus on extradition as simply a tool deployed by prosecutors for bringing serious criminal offenders to justice. This sense of extradition as being purpose-built also explains why reform efforts often push for efficiencies and greater expedition, even though delays are likely inherent in any scheme dealing with jurisdictional differences where fundamental rights are at stake.

This chapter focuses on the making of modern international extradition law. Many experts, dating back to the work of Beccaria, have long believed that extradition plays a role in diminishing crime;[1] a position that encourages engagement in the law's development, although Beccaria recognized the need for a balanced approach that also took into account the liberty interests of the individuals concerned.[2] States make extradition law on a reciprocal basis through the conclusion of bilateral extradition treaties, regional arrangements and multilateral crime suppression conventions. Over time, these efforts have fostered a standard approach

[1] Ivan A Shearer, *Extradition in International Law* (Manchester UP 1971) 10–11 (hereafter Shearer, *Extradition*); Christopher L Blakesley, 'The Practice of Extradition from Antiquity to Modern France and the United States: A Brief History' (1981) 4 BC Intl & Comp LR 39, 49 (hereafter Blakesley, 'Brief History').

[2] Neil Boister, *An Introduction to Transnational Criminal Law* (2nd edn, OUP 2018) 354–55.

Joanna Harrington, *The Making of Modern International Extradition Law* In: *Histories of Transnational Criminal Law*.
Edited by: Neil Boister, Sabine Gless and Florian Jeßberger, Oxford University Press. © Joanna Harrington 2021.
DOI: 10.1093/oso/9780192845702.003.0021

such that certain principles may be said to form an international law of extradition.[3] Examples include the principle of double criminality, the rule of specialty, the optional non-extradition of nationals and the exception to extradition for political offences, although the strict application of these principles has waned, leading to reliance on non-discrimination clauses and human rights protections. It is also clear from an historical perspective that the development of extradition law has been shaped by its interactions with other matters of law, from peace treaties and a sovereign's right to grant asylum, to more recent efforts to encourage regional solidarity, suppress the commission of transnational crime and protect human rights.

## II. Interactions with French and English law

The origins of today's extradition law are well established as being French. France enacted an extradition law in 1830, which through the conclusion of bilateral extradition treaties would be replicated elsewhere, beginning with an 1834 Franco-Belgian arrangement.[4] The French word 'extradition' later became the term used in English law for transfers as between sovereign states,[5] although England was slow to make treaties, unlike France and the United States,[6] likely because of a practice of providing refuge for political offenders.[7] However, later England did recognize a need for an extradition law of general application,[8] with the Extradition Act 1870[9] going on to serve as the legal framework for not just Britain, but also many Commonwealth states. The British also developed a scheme for what was termed the 'rendition' or 'return' of persons as between states with the same overarching sovereign, reflecting the view that the foreign affairs concerns associated with extradition were not applicable within the British Empire where all persons (theoretically) were subject to the same system of justice. The statutory basis for this scheme was the Fugitive Offenders Act 1881,[10] with the bifurcated approach

[3] Described as a 'significant corpus of conventional law' in James Crawford, *Brownlie's Principles of Public International Law* (9th edn, OUP 2019) 465.

[4] Christine van den Wijngaert, *The Political Offence Exception to Extradition: The Delicate Problem of Balancing the Rights of the Individual and the International Public Order* (Kluwer 1980) 4 (hereafter van den Wijngaert, *Political Offence Exception*).

[5] Shearer, *Extradition* (n 1) 12; Ivor Stanbrook and Clive Stanbrook, *Extradition: Law and Practice* (2nd edn, OUP 2000) 4, para 1.05 (hereafter Stanbrook and Stanbrook, *Extradition*).

[6] See Blakesley, 'Brief History' (n 1).

[7] See further Caroline Shaw, *Britannia's Embrace: Modern Humanitarianism and the Imperial Origins of Refugee Relief* (OUP 2015). History shows that public opinion can favour the non-surrender of certain fugitives, such as was the case for escaped slaves who made it to Canada by means of an 'underground railway'.

[8] Previously a separate act was required to implement each treaty: HC Deb 16 June 1870 vol 202 301.

[9] 33 & 34 Vic, c 52.

[10] 44 & 45 Vic, c 69.

it fostered also adopted by many Commonwealth states. Indeed, the two schemes stayed apart for over 100 years, both in Britain and elsewhere.[11]

## III. Interactions with Peace Treaties

An earlier connection can, however, be drawn between extradition and war, with a number of peace treaties providing for the surrender of fugitives. An example often given is that of a 13th-century peace treaty between the Egyptians and the Hittites that contained provisions concerning the surrender of fugitives following a war for control over Syria.[12] Mention may also be made of a peace treaty forced upon King William of Scotland by King Henry II of England in 1174, which provided for the surrender of both traitors and felons.[13]

However, the best example of the development by way of a peace treaty of what we today would call 'extradition' is the 'Jay' Treaty of 1794 between Britain and the United States, with the treaty being named after the American statesman, John Jay, who negotiated its contents while serving as the first Chief Justice of the United States.[14] Jay's Treaty (as it is also known) aimed to avert war through the renewal of trade relations and the resolution of issues arising from the American Revolutionary War, with its proper title indicating clearly that it was a 'Treaty of Amity, Commerce, and Navigation'. However, the 'Jay' Treaty also served in a limited, but practical sense, as the first extradition agreement to be concluded by either state, and as such it established a basic framework upon which each would build in later treaties.[15]

Article 27 of the 'Jay' Treaty was not an elaborate extradition provision. By its terms, it imposed a mutually agreed obligation to 'deliver up to justice, all persons who being charged with murder or forgery committed within the jurisdiction of either', provided 'that this shall only be done on such evidence of criminality as according to the laws of the place, where the fugitive or person so charged shall be found, would justify his apprehension and commitment for trial, if the offence had there been committed'. While rudimentary in nature, article 27 nevertheless shows an early embrace of certain themes that still have purchase within international extradition law, such as the desire for some evidence in support of the criminal charge, as well as some measure of double criminality as between the two states

[11] Consolidation came with the passage of the Extradition Act 1989, c 33 (UK), the Extradition Act 1988, No 4, 1988 (Australia), and the Extradition Act, SC 1999, c 18 (Canada).

[12] See Georg Schwarzenberger, *The Dynamics of International Law* (Professional Books 1967) 40–48, esp 46–47.

[13] Paul O'Higgins, 'The History of Extradition in British Practice, 1174–1794' (1964) 13(2) Indian YB Intl Affairs 78, 80–81.

[14] See further Samuel F Bemis, *Jay's Treaty: A Study in Commerce and Diplomacy* (2nd edn, Yale University Press 1962).

[15] Shearer, *Extradition* (n 1) 12–13, 152.

involved. Indeed, it was this desire for double criminality that later led to the enumeration or 'listing' of what were to be considered extraditable crimes in many bilateral extradition treaties.

Although it was not used to surrender many persons,[16] article 27 did serve as the precursor provision to article 10 of the 1842 Webster-Ashburton Treaty,[17] which extended the British-US extradition relationship to include arson, piracy and robbery. With further additions made in 1899, 1900 and 1905,[18] and Canada's post-independence succession to the Treaty's terms, article 10 would go on to serve as the basis for Canada-US extradition relations until 1976.[19]

A similar example can also be found in the Treaty of Amiens of 1802, which temporarily brought peace during the Napoleonic Wars. Drafted by Britain, France, Spain and the Batavian Republic (Netherlands), article 20 of the Treaty of Amiens contained a reciprocal agreement to 'deliver up to justice' persons accused of 'murder, forgery or fraudulent bankruptcy'. While article 20 was never made operational due to the return to war,[20] it did plant the seed for a mutually beneficial 'deliver up' obligation that later found expression in such bilateral treaties as an 1843 British-French arrangement, which also included a bar on extraditing nationals.[21]

A century later, extradition's connection to conflict resolution would arise again within the most important of the peace treaties bringing an end to World War I.[22] Article 227 of the Treaty of Versailles provided expressly for a request for surrender to be made for the German Kaiser who had found sanctuary in the Netherlands in the final days of the war. The provision prompted much debate within the Netherlands, with some relying on a country's right to provide asylum to those in need, while others posited that acts of war could not be treated as political crimes and thus should be considered extraditable offences.[23] In refusing the request, however, the Netherlands relied upon its status of neutrality during the war and

[16] ibid 14. Canada and the United States, however, continued to surrender fugitives to one another even after the treaty lapsed in 1807: GV La Forest, *Extradition To and From Canada* (Hauser Press 1961) 2.

[17] Treaty to Settle and Define the Boundaries between the Territories of the United States and the Possessions of Her Britannic Majesty in North America; for the Final Suppression of the African Slave Trade; and for the Giving Up of Criminals Fugitive from Justice, in Certain Cases (signed 9 August 1842, entered into force 13 October 1843) TS 119, 8 Stat 572. The treaty is typically known by the surnames of its lead negotiators, US Secretary of State Daniel Webster and the British envoy to the United States, Lord Ashburton.

[18] Shearer, *Extradition* (n 1) 134.

[19] Treaty on Extradition between the Government of Canada and the Government of the United States (signed 3 December 1971, entered into force 22 March 1976) Can TS 1976 No 3, 11 ILM 22 (1972), replacing the use of a list approach with a conduct and punishability standard.

[20] Shearer, *Extradition* (n 1) 14.

[21] Later reflected in the Treaty between Great Britain and France for the Mutual Surrender of Fugitive Criminals (signed 14 August 1876), art II.

[22] Treaty of Peace between the Allied Powers and Associated Powers and Germany (Treaty of Versailles) (opened for signature 28 June 1919, entered into force 10 January 1920) UKTS 1919 No 4.

[23] A summary of the Dutch views can be found in William A Schabas, *The Trial of the Kaiser* (OUP 2018) 75–79.

its lack of a legal obligation to surrender the Kaiser, not being a party to the Treaty of Versailles.[24] The Kaiser remained in the Netherlands until his death in 1941, but a precedent had been set, with the United States announcing in 1942 that the successful close of World War II would have to include provision for the surrender of war criminals to an international tribunal.[25]

## IV. Interactions with Asylum Law

Western European support for the inclusion of a political exclusion clause within extradition law dates back to the 1830s.[26] Its development accords a degree of respect for a state's right to grant asylum to a foreign national, while also embracing a distinction that is often made between what are termed 'ordinary criminals' and another state's political enemies. Over time, however, this distinction has evolved to reflect more accurately the position taken much earlier by Hugo Grotius in 1625, who wrote that '[a]sylum is for the benefit of those who suffer from undeserved hate, and not for those who have injured society or other people.'[27]

First established by Belgium in 1833,[28] and then incorporated into the 1834 Franco-Belgian extradition treaty,[29] the political offence exception to extradition was designed to ensure that the leaders of liberation movements who had escaped from a repressive regime were not handed back to their oppressors. By designating their crimes as ones that were political in nature, a legal basis was created for refusing an otherwise valid extradition request.[30] It did not take long, however, for the need for an 'exception to the exception' to be identified, with Belgium again taking the lead. In 1856, Belgium amended its extradition law so as to add a provision to disapply the political offence exception to attempts on the life of a foreign head of state, having earlier received a French request for the extradition of a would-be assassin of the Emperor Napoleon III.[31] Known as the *attentat* or Belgian clause,[32] the provision makes clear that assassination attempts on foreign heads

[24] ibid 269, 276. Had the Kaiser returned to Germany, the German government would have maintained the constitutional bar to the surrender of a German citizen, then found in art 112 of the Weimar Constitution.

[25] See further Robert G Neumann, 'Neutral States and the Extradition of War Criminals' (1951) 45(3) AJIL 495 (hereafter Neumann, 'Neutral States').

[26] See generally van den Wijngaert, *Political Offence Exception* (n 4). For an Eastern European perpsective, see Martin E Gold, 'Non-extradition for Political Offences: The Communist Perspective' (1970) 11 Harvard Intl LJ 191.

[27] Hugo Grotius, *De Jure Belli ac Pacis* (1625), cited in Stanbrook and Stanbrook, *Extradition* (n 5) 4, para 1.03.

[28] See Neumann, 'Neutral States' (n 25) 505, fn 57.

[29] Shearer, *Extradition* (n 1) 18; van den Wijngaert, *Political Offence Exception* (n 4) 12–13.

[30] van den Wijngaert, *Political Offence Exception* (n 4) 99, 135–36.

[31] ibid 14.

[32] Research in International Law, 'Extradition' (1935) 29 AJIL Supp 15, 114 (hereafter Research in International Law, 'Extradition').

of state, their families or on a member of a foreign government are not to be considered political crimes, with the provision later found duplicated in many extradition statutes and treaties, albeit not without its detractors.[33] The prevalence of syndicalist movements in Europe would later generate another 'exception to the exception' for anarchists, who were deemed the enemy of all governments.[34]

A century later, and with the lessons of World War II at hand, further efforts were made to ensure that the scope of the political offence exception did not lead to the provision of asylum for those who commit the most egregious crimes. To this end, provisions were included within the 1948 Genocide Convention and the 1949 Geneva Conventions to ensure that acts of genocide and war crimes were not to be considered political crimes for the purpose of extradition.[35] States also recognized that the right to seek asylum was a fundamental human right, but one with limits, with article 14(2) of the 1948 Universal Declaration of Human Rights making clear that the right to seek and enjoy asylum 'may not be invoked in the case of prosecutions genuinely arising from non-political crimes.'[36]A similar balancing of interests was also incorporated into the 1951 Refugees Convention, which makes clear that its provisions do not apply to any person who 'has committed a crime against peace, a war crime, or a crime against humanity' or who 'has committed a serious non-political crime outside the country of refuge prior to his admission to that country as a refugee'.[37]

For common law countries, however, the practical impact of the political offence exception was diminished by its absence from the fugitive offenders scheme that was used within the British Empire, which at its height held sway over almost a quarter of the world's population. With everyone living under the broad sweep of the same political authority, it had been thought unnecessary to provide for the grant of asylum for political offenders; an approach that would attract some controversy as former colonies became independent.[38] It was not until 1966, and the

[33] ibid 116–17.

[34] Alona E Evans, 'Reflections upon the Political Offense in International Practice' (1963) 57 AJIL 1, 12–13. See also *In re Meunier*, [1894] 2 QB 415.

[35] Convention on the Prevention and Punishment of the Crime of Genocide (opened for signature 9 December 1948, entered into force 12 January 1951) 78 UNTS 277, art VII; Convention (I) for the Amelioration of the Condition of the Wounded and Sick in Armed Forces in the Field (opened for signature 12 August 1949, entered into force 21 October 1950) 75 UNTS 31, art 49 (hereafter Geneva I); Convention (II) for the Amelioration of the Condition of the Wounded, Sick and Shipwrecked Members of Armed Forces at Sea (opened for signature 12 August 1949, entered into force 21 October 1950) 75 UNTS 85, art 50 (hereafter Geneva II); Convention (III) Relative to the Treatment of Prisoners of War (opened for signature 12 August 1949, entered into force 21 October 1950) 75 UNTS 135, art 129 (hereafter Geneva III); Convention (IV) Relative to the Protection of Civilian Persons in Time of War (opened for signature 12 August 1949, entered into force 21 October 1950) 75 UNTS 287, art 146 (hereafter Geneva IV).

[36] GA Res 217A (111), UN Doc A/810 (1948).

[37] Convention Relating to the Status of Refugees (opened for signature 28 July 1951, entered into force 22 April 1954) 189 UNTS 137, art 1(F).

[38] Stanbrook and Stanbrook, *Extradition* (n 5) 10–11, paras 1.28–1.29.

adoption of a new scheme for the rendition of fugitives,[39] that extradition as between Commonwealth states featured all the standard aspects of modern extradition practice, including the political offence exception.

## V. Interactions with Multilateralism

Although extradition law developed primarily through a large network of bilateral extradition treaties, the possibility of concluding a general extradition convention did attract some interest in the early decades of the 20th century. However, after studying the matter, experts within the League of Nations concluded that 'the difficulties in the way were too great for such solution to be realizable in the near future'.[40] The torch then passed to a group of eminent American academics in the 1930s, who published an extensive study of extradition law under the auspices of the Research in International Law programme at Harvard University, including a text for a proposed convention of intended universal application.[41] The 'Harvard Draft', however, failed to attract support from states, leaving multilateral efforts to be best pursued on a regional basis, among states with a shared respect for their legal traditions.

After World War II, it was the Council of Europe that led the way with the adoption of the multilateral 1957 European Extradition Convention, being an arrangement that today applies as between forty-seven European states and three non-European states (Israel, South Africa and South Korea).[42] This multilateral effort has also encouraged an important change in extradition law, with the Council of Europe states abandoning the 'list approach' in favour of identifying an extraditable offence by reference to the maximum length of the sentence to be imposed. Such an approach allows for the easier inclusion of new offences into an extradition scheme, including those prompted by technological developments. The 1957 European Extradition Convention was also the first multilateral extradition regime to embrace a 'discrimination clause' requiring the refusal of extradition where there are 'substantial grounds for believing that a request ... has been made for the purpose of prosecuting or punishing a person on account of his or her race, religion, nationality or political opinion'.[43] Clearly inspired by the Refugees Convention, it also serves as the precursor for the non-discrimination clause found in the United

[39] Scheme relating to the Rendition of Fugitive Offenders within the Commonwealth, Cmnd 3008, 1966.

[40] See the 'Report on Extradition' adopted by the League's Committee of Experts for the Progressive Codification of International Law in January 1926, reprinted in (1926) 20 AJIL Special Supp 242, 243.

[41] Reproduced in Research in International Law, 'Extradition' (n 32) 21–31.

[42] Art 30 of the Convention expressly permits the accession of non-Council of Europe member states.

[43] Art 3(2).

Nations Convention against Transnational Organized Crime (UNTOC),[44] among others.[45]

As for the evidentiary basis for an extradition request, the 1957 European Extradition Convention also departed from a common past practice by avoiding the imposition of a 'prima facie' case requirement. The latter permits the refusal of an extradition request on the basis that the evidence justifying the individual's committal for trial is considered insufficient under the laws of the requested state. Many common law countries, as well as the Nordic states, had required such protections for extradition to take place, as do the Geneva Conventions,[46] but the drafters of the pan-European scheme saw this requirement as a cause for delay, and a matter to be regulated by national procedures. Later, a smaller sub-set of European states, under the auspices of the European Union (EU), agreed first to simplify their extradition procedures as between themselves to secure greater expedition,[47] and then to replace them entirely with a system of surrender based on a European Arrest Warrant, underpinned by the principle of mutual recognition for each of their legal systems.[48] Concerns, however, remain that the gains for states secured by an EU-wide warrant diminish respect for individual rights.

Success within Europe also helped rekindle earlier efforts within the Americas, leading to the eventual adoption of the 1981 Inter-American Extradition Convention.[49] However, the prospects for a UN-wide extradition treaty remain slim, given the inability of many states to place a sufficient degree of trust in the legal systems of other states. Instead, efforts within the UN have focused on two other routes for the making of international extradition law. One route has focused on the compilation of best practices and the development of a 'Model Treaty' to influence the drafting of future bilateral arrangements,[50] while the other has been concerned with the inclusion of provisions within multilateral crime suppression treaties that serve to deem the proscribed offences as extraditable crimes. Following the lead of the 1970 Hague Hijacking Convention,[51] these provisions

[44] Art 16(14).

[45] See eg United Nations Convention Against Corruption (UNCAC), art 44(15).

[46] Geneva I (n 35), art 49; Geneva II (n 35), art 50; Geneva III (n 35), art 129; Geneva IV (n 35), art 146.

[47] Convention on Simplified Extradition Procedure between the Member States of the European Union [1995] OJ C 78/01, as amended by Convention relating to Extradition between the Member States of the European Union [1996] OJ C 313/02. See further Mark Mackerel and Susan Nash, 'Extradition and the European Union' (1997) 46(4) ICLQ 948.

[48] See further Council Framework Decision 2002/584/JHA [2002] OJ L 190/01, as amended by Council Framework Decision 2009/299/JHA [2009] OJ L 081/24.

[49] Unlike its European counterpart, however, the Inter-American Convention only serves to supplement, not supersede, existing extradition arrangements.

[50] Annexed to UN Doc A/RES/45/116 (1990) then supplemented by UN Doc A/RES/52/88 (1997).

[51] Art 8. A multilateral extradition clause to address crimes on board aircraft had been proposed as early as 1962 to the Royal Aeronautical Society (Air Law Group): Sami Shubber, 'The Destruction of Aircraft in Flight over Scotland and Niger: The Questions of Jurisdiction and Extradition under International Law' (1995) 66(1) BYBIL 239, 263, fn 93.

enable the crime suppression conventions themselves to serve as the legal basis for extradition in the absence of an extradition treaty.[52] In doing so, they both modernize and expand extradition's multilateral reach for a range of offences of global concern, from aircraft hijacking and drug trafficking to transnational organized crime and corruption. Indeed, with their high numbers of ratifications, alongside state reluctance to renegotiate existing bilateral extradition treaties, the multilateral crime suppression conventions serve as the engines for meeting extradition law's double criminality requirement for many of today's crimes.[53]

## VI. Interactions with Counter-Terrorism Law

The deeming provisions of the multilateral crime suppression conventions, as well as their 'extradite or prosecute' obligations,[54] also serve to bolster extradition's role in countering acts of terrorism. In the 1970s and 1980s, a series of conventions were adopted that deemed prohibited acts of violence against civil aviation, the theft of nuclear materials and maritime terrorism to be extraditable crimes. Questions arose, however, as to the application of the political offence exception, which explains why in the 1990s, a 'second generation' of counter-terrorism treaties expressly stipulate (and emphasize) that terrorist bombings and the financing of terrorism 'shall not be regarded as a political offence or as an offence connected with a political offence or as an offence inspired by political motives'.[55]

Similar efforts were undertaken at the regional level resulting in the adoption of a European Convention on the Suppression of Terrorism (ECST)[56] that went further than the first generation of the UN-sponsored conventions by expressly de-politicizing offences involving 'the use of a bomb, grenade, rocket, automatic firearm or letter or parcel bomb if this use endangers persons'.[57] However, unlike the European Convention on Extradition, adherence to the ECST was restricted to Council of Europe states,[58] with the drafters relying on a 'climate of mutual confidence' to justify the imposition of an obligation to disregard, for the purposes of extradition, the political nature of certain odious crimes.[59] The treaty's impact was, however, seriously diminished by a reservation provision which made it far too easy to avoid the de-politicization obligation.[60] Change was later secured by

[52] An innovation instigated by the 1988 Drug Trafficking Convention, art 6(3).
[53] 1988 Drug Trafficking Convention, art 6 (191 states parties); UNTOC, art 16 (190 states parties); UNCAC, art 44 (187 states parties).
[54] A trend for transnational crimes that was also started by the 1970 Hague Hijacking Convention, art 7.
[55] 1997 Terrorist Bombings Convention, art 11; 1999 Terrorist Financing Convention, art 14.
[56] (Opened for signature 27 January 1977, entered into force 4 August 1978) ETS No 90.
[57] ibid art 1.
[58] ibid art 15.
[59] Explanatory Report on the European Convention on the Suppression of Terrorism (1977), para 12.
[60] European Convention on the Suppression of Terrorism (n 56), art 13.

a 2003 Protocol, which introduced a more rigorous reservations regime, while also designating a more extensive list of 'depoliticized' terroristic offences as extraditable crimes.[61] Additional extraditable offences were then added to this list in 2007[62] and 2017.[63]

## VII. Interactions with International Human Rights Law

The newer Council of Europe conventions also make clear that nothing in these treaty regimes imposes an obligation to extradite where there is a substantial risk in the requesting state of persecution on discriminatory grounds, torture or other forms of ill-treatment, the death penalty or life imprisonment without parole.[64] In doing so, these treaties serve to confirm a long-established link between extradition and human rights,[65] which weakens adherence to a strict rule of non-inquiry concerning the conditions in a requesting state.

Internationally, it was the landmark case of *Soering* by the European Court of Human Rights in 1989,[66] which clearly established that extradition is not exempt from human rights considerations. Non-European countries can look to similar guidance from the UN human rights treaty monitoring bodies,[67] which serves to confirm extradition's affinity with matters of immigration and expulsion, where the principle of non-refoulement bars a person's return to a country where there is a substantial risk of torture or mistreatment. Human rights law, however, also allows for the use of conditional extradition,[68] where assurances are obtained to address risks of ill-treatment or the flagrant denial of a fair trial.[69] Indeed, in a recent case, it was the state's rejection of a surrender request that was found wanting on human grounds, since non-cooperation impeded the prosecution of a terrorism offence, with the European Court requiring the requested state to ask for more information

[61] Protocol amending the European Convention on the Suppression of Terrorism (opened for signature 15 May 2003, entered into force on ratification) ETS No 190 (hereafter 2003 Protocol).

[62] 2005 European Terrorism Convention.

[63] 2015 European Terrorism Protocol.

[64] 2003 Protocol (n 61) art 4; 2005 European Terrorism Convention, art 21.

[65] See further Christine van den Wyngaert, 'Applying the European Convention on Human Rights to Extradition: Opening Pandora's Box?' (1990) 39(4) ICLQ 757.

[66] *Soering v United Kingdom*, (1989) Ser A No 161, (1989) 11 EHRR 439.

[67] See *Ng v Canada*, No 469/199, Views of the Human Rights Committee of 7 January 1994, UN Doc CCPR/C/49/D/469/199. See also Joanna Harrington, 'The Absent Dialogue: Extradition and the International Covenant on Civil and Political Rights' (2006) 32 Queen's LJ 82.

[68] See further John Dugard and Christine van den Wyngaert, 'Reconciling Extradition with Human Rights' (1998) 92(2) AJIL 187.

[69] *Othman (Abu Qatada) v United Kingdom*, App No 8139/09, ECHR 2012-I, (2012) 55 EHRR 1, cited with approval in *India v Badesha*, 2017 SCC 44, [2017] 2 SCR 127.

to establish whether, in the specific case, the alleged risk of ill-treatment upon surrender was concrete and real.[70]

## VIII. Conclusion

The idea of sending a wanted person back for trial sounds both simple and sensible, but in many cases, the reality is otherwise. Modern extradition law has long provided for certain exceptions to surrender, from the non-extradition of nationals to the exemption for political offenders, with an historical examination of the law's development and its influences suggesting that states seem engaged in a perpetual search for reforms to make extradition law more efficient and faster. Extradition law, however, must also protect the fair trial and fair treatment interests of the individuals concerned, with further challenges likely to arise with the increased use of extraterritorial jurisdiction in effect extending extradition's reach.

[70] *Romeo Castaño v Belgium*, App No 8351/17, 9 July 2019 ECHR (concerning a European Arrest Warrant request from Spain to Belgium for the alleged ETA terrorist who murdered Colonel Ramón Romeo in Bilbao in 1981).

# 21

# The Historical Development of International Law Enforcement Cooperation—The Case of Interpol

*Saskia Hufnagel*

## I. Introduction

This chapter recounts part of the complex story of transnational policing by focusing on its early days and the institution commonly perceived as its personification: Interpol.[1] The history of Interpol has been told by so many authors from such a number of disciplines that choosing an angle was a difficult task. The simplest for a socio-legal scholar is to focus on the inherent struggle of practice against politics that shaped the organization at its outset and continues to do so. In the early days of Interpol, this battle was won by practitioners and in 1923 they established an apolitical organization that primarily facilitated police-to-police cooperation. However, practitioners partly lost the war to politics over the years. Throughout the 20th century, Interpol gradually developed into a highly bureaucratic institution with an increasingly political mandate—even recognized as an international governmental organization (IGO)—and became more generally perceived as complicating rather than facilitating global policing. Its accountability mechanisms, by contrast, remained predominantly national, with the exception of the Commission for the Control of Interpol's Files (CCF), and relatively weak considering its IGO status. So, one could say that Interpol over time was attributed the organizational worst of both worlds: the accountability mechanisms of a 'policemen's club' and the policing efficiency of an IGO. This chapter aims to shed some light on this development and follows the path of Interpol from an international revolution to an international organization.

[1] See for recent and more comprehensive accounts Cyrille Fijnaut, *A Peaceful Revolution: The Development of Police and Judicial Cooperation in the European Union* (Intersentia 2019) 72–90 (hereafter Fijnaut, *Peaceful Revolution*); James Sheptycki, 'Brand Interpol' in Saskia Hufnagel and Carole McCartney (eds), *Trust in International Police and Justice Cooperation* (Hart 2017) 97 (hereafter Sheptycki, 'Brand Interpol'); Giulio Calcara, 'A Transnational Police Network Co-operating up to the Limits of the Law: Examination of the Origin of INTERPOL' [2020] Transnational Legal Theory 1 (hereafter Calcara, 'Transnational').

Saskia Hufnagel, *The Historical Development of International Law Enforcement Cooperation—The Case of Interpol* In: *Histories of Transnational Criminal Law.* Edited by: Neil Boister, Sabine Gless and Florian Jeßberger, Oxford University Press. © Saskia Hufnagel 2021. DOI: 10.1093/oso/9780192845702.003.0022

## II. Joining Forces: Policing Initiatives Paving the Way for Interpol

Interpol was the earliest international law enforcement cooperation mechanism to be established involving more than a select number of states and is today open for all states of the world to join.[2]

The organization was established in Vienna as the International Criminal Police Commission (ICPC) in 1923 by mainly European nations whereas today it comprises 194 members.[3] However, the road to establishing Interpol was long and rocky and forecasted the problems the organization still faces today. To understand current debates, one is best to start from the beginning of police cooperation—or rather the organization thereof.

Although police cooperation has been said to exist for thousands of years,[4] in Europe a concerted effort to cooperate across borders only became visible in the Napoleonic Empire.[5] A response first to roving gangs of the 18th century, police were aided in their joint investigative efforts by similarities of policing systems. The Napoleonic policing system which had spread throughout Europe during the Empire, for example, facilitated cooperation between forces as did the fact that both the Paris and later the Vienna police forces were used as blueprints to police large cities all over Europe.[6] The French Gendarmerie was, after the French Revolution, even introduced into most Western and Central European jurisdictions.[7] Furthermore, most police had divided their forces into civilian police (cities) and military gendarmerie (countryside) leading to a further harmonization of policing organization and structures across Europe.[8]

After the collapse of the French Empire in 1815 most jurisdictions retained the system introduced during its eleven-year reign. The fight against radical and violent political opponents stimulated the creation of secretive police institutions, which cooperated with other agencies, such as the German 'Polizeiverein' between the German and German-speaking states of Europe or the Russian 'Okhrana'.[9] The fact that these institutions were secretive leads to the conclusion that sovereignty concerns loomed large as a barrier to formal police cooperation across borders.

[2] Bill Hebenton and Terry Thomas, *Policing Europe: Co-operation, Conflicts and Control* (St Martin's Press 1995) 64–69.

[3] ibid; Interpol, *Annual Report 2019* (Interpol 2020).

[4] Calcara, 'Transnational' (n 1) 3.

[5] Fijnaut, *Peaceful Revolution* (n 1) 10.

[6] ibid.

[7] Cyrille Fijnaut 'De la Gendarmerie Hollandaise à la Maréchaussée Royale des Pays-Bas (1805–1815)' in Jean-Noël Luc (ed), *Gendarmerie, Etat et Société au XIXe Siècle* (Publications de la Sorbonne 2002) 423.

[8] Clive Emsley, *Gendarmes and the State in Nineteenth-Century Europe* (OUP 1999).

[9] Mathieu Deflem, *Policing World Society* (OUP 2002) 64 (hereafter Deflem, *Policing*); Richard Johnson, 'Zagranichnaia Agentura: The Tsarist Political Police in Europe' (1972) 7 Journal of Contemporary History 221, 223 (hereafter Johnson, 'Tsarist Political Police').

Apart from being highly secretive, the emerging patterns of police cooperation in the 19th century were also ad hoc and not based on common legal standards and procedures.[10] The political policing at the time was furthermore supported by the police stationed in the big cities of Europe which cooperated through individual officers exchanging information and intelligence, formally visiting each other and jointly attending conferences and events.[11]

At the end of the 19th century, common policing standards and professionalization of policing had started to develop, fostered, in part, by the cooperation related to political crimes. These developments were further facilitated by an increase of personal police contacts because of the distribution of counterfeit currency among the states establishing Interpol.[12] Also, forensic innovations, such as fingerprinting (dactyloscopy) and *bertillonage* (anthropometry, based on the technique of the *portrait parlé*, the study of the physical appearance of a criminal), facilitated cooperation as it led to police visits to learn about the new techniques.[13] Examples of police-to-police cooperation in the 19th century include the information exchange between the Metropolitan Police in London, England and France in relation to French refugees (or political opponents) resident in the United Kingdom, the 'personal correspondence system' between the units of the *gendarmeries* on the borders of individual states, and the distribution of alerts relating to wanted suspects.[14]

It follows that police cooperation had been in the hands of police practitioners with minimal political engagement since the 18th century while the crimes policed were predominantly political in nature. It was hence only logical that governments wanted to get more involved once more coordinated efforts to combat violent political opposition (or, what we would today call 'terrorism') were discussed. One of the first opportunities to do so was the 'Anti-Anarchist' Conference in Rome in 1898, which some commentators see as the birth of Interpol.[15] Another way for governments to get involved in political policing, which developed in parallel to international policing, was fighting political opposition through secret services. The establishment of secret service policing could first be observed in the countries of the British Commonwealth and other European states with strong international (colonial) interests in the 19th and early 20th centuries. Secret services developed initially in these nations as they were facing more prominently international political opposition than states with more domestically focused politics at the time,

[10] Johnson, 'Tsarist Political Police' (n 9) 223.

[11] Fijnaut, *Peaceful Revolution* (n 1) 12.

[12] Peter Andreas and Ethan Nadelmann, *Policing the Globe: Criminalization and Crime Control in International Relations* (OUP 2006) 124–25 (hereafter Andreas and Nadelmann, *Policing*).

[13] ibid 82.

[14] Lindsay Clutterbuck, 'Countering Irish Republican Terrorism in Britain: Its Origin as a Police Function' (2006) 18 Terrorism and Political Violence 95, 97; Fijnaut, *Peaceful Revolution* (n 1) 10; Deflem, *Policing* (n 9) 47.

[15] Fijnaut, *Peaceful Revolution* (n 1) 13.

such as Germany.[16] To date there is still little research on the relationship between Interpol and secret services although initially both types of institutions pursued the same goals. In what follows, the chapter focuses on Interpol and outlines the conferences that led to its establishment and the views presented by both police and government actors while taking into account that secret services were developing and pursuing similar aims at the same time.

## III. From Rome to Monaco and Vienna

The 'Anti-Anarchist' Conference of 24 November 1898 in Rome was the start of a long history of negotiations that had been initiated by the assassination of the Empress Elizabeth in 1898 in Geneva and would eventually result in the establishment of Interpol in 1923.[17] The conference was attended by fifty-two delegates from twenty-one—mainly European—countries. Not only police chiefs, but also diplomats and civil servants attended the conference, a combination that led to legal and political discussions as well as administrative and policing considerations relating to a future initiative.[18] Remarkable for the time were debates on legal harmonization of political crimes that would facilitate the cross-border pursuit of criminals. Concerns were raised relating to extradition and in particular the 'Belgian clause' or 'attentat clause'—this allowed the extradition of a suspect for an attack on a head of state, a procedure that was otherwise prohibited for political offences by the political offence exception.[19] Operationally, the conference discussed mainly the policing of violent political opponents and, more specifically, the distribution of lists detailing suspects and intelligence relating to them.[20] Police furthermore proposed the conclusion of treaty law relating to extradition in particular, as investigations and arrests on behalf of other nations would otherwise be futile.[21] Unlike mutual legal assistance treaties, developed in Europe after the 1920s, bilateral extradition treaties had already been negotiated on a global scale from about the mid-19th century. They were concluded in increasing numbers towards the end of the 19th century (and most of them included the 'attentat clause').[22] While police was

[16] Wolfgang Krieger, *Die Deutschen Geheimdienste—Vom Wiener Kongress bis zum Cyber War* (Verlag C.H.Beck 2021) 8.

[17] Cyrille Fijnaut, 'International Policing in Europe: Its Present Situation and Future' in Jean Paul Brodeur (ed), *Comparisons in Policing: An International Perspective* (Avebury 1995) 115; Malcolm Anderson, *Policing the World: Interpol and the Politics of International Police Cooperation* (OUP 1989) 1.

[18] Fijnaut, *Peaceful Revolution* (n 1) 14.

[19] Julia Jansson, *Terrorism, Criminal Law and Politics: The Decline of the Political Offence Exception to Extradition* (Routledge 2020) 87. See Saul, Chapter 10 and Harrington, Chapter 20 in this book.

[20] Fijnaut, *Peaceful Revolution* (n 1) 14.

[21] ibid 19.

[22] ibid; Bruce Zagaris and Jessica Resnick, 'The Mexico-US Mutual Legal Assistance in Criminal Matters Treaty: Another Step toward the Harmonization of International Law Enforcement' (1997) 14 Ariz J Intl & Comp L 18.

pushing for the conclusion of treaties to facilitate cross-border prosecutions, governments made sure that the treaties would serve their political interests. Mutual legal assistance was seen as 'secondary' or 'minor' legal assistance and therefore not at the centre of the legislators' attention until the political issues relating to extradition had been resolved.[23]

Between the 'Anti-Anarchist' Conference and the 1914 Monaco Conference on the establishment of a joint police commission, the political focus on transnational crime changed dramatically. At the beginning of the 20th century other crimes were pushed to the centre of political attention and, while violent political opposition did not become irrelevant, it was joined by equally important and truly transnational crimes. In a law enforcement officials' meeting held in 1905 and organized by the International Criminalistic Society, participants discussed the legal definition and nature of cross-border crime and proposed the introduction of common police procedures (eg *bertillonage*) and the setting up of national offices tasked with the linking of police services across the member states. While stressing the challenges of joint international policing, it was concluded that a further conference should be convened to discuss its institutionalization.[24]

Among the crimes that were internationally recognized and jointly outlawed at the beginning of the 20th century, or had been created earlier, and were now included in international treaty law were included those relating to the white slave trade, drugs and pornography.[25] Slavery more broadly had been outlawed since 1833—initiated by Britain prohibiting slavery in 1807, but more effectively internationalized by numerous civil society groups. However, the abolitionist movement in relation to the trafficking of women only started in the 1870s and culminated in the 1904 White Slave Agreement.[26] Rather than Britain (until the early 20th century itself heavily involved in the opium trade), the flag bearer of the international anti-drug trafficking campaign was the United States of America.[27] A number of drugs were criminalized in 1912 by the 1912 Hague Opium Convention, which included measures to reduce the trade, but no provisions on cross-border enforcement were introduced until later conventions.[28]

These societal and legislative developments in the field of international proscriptions of transnational crimes led to the 1914 Monaco Conference, which was, unlike the Rome Conference and the event organized by the International Criminalistic Society, a mainly French—or French-speaking—event.[29] Opinions on the Monaco Conference's relevance to police cooperation differ, however, and

[23] Fijnaut, *Peaceful Revolution* (n 1) 20.
[24] ibid 22–23.
[25] ibid 23.
[26] Andreas and Nadelmann, *Policing* (n 12) 35–37. See Askola, Chapter 11 in this book.
[27] Andreas and Nadelmann, *Policing* (n 12) 41–42.
[28] ibid; Fijnaut, *Peaceful Revolution* (n 1) 24.
[29] Fijnaut, *Peaceful Revolution* (n 1) 25.

while some authors assert its importance for policing and its progressive proposals on cross-border law enforcement—such as the drafting of a model extradition treaty, the establishment of an International Bureau of Identification and the permission of mutual legal assistance requests between judicial authorities—a recent account by Giulio Calcara qualifies the event as too state-centric and political.[30] There are several indicators that the Monaco Conference was in fact not particularly practitioner-focused, including that the Monarch of Monaco initiated it and that its attendees were mainly diplomats, legal officers and politicians, rather than police.[31] Calcara interprets the Summary of the Wishes Expressed at the Sessions or Assemblies Held on 15, 16 and 18 April 1914[32] as a proposal that facilitated police cooperation but made it dependent on governmental interference as it relied on diplomats acting as intermediaries.[33] The proposal was therefore doomed to fail, given that police were not accepting of a state-centric approach as they—to operate effectively—wanted to work at a distance from central state authorities.[34] However, the outbreak of World War I interrupted all plans in relation to the 1914 Conference and a new attempt to bring officials together internationally was only considered in 1919, shortly after the end of World War I.[35]

The next conference addressing the establishment of an international police organization was organized in Vienna in 1923 and brought together a considerable number of police practitioners, distinguishing it from its predecessor event in Monaco. Rather than focusing on politicians, diplomats and legal officers, the conference organizers invited 300 chiefs of police from around the world and only thirty political representatives to the Vienna Conference, and it was attended mainly by senior police and judicial officers.[36] The two senior police officials instrumental in organizing the conference were responsible for this focus on practice, one from the Netherlands and one from Vienna.[37] M van Houten was a captain in the Royal Dutch Marechaussée and had lobbied police chiefs around the world regarding international cooperation since 1919.[38] Although his proposals had not fallen on fertile ground at the time, his international awareness-raising campaign appears likely to have paved the way for Johan Schober, police commissioner of Vienna, who organized the practitioner-focused Police Congress that established the ICPC in 1923.

30 ibid 26; Calcara, 'Transnational' (n 1) 1.

31 Calcara, 'Transnational' (n 1) 6.

32 Congress of 1914, Summary of the Wishes Expressed at the Sessions or Assemblies Held on 15, 16 and 18 April 1914, First International Criminal Police Congress (April 2014).

33 Calcara, 'Transnational' (n 1) 7.

34 Deflem, *Policing* (n 9) 47.

35 Fijnaut, *Peaceful Revolution* (n 1) 26–27.

36 Calcara, 'Transnational' (n 1) 8; Fijnaut, *Peaceful Revolution* (n 1) 35.

37 Calcara, 'Transnational' (n 1) 8; Fijnaut, *Peaceful Revolution* (n 1) 27–29.

38 Fijnaut, *Peaceful Revolution* (n 1) 27–28.

The main selling point of the Commission to the practitioner audience at the Congress—leading to the success of the proposal—was a focus on common police professional identity which appealed to the sense of belonging—or 'being blue'—among police officers at the time.[39] Putting practitioners rather than processes in the spotlight also meant that the Commission that was created was independent from the central national authorities and, other than the 1914 proposal, focused on the practicalities and efficiency of police information exchange and assistance.[40] It has been pointed out that the focus of the ICPC at the time of its establishment was still predominantly the prevention of terrorism, in particular in the aftermath of World War I and of the Russian Revolution.[41] However, according to Deflem, the goal of Interpol,[42] as expressed at the Vienna Congress of 1923, was to 'establish and enhance mutual assistance between all police within the framework of the laws of their respective states and to establish all institutions suited to fight against "ordinary crime"'.[43]

## IV. Interpol in the 20th and 21st Centuries

The technical objective of the ICPC at the time of its establishment was to create and enhance mutual assistance between all police within their own legislative frameworks on the basis of national contact points that could connect with each other.[44] According to Deflem the establishment of the ICPC was only possible because political crimes were excluded from the cooperation, representing police independence from the national authorities.[45] However, other commentators, and they are certainly supported by the recent legal changes to article 3 of the Interpol Constitution (allowing for policing of political crimes), found that there was in practice nothing to prevent governments from exercising political policing through Interpol from the beginning.[46] The ICPC's objectives were finally put into practice when each participating country set up National Central Bureaus that acted as gateways between national law enforcement agencies and the Interpol global communication channel. These bureaus were, and still are, tasked

[39] Calcara, 'Transnational' (n 1) 9.
[40] Deflem, *Policing* (n 9) 47.
[41] John Occhipinti, *The Politics of EU Police Cooperation: Toward a European FBI?* (Lynne Rienner 2003) (hereafter Occhipinti, *Politics*).
[42] At the time of its establishment in 1923, the organization was called 'International Criminal Police Commission' or IKK (Internationale Kriminalpolizeiliche Kommission).
[43] Deflem, *Policing* (n 9) 127; W J Leamy, 'International Co-operation through the Interpol System to Counter Illicit Drug Trafficking' (1983) 35 Bulletin on Narcotics 55.
[44] Deflem, *Policing* (n 9) 127.
[45] ibid 47.
[46] Cyrille Fijnaut, *Opdat de Macht een Toevlucht Zij? Een Historische Studie van het Politieapparaat als een Politieke Instelling*, vol 2 (Kluwer 1979) 406.

with handling communication between national police and the police of other participating countries.[47]

After the nazification of the ICPC before and during World War II, the organization ceased operations in its original form and was only re-established in 1946 in Paris. Its nazification was the ultimate politicization of the ICPC and while temporarily leading to the breakdown of operations, some international 'ordinary crime' cooperation still continued with the help of police liaison officers.[48] This chapter of the history of Interpol is indicative of how technical police cooperation against ordinary crimes can coexist up to a breaking point with political policing.

Interpol emerged, in its current form, after 1989 in Lyon[49] and has since then broadly been considered a successful practitioner-led strategy.[50] The establishment of Interpol generally led to a more professional and less political form of police cooperation in relation to information exchange, despite—or because of—its informal nature.[51] Interpol itself fostered little political cooperation between its members and was perceived as lacking high-level political support, being mainly practitioner-driven.[52] However, the support from the practitioner communities does not mean that they accepted the institution uncritically. Indeed, some commentators argue that, at certain times, Interpol lacked both practitioner acceptance *and* political support.[53]

Interpol also reached the limits of its mandate where national sovereignty issues were involved. As a result, the type of information exchanged was only basic and never came close to accessing sensitive classified information generated for national security purposes.[54] These shortcomings of Interpol consequently had a significant influence on the establishment of EU strategies and institutional design in the field of police cooperation. The establishment of the TREVI Group (1975), the Schengen Agreement[55] (1985) and Europol (1992) shared a common goal, namely to address the actual and perceived shortcomings of Interpol.[56] Interpol

[47] Ludo Block, *From Politics to Policing—The Rationality Gap in EU Council Policy-Making* (Eleven International Publishing 2011) 53 (hereafter Block, *Politics to Policing*).

[48] Fijnaut, *Peaceful Revolution* (n 1).

[49] Deflem, *Policing* (n 9) 179; Occhipinti, *Politics* (n 41) 29.

[50] Malcolm Anderson, *Policing the World: Interpol and the Politics of International Police Co-operation* (OUP 1989) 37–42.

[51] Paul Swallow, 'Of Limited Operational Relevance: A European View of Interpol's Crime-fighting Role in the Twenty- first Century' (1996) 2 Transnational Organised Crime 106, 121 (hereafter Swallow, 'Limited Operational Relevance').

[52] ibid 121.

[53] ibid 117–19.

[54] See Cyrille Fijnaut, 'International Policing in Europe: Present and Future' (1994) 19 European Law Review 601; see also James Sheptycki, 'The Accountability of Transnational Policing Institutions: The Strange Case of Interpol' (2004) 19 Canadian Journal of Law and Society 116, 117.

[55] Agreement between the Governments of the States of the Benelux Economic Union, the Federal Republic of Germany and the French Republic on the Gradual Abolition of Checks at their Common Borders, signed 14 June 1985, [2000] OJ L 239/19 (hereafter 'Schengen Agreement').

[56] Swallow, 'Limited Operational Relevance' (n 51) 109–10.

has therefore done much more to advance legal harmonization of European Union (EU) police cooperation than is usually credited.

Interpol is today a significant police cooperation institution with nearly global membership and its core business is facilitating informal information exchange on a case-by-case basis. However, despite its usefulness in international law enforcement cooperation, two aspects of the organization have been debated since its establishment: first, its status as an IGO, and second, its responsibilities in the facilitation of cooperation on political crimes.

In relation to the first point of contention, while the UN today recognizes Interpol as an IGO, legally its status is still highly debated.[57] As governments were not members of Interpol (being a police-led initiative), a constitution had to be selected as its legal basis rather than an international treaty. Article 4 of the Interpol Constitution consequently states that '[a]ny country may delegate as a Member to the Organization any official police body whose functions come within the framework of activities of the Organization'; '[t]he request for membership shall be submitted to the Secretary General by the appropriate governmental authority',[58] but the 'appropriate governmental authority' is not defined.[59] While Interpol was gradually recognized under customary international law as an IGO during the second half of the 20th century, the organization had also applied to ECOSOC for recognition as an NGO in 1947. Though initially turned down, NGO status was granted later that year but the relationship between Interpol and the UN remained uneasy because the agents of the organization were police officials. In 1971, a new 'special relationship' was constituted between the UN and Interpol through which Interpol would, under certain circumstances, be treated *as if* it were an IGO.[60] The two organizations would cooperate for the purposes of the prevention and repression of commonly recognized crimes, exchange information and documentation and collaborate in various other ways. Interpol was from then on recognized as a global IGO by the United Nations Secretary-General.[61] Interpol's mandate today is mainly the facilitation of information exchange and execution of certain types of searches and warrants internationally. As distinct from regional cooperation mechanisms, Interpol only works on a case-by-case basis, although this could be debated with a view to the Interpol-wide distribution of red and other notices. It follows that although Interpol is not an association of governments, its status has been recognized as such. Hence an organization that was meant to be police-led is now de facto considered to be 'governmental'.

[57] See on this debate Julia Jansson 'Different Centuries, Similar Strategies? Opposing Terrorism in 1898 and 1998' in MH Conley Tyler (ed), *Australian Institute of International Affairs. Emerging Scholars 2009–2010* (Australian Institute of International Affairs 2010) 70–86.

[58] ibid.

[59] Interpol, 'Legal Materials' <www.interpol.int/Public/ICPO/LegalMaterials/constitution/constitution GenReg/constitution.asp#constitution>.

[60] See the Economic and Social Council, Res 1579 (L) 288 (3 June 1971).

[61] Sheptycki, 'Brand Interpol' (n 1) 115.

In relation to the second point of contention, under article 3 of its Constitution, Interpol has competences in the area of 'ordinary crime' and not 'political crimes'. However, as priorities shifted in the 1970s and 1980s with a surge of terrorism in Europe and after the events of 9/11 in the United States so too have the competences of Interpol, although article 3 has not been amended. In 1983 the Interpol General Assembly reviewed the restriction in relation to political crimes and the following year two resolutions were passed in the Interpol General Assembly. These resolutions changed the interpretation of article 3,[62] which since then has been interpreted as permitting the use of Interpol mechanisms in the fight against terrorism.[63] This was specifically recognized in the United Nations Security Council Resolution 2178 (2014) and highlights the use of Interpol's I-24/7 secure police communications network, global databases and system of advisory notices, in addition to its counter-terrorism efforts and procedures to track stolen, forged identity papers and travel documents.[64] Interpol mechanisms preventing the international travel of foreign fighters include its Stolen and Lost Travel Documents (SLTD) database, as well as I-Checkit.

Despite political limitations,[65] Interpol has over time developed many functions to support international law enforcement, such as criminal databases, analytical services and operational support and has become a meeting platform for experts in different areas of crime.[66] Interpol's most important function is, however, information exchange with a view to facilitating cross-border criminal investigations.[67] As there is generally no legal obligation to answer requests, whether a request made through Interpol is responded to by the requested member state depends on the relationship with the requesting country's law enforcement agencies, the current political climate between requesting and requested country, human rights standards of both parties and many other variables. While the usefulness of the organization could therefore be debated and many regions around the world have created specialist information channels that circumvent Interpol, at a truly global level, Interpol is still needed to connect countries across the world. Here, membership of Interpol can enhance cross-border law enforcement cooperation and the locating of suspects.[68] In addition, the Interpol I-24/7 Global Police Communications

[62] Res No AGN/53/RES6, 1984 Subject: Violent Crime Commonly Referred to as Terrorism; subject heading Constitution, Application of art 3; Res No AGN/53/RES/7, 1984 Subject: Application of art 3 of the Constitution, Sub-heading: Constitution, Application of art 3.

[63] Sheptycki, 'Brand Interpol' (n 1) 97–124.

[64] UNSCR Res 2178, S/Res/2078 (2014).

[65] Art 3 of the Interpol Constitution excludes political crimes from its competences, thereby making it until recently impossible for member states to use the Interpol channel in terrorism cases. This has, however, changed with the reinterpretation of art 3 (after the 11 September 2001 attacks in particular) to include terrorism related offences within Interpol's competences.

[66] Ludo Block, 'European Police Cooperation on Art Crime: A Comparative Overview' (2011) 4(1) Journal of Art Crime 13.

[67] Block, *Politics to Policing* (n 47) 54.

[68] ibid.

System is a useful tool for the sharing of information on criminals and criminal activities worldwide in a timely and secure manner.[69] I-24/7 enables authorized users around the world to exchange information twenty-four hours a day, seven days a week through a secure network providing direct access to a number of databases relevant to law enforcement operations.[70]

Many scholars researching international police cooperation have been critical of the Interpol mechanism. In particular, Interpol Red Notices have been blamed for leading to human rights breaches.[71] While only few such cases have been discussed in detail in the media,[72] probably because very few if any were subject to court decisions,[73] their impact can be felt in relation to political abuses of Red Notices in particular.[74] While some breaches happen 'negligently', such as cases of mistaken identity or through lack of detailed information contained in the Red Notice, others have been labelled as political abuse and the facilitation of oppression. A UK-based NGO, Fair Trials International, has produced a highly critical report, pinpointing cases where individuals were targeted by governments, who had Red Notices put up against them, with no scrutiny of the credibility of the request.[75] In their reports, Fair Trials International point to the steep increase in the numbers of Red Notices being issued since 2008 (when electronic systems were introduced).[76] Countries found to be using the system against political activists include Russia, Sri Lanka, Turkey, Belarus, Indonesia, Iran and Venezuela. People subject to such notices are unable to travel and are effectively exiled. While article 3 of Interpol's Constitution forbids any political, military, religious or racial intervention or activities, the Interpol mechanism does not allow for the monitoring of the quality of national-level information, therefore leaving the system open to potential abuse.[77] Without wanting to downplay the use and value of the Interpol platform for police cooperation, it is important to also acknowledge its shortfalls. States should today

[69] UNODC, *State of Implementation of the United Nations Convention against Corruption: Criminalization, Law Enforcement and International Cooperation* (UNODC 2015) 209–10.

[70] Interpol, 'I-24/7 Secure Network' <www.interpol.int/fr/INTERPOL-expertise/Data-exchange/I-24-27>.

[71] See eg Ben Bowling and James Sheptycki, *Global Policing* (Sage 2012) 9–11 (hereafter Bowling and Sheptycki, *Global Policing*); Bruce Zagaris, 'International Organizations and International Police Cooperation—Bill to Curb INTERPOL Abuse Follows Helsinki Commission Hearing' (2019) 35(9) International Law Enforcement Reporter 354.

[72] Tim Butcher and Sally Pook, 'Wine Tasting Pensioner Finds Himself in Jail and Wanted by the FBI' (*Daily Telegraph*, 26 February 2003).

[73] Bowling and Sheptycki, *Global Policing* (n 71) 8–11.

[74] Fair Trials International, 'Fair Trials Highlights Abuses of INTERPOL's Systems by Former Soviet States' (19 December 2017) <www.fairtrials.org/news/fair-trials-highlights-abuses-interpol%E2%80%99s-systems-former- soviet-states>.

[75] ibid.

[76] Fair Trials International, 'Defending Human Rights, Strengthening INTERPOL: INTERPOL is Being Used as a Weapon against Journalists, Human Rights Defenders and Refugees' <www.fairtrials.org/wp- content/uploads/INTERPOL-Summary.pdf>.

[77] Fair Trials International, 'Abuses of Interpol's System Must Be Stopped' (3 November 2017) <www.fairtrials.org/news/abuses-interpol%E2%80%99s-systems-must-be-stopped>.

not, for example, execute Red Notices on the basis of trust in the Interpol system alone. While Interpol does have a CCF that can remove Red Notices upon request of individuals, their decision cannot be appealed.[78] It is hence advised to turn to the state issuing the Red Notice to ask for its removal or to ask the authorities of the state where the person lives to remove the notice.[79] Other than the CCF, there is no inbuilt legitimacy/accountability/human rights mechanism for the content of Red Notices and states should be encouraged to question their content before executing them. If the notice is executed by the country that issued it 'illegally' under international human rights standards, Interpol should have the responsibility to check whether the notice is legitimate and to take it down if it is not. A mechanism that would enable such scrutiny before a notice is published does not, however, exist within Interpol procedure and it can be doubted whether the CCF is an appropriate mechanism to eliminate political abuse from the organization's work. It follows that, as has been the case historically, in Interpol 'ordinary' police cooperation has to coexist with political policing and its IGO status has not and cannot generally introduce higher standards of due diligence today. However, more detailed legal provisions would likely not be able to eliminate the existing dilemma.

## V. Conclusion

This chapter could not be remotely exhaustive of the historical developments that led up to the establishment of Interpol or the current problems it faces. Its particular focus has been to show why the organization is problematic from both a practitioner and a political point of view. The chapter hence provided a brief discussion of the practitioner and the political focus of Interpol and came to the conclusion that a practitioner initiative had been hijacked for governmental and political purposes while not providing the safeguards required of a governmental organization.

However, the history of this institution is not that clear cut and although not considered by the practitioners involved in Interpol's establishment, the possibility for political involvement existed from its very beginnings. The creation of Interpol for police at the time must have been an emotional moment. Feeling united, even understood, by colleagues across the world, the thought that they could be used to make the lives of political dissidents miserable was probably not uppermost in their minds.

[78] Interpol, 'Commission for the Control of Interpol's Files (CCF)' <www.interpol.int/en/Who-we-are/Commission-for- the-Control-of-INTERPOL-s-Files-CCF>; see generally, Cheah Wui Ling, 'Policing Interpol: The Commission for the Control of Interpol's Files and the Right to a Remedy' (2010) 7(2) International Organizations Law Review 375.

[79] Fair Trials International, 'Asking for the Removal of Information from Interpol's Files' <www.fairtrials.org/asking- removal-information-interpols-files>.

Finally, the possibility of governments to assert—both legitimate and illegitimate—power through Interpol does not make this organization generally less useful in practice. Interpol was, and still is, for many countries and even regions and neighbouring states around the world the primary point of contact for police cooperation. What should be considered, however, is how Interpol can and should be made accountable for misuses of its system, so that abuses are prevented not only at national, but also at institutional levels.

# 22

# The Acquisition of Legal Status by Individuals in Transnational Criminal Proceedings in Europe

*Sabine Gless*

## I. Introduction

Scholars of domestic criminal procedure—in addressing the legal status of a defendant in a criminal justice system—have sometimes argued that the rights and remedies given to an alleged offender indicate the overall respect that a particular legal system shows towards individual rights and the rule of law.[1] Applying this perspective to transnational criminal law leads to troubling findings: if the legal status of the individual sought for prosecution[2] by a foreign state is a benchmark for the international community's respect for individual rights, we might find that many Western jurisdictions have, until recently, been geared to prioritize state interests over the individual's.[3] It appears that the individual's legal status in transnational criminal law has significantly lagged (and, in some respects, still lags) behind his or her status in domestic criminal justice systems, though defendants, in general, are in a vulnerable position, regardless of whether they are suspected to have violated the law of the land or are sought for prosecution abroad.

Defendants in domestic criminal trials traditionally enjoy (often strong) defence rights to protect them against the state.[4] In contrast, individuals subject to extradition proceedings to stand trial abroad still do not typically benefit from

[1] Claus Roxin and Bernd Schünemann, *Strafverfahrensrecht* (29th edn, CH Beck 2017) 10, 258; Astrid Liliana Sánchez- Mejía, *Victims' Rights in Flux: Criminal Justice Reform in Colombia* (Springer 2017) 70.

[2] This chapter does not include observations on the legal situation of victims or witnesses to a crime.

[3] Ann Powers, 'Justice Denied? The Adjudication of Extradition Applications' (2002) 37 Tex Intl LJ 277, 286; Otto Lagodny, 'Comparative Overview' in Albin Eser, Otto Lagodny and Christopher L Blakesley (eds), *The Individual as Subject of International Cooperation in Criminal Matters* (Nomos 2002) 746.

[4] Stefan Trechsel, 'Why Must Trials Be Fair?' (1997) 31 Is LR 94, 100; Andrew Ashworth, *Sentencing and Criminal Justice* (5th edn, CUP 2010) 74; RA Duff, 'Responsibility, Citizenship, and Criminal Law' in RA Duff and Stuart P Green (eds), *Philosophical Foundations of Criminal Law* (OUP 2011) 131.

Sabine Gless, *The Acquisition of Legal Status by Individuals in Transnational Criminal Proceedings in Europe* In: *Histories of Transnational Criminal Law*. Edited by: Neil Boister, Sabine Gless and Florian Jeßberger, Oxford University Press. © Sabine Gless 2021. DOI: 10.1093/oso/9780192845702.003.0023

similarly comprehensive safeguards in transnational criminal proceedings.[5] Criminal law scholars—traditionally oriented inwardly at their domestic criminal justice system—started to sporadically point out legal shortcomings regarding the legal status of the individual at the turn of 20th century.[6] However, it took another century for a more systematic approach to emerge, which finally came to examine and determine the legal position of the individual in transnational criminal proceedings.[7]

The historical review in this chapter is rather fast-motioned and condensed, as it zooms in on two central European neighbours, Germany and Switzerland, who—since the end of the 19th century—have shared legal developments and maintained close contact, yet opted for different stances on individual rights in mutual legal assistance. The study begins after central European states established written procedures among themselves for more formalized transboundary cooperation in the 18th century,[8] highlighting the conversion of these procedures into legal institutions by certain central European states that had adopted legislation by the end of the 19th century. This would ultimately become known as mutual legal assistance (MLA) in criminal matters. As a body of law, it was merged into today's MLA legislation, which, in a broad way, determines the legal status of the individual. Beginning in the mid-19th century and occurring at divergent speeds, change in Europe took well over a century. Belgium and Switzerland were forerunners, while the German Confederation lagged behind. Even when the German Empire had been established, authorities retained the view that cooperation in criminal matters was a part of dealings between states and not law enforcement affecting the individual. From this perspective, transnational criminal law formed part of public international law—with rights and obligations granted to states only—rather than criminal law, with its formal defence rights. Overall, the individual's position remained vague and was rarely considered worthy of legal debate. In particular, in Germany the individual was depicted as an object rather than a subject in the proceedings.[9] Thus when an individual received protection, it was deemed a 'reflex' that derived from states' rights, rather than a legal entitlement of their own.[10]

[5] For Switzerland, see Daniel Schaffner, *Das Individuum im internationalen Rechtshilferecht in Strafsachen* (Helbing & Lichtenhahn 2013) *passim* (hereafter Schaffner, *Das Individuum im internationalen Rechtshilferecht).*

[6] Josef Kohler, 'Der Savarkar-Streitfall zwischen Frankreich und England' in Walther Schücking (ed), *Das Werk vom Haag, Die gerichtlichen Entscheidungen,* vol 1 pt 3 (Dunker & Humblot 1914) 65 (hereafter Kohler, 'Der Savarkar-Streitfall zwischen Frankreich und England').

[7] See Otto Lagodny, *Die Rechtsstellung des Auszuliefernden in der Bundesrepublik Deutschland* (Max Planck-Institut für ausländisches und internationales Strafrecht 1987) at various places (hereafter Lagodny, *Die Rechtsstellung des Auszuliefernden*); John Dugard and Christine Van den Wyngaert, 'Reconciling Extradition with Human Rights' (1998) 92 AJIL 187 (hereafter Dugard and Van den Wyngaert, 'Reconciling Extradition with Human Rights').

[8] See Härter, Chapter 1 in this book.

[9] Meinhard Schröder, 'Staats- und völkerrechtliche Fragen der Auslieferungsbewilligung' (1979) 110 Bay V Bl 231 (hereafter Schröder, 'Staats- und völkerrechtliche Fragen der Auslieferungsbewilligung').

[10] Malcolm N Shaw, *International Law* (8th edn, CUP 2017) 743.

Only in the second half of the 20th century did the notion of legal rights exercised by the individual arise as a global issue of mutual legal assistance. At that time, the individual's position in domestic criminal justice had been consolidated and was, in many respects, strong in European states. These states shared legal reformist concepts for decades—as Pifferi illustrates in Chapter 2 of this book. Scholars engaging in those international debates exchanged ideas, not only on amelioration of domestic law, but also for transborder cooperation.[11] Yet the early ideas of 'international defence rights' were lost, and even countries that were pioneers with regard to individual rights in mutual legal assistance and were home to scholars engaged in law reform—like Switzerland with Carl Stooss—did not take up these ideas.

Overall, it was the human rights narrative that caused the paradigm shift to transform transnational cooperation, figuratively speaking, from a two-dimensional dealing (from state to state) to a three-dimensional approach, with the individual able to raise legal concerns before being extradited from one state to the other. According to this new approach, not only the states involved in MLA held a legal position (in their mere two-dimensional relationship), but the individual concerned could also assert rights—creating a new third dimension. The late 20th century debate on constitutional and human rights clearly encouraged this approach.[12] Case law acknowledged the impact of human rights with the landmark European Court of Human Rights' (ECtHR) decision in the *Soering* case.[13] The way had been paved by other Strasbourg judgments, however, emphasizing the all-pervasive power of the European Convention on Human Rights (ECHR).

Today, with EU member states cooperating closely in cross-border matters based on the principle of mutual recognition, the legal position of individuals sought for prosecution in another country is again under review as EU states are increasingly granted permission to infringe individuals' rights across borders.

## II. Terminology

This chapter starts out with a broad definition of transnational criminal law, explained in the introduction to this book, as 'suppression by international law through domestic penal law of criminal activities that have (i) actual or (ii) potential transboundary effects or (iii) transboundary moral impact'. While the description often used by scholars, based on a definition introduced by Neil Boister,[14]

[11] See Pifferi, Chapter 2 in this book.

[12] See Kate Parlett, *The Individual in the International Legal System* (CUP 2011) at various places; Anne Peters, *Beyond Human Rights. The Legal Status of the Individual in International Law* (CUP 2016) at various places (hereafter Peters, *Beyond Human Rights*).

[13] *Soering v the United Kingdom*, App No 14038/88, 7 July 1989.

[14] Neil Boister, 'Further Reflections on the Concept of Transnational Criminal Law' (2015) 6 Transnational Legal Theory 9, 10–12.

recounts the state-centred way of capturing cross-border cooperation, the perspective of individuals affected by transnational prosecution is important in this chapter: it shifts attention from the bird's-eye view to the worm's-eye view.[15] This change in perspectives is necessary as, historically, little attention has been paid to the legal position of individuals affected by the implementation of international conventions aimed at the suppression of crime. In particular, this chapter focuses on individuals sought for extradition to stand trial abroad and at risk of losing legal protections provided by a particular jurisdiction.

Following the classic approach to public international law, crime suppression conventions regulate rights and obligations of the states. In contrast, the legal position of the individual has often been assessed on the basis of domestic legislation governing MLA, that is the legal rules determining the process by which states seek and provide assistance to other states, and thus must infringe the legal position of the individual when extraditing a person or gathering evidence for criminal proceedings. This two-level approach reflects the traditional stance that states define the legal status of individuals with domestic law.[16] However, government reservations against judicial cooperation, for instance, the political offence proviso, provided early indications as to whether individuals only benefited from a derivative of state rights or whether they held rights themselves.[17]

Central to this chapter is the perception that individual rights invoke and enforce a legal claim, regardless of whether they invoke a right at the international or national level.[18] In criminal proceedings, with historical roots dating back to canon law, individual rights often have very different origins, ambits and alignments, but today jointly establish the legal status of the individual against state power.[19] Switzerland and Germany share a common heritage with other Western jurisdictions that has seen rights—like the *nullum crimen* principle[20] or the political offence caveat—gain a constitutional or human rights link over time, without losing

[15] Sabine Gless, 'Bird's-Eye View and Worm's-Eye View: Towards a Defendant-Based Approach in Transnational Criminal Law' (2015) 6 Transnational Legal Theory 117 (hereafter Gless, 'Bird's-Eye View and Worm's-Eye View').

[16] Nguyen Quoc Dinh, Patrick Daillier, Mathias Forteau and Alain Pellet, *Droit International Public* (8th edn, LGDJ 2009) 422–26.

[17] Alona E Evans, 'Reflections upon the Political Offense in International Practice' (1963) 57 AJIL 1. One must, however, not forget that many treaties would not carry such a caveat, but aim at the extradition of political dissidents, see Heinrich Lammasch, *Das Recht der Auslieferung wegen politischer Verbrechen* (Mainz 1884) 29–30 (hereafter Lammasch, *Das Recht der Auslieferung*) and Harrington, Chapter 20 in this book.

[18] See Peters, *Beyond Human Rights* (n 12) 472–74, 485–87.

[19] Carl-Friedrich Stuckenberg, 'Double Jeopardy and Ne Bis In Idem in Common Law and Civil Law Jurisdictions' in Darryl K Brown, Jenia Iontcheva Turner and Bettina Weisser (eds), *The Oxford Handbook of Criminal Process* (OUP 2019) 463–64 (hereafter Brown and others, *The Oxford Handbook of Criminal Process*).

[20] See International Covenant on Civil and Political Rights (ICCPR), art 15(1) and ECHR, art 7; see Peters, *Beyond Human Rights* (n 12).

their historical roots.[21] Yet the translation of these rights into daily court proceedings can differ widely, in particular, with regard to transnational cases.

Legal scholars quite naturally refer to the common European heritage[22]—and world-wide recognition[23]—of certain judicial rights that have come to constitute human rights, such as the right to confront an incriminating witness, the right to a fair hearing, the right to remain silent and the right to a lawyer.[24] Regardless of whether these are human rights, or a derivate thereof, they are individual rights addressed at states and the corresponding obligations of states endow the persons concerned with rights. In practice, such rights are determined by domestic procedural rules, not least because they have to be granted in line with a particular jurisdiction's criminal procedure. For this reason, capturing the legal position of the individual in a form of cross-border law enforcement is a challenge.[25] A mapping of transnational criminal law from the perspective of the individuals affected ought to reflect the overall shift in recent decades from a sovereignty-centred to individual-oriented system.[26] Looking at the overall historical development traced in this book, one sees that states did not consider transnational criminal law as a system that ought to follow certain principles protecting individuals' interests until the end of the 20th century. With the rise of human rights, awareness of a possible legal shortfall developed; but at the same time, a belief evolved that the acknowledgement of certain judicial rights in a separate human rights convention could sufficiently protect the individual. Yet individuals prosecuted across borders still miss out on certain rights.[27] It is the aim of this chapter to integrate the bird's eye view of transnational criminal law—as treaty obligations in international crime suppression conventions that determine states' rights and obligations—with the

[21] Hans Schultz, 'Aktuelle Probleme der Auslieferung: Vorläufiger Generalbericht zum vorbereitenden Kolloquium' (1969) 81 Zeitschrift für die gesamte Strafrechtswissenschaft 199, 220 (hereafter Schultz, 'Aktuelle Probleme der Auslieferung').

[22] Bettina Weisser, 'The European Convention on Human Rights and the European Court of Human Rights as Guardians of Fair Criminal Proceedings in Europe' in Darryl K Brown, Jenia Iontcheva Turner and Bettina Weisser (eds), *The Oxford Handbook of Criminal Process* (OUP 2019) 90 (hereafter Weisser, 'The European Convention on Human Rights') with reference to ECHR.

[23] Ed Cape, 'Defense Rights, Duties, Norms, and Practices in Common Law and Civil Law Jurisdictions' in Darryl K Brown, Jenia Iontcheva Turner and Bettina Weisser (eds), *The Oxford Handbook of Criminal Process* (OUP 2019) 189, 193–97 with reference to the ICCPR (hereafter Cape, 'Defense Rights, Duties, Norms and Practices').

[24] Weisser, 'The European Convention on Human Rights' (n 22) 90; Cape, 'Defense Rights, Duties, Norms, and Practices' (n 23) 193–97; Richard Friedman, 'The Confrontation Right' in Brown and others, *The Oxford Handbook of Criminal Process* (n 19) 865, 870–71.

[25] For a European approach, see Martin Böse, 'International Law and Treaty Obligations, Mutual Legal Assistance, and EU Instruments' in Brown and others, *The Oxford Handbook of Criminal Process* (n 19) 611 (hereafter Böse, 'International Law and Treaty Obligations').

[26] Christian Tomuschat, 'International Law: Ensuring the Survival of Mankind on the Eve of a New Century: General Course on Public International Law' (1999) 281 RdC 9, 237.

[27] Monique Mann, Ian Warren and Sally Kennedy, 'The Legal Geographies of Transnational Cyber-Prosecutions: Extradition, Human Rights and Forum Shifting' (2018) 19(2) Global Crime 108; Radha Ivory, 'Corruption Gone Wild: Transnational Criminal Law and the International Trade in Endangered Species' in Anne Peters (ed), *Studies in Global Animal law* (Springer 2020) 88–89.

worm's eye view that individuals are empowered to demand something from a state or invoke something in relation to a state regarding transnational cooperation in criminal justice.[28]

## III. The Acquisition of Legal Status by Individuals

As the acquisition of legal status by individuals in transnational criminal law is rather new, the practice of including the testimony of an individual who is capable of invoking a double criminality proviso or a territoriality matter is often a challenge to traditional proceedings in MLA. This contrasts markedly with that of defendants in domestic criminal justice systems. In Germany, for instance, defendants in criminal trials gained subjective defence rights throughout the 18th and 19th centuries, with legal ideas of the Enlightenment finally replacing notions of criminal procedure that were based on canon law.[29] In addition, subjective rights emerged as a protection against feudal systems.[30] However, only in the 1950s did the general notion of individuals having 'subjective' international rights surface globally, and only during the following decades did the concept of an individual being entitled to international legal subjectivity in virtue of personhood emerge on a well-founded theoretical basis.[31]

The differences in the definition of an individual's standing in transnational cases resulted from scholarship and analysis of treaties—which focused on whether states had entered into treaties for the benefit of a 'third party' or not (*pactum in favorem tertii*).[32] Today, the European acceptance of human rights as individual entitlements beyond state power is undisputed,[33] providing individuals with a key to accessing rights that exist independent of state power.[34]

[28] Gless, 'Bird's-Eye View and Worm's-Eye View' (n 15) 117.

[29] Hinrich Rüping and Günter Jerouschek, *Grundriss der Strafrechtsgeschichte* (6th edn, CH Beck 2011) 87.

[30] Marietta Auer, 'Subjektive Rechte bei Pufendorf und Kant' (2008) 208 Archiv der civilistischen Praxis 584, 633; Christian Reus-Smit, *Individual Rights and the Making of the International System* (CUP 2013) 41–50.

[31] See Peters, *Beyond Human Rights* (n 12) 27–32 pointing out earlier scholars and courts that phrased such ideas.

[32] Christian Dominicé, 'L'emergence de l'individu en droit international public' in Christian Dominicé, *L'ordre juridique international entre tradition et innovation* (Graduate Institute Publications 1997) 109, 123 (hereafter Dominicé, 'L'emergence de l'individu').

[33] See Peters, *Beyond Human Rights* (n 12) 430–31.

[34] For an analysis of the weaknesses of state dependent rights, ie citizenship as the 'right to rights', see Hannah Arendt, *The Origins of Totalitarianism* (Harcourt, Brace and Co 1951) 287–98, especially 294.

## 1. Pragmatic Cross-Border Cooperation

Metternich's Europe, a heyday of pragmatic cross-border cooperation between allies, seems the appropriate starting point to consider the journey of the individual. From this juncture, the individual's status evolved in Continental Europe from that of an object without legal protection, susceptible to the whims of state power and arrestable on a foreign warrant, to a legally protected defendant in transnational proceedings. At that time, allied governments cooperated across borders to assist each other's law enforcement based on so-called requisition proceedings that could include the exchange of search and arrest warrants, court records and interrogation protocols,[35] while also using pragmatic policing approaches.[36] The legal procedures were as varied as the fates of the persons affected. Among those taking advantage of the legal boundaries and the low level of border protection were individuals who fled after committing thefts and robberies, offenders running from (arbitrary) law enforcement or political dissidents seeking sanctuary. This chapter's focus is predominantly on the latter, a group whose acquisition of a legal status is suitable for investigation as their stories are often documented.

The Congress of Vienna produced authoritarian states in central Europe—such as Prussia and Austria—with few civil liberties and an internationally connected police and intelligence system.[37] Meanwhile, smaller and politically neutral states—for instance, Switzerland (which regained sovereignty in 1815) or Belgium (after its struggle for independence in 1830)—fulfilled their promise of providing a sanctuary. To this day, the age of Metternich is known for notorious surveillance of dissidents and cross-border policing with the help of spies. His various *Beobachtungs-Anstalten* (though, legally, little more than private intelligence) formed part of police services, which worked internationally and played a pivotal role in the Restoration. It enabled surveillance of liberal dissidents along with cross-border reporting, extraditions and expulsions.[38] This cooperation, however, was based more on police practice and power politics than on law.[39] Extraditions

[35] See eg Christoph Carl Stübel, *Das Criminalverfahren in den deutschen Gerichten mit besonderer Rücksicht auf das Königreich Sachsen wissenschaftlich und zum praktischen Gebrauche dargestellt*, vols 1–5 (Leipzig 1811) vol 1, 189–200, vol 3, 223–89, vol 5, 106.

[36] Hsi-Huey Liang, *The Rise of Modern Police and the European State System from Metternich to the Second World War* (CUP 1992) 18–19, 33–34.

[37] For the impact on cross-border cooperation, see Jean Conrad Tyrichter, 'The Formation of Transnational Criminal Law within the German Federation: A Normative Order?' in Karl Härter, Tina Hannappel and Jean Conrad Tyrichter (eds), *The Transnationalisation of Criminal Law in the Nineteenth and Twentieth Century* (Vittorio Klostermann 2019) 21, 21–24.

[38] Ido de Haan and Jeroen van Zanten, 'Constructing an International Conspiracy' in Beatrice de Graaf, Ido de Haan and Brian Vick (eds), *Securing Europe after Napoleon: 1815 and the New European Security Culture* (CUP 2019) 185.

[39] See Albert Billot, *Traité de l'extradition suivi d'un recueil de documents étrangers et des conventions d'extradition conclues par la France et actuellement en vigueur* (Plon 1874) 39 (hereafter Billot, *Traité de l'extradition*); Lammasch, *Das Recht der Auslieferung* (n 17) 203–06; Schultz, 'Aktuelle Probleme der Auslieferung' (n 21) 199. For details on the history of deportation and extradition before the 19th century, see Karl Härter, 'The Transnationalisation of Criminal Law in the Nineteenth and Twentieth

and expulsions were a practical element of police prevention of public dangers and maintenance of order that excluded the protection provided to alleged criminals in domestic proceedings.[40] The juridification of pre-modern practices—like the granting of criminal asylum by churches, cities or other privileged jurisdictions—demonstrates that the lack of rights of the individuals affected continued deep into the 19th century.[41]

As we know today, the Restoration period did not prevent modern ideas about the rule of law and liberalism from circulating Europe; certain countries—like Belgium—were able to pass legislation on refugee rights, while others—such as Switzerland—came to tolerate an influx of political dissidents.[42]

In Europe, notions of an individual's rights and remedies with respect to the government strengthened over the 19th century and became entrenched, in particular, in criminal justice, where classic state-citizen conflicts arose. In Germany, for instance, legal scholars refined Enlightenment principles, like *nullum crimen sine lege* and procedural defence rights to the level of sophistication that resulted in the widespread reputation of German criminal legal theory in the 20th century. Criminal justice, in that respect, grew into a citizen's bastion against the omnipotent state.[43] Prominent examples of such pioneering work were Ludwig Feuerbach's Penal Code of 1813 or Heinrich Zachariae's *Grundlinien des gemeinen deutschen Criminalprozesses* of 1837. By pointing out the crucial function of formal rights and clear remedies (*schützende Formen des Prozessrechts*),[44] the latter illustrated how the legal status of the individual in criminal proceedings transformed with the advent of constitutionalism.

In central Europe, these ideas on criminal justice were exchanged across borders, first between individual scholars,[45] and later between international organizations.[46]

Century' in Karl Härter, Tina Hannappel and Jean Conrad Tyrichter (eds), *The Transnationalisation of Criminal Law in the Nineteenth and Twentieth Century* (Vittorio Klostermann 2019) 1, 12 (hereafter Härter, 'The Transnationalisation of Criminal Law'). Certain remedies and notions can be traced back to the Middle Ages, when the expulsion of individuals was basically an act of political power, see eg Hugo Grotius, *De jure belli ac pacis* (first published Paris 1625) Liber II Caput XXI ('extradition chapter').

[40] Mathieu Deflem, 'International Policing in Nineteenth-Century Europe: The Police Union of German States, 1851–1866' (1996) 6 International Criminal Justice Review 36, 39–40.

[41] See Härter, Chapter 1 in this book.

[42] Herbert Reiter, *Politisches Asyl im 19. Jahrhundert* (Duncker & Humblot 1992) 170, 216.

[43] Franz von Liszt, 'Die deterministischen Gegner der Zweckstrafe' (1893) 13 Zeitschrift für die gesamte Strafrechtswissenschaft 325, 357.

[44] Heinrich Albert Zachariae, *Handbuch des deutsches Strafprocesses*, vol 1 (Dietrich'sche Buchhandlung 1861) 145–46.

[45] Lieselotte Jelowik (ed), *Briefe deutscher Strafrechtler an Karl Josef Anton Mittermaier 1832–1866* (Vittorio Klostermann 2005); Lars Hendrik Riemer (ed), *Das Netzwerk der "Gefängnisfreunde" 1830–1872. Karl Josef Anton Mittermaiers Briefwechsel mit europäischen Strafvollzugsexperten* (Vittorio Klostermann 2005).

[46] Härter, 'The Transnationalisation of Criminal Law' (n 39) 1, 16–17; Diego Nunes, 'The Extradition and Political Crimes in the "International Fight Against Crimes": Western Europe and Latin America, 1833–1933' in Karl Härter, Tina Hannappel and Jean Conrad Tyrichter (eds), *The Transnationalisation*

Over time, these debates included issues in international criminal law and often resulted in reform proposals, such as the Oxford Institute of International Law's recommendations on extradition of 1880.[47]

## 2. Juridification of Domestic Proceedings and Cross-Border Cooperation

Germany presents an interesting example of the juridification of domestic criminal proceedings and the lack of such a process transnationally. The core ideas of constitutionalism in Germany had shaped many areas of law—such as the adoption of the so-called *Reichsjustizgesetze* in 1877, which legislated on the constitution of courts, civil procedure, bankruptcy and criminal procedure—and, most importantly, acknowledged the individual as the bearer of rights and obligations. Nonetheless, it would take Germany more than fifty years to adopt legislation on MLA in criminal matters.[48] A draft extradition law, first presented to parliament in 1892,[49] remained an object of intense scholarly[50] and legislative debate for four decades,[51] with the legislator unable to pass the law. Criminal law scholars addressing issues of transnational cooperation clearly drew a line at that time. In their thinking, the rule of law and defence rights were meant for criminal trials *in* Germany; extraditions, however, followed different rules.[52] While criminal charges in the country had to be presented in the formal way of the judiciary, extradition and deportation proceedings often lacked a legal basis and were handled as a police matter.[53]

*of Criminal Law in the Nineteenth and Twentieth Century* (Vittorio Klostermann 2019) 41, 59 (hereafter Nunes, 'The Extradition and Political Crimes').

[47] Ivan A Shearer, *Extradition in International Law* (Manchester UP 1971) 124 (hereafter Shearer, *Extradition in International Law*).

[48] Deutsches Auslieferungsgesetz of 23 December 1929 in Reichs-Gesetzblatt (RGBl) 1929, pt 1, 239–44.

[49] RT-Drucks 1890/92, no 627; Wolfgang Mettgenberg and Karl Doerner (eds), *Deutsches Auslieferungsgesetz* (2nd edn, F Vahlen 1953) 15 et seq.

[50] See von Liszt's report on a Codification of Extradition Law at the German Jurists' Conference in Leipzig 1880, in Franz von Liszt, 'Sind gleiche Grundsätze des internationalen Strafrechts für die europäischen Staaten anzustreben? Und eventuell welche?' (1882) 2 Zeitschrift für die gesamte Strafrechtswissenschaft 50.

[51] Stenographische Berichte über die Verhandlungen des Reichstags, 164. Sitzung 5 February 1892, vol 119, 4013 et seq <https://daten.digitale-sammlungen.de/~db/0001/bsb00018669/images/>. For a contextualization, see Jochen Oltmer, 'Protecting Refugees in the Weimar Republic' (2016) 29 Journal of Refugee Studies 318. See excerpts from the parliamentary debate, eg contributions of Dr Ludwig Marum (SPD) and Dr Eduard Ludwig Alexander (KPD) in Verhandlungen des Deutschen Reichstags, Stenographische Berichte 4. Wahlperiode 1928, 106. und 107. Sitzung 2 December 1929, vol 426, 3375–81 < https://www.reichstagsprotokolle.de/Blatt2_w4_bsb00000110_00267.html >.

[52] See Delius, 'Das Auslieferungsverfahren in Preussen, insbesondere die Mitwirkung der Gerichte bei demselben' (1891) 11 Zeitschrift für die gesamte Strafrechtswissenschaft 677, 684 (hereafter Delius, 'Das Auslieferungsverfahren in Preussen').

[53] See Franz von Liszt, *Lehrbuch des Deutschen Strafrechts* (9th edn, Guttentag 1899), who emphasizes the legal position of individuals in a domestic criminal trial 72–73, but sees no problem in an extradition without a legal basis 103.

Germany was among the latecomers, with other Continental European countries—for example, Belgium (after having gained independence) in 1833, the Netherlands in 1849, Luxembourg in 1870 and Switzerland in 1892—having already adopted extradition laws during the 19th century.[54] These laws spelled out specific reservations against extradition, for instance, the political crime caveat.[55] Belgium became known for linking rights relevant to mutual legal assistance to its constitution of 1831 and thus provided a basis for legislation that aimed to offer protection, even to the politically persecuted.[56] However, the Belgian law and its endorsement in other states did not open a pathway for all individuals to be equally vested with rights in the extradition proceeding. *Raison d'état* and specific historic developments time and again threatened to derail the individual's legal position in extradition proceedings. In the second half of the 19th century, governments in many European countries were extremely wary of anarchists and implemented measures such as the 'assassination clause', which refused political asylum to anyone who attempted to kill the monarch or his or her representatives.[57]

However, some countries remained on a liberal course. Switzerland—diminutive by nature and bordered by many neighbouring states—took a procedural approach as reflected by the law of 1892.[58] With the legal diversity inherent in federalism, it often aimed at pragmatic solutions, but stood firm on its strong commitment to remain non-monarchical, refusing to implement the assassination clause.[59] Swiss scholars at the time addressed the precarious legal situation of individuals sought for extradition,[60] pointing out that individuals were able to raise objections in Swiss courts against their extradition. The grounds for such objections were that states involved had not complied with treaty requirements[61] such as the political offence caveat or the requirement for dual criminality in extradition proceedings.[62]

[54] Shearer, *Extradition in International Law* (n 47) 8, 18; Lagodny, *Die Rechtsstellung des Auszuliefernden* (n 7) 33–37.

[55] For the link between a liberal approach and the acceptance of a 'political crime' as an exception to the duty to extradite, see Nunes, 'The Extradition and Political Crimes' (n 46) 47–62.

[56] See art 128 of Belgium's Constitution of 1831 <https://www.constituteproject.org/con-stitution/ Bel- gium_2014.pdf?lang=en>; Loi du 1er octobre 1833 sur les extraditions. <http://www.ejustice.just.fgov.be/eli/loi/1833/10/01/1833100150/justel>; the law raised international interest, even centuries later, eg Heinrich Grützner, 'Staatspolitik und Kriminalpolitik im Auslieferungsrecht?' (1956) 68 Zeitschrift für die Gesamte Strafrechtswissenschaft 504.

[57] Peter Reisner, *Die Voraussetzungen der Auslieferung wegen strafbarer Handlungen nach Erlass des Auslieferungsgesetzes* (Noske 1932) 80 (hereafter Reisner, *Die Voraussetzungen der Auslieferung*); for more details on the assasination clause see Lammasch, *Das Recht der Auslieferung* (n 17) 309–12.

[58] Bundesgesetz der Schweiz betreffend die Auslieferung gegenüber dem Auslande vom 22. Januar 1892, printed in (1892) 7 Archiv des öffentlichen Rechts 565. Cantonal laws granted access to court before an extradition, see Jacques Berney, *De la procédure suivie en Suisse pour l'extradition des malfaiteurs aux pays étrangers* (C Detloff 1889) 4 (hereafter Berney, *De la procédure suivie en Suisse*).

[59] Reisner, *Die Voraussetzungen der Auslieferung* (n 57) 80.

[60] Berney, *De la procédure suivie en Suisse* (n 58) 126–27.

[61] Swiss Federal Court (Schweizer Bundesgericht) Judgment of 7 December 1877, Entscheidungen des Bundesgerichts Vol 3, no BGE 3 I 708 (1877) 708–13.

[62] Art II and VII Auslieferungsvertrag zwischen der Schweiz und Grossbritannien, Swiss Federal Gazette Bundesblatt (BBl) 1874 303.

Swiss judges acknowledged the legal interests of individuals in mutual legal assistance, even when alleged anarchists were sought for involvement in an assassination plot,[63] while petty criminals who had eventually settled in Switzerland and faced extradition to face a potential sentence abroad that seemed excessive were also afforded protection.[64]

In contrast, the German *Reichsgericht* maintained in 1909 that, in principle, extradition took place from government to government, and the individual was a mere object to be delivered.[65] This approach, however, sparked criticism at the time among scholars with regard to the language and the lack of rights of the individual: 'Thus the delivered humans are objects, *vilis materia*, who are pushed back and forth without personal rights! ... Mind the language [of the court]: The person is an object, nothing but an object! ... The delivered person of course has no rights, he is a mere object.'[66] This rather technocratic approach was reflected in teaching and in extradition procedures. Authorities did not necessarily need an arrest warrant to imprison someone pending their extradition. Governments could simply revert to police detention in order to hold someone prior to delivering them abroad.[67] Although some scholarly voices maintained criticism,[68] the belief that states are the stakeholders and individuals mere objects in international law was deeply rooted. A fundamental shift in assessing the legal position of the individual only took place during the late 20th century, with the acknowledgement of human rights in Germany.[69]

## IV. The Lost Idea of a 'Doctrine Cosmopolite'

The idea of the individual as a stakeholder in cross-border cooperation for criminal justice, however, had already surfaced at the end of the 19th century among international scholars. They advocated for a transformation of criminal law based on their ideas of rational criminal justice and 'social defence' as well as prevention measures tailored to individual offenders.[70] The criminological reformists aiming

[63] An alleged anarchist faced prosecution in Italy for a presumed part in killing the King, see Swiss Federal Court, Judgment of 30 March 1901, Entscheidungen des Bundesgerichts, no BGE 27 I 52 (1901).

[64] The individual had been sought by Germany for petty theft dating years back. See Swiss Federal Court, Judgment of 6 February 1894, Entscheidungen des Bundesgerichts, no BGE 20 I 52 (1894).

[65] German Reichsgericht Decision of 23 April 1909, RGSt 42 309, 310. For a broader discussion, see Dugard and Van den Wyngaert, 'Reconciling Extradition with Human Rights' (n 7) 188–90.

[66] Kohler, 'Der Savarkar-Streitfall zwischen Frankreich und England' (n 6) 130 (translation provided by author).

[67] For details, see Delius, 'Das Auslieferungsverfahren in Preussen' (n 52).

[68] Reisner, *Die Voraussetzungen der Auslieferung* (n 57) 9.

[69] For an example of the longevity of the traditional view, see Schröder, 'Staats- und völkerrechtliche Fragen der Auslieferungsbewilligung' (n 9) 231: 'Der Verfolgte ist blosses Objekt des Auslieferungsverfahrens.'

[70] See Pifferi, Chapter 2 in this book; Ignacio de la Rasilla del Moral, 'International Criminal Justice as Universal Social Defence. Quintiliano Saldaña (1878–1938)' in Frédéric Mégret and Immi Tallgren

at an amelioration of domestic institutions of criminal justice at home, while also developing rational and coherent criminal legislation worldwide, included, among many other scholars from all over Europe, von Liszt from Germany and Stooss from Switzerland. The debates enabled by the International Union of Penal Law and, later, the Association Internationale de droit Pénal (AIDP) acknowledged new ideas, including support for the position of the individual in transnational criminal proceedings, with divided responsibilities among the involved states, as Pifferi shows in Chapter 2 of this book.[71] These exchanges situated the individual not only in a new approach on the domestic level, but also within transnational developments. In Switzerland, for instance, Stooss vividly advocated von Liszt's 'special preventive punishment theory' based on deterrence, rehabilitation and societal protection and, on that basis, argued that deportation was not an acceptable punishment.[72] It appears, however, that German and Swiss scholars were much more concerned with the doctrinal issues at the heart of traditional criminal law—for instance, the acknowledgement of freedom of will in penal law or the purpose of punishment—than with a true international perspective on criminal justice.[73]

It was other scholars and, in particular, Saldaña, deeply influenced by the teaching of von Liszt, who pointedly demanded a new approach of 'non-territoriality' based on a more universal idea of criminal jurisdiction, able to protect any individuals adversely affected by transnational law enforcement.[74] In the spirit of the ideas for reform, Saldaña proposed that states in their domestic legislation as well as in international treaties ought not to aim for the surrender of the individual, but for the guarantee that he or she would face a fair trial and rational and humane treatment.[75] Therefore, he demanded the replacement of 'extradition systems' with a new approach to jurisdiction and a kind of international penal guarantee that ensured alleged offenders would receive adequate treatment. In particular, he based his 'doctrine cosmopolite' on universal jurisdiction of the *iudex deprehensionis* with certain judicial guarantees, replacing traditional extradition procedures that lacked adequate legal entitlements.[76]

(eds), *The Dawn of a Discipline: International Criminal Justice and Its Early Exponents* (CUP 2020) 118 (hereafter de la Rasilla del Moral, 'International Criminal Justice').

[71] See eg Paul Knepper, *The Invention of International Crime. A Global Issue in the Making, 1881–1914* (Palgrave Macmillan 2010) 159–87; Willem Hendrik Nagel, 'International Collaboration in the Field of Criminology' in *Le droit pénal international. Recueil d'études en hommage a Jacob Maarten Van Bemmelen* (Brill 1965) 193.

[72] Carl Stooss, 'Welche Anforderungen stellt die Kriminalpolitik an ein eidgenössisches Strafgesetzbuch' (1891) 4 Zeitschrift für Schweizer Strafrecht 245.

[73] See further intervations of Carl Stooss and Franz von Liszt, 'Die Internationale Vereinigung und ihre Zielpunkte' (1894) 14 Zeitschrift für die gesamte Strafrechtswissenschaft 611.

[74] de la Rasilla del Moral, International Criminal Justice (n 70) 123.

[75] Quintiliano Saldaña, 'La Justice Pénale Internationale' (1925) (10) RdC 228 (hereafter Saldaña, 'La Justice Pénale Internationale').

[76] See further Quintiliano Saldaña, *La Défence Sociale Universelle* (Conference donné à la Faculté de Droit de l'Université de Paris le 29 Mars 1924, Roma y La Haya) (Góngora 1926) 15–16, 21.

Disruptions caused by war, with their nationalist movements, obviously interrupted the European exchange of ideas for reform. Despite the efforts to restore academic exchange in new international organizations and to have an international approach endorsed, with World War II many ideas were, seemingly, lost. Among these was that of international penal guarantees.[77] This comes as no surprise with his thinking being contrary to the prevailing approach to the kind of instrumental transfer prevailing at that time.

## V. The Paradigm Shift Empowering the Individual

After World War II, states which took part in extraditions were concerned only with the allocation of the rights and obligations of the other state party, and ignored the individuals affected.[78] In retrospect, it is interesting to note how few voiced their concern about the traditional state-centric approach of public international law, especially considering the devastation wreaked by World War I. Indeed, the idea that states had lost their legitimacy as stakeholders in international matters to the benefit of an individual's subjectivity in transnational affairs was rarely proffered.[79] But slowly, the reading of international treaties—including those on MLA—changed. After World War II, European countries embraced the idea of human rights, including judicial rights. In particular, with the adoption of the ECHR, states promised the right to a fair trial (along with the right to an interpreter, to confront or cross-examine witnesses etc) that went beyond domestic law. But again, this transnational promise aimed at compliance with a minimum standard in domestic proceedings rather than cultivating subjective rights in transnational criminal law or, in other words, the idea of human rights.[80]

### 1. Reading of Treaties

MLA treaties were international treaties with many purposes. They defined rights and obligations of states, but also divided powers between governments and houses of parliament when entering into obligations with other states. The least likely motivation, in most jurisdictions, was to empower the individual. The lack of recognition for subjective rights in cross-border cooperation corresponded with

[77] See further de la Rasilla del Moral, 'International Criminal Justice' (n 70) 124–28.

[78] For Switzerland, see Schultz, 'Aktuelle Probleme der Auslieferung' (n 21) 199.

[79] See, however, Jean Spiropoulos, 'L'individu et le droit international' (1929) 30 RdC 191, 197 or Nicolas Politis, *Les nouvelles tendances du droit international* (Hachette 1927) 55–93, 76.

[80] Schaffner, *Das Individuum im internationalen Rechtshilferecht* (n 5) 83–85; with reference to Stephan Breitenmoser and Gunter E Wilms, 'Human Rights v. Extradition: The Soering Case' (1990) 11 Mich J Intl L 845, 846 (hereafter Breitenmoser and Wilms, 'Human Rights v. Extradition').

the prevailing theory of international law in the 19th century that saw states as the sole beneficiaries of international treaties and acknowledged a 'third party' right only in case of a *pactum in favorem tertii*.[81] Thus, even where international treaties established a political offence caveat or required double criminality as a precondition for extradition, the individual could not invoke it, unless domestic law assigned the right.[82]

That is the very reason why the Belgian approach caused a sensation, even though it was in line with earlier ideas, like provisions adopted after the French Revolution.[83] Around the middle of the 19th century, France embraced Belgium's notion of granting rights to individuals sought for extradition and concluded international treaties to reflect this.[84] With a significant player on the international stage like France accepting it, the idea gained importance.

At the beginning of the 20th century, manifold MLA treaties connected European countries. Underpinned by domestic legislation, it is difficult to determine what their respective obligations were regarding rights related to foreign policy, the internal legislative powers and the authority to infringe individual rights. Each nation seemingly developed its own unique understanding.[85] But there is sufficient evidence for a general claim to be made that extradition treaties never in fact granted rights to individuals.[86]

German courts strongly rebuked the legal status of the individual in cross-border cooperation, arguing that any protection granted was merely a derivative of a state right to refuse cooperation with a foreign state.[87] As late as the second half of the 20th century, some scholars still reaffirmed the notion that: '[t]he individual affected [was] merely the object of extradition proceedings'.[88] But such opinions actually corresponded with the legal situation: the Act on International Cooperation in Criminal Matters (AICCM),[89] adopted in the 1980s, maintained the traditional

[81] Dominicé, 'L'emergence de l'individu' (n 32) 109, 123.

[82] For a more detailed account, see Robert Kolb, 'The Protection of the Individual in Times of War and Peace' in Bardo Fassbender and Anne Peters, *The Oxford Handbook of the History of International Law* (OUP 2012) 317, 318–19.

[83] Schultz, 'Aktuelle Probleme der Auslieferung' (n 21) 220.

[84] See Billot, *Traité de l'extradition* (n 39) 471; Reisner, *Die Voraussetzungen der Auslieferung* (n 57) 9; Lagodny, *Die Rechtsstellung des Auszuliefernden* (n 7) 37–40.

[85] For Germany, see Lagodny, *Die Rechtsstellung des Auszuliefernden* (n 7) 29–62; for Switzerland, Schaffner, *Das Individuum im internationalen Rechtshilferecht* (n 5) 43–70.

[86] Haro F van Panhuys, 'Le traité d'extradition en tant que source de droits pour les individus' in Jacob Maarten van Bemmelen (ed), *Le droit pénal international: recueil d'études en hommage à Jacob Maarten van Bemmelen* (EJ Brill 1965) 57, 58 et seq; John G Kester, 'Some Myths of United States Extradition Law' (1988) 76 Geo LJ 1441, 1465 et seq; Michael P Shea, 'Expanding Judicial Scrutiny of Human Rights in Extradition Cases After Soering' (1992) 17 Yale J Intl L 85, 86 (hereafter Shea, 'Expanding Judicial Scrutiny').

[87] Federal Court, Bundesgerichtshof in Strafsachen (BGH, Decision of 16 January 1963, BGHSt 18 218, 220 (1963)).

[88] Schröder, 'Staats- und völkerrechtliche Fragen der Auslieferungsbewilligung' (n 9) 231.

[89] Act on International Cooperation in Criminal Matters of 23 December 1982 (Gesetz über die Internationale Rechtshilfe in Strafsachen) <https://www.gesetze-im-internet.de/englisch_irg/index.html>.

idea that MLA was primarily to secure government interests in state dealings—what was later called a 'two-dimensional system'.[90]

## 2. The Turn towards Human Rights

The 20th century, with its general turn towards human rights, fundamentally changed the understanding of the legal status of the individual. This development can be understood as a derivative of a modern perception of the individual in public international law.[91] The new approach probably resulted from the participation of criminal law scholars in an international debate and a 'cross- fertilization of courts'.[92]

The latter culminated with the ECtHR decision in *Soering v United Kingdom*,[93] a landmark case for the establishment of the legal status of the individual in extradition proceedings in Europe. The Strasbourg court ruled that extradition from a European country to the United States to face charges of capital murder violated article 3 of the ECHR, which protected against inhuman and degrading treatment. The ECHR's acknowledgement that a person wanted for extradition may invoke article 3 of the ECHR to fight extradition (in the requested state) on the grounds that punishment in the requesting state infringes human rights is seen as an implicit rejection of the traditional concept that mutual legal assistance is a purely intergovernmental law granting rights only to states.[94] Certain lawyers and government officials were surprised by the *Soering* decision, although they could have seen it coming with the ECtHR's encouragement for an expansive reading of article 6 of the ECHR:

> the Convention is intended to guarantee not rights that are theoretical or illusory but rights that are practical and effective; this is particularly so of the rights of the defence in view of the prominent place held in a democratic society by the right to a fair trial, from which they derive.[95]

[90] Nadeschda Wilkitzki, *Entstehung des Gesetzes über die Internationale Rechtshilfe in Strafsachen (IRG)* (De Gruyter 2010) 241–44.

[91] See Breitenmoser and Wilms, 'Human Rights v. Extradition' (n 80) 879.

[92] Anne-Marie Slaughter, 'A Global Community of Courts' (2003) 44 Harv Intl LJ 191, 193.

[93] *Soering v United Kingdom*, App no 14028/88, 7 July 1989.

[94] See Breitenmoser and Wilms, 'Human Rights v. Extradition' (n 80) 879; but subsequent case law does not grant a straightforward entitlement of all persons affected by cross-border law enforcement, nor do scholars agree on the shape of particular entitlements. See eg *Sanchez-Reisse v Switzerland*, App no 9862/82, 21 October 1986, para 47; *Mamatkulov and Askarov v Turkey*, App no 46827/99 and 46951/99, 4 February 2005, para 82; *Buijen v Germany*, App no 27804/05, 1 April 2010, para 42; *Gallardo Sanchez v Italy*, App no 11620/07, 24 March 2015, paras 39 et seq.

[95] *Artico v Italy*, App no 6694/74, 13 May 1980, para 33.

This understanding almost inevitably led to acknowledgement of certain individual rights in transnational criminal law. It was underscored by the court's view that the ECHR, unlike other international treaties, creates an objective obligation to enforce the established individual rights for anyone within the jurisdiction of the contracting states and to prevent a breach at all levels.[96]

When the Strasbourg court decided *Soering*, many scholars simply embraced the judgment,[97] creating the 'three-dimensional approach'. In 1987, German scholar, Otto Lagodny, published a monograph on the legal position of individuals wanted for extradition (*Die Rechtsstellung des Auszuliefernden in der Bundesrepublik Deutschland*), which contrasted the traditional doctrine with a new vision: a three-dimensional legal assistance procedure, with the individual vested with rights and remedies.[98]

Thus the individual involved in a transnational criminal case developed into a subject and not the object of negotiation between two states; the individual came to hold a legal position vis-à-vis both the requesting and the requested state.[99]

Others remained more cautious. Some pointed to legal hurdles like the *ordre public* reservation,[100] the invocation of which must be reserved for states, or insisted that criminal proceedings and mutual legal assistance are 'two different things' and individuals sought for extradition could not claim the legal status of a defendant.[101] Some criticized the turn to humanitarianism and claimed that the acknowledgement and application of individual rights in MLA would lead to an unwanted 'extraterritorial export' of domestic constitutional rights.[102]

Nevertheless, it is now generally accepted that, in Germany, MLA caveats protect the individual, for instance, where the death penalty might be threatened or where political persecution may eventuate.[103]

96 *Ireland v United Kingdom*, App no 5310/71, 18 January 1978, para 239.

97 Christine van den Wyngaert, 'Applying the European Convention on Human Rights to Extradition: Opening Pandora's Box?' (1990) 39 ICLQ 757; Otto Lagodny, 'Human Rights in the Field of Extradition' (1991) 62 RiDP 45; Shea, 'Expanding Judicial Scrutiny' (n 86) 85; Sharon A Williams, 'Human Rights Safeguards and International Cooperation: Striking the Balance' (1992) 3 Crim LF 191.

98 Lagodny, *Die Rechtsstellung des Auszuliefernden* (n 7) 1, 9, 98, 259.

99 Albin Eser, 'Common Goals and Different Ways in International Criminal Law: Reflections from a European Perspective' (1990) 31 Harv Intl LJ 117, 125.

100 Böse, 'International Law and Treaty Obligations' (n 25) 613.

101 Ferdinand von Maritz, *Internationale Rechtshilfe in Strafsachen. Beiträge zur positiven Theorie des Völkerrechts der Gegenwart*, vol 1 (H Haessel 1888) 451: 'durch Auslieferung wird man nicht bestraft; vielmehr ist es ein Mittel, um die rechtlichen Interessen des Auslandes zu realisieren'.

102 Theodor Vogler, 'Grundrechte und grenzüberschreitende Sachverhalte. Besprechung des gleichnamigen Buches von Rainer Hoffmann' (1996) 143 Goltdammer's Archiv 569, 575–76, upheld in BVerfG NJW 1979, 1285.

103 Wolfgang Schomburg, 'Die Rolle des Individuums in der Internationalen Kooperation in Strafsachen' [1998] Strafverteidiger 153.

## 3. Roll-Back to Be Feared?

Today, the legal status of the individual appears to be established, even beyond state reproach: international law aims to prevent states from exposing individuals to situations that would result in the violation of certain fundamental rights.[104] However, protection of the legal status of the individual is not spread evenly to all areas of transnational criminal law: while interest has centred on extradition,[105] individual rights in other areas—like evidence and information sharing among states—remain less protected. Furthermore, the individual's legal status is not immune to roll-backs. Extrajudicial renditions for interrogation purposes[106] and the establishment of 'black site' prisons where inmates are subjected to torture, provide recent examples.[107] The future will present novel challenges, for instance, with regard to automated data sharing and profiling.[108]

The individual's legal status in European cross-border cooperation has come under scrutiny with the EU's adoption of the principle of mutual recognition. As a consequence, extraditions have developed legally from the 'external' handing over of a person to another state for an 'internal' procedure (leading to a person standing trial in another EU state) on the presumption that criminal justice works under comparable conditions throughout the EU.[109] The European Arrest Warrant provides a prominent illustration of this with 'extradition' reworded to 'surrender' and traditional reservations protecting individual interests in extradition proceedings erased.[110] However, European courts seem to have learned their lesson, with domestic courts as well as the European Court of Justice cautiously implementing a human rights standard in the system of mutual recognitions of judicial decisions

[104] For a detailed comparative overview, see Albin Eser, Otto Lagodny and Christopher L Blakesley (eds), *The Individual as Subject of International Cooperation in Criminal Matters* (Nomos 2002). The consensus has had an impact on international criminal law too, see eg *Prosecutor v Anto Furundzija*, Case no IT-95-17/1-T, 10 December 1998, paras 143–57.

[105] John Quigley, 'The Rule of Non-Inquiry and the Impact of Human Rights on Extradition Law' (1990) 15 NCJ Intl L & Comm Reg 401.

[106] Council of Europe (CoE) Parliamentary Assembly, Committee on Legal Affairs and Human Rights (Rapporteur: Dick Marty), Information Memorandum II, AS/Jur (2006) 03 rev, 22 January 2006; Memorandum from the CoE Commissioner for Human Rights (Thomas Hammarberg), Advancing Accountability in Respect of the CIA Black Site in Romania, CommDH (2012) 38, 30 March 2012.

[107] See *Al Nashiri v Poland*, App no 28761/11, 24 July 2014; *Husayn (Abu Zubaydah) v Poland*, App no 7511/13, 24 July 2014.

[108] Paul de Hert and Serge Gutwirth, 'Interoperability of Police Databases Within the EU: An Accountable Political Choice?' (2006) 20 Intl Rev L Comp & Tech 21, 30.

[109] Böse, 'International Law and Treaty Obligations' (n 25) 613–14.

[110] Böse, 'International Law and Treaty Obligations' (n 25) 615–16; for a policy evaluation, see Karin Landgren, 'Deflecting International Protection by Treaty: Bilateral and Multilateral Accords on Extradition, Readmission and the Inadmissibility of Asylum Requests' (1999) New Issues in Refugee Research, UNHCR Working Paper No 10, 31–42. See also Steve Peers, 'Proposed Framework Decision on European Arrest Warrants' Statewatch post 11/9/2001 analyses no 3, 8–10 <http://www.statewatch.org/analyses/no-3-ewarrant.pdf>.

established among EU states,[111] with individuals permitted to raise alleged violations even when domestic law did not explicitly entitle them to do so.[112]

## VI. Conclusion

Today, the individual's legal status seems firmly embedded in legal practice and theory. It has been a long journey for fugitives, foreigners and emigres, with protections by European countries having been introduced at divergent speeds across the Continent. Ultimately, with transnational criminal law being considered more a system than a compilation of special treaties (driven by diplomacy and transnational concessions), along with the rise of human rights and a new reading of treaties that reflected the generally increasing status of the individual under international law, domestic legislators adopted corresponding laws. Eventually, it seems that the significance of human rights has settled the legal status of the individual in transnational criminal law, not only in Europe, but globally.[113]

Why did it take so long for the individual to acquire a legal status in transnational criminal proceedings? There is no mono-causal answer to this question. Many factors have had an impact: the traditional understanding of criminal law as a local matter which prevented transnational criminal law from gradually building up as a legal system, along with the disruptions to the international debate among criminal law scholars who were unsuccessful in materializing the idea of international penal guarantees that had surfaced at the beginning of the 20th century. Only after a general turn towards human rights did scholars and courts use this line of argument to underpin individual rights in transnational criminal law at the end of the 20th century.

Perhaps individual rights would have been established earlier if fear of cross-border prosecution and extradition had concerned the population evenly. In civil law jurisdictions, citizens did not have to fear extradition; most individuals sought for prosecution abroad were, by definition, the 'other'. This demarcation and insularity—that failed to go behind the 'veil of ignorance'—reduced human beings

[111] Martin Böse, 'The European Arrest Warrant and the Independence of Public Prosecutors: OG & PI, PF, JR & YC' (2020) 57 CML Rev 1259; Valsamis Mitsilegas, 'The European Union and the Rights of Individuals in Criminal Proceedings' in Brown and others, *The Oxford Handbook of Criminal Process* (n 18) 131–34.

[112] See *Aranyosi und Căldăraru* [2016] ECLI:EU:C:2016:198; *Bob-Dogi* [2016] ECLI:EU:C:2016:385; *Poplawski* [2017] ECLI:EU:C:2017:503; *Ardic* [2017] ECLI:EU:C:2017:1026; *Piotrowski* [2018] ECLI:EU:C:2018:27; *LM (Deficiencies in the system of justice)* [2018] ECLI:EU:C:2018:586.

[113] See *Cox v Kanada*, Human Rights Committee Meeting 31 October 1994, CCPR/C/52/D/539/1993, No 539/1993, para 16.1: '[I]f a State party to the [UNO-Pakt II] takes a decision relating to a person within its jurisdiction, and the necessary and foreseeable consequence is that that person's rights under the [UNO-Pakt II] will be violated in another jurisdiction, the State party itself may be in violation of the [UNO-Pakt II]'; *LaGrand (Germany v United States of America)* (Judgment) [2001] ICJ Rep 466, para 77.

affected by cross-border cooperation to a sort of non-citizen and left individuals sought for prosecution in another jurisdiction outside the 19th century process of juridification that shaped the legal status of individuals in domestic criminal proceedings. It could act as a reminder of the fundamental principle that captures the legal status of the individual in transnational criminal law today: the ultimate normative source of all law—criminal as well as international—is not authority, nationality or sovereignty, but humanity.[114]

[114] Saldaña, 'La Justice Pénale Internationale' (n 75) 228–42; Anne Peters, 'Membership in the Global Constitutional Community' in Jan Klabbers, Anne Peters and Geir Ulfstein, *The Constitutionalization of International Law* (OUP 2009) 153, 155, 157: 're-introduction of the individual'.

# Index

*For the benefit of digital users, indexed terms that span two pages (e.g., 52–53) may, on occasion, appear on only one of those pages.*

Tables and figures are indicated by *t* and *f* following the page number.


**African Court of Justice and Human and Peoples' Rights**
  criminal jurisdiction 101–2
  proposal to establish 112–13, 114
**aggression**
  concept 107
  definition 107
**anarchism**
  growth (1870s to 1914) 140
  modernization of policing, stimulus to 141
  terrorism, as 140
**anarchy**
  anarchist act, definition 141
  extradition, and 280–81
  national laws, against 141
  police cooperation 141–42
  *portrait parlé* 142
  propaganda by deed 140
  transnational cooperation, against 140–42
**Anti-Anarchist Conference 1898** 141–42, 149–50
**Anti-Anarchist Protocol of 1904 (St Petersburg)** 142, 149–50
**anti-corruption law** *see* **international anti-corruption law**
**anti-human trafficking**
  conclusion 161
  history, of 151–61
  International Abolitionist Federation 156, 158
  International Bureau for the Suppression of the White Slave Traffic 155–56, 157
  International Conference on the White Slave Traffic 1902 154–55, 157–58
  International Congress on the White Slave Trade 1899 157–58
  introduction 151–52
  League of Nations
    Advisory Committee on Traffic in Women and Children 159
    role 158–61
  moral panic 152–53, 154
  National Vigilance Association (NVA) 153–54, 155–56, 157
  overview 152–54
  prostitution 151, 152–54, 160–61
  regulationism, abolition of 153–54, 155, 156, 161
  sexual exploitation 151
  sexual morality
    attitudes, to 159
    regulationism, comparative analysis 154–58
  suppression, (post 1918) 158–61
  'white slavery' 152–53, 154–55
***Anwendungsbereich*** 261–62
**Apartheid Convention 1973**
  transnational criminal court, establishment 109, 113–14
**Association International de Droit Pénal (AIDP)**
  extradition law reform
    advocacy, for 4–5
  influence on international penal reformism 28, 30–31, 310–11
  international court
    advocacy, for 4–5
  international penal code
    advocacy, for 4–5, 49–50, 143–44
  police cooperation
    advocacy, for 4–5
**asylum**
  abrogation 25
  criminal asylum 20–21
  extradition, relationship with 20–21, 280–82
  political asylum 20–21
  pre-modern transnational criminal law 20–22
***attentat* clause** 25, 139–40, 280–81
***aut dedere aut iudicare***
  principle 15, 17, 268, 270–71

**'boat people'** 164–65

**British anti-slave-trade treaties**
abolition of slave trade 131–32, 137
action for non-compliance 134
adhesion treaties, as 135–36
bilateral suppression treaties with African and Arab leaders 128–29
conclusion 136–37
criminalization 133–34
introduction 128–30
manuscripts of treaties 129, 129n.8
mutual cooperation 135
nationality jurisdiction 133n.23
obligations on leaders 130
punishment 133–34
resources devoted, to 129–30
sample of treaties to 1850 132–36
suppression obligation 135
**Butler, Josephine**
Contagious Diseases Act, work against 154
regulationism, work to abolish 154, 155, 157n.39

**Cambridge Commission** 64
**Chile**
international anti-corruption law
ITT covert activities 189–91, 195
**Commission for the Control of Interpol's Files (CCF)**
role in Interpol 287, 297–98
**Committee of Experts on Crime in Cyber-Space (PC-CY)** 241–42
**common danger** *see also* **terrorism**
crimes, constituting 142, 143, 144
limits to offences 146
terrorism, and 145–46, 147, 148–49, 150
**Conference on Indochinese Refugees 1979** 164–65
**Convention on the Means of Prohibiting and Preventing the Illicit Export, Import and Transfer of Ownership of Cultural Property (1970 UNESCO Convention)**
measures against illicit trade 227–28
**core crimes** *see also* **crimes under international law**
apartheid, as 109
concept 4, 4n.13
International Criminal Court 109–10, 114
piracy, distinguished 122–23
transnational crimes, evolution into 75
**corporate liability** *see also* **economic crimes; international anti-corruption law**
anti-corruption agenda of US 207–10
conclusion 217–19
economic crimes, for 202–19
Financial Action Task Force (FATF) 208, 209
Foreign Corrupt Practices Act (FCPA) 202, 205–7
amendment 207
corporate criminal liability 205–6
globalization of local developments 217
governance
global South governments, delegitimization of 202, 203–4, 207–10, 217, 219
international development
pre-treaty phase 203–10
introduction 202–3
meaning 202
multilateral treaties
corporate liability standards 202–3, 210–12
non-binding international instruments 215–16
norm diffusion 203n.3, 217–18
post-treaty phase 212–14
pre-treaty phase
1970s 204–7
1980s–1990s 207–10
private transnational governance 218
standards
economic crime treaties, emergence in 210–12
post-treaty developments 212–14
test to limit of transnational criminal law 218–19
transnational corporations
code of conduct 204–5
Foreign Corrupt Practices Act (FCPA) 202, 205–7
legitimization of power 202, 203–7, 219
'moral actors', as 209
self regulation 208–9
treaty phase 210–12, 217
**corruption**
meaning under international law 187
**Council of Europe (CoE)**
jurisgenerative processes
role in policy cycle 89, 89n.13, 90
Recommendations of the CoE Committee of Ministers 90, 90n.19
**Courts of Mixed Commission** 104–5
**crime**
internationalization, of v
local matter, as v
**crime types**
trajectory 75, 75*f*
***crimen publicum*** 23
**crimes against humanity**
concept 57, 63–64
core crime, as 4

**crimes under international law**
definition 4
**criminal asylum** *see also* **asylum**
abrogation 25
extradition, relationship with 20–21
pre-modern transnational criminal law 20–22
**criminal justice**
nationalization 25
**criminological positivism** *see also* **criminological reformism**
basis 31
indirect effect on transnational criminal justice 31
nationality principle 32–33
natural crimes 32
transnational criminal law, influence on 31–36
**criminological reformism (1870s–1930s)** 27–38
conclusion 38
international social defence criminal policy 31–36
*Internationale Gemeingefärlichkeit* 34–35
introduction 27–28
*iudex deprehensionis* 34, 36
transnational criminal law, influence on 28–31, 310–11
unification of international criminal law 36–38
universal social defence 34, 143–44
**criminologists**
meaning 27n.1
**criminology**
meaning 27n.1
**cultural heritage** *see* **illicit trade in cultural objects**
**cybercrime** *see* **transnational cybercrime**

***delictis extra territorium*** 23
***delictis gravibus*** 21
**Delphi Convention** *see* **European Convention on Offences Relating to Cultural Property**
***derecho internacional penal*** 3
***doctrine cosmopolite*** 310–12
***droit international pénal***
definition 3
*ius commune* 15
***droit pénal international***
*ius commune* 15

**economic crimes** *see also* **corporate liability**
committal 203
corporate liability, for 202–19
**European Committee on Crime Problems (CDPC)**
jurisgenerative process, example of 88
**European Convention on Offences Relating to Cultural Property 1985 (Delphi Convention)** 229–30
**European Convention on Offences Relating to Cultural Property 2017 (Nicosia Convention)** 232
**European Court of Human Rights** 94–95
access, to 94n.30
extradition 314
jurisgenerative processes 94–95
**European Cybercrime Convention 2001** 241–42
**European Union**
harmonization of laws 92–93, 294–95
individual rights, protection of 316–17
Interpol, interaction with 294–95
jurisgenerative processes
conversion into legal content 92–93
input into policy cycle 89, 90
Security Agenda 90
smuggling migrants 173–74
supranationalization 92–93
**Europol**
establishment 294–95
**Evian Conference 1938** 164
**extradition**
anarchists, exception 141–42, 280–81
asylum, interactions with 20–21, 280–82
bilateral agreements 21–22
conclusion 286
counter-terrorism law, interactions with 147, 284–85
criminal asylum, relationship with 20–21
depoliticalization of political offences 139–40
development 20–22
French/English law, interaction between 277–78
Harvard Draft 282
historiography 22n.34
international human rights law, interactions with 285–86
introduction 276–77
making of modern international law 276–86
multilateralism, interactions with 282–84
peace treaties, interactions with 302–280
political offence exception 11, 25, 142, 149–50, 281–82
definition of political offences 139–40
depoliticalization, of 139–40
meaning 139
pre-modern transnational criminal law 20–22

**extraterritorial crime**
transnational crime, as 3

**Falcone, Judge Giovanni**
international cooperation against organized crime 180–81, 181n.22, 181n.23
**Fedozzi, Prospero**
positivism and the nationality principle 32–33
***forum delicti commissi***
jurisdiction 16
***forum deprehensionis***
extent 17
jurisdiction 16–17, 23, 267
transnational criminal law, relevance for development 16–17
universal jurisdiction, characterization as 17
***forum domicilii***
jurisdiction 16
**French Revolution**
establishment of national criminal justice system 25
terrorism, origin of term 138

**Garofalo, Raffaele**
international penal code, draft 32
***Geltungsbereich*** 261–62
**genocide**
concept 57
core crime, as 4
**'Gentleman's Club'** 48
**global justice**
development, of 57
**globalism**
statism, tension between 13
**globalization**
scope of international criminal law 84n.1, 84n.2, 250–51
***Golden Venture***
smuggling of migrants 166–67
**Gunzburg, Niko**
terrorism 145–46

**Harvard Draft**
extradition 282
piracy 118–19
**Hijacking Convention 1970**
jurisdiction, as model framework 268–69
**historical terms** 15n.6
***hostes humani generis***
piracy, as 115, 118n.15
**human rights** *see* **international human rights**

**illicit trade in cultural objects**
Convention on the Means of Prohibiting and Preventing the Illicit Export, Import and Transfer of Ownership of Cultural Property (1970 UNESCO Convention) 227–28
criminal policy strategies 235
criminalization 225–26
cultural heritage and laws of war 221–26
cultural heritage protection
early twentieth century 222–23
late twentieth century 225–26
post World War II 223–25
Enlightenment thinking 203–5
EU law 232–33
European Convention on Offences Relating to Cultural Property 1985 (Delphi Convention) 229–30
European Convention on Offences Relating to Cultural Property 2017 (Nicosia Convention) 232, 233
implementation of measures 235
introduction 220–21
marginalization of criminalization 226–28
Model Treaty 228–29, 231
money laundering 232–33
Napoleonic wars 222
organized crime 230, 231, 232–33, 234–35
systematic criminal justice responses 228–30
terrorist financing 231, 232–33, 234–35
United Nations Office on Drugs and Crime, role 230–31
war crime
proportionate penalty 226n.43
**incrementalism** 12
**individual rights** *see also* **international human rights**
conclusion 317–18
*doctrine cosmopolite* 310–12
human rights, influence on individual legal status 314–15
individuals, empowerment of 312–17
introduction 300–2
juridification of domestic proceedings 308–10
legal status acquisition, of 305–10
mutual legal assistance caveats 301, 308, 312, 315
mutual legal assistance treaties 312–14
pragmatic cross-border cooperation 306–8
protection, extent of 316–17
terminology 302–5
transnational criminal law, and 5–6, 300–18
definition 302–3
**Indochina**
'boat people' 164–65
smuggling migrants 164–65
**influence**
transnational criminal laws, effect of 12–13
**inquisitorial system**
categories of suspects 16–17

*ius commune* 15–17
**internalization of external ideas**
concept 89
**International Abolitionist Federation** 156, 158
**International Anti-Corruption Court (IACC)**
proposal to establish 101–2
**international anti-corruption law**
bribery 187–88, 195, 196, 197
corrupt practices 196
corruption
competing conceptions 195–98, 205–6
international law, meaning 187
historical context 188–94
illicit payments 196–97
international agreement on 'illicit payments'
code of conduct 198–99, 200
criminal law approach 198
failed negotiation (1970s) 188–89, 195–200
legacy 199–200
scope of treaty 195–98
misconduct by US companies
ITT covert activities in Chile 189–91, 195
Watergate scandal 191–93, 195
OECD Bribery Convention 200, 201
origins 187–201
regional anti-corruption instruments 200–1
sanctions and southern Africa 193–94, 195, 197–98
United States, role 187–88
**International Association of Penal Law** *see* **Association International de Droit Pénal (AIDP)**
**International Bureau for the Suppression of the White Slave Traffic** 155–56
**International Bureau for the Unification of Criminal Law (IBUCL)**
foundation 138–39
terrorism, suppression, of 138–39, 144–45
**International Commission for Penal Reconstruction and Development** 64
**International Conference on the White Slave Traffic 1904** 154–55
**International Congress on the White Slave Trade 1899** 157–58
**international cooperation**
procedural modes, of 2
**international courts** *see also* **transnational criminal courts**
development, of v
**international crime** *see also* **transnational crime**
crimes of inter-connectedness 47
definition 4, 4n.17
development of responses, to v
forms, of v
**International Criminal Court**
establishment 109–11
**international criminal law**
ambiguity in term 48–49
definition, *lato sensu* 4, 4n.18
definition, *stricto sensu* 3
*derecho internacional penal*, distinguished 3n.12
*droit international penal*, distinguished 3n.11
*Internationales Strafrecht* 4n.18
principles 39
transnational criminal law, distinguished 3, 40
unification 36–38
*Völkerstrafrecht*, same meaning as 3
**International Criminal Police Commission (ICPC)** *see also* **Interpol; transnational police cooperation**
establishment 28–29, 288, 293
nazification 294
objectives 293–94
re-establishment 294
**international drug suppression**
League of Nations, role 45–46
**international extradition** *see* **extradition**
**international human rights law** *see also* **individual rights**
extradition, interactions with 285–86
protection of individual rights 185–86, 302, 314–15
**international legal frameworks**
history, of 1–2
**International Law Commission**
aggression, concept of 107
Draft Code of Offences against International Peace and Security 106–7, 108
role in establishing international criminal jurisdiction 106–8, 113–14
**international law enforcement cooperation** *see also* **Interpol**
historical development 287–99
**international organizations** *see also* **jurisgenerative processes**
analytical basis of research into 85–86
emergence of criminal law norms, in 84–100
introduction 84–86
jurisgenerative processes 84–85, 88–98
methodological challenges 87
**International Prison and Penitentiary Commission**
influence on international penal reformism 28–29
**International Union of Penal Law**
crimes constituting a common danger 144
foundation 29
influence on international penal reformism 29–30, 144
***Internationale Kriminalistische Vereinigung* (IKV)** *see* **International Union of Penal Law**

***Internationales Strafrecht***
international criminal law, as 4n.18
*ius commune* 15
**internationalism**
external sovereignty/peace 6
transnationalism, division between 6
**Interpol** *see also* **transnational police cooperation**
accountability mechanisms 287
Commission for the Control of Interpol's Files (CCF) 287, 297–98
conclusion 298–99
criticism of Red Notices 296–97
establishment 288, 294
EU harmonization, effect on 294–95
functions 296–97
information sharing 296–97
International Criminal Police Commission (ICPC)
establishment 288, 293
Nazification 294
objectives 293–94
re-establishment 294
international government organization, status as 287, 295
introduction 287
limits to mandate 294–95
membership 295
political crimes, facilitation of cooperation 295, 296
preceding mechanisms 288–90
shortfalls 297–98
terrorism 296
**isolationism** 12
***ius commune***
abrogation by nation states 25
inquisitorial system 15–17
introduction 14–15
pre-modern transnational criminal law, relationship with 25–26
systematization 25–26
***ius gentium*** 42–43
***ius puniendi*** 90–91, 92–93, 98–99, 261–62

**jurisdiction** *see also* **multilateral suppression conventions**
*Anwendungsbereich* 261–62
*aut derdere aut iudicare* clause 268, 270–71
basic structures 265–68
conclusion 274–75
derivative jurisdiction 262–63
duty to notify other states 269
format 272–73
*forum* 261–62
*forum deprehensionis* 267
*Geltungsbereich* 261–62
Hijacking Convention 1970, as model framework 268–69
history in transnational criminal law 261–75
individual right-based limitations 261–62
innovations in jurisdiction 266–67, 268, 273
international law requirements 261–62
introduction 261–64
*ius puniendi* 261–62
jurisdictional principles 139
legal interests 262–63
*lex fori* 261–62
mandatory jurisdiction 270–71
model framework, crystallization of 268–70
nationality principle 266–67
application, of 142, 267
non-extraditability, and 267–68
optional resident jurisdiction 269–70
original jurisdiction 262–63
passive personality jurisdiction 269–70
permissive jurisdiction 270–71
personality jurisdiction 262–63
protection principle 267–68
regional agreements 264–65
regulation of transnational jurisdiction 264–65
sectoral suppression conventions 265
substance 273
suppression conventions 265–72
basic structures 265–68
consolidation and extension (1990s, early 2000s) 270–72
jurisdictional pillar 265–66
model framework 268–70
terminology 261–62, 262n.5, 262n.6
*territoire flotant* 265–66
territoriality 262–63, 263n.15, 265–66, 269–70
application of principle 142, 267
transferred jurisdiction 262–63
trends and directions 272–73
ubiquity principle 266–67
uniformity of domestic criminal law 263–64
vicarious administration of justice principle 267
**jurisgenerative processes**
best practice, identification and promulgation of 96, 97
Compendium of United Nations standards and norms 90
conclusions 99–100
conversion 92–96
best practice, identification and promulgation of 96
customary law, constructive creation of 93
explanatory memoranda 92–93

guidance notes 92–93
multilateral treaties 92
policy evaluation 95–96
transformation of input into legal content 92–96
value standardization and enforcement by courts based on human rights 94–95
Council of Europe, role 89, 89n.13, 90, 90n.19
epistemic communities, role 89
European Court of Human Rights 94–95
access, to 94n.30
European Union
Court of Justice of the EU 95
harmonization 92–93
Security Agenda 90
supranationalization 92–93
implementation 96–98
judicial enforcement 98
monitoring 97
mutual evaluation 97
policy evaluation 97–98
influence on development of transnational criminal law 84–85
input 88–92
drafting and adoption of policy guidelines 90
examples 88–89, 90–91
framing (of issues) 88
preparation of treaties, resolutions, legal documents 90–91
typical features of input phase 92
value communication 91–92
international terrorism, effect 88, 89
internalization of external ideas 89
legitimacy 98–99
OECD, role 89
overview 88–98
policy-cycle stages, of 88
Recommendations of the CoE Committee of Ministers 90, 90n.19
resolutions as soft law 91–92
Tampere Conclusions 90
United Nations Congress on Crime Prevention and Criminal Justice, role 88
United Nations Security Council
Chapter VII resolutions 92–93, 97, 98–99
diversification of concept of 'peace' 93

***Landfriedensbruch*** 23
**Latin American and Caribbean Criminal Court Against Transnational Organized Crime (COPLA)**
proposal to establish 101–2, 114
**League of Nations**
access to power 59
Advisory Committee on Traffic in Women and Children 159
Commissions 59–60
crimes against civilians 57–63
disarmament 60–61
establishment 59
global role in crime control 44, 45
international drug suppression 45
learning system, formation of 57, 60
nature, of 59
Opium Advisory Committee 45–46, 48
personal cooperation among delegates 60, 61–62
purpose 59–60
small states
access to power 59, 62–63
World Disarmament Conference, failure 63
**League of Nations Convention for the Creation of an International Criminal Court 1937**
transnational criminal courts 105–6, 113–14
***lex fori*** 261–62
**London 'hub'** 63–64
**London International Assembly (LIA)** 64

**Malabo Protocol**
African Court of Justice and Human and Peoples' Rights
proposal to establish 101–2, 112–13, 114
critiques 113
progress 113
subject-matter jurisdiction 112–13
**maritime piracy *see* piracy**
**modes of liability *see also* transnational criminal law**
collective criminality 249–50, 260
conclusion 260
corruption 258–60
historical perspectives 249–60
individual liability
criminal activities, addressed 251–52
forms 250–60
forms, generally 253
general background 250–51
group responsibility 255–56
historical development 256–60
participation 254–55
perpetration 253–54
transnational treaty obligations 252–53
introduction 249–50
trafficking in human beings 257–58
**Mueller, Gerhard**
categories of transnational crime 79
conclusion 82–83
intellectual background 71–75
international bodies, membership of 76–77

**Mueller, Gerhard** (*cont.*)
introduction 70–71
organized crime
definition 45–46
elements 82*t*
organized group
definition 45–46, 81
elements 82*t*
Survey of Crime Trends and Operation of Criminal justice Systems (UN-CTS) 79
transnational crime
categories 79
container concept 78
definition 81–82
elements 82*t*
role in development of concept for UN 70–83
transnational organized crime
definition 81
elements 82*t*
UN Congresses on Crime Prevention and Criminal Justice 77–78, 80*t*
UN Crime Prevention and Criminal Justice Branch
appointment as head 70, 76
**multilateral suppression conventions** *see also* **jurisdiction**
categorization, of (inter-war) 48–52
conceptualization, of (inter-war) 42–44
conclusion 55–56
criticism, of 53–54
development phase 1 (late 19th and early 20th centuries) 40–44, 250–51
development phase 2 (inter-war period) 44–47
growth (1900s to 1950s) 39–56
indirect enforcement system 251
inductive nature of development 47
institutionalization of transnational crime suppression 44–47
international criminal law
principles 39
introduction 39–40
maximalist/minimalist views of cooperation 44–45, 46–47, 52
nature of inter-war development 47–48
'omnibus' international criminal law, and 52–54, 55–56
post-war, 52–54
suppression of crime as multilateral issue 40–42
transnational criminal law
principles 39
United Nations Convention against Transnational Organized Crime, as 178
utilitarian law enforcement rationale 47–48

**national criminal justice systems**
establishment 25
**National Vigilance Association (NVA)** 153–54, 155–56
**Nicosia Convention** *see* **European Convention on Offences Relating to Cultural Property 2017**
**norm dispersion**
changing methods, of 13
***nullum crimen sine lege***
respect for in transnational context 5–6, 49–50, 307

**OECD Bribery Convention**
anti-corruption mechanism 200, 201
**Opium Advisory Committee**
'Gentleman's Club' 48
International drug suppression 45–46, 48
**organized crime** *see also* **United Nations Convention against Transnational Organized Crime (UNTOC, 2000 Palermo Convention)**
criminal networks 184n.45
EU/US coincidence of interests 183
flexible and integrated approach, against 183–86
freedom of movement facilitating expansion 182
international cooperation against 180–82
introduction 177–78
national security interests 182–83
organized criminal group, definition 184–85
serious crime 185
structured criminal group 179n.11, 184–85
world-wide problem, as 181–82

**Palermo Convention** *see* **organized crime; United Nations Convention against Transnational Organized Crime**
**peace**
diversification of concept 93
**peace treaties**
extradition, interactions with 302–280
**Pella, Vespasian**
AIDP, role 30–31
'inter-state' criminal law 4–5
social defence 33–34
suppression conventions 54
terrorism 144, 145
unification of penal law 49–50, 143
**piracy**
*communis hostis omnium* 115n.1, 122–23
conclusion 126–27
duty to cooperate 119

duty to criminalize 116–22, 126, 127
conventional basis, for 117–20
customary basis, for 120–21
first steps towards 116
UN Security Council resolutions 121–22
historical factors affecting transnational criminal law 122–25
history, of 115–27
*hostes humani generis*, as 115, 118n.15
introduction 115–16
nature of crime 122–23
reoccurrence as factual phenomenon 125
sovereign powers' interests and needs operating at sea 123–25
transnational criminal courts, establishment 111–12, 120–21
UN Convention on the Law of the Sea (UNCLOS), relevance 117
**policy decisions**
UN Security Council resolutions 121–22, 126
transformation into law v
**pre-modern transnational criminal law**
categories of suspects 16–17
core elements, of 15–16
extradition 20–21
*forum delicti commissi* 16–17
*forum deprehensionis* 16–17
*forum domicilii* 16
hot pursuit 19, 20
inquisitorial system 15–17
*ius commune* 15–16
police cooperation 19, 20
requisition proceedings 18
transnational threats to security 16–17
**prostitution** *see* **anti-human trafficking**
**pursuit**
hot pursuit 19
regulation 19
requisition proceedings, exception to 19

**Radhabinod, Pal**
crimes under international law 54
**Rappaport, Emil Stanislaw**
AIDP, role 30–31
**regulationism**
campaign to abolition 153–54, 155, 156
***remissio delinquentium ad locum commissi delictis*** 21
**remission**
principle 20–22
***remission ad locum delicti*** 21
**requisition proceedings**
form in early modern period 18
**roots in law enforcement** 11–12

**Saldaña, Quintiliano**
AIDP, role 30–31
universal social defence 4–5, 34–36, 311
**Schleich, Josef** 163–64
**slavery** *see also* **anti-human trafficking**
transnational criminal courts 104–5
UK Slavery Courts 104–5
**smuggling of migrants**
'alien smuggling' 167–68
'boat people' 164–65
Cold War period 165–66
Europe, regional developments 173–74
future of international law, concerning 174–76
Global Compact for Safe, Orderly and Regular Migration 2018 176
*Golden Venture* 166–67
history, of 162–76
Holocaust and Nazi Germany 163–64
Indochina 164–65
initiatives by Italy and Austria 168–69
international agreement, progress towards 167–69
introduction 162–63
post-Cold War period 166–67
problems created, by 175
Smuggling of Migrants Protocol 169–73
criminal justice instrument, as 171
criminal prosecution, liability to 172
criminalization of smuggling of migrants 171–72
final text 171–73
objectives 170–71
prevention and suppression by sea 172–73
purpose 171
smuggled migrants, protection of rights 172–73, 176
support, for 174–75
twentieth century, during 163–67
United Nations, role 167–68
**social defence**
criminological reformism 31–36
influence on AIDP 143–44
**Southern Africa**
international anti-corruption law
influence of economic sanctions 193–94, 195
**St Petersburg Anti-Anarchist Protocol of 1904** 142, 149–50
**statism**
globalism, tension between 13
**suppression**
turn towards 12

**suppression conventions** *see also* **British anti-slave-trade treaties; multilateral suppression conventions**
list 3n.7, 250–51
meaning 3

**Tampere Conclusions**
jurisgenerative process, example of 90
***territoire flotant*** 265–66
**territoriality**
cybercrime, and 247–48
jurisdiction, and 140n.15, 262–63, 265–66, 267, 269–70, 270n.39, 274n.53
legal status of individuals 305
multilateral suppression treaties 44
non-territoriality principle 34
principle 25
*territoire flotant* 265–66
**terrorism** *see also* **anarchism; anarchy**
anarchism, as 140
common danger, crimes constituting 145–46, 147, 148–49, 150
conclusion 149–50
definition 146–48, 149
depoliticalization of political offences in extradition 139–40, 143–44
extradition, interactions with 284–85
international criminal justice, and 143–44
Interpol 296
introduction 138–39
legal concept, as 138
model laws 148
national criminal laws, unification 144–49
police cooperation 141, 142–43
political offences, definition 139–40, 149
political origins of term 138
special intent element 147
transnational legal suppression, of 138–50
unification of criminal laws, against 142–49
**Trainin, A N**
suppression conventions 53–54
**transborder crime**
transnational crime, as 3
**transboundary crime**
transnational crime, as 3
**transboundary practices**
pre-modern transnational criminal law 18–20
**transnational crime**
concept 252
development by Gerhard Mueller for the UN 70–83
definition 1, 3
development of responses, to 1
distinctions 1
early concepts, of 23–24
flexible and integrated approach, against 183–86
pervasive nature, of v
principles 39
transnational treaty obligations 254–53
**transnational criminal courts** 101–14
African Court of Justice and Human and Peoples' Rights 101–2
Apartheid Convention 1973 109
introduction 101–2
International Law Commission, role 106–8
Latin American and Caribbean Criminal Court Against Transnational Organized Crime (COPLA) 101–2
legal practicality 102–3
Malabo Protocol 112–13
piracy 111–12
reasoning, for 102–4
UK Slavery Courts 104–5
**transnational criminal law** *see also* **jurisdiction; modes of liability; pre-modern transnational criminal law**
18th and early 19th century Europe 14–26
collective criminality 249–50
concept 4–7
criminal phenomena, addressed in 265–52
definition 3, 14, 302–3
globalism/statism, tension between 13
incrementalism 12
individual rights, and 5–6
influence 12–13
international criminal law, distinguished 3, 40
international organizations, role 84–86
isolationism 12
jurisgenerative processes 84–85, 88–98
norm dispersion, changing methods of 13
ontological beliefs, and 2
principles 39
statism/globalism, tension between 13
suppression, turn to 12
transnational treaties, transposition to domestic law 254–53
treaty-based crimes 84–85
unification of criminal laws 4–7, 49–50
**transnational criminals**
early concepts 23
**transnational cybercrime**
activity for the masses, as 239–40
ambiguity of term 237
common problem, as 238–39
criminal activities affecting information technology 236–37
criminalization of features/risks of information technology 236–37
definition 236–37, 236n.1
European Cybercrime Convention 2001 241–42

evolution 236–40
'flat e-commerce business model' 239
global convention 244–45
history, of 236–48
information technology as tool to commit crime 236–37
international 'soft law' 240–41
introduction 236
multi-dimensional and global challenge, as 245–46
parallel problem, as 238
regional conventions 241–44
regional initiatives 243
territoriality 247–48
transformative power, of 247–48
transnational criminal justice responses, to 240–45, 246–47
transnational problem, as 239
US CLOUD Act 243–44, 247

**transnational epistemic communities** *see also* **League of Nations; United Nations War Crimes Commission (UNWCC)**
common goal 60, 69
conclusion 68–69
crimes against civilians, conceptual development 57–59
definition by shared understanding of terms 65
exile lawyers, role 63–64, 66
Geneva network 59, 61, 63, 68–69
introduction 57–59
jurisgenerative processes 89
League of Nations 59–63
learning system, formation of 57, 60, 68
London 'hub' 63–64
notion of group 65
personal cooperation among delegates 60, 61–62
transnational intellectual network 63–64, 66, 68
United Nations War Crimes Commission (UNWCC) 63–68

**transnational institutions**
development, of 2

**transnational police cooperation** *see also* **Interpol**
'Anti-Anarchist' Conference 118–19, 290–91
common standards, development of 289, 291
historical development 287
legislative developments 291–92
Monaco conference 1914 291–92
Napoleonic policing system 288–89
Okhrana 288–89
police-to-police cooperation ($19^{th}$ century) 289
political engagement, in 289–91
Polizeiverein 288–89
secretive police institutions ($19^{th}$ century) 288–89
Vienna Conference 292, 293

**transnationalism**
internal sovereignty/crime control 6
internationalism, division between 6

**UK Slavery Courts**
transnational criminal courts 104–5

**UNESCO Convention 1970** *see* **Convention on the Means of Prohibiting and Preventing the Illicit Export, Import and Transfer of Ownership of Cultural Property**

**unification of criminal law**
advocacy, for 4–7, 49–50
criminological reformism 36–38
suppression conventions, and 48–52

**United Nations Congresses on Crime Prevention and Criminal Justice**
jurisgenerative process, example of 88
occurrences 80*t*
transnational crime, development of concept 77

**United Nations Convention against Illicit Traffic in Narcotic Drugs and Psychotropic Substances 1988**
continuity, between 179–80

**United Nations Convention against Transnational Organized Crime (UNTOC, 2000 Palermo Convention)** *see also* **organized crime**
adoption 177, 180–81
antecedents 178–79
basis 179
conclusion 186
contracting parties 177
definition of transnational organized crimes 81–82, 82*t*, 184–85
driving forces behind adoption 180–83
Drug Trafficking Convention 1988, continuity between 179–80, 186
flexible and integrated approach 183–86
force, in 177
general criminal policy 184
harmonization of domestic law 184
individual rights, protection of 185–86
jurisdiction 270–72
preceding materials 177–78
prevention obligations 185–86
purpose 180
serious crime 185
sovereignty, protection of 179
suppression convention, as 178, 186
transnational criminal law, and 178–80
transnationality, requirement for 179n.11

**United Nations Crime Prevention and Criminal Justice Branch**
transnational crime
development of concept by Gerhard Mueller 70–83
**United Nations Office on Drugs and Crime**
illicit trade in cultural objects 230–31
**United Nations Security Council**
Chapter VII resolutions 92–93, 97, 98–99, 121–22
diversification of concept of 'peace' 93
jurisgenerative process, example of 92–93, 97, 98–99
piracy, duty to criminalize 121–22
**United Nations War Crimes Commission (UNWCC)**
composition 65
crimes against humanity 63–64, 66–67
epistemic community, as 63–64
establishment 65
Faculty of Law at the University of Cambridge (Cambridge Commission) 64
'London hub' 63–64
London International Assembly 64
objectives 65
Pacific sub-commission, failure 67–68
preceding bodies 64–65
war crimes, role 65–68
**United States**
anti-corruption agenda 207–10
CLOUD Act 243–44
Foreign Corrupt Practices Act (FCPA) 202, 205–7
amendment 207
corporate criminal liability 205–6
international anti-corruption law
ITT covert activities in Chile 189–91
role 187–88
Watergate scandal 191–93
**universal social defence**
concept 4–6, 5n.22
criminological reformism 34–36

***Völkerstrafrecht***
definition 3
*ius commune* 15

**war crimes**
core crime, as 4
criminalization, of 6
**Watergate scandal**
international anti-corruption law 191–93, 195
**white slavery** *see* **anti-human trafficking**
**World Disarmament Conference**
failure 63